RETHINKING DEATH IN AND AFTER HEIDEGGER

Iain D. Thomson is renowned for radically rethinking Heidegger's views on metaphysics, technology, education, art, and history, and in this book he presents a compelling rereading of Heidegger's important and influential understanding of existential death. Thomson lucidly explains how Heidegger's phenomenology of existential death led directly to the insights that forced him to abandon *Being and Time*'s guiding pursuit of a fundamental ontology, and thus how his early, prometaphysical work gave way to his later efforts to do justice to being in its real phenomenological richness and complexity. He also examines and clarifies the often abstruse responses to Heidegger's rethinking of death in Levinas, Derrida, Agamben, Beauvoir, and others, explaining the enduring significance of this work for ongoing efforts to think clearly about death, mortality, education, and politics. The result is a powerful and illuminating study of Heidegger's understanding of existential death and its enduring importance for philosophy and life.

IAIN D. THOMSON is Professor of Philosophy at the University of New Mexico. He is the author of *Heidegger on Ontotheology: Technology and the Politics of Education* (Cambridge, 2005) and *Heidegger, Art, and Postmodernity* (Cambridge, 2011), and coeditor (with Kelly Becker) of *The Cambridge History of Philosophy: 1945–2015* (Cambridge, 2019).

RETHINKING DEATH IN AND AFTER HEIDEGGER

IAIN D. THOMSON
University of New Mexico

CAMBRIDGE
UNIVERSITY PRESS

Shaftesbury Road, Cambridge CB2 8EA, United Kingdom

One Liberty Plaza, 20th Floor, New York, NY 10006, USA

477 Williamstown Road, Port Melbourne, VIC 3207, Australia

314–321, 3rd Floor, Plot 3, Splendor Forum, Jasola District Centre, New Delhi – 110025, India

103 Penang Road, #05–06/07, Visioncrest Commercial, Singapore 238467

Cambridge University Press is part of Cambridge University Press & Assessment, a department of the University of Cambridge.

We share the University's mission to contribute to society through the pursuit of education, learning and research at the highest international levels of excellence.

www.cambridge.org
Information on this title: www.cambridge.org/9781009480031

DOI: 10.1017/9781009480048

© Iain Thomson 2024

This publication is in copyright. Subject to statutory exception and to the provisions of relevant collective licensing agreements, no reproduction of any part may take place without the written permission of Cambridge University Press & Assessment.

When citing this work, please include a reference to the DOI 10.1017/9781009480048

First published 2024
First paperback edition 2025

A catalogue record for this publication is available from the British Library

ISBN 978-1-009-48008-6 Hardback
ISBN 978-1-009-48003-1 Paperback

Cambridge University Press & Assessment has no responsibility for the persistence or accuracy of URLs for external or third-party internet websites referred to in this publication and does not guarantee that any content on such websites is, or will remain, accurate or appropriate.

In memory of my father
and all those who went before,
let fear turn to wonder,
and so helped light another way.

CONTENTS

Preface xi
Acknowledgments xviii
A Note on the Notes (da capo) xxi
Abbreviations Used for Works by Heidegger xxii

PART I **Rethinking Death in Heidegger** 1

1 Death and Demise in *Being and Time* 3
   1.1 Introduction: The State of the Debate 3
   1.2 What It Means for Us to *Be*: Dasein (Preliminary Excursus) 10
   1.3 Rethinking Death: Distinguishing Perishing, Demising, and Dying 15
   1.4 Death as the Possibility of Dasein's Impossibility Par Excellence 36
   1.5 Heidegger's Phenomenological Bridge from Demise to Death: Formal Indication 48
   1.6 Preliminary Conclusions: Fear of Demise and Anxiety about Death 57
   1.7 Ontological Futurity: Situating *Being and Time*'s Phenomenology of Death 62

2 The Death of Metaphysics and the Birth of Thinking, or Why Did *Being and Time* Fail to Answer the Question of Being? 74
   2.1 Introduction: Thinking Philosophical Failure 74
   2.2 Fundamental Ontology as the "Onto-" of Ontotheology 76
   2.3 Beneath Fundamental Ontology: The Temporal Abyss of Being 85
   2.4 Being Unfinished 95

3 Heidegger on Death and the Nothing It Discloses 100
   3.1 Death: A Phenomenological Ontology 100
   3.2 What Does It Mean to Approach Death Phenomenologically? 102
   3.3 Death and Existential Possibility 107
   3.4 Existential Death and the Noth-ing of the Nothing 113
   3.5 Understanding Heidegger's Phenomenology of Noth-ing 115

4 Death and Rebirth in *Being and Time*'s Perfectionist
   Philosophy of Education   130
   4.1 *Being and Time*'s Philosophy of Education?   130
   4.2 What Is Philosophical Perfectionism?   132
   4.3 Heidegger's Perfectionism in *Being and Time*   136
   4.4 How We Become What We Are: *Being and Time*'s Answer to the
       Bildungsfrage   142
   4.5 Philosophical Education as Preparation for Existential Death – and
       Rebirth: Authenticity   148

   PART II   **Rethinking Death after Heidegger**   157

5 White's *Time and Death*: On the Advantages and
   Disadvantages of Reading Heidegger Backward   159
   5.1 Introduction   159
   5.2 White's Reading: Unorthodox Orthodoxy   161
   5.3 Reading White   168

6 Rethinking Levinas on Heidegger on Death   181
   6.1 Heidegger and Levinas: Beyond the Standard View   181
   6.2 From Heidegger to Levinas: The Basic Terms
       of the Dispute   189
   6.3 Thinking through Levinas's Challenge   193

7 Critical Afterlives of Heidegger's Phenomenology
   of Existential Death in Sartre, Beauvoir, Levinas, Agamben,
   and Derrida   208
   7.1 Existential Death in Sartre's Look of the Other and Beauvoir's Crisis
       of Adolescence   208
   7.2 Levinas's "Other" Phenomenology of Existential Death:
       Political Afterthoughts   218
   7.3 Agamben on How Existential Death Discloses the Phenomenon of
       "Bare Life"   225
   7.4 Derrida's Deconstructive Thinking of Demise as Aporia and Death as
       Survivance   229

8 Heidegger's Mortal Phenomenology of Existential
   Death and the Postmetaphysical Politics of
   Ontological Pluralism   239
   8.1 The Serious Issue of Philosophical Facetiousness   242
   8.2 Disclosing Technological Nihilism through
       Hermeneutic Phenomenology   245
   8.3 From the Righteous Lure of Good Conscience toward the Creative
       Peace of Ontological Pluralism   250

	8.4	Wrestling with Nietzsche and the Mortal Politics of Ontological Technologization 258
	8.5	The Future beyond Spinoza: Toward a Free Thinking of Death and the Nothing 262
9		Why It Is Better for a Dasein Not to Live Forever, or Being Pro-Choice on the Immortality Question 267
	9.1	To Be or Not to Be – Forever? 268
	9.2	The Finitude of Being within the Infinitude of Time 274
10		Concluding Recapitulations: Lessons from Rethinking Heidegger's Phenomenology of Existential Death and the Irreducible Nothings It Discloses 286

References   305
Index   317

PREFACE

The centenary of *Being and Time*'s original 1927 publication is rapidly approaching, yet some of the central concepts Heidegger developed in his early and unfinished magnum opus remain shrouded in controversy and confusion and so are still widely misunderstood, including what he means by *death*. Indeed, even calling "death" one of *Being and Time*'s "central concepts" downplays its importance: Heidegger's existential phenomenology of death is not just central to the structure and argument of *Being and Time* (as the transitional concept that helps bridge the text's two published divisions, enabling Heidegger to uncover the temporal horizons beneath the existential structures); it is also the pivotal phenomenological insight on which some of the text's other most important and influential phenomenological concepts turn, including (most notably) *authenticity*, *temporality*, and *nothingness*. That would already be sufficient to warrant a careful rethinking of Heidegger's existential phenomenology of death.

But Heidegger's phenomenological reconceptualization of death also enjoyed its own extremely influential philosophical afterlife, so rethinking it facilitates an illuminating reexamination of the often fascinating role it came to play in the work of such philosophers as Sartre, Beauvoir, Levinas, Derrida, and Agamben, among others. Moreover, I shall suggest, rethinking Heidegger on death also encourages us to rethink some other dubious orthodoxies that are currently taking shape or have already hardened into misleading prejudices. These include, first, that old (but recently resurgent) claim that Heidegger advances essentially the same philosophical views in both his early and later work; second, the idea (which goes well beyond Heidegger scholarship) that thinking about death is pointless, irrational, or even unfree; and third, the belief that living forever would be preferable to ever undergoing mortal demise.

In other words, *rethinking Heidegger on death* also means *rethinking death after Heidegger*. To suggest both, I have taken *Rethinking Death in and after Heidegger* as the title for this book, where "rethinking" expresses my hope to contribute to these interconnected projects rather than try to settle them once and for all. For, while I certainly have my own philosophical views on the meaning and significance of death in and after Heidegger and unabashedly present and defend those views here (as clearly and convincingly as I can), two and a half decades working on this difficult issue has taught me that death's meaning is not the sort of thing that can ever be settled once and for all – and, moreover, that this turns out to be a good thing in several important ways, or so I shall try to show in this book.

If the mass deaths of the two World Wars drove mortality and finitude into the forefront of the consciousness of Heidegger's existential generation, our own global pandemic has similarly forced death back into our thoughts.[1] While undeniably terrible in many respects, this derepression of death is also fitting from the perspective of existential phenomenology, since "pandemic" literally means something that affects *all people* (from the Greek *pán-*, "all" + *dêmos*, "people"), suggesting that our fear of mortality may well be the original *pandemic*. But is our common fear of mortality really so self-explanatory that we are right to flee and repress our fleeting awareness of it – or else try to escape it through fantasies of *immortality* – rather than seeking out and thinking through its deepest sources in our experience, however uncomfortable doing so might be? What if such a rethinking of death could help liberate us in our relation to mortality, and could do so precisely by encouraging us to confront and *rethink* rather than deny and repress our defining existential finitude?

As we shall see in Chapter 1, Heidegger thought that the search for an existential ontology of death capable of coming to grips with its sources and significance was deeply worthwhile.[2] *Being and Time* uncovers and articulates what he takes to be the deepest motivations behind our ordinary fear of demise

---

[1] See Kelly Becker and Iain Thomson, "Introduction: Philosophical Reflections on the Recent History of Philosophy," in K. Becker and I. Thomson, eds, *The Cambridge History of Philosophy* (Cambridge: Cambridge University Press, 2019),1–12.

[2] In 1936, Heidegger goes so far as to suggest that what made "that great era of the German spirit" that runs from Hegel and Schelling to Nietzsche so great was that these philosophers "dared to think the negative as belonging to being," and so were able to recognize (each in their own way) that "the noth-ing [*das Nichtige*] belongs to the essence of being." Along with Schelling's rethinking of *evil* and Nietzsche's reconception of creation as requiring *destruction* (see Iain Thomson, *Heidegger, Art, and Postmodernity* (Cambridge: Cambridge University Press, 2011), ch. 5), Heidegger celebrates the philosophical fortitude Hegel needed to "look the negative in the eye and linger [or "tarry," *verweilt*] with it," a spiritual strength Hegel believed enabled him to recognize the "monstrous power" of this negativity as the very "energy of thinking, the pure I," as Hegel famously wrote in the preface to his *Phenomenology of Spirit*. There Hegel continues (and Heidegger quotes him): "Death, if we wish to so name this unreality [*Unwirklichkeit*], is the most fearsome [*das Furchtbarste*], and to hold fast to death requires the greatest force." Yet, such holding fast in the face of death, Hegel adds, is precisely what "the understanding [unreasonably] demands [*zumutet*]"; true philosophical understanding must "endure death and maintain itself in death" (N1 61–3/NI 73–5). Heidegger does not explain himself here, but we will see that his view remains different from the one Hegel conveys in this famous passage. (Hegel's point, put simply, is that to understand self-

in a way that is meant to help free us from that fear – albeit inter alia and almost in passing (pun not intended) on the way to grander philosophical goals. To recognize not only *that* Heidegger does this but also to understand *why* and *how* – and so to begin to understand what he thinks an unflinching phenomenological examination of our ordinarily fearful relation with mortal demise can help *teach* us – we need to *rethink* what Heidegger means by "death," carefully understanding *Being and Time*'s existential phenomenology of our "anxiety in the face of death" in both its connections to and differences from our common fear of mortal demise.

By calling this a *rethinking* of Heidegger on death (and thereby calling for a *rethinking* of death after Heidegger), I mean "rethinking" in both the ordinary and the literal sense: *reconceiving* as well as *making thoughtful again*, and each in relation to the other. In my own philosophical development I had to *rethink* death in both senses, because my first two publications on Heidegger on death (both from the twentieth century) misunderstood Heidegger on "death" in the same way almost everyone else still does, by too closely conflating existential death with mortal demise.[3] This *fatal* misunderstanding (pun intended this time) was a bit of a shame, since those articles contained some significant insights of enduring importance to me (including my reading of Jonathan Demme's *The Silence of the Lambs* (1991) as a filmic work of art that profoundly resonated with audiences precisely because it led us through a

---

consciousness we must understand the logic governing its historical emergence, subsequent unfolding, and ultimate intersubjective destiny. Such understanding requires us to explain why each of the consecutive and partial forms of historical self-consciousness must repeatedly *die* and then be reborn differently, so that we can reconstruct the logic governing this overarching dialectical sojourn of "spirit" – that is, *social subjectivity*, humanity's collective self-awareness – through all the disparate historical moments into which it otherwise stands "torn asunder," this reconstruction being the very task of Hegel's *Phenomenology*.) On the basis of the views I explain in Chapters 1 and 3, we will be able to understand Heidegger's provocative claim that confronting death discloses the core of the self – not as a "pure I" (as Hegel has it), perhaps, but still as an intentional structure that establishes the "mineness" of Dasein's world or fails to do so (in *authenticity* or in the reactionary rejection that flees death into the thoughtless conformism of *inauthenticity*, respectively). Indeed, we will see that for Heidegger death discloses the very core of the self as a worldless "*solus ipse*" (or "self alone") which is nevertheless constitutively open to "the noth-ing [*das Nichtige*]" that "belongs to the essence of being itself" (as he so laconically puts it here). Heidegger's (initially strange) terminology will obviously take some explaining, but by the end of Chapter 1 we should be able to understand what he means when he says that death phenomenologically discloses the temporal horizon of "futurity," whereby *what is not yet* repeatedly comes toward us, and thereby enables us to discover a "nothing" built into the temporal arrival of our ontological world.

[3] See Chapter 1, Iain Thomson, "Can I Die? Derrida on Heidegger on Death," *Philosophy Today* 43:1 (1999), 29–42 and "The Silence of the Limbs: Critiquing Culture from a Heideggerian Understanding of the Work of Art," *Enculturation* 2:1 (1998). www.enculturation.net/2_1/thomson.html (accessed January 22, 2023).

vicarious repression of our fear of mortal demise, an interpretation I still believe to be *true* in the deepest Heideggerian sense), even if I now find their youthful style rather too quick and exuberant. But this sometimes painful history of learning-in-public also means that I know first-hand some of the ways we tend to resist coming to terms with Heidegger's existential-ontological interpretation of death, ignoring or repressing rather than carefully reconstructing his all-too-hastily sketched views on existential death and mortal demise in their relations as well as their differences. That task is exactly what we need, however, to begin to understand Heidegger's philosophical views on death in their full complexity, phenomenological depth, and enduring provocativeness.

Of course, as such assertions already suggest, my efforts to be clear sometimes encourage me to state my views before fully supporting or developing them, so I must ask readers to bear with me even (indeed *especially*) where some might be tempted to close the page on any book that would advance views about death that seem to run so obviously counter to common sense. That is not always easy, I recognize, but perhaps it will help here to remember that much of our shared common sense on truly difficult and fundamental philosophical issues (like the meaning and significance of death) is just the superficial and self-protective residue of earlier philosophical interpretations. (*Common sense is written by the winners*, we could say, who do not always win because they were right, let alone because they demonstrated their view's exclusive monopoly on the truth.) Heidegger is rightly famous for carefully deconstructing such seemingly self-evident philosophical views in ways that expose their contingency and reductive one-sidedness, thereby helping us discover what continues to make the deeper questions they conceal so enduringly important.[4]

The struggle against our own hermeneutic prejudices proves genuinely worthwhile in this case, I shall suggest, because Heidegger's existential phenomenology of death turns out to be much more original, insightful, influential, and philosophically *provocative* than we would recognize otherwise. In the face of such clear provocations, can we allow ourselves to be provoked into rethinking our preexisting views (and those of the tradition), instead of turning away from seemingly obvious falsehoods? I think doing so can help us discover, in turn, that the resistance we sometimes feel to being disabused of such one-sided prejudices is also a problematic resistance to *learning* (and so

---

[4] On Heidegger's "deconstruction" of the way the metaphysical tradition of *ontotheology* establishes the deepest and most widely shared presuppositions that tacitly shape Western humanity's shared view of what is and what matters (a seemingly fixed view that in fact varies dramatically throughout history), see Iain Thomson, *Heidegger on Ontotheology: Technology and the Politics of Education* (Cambridge: Cambridge University Press, 2005), Ch. 1.

to *growing* and *becoming*). But as Einstein famously observed: "*Once you stop learning, you start dying.*" So perhaps our fear of demise can be mobilized and channeled back into the very rethinking and relearning of what Heidegger means by "death" now called for – not least to help us think our way free of that mortal fear and so, perhaps, some of its most devastating consequences for ourselves and our worlds.

This book is organized into a longer first chapter that presents and explains what Heidegger means by death in great detail (while also responding to the most common objections to this interpretation), followed by shorter chapters that often reiterate and delve deeper into aspects and implications of this view to develop them further, redeploy them in other contexts, or contrast them with their subsequent use (and misuse) by other philosophers. In general terms, the first four chapters primarily rethink death *in* Heidegger, while the last five predominantly rethink death *after* Heidegger. These two main parts of the book support and illuminate one another, with later chapters recapitulating enough from earlier ones to be able to be read independently. I shall not seek to summarize each of these chapters schematically here, but the table of contents provides a thematic and topical map that should prove helpful for those uninterested in a linear reading. Since that seems to be most readers today, I have sought to make each chapter capable of standing on its own (at the undeniable cost of the occasional repetition and intertextual self-citation, but always in the service of going further, deeper, or in other directions) while also contributing to this larger project of rethinking death in and after Heidegger.[5] I have not sought to conceal the fact that these chapters began as independent works, and those looking for a single, overarching line of argumentation will find it primarily in the hermeneutic reading of death articulated, developed, and advanced in every chapter. If this work helps move this interpretation of death from its current minoritarian position into the scholarly mainstream (by showing it to be much more plausible and illuminating than it might initially appear), then it will have succeeded, whether or not all readers ultimately find it convincing (that, on a topic like this, is just too high a bar). I am convinced, of course, but looking back over this work as a whole I feel confident that this rethinking of Heidegger's views on death helps open (or reopen) more difficult issues and enduringly engaging questions than it closes old superficial answers. It is thus my hope that the chapters revised

---

[5] I try to provide sufficient textual evidence and philosophical argument for the interpretive claims about death advanced herein. As we will see, however, these issues frequently open onto some of the largest topics Heidegger takes up in his later work, complex topics I explain with more of the requisite philosophical care elsewhere. To briefly explain my views on that later thinking, I felt it necessary to refer to my own previous work more than might properly be ideal (a practice both required and bemoaned by my philosophical conscience).

and collected here will contribute in some small ways to a thoughtful rebirth of our philosophical thinking about death – a thinking and rethinking philosophers have never entirely left behind, but which nevertheless waxes and wanes with the tenor of the times.

Rethinking Death in and after Heidegger, as I intend it, also seeks to suggest both thinking *into* and *from* existential death – that is, repeatedly entering into and returning from a careful rethinking of this core existential phenomenon in its complex philosophical significance. The kind of "return from death" I have in sight turns out to be *authentic* and *phenomenological* rather than *oxymoronic* (as are attempts to efface or deny the undeniably strange and troubling reality of our experiences of our own death) or *faithful* (at least insofar as such faith commits the phenomenological heresy of letting second-hand hearsay trump first-personal acquaintance in eminently questionable matters each of us remain capable of thinking through for ourselves). Thinking through this phenomenological and therefore (as available to experience here in this world) *secular* rebirth from death does not seek to put to death all thought of rebirth. But the thoughts of rebirth articulated herein remain akin to that mythical serpent who must shed its old skin in order to grow, while categorically rejecting that reactionary tide of thanatological forces rising around the globe today, some still fanatically hoping for some global apocalypse that will mark the end of all time on earth, others sadistically happy to kill off our world's newest and so most vulnerable existential growths in vain hopes of moving backward in time – that most *ressentiment*-fueling impossibility, as Nietzsche helped teach Heidegger.[6]

Yet, if we cannot ever go backward in time, then why gather so much of my previous work rethinking death in and after Heidegger together, revise and develop it, and publish it as this book? Precisely to try to go forward in thought, if only by repeatedly taking a few halting steps into blustery headwinds of interpretive resistance. (Fortunately, these hermeneutic headwinds often turn out to be less formidable than they sought to appear, or so I have found.) Besides the luxury of being able to slow down and develop details that often had to be dropped or treated too quickly in independent essays, my motivation for publishing this book also comes from my recognition that some of the strongest support for the rethinking of death advanced here comes from the sometimes surprising ways it helps illuminate a wide nexus of

---

[6] "'This, indeed, this alone is what *revenge* is: the will's ill-will against time and its 'it was.'" (Friedrich Nietzsche, *Thus Spoke Zarathustra*, in W. Kaufman, ed. and trans., *The Portable Nietzsche* (New York: Viking Penguin Books, 1954), 252.) Nietzsche diagnoses the way our will-frustrating inability to change the past can turn us against the present and future. Heidegger painfully learns the same point not just about time but about history: human beings cannot move backward, and our vain attempts to do so unhappily degenerate into reactionary nihilism.

interconnected philosophical issues and thinkers. Plus, I have always found that the best way to write a book is to realize one day that you have already written most of it, a realization that perhaps provides some consolation for making the same less happy recognition about one's life (namely, that one has already lived most of it). If I find this *consoling*, at any rate, that is both because the rethinking of death undertaken throughout this work seems likely both to continue for as long as I do (since it has already accompanied almost every step of my existential journey thus far) and also to be carried on by others in their own ways long after I *am here* (as a *Dasein*). I think this hope is reasonable, especially since I happily acknowledge that I cannot foresee the directions such work will take. But such hopes and consolations should sound less strange *after* reading this work, so let this rethinking of death in and after Heidegger commence without further prefatorial preamble (or apparent peregrination).

ACKNOWLEDGMENTS

Thinking is thanking, as Heidegger said, that is, inevitably a *response* to what we have been given, gifts we can never fully count nor account for but which we do well to acknowledge with gratitude nonetheless. For all the genuinely helpful comments, criticisms, and encouragement on earlier versions of this work over the last two decades (and more) from so many friends, family, colleagues, and students, I would especially like to thank Jessica Avery, Anne Margaret Baxley, Kelly Becker, Jim Bodington, Albert Borgmann, William Bracken, Lee Braver, Adam Buben, Haley Burke, Taylor Carman, David Cerbone, Suraj Chaudhary, Susanne Claxton, Daniel Conway, Kaity Creasy, Ben Crowe, Steve Crowell, Jerry Doppelt, Ingo Farin, Arnold Farr, Megan Flocken, Rick Furtak, Francisco Gallegos, Hilary Gaskin, Theodore George, Charlie Guignon, West Gurley, Martin Hägglund, Beatrice Han-Pile, P.-J. Harter, John Haugeland, Kevin Hill, Piotr Hoffman, John Hughes, Tal Ben Itzhak, Brent Kalar, Charley Kalm, Eric Kaplan, Claire Katz, Stephan Käufer, Sean Kelly, Chad Kidd, Yong Du Kim, Cristina Lafont, Jonathan Lee, David Liakos, Paul Livingston, Leslie MacAvoy, Simone Mahrenholz, Wayne Martin, Denis McManus, Ian Moore, Stephen Mulhall, Ann Murphy, Achim Oberst, Mark Okrent, Raoni Padui, Mariah Partida, Geoffrey Pfeifer, Robert Pippin, John Preston, Mark Ralkowski, James Reid, John Richardson, Idris Robinson, Joe Rouse, Tao Ruspoli, Rajesh Sampath, Carlos Sánchez, Bob Sandmeyer, Joseph Schear, B. Scot Rousse, Robert Shafer, Ted Schatzki, Phil Schoenberg, Charles Siewert, Bob Stolorow, Kristi Sweet, Charles Taylor, Carolyn Thomas, Cap Thomson, Darian Thomson, Kirsten Krebs Thomson, Mungo Thomson, Tamsin Thomson, Marc Vinciguerra, Simon Walker, Aaron Wendland, Amy Wendling, Dale Wilkerson, Christian Wood, Julian Young, Nate Zuckerman, and my two anonymous referees for Cambridge. I also want to particularly express my gratitude for the way Bert Dreyfus and Jacques Derrida both generously encouraged this work from its very earliest inception (back in the twentieth century), to Bill Blattner for doing so much to inspire and improve it along the way, and to Mark Wrathall for consistently provoking me to go further with deep questions that initially seemed unanswerable and so repeatedly called for my authentic response. (I own the many flaws that remain, with resolve, but I also take some of the unresolved differences between our views as vouchsafing my postmodern hope that the great philosophical conversations and debates that helped shape and reshape all our work should never end.)

As that long (but inevitably incomplete) list of grateful acknowledgments suggests, *Rethinking Death in and after Heidegger* is largely composed of significantly revised and expanded versions of work that was first presented, discussed, and published elsewhere, and I want to thank all those whose thoughtful invitations and responses helped improve this work along the way as well as those who originally published my work and allowed me to make use of it here. An earlier version of Chapter 1 was given as a Philosophy Colloquium at the University of South Florida (January 11, 2013) and published in Mark A. Wrathall, ed., *The Cambridge Companion to Heidegger's* Being and Time (Cambridge: Cambridge University Press, 2013). Chapter 2 was first presented to the Southwest Seminar in Continental Philosophy (Colorado College, June 8, 2014) and the American Society for Existential Phenomenology (UC Berkeley, April 10, 2015) and published in Lee Braver, ed., *Division III of Heidegger's* Being and Time: *The Unanswered Question of Being* (Cambridge, MA: The MIT Press, 2015). Chapter 3 is composed of two earlier works, on the related topics of Heidegger's thinking on death and the nothing: The former was first presented at the American Society for Existential Phenomenology's "Bert Dreyfus Memorial conference" (Wake Forest University, September 23, 2017) and revisited for a Philosophy Department Colloquium at the University of Manitoba (October 13, 2017); the latter was first presented at the Southwest Seminar in Continental Philosophy (California State University Northridge, June 8, 2017). The two were delivered in a combined form as a keynote address to the North Texas Philosophical Association (Dallas, March 30, 2019) and in revised form as a lecture to the Post-Kantian European Philosophy Seminar at Oxford University (March 10, 2020). The two were then published separately as "Death (*Tod*)" and the "Nothing (*Nichts*)" in Mark Wrathall, ed., *The Heidegger Lexicon* (Cambridge: Cambridge University Press, 2021).

Chapter 4 was first presented to the International Society for Phenomenological Studies (Asilomar, California, July 17, 2004), then repeatedly revised for the World Congress of Phenomenology (Oxford University, August 20, 2004), a keynote address to the Graduate Student Philosophy Conference on "Philosophy as a Way of Life" (UNM, June 3, 2005), and finally as a Dean's Lecture at St. John's College (Santa Fe, New Mexico, April 20, 2006); an earlier version was published as "Heidegger's Perfectionist Philosophy of Education in *Being and Time*" in *Continental Philosophy Review* 37:4 (2005 [and that official date is backdated: it was actually first published in 2006]). Chapter 5 was first presented to the International Society for Phenomenological Studies (Asilomar, California, July 14, 2006), revised for a memorial conference for Carol White on "Time and Death" at Santa Clara University (California, April 28, 2007), and first published as "On the Advantages and Disadvantages of Reading Heidegger Backwards: White's *Time and Death*," *Inquiry* 50:1 (2007). An earlier version of Chapter 6 was first presented to the International Society for Phenomenological Studies (Asilomar, California, June 28, 2005), revised for the Colloquium on Contemporary European Philosophy (Brigham Young University, December 1, 2005), and first published as "Rethinking Levinas on Heidegger on Death," in *The Harvard Review of Philosophy*, Vol. XVI (Fall 2009). Chapter 7 was first delivered as a Keynote Address to the Southwest Society in Continental Philosophy (hosted virtually during the Pandemic by Texas A&M, CSU San Bernadino, and Pomona College, May 9, 2021); it is published here for the first time. Chapter 8 was never delivered but an earlier version was published as "Heideggerian Phenomenology and the Postmetaphysical Politics of Ontological Pluralism," in S. West Gurley and Geoffrey Pfeifer, eds., *Phenomenology and the Political* (London: Rowman & Littlefield, 2016). Chapter 9 first met the public as a Philosophy Colloquium at Denver Metropolitan University (November 14, 2014); an earlier version was published as "Against Immortality: Why Death Is Better than the Alternative" (coauthored with Jim Bodington), in Russell Blackford and Damian Broderick, eds., *Intelligence Unbound* (Oxford: Wiley-Blackwell, 2014).

If I would not wish the writing of this book on my worst enemies, that is only because I enjoyed and learned so much from it along the way – and why should they have all the fun? Instead, I commend it to the care of my friends (in the *philosophical* sense), all those who find *their own ways* of drawing its lessons, implications, flaws, and unfinished tasks and so come to participate in this ongoing philosophical conversation about the significance of death for themselves. (Whether we ever meet in person, our thinking will have met here. And that, I shall suggest, is something that remains worthwhile.)

A NOTE ON THE NOTES (*DA CAPO*)

For those new to my work, allow me to repeat my now standard warning: Some of us are footnote people, but many are not. For those who find detailed footnotes too distracting from the flow of the text, my perhaps obvious suggestion is: *Please do not feel compelled to read every note as you go.* If you have an unanswered question about a sentence, paragraph, or section that includes a note (or simply want to consult the secondary references), then you should read that note. With any luck your question will be answered there (and if it is not, then you will see that in fact I do not have *enough* notes). Otherwise, I invite you to read through the remaining notes at your leisure. Supplemental and specialized argument often gets conducted in the notes, and some *Holzwege* – other paths and views – can be found there as well. (The received view that by *Holzweg* Heidegger means "dead-end" is mistaken. In the prefatory epigraph to the collection of essays he titled *Holzwege*, Heidegger explains these as forest paths made by backwoods loggers and known to back-country hikers, meaning that a *Holzweg* is a path that leads to a place in the forest from which trees have been removed – in other words, to a *clearing*, a place where we can see the light through which we ordinarily see.)[1]

---

[1] On the full meaning of *Holzwege* (a crucial later Heideggerian term of art), see Chapter 2 and Thomson, *Heidegger, Art, and Postmodernity*, 83–4.

ABBREVIATIONS USED FOR WORKS BY HEIDEGGER

(Translations frequently amended)

AED	*Aus der Erfahrung des Denkens*. Neske: Pfullingen, 1954.
BaT	*Being and Truth*. G. Fried and R. Polt, trans. Bloomington, IN: Indiana University Press, 2010.
BC	*Basic Concepts*. G. E. Aylesworth, trans. Bloomington, IN: Indiana University Press, 1993.
BH	*Becoming Heidegger: On the Trail of His Early Occasional Writings, 1910–1927*, eds. Theodore Kisiel and Thomas Sheehan. Evanston, IL: Northwestern University Press, 2007.
BQP	*Basic Questions of Philosophy: Selected "Problems" of "Logic."* R. Rojcewicz and A. Schuwer, trans. Bloomington, IN: Indiana University Press, 1994.
BT	*Being and Time*. J. Macquarrie and E. Robinson, trans. New York: Harper & Row, 1962.
BTS	*Being and Time*. J. Stambaugh and D. Schmidt, trans. New York: SUNY Press, 2010.
CP	*Contributions to Philosophy (From Enowning)*. P. Emad and K. Maly, trans. Bloomington, IN: Indiana University Press, 1999.
CPC	*Country Path Conversations*. B. Davis, trans. Bloomington, IN: Indiana University Press, 2010.
CT	*The Concept of Time*. Ingo Farin, trans. London: Continuum, 2011.
DT	*Discourse on Thinking*. J. Anderson and E. Freund, trans. New York: Harper & Row, 1966.
EB	*Existence and Being*. W. Brock, trans. Washington, DC: Gateway, 1949.
EHP	*Elucidations of Hölderlin's Poetry*. K. Hoeller, trans. New York: Humanity Books, 2000.
EP	*The End of Philosophy*. J. Stambaugh, trans. New York: Harper & Row, 1973.
ET	*The Essence of Truth*. T. Sadler, trans. London: Continuum, 2002.
FCM	*The Fundamental Concepts of Metaphysics: World, Finitude, Solitude*. W. McNeill and N. Walker, trans. Bloomington, IN: Indiana University Press, 1995.

FS	*Four Seminars*. A. Mitchell and François Raffoul, trans. Bloomington, IN: Indiana University Press, 2003.
G	*Gelassenheit*. Pfulligen: Neske, 1959.
GA1	*Gesamtausgabe*, Vol. 1: *Frühe Schriften*. F.-W. von Herrmann, ed. Frankfurt: V. Klostermann, 1978.
GA2	*Sein und Zeit*. F.-W. von Herrmann, ed., Frankfurt: V. Klostermann, 1977.
GA3	*Gesamtausgabe*, Vol. 3: *Kant und das Problem der Metaphysik*. F.-W. von Herrmann, ed. Frankfurt: V. Klostermann, 1991.
GA4	*Gesamtausgabe*, Vol. 4: *Erläuterungen zu Hölderlins Dichtung*. F.-W. von Herrmann, ed. Frankfurt: V. Klostermann, 1981.
GA5	*Gesamtausgabe*, Vol. 5: *Holzwege*. F.-W. von Herrmann, ed. Frankfurt: V. Klostermann, 1977.
GA7	*Gesamtausgabe*, Vol. 7: *Vorträge und Aufsätze*. F.-W. von Herrmann, ed. Frankfurt a. M.: V. Klostermann, 2000.
GA8	*Gesamtausgabe*, Vol. 8: *Was Heißt Denken?* P.-L. Coriando, ed. Frankfurt a. M.: V. Klostermann, 2002.
GA9	*Gesamtausgabe*, Vol. 9: *Wegmarken*. F.-W. von Herrmann, ed. Frankfurt a. M.: V. Klostermann, 1976.
GA11	*Gesamtausgabe*, Vol. 11: *Identiät und Differenz*. F.-W. von Herrmann, ed. Frankfurt a. M.: V. Klostermann, 2006.
GA12	*Gesamtausgabe*, Vol. 12: *Unterwegs zur Sprache*. F.-W. von Herrmann, ed. Frankfurt a. M.: V. Klostermann, 1985.
GA13	*Gesamtausgabe*, Vol. 13: *Aus der Erfahrung des Denkens, 1910–1976*. H. Heidegger, ed. Frankfurt a. M.: V. Klostermann, 1983.
GA14	*Gesamtausgabe*, Vol. 14: *Zur Sache des Denkens*. F.-W. von Herrmann, ed. Frankfurt a. M.: V. Klostermann, 2007.
GA15	*Gesamtausgabe*, Vol. 15: *Seminare*. C. Ochwadt, ed. Frankfurt: V. Klostermann, 1986.
GA16	*Gesamtausgabe*, Vol. 16: *Reden und andere Zeugnisse eines Lebensweges, 1910–1976*. H. Heidegger, ed. Frankfurt: V. Klostermann, 2000.
GA18	*Gesamtausgabe*, Vol. 18: *Grundbegriffe der aristotelischen Philosophie*. Mark Michalski, ed. Frankfurt: V. Klostermann, 2002.
GA20	*Gesamtausgabe*, Vol. 20: *Prolegomena zur Geschichte des Zeitbegriffs*. P. Jaeger, ed. Frankfurt: V. Klostermann, 1979.
GA22	*Gesamtausgabe*, Vol. 22: *Die Grundbegriffe der antiken Philosophie*. Franz-Karl Blust, ed. Frankfurt: V. Klostermann, 1993.
GA24	*Gesamtausgabe*, Vol. 24: *Die Grundprobleme der Phänomenologie*. F.-W. von Herrmann, ed. Frankfurt: V. Klostermann, 1975.
GA26	*Gesamtausgabe*, Vol. 26: *Metaphysische Anfangsgründe der Logik im Ausgang von Leibniz*. K. Held, ed. Frankfurt: V. Klostermann, 1978

GA29-30	*Gesamtausgabe*, Vols. 29-30: *Die Grundbegriffe der Metaphysik: Welt, Endlichkeit, Einsamkeit*. F.-W. von Herrmann, ed. Frankfurt: V. Klostermann, 1983.
GA33	*Gesamtausgabe*, Vol. 33: *Aristoteles, Metaphysik Θ 1-3. Von Wesen und Wirklichkeit der Kraft*. Heinrich Hüni, ed. Frankfurt: V. Klostermann, 1981.
GA34	*Gesamtausgabe*, Vol. 34: *Vom Wesen der Wahrheit*. H. Mörchen, ed. Frankfurt: V. Klostermann, 1988.
GA38	*Gesamtausgabe*, Vol. 38: *Logik als die Frage nach dem Wesen der Sprache*. G. Seubold, ed., Frankfurt: V. Klostermann, 1998.
GA39	*Gesamtausgabe*, Vol. 39: *Hölderlins Hymnen "Germanien" und "Der Rhein."* S. Ziegler, ed., Frankfurt: V. Klostermann, 1980.
GA40	*Gesamtausgabe*, Vol. 40. *Einführung in die Metaphysik*. P. Jaeger, ed. Frankfurt: V. Klostermann, 1983.
GA43	*Gesamtausgabe*, Vol. 43. *Nietzsche: Der Wille zue Macht als Kunst*. B. Heimbüchel, ed. Frankfurt: V. Klostermann, 1985.
GA45	*Gesamtausgabe*, Vol. 45. *Grundfragen der Philosophie: Ausgewählte "Probleme" der "Logik."* F.-W. von Herrmann, ed. Frankfurt: V. Klostermann, 1984.
GA50	*Gesamtausgabe*, Vol. 50: *Nietzsches Metaphysik*. P. Jaeger, ed. Frankfurt: V. Klostermann, 1990.
GA51	*Gesamtausgabe*, Vol. 51: *Grundbegriffe*. P. Jaeger, ed. Frankfurt: V. Klostermann, 1981.
GA53	*Gesamtausgabe*, Vol. 55: *Hölderlin's Hymne "Der Ister."* W. Biemel, ed. Frankfurt: V. Klostermann, 1984.
GA61	*Gesamtausgabe*, Vol. 61: *Phänomenologische Interpretetationen zu Aristotles: Einführung in die Phänomenologische Forschung*. W Bröcker and K. Bröcker-Oltmanns, eds. Frankfurt: V. Klostermann, 1985.
GA65	*Gesamtausgabe*, Vol. 65: *Beiträge zur Philosophie (Vom Ereignis)*. F.-W. von Herrmann, ed. Frankfurt: V. Klostermann, 1989.
GA66	*Gesamtausgabe*, Vol. 66: *Besinnung*. F.-W. von Herrmann, ed. Frankfurt: V. Klostermann, 1997.
GA67	*Gesamtausgabe*, Vol. 67: *Metaphysik und Nihilismus*. H.-J. Friedrich, ed. Frankfurt: V. Klostermann, 1999.
GA69	*Gesamtausgabe*, Vol. 69: *Die Geschichte des Seyns*. P. Trawny, ed. Frankfurt: V. Klostermann, 1998.
GA75	*Gesamtausgabe*, Vol. 75: *Zu Hölderlin - Greichenlandreisen*. C. Ochwadt, ed. Frankfurt: V. Klostermann, 2000.
GA77	*Gesamtausgabe*, Vol. 77: *Feldweg-Gespräch*. I. Schüßler, ed. Frankfurt: V. Klostermann, 1995.
GA79	*Gesamtausgabe*, Vol. 79: *Bremer und Freiburger Vorträge*. P. Jaeger, ed. Frankfurt: V. Klostermann, 1994.

LIST OF ABBREVIATIONS   xxv

GA90   *Gesamtausgabe*, Vol. 90: *Zu Ernst Jünger.* P. Trawny, ed. Frankfurt:
        V. Klostermann, 2004.
GA96   *Gesamtausgabe*, Vol. 96: *Überlegungen XII–XV (Schwarze Hefte
        1939–1941).* P. Trawny, ed. Frankfurt: V. Klostermann, 2014.
GA97   *Gesamtausgabe*, Vol. 97: *Anmerkungen I–V (Schwarze Hefte
        1942–1948).* P. Trawny, ed. Frankfurt: V. Klostermann, 2015.
GA99   *Gesamtausgabe*, Vol. 99. *Bremer and Freiburger Vorträge*, ed. P. Jaeger.
        Frankfurt a. M.: Vittorio Klostermann, 1994.
GA102   *Gesamtausgabe*, Vol. 102. *Vorläufiges I–IV (Schwarze Hefte
        1963–1970).* P. Trawny, ed. Frankfurt a. M.: Vittorio
        Klostermann, 2022.
H   *Holzwege.* Frankfurt: V. Klostermann, 1994.
HB   "Selected Letters from the Heidegger-Blochmann Correspondence."
        F. Edler, trans. *Graduate Faculty Philosophy Journal* 14–15 (1992):
        559–77.
HBC   Heidegger, Martin, and Blochmann, Elisabeth. *Martin Heidegger,
        Elisabeth Blochmann, Briefwechsel 1918–1969.* J. W. Storck, ed.
        Marbach: Deutsche Literaturarchiv, 1989.
HCE   *Hegel's Concept of Experience.* Gray, trans. New York: Harper &
        Row, 1970.
HHI   *Hölderlin's Hymn "The Ister."* W. McNeill and J. Davis, trans.
        Bloomington, IN: Indiana University Press, 1996.
HCT   *History of the Concept of Time.* T. Kisiel, trans. Bloomington, IN:
        Indiana University Press, 1985.
HHGR   *Heidegger, Hölderlin's Hymns "Germania" and "The Rhine."*
        Bloomington, IN: Indiana University Press, 2014.
HR   *The Heidegger Reader.* G. Figal, ed. J. Veither, trans. Bloomington, IN:
        Indiana University Press, 2009.
ID   *Identity and Difference.* J. Stambaugh, trans. New York: Harper &
        Row, 1969.
IM   *Introduction to Metaphysics.* G. Fried and R. Polt, trans. New Haven,
        CT: Yale University Press, 2000.
KPM   *Kant and the Problem of Metaphysics.* R. Taft, trans. Bloomington, IN:
        Indiana University Press, 1997.
LQ   *Logic as the Question Concerning the Essence of Language.* W. T.
        Gregory and Y. Unna, trans. Albany, NY: State University of New
        York Press, 2009.
M   *Mindfulness.* P. Emad and T. Kalary, trans. London: Continuum,
        2006.
MFL   *Metaphysical Foundations of Logic.* M. Heim, trans. Bloomington, IN:
        Indiana University Press, 1984.
N1   *Nietzsche: The Will to Power as Art.* David Farrell Krell, ed. and trans.
        New York: Harper & Row, 1979.

N3	*Nietzsche: The Will to Power as Knowledge and as Metaphysics*. David Farrell Krell, ed. J. Stambaugh, D. F. Krell, and F. Capuzzi, trans. New York: Harper & Row, 1987.
N4	*Nietzsche: Nihilism*. David Farrell Krell, ed. F. Capuzzi, trans. New York: Harper & Row, 1982.
NHS	*Nature, History, State*. London: Bloomsbury, 2013.
NI	*Nietzsche*, Vol. I. Pfullingen: G. Neske, 1961.
NII	*Nietzsche*, Vol. II. Pfullingen: G. Neske, 1961.
OBT	*Off the Beaten Path*. J. Young and K. Haynes, eds. and trans. Cambridge: Cambridge University Press, 2002.
OWL	*On the Way to Language*. P. Hertz, trans. San Francisco: Harper & Row, 1971.
P	*Pathmarks*. William McNeill, ed. Cambridge: Cambridge University Press, 1998.
PIA	*Phenomenological Interpretations of Aristotle: Initiation into Phenomenological Research*. R. Rojcewicz, trans. Bloomington, IN: Indiana University Press, 2001.
PLT	*Poetry, Language, Thought*. A. Hofstadter, trans. New York: Harper & Row, 1971.
Pre	"Preface" to William Richardson, *Through Phenomenology to Thought*. The Hague: Martinus Nijhoff, viii–xxiii, 1967
PXII–XV	*Ponderings XII–XV: Black Notebooks 1939–1941*. R. Rojcewicz, trans. Bloomington, IN: Indiana University Press, 2017.
QA	*Martin Heidegger and National Socialism: Questions and Answers*. Günther Neske and Emil Kettering, eds. L. Harries, trans. New York, Paragon House, 1990.
QCT	*The Question Concerning Technology*. W. Lovitt, trans. New York: Harper & Row, 1977.
SZ	*Sein und Zeit*. Tübingen: M. Niemeyer, 1993.
TB	*On Time and Being*. J. Stambaugh, trans. New York: Harper & Row, 1972.
TTL	"Traditional Language and Technological Language." W. T. Gregory, trans. *Journal of Philosophical Research* XXIII (1998), 129–45.
UK1	"Vom Ursprung des Kunstwerks: Erste Ausarbeitung." *Heidegger Studies* 5 (1989), 1–22.
USTS	*Überlieferte Sprache und Technische Sprache*. H. Heidegger, ed. St. Gallen: Erker-Verag, 1989.
WBGM	"The Way Back into the Ground of Metaphysics" (orig. 1956). In *Existentialism from Dostoevsky to Sartre*. Kaufmann, ed. New York: Penguin, 1975.
WCT	*What Is Called Thinking?* J. G. Gray, trans. New York: Harper & Row, 1968.

PART I

Rethinking Death in Heidegger

1

Death and Demise in *Being and Time*

> Mortals die their death in life.
>
> Martin Heidegger[1]

1.1 Introduction: The State of the Debate

This introductory chapter seeks to answer the question of what Heidegger means by "death" (*Tod*) in *Being and Time* – and *begin* to justify that answer.[2] I take up this weighty topic with some trepidation (if not quite fear and trembling) in part because to say that the meaning of "death" in *Being and Time* is controversial is to strain the limits of understatement. In addition to the emotionally freighted nature of the topic itself (to which we will return), I think four main factors contribute to and perpetuate this controversy: (1) Heidegger's confusing *terminology*; (2) the *centrality* of the issue to the text as a whole; (3) the *demanding* nature of what is required to adjudicate the matter; and (4) the radically *polarized* scholarly literature on the subject. One of my main goals here is to suggest a way to move beyond the controversy that currently divides the field, so let me begin by saying a bit about its four main contributing factors.

The first and most obvious cause of the controversy is that those passages in *Being and Time* where Heidegger describes phenomenologically what he means (and does not mean) by "death" are initially quite obscure. Heidegger deliberately employs a non-commonsensical terminology, for example, when he *formally defines* "the full existential-ontological concept of death" in the following important but initially ambiguous terms: "*death, as the end of Dasein, is Dasein's ownmost, non-relational, certain and as such indefinite, and non-surpassable possibility*" (BT 303/SZ 258–9), and again, more notoriously,

---

[1] "*Die Sterblichen sterben den Tod im Leben.*" Martin Heidegger, "Hölderlin's Earth and Heaven [1959]" (EHP 190/GA4 165).

[2] I say "begin" because I think some of the best evidence for the reading advanced here is the revealing light it casts on the interconnected issues taken up in subsequent chapters, which develop and extend aspects of this analysis while also focusing on details and implications of the view not addressed here (as well as addressing some critical responses to it).

when he characterizes death "*as the possibility of the impossibility of existence in general*" (BT 307/SZ 262 [translations frequently emended]). Conversely, and even more confusingly (at least for unwary readers), he also misleadingly employs an only apparently commonsensical terminology, using ordinary words such as "death," "demise," "perishing," "possibility," and "existence [that is, *Dasein*]" in ways that turn out to have decidedly non-commonsensical meanings. We will therefore need to spend a significant amount of time clarifying some of Heidegger's crucial philosophical terms of art in what follows.

The second source of the controversy is that a great deal turns on Heidegger's phenomenological analysis of death. John Haugeland rightly observes that "death, as Heidegger means it, is not merely relevant but in fact the fulcrum of Heidegger's entire ontology."[3] The main reason death plays such an important part in the overarching ontological project of *Being and Time*, in a nutshell, is that the experience of the phenomenon Heidegger calls "death" discloses "futurity," which (as we will see at the end of this chapter) is itself the first horizon we encounter of *originary temporality*, that most fundamental structure of intelligibility that makes possible any understanding of being at all (or so the early Heidegger of *Being and Time* believes).[4] Even more to the point for us here, death is also crucial to the text's existential ambitions because readers must understand death in order to understand *authenticity* (as well as such other interconnected notions as *anxiety*, *conscience*, *guilt*, and the *solus ipse* or "self alone").[5] This doubly pivotal role played by Heidegger's phenomenology of death in *Being and Time* means that

---

[3] See John Haugeland, "Truth and Finitude: Heidegger's Transcendental Existentialism," in *Heidegger, Authenticity, and Modernity: Essays in Honor of Hubert L. Dreyfus*, Volume 1, ed. by Mark Wrathall and Jeff Malpas (Cambridge, MA: MIT, 2000), 44.

[4] *Temporality* is the most fundamental structure of intelligibility *accessible to phenomenology*, in the early Heidegger's view. (See also William Blattner, *Heidegger's Temporal Idealism* [Cambridge: Cambridge University Press, 1999].) As we will see later, in "genuine anxiety," our being is, or becomes, sheer becoming; we exist as a pure or empty existing, deprived of the practical world. ("As we will see later" – as a phrase by which something still to come enters into and makes itself felt in our present – is not itself a bad indication of what "futurity" means.)

[5] Such "understanding" is not meant by Heidegger to be merely cognitive or intellectual but, rather, primarily something we personally instantiate or *stand-under* (such that our intelligible worlds are implicitly organized in its terms). Indeed (at the risk of being too provocative at the outset), *Being and Time* repeatedly contends that *each of us must pass through existential death in order to reach authenticity*. (But because this is a death of the lived possibilities that organize our worldly selves rather than a mortal demise, Heidegger does not thereby presuppose any kind of metaphysical afterlife.) What is more, I show below (and would try to demonstrate thoroughly, were I offering a broader interpretation of *Being and Time* here) that the multifaceted phenomenon disclosed by death turns out to be absolutely central to almost all of the subsequent phenomenological analyses in Division II of *Being and Time*, many of which disclose interconnected aspects of the same phenomenon (see n. 6) or trace its roots and subsequent implications.

1.1. INTRODUCTION: THE STATE OF THE DEBATE

critical readers of the text cannot indefinitely postpone the difficult task of coming to terms with Heidegger's understanding of the phenomenon.

That brings us directly to the third reason for the controversy surrounding the meaning of death in *Being and Time*, which is that the phenomenological method we are supposed to use to adjudicate the matter is particularly difficult to employ in this crucial case. The problem, put simply, is that many readers seem to have trouble experiencing the *phenomenon* that Heidegger describes as "death" for themselves. Without such first-personal experience, however, readers can neither contest nor confirm *Being and Time*'s existential phenomenology of death. It is worth emphasizing that this is a general problem for critical readers of phenomenological works: Absent our own experience of the phenomenon at issue, we can neither attest to that phenomenon and its purported significance (and so confirm or develop it for ourselves) nor testify against it (and so seek to contest, refine, or redescribe it). This general phenomenological problem is greatly exacerbated in the case of death, however, because unlike phenomenological descriptions of more mundane phenomena (such as using a hammer, staring at a Gestalt figure or optical illusion, or even such unsettling experiences as being stared at by a stranger or feeling the pangs of a guilty conscience), the phenomenon by means of which we first encounter what Heidegger means by "death" – namely, the affective attunement of "'real' or 'authentic' anxiety" (*"eigentliche" Angst*), in which, as we will see, we experience ourselves as radically "not-at-home" in the world of our everyday projects – is both quite "rare" (BT 234/SZ 190) and extremely difficult to endure.[6]

The requirement that we must personally undergo an anguished experience of the utter desolation of the self in order to be able to testify for or against the adequacy of Heidegger's phenomenological analysis of death thus seems

---

[6] As Heidegger puts it, "this primordial anxiety . . . clears away everything covering over the fact that Dasein has been abandoned to itself. The 'nothing' with which anxiety brings us face to face unveils the nullity [or "emptiness," *Nichtigkeit*] by which Dasein, in its very *basis*, is defined; and this basis itself *is* as thrownness into death" (BT 356/SZ 308). Hence: "Being-toward-death is essentially anxiety" (BT 310/SZ 266; see also BT 295/SZ 251). Blattner nicely articulates this connection in terms of Heidegger's three inextricably interconnected *existentials* (that is, structures that condition all existence): "Death is the self-understanding that belongs to this experience, anxiety is the mood, and conscience its discourse" (see William Blattner, *Heidegger's Being and Time: A Reader's Guide* [London: Continuum, 2006], 140). By "primordial" (*ursprüngliche*) or "real or authentic anxiety," Heidegger means anxiety that stems not from individual physiological peculiarities or unrelated neurochemical imbalances but, instead, from the ontological structure of the self, specifically, from what I shall explain as the "uncanny" lack of fit between the empty self at our volitional and intentional, existential core, on the one hand, and the practical world of particular ontic and existentiell choices by which we give this self concrete, worldly meaning, on the other (see also n. 74). This lack of any perfect fit between self and world is common to everyone whether we realize it or not, Heidegger suggests (we will see), and so the source of an ineliminable undercurrent of existential anxiety in all our everyday lives.

excessively demanding. Indeed, Heidegger recognizes this and acknowledges that this demand "remains, from the existentiell point of view [that is, from the ordinary perspective of our individual lives and everyday concerns], a fantastically unreasonable demand [*eine phantastische Zumutung*]" (BT 311/SZ 266).[7] Nonetheless, without experiencing the phenomenon at issue for ourselves, we can at best approach Heidegger's phenomenological descriptions of death from the outside, and so find them, for example, suggestive, impressive, or deep-sounding, or else fanciful, idiosyncratic, or even absurd – all surface-level reactions with which no true *philosopher* (as a literal "lover of wisdom," that is, of *practical*, life-guiding knowledge) and certainly no existential phenomenologist should ever rest content.[8]

I find it revealing to contrast those kinds of superficial evaluations – typical of but not limited to neophyte readings of *Being and Time* – with the critical interpretations advanced in the late 1940s by Heidegger's first "existentialist" readers, especially Levinas but also, to a lesser degree, Sartre. As we will see (in Chapters 6 and 7), both Levinas and Sartre sought to contest and revise Heidegger's phenomenology of death by drawing on their own experiences of the phenomenon at issue (or, in Sartre's case, his experience of an alternative but arguably analogous phenomenon, namely, "the look of the other [person]," which is similarly supposed to result in "the death of my [lived] possibilities").[9] Perhaps the commendable quest for scholarly objectivity, which has yielded important advances in clarity and argumentative precision

---

[7] Heidegger's use of this term has faint Kierkegaardian echoes, since a *Zumutung* is the kind of completely "*unreasonable* demand" that the Judeo-Christian God legendarily requires of Abraham by commanding him to sacrifice his only son (who is still a child) after having promised the now elderly Abraham that his descendants would one day be as plentiful as grains of sand on the beach or stars in the sky (that is, a demand that goes against the rationality of our preexisting worldly cares and concerns).

[8] For the Heidegger of *Being and Time*, philosophy must be phenomenological: "Ontology and phenomenology are not two distinct philosophical disciplines among others. These terms characterize philosophy itself with regard to its object and its way of treating that object. Philosophy is universal phenomenological ontology" (BT 62/SZ 38). (We return to this point in the Concluding Recapitulations.) As we will see in Chapter 2, Heidegger will later abandon this project of fundamental ontology (the attempt to understand "the meaning of being in general") and, with it, "philosophy" itself (which he will then identify with the pursuit of the very "metaphysics" he later tries to help us *think* beyond).

[9] (See Jean-Paul Sartre, *Being and Nothingness: A Phenomenological Essay on Ontology*, trans. by H. E. Barnes [New York: Philosophical Library, 1956 [original 1943]], 271, 288; and Emmanuel Levinas, *Time and the Other*, trans. by R. A. Cohen [Pittsburgh: Duquesne University Press, 1987].) When a stranger stares at me, Sartre will argue (using his famous phenomenological example of being caught looking through a keyhole), my subjectivity temporarily becomes objectified by this stranger's gaze; that is, I implicitly experience myself not as stretching out into a world of practical projects that implicitly define me but, instead, as caught and frozen by this stranger's stare like a bug on a pin, transformed by a subjectivity outside myself into one (for me inaccessible and so

1.1. INTRODUCTION: THE STATE OF THE DEBATE 7

over the last century, has also rendered us much more reluctant to inject ourselves into the discussion by testing Heidegger's descriptions for ourselves (where that also means testing them *on* ourselves, that is, comparing them to our own first-personal encounters with the phenomenon at issue). Or perhaps Heidegger's own appalling misadventure with Nazism has led interpreters to distance themselves from the fact that, as he acknowledged in *Being and Time*, "a definite ontic interpretation of authentic existence, a factical ideal of Dasein, underlies our ontological interpretation" (BT 358/SZ 310).[10]

---

unknowable) objective moment, my lived possibilities suddenly reduced to nothing but an actuality from which I remain alienated. ("In the look, the death of my possibilities makes me experience the other's freedom; . . . and I am myself, inaccessible to myself and yet myself, thrown and abandoned within the other's freedom." Jean-Paul Sartre, *Being and Nothingness: An Essay in Phenomenological Ontology*, trans. by Sarah Richmond [New York: Washington Square, 2021[original 1943]], 369.) Levinas, for his part, still explicitly discusses "anguish" and "death" in terms very close to Heidegger's – indeed, much closer than is usually recognized.

[10] This important and often overlooked passage runs, in full (with my explanatory gloss in brackets): "Is there not, however, a definite ontic way of taking authentic existence, a factical ideal of Dasein, underlying our ontological interpretation of Dasein's existence? That is in fact the case. [Here Heidegger is acknowledging that *Being and Time*'s description of the ontological structure of authentic existence is in fact an idealized portrayal drawn from his own particular way of experiencing such a transformation from inauthenticity to authenticity himself.] But this fact is not only one which must not be denied and which we are forced to concede; it must also be conceived in its *positive necessity*, in terms of the object that we have taken as the theme of our investigation. [In other words, phenomenology *always* draws on our own individual experiences of things. Just as we can only work to uncover the fundamental ontological "meaning of being in general" by first drawing on the unthematized, "pre-ontological" understanding of what things are that remains implicit in our own practical knowledge, so, he is suggesting here, we can only develop a formal description of authenticity as a possible existential structure by drawing on our own individual ways of experiencing such a transition to authenticity for ourselves.] Philosophy will never seek to deny its 'presuppositions' [that is, phenomenology should never deny that its insights emerge from the phenomenologist's own individual life and hence particular way of experiencing things], but neither may philosophy simply admit them [in that individual form, because that would risk introducing merely idiosyncratic elements into phenomenology. Rejecting both those options, Heidegger's phenomenology instead pursues the following third path.] Philosophy conceives these presuppositions themselves [that is, phenomenology seeks to rigorously *conceptualize* the basic structures that underlie and condition the phenomena it examines, "ontological" structures that make possible our most common ways of experiencing and describing these everyday "ontic" phenomena] and it unfolds these [ontological structural] presuppositions with increasing vividness together with that for which they are presuppositions [namely, the ordinary, ontic phenomena that these structures purportedly condition]. This is the function that the methodological considerations demanded of us now have" (BT 358/SZ 31. See also BT 360/SZ 312: "Unless we have an existentiell [or particular individual] understanding, all analysis of existentiality will remain groundless.") As a result, there is a (self-enriching) *feedback loop* between individual life and phenomenology (so that everyday life informs phenomenology, which

Yet, should not Heidegger's admission that his phenomenological analyses derive ultimately from his own idealized personal experiences have precisely the opposite effect? That is, should not Heidegger's demonstration of his own susceptibility to the grossest errors of judgment instead encourage us to subject his phenomenological analyses to the most careful scrutiny for ourselves, as his early existentialist readers undoubtedly sought to do, in part for this very reason?[11] Because it is only by relying on such personal experience that one can develop either an internal confirmation or an immanent critique of Heidegger's phenomenology of death, the post-existentialist interpretations of Heidegger seem to me to have made a significant step backward in this critical regard (with a few important exceptions that we will note along the way), so it will thus be worthwhile to examine those earlier interpretations in some detail.

Finally, the fourth reason for the persistent controversy about the meaning of "death" in *Being and Time* is that, owing to the combined effect of the aforementioned factors, the interpretive field is now radically polarized, with the secondary literature starkly divided into two diametrically opposed and seemingly incommensurable camps. In the first (and much larger) camp, most traditional scholars, critics, and readers of *Being and Time* adopt the straightforward view that, by "death," Heidegger must mean the same sort of things that we normally mean when we talk about "death," such as *demise* (Edwards), *decease* (Hoffman), or *mortality* (Mulhall). In the second (and significantly smaller) camp, a number of cutting-edge Heidegger scholars think that what *Being and Time* means by "death" has almost nothing to do with the ordinarily sense of the word (or that the two senses of "death" share a merely "metaphorical" connection, as Haugeland believes). Instead, Heidegger means something like *the global collapse of significance* typified by a depressive episode (Blattner), *the collapse of an understanding of being* exemplified by a scientific paradigm shift (Haugeland), or *the end of an historical world*, which allows a new historical epoch to take shape (White).[12]

---

then conceptualizes its conditioning structures in ways that should deepen, enrich, and transform life). Thus, part of the test of any phenomenological analysis will be how well it deepens, enriches, or transforms our everyday experience of the phenomenon whose underlying structures it seeks to conceptualize (as we shall see in the case of death here, and as I showed in the case of art in Iain Thomson, *Heidegger, Art, and Postmodernity* [Cambridge: Cambridge University Press, 2011], chs. 3–4).

[11] On the relation of Heidegger's Nazism to his philosophy, see esp. Iain Thomson, *Heidegger on Ontotheology: Technology and the Politics of Education* (Cambridge: Cambridge University Press, 2005), chs. 3–4, and "Heidegger's Nazism in the Light of His Early *Black Notebooks*: A View from America," in *Zur Hermeneutik der 'Schwarzen Hefte': Heidegger Jahrbuch 10*, ed. by Alfred Denker and Holger Zaborowski (Freiburg: Karl Alber, 2017). (Some of these issues will come back in Chapters 6–8.)

[12] See Paul Edwards, *Heidegger's Confusions* (New York: Prometheus, 2004) (which reprints Edward's incredibly confused articles from 1975 and 1976); Piotr Hoffman, "Death, Time, History: Division II of Being and Time," in *The Cambridge Companion to*

Despite the hermeneutic liberties taken by Haugeland and White (and consequent problems with their readings), I shall argue that the second camp is much closer to Heidegger's understanding of death as an existential phenomenon that stands revealed when the practical intelligibility of our everyday worlds collapses. Still, the interpretations of death in terms of existential world-collapse advanced by this second camp leave it largely baffling why Heidegger should call the phenomenon he is interested in "death." Indeed, his doing so only seems to muddy the waters of *Being and Time*, thereby encouraging the much more commonsensical misreadings of death as mortal demise that are typical of the first camp. To such a charge of misreading, moreover, those in the first camp will respond forcefully that (as Hoffman once objected to me): "One can stretch the meanings of words, but only so far: *Up* cannot mean *down*; *black* cannot mean *white*, and *death* cannot mean *something that you can live through!*"

Though the endeavor might initially seem rather unlikely, in what follows I would like to suggest a way beyond the current deadlock over the meaning of "death" in *Being and Time*. What I shall show is that if we understand the phenomenological method *Being and Time* employs, then we can see exactly how Heidegger is able to move from our relation to the event we ordinarily call *death* (which *Being and Time* calls "demise") to that ontological phenomenon, revealed in world-collapse, which he calls "death." To follow this path, we need to avoid conflating Heidegger's existential conception of death with that experience of the end of our lives that he calls "demise," as the first camp tends to do, but we also cannot treat demise and death as radically heterogeneous phenomena, as those in the second camp tend to do. Instead, we need to understand how "death" is *both distinguished from and related to* "demise" if we want to transcend these long-standing hermeneutic controversies and begin to grasp the full existential-ontological significance of "death" in *Being and Time*. That will be the main goal of this introductory chapter.

Heidegger, ed. by Charles Guignon (Cambridge: Cambridge University Press, 1993), 195–214; Stephen Mulhall, "Human Mortality: Heidegger on How to Portray the Impossible Possibility of Dasein," in *Dreyfus and Wrathall, A Companion to Heidegger* (Oxford: Blackwell, 2005), 297–310; William Blattner, "The Concept of Death in *Being and Time*," *Man and World*, 27:1 (1994), 49–70 (Blattner's 1994 article is the seminal work for this way of reading Heidegger); Haugeland, "Truth and Finitude"; and Carol J. White, *Time and Death: Heidegger's Analysis of Finitude*, ed. by Mark Ralkowski (Aldershot: Ashgate, 2005). With the exception of Edwards's confused polemics, these are all serious and informed scholars, and a detailed response to their views (which I am simplifying here) would be a worthy but massive undertaking. But for a detailed critique of White's interpretation, see Chapter 5.

1.2 What It Means for Us to *Be*: Dasein (Preliminary Excursus)

Repeatedly in *Being and Time*, "'death' is *defined* as the end of Dasein" (BT 292, my emphasis/SZ 247). In other words, the phenomenon Heidegger calls *death* refers to the particular type of "end" that is distinctive to "Dasein" as the living embodiment of an intelligible world. It will thus help to briefly remind ourselves what Heidegger means by "*Dasein*" (so that we will then be able to understand what it means for our own Dasein to end). It has become standard practice to leave Heidegger's German term untranslated in English, but "Dasein" is his famous term of art for our distinctive kind of "existence" (*existence* is the ordinary meaning of the German word *Dasein*), and he deliberately uses the term to characterize the nature of our existence (in a minimally question-begging way) as an intelligible world disclosing "being-here" (or "*Da-sein*"). As Dreyfus nicely explains, *Being and Time*'s "primary concern is to raise the [ontological] question of being" (that is, "to make sense of our ability to make sense of things"), and Heidegger focuses on our "being-here" as "Dasein" in order to broach "ontological questions concerning the sort of beings we [human beings] are and how our being is bound up with the intelligibility of the world."[13]

As Heidegger's thought develops, he will increasingly hyphenate "*Da-sein*" to emphasize the significance of the two semantic elements from which the word is composed, "here-" (*Da-*) and "being" (*Sein*); as he later liked to put it, we are both *the here of being* and *the being of the here*.[14] In other words, *Dasein* names both (1) the existential place where being takes place (the site where intelligibility becomes an issue for itself, or metaphorically put, where being looks at itself in the mirror and tries to understand itself) and also (2) the specific way

---

[13] (Hubert L. Dreyfus, *Being-in-the-World: A Commentary on Heidegger's Being and Time, Division I* [Cambridge, MA: The MIT Press, 1990], 3, 10.) As Dreyfus suggests, the English "human being" (which can designate both a way of being and an individual) comes closest to Heidegger's use of "Dasein" and "a Dasein" in *Being and Time* (ibid., 14). As is well known, however, Heidegger vociferously rejected "anthropological" misunderstandings of *Being and Time* (which would reduce his work to an attempt to understand "the being of the human," an effort that Heidegger – insofar as he did indeed engage in it – always meant to serve the larger ambition of "fundamental ontology," viz., the attempt to understand "the meaning of being in general," as we will see in Chapter 2). But for this and other reasons, it has now become common to misunderstand Heidegger in almost the opposite terms, as an "anti-humanist." In truth, however, from beginning to end, "*Heidegger is an affirmative thinker of the ontological essence of the human being,* that is, *an ontological humanist* dedicated to disclosively thinking the being definitive of the human being" (as I show in Chapter 4 and in Iain Thomson, "Hearing the Pro-Vocation within the Provocation: Heidegger on the Way to Post-Metaphysical Humanism," *Gatherings: The Heidegger Circle Annual*, XII [2022], 187).

[14] "To characterize with a single term both the involvement of being in human nature and the essential relation of humanity to the openness ('here' [*Da*]) of being as such, the name 'being-here' [Dasein] was chosen" (WBGM 270).

1.2. WHAT DASEIN MEANS

this existential place becomes intelligible to itself (for example, by subconsciously employing a set of universal existential structures, or "existentials," the detailed articulation of which forms the main subject matter of the "existential analytic" in *Being and Time*'s first division, which thereby analyzes the structure of Dasein's "being-in-the-world," to which we will return).[15]

"Dasein" is thus Heidegger's philosophical shorthand for a detailed story in which the intelligibility of the "here" that we *are* (as a first-personal disclosure of an intelligible world) both helps constitute and is partly constituted by our preexisting sense of what it means to *be* anything at all (a prior "understanding of being" that ordinarily passes unnoticed, like the prescription on the lenses through which we see).[16] In *Being and Time*, the early Heidegger shows that

---

[15] ("Division I" makes up roughly the first half of *Being and Time* as it was published, albeit not as it was planned – an important proviso I will explain in Chapter 2.) Heidegger clearly employs the tools of conceptual analysis in *Being and Time*. He does so, however, not to try to define some new philosophical position into existence out of the logical space of possible options but, instead, to help analyze and develop the larger significance of a momentous phenomenon he has experienced in his own life, since Heidegger's version of existential phenomenology is empty and pointless without such first-personal experience, as we will see repeatedly (see also n. 10).

[16] In fact, Heidegger's account of the relation of mutual conditioning between Dasein and being will turn out to be considerably more complex than he initially recognized in *Being and Time* (though we can bracket most of these complications until Chapters 2 and 4). Put simply, the (more idealistic) early Heidegger of *Being and Time* thinks of our understanding of being as something we unknowingly constitute by subconsciously employing temporal structures as necessary and sufficient *transcendental conditions* that most deeply shape our intelligible worlds (thus Heidegger describes *Being and Time*'s goal to "expose primordial time ... as the condition which makes the everyday experience of time *both possible and necessary*" [BT 381, my emphasis/SZ 333], although this ambitious goal fails, as we shall see in Chapter 2), whereas the (more realistic) later Heidegger thinks of our understanding of being as shaped by historically changing ontotheological structures that are largely inherited from our historical tradition. But *Being and Time* already begins to recognize that we Dasein are entities whose existence as embodied ways of being implicitly answer the question of what it means for us to be, and also that these particular existential answers always borrow (in multiple ways) from our preexisting answer to the larger ontological question of what it means to be anything at all. Most importantly, for example, *Being and Time* argues (in Division One) that our taken-for-granted *modern* answer to the ontological question (in which we understand ourselves as "subjects" ontologically separated from and so *standing-over against* "objects" [*Gegenstand*]) "disastrously" misunderstands (BT 46/SZ 25) and so obscures our deeper nature *as* Dasein (that is, entities whose "usual and ordinary" practical ways of disclosing being in time "always-already" bridge and so undermine the supposed ontological gulf that post-Cartesian modernity posits between subjects and objects). In *Being and Time*, however, this "disaster" seems to be primarily for our philosophical self-understanding, whereas for the later Heidegger, the broader (and ever more pervasively embodied) ramifications of this philosophical disaster of modern "subjectivism" take on increasingly world-historical proportions, especially as such modern "subjectivism" continues to evolve historically into the late-modern epoch of technological "enframing" in which we now find ourselves

every Dasein already embodies an answer to the question of the meaning of its own being. This largely implicit *existential answer* to the question of the meaning of my own being may or may not be recognized as such, but it is nevertheless embodied concretely in the ways I go about *being* a teacher, father, husband, friend, brother, citizen, nature-lover, bike-rider, and so on. This embodied stand each of us takes on what it means to be can of course be more or less coherent, honest, thoughtful, unique, and so on, but for the early Heidegger the crucial issue here is just whether or not we *own up to* being this

trapped (see Iain Thomson, "Post/Modernity? How to Separate the Stereo from the Styrofoam," *Gatherings: The Heidegger Circle Annual*, XI [2021], 183–97). As a result, *for the later Heidegger (beginning in the late-1930s), Dasein increasingly becomes a prescriptive existential achievement* (and eventually even a literally "postmodern" way of being-in-the-world) *rather than just an unbiased phenomenological description of our distinctive way of being*. In other words, as we will begin to see in Chapter 4 (and I argue in Thomson, *Heidegger, Art, and Postmodernity*), Dasein becomes something we need to understand ourselves in terms of – and so progressively transform ourselves into – in order to find our way beyond the historical "epochs" of modern "subjectivism" and late-modern "enframing," in whose reductive and nihilistic ontologies we all tend initially to understand ourselves, owing to our current place in the "history of being" (*Seinsgeschichte*), the historical succession of different ways of understanding "the being of entities" that the later Heidegger discovers at the metaphysical core of the West. (Heidegger's later *history of being* designates the succession of historical epochs that take shape around the different answers metaphysics gives us to the question of what it means to be anything at all. These typically taken-for-granted, metaphysical answers to the question of what it means to be profoundly shape the history of the West, in which, put simply, to *be* an entity means, successively, to be a presocratic "whooshing-up" [*phusis*], a medieval "creature" of God, a modern "object" for a subject to master and control, a late-modern "resource" ["*Bestand*"] on standby for efficient ordering and enhancement, or even a postmodern, polysemic world-discloser, in tune with being's inexhaustibility and so seeking poetically to compose its polysemic disclosures meaningfully.) In *Being and Time*, Heidegger has not yet situated his existential analysis "ontohistorically" (that is, in terms of that later "history of being"), so his most famous early work suggests that all typical adult humans are basically *already* Dasein (and just need to recognize that to correct the philosophical errors that follow from modern subject/object dualism). The early Heidegger thus lacks most of his later story about the transformative power of metaphysics to reshape entire epochs of intelligibility (as I show in ch. 1 of Thomson, *Heidegger on Ontotheology*). But for Heidegger, both early and late, there is still a sense in which we need to doubly *realize* that we are Dasein (that is, both *recognize* what that means and also *embody* that truth in our lives, so that we transformatively "become what we are"), though the difficulties for and consequences of that double realization continue to ramify dramatically as his thinking develops. In the end, however, these two views of what it means to be "Dasein" (that is, his earlier, more *descriptive* view and his later, more *prescriptive* one) are largely compatible, since the later view dramatically builds on and complicates the earlier one. (If that were all the orthodox Heideggerians meant when they asserted that the early and later Heidegger were just saying identical things in different ways, then I would partly agree with them. They go much further, however, and assert that Heidegger never changed his mind about what "being" [*Sein*] means, which is not only false but deeply misleading, as we will see in Chapters 2 and 5.)

1.2. WHAT DASEIN MEANS

individual stand on what it means to be, taking *ownership* of (and so responsibility for) who we are in transformative moments of what *Being and Time* calls "ownedness or authenticity [*Eigentlichkeit*]."

Being and Time's "existential analytic" endeavors primarily to explicate a tripartite group of the universal "existential structures" ("existentials" or "*existentialia*" for short) that underlie and condition *all* our different, particular individual (or "*existentiell*") ways of embodying living answers to this existential question of what it means for us to be.[17] Despite the enduring importance of *Being and Time*'s analyses of Dasein's hidden existential structure, Heidegger originally intended their discovery and articulation to serve primarily as a stepping-stone to his grander *ontological* ambition.[18] Ultimately, *Being and Time*'s guiding hope is that uncovering the three main existential structures that condition all our specific ways of existing (and then tracing these existentials back to the even deeper "temporal horizons" that underlie and condition the existentials in turn) would "prepare" him to answer the most *fundamental ontological* question of "the meaning of being in general," that is, the metaphysical question of what it means to *be* anything at all.

As we will see in Chapter 2, Heidegger is quite clear in *Being and Time* that his ultimate goal is to uncover a "fundamental ontology" that finally answers

---

[17] I put it this way here because *Being and Time* suggests that this existential question ("What is the meaning of my own being?") is something especially conformist people (for example, those who manage to go about doing everything the way *one is expected* to do things) may never confront at all (see, for example, the first sentence of section 8 [BT 63/SZ 39]). But this embodied question of the meaning of my own being (Heidegger also argues) is rendered not just salient but virtually unavoidable in existential death. That is because (we will see) existential death is a stark, desolate, and aporetic condition of existential breakdown in which we find ourselves at least temporarily unable to be the self that we were *and yet still exist* and *must thus find a way to go on*, a condition that *presses* us into taking an embodied stand on the meaning of our own being – that very stand whereby we achieve "authenticity" (*Eigentlichkeit*, literally "ownedness") by taking ownership of our own existences (however temporarily). The provocative conclusion that suggests itself here is that *das Man* as such never dies in Heidegger's existential sense. (*Das Man* is Heidegger's name for the ubiquitous and superficial understand of things reinforced by "the [anonymous] anyone.") White, Haugeland, and (building on Haugeland's work) Lear (in *Radical Hope*) all rightly recognize that during times of radical historical crisis, the entire understanding of being implicitly guiding an age can break down, but Heidegger's view of *das Man* nevertheless suggests that not everyone living through such a historical crisis will recognize and confront that breakdown individually – although most of them will demonstrate a repressed awareness of the crisis by reactively seeking to deny or prevent it. (We shall come back to some of these issues in Chapter 5.)

[18] This also helps explain why Heidegger often resisted the label of "existentialist" (despite its obvious applicability to his work in many respects); his existential analyses were meant to be in the service of his *ontological* inquiries, and he did not want the former to eclipse the latter. Indeed, even his definition of existence as a "being-here" *is* ontological (as we will see in detail in Chapter 4).

"the question of the meaning being in general." It was only subsequently that the hermeneutic waters were muddied by the facts that (1) Heidegger never delivered that fundamental ontology he sought in *Being and Time* (1927), and (2) by the end of the dramatic "metaphysical decade" that followed he comes to reject *Being and Time*'s guiding project of fundamental ontology as unknowingly committed to an *impossible* metaphysical ambition – indeed, to that same metaphysical ambition which has shaped the core tradition of Western philosophy since its first beginnings.[19] (As Heidegger himself later recognizes: "The Heidegger of *Being and Time* . . . is still stuck in metaphysics, attempts 'ontology' and does not yet clearly see that wherein he moves" [GA102 94].) Indeed, Heidegger's notorious "turn" revolves around his own transformative realization that such metaphysical ambitions need to be transcended and moved beyond (rather than finally vindicated, as *Being and Time* sought to do), thereby giving rise to the "post-metaphysical" (and literally *postmodern*) project that becomes the guiding mission of Heidegger's "later" (c. post-1937) thought (as I have shown in detail elsewhere).[20]

Without downplaying such dramatic transformations in Heidegger's philosophical development (as too many orthodox Heideggerians continue to do, for reasons we will explore in Chapter 5), we can say that for Heidegger, both early and late, "Dasein" designates our distinctive, *ontological* "existence" as beings who implicitly understand what it means to be (both the meaning of our own being and the meaning of anything that in anyway "is"). Such an ontological understanding always plays a fundamental role in constituting the intelligible worlds that we Dasein are as we go about charting our courses through time and history.[21] For both early and later Heidegger, then, to be a Dasein means to be a particular kind of intelligible world that makes sense of itself, its world, and others by building on its own tacit answers to ontological questions about what it means to be.[22]

---

[19] "Metaphysical decade" is Crowell's apt term (see, for example, Steven Crowell's "Metaphysics, Metontology, and the End of *Being and Time*," *Inquiry*, 44:4 [2001], 433–54).

[20] See, for example, Thomson, *Heidegger on Ontotheology*, ch. 3 and *Heidegger, Art, and Postmodernity*, ch. 1.

[21] The basic difference here, put simply, is that our sense of what it means to *be* anything at all is predelimited by our subconscious employment of (1) a linked triumvirate of temporal horizons in *Being and Time*, as opposed to (2) a tacit ontotheological framework that shapes our shared historical sense of what is and what matters in Heidegger's mature work.

[22] In *Being and Time*, "Dasein" is also synonymous with our "being-in-the-world," another term of art that itself serves as shorthand for his detailed account (in the "existential analytic") of how our living understanding of being is inextricably entwined with the embodied ways we project ourselves into the practical life-projects that implicitly organize the intelligibility of our worlds. Hence the fuller line quoted at the beginning of this section reads: "'death' is defined as the end of Dasein, that is to say, of being-in-the-

Beneath the other changes in Heidegger's thought, our being such a first-personal disclosure of an *ontological* world – in which we *exist* or "stand-out" (from the Latin *ek-sistere*) into "intelligibility" (BT 193/SZ 151) by relating ourselves to the "being" of all the things we encounter (that is, to their ontologically disclosive meaning, sense, or truth) – is what characterizes our distinctive *being-here* as "Dasein." It should thus not be too surprising that this *existential world-disclosure* is precisely what "demise" and "death" both crucially interrupt and bring to an end – as we shall now go on to see by untangling and explaining he specific technical terms Heidegger uses to articulate and develop what he means by "death."

1.3 Rethinking Death: Distinguishing Perishing, Demising, and Dying

Section 49 of *Being and Time* is titled "How the Existential Analysis of Death is *Distinguished from* other Possible Interpretations of that Phenomenon" (BT 290, my emphasis/SZ 246). Here Heidegger first introduces his "existential analysis of death" by acknowledging the need to explicitly disambiguate his own "ontological interpretation of death" from other possible interpretations of the phenomenon. *Being and Time*'s turn toward death starts with the obvious observations that death is something that can only happen to the living ("death, in the widest sense, is a phenomenon of life" [ibid.]) and that, of course, Dasein is a living being too, although for Heidegger being alive cannot define Dasein, not only because lots of entities other than Dasein are alive (including the entire plant and animal kingdoms) but also because it is Dasein that defines what "being alive" *means*.[23]

Moving very quickly,[24] Heidegger points out that all biological accounts of death necessarily presuppose some *ontological* understanding of what death *is*,

---

world" (BT 292/SZ 247). For Dasein to be at its *end* in death (we will see) is thus for our practical "being-in-the-world" to be at an end. That can happen in a way that is still *conceptually* intelligible to us (and hence describable by existential phenomenology), precisely because that "in" (in "being-in-the-world") primarily designates practically "involved with" (in a "ready-to-hand" or *zuhanden* way), *not* cognitively related to (in a "present-at-hand" or *vorhanden* way). To say that death is the end of our Dasein as a "being-in-the-world" thus turns out to mean that death is the end of our being-in-the-world only in its primary, *practically engaged* significance. In death we can no longer connect to our practical projects or relate meaningfully to "ready-to-hand" equipment, but we can still make sense of such objects in a present-at-hand way; their intelligibility does not simply disappear, leaving us in an empty void (as Heidegger will stress when he distinguishes his view of the core of the self from that of Descartes).

[23] As that begins to suggest, Heidegger's consistent critique of Nazi "biologism" develops out of his early critique of the neo-Darwinistic "life-philosophy" of Nietzsche and others. (See Thomson, "Heidegger's Nazism in the Light of His Early *Black Notebooks*.")

[24] We should not allow the fame of the text to make us forget that *Being and Time* was a work written under immense time pressure (dramatic exigencies that mark the text with

simply in order for biologists to have some idea of what to focus on in their empirical investigations of the biological processes involved in "death."[25] But biologists tend to understand death merely as the cessation of life, and do not (at least not as biologists) try to explain what death itself *is* as a positive phenomenon, let alone begin to explain the broader meaning death holds for us Dasein, the very beings who develop such ontological conceptions of what "life" and "death" *are* as we go about seeking to make sense of the intelligible worlds that *we* are.[26] Dasein must already exist (or "stand-out" into an intelligible world) in order to be able to devise or employ any *concepts* of life or death, and even our most culturally pervasive ways of making sense of death are much broader (and suggestively richer, as we will see) than the strictly functional accounts provided by biology. Indeed, Heidegger boldly asserts, we need to understand what death most fundamentally *is* for us Dasein so that future academic researchers into death's myriad meanings can ground their broad-spectrum investigations in this clear and unambiguous *ontological* interpretation of death.

This missing ontological conception of death will be "*formal* and empty" compared to the specialized research it will ground in such subordinate academic fields as the biology, history, ethnography, psychology, and theodicy of death (*subordinate* fields because they will take over their guiding understanding of what death *is* from Heidegger's ontological conception, which their broad-spectrum investigations will expand and explore).[27] But Heidegger also warns readers that the comparative emptiness and formality

---

myriad unclarities), as the 37-year-old Heidegger sought finally to publish a major work and so secure (the German equivalent of) his first full professorship. (We return to this point at the end of Chapter 2.)

[25] In fact, this is true of *all* accounts of death, not only biological ones. (For an explanation and critical analysis of Heidegger's general argument in *Being and Time* for the priority of phenomenological ontology over all of the other sciences, see Thomson, *Heidegger on Ontotheology*, ch. 3.)

[26] "Life is its own kind [or mode] of being [*eigene Seinsart*], but essentially accessible only through Dasein. The ontology of life is accomplished by way of a privative interpretation; it determines what is the case if there can be anything like mere aliveness. ... Dasein is never to be defined by regarding it as life ... plus something else" (BT 75/SZ 50). (The early Heidegger is deeply influenced by his reading of Aristotle, as we will see in Chapter 4, but here he also marks his distance from the way Aristotle's view of humanity – as a *zoon logon echon* – is traditionally understood, viz., as living being distinguished by its possession of language or rationality.)

[27] It is this move that Derrida seeks to challenge in *Aporias*, which suggests that anthropological studies of death across different cultures, times, and places (like those painstaking efforts carried out by Philippe Aries, *The Hour of Our Death: The Classic History of Western Attitudes Toward Death over the Last One Thousand Years*, trans. by H. Weaver [New York: Vintage, 2008]) cannot be fully subordinated to Heidegger's phenomenological analysis of death as Dasein's distinctive end. (We return to Derrida's reading in Chapter 7.)

of his phenomenological interpretation of what death *is* for Dasein "must not blind us to the rich and complicated structure of the phenomenon" (BT 292/ SZ 248).[28] Heidegger never comes back to address any specific questions concerning how his "superordinate" existential analysis of the being of death will ground and unify all subsequent academic research into death, but he clearly does believe that *Being and Time succeeds* in "defining" just such a "full existential-ontological conception of death" (BT 303/SZ 258), as we will see in detail in this chapter.[29] But in order to articulate this existential interpretation of what death *is* (which can then ontologically *ground* the broader academic study of death), Heidegger points out, we first need to understand Dasein's "basic state or fundamental condition [*Grundverfassung*]," so that we can understand how death (as what Karl Jaspers calls an extreme "limit situation") disrupts, modifies, and so reveals this fundamental condition of our *existential* "being-here" (BT 291/SZ 247).[30] To understand what death *is* as the end of our being, in other words, we first have to understand the nature of that being (namely, our distinctive type of *existence* as "Dasein" or a *being-in-the-world*).

The preliminary goal of Heidegger's "existential analysis of death," in sum, is to understand what death *is* (that is, to develop an "ontological interpretation" of death) by examining *phenomenologically* how death most fundamentally shows up and becomes intelligible for us Dasein (as the *end* of our distinctive being-in-the-world). Such an ontology of death should then be able to serve as the foundation for a much broader academic study of death in the future. (*Being and Time* contains only a few hints on that last score, but the enduring importance of the project to Heidegger is suggested by the fact that when he sketches his vision for an ontologically unified university in the mid-1930s, it includes a new academic field dedicated entirely to the study of

---

[28] "The existential interpretation of death takes precedence over any biology and ontology of life. But it is also the foundation for any investigation of death which is biographical, or historiographical, ethnological, or psychological" (BT 291/SZ 248). That first sentence suggests that we must understand what death *is* for Dasein in order to understand what life *is* for us, rather than the reverse, as biology assumes. (That follows, in part, because what Heidegger means by "death" turns out to be rather distantly related to life and death in a biological sense, and also because he makes the case that even our ordinary thinking about death as the end of our lives is a kind of motivated confusion.)

[29] We will return to *Being and Time*'s "full existential-ontological conception of death," according to which: "*death, as the end of Dasein, is Dasein's ownmost, non-relational, certain and as such indefinite, and non-surpassable possibility*" (BT 303/SZ 258–9). *Being and Time* also casts some light on the question of why our culture's general understanding of death has taken on some of its specific meanings, including, most importantly, the pervasive view according to which death is anxiety-provoking, something to be fled, repressed, and thought about as little as possible (as we shall see in Chapter 8).

[30] As Heidegger thus schematically explains: "Within the ontology of Dasein, which is *superordinate* to the concept of life, the existential analysis of death is, in turn, *subordinate* to a characterization of Dasein's basic state or condition" (BT 291/SZ 247).

death.)³¹ Other than being so highly condensed, Heidegger's ambitious preliminaries should not surprise careful readers of *Being and Time*, because they are perfectly in keeping with the text's grand ambitions for the future of the phenomenological movement, the very movement the early Heidegger still hoped to inherit and helm.³²

With these ambitious preliminaries quickly sketched and unceremoniously set aside, *Being and Time*'s very next sentence launches into a dense but extremely important passage on death (which I shall refer to subsequently as "D1"), in which Heidegger distinguishes between three terms we might otherwise tend to use interchangeably, namely, "perishing" (*Verenden*), "demising" (*Ableben*), and "dying" (*Sterben*):

> [D1] The ending of that which [merely] lives we have called *perishing* [Verenden]. Dasein too "has" its physiological death of the kind appropriate to anything that lives; however, [the way Dasein "has" (i.e., experiences) such physiological perishing is] not in ontic isolation [like one rock merely bumping into another, or a blood clot blocking the flow of blood to the heart] but, instead, as co-determined by its primordial way of being [namely, "existence," Dasein's distinctive way of "standing-out" (*ek-sistere*) into an intelligible world; in other words, we Dasein *experience* the "perishing" of our physiological systems only insofar as such a strictly organic failure makes itself felt in the intelligible worlds that we *are*].³³ Dasein can also end without genuinely dying [*eigentlich stirbt*], although in this latter case it does not, *qua* Dasein, simply perish. We designate this intermediate phenomenon as *demise* [Ableben]. [Demise is intermediate *between* "perishing" and "death," because in demise we experience our physiological perishing as the approaching end of our intelligible worlds

---

³¹ See Thomson, *Heidegger on Ontotheology*, ch. 3.
³² I cannot recapitulate it here, but I have elsewhere detailed *Being and Time*'s ill-fated plan to make good on Husserl's project of restoring philosophy, as phenomenology, to its role as "the queen of the sciences," the "torch-bearer" who goes first, lighting the way for other academic "sciences" [or "fields of knowledge," *Wissenschaften*] to follow, rather than the "hand-maiden" or "train-bearer" who follows along behind, straightening out the puzzling tangles these sciences leave in their wake. This ambitious view risks (what I have called) the *ontological imperialism* of a top-down, phenomenological approach (too easily aligned with the rigidly hierarchical political vision of a Führer-Rector), so it is worth pointing out that Heidegger believes that, once the fields researching death have been grounded in his ontological interpretation of death, at least some of them "can obtain results that may be able to become significant ontologically," by feeding back into and reshaping our existential self-understanding (see Thomson, *Heidegger on Ontotheology*, ch. 3).
³³ The scare quotes Heidegger puts around "has" here signal his awareness of the Epicurean paradox concerning our experience of demise. The paradox (see n. 39 and below), put simply, is: If demise designates the absence of all experience, then how could we experience the absence of all experience? Heidegger frequently uses scare quotes to signal such Epicurean worries [see for example, SZ 251]).

and yet we do not experience such an *end* itself and so "die" in Heidegger's "genuine or authentic" sense.] Let the term *dying* [Sterben] designate the *way of being* in which Dasein *is toward* its death [*Tod*]. [As we will see, "being-toward" (*Seins zum*) means "pressing" or "projecting" (*Entwurf*) oneself into that existential possibility or project and so existing in terms of it; it does not mean simply thinking about, imagining, or otherwise relating oneself to one's eventual demise.]³⁴ We must thus say: Dasein never perishes. Demising, however, is something Dasein can do only so long as it dies [i.e., dying turns out to be a necessary condition of demising].³⁵ (BT 291/SZ 247, all emphases in the original)

My bracketed insertions begin to explain Heidegger's deliberately chosen but idiosyncratic (and so initially confusing) philosophical terminology. But we will need to slow down and carefully unpack the phenomenological concepts at work in this dense but important passage in order to understand what

---

³⁴ Heidegger explicitly clarifies that "being toward death" does not mean "actualizing" death in the sense of "bringing about one's demise" (as in suicide), nor merely "thinking about death" by "dwelling upon the end in its possibility" or "brooding over death"; instead, death "must be understood *as a possibility*, it must be cultivated *as a possibility*, and we must *put up with* it as a possibility in the way we comport ourselves toward it (BT 305–5/SZ 261). We will see that by "possibility," Heidegger means *existential* (not logical) possibility; that is, such a *possibility* is an existential project into which we project ourselves and in terms of which we thereby come to understand our being. As he explains, "any Dasein has, as Dasein, already projected [*entworfen*] itself and, as long as it is, it is projecting [*entwerfend*]. As long as it is, Dasein always has and always will understand itself in terms of possibilities. [Notice that those two sentences say the same thing in two ways; Heidegger is making clear that *projecting into projects* is Dasein's way of being its existential possibilities.] Furthermore, ... the understanding does not thematically grasp [that is, conceptually, propositionally, or representationally relate to] that upon which it projects – that is to say, possibilities. ... As projecting, it *is* its possibilities as possibilities" (BT 185/SZ 145). Hence, being-toward-death means existentially projecting oneself into the phenomenon Heidegger calls *death* (that is, the being at an *end* of Dasein's distinctive being as a primordially practical "being-in-the-world"); it does not mean imagining or adopting some attitude toward one's eventual *demise* (let alone actualizing that mortal demise by committing suicide or otherwise demising [that is, "croaking" or "kicking the bucket"]). This, however, does not negate the fact that Heidegger believes these two phenomena – existential death and mortal demise – remain closely related, and in such a way that understanding death can and should help transform our relationship toward our demise (for reasons we will examine).

³⁵ I shall suggest that dying (that is, the phenomenon disclosed by death) conditions demising in two related senses (in which the second reiterates and deepens the first): (1) Dasein can experientially approach the end of its own life only insofar as Dasein can experience itself being at an end; for, one can approach something only up until that point at which one has arrived at it. (2) Death discloses the core of the self as a projectless *projecting*, a sheer *projecting* that must be in place in order for Dasein to be able to *project into* the final terminal collapse of its world in demise at all.

exactly *Being and Time* says about the relations between perishing, death, and demise.

Over the last two decades of teaching and writing about this issue, I have found that the primary stumbling block to understanding Heidegger's phenomenology of "death" in *Being and Time* comes from the fact that the phenomenon he is referring to (as the "*way of being*" in which Dasein "*is toward*" its own death) is *not* what we ordinarily mean by *death*.[36] For Heidegger, "death" means *neither* the "physiological" ending of our biological lives, which he calls "perishing," *nor* even our experience of that biological ending of our lives as a terminal collapse of our intelligible worlds, an experience of our lives ending which he calls "demise." Just to make clear that he is indeed drawing this initially strange distinction between *existential death* and *mortal demise*, Heidegger almost immediately adds [and we will call this sentence "D2"]: "Dasein does not only, first, or really die [*erst stirbt*], nor even genuinely or authentically die [*eigentlich stirbt*], in and with an experience of its factual demise [*Ableben*]" [BT 291/SZ 247].[37] *Demise* is Heidegger's term for our experience of that terminal collapse of our intelligible world which (as far as we know and can tell) accompanies our physiological *perishing*, the final cessation of our biological functions.[38] We reach the end of our lives when the

---

[36] On the meaning of "being-toward" in "being-toward death," see n. 34 and Section 1.4 below.

[37] (Translation emended; the existing English translations have dropped Heidegger's "*erst* [only, first, or really]," a word which rightly suggests that Heidegger thinks of *death* not as that singular end of our lives but, instead, as something each of us can go through multiple times in our lives, an idea apparently too strange for the translators.) Heidegger adds this provocative line to explain his immediately prior claim that "a psychology of 'dying' gives information about the 'living' of the 'dying person,' rather than about the dying itself" (BT 291/SZ 247). In other words, psychological (and other) studies about how we approach the end of our lives are told entirely from the side of life, and so can only illuminate what life is like (as it *approaches* its end); such studies (of *demise*) tell us nothing about *what it is like for our existence as Dasein to be at an end* (which, we will see, is precisely what Heidegger's notion of "genuine or authentic death" seeks to explain). Hence Heidegger's claim that this point (that a "psychology of death" is really a misnamed aspect of a psychology of life) follows from the fact that we do not have to demise (or experience the approach of mortality) in order to experience our Dasein being at an end (in the phenomenon *Being and Time* calls *genuine* or authentic death, that is, the direct phenomenological experience of the end of our distinctive kind of being).

[38] Dasein "demises" insofar as the perishing of its physical body leads it to experience its own terminal world-collapse. The precise physiological mechanisms at work in each case will of course vary, but the general relation between *perishing* and *demise* is suggestively illustrated by a scene in the Wachowski sisters' *The Matrix* (1999) when several minor characters are murdered by being "unplugged" while still in the Matrix world. Their Daseins, cut off from their actual physical bodies, suddenly "demise" in the world of the Matrix, and shortly thereafter their physical bodies "perish," having thus "given up the ghost." (That is, perhaps an intentional pun in this scene, as one of the characters is named "Ghost." Yet, the fact that one's physical body would perish so quickly after being deprived of its Dasein suggests, in good Heideggerian fashion, that being Dasein in the

organic systems that kept us alive "perish" and – if we are awake, aware that our life is coming to an end, and the event is not too sudden – we experience our intelligible worlds terminally collapsing in "demise."

The basic premise underlying Heidegger's strict terminological distinction between *perishing* and *demise*, then, is that we Dasein do not directly or immediately experience the failure of the physiological systems that had been keeping us alive. Instead, we experience the collapse of our sheer physiological functioning only insofar as it is "codetermined by" (*mitbestimmt durch*, that is, "contributes to" or gets taken up into and experienced in terms of) the intelligible worlds that we Dasein are. So, for example, we would not directly experience the capillaries in our lungs failing to adequately oxygenate our blood; what we might experience, instead, are such phenomena as "fatigue," "light-headedness," "shortness of breath," or – less clinically and more aptly in terms of Dasein's existential world – a sudden inability to breathe or sit up in bed, which we might rightly take as heralding the end of our life. In Heidegger's terms, then, we Dasein never directly experience our own biological perishing at all; instead, we experience such perishing only indirectly (that is, as *mediated through* the intelligible worlds that we are) *as* our demise, that is, as an apparently final collapse of the intelligible worlds we *are*.[39] Put simply, *Dasein experiences its perishing only indirectly – as its demise.*[40] So much for Heidegger's distinction between *perishing* and *demise*.

How, then, does Heidegger distinguish his "genuine or authentic" conception of "dying" (*Sterben*) both from "perishing" (*Verenden*) and from "demising" (*Ableben*)? First, he distinguishes dying from perishing in the same way

---

Matrix world involves much more than what mind/body dualism imagines as the "mind," including all sorts of subconscious and even apparently "autonomic" processes without which the body cannot maintain even its minimal life functions.) The same relation is then enacted in reverse later, when Neo demises in the Matrix but is then "resurrected" there, apparently jump-started (in some unexplained way) when Trinity kisses his physical body, still living outside the Matrix world from which he has been disconnected. (I remain grateful to Hubert Dreyfus and Mark Wrathall for a helpful conversation about this and related matters.)

[39] I briefly defer its discussion for the sake of clarity, but there is an important further complication implicit here: Demise, as "an 'experience' of ceasing to live [*ein "Erleben" des Ablebens*]" (BT 295/SZ 251), turns out to be phenomenologically paradoxical. (Put simply: How can we fully "live-through" [*Er-leben*] our "ceasing to live" [*Ableben*]? How can we Dasein *be* at the very end of our lives?) This apparent experiential *impossibility* will in fact help motivate Heidegger to distinguish our ordinary thinking of death *as mortal demise* from his "authentic or genuine" *phenomenological* conception of death, as our way of being at the end of the world which we are (which he thinks we *can* experience in an extreme and desolate "way of being," and indeed *must* endure the experience of, in order to be able to phenomenologically disclose such crucial structures as *futurity*, and thereby *temporality*, as we will see at the end of this chapter).

[40] I will criticize the overly rigid boundary that Heidegger draws between perishing, on the one hand, and death and demise, on the other, in Chapter 7.4.

he distinguished demising from perishing. We Dasein can demise and die (because, as we will see, terminal world-collapse and world-collapse are both phenomena we Dasein can encounter, at least to some extent, in the intelligible worlds that we are), while our perishing is not something we can experience directly, in its own sheerly physiological terms (for the reasons just explained). Hence Heidegger's stark *provocation* (in D1 above): "Dasein never perishes." *Pace* Derrida, "Dasein never perishes" does not mean that "I do not end, I never end" (regardless of whether this alleged inability to experience our own end is recited as a calming mantra, with Epicurus, or as a heartbroken lament, with Kierkegaard and Blanchot). Here, in fact, Derrida misses a crucial point: Even though Heidegger thinks we Dasein *cannot* experience our lives having *come to an end* in demise (because Heidegger holds that *there is nothing that it is like for me to be demised*, for phenomenological reasons we will soon explore), Heidegger will argue that a living Dasein *can* experience its own intelligible world having come to an end. Indeed, we will see that this crucial experience of my existential world being ended and yet my somehow still being here (like a living witness to the end of the practical world that I was) is the very phenomenon Heidegger designates in D1 as "genuine or authentic dying," Dasein's way of *first* or *genuinely* "being toward" – that is, existentially "projecting into" and thereby undergoing and phenomenologically encountering – its own *death*.[41]

So, "Dasein never perishes" does not mean that Dasein *is endless* (or that I can never experience my own intelligible world having come to an end) but, instead, that to describe the distinctive type of ending that is proper to Dasein as "perishing" is to make the *category mistake* of trying to conceive of the distinctive end of Dasein's existence, the end of our standing out into an intelligible world, in terms drawn from the "worldless" occurrence of objects – which can occur "in ontic isolation" (as D1 put it), that is, without entering into the ontological intelligibility of Dasein's existential world.[42] Put

---

[41] (On the meaning of Heidegger's "being-toward," see n. 34.) See Jacques Derrida, *Aporias: Dying – Awaiting* (One Another at) 'the Limits of Truth," trans. by T. Dutoit (Stanford, CA: Stanford University Press, 1993), 40; Derrida gets this point from Blanchot (see Iain Thomson, "Can I Die? Derrida on Heidegger on Death," *Philosophy Today*, 43:1 [1999], 29–42, a problematic text written while I was still unknowingly in that first interpretive camp discussed in Section 1.1). As I shall show when we return to this issue in detail in Chapter 7, Heidegger is quite right to distinguish Dasein's distinctive mode of being, *existence*, from the on-hand occurrence of objects and the hands-on availability of equipment, but Derrida is also right that these distinct realms obviously interpenetrate and act on one another in a wide variety of ways (to which Heidegger, in his quest for clear philosophical distinctions, does not fully do justice).

[42] This is also why Heidegger argues that if "*death must be conceived as the ending of Dasein*" (BT 289/SZ 244), then we must also recognize that the intelligible world of a Dasein *ends* in a very different *kind* of way than an unfinished road ends, the rain stops, or any other objective entity or process reaches its end (BT 289/SZ 245).

differently, the logic behind Heidegger's distinction between *perishing*, on the one hand, and both *death and demise*, on the other, is that objective processes such as the sheer physiological functioning of our biology can *occur in* us without *happening for* us. When such objective processes both occur in us *and* happen for us, moreover, that phenomenological *happening*, as variously inflected by the light of Dasein's intelligible world, will always be different in kind from their sheer ontic *occurrence* (the very objective functioning that biologists and other natural scientists seek to isolate and study).[43]

For pedagogical expediency, we could thus express Heidegger's first crucial distinction here with a simple mnemonic formula: *Pear trees perish, but Daseins demise and die.* The physiological systems that maintain the life of a pear tree can run their course without anyone taking any notice (say, in the case of a wild pear tree that reaches the end of its life cycle without anyone ever noticing). But when the "physiological" systems that support Dasein's life functions perish, Dasein, as Dasein, does not perish; it *demises*, if this Dasein is conscious, aware of what is happening, and the event is not too sudden. Indeed, in what Heidegger treats as the *paradigmatic* case in which we Dasein are awake, aware, and undeceived, the way we *experience* the final "perishing" of our physiological systems is precisely by "demising," undergoing the terminal collapse of our intelligible worlds (as mentioned earlier). But if a person never experiences their own perishing – for example, if they are in a dreamless sleep when their physiological systems suddenly and unexpectedly stop functioning (and they never wake up) – then this Dasein will have ceased to be without ever experiencing the terminal collapse of its world in demise.

Ironically, our culture euphemistically calls that "passing away peacefully" and presents it as an ideal way to "shuffle off this mortal coil" (without risk of any indecorous last-minute drama to inconvenience the living or embarrass the reputation of the soon-to-be-dead). From the perspective of Heidegger's existential phenomenology, however, that kind of *non-demise* looks more like a thief in the night who steals not just our life but also our demise, along with our ability ever to notice that theft. The wide resonance of this "passing peacefully" euphemism in our culture thus inadvertently testifies to our pervasive fear of demise, subtly reinforcing the existentially cowardly message that it would be better never to experience anything of that final foreclosure of our worlds in demise.[44] Heidegger's suggestion is not that it would be better to go out the way we came in ("kicking and screaming," as it were) but, rather, that our cultural idealization of "passing quietly in your sleep" conveniently

---

[43] For example, the sheer *occurrence* of a tree falling in the woods (whether or not anyone hears it) generates acoustic waves that could in principle *happen* for a suitably placed and enabled Dasein, and not just as a mere sound but as alarming, gratifying, puzzling, loud, etc.

[44] I return to this point in detail in Chapters 8 and 9.

excuses many people from ever taking up the existential struggle to face up to and reconcile ourselves with a difficult fact: Our inevitable perishing will ordinarily (in the aforementioned paradigm cases) lead to our experience of demising, a final "appointment in Samarra" we certainly cannot count on sleeping through or otherwise dodging entirely (myriad cultural fantasies to the contrary notwithstanding).[45]

In sum, then, our physiological perishing is experienced *as* our mortal demise in the ordinary or paradigmatic case, even though Dasein can also perish without demising (as in that euphemistic ideal of "passing peacefully" while asleep). This ordinary (but contingent) connection between perishing and demise gets mirrored in the relation between demise and death: Just as one can perish without demising, one can also demise without genuinely or authentically dying (as Heidegger directly states in D1). (Thus, neither perishing nor demise is required for what Heidegger calls "death," as we will see.) In the paradigm case, however, perishing leads to demise (that is, the breakdown of our physiological functioning leads to the experience of terminal world-collapse), and demise leads *toward* death (that is, the experience of terminal world-collapse leads *toward* the experience of my intelligible world being at an end). But to understand why I deliberately emphasize "*toward*" here, we need to understand why Heidegger (in D1) calls *demise* "the intermediate phenomena" *between* the physiological occurrence of perishing and the experience of Dasein's being at its own end in the existential world-collapse of *death*.

Put simply, Heidegger's provocative claim is that only existential death gives phenomenology the full experience that demise seems to lead inexorably toward and yet cannot itself deliver (at least not *to phenomenology*), namely,

---

[45] Of course, this is not to deny that the experience of demising can often be filled with unbearable pain and suffering (although some of that suffering comes from our culture's unfortunate tendency to reduce death to demise, Heidegger will suggest, in a way that leaves us unnecessarily terrified about demise and so often unequipped to be there to support one another with it). There may also be many pain-dominated demises that it might be better to dodge than undergo, and yet the point remains: Absent such an experience of the terminal collapse of our intelligible worlds (in the paradigm case), we will not have experienced our own *demising*, that is, we will not have experienced the approaching terminal collapse of our intelligible world but, instead, will simply have ceased to be (our physiological systems merely perishing, much like that unwitnessed pear tree in the wilderness). Still, the Epicurean paradox implicit in the very idea of *experiencing* our own *demise* helps motivate Heidegger's distinction between such mortal demise and existential death, the latter giving us a way of experiencing our intelligible worlds having come to an end, something we apparently cannot do in the case of our demise, which nevertheless seems to lead inexorably toward such an end. This means, crucially, that only existential death gives us an experience of that end which demise promises and yet cannot deliver (an experience of being at our end that can subtly but profoundly transform our relationship toward demise), as we shall see.

the experience of the intelligible world that we are having reached its own distinctive end. Indeed, that claim is precisely what explains Heidegger's otherwise puzzling assertion (at the end of D1): "Demising, however, is something Dasein can do only so long as it dies." Only existential death allows phenomenology to experience that end of our distinctive kind of being, an end which demise is oriented toward and yet seemingly cannot actually reach (owing to the Epicurean paradox we will address momentarily). Only what Heidegger calls "genuine or authentic death" – "the end of Dasein, that is to say, of [our own] being-in-the-world" (BT 292/SZ 247) – can ultimately show us what it genuinely means for our first-personal existence as a world-disclosive being-here to reach its own end, by undergoing (and subsequently being able to attest to phenomenologically) the experience of its existence as a practical "being-in-the-world" having *ended*.

One of *Being and Time*'s most provocative insights, in other words, is that death and demise come apart phenomenologically. We Dasein can live through our own intelligible worlds having come to an end (in the existential phenomenon Heidegger calls genuine or authentic death) without having to undergo the experience of terminal world-collapse (in mortal demise).[46]

[46] We have seen that one can perish without demising (as in the case of perishing while in a dreamless sleep and never awaking), but can one demise without perishing? That would require a scenario in which one undergoes the terminal collapse of one's intelligible world and yet one's physiological systems somehow continue functioning to support the biological life of their organic system. That might indeed happen if, for example, one experienced some physiological crisis sufficient to catalyze one's demise (so that one rightly recognized that one is demising and one's intelligible world never subsequently comes back "on-line," so to speak) and yet one's physiological systems somehow remain functionally "alive." (This could occur in some subset of those cases typically referred to as "brain death.") Analogously, we have just seen that Heidegger thinks we can die without demising. But can one demise without dying? Heidegger's answer here is "no," because he thinks (as just explained) that "[d]emising ... is something Dasein can do only so long as it dies." We can demise, or undergo the terminal collapse of the intelligible worlds we are, only so long as we die, or undergo the collapse of these worlds we are *and yet continue to be there*, witnessing this collapse of our world. The basic point is clear (albeit initially strange): We can only experience the *terminal* collapse of our worlds so long as we can experience the collapse of our worlds at all. But the deeper question that seems to motivate this one remains: Can we experience demise without experiencing existential world-collapse in a traumatic way? I shall later suggest reasons for thinking that the answer is yes: if one has completely relinquished one's strictly personal attachments to one's world-defining projects, instead identifying entirely with projects that will survive one's own personal demise (as *Being and Time* suggests existential death should indeed help encourage us to do), then the experience of undergoing terminal world-collapse need not lead to one final traumatic collapse of my practical identity (no more than our practical identities must collapse traumatically in order for us to fall asleep). For, if I have come to identify myself with defining projects that will outlive my demise, then I need not experience my final inability to connect practically, ever again, to those projects as a traumatic collapse of my identity. This may well be the best way of

That proves highly fortunate for existential phenomenology since, by all appearances, we *cannot* live through our own *demise* to experience *that* end.[47] With this latter point, Heidegger incorporates his understanding of Epicurus's famous paradox – that I never experience my own demise, since "When I am, death is not, and when death is, I am not" – into his discussion of "demise." As his German nicely suggests, "an 'experience' of [one's own] demise [*ein "Erleben" des Ablebens*]" literally (and paradoxically) means "a 'living-through' of [one's own] ceasing to live" (BT 295/SZ 251), an apparent absurdity.[48] For Heidegger, "demise" designates this ultimately paradoxical "experience" of the end of one's own life (that is, an "experience" of the approaching cessation or *absence of all experience*), a final event that we seem to be able to experience as it approaches but not once it has arrived, because once demise arrives our Dasein is no longer "here" to be anything. From the phenomenological perspective, put simply (albeit provocatively), *our own Dasein cannot be demised*. (Dasein and its own demise are ultimately incompatible, because we cannot both "be here" and *be demised*; to be demised is not to "be here" at all.)[49]

describing what Heidegger will suggest is an authentic relation to demise, a relation that (having passed through and drawn the lessons from existential death) finds a nontraumatic way to integrate the terminal world-collapse of mortal demise into one's practical identity. And yet, the later Heidegger suggests (*pace* the earlier), perhaps we should not invest ourselves so heavily in *surviving* in any form but, instead, find ways to embrace the "letting go" of our worlds one last time, as we turn to welcome the coming immersion into being's inexhaustible riches. I would suggest that the former is close to Heidegger's early view, the latter closer to his later (in which a letting go of the ego turns anxious fear into wondrous openness to the excessiveness of being), and I return to this fascinating issue in detail in Chapter 9. (Thanks to Mark Wrathall for repeatedly pushing me to respond to this difficult but important existential question, which to my recollection Heidegger never takes up explicitly himself and yet does help us think about.)

[47] We will see that Heidegger is aware of the worry that this may seem a little too convenient for more than one reason. (If all you have is a hammer, then everything looks like a nail, as one says; if all one has is phenomenology, then everything shows up as an experience to be entered into and undergone.)

[48] See also n. 39.

[49] It is for this reason that Levinas criticizes Heidegger's phenomenology of death for deliberately remaining one-sidedly "this-worldly," thereby alleging that Heidegger (in an implicit *atheism*) ignores the possibility that one might look back on one's life from some eternal beyond (or perhaps receive divine prophecy about such an afterlife while still alive). But here Levinas seems to confuse death with demise (as we shall see in Chapter 7), and, even if we restrict the question to the phenomenology of demise, is not clear how Heidegger – as *a phenomenologist who must deliberately confine himself to what we are capable of personally experiencing of the phenomenon at issue* – could avoid restricting himself to what Dasein can experience *here*, in *this* world. ("Near-death" experiences, for example, – precisely as *experiences* – *show* that Dasein has not yet reached the end of its experiences and so has not yet demised in Heidegger's sense; such experiences thus cannot settle the question of whether there is any other-worldly beyond

1.3. PERISHING, DEMISING, AND DYING

This paradox means, Heidegger repeatedly points out, that if death is understood only as demise (that is, as our relation to or experience of our impending mortality), then our being-here as Dasein can *never* comprehend itself *as a whole*. For it appears that, up until we demise, our intelligible worlds will always be constituted by worldly projects that stretch into an unknown future[50] (so that our sense of self will never be fully "transparent to itself [*durchsichtig*]" in a way that enables Dasein to *see through* itself completely – without being stretched out into some always partly unseen future – and so grasp itself in its entirety), but then, once we demise, we will no longer *be here* at all (that is, we will no longer be Dasein). *Being and Time*'s discussion of death begins (§§46-7) by setting up this very problem at great length. In fact, this is the problem that motivates Heidegger's phenomenological distinction between death and demise in the first place: How can Dasein – an entity whose being (or intelligible world) is constitutively organized by life-projects that stretch into an unknown future – ever comprehend itself as a whole?[51] What

---

on the far side of demise.) For these very reasons, in fact, Heidegger is careful to acknowledge that the phenomenological necessity of methodologically privileging what Dasein can experience (in our *being-here*) with respect to death and demise remains neutral on the religious question of whether or not there is any life after demise (BT 292/ SZ 247-8), an issue in terms of which *Being and Time* thereby remains methodologically *agnostic* (rather than either theistic or atheistic, which as would-be philosophical positions – Heidegger provocatively maintains – both equally commit themselves untenably to knowing something unknowable, such as whether or not some afterlife might be found on the far side of Dasein's great experiential beyond). (We return to related issues further in the text and in Chapters 6, 7, and 9.)

[50] This remains true, I think, even if our last remaining existential project is not even tonight's sleep or tomorrow's breakfast but nothing more than demising itself (undertaken, for example, as our last great existential adventure into the unknown – before the undertaker takes our corpse six feet under, as it were).

[51] The issue Heidegger uses to transition from Division I to Division II of *Being and Time* is the question of whether Division I's existential analytic has grasped Dasein in its "most primordial totality" by setting out Dasein's three main "existential structures" (namely, Dasein's affective attunement [*Befindlichket*], conversance [*Rede*], and understanding [*Verstehen*], to which we will return) [BT 273/SZ 230]. Division II of *Being and Time* eventually answers this question in the negative, by phenomenologically discovering a deeper layer of Dasein's structure in the three interconnected temporal horizons that directly underlie these three existential structures. But the way Heidegger tries to motivate this transitional question (of whether he has yet plumbed the bottom of Dasein's existential structure phenomenologically) is by connecting this issue of "primordiality" (*Ursprünglichkeit*) to the issue of Dasein's "wholeness or totality" (*Ganzheit*). His suggestion is that the existential analysis will have hit bottom, as it were, only once we get Dasein's totality in sight (or into our "hermeneutic fore-having," in his terminology). (As he writes: "If ... the ontological interpretation is to be a *primordial* one, this ... requires explicit assurance that the *whole* of the entity which it has taken as its theme [viz., Dasein] has been brought into the fore-having" [BT 275/SZ 232, Heidegger's italics].) Taking *wholeness* as a guarantor of *primordiality* is a strange move, for which the best analogue is

most readers seem to miss, however, is that Heidegger is able to solve this problem only by introducing his existential-ontological conception of death – in distinction from our ordinary understanding of death as mortal demise.

The unfortunate fact that Heidegger does not clearly distinguish existential death from demise while setting up the problem is part of what misleads most readers into conflating existential death with mortal demise. It is probably a sign of the speed with which the text was written that Heidegger gets almost halfway through his introductory treatment of death before finally acknowledging that his "analysis cannot keep clinging to an idea of death which has been devised accidentally and at random" (BT 292–3/SZ 248), and so begins to develop existential death in its relation to and difference from mortal demise. Even then, however, the fact that death and demise share the same formal structure (as we will see in Section 1.4), coupled with the strangeness and subtlety of his twofold examination of existential death and mortal demise, makes it less likely that readers who already have conflated existential death with mortal demise will understand how he eventually disambiguates the two

---

probably weeding: You can rest assured that you have reached the very bottom of the plant you are seeking to unearth only once you can see the entire plant before you (roots and all). It is precisely this "task of putting Dasein as a whole into our fore-having" (BT 276/SZ 233) that allows Heidegger to introduce death and motivate the distinction between death and demise, because that missing wholeness is possible only in existential death and not in mortal demise. Nonetheless, I should also note that I have never found this way of motivating the transition convincing. It works structurally as a convenient way to connect the Kantian-pragmatic analyses of the first Division to the Kierkegaardian-existential ones in Division II, and then to vindicate the turn to temporality as finally securing that promised primordiality and wholeness (all on the way toward the promised fundamental ontology). Nonetheless, *Being and Time*'s strange faith in the connection between primordiality and totality is redolent of *ontotheology* (in which Western metaphysics repeatedly connects the deepest *ontological* ground and the furthest *theological* horizon; see also BT 49/SZ 26). I am not surprised that this way of thinking about Dasein as the temporal ground of being disappears from his later work, as metaphysics (understood as ontotheology) becomes the problem rather than the solution (as I first showed in Thomson, *Heidegger on Ontotheology*, chs. 1 and 3), but we shall come back to this important issue in detail in Chapter 2. Moreover, Heidegger's focus on Dasein's "wholeness" is potentially quite misleading, as it risks suggesting that he is trying to give an *exhaustive* analysis of Dasein's existential structure, which he is not. Heidegger's articulation of Dasein's existential structures is not meant to be *complete* (in the way Kant's categories are, now rather notoriously). The three main existentials (listed above) are not Dasein's only existentials (in fact, he lists numerous others); they are just the three interconnected existential structures that sit directly atop the three interconnected temporal horizons (which Heidegger is still hoping to leverage in order to disclose a *fundamental ontology*, as we shall see in Chapter 2). This means that it is not, *prima facie*, a telling critique to point out that *Being and Time* ignores or downplays existential structures like embodiment, sex, gender, etc., since his analysis is not striving for completeness in that sense. (See also n. 55 for another sense in which his talk of "wholeness" is misleading.)

phenomena.⁵² (For better and for worse, Heidegger is a subtle thinker and writer, and often leaves important philosophical lessons implicit and unstated in his texts for readers to draw out for themselves – lessons and insights that his most careful readers will likely discover, excavate, and debate for years – which is part of what *continues* to make him such an engaging thinker, numerous problems notwithstanding.)⁵³ Although I do think he should have been much clearer here, I shall also explain the reasons why his phenomenological method leads him deliberately to couple death and demise together so closely, as the two phenomena are indeed related closely (though not inextricably, as we have already seen).

By definition, we living beings cannot experience all our experience having ended in our mortal demise (and so cannot do any phenomenology of our own *being demised*). But Heidegger remains convinced that there is an end proper to (or distinctive of) our Dasein – as a primordially practical "being-in-the-world" embodied in and organized by our life-projects – which we *can* experience, and, moreover, that this is an experience in which Dasein can grasp itself as a whole. As he will thus put it: "In such being-toward-its-end, Dasein exists in a way which is genuinely whole, as that entity which it can be when 'thrown into death.' Dasein does not have an end at which it is simply stops but instead [Dasein has an end in which it] *exists finitely* [existiert endlich]" (BT 378/SZ 329).⁵⁴ Dasein "exists at an end" or experiences an

---

⁵² Let me thus emphasize that scholars like me owe a deep debt of gratitude to William Blattner (along with Heidegger's earliest phenomenological readers like Levinas, Sartre, and de Beauvoir, see Chapter 7), for recognizing and first helping clearly to explain the difference (despite the many divergences between our views).

⁵³ To me, some obvious (if still not widely recognized) examples of Heidegger's subtlety (and perhaps excessive faith in his readers' phenomenological and hermeneutic skills) include Heidegger's widespread, deliberately ambiguous use of "the nothing" (to which we return in Chapter 3), as well as his phenomenological unearthing of a farming woman in Van Gogh's painting of "A Pair of Shoes" (1886); for a detailed treatment of both examples, see Thomson, *Heidegger, Art, and Postmodernity*, ch. 3.

⁵⁴ On "being toward death," notice that Heidegger equates it here with "thrown into death" (and see n. 36). As *Being and Time* explained earlier, Dasein is always already "thrown" into "projection" (BT 185/SZ 145), and, in death, we experience ourselves as thrown into *projectless* projecting. In the full experience of existential death, Dasein is still a *thrown projection* structurally, but it discovers itself as "the null-basis of a nullity," that is, as having to take over its own ungrounded facticity (the "null-basis" that it is as *thrown*, that is, as unable ever to understand itself from the ground up and so fully justify its existential choices) in order to resolutely reconnect to a worldly project, inevitably negating (or "nullifying" in its finite *projecting*) all the other projects it could have been (see also n. 56). Just as the ineliminable lack-of-fit between self and world that we discover in *anxiety* helps explain that ungroundedness which Dasein is as a "null-basis" in existential death, so Heidegger's phenomenology of guilt encourages the *solus ipse* we most fundamentally are to embrace its defining finitude by nullifying all that it has chosen not to be so as to become what it is choosing, in Dasein's return to the practical world in resolve (see BT

"end-like existence" in the strange phenomenon of existential death – in which we continue to *exist* and yet find ourselves radically estranged from the practical projects and identities that ordinarily allow us to make sense of our ourselves (as a practically engaged "being-in-the-world"). Existential death's experience of radically *finite existing* – that is, of existing as "a whole," as "transparent" to ourselves, because no longer projecting into worldly projects that (as "something still outstanding" [BT 276/SZ 233]) would conceal our own existence from us – is what Heidegger means when he says that existential death "delimits and determines in each case the possible wholeness of Dasein" (BT 277/SZ 234).[55]

Heidegger's solution to the Epicurean paradox, in other words, is that in the desolate experience he calls "death," the self – temporarily cut off from the world of practical projects in terms of which it usually understands itself – finds itself radically alone with itself (a worldless *solus ipse*), and so can lucidly comprehend itself in its entirety for the first time, since there is no worldly, futural component of itself to elude its self-transparent grasp.[56] When Dasein

---

333/SZ 287; BT 354/SZ 306). (For a detailed reconstruction of Heidegger's phenomenological move from ontic to ontological guilt, see also Guy Elgat, "Heidegger on Guilt: Reconstructing the Transcendental Argument in *Being and Time*," *European Journal of Philosophy*, 28:4 [2020], 911–25).

[55] For some individuals, it may well be that undergoing this experience of the radical wholeness of the finite self can powerfully carry over into the felt task of conferring some narrative or other unified understanding on one's life as a whole (as Guignon often suggests, and Beauvoir similarly "assumes"; Simone de Beauvoir, *Ethics of Ambiguity* [New York: Open Road, 2018], 26), but I do not see Heidegger specifically making *that* argument in *Being and Time*, which instead suggests that authenticity involves *repeatedly* reconstituting my dynamic becoming in lucidly *coherent* ways (disclosively constituting the "constancy" of my self by repeatedly taking a stand on the meaning of my life and its place in history "as a fateful whole" [BT 463/SZ 410]), an enduring struggle which is never accomplished once and for all time (see BT 388/SZ 339, BT 443/SZ 391, and Chapters 4 and 7.4). Indeed, as a later-Heidegger inspired postmodernist incredulous toward the exclusive claims of any such metanarrative, I do not believe we can ever finally tell ourselves our own life stories (especially in their intersections with history) in terms of some single, overarching account (although we can repeatedly learn a great deal from the attempt, and, moreover, Heidegger's own efforts "to sum it all up" conceal as much as they reveal [see, most famously, PLT 4/AED 7]). I think the more direct uptake of this experience of radical wholeness in existential death can be felt in the liberating *wholeheartedness* and "unshakable joy" (BT 358/SZ 310) of the *resolute* decision or lucid commitment that brings us back from such death to the world of projects in *authenticity*. (I am grateful to Charles Guignon, Taylor Carman, and Mark Wrathall for encouraging me to clarify this point.)

[56] One might well object here that, even when (in existential death) the collapse of my defining projects leaves me bereft of that practical world that ordinarily allows me to make sense of myself by pressing forward or projecting into projects that stretch into a partly unknown future, I am still shaped by a past (a "having-beenness") that stretches into distant mists I can never fully comprehend, such that Dasein also disappears (not just ahead of itself in projection but also back behind itself) into a "thrownness" that similarly prevents me from

1.3. PERISHING, DEMISING, AND DYING

experiences itself as desperately unable to project into the worldly projects in terms of which it normally makes sense of itself, then "the future itself is closed" for Dasein (even though objectively "time goes on"). Bereft of all its worldly projects in existential death, Dasein can fully grasp itself in its own "finitude" for the first time – and thereby come to understand itself as a "primordial existential projecting" (BT 379/SZ 330), a sheer *existing* (from the Latin *ek-sistere*, a literal "standing-out" toward a world I cannot connect to practically or project into), a desolate condition I call *projectless projecting* (for terminological reasons I shall explain in Section 1.4).[57]

---

ever being fully "transparent" (*durchsichtig*) to myself in the way Heidegger seeks (in order to get *all* of Dasein into his hermeneutic "fore-having"; see n. 51). But Heidegger is cognizant of this point (see GA2 310, note a) and his response (which he articulates in his related phenomenology of *guilt* and *conscience*) is that my embodied past thrownness shows up not in my practical or conceptual self-understanding (*Verstehen*, since death is primarily the breakdown of such understanding) but, instead, in my affective attunement (*Befindlichkeit*) to the world, which in anxiety and guilt (combined) manifest me to myself as cut off from that past which has shaped me (because I experience my own defining having-beenness as no longer sufficient to tell me how specifically to reconnect to the practical world). Experiencing my having-beenness as no longer determining my to-come (to put it in Heidegger's terms) encourages me to recognize myself *as* the groundless (or "null") ground of my own existential decisions about what to be henceforth, a recognition which helps enable me to forge my own path back to the world of identity-bestowing practical projects in what Heidegger calls resolve (or un-closedness, *Entschlossenheit*). Now, that answer, in turn, raises the oft-discussed problem of Heidegger's apparent *decisionism* (or *voluntarism*), but it also allows us to glimpse a crucial part of his response: Dasein's resolute decisions are *contingent* (hence *free*) but not *arbitrary* (hence meaningless). Dasein's defining decisions (by which we reconnect to the world lost in death) are *neither determined nor completely indeterminate*, because the world of projects that impends toward us (when death discloses futurity as a coming-toward which brings us back before our making present in resolve [as we will see in the final section of this chapter]) is still *partly* shaped or pre-delimited by the "facticity" that we are (the typically unnoticed effect of our pasts upon us), the "having-beenness" still embodied in our affective attunements and dispositions. Hence, as we "open ourselves" (in *Ent-schlossenheit*, "un-closedness" or "resolve") toward the beckoning worlds of those practical projects we *can* become, not every logically possible project shows up (so we are not simply numbed by some overwhelming array of options). Thanks to the enduring effects of our thrownness (not primarily cognitive but attuned and embodied), this finite array of futural projects does not come toward us as all equally attractive, desirable, worthy, and so on, so that we are not permanently paralyzed by existential death – as could happen if those resolute decisions whereby the *solus ipse* reforges its connection to the practical world were just some "frictionless spinning in a void" (to borrow McDowell's famous phrase for the Cartesian divide between mind and world). Instead (to put it in the simplest terms), although I genuinely might not know if I want to be a writer or a philosopher, for example, that decision would take place against a background in which being a lawyer or stockbroker, say, simply do not present themselves to me as live-options (for good or for ill, in cases of entrenched disenfranchisement).

[57] (See also n. 34.) Understanding this point allows us to answer another difficult question careful readers often pose, namely: Why does Heidegger think that the collapse of projects we experience in what he calls "death" has to be *global*? It is necessary that *all* Dasein's projects break down because, as we have just seen, existential "death" is introduced in *Being*

As that suggests, Heidegger's conviction that there is a kind of end that is distinctive of Dasein – that we *can* experience our intelligible world as having ended and so exist in a way that is radically "finite" (*endlich*) – is what leads him to distinguish this "existential conception of death [*die existenziale Begriff des Sterbens*]" from demise (BT 295/SZ 251). Recall his clear (if initially puzzling) statement (in D2): "Dasein does not only, first, or really die [*erst stirbt*], nor even genuinely or authentically die [*eigentlich stirbt*], in and with an experience of its factical demise [*Ableben*]" (BT 291/SZ 247).[58] The main point behind this provocative assertion that *we can die without demising* is that neither "death" nor "dying" (nor even "genuinely or authentically dying," a

---

and Time to solve the puzzle of how can have a *complete* phenomenological grasp of our Dasein (or "being-here"), given that there always seems to be something still outstanding about Dasein so long as it exists in the world, and once Dasein demises, it is no longer here at all. A phenomenological grasp of Dasein "as a whole" is only possible, then, if Dasein undergoes an experience in which *all* its existentiell possibilities have collapsed so that it finds itself retracted from the world like a turtle into its shell. (A second reason, I shall suggest, is that fear of demise is ultimately driven by our fear of not being at all, not our anxiety about being diminished – although that can be a real concern too.) It is natural to worry that the idea of total world-collapse is problematic phenomenologically, and so to suspect that Heidegger is either generalizing from his own depressive nature or else letting the hermeneutic dictates of the existential analysis trump phenomenology – which, I think, should instead have led him to recognize that *all* our projects do not need to collapse in order for us to come to understand the existential structure of the self. Nonetheless, undergoing such a global collapse is possible and seems to yield precisely the insight Heidegger suggests, which is all he needs. I think he believes in such global collapse not only because he himself experienced it repeatedly (on this point see my philosophical biography of Heidegger, in progress), but also because he thinks that if Dasein experiences the collapse of its "ultimate for the sake of which" – that is, the single project which ultimately organizes all Dasein's other projects (that is, the project we would give up last) – then its whole world will collapse like a house of cards. (See also the analogy from Gestalt psychology that Sartre uses to argue for Heidegger's same point in Sartre, *Being and Nothingness*, 469-70.) As this suggests, Heidegger is committed to a robust neo-Kierkegaardian notion of a unified self, not a late-modern fractured self whose identity transforms from one context to the next as it seeks to optimally respond to the shifting demands of its life with maximal flexibility and efficiency (as our technological age of *enframing* increasingly challenges us to do). At any rate, Heidegger seems right that the collapse of our defining projects can easily paralyze our peripheral projects, making us feel like our world has ended (whereas the collapse of peripheral projects will probably only completely paralyze the most neurotic of individuals). (See also n. 72.)

[58] Macquarrie and Robinson render this line more telegraphically (and leave out the important word in brackets, see n. 37): "[W]hen Dasein [first or really, *erst*] dies – and even when it dies authentically – it does not have to do so with an experience of its factical demising, or in such an experience" (BT 291/SZ 247). What is nice about this translation is that their "does not have to" clearly implies *but can*. Death can take place without demise, but the two can at least partly coincide and, by all appearances, will if one is conscious when one demises and one's demise is not too sudden. In such cases, it seems to me that demise and death will at least temporarily coincide in the experience of terminal world-collapse. (But see also n. 46.)

1.3. PERISHING, DEMISING, AND DYING

repeated enduring of existential death, to which we will return) requires us to undergo the *terminal* world-collapse of demise. (This is fortunate for phenomenology, because if experiencing "death" in Heidegger's sense required us to experience the permanent foreclosure of our intelligible worlds in demise, then we would have to write our phenomenologies of death from beyond the grave, by séance or Ouija board!)[59]

Heidegger's distinctive contribution here – that we do not need to experience our mortal demise in order to "first or really die" existentially – is so contrary to our commonsensical notions of death that most traditional readers of *Being and Time* seem simply to repress and ignore it; for it suggests that what Heidegger calls "death" is in fact something we can live through. Indeed, despite the forceful protestations of Hoffman and the first camp (described earlier), Heidegger himself is quite clear that existential death does not require mortal demise, our ultimately paradoxical experience of the "event" of the end of our lives (BT 284/ SZ 240). Instead, as *Being and Time* plainly states: "Death is a way to be, which Dasein takes over as soon as it is" (BT 289/SZ 245).[60] In other words, undergoing the phenomenon of existential "death" discloses and designates a fundamental modality of existence that is ordinarily filled-in – and so covered over – by our everyday worldly experience (as we will see in detail in Section 1.4).

To help accustom his audience to this strange use of the word "death," Heidegger immediately quotes a famous line from the Christian mystic, Jakob Böhme (1575–1624): "As soon as a human being comes to life [*zum Leben kommt*], he is at once old enough to die" (BT 289/SZ 245). Stambaugh translates this important quotation as follows: "As soon as a human being is born, he is old enough to die right away" (BTS 228), but that is a bit misleading

---

[59] The distinction between the *ends* involved in death and demise, put another way, is that the first-person phenomenology of demise – of terminal world-collapse – leaves no phenomenological record. We might be able to *witness* the terminal collapse of our worlds (Epicurean paradoxes notwithstanding), but we Dasein (or being-here) cannot subsequently bear witness to the "final moment" of our lives, since we will no longer *be here* to do so. (However far we might go into demise, as it were, there is ultimately no phenomenological testimony of what it is like to *be demised*. For, there is nothing that being demised is like, as far as we can tell; being demised is not an *end* at which we Dasein can be here. [On the worry that this entails atheism, see n. 49.]) The search for some intelligible position beyond demise from which to narrate its entire content (*up to and including what it is like to be demised*) probably helps explain the interest in (so-called) "near death experiences," which are really (in Heidegger's terms) *near-demise experiences*. My own favorite example from a neighboring genre (of these experiences on the verge of *nothing*, in Heidegger's dual sense) can be found in Yoel Hoffman's wonderful collection, Yoel Hoffman, *Japanese Death Poems: Written by Zen Monks and Haiku Poets on the Verge of Death* (Rutland, Vermont: Tuttle, 1986), which contains such gems as the fourteenth-century Giun's final lines: "The sky now cracks and falls / The earth cleaves open— / In the heart of the fire / Lies a hidden spring" (98).

[60] See also: "Dasein is dying, factically and indeed constantly, as long as it has not yet come to its demise" (BT 303/SZ 259). Or, as Heidegger wrote in 1925, "I myself am my death precisely when I live" (BH 263; see also Chapter 3).

because Heidegger is not using Böhme to make the morbid suggestion that newborns can die in a way that late-term fetuses cannot. Instead of being born biologically, Böhme's "coming to life" means *entering into the life of the spirit* (or becoming aware of oneself as existing before God, that is, as this particular individual). Heidegger is thus suggesting that one is capable of experiencing the collapse of one's intelligible world as soon as one *has* such a world to collapse, that is, as soon as one has come to embody an existential stand on oneself and thereby become a full-fledged Dasein (which is something a newborn infant has yet to do). As this reference to Böhme indicates, Heidegger's conception of existential death is influenced by the idea of "dying with Christ" or "dying to the world" long familiar to Pauline Christianity (in which, in the archetypal myth of spiritual *conversion*, Saul must *die* to his defining identity as a zealous persecutor of Christians in order to be *reborn* as Paul, the sainted evangelist of Christian faith).[61] Kierkegaard elaborates and describes this same spiritual passage through despair philosophically in *The Sickness Unto Death*. The basic point, *The Sickness Unto Death* explains, is that "in the Christian understanding, *death is itself a passing into life*."[62] To anyone familiar with Kierkegaard's brilliant text (as Heidegger was), it is clear that *Being and Time*'s phenomenology of existential death seeks to secularize the mystical Christian idea that, in order for one to be born truly into the life of the spirit, one must first die to the material

---

[61] Here, of course, Paul takes himself to be following in the spiritual footsteps of Christ. As Böhme describes his vision of spiritual death and rebirth, Christ's resurrection "is the original of the eternal death or devoration [that is, the *devouring* of the preceding life]; and in this devoration is the highest arcanum or secret, for the true essential lively spirit and understanding proceedeth out of this devoration, and maketh another beginning" (Jakob Böhme, *Mysterium Magnum*, trans. by John Sparrow [San Rafael, CA: Hermetica, 2007 [original 1623]], 15). Such spiritual death and rebirth is thus the "highest secret" of Böhme's *Great Mystery*, and thus a central teaching of Christian mysticism. In so far as this mystery describes a death and rebirth *within life*, Christian mysticism can be thought of as already moving toward phenomenology. (In 1940, Heidegger emphasizes that such a *secularization* of Christian wisdom was not simply a translation of other-worldly myths into the terms of a preexisting secular world; rather, this translation of Christian insights into "this worldly" wisdom helped historically to create and expand the very secular world we now take for granted as having been there all along. (See N4 100/NII 146; cf. Charles Taylor, *A Secular Age* [Cambridge, MA: Harvard, 2007], part 1.)

[62] (See Søren Kierkegaard, *The Sickness Unto Death*, trans. A. Hannay [London: Penguin Books, 2004], 47, my emphasis.) As I showed in Thomson, *Heidegger on Ontotheology*, ch. 4, there is also a structurally analogous conversion narrative in Plato's famous parable of the cave, at least as Heidegger understands and elaborates it. Heidegger's vision of authenticity as entailing a death and rebirth of the self is thus influenced by both the deepest Christian and Greek traditions (as well as by his own personal experience, as I will show in *Heidegger: A Philosophical Biography*).

1.3. PERISHING, DEMISING, AND DYING 35

world – so that one can be *reborn* to this world in a way that will unify the spiritual and material aspects of the self.[63]

Indeed, the influence of Kierkegaard on Heidegger's thinking about death is profound and important. According to the view Kierkegaard (or, more precisely, his spiritually elevated pseudonym, "Anti-Climacus") presents in *The Sickness Unto Death*, when we acknowledge and confront our own despair, we are led to abandon our familiar, everyday self, "the fully clothed self of immediacy" that is constituted by all our worldly "projects." This seemingly disastrous loss of our "actual self" turns out to be our salvation, however, because when despair alienates us from the world of our ordinary projects, we discover that what survives this expulsion from the world is our true or "infinite" self. This infinite self, the "naked and abstract" self at our volitional core, is then able explicitly to repossess its "actual self," the world of its immediate projects, from the perspective it discovers in that very expulsion from the world.[64]

There are significant differences between Kierkegaard's profoundly religious and Heidegger's rigorously phenomenological and thus thoroughly secularized versions of conversion. Grasped in their broad outlines, however, there can be no mistaking the momentous influence on *Being and Time* of Kierkegaard's view that confronting the despair intrinsic to the structure of the self can allow us to pass through a kind of salvific death and rebirth to the public world. It is thus not surprising that Heidegger's notoriously ambivalent acknowledgments of Kierkegaard in *Being and Time* should be so colored by (what Bloom called) "the anxiety of influence" (which leads us to overemphasize our differences from those who shape us most deeply) because Kierkegaard's religious view provides the obvious philosophical prototype for Heidegger's secularized conversion narrative. Kierkegaard paved the way for Heidegger's phenomenological account of the how confronting our inescapable anxiety can allow us to turn away from the world, break its grip on us (in death), so that we can turn back to the world (in resoluteness), and thereby gain (or regain) our grip on the world – which is precisely Heidegger's vision of how Dasein transitions from inauthenticity to authenticity (however temporarily), as we will see in Section 1.4.[65]

---

[63] As White and others have observed, Heidegger's notion of "being toward death" (*Sein zum Todes*) seems deliberately to echo the title of *The Sickness Unto Death* in its German translation (*Krankheit zum Todes*); see White, *Time and Death*, 61. As White also rightly suggests (60), *The Sickness Unto Death* advances the view that "in 'Christian terminology,' the word 'death' means 'spiritual wretchedness,' not physical dying."

[64] "This self, naked and abstract, in contrast to the fully clothed self of immediacy, is the first form of the infinite self and the progressive impulse in the entire process through which a self infinitely takes possession of its actual self along with its difficulties and advantages" (Kierkegaard, *The Sickness Unto Death*, 86).

[65] Interestingly, Kierkegaard's version of conversion seems to leave the world just as it was (as if "rendering unto Caesar what is Caesar's"), whereas Heidegger's core self (the *solus*

In other words, Kierkegaard's view that it is necessary to confront one's own despair and so pass through such spiritual death in order to "become oneself" clearly had a formative impact on what I shall characterize (in Chapter 4) as Heidegger's *perfectionist* account of "how we become what we are."[66] The crucial point for us here is that recognizing Kierkegaard's subterranean but unmistakable influence on Heidegger's thinking helps us to see that Heidegger too conceives of death as something we can live through.[67] So, with Böhme and Kierkegaard having primed the pump, let us delve more deeply into our main question: What exactly does Heidegger mean to designate by the phenomenon of "death" in *Being and Time*? In what sense can Dasein live through such death, and what role does doing so play in *Being and Time*? Why, specifically, does Heidegger say not only that "Death is a way to be, which Dasein takes over as soon as it is" but, also (repeatedly, and much more famously), that: "Death is the possibility of the ultimate [in the sense of *quintessential*] impossibility of Dasein [*schlechthinnigen Daseinsunmöglichkeit*]" (BT 294/SZ 250) – that is, more clearly translated, "the possibility of Dasein's impossibility *par excellence*"?

1.4 Death as the Possibility of Dasein's Impossibility Par Excellence

We still need to know what exactly Heidegger means by *possibility* (and hence *impossibility*), so that we can understand what phenomenon he is designating when he calls *death* "the possibility of Dasein's impossibility *par excellence*" (BT 294/SZ 250). How are we to understand the phenomenon – of Dasein's being at its own distinctive *end* (let us recall) – that *Being and Time* repeatedly characterizes as the possibility of Dasein's quintessential or defining impossibility? As *Being and Time* famously maintains, "Higher than actuality stands possibility" (BT 63/SZ 38). The sense of "possibility" celebrated here is not

---

ipse) can (but, *pace* White, need not) choose quite different projects, and so a quite different world, for itself. Sartre notoriously exaggerates this difference even further in his appropriations of Heidegger (which, like Heidegger's appropriations of Kierkegaard, are similarly creative and, when not explicitly critical, typically underacknowledged). Such debts are not terribly important *philosophically* (as I argued in Thomson, *Heidegger, Art, and Postmodernity*), unless noticing them can help us to better understand their views (but cf. Harold Bloom, *The Anxiety of Influence: A Theory of Poetry* [Oxford: Oxford University Press, 1997]).

[66] On Heidegger's (Plato-influenced) thinking of such a spiritual transformation as the very heart of a genuinely philosophical education (and the pedagogical method whereby we can transcend the nihilism of technological enframing), see Chapter 4 (as well as Thomson, *Heidegger on Ontotheology*, ch. 4 and "Heidegger's Mature Vision of Ontological Education, or: How We Become What We Are," *Inquiry*, 44:3 [2001], 243–68).

[67] Like Heidegger, moreover, Kierkegaard also uses paradox to distinguish what he means by *death* from our ordinary use of the term – for example, when Anti-Climacus tells readers that "to die death itself means to live to experience dying" (Kierkegaard, *The Sickness Unto Death*, 48).

1.4. THE POSSIBILITY OF DASEIN'S IMPOSSIBILITY

"logical possibility," mere alternatives arrayed in a conceptual space, but rather *existential possibility*, "being-possible" (*Möglichsein*), which is for Heidegger "the most primordial and ultimately positive way in which Dasein is characterized ontologically" (BT 183/SZ 143–4).[68] As the always specific and practical "way in which Dasein is in every case ... what it can be" (ibid.), our existential possibilities are what we *forge ahead* into: the roles, identities, and commitments that shape and circumscribe our comportmental navigation of our lived environments. Dasein *exists – that* is, "stands out" (*ek-sistere*) into intelligibility in a meaningful way – through such a charting of "live options," choices that matter and are made salient to us by these fundamental life-projects, this sense of self embodied and reflected in our practical worlds.

It is important to recognize that Heidegger subtly distinguishes between our "being-possible" (*Möglichsein*) and our "ability-to-be" (*Seinkönnen*) in order to mark a crucial difference between these life-*projects*, on the one hand, and our *projecting* ourselves into those life-projects, on the other. Dasein cannot *be* something the way a physical object like a chair can be a chair (in a continuous substantive identity with itself); instead, Dasein "*is* what it becomes" (BT 186/SZ 145). That is, we can only "be" something – a teacher, father, husband, brother, friend, environmentalist, bicyclist, citizen – by continuing to *become* that, repeatedly "projecting" or pressing ahead existentially into that "project" (*Entwurf*) or practical identity as we go about our lives.[69] This explains why Heidegger writes that "Dasein, as being-possible [*Möglichsein*], *is* existentially that which, in its ability-to-be [*Seinkönnen*], it is *not yet*" (BT 185–6/SZ 145). For example, when I project into the project of being a teacher (by preparing for and teaching a class, meeting with students, carefully responding to their work, answering their emails, and so on), that is my way of *being* a teacher. In Heidegger's terms of art, I *am* that teacher (as the "being-possible" of my defining *life-projects*) which I am thereby *becoming* (in the "ability-to-be"

---

[68] As Guignon puts it: "What I *am* at the most basic level is a reaching forward into possibilities, not an actualizing of possibilities." (See Charles Guignon, "Heidegger and Kierkegaard on Death: The Existentiell and the Existential," in *Kierkegaard and Death*, ed. by P. Stokes and A. Buben [Bloomington, IN: Indiana University Press, 2011], 197.) In existential death, this "reaching forward" (or "projecting," the term Heidegger and I most often employ) can *fail* to reach into our projects, constituting an experience in which this existential reach that fundamentally defines us completely exceeds our actual worldly grasp (to redeploy Guignon's terms), thereby helping us grasp that reaching out itself.

[69] Because "the being of the here" ("*das Sein des Da*" that defines "Dasein") "receives its constitution through the understanding and its character as projection, it [Dasein] *is* what it becomes" (BT 186/SZ 145). Existential death, we will see, is primarily described as a collapse of the understanding as the existential structure of projecting into projects (though it will also be crucial to recognize that, since the three existential structures are inextricably entwined, the phenomenon death discloses is also felt via our affective attunement as *Angst* and articulated through our *Rede* as conscience [see n. 6]).

whereby I *project into* those roles, goals, and embodied ways of understanding my own being).[70]

Now, usually we project ourselves into our life-projects by skilfully navigating, rather than theoretically deliberating over, the live-options these projects implicitly delimit and render salient for us – except in cases when something goes wrong or breaks down, and we become explicitly aware of what we were previously trying to do. Heidegger thinks it is possible, however, for all of our projects to break down simultaneously; indeed, this is precisely what he thinks will happen to anyone who endures a true confrontation with their existential *Angst*. Rather than acknowledging and confronting the underlying *Angst* that subtly accompanies the thought of death throughout our lives, Heidegger points out, we normally flee this "anxiety" (or "dread") by seeking to adopt *das Man*'s "indifferent tranquillity as to the 'fact' that one dies" (telling ourselves, for instance, that "everyone dies, of course, some day," by which we really try to assure ourselves "but not me, not today"). This repression transforms the existential anxiety that continually accompanies us "into fear in the face of an oncoming event" (namely, *demise*), an event we thereby push off as far as possible into the distant future (BT 298/SZ 254) – as if death could thereby be safely cordoned off from our own existing world. But if we can confront and endure our existential anxiety instead of seeking to deny and tranquillize it (by adopting such common strategies as "hurrying" and "keeping busy"),[71] then it becomes possible, *Being and Time* suggests, for us to trace this baseline anxiety back to its source in our basic "uncanniness" (or *Unheimlichkeit*), the fundamental existential *homelessness* that follows from the fact that there is no life-project any of us can ever finally be at home in, because there is ultimately nothing about the ontological structure of the self that could tell us what specifically we should do with our lives. There is, in other words, no one correct answer about what to do when facing any of the important existential cross-roads in our lives, and insofar as we had been living with the naïve sense that we were indeed doing the right thing simply by doing "what one does" (that is, just following along with *das Man*, the anonymous "anyone"), then recognizing the contingency of our life-defining choices is likely to prove at least temporarily paralysing.[72]

---

[70] Heidegger's idea that *our being is a becoming* means that, through our existence-defining projecting into projects, we repeatedly change and grow in our very ways of being what we are, sometimes even dying to our defining projects, whether temporarily or permanently (as we shall see in Chapter 4).

[71] Here Heidegger nicely begins to anticipate that widespread and multivalent anxiety-avoidance behavior that has metastasized technologically into our current cultural addiction to micro-dosing miniscule amounts of dopamine via the unsteady drip of the new, endlessly arriving via social media, "the news," etc.

[72] Like Kierkegaard, who famously proclaimed that "purity of the heart is to will one thing" and so believed he had to choose between *either* being a philosopher *or* a husband,

1.4. THE POSSIBILITY OF DASEIN'S IMPOSSIBILITY

As Heidegger puts it, when we confront our existential *Angst* (that is, when we "pursue what such moods disclose and ... allow ourselves to confront what has been disclosed" through them [BT 173/SZ 135]), we can come to recognize our essential *Unheimlichkeit*, that is, our "not being at home" in the world, the fundamental lack of fit between our underlying existential projecting and the specific existentiell (or particular individual) worldly projects in terms of which we each flesh out our existence and so give shape to our worlds. (Here again we can see the influence of *The Sickness Unto Death*, which insists on the radical heterogeneity of our "naked and abstract" self before God and our "fully clothed" self of worldly immediacy.[73] More generally, Heidegger's insistence on Dasein's essential "uncanniness" or "not-being-at-home" in the world seems to be his way of secularizing – and so preserving the core phenomenological insight contained in – the Christian idea that we are *in* but not *of* the world.) Heidegger's basic idea here is that there can be no seamless fit between Dasein's existing and the projects that allow us to make

---

Heidegger too thinks Dasein is implicitly guided (at least in times of great difficulty, when we become like a cutter ship seeking to break through an ice-field) by a singular life-project that all our other projects ultimately serve. (*Being and Time*'s terminology for this life-defining project is Dasein's "ultimate for-the-sake-of-which.") In the case of a self structured according to such a quasi-teleological hierarchy of life-projects, it is not unreasonable to think that if our leading life-project collapses, then all our other projects that exist primarily to support it will come cascading down in its wake, like a house of cards. (This is indeed what happened to Heidegger when he experienced the existential death of what had been his defining life-project of becoming a Jesuit Priest, as I will show in *Heidegger: A Philosophical Biography*). Of course, as Dreyfus often pointed out to his students, we live in a late-modern age too rational and risk-averse to admire this Kierkegaardian ideal, which to us looks like that infamous investment strategy of "putting all your eggs in one basket" – a perilous strategy precisely because it makes it possible for *all one's eggs to break at once* (which here nicely suggests undergoing *existential death*). And yet this is the very mark of Kierkegaardian faith – to see the sword hanging over the head of the beloved and yet risk loving her unreservedly nonetheless – that is, to make just such a risky commitment unconditionally, risking everything and receiving a *meaningful* life in return for this vulnerable but wholehearted commitment, at least for as long as it lasts. (It may be out of fashion today, but Dreyfus makes a strong, Heidegger-inflected case for the thorough secularizability and growing relevance of this Kierkegaardian ideal in Hubert L. Dreyfus, *On the Internet*, 2nd ed. [London: Routledge, 2008].)

[73] Kierkegaard similarly suggests that confronting despair "begins that act of separation in which the self becomes aware of itself as essentially different from the environment and the external world and their effect on it." (See Kierkegaard, *The Sickness Unto Death*, 85.) The uncanny "lack of fit" I have in mind between Dasein and its world, to develop the Kierkegaardian metaphor, is a bit like the blob trying to find clothing off the rack that fits, or like trying to fit a water-balloon into a keyhole. But the blob or water-balloon here is what Heidegger describes phenomenologically as the positive *nothingness* of the self, an existing that *is* always more than it can express in worldly terms, as we shall see. (I thank an anonymous reviewer for pressing me to clarify this difficult but crucial point.)

sense of our existing by bestowing our being-here with the shape and content of specific worldly projects (teacher, student, friend, father, brother, citizen), and thus no one right answer to the question of what we should do with our lives. (Our anxiety stems from and so can help reveal this fact that there is no one correct answer about *what* projects to project ourselves into, nor about *how* to project ourselves into whatever projects we have thereby chosen to understand ourselves in terms of.)

Our sense of *uncanniness* or "not-being-at-home" in the world thus derives from and testifies to this anxiety-provoking lack of a fit between Dasein and its world (between, that is, the sheer "projecting" of *existence* as a "standing-out" into intelligibility and the specific worldly projects that shape and circumscribe our existential worlds, rendering these worlds *significant*, as we will see).[74] This means that, insofar as one has been blithely living with an unquestioned sense that one is simply doing what one should be doing with one's life (whether by following the path of least resistance, the guidance of the authority figures in one's life, or the various exemplars our cultures hold up as successful role models to be emulated), confronting one's *Angst* will expose one's fundamental lack of fit with one's practical world and can thereby catalyze the temporary collapse of the life-projects one has been pursuing with a sense of naïve good conscience. Just such a scenario, in which I pursue my anxiety to the point where all my life-projects, foundering on the reef of their own contingency, forfeit their unquestioned inertia and so temporarily break down or collapse – no longer allowing me to project (or "press-ahead") into them and so make sense of myself in their worldly terms – is what Heidegger means by "anticipation" of (or "running-out" toward) death, and it forms the first structural component of *authenticity* understood in its two successive moments as *anticipatory resolution*.[75]

To bootstrap our way into understanding why Heidegger calls death "the possibility of Dasein impossibility *par excellence*," it helps to think, first, of someone whose fundamental life-project was being a teacher (or a priest,

---

[74] This means, I think, that if one could imagine a Dasein-like being (a kind of android, say) who fit perfectly into its world without leaving any remainder of self (a being for whom one and only one life-project made perfect sense), then this being would not experience any anxiety. Of course, if the world changed, or such a being changed (think, for example, of *Wall-E*), then even such a being could find itself no longer entirely at home in the world (and so subject to existential anxiety).

[75] Heidegger's heroic image of "charging forward into death [*Vorlaufen in den Tod*]" seems to have been drawn from Ernst Jünger's grim yet romantic description of German soldiers charging blindly from the trenches through clouds of poisonous gas meant to cover and aid their *Blitzkrieg* – gas attacks that Heidegger's own "weather service" unit helped plan. (See Ernst Jünger, *Storm of Steel*, trans. by M. Hofmann [New York: Penguin, 2004] and chs. 3 and 4 of Thomson, *Heidegger on Ontotheology*. I thank Taylor Carman for originally suggesting this connection to me.)

1.4. THE POSSIBILITY OF DASEIN'S IMPOSSIBILITY   41

husband, son, communist, pet owner, or any other identity-defining self-understanding) but who then experiences the catastrophic collapse of this embodied life-project. What is crucial to recognize is that when such world-collapse occurs, we do not instantly forfeit the skills, capacities, and inclinations that this identity previously organized. Instead, in such a situation, we tend to continue projecting ourselves upon an absent project (for a time at least – the time it takes to mourn that project or else replace it, redirecting or abandoning the drives it organized). After that world collapses, we tend to keep pressing blindly ahead (absentmindedly moving to fill the food bowl of a recently deceased pet, for example), even though the project that previously organized this projection is no longer there for us to press-ahead into (since, in this example, one no longer has that pet). Thinking about such a paradoxical (and yet quite common) situation – in which we project ourselves toward a life-project we can no longer project ourselves into – helps us grasp what Heidegger means when he calls death "the possibility of Dasein's *impossibility* par excellence" (that is, the existential impossibility that shows us both what we Dasein essentially are and what "impossibility" most fundamentally means for us, at the very structural core of our existential "being-here"). For when not just one but all of our life-projects break down in what Heidegger calls "anticipation" or "running-out" (*Vorlaufen*) toward death, we experience ourselves as a kind of bare existential projecting without *any* existentiell projects to project ourselves into (and so understand ourselves in terms of). We can thereby come to understand ourselves as, at bottom, a "primordial existential projecting" (BT 379/SZ 330), a brute projecting (or sheer *ek-sisting*) that is more basic than – and independent of – any of the particular projects that usually give our lives content and significance.

To grasp what Heidegger thinks the self ultimately boils down to (in this existential version of Husserl's phenomenological reduction), it is crucial to remember that when my projects all break down or collapse, leaving me without any life-project to project myself into, projection itself does not cease. When my being-possible becomes impossible, I still am; my ability-to-be becomes insubstantial, unable to connect to the world practically, but *not inert*. My projects collapse, and I no longer have a concrete self I can be, but I still *am* this inability-to-be. Heidegger calls this paradoxical condition (of projectless projection) revealed by anticipation "the possibility of Dasein's impossibility," or *death*. In his words:

> Death, as possibility [that is, as something we project ourselves into practically], gives Dasein nothing to be "actualized," nothing which Dasein could itself actually *be*. [I do not experience the messy bed or the coffee beans as things that demand making, for example, because in existential death I can no longer actually project myself into my previous life-guiding project of being a teacher – or whichever practical life-project had previously been my "ultimate for-the-sake-of-which" – so all my

other subordinate projects, like taking care of my home or preparing coffee for school, no longer solicit my practical engagement.] Death is the possibility of the impossibility of every way of *comporting* oneself toward [*Verhaltens zu*, which in *Being and Time* means *practically engaging with* and thereby relating to] anything, of every [practical or worldly] way of existing. (BT 307, my emphasis/SZ 262)

We can see the phenomenon Heidegger has in mind when we generalize from the case in which one project breaks down to the catastrophic collapse of them all. A student can explicitly encounter his computer, a carpenter her hammer, and a commuter their car as a tool with a specific role to play in an equipmental nexus organized by their self-understanding, precisely when this tool breaks down – when the hard drive crashes the night before a paper is due, the hammer breaks and cannot be fixed or replaced in the middle of a job, or the car breaks down on the way to an important meeting, leaving the commuter stranded by the side of the road. Just so, Dasein can explicitly encounter its structure as the practical embodiment of a self-understanding when its projects all break down in death. Dasein, stranded (as it were) by the global collapse of its practical projects, can come explicitly to recognize itself as, at bottom, not any particular self or life-project but, rather, as a projecting into projects, that is, as *a being who fundamentally takes an engaged stand on its being and is defined by that stand*. Thus, by severing all my practical relations to my world-defining projects, existential death brings the existential structure of my usually implicit and embodied being-in-the-world into focus, allowing me to understand explicitly what usually I am implicitly in my comportmental engagement with things and other people.

Now, among the relatively few who get this far in understanding Heidegger's phenomenological depiction of existential death as a global collapse of my practical being-in-the-world, a fairly common worry is that such a situation is not just extremely rare or unrealistic but, worse, phenomenologically *incoherent*, since (those who advance this objection suppose) such a situation would leave me completely unable even to make sense of the objects surrounding me. Here it is illuminating to see how this objection is based on a subtle but important misreading. The total breakdown of Dasein's being-in-the-world in existential death incapacitates Dasein's "ready-to-hand" (or "hands-on," *zuhanden*) comportmental relations to those networks of equipmental paraphernalia rendered "*significant*" by Dasein's practical world (BT 231/SZ 187); it does not entail a breakdown of our "thematic" or conscious ability to comprehend what entities are as "present-at-hand" (or "on-hand," *vorhanden*) objects (BT 393/SZ 343). So, for example, in the total breakdown of my life-projects in existential death, I can still understand "thematically" (that is, cognitively or representationally) what an alarm clock or an espresso machine is as a "deworlded" *object* (*Gegenstand*) merely *standing* there over *against* me. The real problem is that I cannot "press-ahead" or *project into* any of my usual practical life-projects –

1.4. THE POSSIBILITY OF DASEIN'S IMPOSSIBILITY 43

such existential possibilities as being a father or teacher – that would ordinarily make those entities part of my world by endowing them with "significance" (that is, practical relevance for the existential projects I am projecting into, like teacher, father, or homeowner).

As *Being and Time* famously argues (in division one), "ordinarily and usually," the entities that implicitly populate my world have "hands-on" (*zuhanden*) practical *"significance"* as nodal points of engagement in holistically interconnected equipmental nexuses that are implicitly organized by my life-projects. For example, while implicitly projecting into the existential possibility of being a *teacher*, I encounter my bedroom as a quiet place full of useful paraphernalia for sleeping and waking so as to be rested from today's teaching and ready for tomorrow's classes, whereas the "kitchen" shows up as the place full of equipment for preparing the meals or making the coffee I bring with me to school. Deprived of such practical significance in existential death, all such entities become radically "de-worlded" objects – and so merely stand there in their "empty mercilessness" (BT 393/SZ 343), as if their sudden loss of saliency and relevance constituted a silent mockery of my existence as a being who *cares* about its own being. (It is this very same "care" [*Sorge*] that I ordinarily manifest by implicitly taking an embodied stand on what it means to be, a practical stand that discloses entities not as mere *objects* standing over against me but as interconnected nexuses of practical *equipment* implicitly playing some significant role for my projects and thereby soliciting my engagement.)[76]

---

[76] As Heidegger writes: "The world in which I exist has sunk into insignificance; ... but this does not mean that in anxiety we experience something like the absence of what is present-at-hand within the world" (BT 392/SZ 343). To briefly address another likely objection here, let me just note that, while it is quite right to point to that Heidegger is describing the phenomenon *anxiety* discloses in some of the passages I draw on here, it is wrong to think that this counts as a telling *objection* to incorporating those insights into my view of *death*. The simple reason for this is that the basic phenomenon Heidegger describes in existential death is *three-sided*, as it were, showing three *inextricably interconnected* and "equiprimordial" aspects, which can nevertheless be analytically articulated in terms of *death, anxiety,* and *conscience*. Like any existential phenomenon that discloses Dasein to itself in its inextricably tripartite existential structure, the desolate *"solus ipse* [or self alone]" at Dasein's existential core can be approached through *all three* of Dasein's main existential structures – showing up as *death* when disclosed through the understanding, as *uncanniness* when revealed through our "affective attunement" (or *Befindlichkeit*) of *Angst*, and as *conscience* when encountered through Dasein's "conversance" [or *Rede*]. Dasein's equiprimordial and interconnected tripartite existential structure (along with the similarly interlinked temporal horizons that underlie and condition its existential structure) explains why Heidegger ultimately thinks all three of these existential phenomena *together*, referring, for example, to "anxiety in the face of death" (BT 295/SZ 251), then turning to conscience (which ultimately stems from the *solus ipse*, as we will see at the end of this chapter; see also n. 6 and Chapter 7). (I am grateful to an objection from Mark Wrathall that encouraged me to clarify this point.)

Hence, qualifying his description of Dasein – radically individualized by its confrontation with "anxiety in the face of death" – as a "self alone" (or *solus ipse*), Heidegger distinguishes the existential reduction he is describing from the famous Cartesian reduction of the self to an isolated thing certain only of its own thinking:

> But this existential "solipsism" is so far from transposing an isolated subject thing into the harmless emptiness of a worldless occurring [here "subject thing" is a jab at Descartes' paradoxical conception of the self as a *res cogitans* or "thinking substance"], that what it does is precisely to bring Dasein in an extreme sense face to face with its world as world, and thus face to face with itself as being-in-the-world. (BT 233/SZ 188)

That is, when our worlds collapse in death, we discover ourselves not as a worldless *cogito* (cast out into an empty void of cognitive uncertainty, all objects having dissolved into epistemic uncertainty) but as a "world-hungry" Dasein (as Dreyfus nicely puts it), a "world hunger" we discover explicitly when we find ourselves utterly unable to 'eat' anything – unable, that is, to project into any of the life-projects that ordinarily constitute our worlds (BT 231/SZ 189) – despite our desperate desire to do so.[77] Hence Heidegger's description of this radically individuated "self" of pure "mineness" as "a naked 'that-it-is-*and-has-to-be*'" (BT 173, my emphasis/SZ 134), a being that *must* find a way to go on practically and yet, at least temporarily, cannot.

This strange and dreadful experience of our own *being completely unable* (or *projectless projecting*) explains the phenomenology of existential death as "the possibility of Dasein's impossibility *par excellence*," because it is only through such a collapse of the practical world that we usually are that we first come to *understand* (in Heidegger's primary sense, that is, "stand-under" or encounter for ourselves) the structure of our own being as an existential projecting into worldly projects. Or, to take another example, a student does not usually experience their pen in its implicit worldly significance as an item of equipment they are writing with, in their green notebook, so as to take notes on today's lecture on *Being and Time*, in order to help learn about Heidegger, for the sake of being a good student – until, say, that pen runs out of ink and cannot be replaced in the middle of an illuminating explanation of a difficult and important passage. Similarly, we only *recognize* that we are beings who take such engaged, worldly significance disclosing stands on the meaning of our own being by projecting into life-projects when these projects collapse in existential death.

When we *find ourselves* (pun intended) in this desolate condition – existing as a projectless *solus ipse* deprived of any world of practical life-projects

---

[77] See Hubert L. Dreyfus, "Foreword" to Carol J. White, in *Time and Death: Heidegger's Analysis of Finitude*, ed. by Mark Ralkowski (Aldershot: Ashgate, 2005). See also Steven Crowell's iconoclastic, insightful, and increasingly influential essay, "Subjectivity."

1.4. THE POSSIBILITY OF DASEIN'S IMPOSSIBILITY

(a world of projects to which we seek desperately to return) – what do we do? Here again Heidegger follows Kierkegaard (and the insight from Christian mysticism portrayed by Dante): *The only way out is through*. (Or as Winston Churchill famously put it: "When you are going through hell, keep going!") By anxiously "running-out" toward death and so embodying this possibility of impossibility par excellence (an embodied existential *possibility* in which we discover what it truly means for our worldly existence to become *impossible*), "Dasein is taken back all the way to its naked uncanniness, and becomes fascinated by it. This fascination, however, not only *takes* Dasein back from its '*worldly*' possibilities, but at the same time *gives* Dasein the possibility of an *authentic* ability-to-be" (BT 394/SZ 344). This idea that anxiously running-out toward death not only radically individuates Dasein but, in so doing, also gives Dasein an authentic ability-to-be brings us back to the point that, for Heidegger, death is something I can live through. (Remember that Heidegger himself stresses the paradox that Dasein lives through its death when he writes, "Death is a way to be, which Dasein takes over as soon as it is.") Heidegger's point is that the pure, world-hungry projecting we experience when we are unable to connect to our projects is what is most basic about us. For, this fundamental existential projecting is implicit in all of our ordinary *projecting* into projects, and it also inalienably survives the nonterminal loss of Dasein's any and every particular worldly project.

This is what explains the otherwise puzzling fact that Heidegger often refers to the *projectless projecting* of existential "death" as Dasein's "ownmost ability-to-be" (*eigenste Seinkönnen*); this sheer existential *projecting* is something no Dasein can forfeit so long as it is. Remember that Heidegger distinguishes between our "being-possible" (*Möglichsein*) and our "ability-to-be" (*Seinkönnen*) to mark this crucial difference between our life-*projects*, on the one hand, and our *projecting* ourselves into those life-projects, on the other. Heidegger *frequently* refers to existential "death" in *Being and Time* by calling it Dasein's "ownmost ability-to-be [*eigenste Seinkönnen*]."[78] Why is existential death the "ability-to-be" (that is, the existential *projecting* or pressing-forward) that is *most Dasein's own*? Because existential death phenomenologically discloses that sheer *projecting* or existing (*ek-sisting* as "standing-out" toward a world) that Dasein cannot forfeit without thereby ceasing to be Dasein. Every particular life-project that constitutes our being-possible (*Möglichsein*) can be lost, but this brute projecting or *existing* cannot (so long as we have not demised but are still here as *Dasein*). I thus take Heidegger's frequent use of "Dasein's ownmost ability-to-be" to designate *death* as strong evidence for my phenomenological reconstruction of existential death as *projectless projecting*.

But how, to return to the crucial question, can we "live through" such death? The passage through existential death (and back to the world of

---

[78] See, for example, SZ 144, 178, 181, 191, 228, 262, 263, 276, 278, 300, 306, 307, and 339.

practical life-projects) is what Heidegger calls "resolve or resoluteness" (*Entschlossenheit*) and it is the *second* part of his full phenomenological account of *authenticity* in its two connected structural moments as *anticipatory resoluteness*. Resoluteness is just as complex a phenomenon as anticipation (or "running-out" into death), and we will explore it in more detail in subsequent chapters. But at its core *resolve* designates Dasein's accomplishment of a reflexive reconnection to the world of projects lost in death, a recovery made possible by the lucid encounter of the self with its own unsinkable core in existential death. On the basis of the insight gained from this radical self-encounter, it becomes possible for us to recover ourselves (from *das Man*'s superficial and homogenizing ways of doing *what one does*) and then reconnect to the practical world we are usually connected to effortlessly and unreflexively. This reconnection turns on our giving up the unreflexive, paralyzing belief that there is a single correct choice to make (about what or how to be), since recognizing that there is no such single correct choice (because there is no sufficiently substantive self to *determine* such a choice) is what gives us the *freedom* to choose among the existential possibilities (the roles, goals, and life-projects) we face as live-options (their full range ordinarily "dimmed-down" by the pervasive conformity of *das Man*), and also what gives us the subsequent "responsibility" for having so chosen (by making us "answerable" for the lives we have thereby made our own).

As Heidegger dramatically puts it:

> If Dasein, by anticipation, lets death become powerful in itself, then, as free for death, Dasein understands itself in its own *greater power*, the power of its finite freedom, so that in this freedom, which "is" only in its having chosen to make such a choice, it can take over the *powerlessness* of abandonment to its having done so, and can thus come to see clearly what in the situation is up to chance [and, correlatively, what is up to Dasein]. (BT 436/SZ 384)

"Resoluteness" (*Entschlossenheit*) is Heidegger's name for such free decisions, by which we recognize that the core of the self, as a projectless projecting, is more powerful than (that is, *survives*) death (the collapse of its projects), and so become capable of "choosing to choose," of making a lucid or deliberate reconnection to the world of our existential projects. The freedom of such lucid or meta-decisions is "finite" because it is always constrained: by Dasein's own *facticity* and *thrownness* (the fundamental fact that each Dasein is, and has to continue to be, as "thrown" into a world that predates and shapes us such that we "always-already" possess a variety of particular talents, cares, and predispositions, an orienting "facticity" that partly constitutes our being and can often be altered piecemeal but not simply thrown off in some Sartrean "radical choice"); by the preexisting concerns of our time and "generation" (to which we cannot but respond in one way or another); by the facts of the specific situation we confront (and which of these facts can be altered, Heidegger stresses, we cannot fully appreciate until we act and so enter into this situation concretely); as well as by that which remains unpredictable about the future (including the responses of others).[79] Nevertheless, it is by embracing this finitude – giving up our naïve desire for either absolute freedom or a single correct choice between (and within) defining life-projects and instead accepting that our finite freedom always operates against a background of constraint (in which there is usually more than one "right" answer for us, rather than none at all) – that we are able to overcome that paralysis of projects experienced in death. It is thus important that Heidegger increasingly hyphenates "*Ent-schlossenheit*" (literally "un-closedness") to emphasize that the existential "resoluteness" whereby Dasein freely chooses the existential commitments that define it does not entail deciding on a particular course of action ahead of time and obstinately sticking to one's guns come what may but, instead, requires an "openness" whereby one continues to be responsive to the emerging solicitations of, and unpredictable elements in, the particular existential "situation," the full reality of which only the actual decision itself discloses.

In resolve's decisive "moment of insight," Dasein is (like a gestalt switch) set free rather than paralyzed by the contingency and indeterminacy of its choice of projects, and so can project itself into its chosen project in a way that expresses its sense that, although this project is appropriated from a storehouse of publicly

---

[79] It is that third point that L. A. Paul mainly focuses on in L. A. Paul, *Transformative Experience* (Oxford: Oxford University Press, 2016). Paul argues for an extreme view of such future uncertainty, which brings her position closer to that of Sartre or even Derrida (for whom any truly free decision must pass through its own radical undecidability) than Heidegger (see Chapters 6 and 9 and Jacques Derrida, *The Gift of Death* [Chicago, IL: University of Chicago Press, 1996]). In Heidegger's view, when we face important existential decisions such as whether to become a parent, it is true that we cannot fully know what that will mean for us unless we do it. But we will in fact have *some sense* of how attractive (or repulsive) such a project is for us in particular (given the "thrown facticity" that always already shapes our own talents, cares, and affective predispositions), so we do not face such decisions from a position of radical ignorance or rational neutrality. (We do not even face the hypothetical decision about whether to choose *immortality* from a position of total ignorance, I argue in Chapter 9, since we can easily imagine how immortality can go terribly wrong, while we cannot convincingly envision how it could possibly go well for us.) Paul, like Derrida, seems to over-correct in response to the type of mistake *one* (as *das Man*) typically makes, which is to blithely assume that important life-decisions are simply obvious or else can be rationally determined ahead of time (or even optimized through some strictly rational calculus). Indeed, that kind of rationalistic confidence is typical of the false "good conscience" we possess (as *das Man*) before recognizing the anxiety-provoking absence of any single correct answers about who or how we should be, that very anxiety which first throws us back upon our *finite* freedom in existential death. From the perspective of the finite freedom of that thrown projecting we are in death, which way to go at the existential cross-roads we come to is *neither* obvious or predetermined and so illusory *nor* merely arbitrary and so relativistic (as explained in n. 56). Instead, our finite but ineliminable margin of freedom is precisely what makes us *answerable* for what and how we ourselves decide to do and be.

intelligible roles inherited from the tradition, it nevertheless matters that this particular role has been chosen by this particular Dasein and updated, *via* a "reciprocative rejoinder" (BT 438/SZ 386), so as, ideally, to develop its particular ontic and factical aptitudes and predispositions as these intersect with the pressing needs of its time and "generation," doing so in a way that is uniquely this Dasein's own even as it reaches back into that public world and thereby connects with the defining projects of other Dasein. (Indeed, *Being and Time* suggests, existential death encourages us to find our own ways of aligning our defining existential projects with the needs of a larger community, our "generation," so that the practical projects we project into and so understand ourselves in terms of do not remain strictly individual and hence cease to be with our own eventual demise (BT 308/SZ 263–4). For, insofar as the existential projects we understand ourselves in terms of can survive our demise by living on in the existential projects of those who survive us, our own demise loses some of its fearsomeness, as we will see.)[80]

Instead of simply taking over our projects from *das Man* (by going with the flow, following the path of least resistance, or simply doing "what one should do"), it thus becomes possible, through resolve, to take over a project reflexively (whether lucidly or explicitly), and so to reappropriate oneself (taking or retaking *ownership* of our own existence), thereby "becoming what we are" by breaking the previously unnoticed grip arbitrarily exerted upon us by *das Man*'s ubiquitous norms of social propriety, its pre- and proscriptions on *what one does and how one should do it*.[81] In sum, then, "authenticity or ownedness [*Eigentlichkeit*]," as *anticipatory resoluteness*, names this double movement in which the world lost in anticipating or running-out into death is regained in resolve, a (literally) revolutionary movement by which we are involuntarily turned away from the world and then voluntarily turn back to it, in which the grip of the world upon us is broken in order that we may thereby gain (or regain) our grip on this world.

1.5 Heidegger's Phenomenological Bridge from Demise to Death: Formal Indication

With this detailed overview in place, let us return to the specific question of how the existential phenomenon Heidegger calls "death" is *both related to and distinguished from* our ordinary notion of "demise." By "death," we have seen,

---

[80] See also n. 46.
[81] (I develop this line of thinking much further in Thomson, *Heidegger, Art, and Postmodernity*, as well as in subsequent chapters here.) Heidegger's understanding of "finite freedom" is bolstered by Bernard Williams's suggestive speculation concerning the roots of the very idea of "liberty," viz., that "it is a plausible guess at a human universal that people resent being, as they see it, arbitrarily pushed around by others." (See Bernard Williams, "Liberalism and Loss," in *The Legacy of Isaiah Berlin*, ed. by Mark Lilla, Ronald Dworkin, and Robert B. Silvers [New York: New York Review of Books, 2001], 93.)

1.5. HEIDEGGER'S BRIDGE FROM DEMISE TO DEATH

Heidegger means the experience of existential world-collapse that first occurs when we confront the ineliminable anxiety that stems from the basic lack of fit between Dasein and its world, an anxiety that emerges from the uncanny fact that there is nothing about the structure of the self that can tell us specifically to do with our lives. By "dying," I have suggested, Heidegger means the mere *projecting, disclosing,* or *ek-sisting* ("standing-out") that we lucidly experience when our projects collapse in death (and we encounter ourselves as a projectless projecting). By "genuinely or authentically dying," let me now suggest, he means the *explicit* experience of undergoing such world-collapse and thereby coming to understand ourselves phenomenologically as, at bottom, a mere projecting, that is ("ordinarily and usually"), a *projecting* into projects, a fundamental existential projecting that survives even the (non-terminal) global collapse of the worldly projects that normally constitute and organize our being-here.[82]

If this is right, then (to come back to passage D1 for a final time) Heidegger's claim that "Dasein can demise only as long as it is dies" must also mean that only so long as one is dying, that is, simply projecting, existing, or disclosing at all, can one demise, that is, project into, disclose, or move toward the terminal collapse of one's world. Indeed, we can move *toward* that end of the being that we are in *demise* only so far as we are capable of experiencing that end of our own distinctive being (as a practical being-in-the-world) in the "finite existing" of *death's* projectless projecting. It is thus existential death that lets us experience that distinctive *end* of our own being – that "being here" at an end of our being-in-the-world – which we can only move asymptotically *toward* in demise (at least as far as we can tell phenomenologically, confined as we are in our experience to this side of life's "great beyond").

We have been driven to such an initially strange view of what Heidegger means by "death" by the fact that Heidegger claims not only that we can "die" in his existential sense without having to undergo mortal demise but also, conversely, that most human beings reach their demise without ever undergoing his kind of "death." This functional independence of death from demise (that is,

---

[82] In "authentic [or *genuine*] death" (Heidegger's potentially misleading name for undergoing an experience with the intention of checking one's phenomenological account of it), I explicitly *repeat* the experience I have previously undergone lucidly (in death); that is, I explicitly project myself into my own brute projecting and (by "enduring" this experience of existential death) I not only come to exist my own existing or become my own becoming but can also come to disclose the temporal horizons conditioning my existence at the very deepest level phenomenology is capable of uncovering. (I explore this difficult view of Heidegger's in the final section of this chapter.) See, for example, §61, where Heidegger rhetorically asks: "What if resoluteness ... should bring itself into its authenticity only when it projects itself ... upon the uttermost possibility which lies ahead of Dasein's every factical ability-to-be [viz., the possibility of our impossibility, or death]?" (BT 349/SZ 302). Such "authentic or genuine dying" is thus something one needs to undergo (again) and endure if one is seeking phenomenologically to describe (or check one's own or someone else's previous description of) what exactly the experience of world-collapse discloses about the structure of the selves that we are.

the fact we can die without demising and demise without dying) justifies distinguishing the two phenomena in even a non-commonsensical way, as Blattner, Haugeland, and White have long done well to argue against numerous critics who, like Hoffman, simply cannot accept that Heidegger would be so confusing as to use the word "death" to refer to something we can live through. This is precisely what Heidegger is doing, however, thereby generating the almost inevitable confusion experienced by the legion of readers who enter his hermeneutic circle already armed with the commonsensical (and yet nonetheless false) conviction that "death" *must* mean demise, such that when Heidegger writes about "death," he must surely be describing the phenomenon we colloquially (and euphemistically) call "kicking the bucket," "taking a dirt nap," "buying the farm" (as if finally making good on our "*mort-gage*," our *promise* to demise), or simply "passing away." As we have seen, however, he is not, and Heidegger is quite explicit that his "existential analysis" of such phenomena as Dasein's death "constantly has the character of doing violence [*Gewaltsamkeit*]" to "the everyday way in which Dasein is interpreted" (BT 359/SZ 311). The goal of this acknowledged hermeneutic "violence" (or "forcing-open") is to discover the constitutive ontological structures that underlie and condition our "everyday" interpretations, everyday views that cover over and obscure these structures and so close them off from our understanding. It is thus not to sound radical, different, or original that Heidegger's phenomenological interpretations do "violence" to our ordinary ways of interpreting phenomena like death; instead, that hermeneutic violence results from *Being and Time*'s deeper goal of "*freeing*" the "undisguised" ontological truth of phenomena like death from their concealment beneath our widespread but superficial and confused ways of understanding their meaning (BT 360/SZ 313).

At the same time, however, rightly insisting on the difference between existential death and mortal demise should not lead us to err in the opposite direction (as Haugeland and White clearly do), prying death and demise so far apart that they entirely overlook the crucial interconnections linking the two phenomena together.[83] For, I now want to show, demise and death remain intimately related, of methodological necessity, and these connections are what rightly generate the undeniable *existential pathos* that has led generations of readers to expect to find a discourse about the ontic event of demise (or kicking the bucket) in Heidegger's ontological analysis of death as the type of end most proper to and distinctive of Dasein's being.

We can begin to understand the crucial connection between death and demise if we notice that the six structural characteristics that "define" Heidegger's "full existential-ontological conception of death" – namely, that

---

[83] Haugeland asserts that: "What is important about these ["demise and perishing"] is *only* that neither is to be identified with death, *existentially* conceived." See Haugeland, "Truth and Finitude," 66 (first emphasis mine). Although I think Haugeland is wrong on this important point, many of his other observations about death remain insightful and suggestive.

1.5. HEIDEGGER'S BRIDGE FROM DEMISE TO DEATH 51

"*death*, as [1] *the end of Dasein, is* [2] *Dasein's ownmost,* [3] *non-relational,* [4] *certain and* [5] *as such indefinite, and* [6] *non-surpassable possibility*" (BT 303/SZ 258-9) – are all drawn from a formal analysis of demise. This, I submit, is no accident but rather the deliberate result of Heidegger's phenomenological method. The fulcrum of Heidegger's broader method of *phenomenological attestation* is what he calls "formal indication"; formal indication is the pivot that allows Heidegger to move from the ontic to the ontological level of phenomenological analysis (as he does, for example, with ontic and ontological guilt, ontic and ontological conscience, demise and death, and time and temporality). In a formal indication, Heidegger explains, "The empty content, viewed with respect to the structure of its meaning [*das leer Gehaltliche in seiner Sinnstruktur*], is at the same time that which indicates the direction of its fulfilling enactment [*die Vollzugsrichtung*]" (PIA 26/GA 61 33).[84] In other words, "formal indication" enables Heidegger to extract from the ontic phenomenon under consideration only its formal *structures*, which he then fleshes out in quite different senses in his analysis of the corresponding ontological phenomenon (BT 362/SZ 314-5). We then have to project ourselves into this ontological phenomenon in order to be able to understand (in this "fulfilling enactment") both (1) the ontological phenomenon underlying our ordinary ontic and existentiell experience and (2) how that ontological phenomenon actually conditions that ontic one (which ordinarily covers it over and so obscures it from view).

When Heidegger deploys formal indication in *Being and Time* (as he does to describe the formal structures of our ordinary understanding of demise),

---

[84] (These lectures intended to "initiate" students into the methods of "phenomenological research" are from 1921 to 1922.) As Karin de Boer recognizes, "Heidegger emphasizes that the formal indication, despite its formal character, must *intimate something* about the concrete possibilities that inhere in the concept." (Karin De Boer, *Thinking in the Light of Time: Heidegger's Encounter with Hegel* [Albany, NY: SUNY Press, 2000], 88, my emphasis, see also 91.) Theodore Kisiel even speculates (a bit wishfully, in my view) that: "Formal indication, as hermeneutic phenomenology's guiding method … would have become a main theme of the [unwritten] third division" of *Being and Time*. (Theodore Kisiel, "The Demise of *Being and Time*: 1927-1930," in *Heidegger's Being and Time: Critical Essays*, ed. by Richard Polt [Lanham, MD: Rowman & Littlefield, 2005], 192.) Kisiel also points to the connection between formal indication as a method and what I call Heidegger's *perfectionism* (see Chapter 4), quoting Heidegger's 1929-30 view that: "The meaning content of these [formally indicating] concepts [and here Heidegger mentions "death," *Tod*, as his first example!] does not directly intend or express what they refer to, but only gives an indication, a pointer to the fact that anyone who seeks to understand is called upon by this conceptual context *to undertake a transformation of themselves in their Dasein*." (See GA 29/30: 428-30; quoted by Kisiel, ibid., 208, my emphasis.) Using formal indication to pass from the ontic to the ontological level of analysis thus requires us to practice existential phenomenology ourselves, moving back-and-forth from the ontic (and existentiell) and ontological (and existential) levels in a way that first points us from the ontic and existentiell structures to the ontological and existential ones, which we must enact and experience for ourselves, and then brings us back, *transformatively*, to the ontic and existentiell level of our ordinary lives (as I shall now show).

doing so gives us "a non-binding *formal indicator* of something that, in its actual phenomenal context of being, may perhaps reveal itself [*enthüllt*, that is, stand fully revealed only when we encounter the phenomenon for ourselves] as being the 'opposite'" (BT 152/SZ 116) – the opposite, that is, of what we will at first naturally assume if we fall into "the trap of starting with the givenness of Dasein and its obvious self-interpretation" (BT 151/SZ 116). Whether the phenomenon initially indicated in its formal structures is selfhood, death, or guilt, we must thus beware of simply relying on the seeming obviousness of our ordinary understanding of it and instead pay maximally unbiased attention to how the phenomenon actually discloses itself to us when we encounter it for ourselves, rather than relying on the hearsay of received wisdom, from which we must nevertheless begin (a common sense view to which the ontological interpretation does that aforementioned hermeneutic "violence" that breaks it open as it frees the deepest structures that condition it).

By providing a bridge from the ontic to the ontological in this way, formal indication allows Heidegger to present an ontological interpretation that is not simply arbitrary, groundless, or idiosyncratic. On the contrary, Heidegger's ontological interpretations may be judged compelling only insofar as we too can experience the phenomenon in a way that enables us to recognize and personally attest that this allegedly more basic but previously unnoticed ontological phenomenon Heidegger describes does indeed condition our own experience of the everyday ontic phenomenon with which we are all familiar and from which the formal features of the more fundamental ontological phenomenon are first drawn.[85] Like Aristotle, who thought philosophy should begin by surveying the expert wisdom of the past that is preserved in common sense, Heidegger maintains that "All ontological investigations of such phenomena as guilt, conscience, and death must start with what the everyday interpretation of Dasein 'says' about them" (BT 326/SZ 281).

Heidegger's phenomenological attestation of *death* thus begins with an analysis of our everyday understanding of *demise*. After isolating and "formally indicating" the most significant structural characteristics of the ordinary ontic phenomenon of demise (formal structures which, when we project ourselves into them, we discover to have quite different meanings), Heidegger then seeks to flesh out these structural characteristics, individually and collectively, in a way that will reveal the heretofore unnoticed ontological phenomenon of "death" that *conditions* the phenomenon of ordinary ontic demise. I try to summarize this rather complex analysis in the following table:

---

[85] I shall suggest at the end that the force of such an ontological and existential recognition comes from the way that it simultaneously illuminates and transforms our ordinary ontic and *existentiell* experience, that is, our everyday individual experience of the being (or meaning) of that entity which is being formally indicated – in this case, *death*. (See also n. 84.)

1.5. HEIDEGGER'S BRIDGE FROM DEMISE TO DEATH

Shared formal structures	Demise (ontic)	Death (ontological)
1. End	In demise, I experience the terminal collapse of my world. But this experience is ultimately paradoxical, because I do not live through demise to be there at the end.	Death is the stark phenomenon revealed by a global collapse of my worldly projects, in which, unable to project myself into the projects that ordinarily give my world significance, I experience myself as a mere *projecting*. I do live through death (constantly in my ordinary *projecting* into projects, repeatedly in authentic death – a periodic re-confrontation with the inauthentic one-self I continually accrue, by which I can repossess myself and also subsequently verify my description of the phenomenon).
2. Ownmost	No one can take demise away from me, in the sense that no one can demise in my place. (Even if someone sacrifices his or her own life for me, I still find myself faced with my own demise at the end of my life.)	My very being is at issue in death. When my worldly projects break down in existential death, I can experience myself (lucidly in death or explicitly in genuine or authentic death) as a being whose world is made significant by *projecting* into projects. In death, I discover this *projecting* (existing, or *disclosing*) as the most basic aspect of my self (as "stronger than death"), for I recognize that this projecting can survive the collapse of any and all of my particular projects.
3. Non-relational	No one else can directly experience my demise with me; I demise alone.[1]	In death, I encounter myself as having to project into projects, and thereby choose myself, of my own resources, experiencing the fact that no one else can do this for me. In this moment (of world-collapse), I am radically individuated (as a *solus ipse* or "self alone").
4. Certain	Demise is empirically certain: We know no exceptions to the proposition that "all men are	Death is transcendentally or ontologically certain. The projecting it reveals as my ownmost self is the baseline horizon of all experience, and experiencing this projectless

(cont.)

Shared formal structures	Demise (ontic)	Death (ontological)
	mortal." *Das Man* reduces this to the certainty that *one dies* (someday), or that *we all die* (but not me, not now).	projecting supplies us with the very benchmark of phenomenological certainty. (All worldly significance requires projecting into projects, which in turn presupposes mere projection; so, phenomenologically, nothing could be more certain.)[2]
(and as such)	(and, experienced as the empirical certainty that *one dies* (someday), demise takes on the inevitability of)	(and, recognizing death's sheer *projecting* as the greatest certainty Dasein can ever encounter), we also experience
5. Indefinite[3]	An impending event ("indefinite as to its 'when'"). The *imminence* of demise (in its unpredictable and often sudden arrival) is obscured by the *indefiniteness* of "one dies."	this core of the self (the *solus ipse*) first *come-toward* the worldly self (in the world-collapse of death) and then, second, we can encounter our partly inchoate possible selves *coming toward* this core of the self (in resolve), in both ways experiencing the pure temporal horizon of "futurity" (as the final section will explain). Here, the *indefiniteness* of demise becomes the *immanence* of death, the fact that the sheer *projecting* existential death discloses as the indefinite core of the self underlies and enables all worldly experience (as a projecting into projects).
6. Unsurpassable	Nothing comes after demise; it is the last moment of my life.	Death is not something I can get beyond; rather, I live through what it discloses – again, constantly in my ordinary *projecting* into projects (BT 185/SZ 145), and repeatedly in genuine or authentic death.[4]

---

[1] Amusingly, this is the reading of Heidegger advanced by Ethan Hawke's character in Ben Stiller's film *Reality Bites* (1994), in response to which Stiller's character suggests that this belief that we all demise alone explains why Hawke's character does not deserve to be in a romantic relationship with Winona Ryder's character. (This problem disappears, however, if one does not reduce death to demise; see n. 39.)

(*cont.*)

² (For more on Heidegger's underexplored view of the paradigmatic *certainty* of death, see below and Thomson, "Can I Die?") It may also be that this recognition empowers the self's meta-choice of its defining project in resolve and is carried over into the joyful "wholeheartedness" of its commitments, as Taylor Carman suggests in Carman, *Heidegger's Analytic* (Cambridge: Cambridge University Press, 2003), thereby working in tandem with Dasein's experience of its own radical finitude in existential death (see also n. 55).

³ By formally "indefinite," Heidegger specifies "the *indefiniteness* of its when [*die Unbestimmtheit seines Wann*]," meaning both that it is *imminent*, or always capable of befalling us (even when everything seems to be going smoothly), and also *immanent*: "*that it is possible at every moment*" (BT 302/SZ 258), which (understood as *existential possibility*) means that we are *always* in the core *projecting* that death discloses, though this "undetermined" existential projecting can be filled in (or clothed) variously by our worldly projects (as we see in the *Augenblick* of resolve).

⁴ Heidegger suggests that experiencing authentic death teaches me a kind of existential humility by reminding me that my projects are vulnerable – not just because a successful reconnection to the world through resolve is not guaranteed but, more importantly, because my existence is finite and will predictably end with a terminal world-collapse that will separate me from my incomplete projects for a final time. Recognizing this helps me to acknowledge that others' projecting into projects will continue after mine has ended, thereby encouraging me to recognize the independence of others and treat them as potential collaborators in or heirs to shared projects I cannot complete (BT 308/SZ 264). (On this ideal of existential community made possible by an authentic "being-together" or *Mitsein*, see also the conclusion of Thomson, *Heidegger on Ontotheology* and the opening acknowledgments of Thomson, *Heidegger, Art, and Postmodernity*.) Moreover, the fact that *what* resolve resolves (beyond any particular project) is *to repeat itself* suggests that this repeated reconnection to the ontological core of the self (a kind of return to dry-dock to remove the barnacles of worldly habit) is part of what makes it possible and important to seek some sense of continuity and coherence in my life as a whole (BT 351/SZ 303–4), a requirement Heidegger also *inherits* from Kierkegaard. (See n. 55.) How frequently, then, is existential death supposed to occur? If we recall the reason that confronting one's *Angst* leads one's world to collapse in the first place – namely, because the confrontation with *Angst* reveals the uncanny lack of fit between the self and its world, revealing a contingency that undermines one's naïve sense that one is doing the right thing with one's life – then we can see that this kind of global collapse can only happen to one *again* insofar as one has settled back into this kind of naïve (or even *righteous*) "'good' conscience" that one is doing the right thing with one's life (BT 338/SZ 189). But that is exactly what we do tend to do (living in the everyday public world of *das Man*), which helps explain why Heidegger specifies that "*authentic resoluteness . . . resolves to keep repeating itself*" (BT 355/SZ 308). This means that we must hold ourselves open to the occasional experience, typically in a moment of radical breakdown, of

experiencing a certain distance with respect to our defining existential projects, a distance from which we can reevaluate, recommit to, or reject them (BT 443/SZ 391). This commitment to such reevaluation is not paralyzing or alienating, I think, both because it is only periodic, dictated by the accumulation of the conformist "one-self" that actually alienates us from *leading* our own unique lives, and also because it is only required for our "ultimate for-the-sake of which," not for every project organized by that ultimate, life-guiding project. (I do, however, think this is a problem for Haugeland and Blattner's belief in the centrality of such defeasibility to our guiding existential projects.) In authentic death and resoluteness, we explicitly re-experience ourselves as a projectless projecting that makes sense of itself by projecting into projects, and we can thereby *explicitly* experience that disconnection from and reconnection to the world that we tend to experience only *lucidly* the first time we undergo it, which is part of why Heidegger suggests that this repetition (of "authentic resolve") is needed in order "genuinely or authentically" to check or evaluate his phenomenology for ourselves. Nonetheless, this methodological requirement of Heidegger's view seems phenomenologically problematic to me; I think we need only live through death at least once, lucidly (and, moreover, that this world-collapse can be partial), to be able, in retrospect, to begin to explicitly understand the structures revealed by the experience thus lived through.

Obviously, this sketch remains incomplete, but I hope it is sufficient to illustrate Heidegger's method and so show that he does not arbitrarily choose to rechristen some unrelated phenomenon "death" and analyze it outside of any relation to what the rest of us normally mean by the word. This is important because it helps us see that, here as elsewhere, the ontic and the ontological are not *heterogeneous* domains (*pace* orthodox Heideggerians and influential critics like Habermas) but, instead, necessarily overlap and interrelate, and must, in order for the method Heidegger uses in *Being and Time* (which I have called *phenomenological attestation*) to work, that is, to be convincing. Indeed, Heidegger's phenomenological method can only be *convincing*, I shall now suggest, by moving back and forth in the right (affectively and cognitively resonant) way between our own individual, everyday (existentiell and ontic) understanding of death as mortal demise and the phenomenological discovery of the ontological structure underlying and conditioning our ordinary relation to demise, as that structure is disclosed in the phenomenon of existential death.[86]

---

[86] For a detailed explanation of the phenomenological argument that allows Heidegger to move from an ontic work of art (Van Gogh's painting of "A Pair of Shoes" [1886]) to the ontological truth of art in general, see Thomson, *Heidegger, Art, and Postmodernity*, ch. 3. There I also develop Heidegger's later view that art can teach us to embrace the nothing that death discloses (by helping us see this dynamic "noth-ing" as the source of meaningful possibilities for the future), instead of anxiously fearing it (as what reveals the limits of our subjectivistic fantasies of extending total control over our worlds). We return to this topic in Chapter 3.

1.6 Preliminary Conclusions: Fear of Demise and Anxiety about Death

I mentioned at the beginning that a significant obstacle to checking the phenomenological evidence for Heidegger's analysis of death comes from the fact that what he calls "death" – namely, the projectless *projecting* we experience in the wake of the global collapse of the inauthentic one-self each of us continually accrues – seems to be an extremely difficult experience for most people to endure. The magnitude of this difficulty is conveyed by Heidegger's aforementioned acknowledgment that requiring his readers to undergo what he means by death in order to be able to evaluate his account of the phenomenon seems, from the ordinary perspective of our everyday concerns, to be a "fantastically unreasonable demand" (BT 311/SZ 266), as well as by *Being and Time*'s suggestion that the avoidance of a confrontation with our anxiety before death may be the real engine of Western history.[87]

By *anxiety before death*, however, it is crucial to recognize that Heidegger means anxiety about the core self revealed in the collapse of my world, not fear concerning my eventual demise. In fact, Heidegger considers such fear of demise – which "perverts anxiety into cowardly fear" (BT 311/SZ 266) – to be one of the main ways we flee from our real anxiety about death. He goes so far as to assert that even those who seek heroically to confront and overcome their fear of demise (like Spinoza, as we shall see in Chapter 8), in so doing, merely reveal their "own cowardliness in the face of anxiety" (ibid.). Heidegger's startling claim – that our fear of our eventual demise is really just a way of fleeing our anxiety about the core self laid bare by the global collapse of worldly projects in what he calls "death" – is so strange that, as far as I know, no interpreter has explicitly thematized and addressed it. Instead, it is most often miscognized: existential death is misunderstood as mortal demise, and Heidegger's view is thereby reduced to that of Ernest Becker (a later sociologist who taught that we human beings are driven to construct all our systems of meaning in order to deny the demise we nevertheless cannot escape).[88] Upon grasping Heidegger's strange claim, moreover, many readers will suspect the very opposite, namely, that Heidegger himself has just reinterpreted "death" so as to transform it into

---

[87] On this phenomenological demand, see n. 7. (See also Haugeland, "Truth and Finitude," 74; Robert Pippin, *Idealism as Modernism* [Cambridge: Cambridge University Press, 1997], 383, n. 16. I think the larger point Pippin makes here is right and insightful, but we need to emend the details so as not to equate "death" with "mortality," the latter having to do with "demise," because, as I shall now explain, Heidegger himself insists that our fear of demise is a way of fleeing from our anxiety before death.)

[88] Heidegger believes something similar to Becker's "terror management" theory but thinks that this denial of demise is itself motivated by our flight before what Heidegger calls death. (See below and Ernest Becker, *The Denial of Death* [New York: Free Press, 1973].)

an experience that can be survived, thereby inadvertently exposing his own fear of demise. Further evidence that Heidegger is indeed making the initially strange claim I am attributing to him can thus be found in the fact that he anticipates that table-turning suspicion and goes out of his way to deny it as one of "the grossest perversions," explicitly asserting that: "Anticipatory resoluteness [that is, "authenticity" understood as existential death and rebirth to the world through resolve] is not a way of escape, fabricated for the 'overcoming' of death" (BT 357/SZ 310). Instead, Heidegger thinks, we usually live superficially with an uneasy sense that we are doing the right thing with our lives simply by doing what one should do, and if we dare to endure a genuine confrontation with that underlying existential *Angst*, rather than fleeing it back into *das Man*'s "indifferent tranquillity as to the 'fact' that one dies" – a flight by which we displace "this anxiety into fear in the face of an oncoming event" (BT 298/SZ 254) – then we will end up experiencing a global collapse of our identity-defining life-projects in existential "death."

In my view, then, what will ultimately be decisive in evaluating Heidegger's phenomenological attestation of death is that we be able to recognize the phenomenon he calls *death* as ontologically *conditioning*, and so explaining at a deep experiential level, the main features of our relationship to ordinary demise, including not only the six formal features they share (in the way outlined in the table above) but also, and perhaps most saliently, the widespread *fear* of demise from which, he recognizes, we habitually flee into diversions that keep us busy or otherwise tranquillize that fear and the anxiety beneath it. Accordingly, I want to suggest that the strange provocations on the subject of the relation between death and demise just rehearsed are best understood as Heidegger's attempt to show that our anxiety in the face of *what he calls "death" is what really drives our fear of demise*, and thus that *fleeing demise* is really just a distorted way of *repressing death*. But what exactly does this mean?

We might think that Heidegger is suggesting that what scares us about demise is the fact that, insofar as we experience demise, we will experience a world-collapse without any subsequent reconnection to the world. In this case, we would fear and so flee demise because in it we will suffer an irreversible world-collapse, undergoing the apparently permanent foreclosure of our worlds. If this were what Heidegger meant, then he would be suggesting that our fear of such demise is ultimately a cover for our deeper *Angst* about running-out into death and then failing subsequently to reconnect to the world in resolve. In other words, Heidegger might seem to be suggesting that what drives our fear of demise is our underlying anxiety that (much like the legendary shark that must keep swimming to stay alive) should we ever lose that unquestioned existential inertia driving us through our daily lives, should we ever stop and step back from our worlds in a radical way, we might lose our worlds never again to regain them.[89]

I do not want to deny that this is a real worry (perhaps even one to which Heidegger's own anxious and depressive nature might have inclined him). But I think it cannot be correct as an attempt to reconstruct Heidegger's analysis of the ultimate motivations behind our own fear of demise. For, if it were correct, then this would actually be an argument in favor of the interpretation Heidegger dismissed as "the grossest of perversions," namely, the view that Heidegger's call for us confront our *Angst* before death is really just his way of repressing his fear of demise. Because demise looks like *terminal* world-collapse, any dread we might feel about *permanently* losing our unquestioned existential inertia seems to stem from our fear of demise, that is, our fear of our intelligible world coming to an *irreversible* end, never to return again. (This haunting fear of demise as eternal nothingness – "faintly ... tapping at my chamber door... / here I opened wide the door; / —Darkness there and nothing more" – is what Edgar Allan Poe captures so brilliantly in his famous poem's discomfiting refrain: "Quoth the raven, 'Nevermore.'" Poe's portentous "*nevermore*" succinctly expresses our mortal fear that demise will indeed turn out to be absolutely nothing, just like it appears to be from here.)[90] That, however, is to derive *Angst* in the face of death from our fear of demise, which is exactly the reverse of what Heidegger seeks to do.

For Heidegger to make his case that our fear of demise is ultimately motivated by our anxiety in the face of death, then, his view must be that what we are really afraid of about demise *is* what he calls death, namely, *losing our world and still being here to experience that loss*. In other words, Heidegger is suggesting that what we fear about demise is the same thing that suicidal people desperately hope to gain from it, namely, that in demise we will *be rid of ourselves*, as it were. Yet, as Epicurus pointed out long ago (and as Heidegger

---

[89] This is close to Thomas Nagel's reason for thinking life absurd. As Nagel puts it: "What sustains us, in belief as in action, is not reason or justification, but something more basic than these ... If we tried to rely entirely on reason, and pressed it hard, our lives and beliefs would collapse – a form of madness that may actually occur if the inertial force of taking the world and life for granted is somehow lost" (Thomas Nagel, *Mortal Questions* [Cambridge: Cambridge University Press, 1979], 20).

[90] Taken out of context, one might similarly misinterpret Heidegger's famous description of death as "the possibility of Dasein's impossibility" to mean something like facing up to the very possibility of this atheistic *nevermore* – *as* if existential death were merely Dasein's confrontation with the possibility that demise might not be followed by an afterlife – a thought that, admittedly, might indeed catalyze the genuine existential death of a certain kind of unquestioned religious belief (as well as its possible rebirth as *faith*, or its lack). (This seems, for example, to be the way Martin Hägglund misunderstands Heidegger on death.) But in fact the question of a possible afterlife is something about which Heidegger remains deliberately *neutral* or *agnostic* (as we saw in n. 49), since phenomenology must confine itself to what it can experience (here, on this side of the mortal veil).

repeatedly stresses in *Being and Time*), we will not be rid of ourselves in demise because, once we demise, we will not *be* at all.[91] If Heidegger is right, in other words, our fear of demise is really our fear of a paradoxical state in which we *are not* – or, more precisely, in which we are not and yet somehow are in order to be aware that we are not. Our fear of demise is thus a *misplaced* fear, but it is not (*pace* Nagel) an *unfounded* one.[92] For there is an experience in which what we are afraid of about demise – namely, not being, or, more precisely, being our own not being – can actually happen to us. As we have seen, this strange experience of *being in a way in which we are not able to be anything worldly* is precisely what Heidegger calls *death*. When all our worldly projects collapse in existential death, leaving a projectless projecting as the sole survivor of the shipwreck of the self, we do indeed experience the paradoxical "possibility of an *im*possibility of existence – that is to say, the utter nullity [*Nichtigkeit*] of Dasein" (BT 354/SZ 306), as Heidegger provocatively puts it – that is, the sheer *nullification* of all the defining life-projects which Dasein suddenly finds itself unable to project into in existential death.[93]

[91] As far as we can tell phenomenologically, in demise we will not "be here" (as Dasein) either to enjoy or to suffer from not being here. Here we come close to the Epicurean argument that we should no more fear our demise than we fear the time before we existed, and also to Kierkegaard's argument for the inevitable failure of suicide. In the view Anti-Climacus presents, the suicidal person does not want to not be, full stop; instead, the would-be suicide really wants to *be* without those aspects of experience that torture them (in "despair"). Moreover, we are all in a similar situation, even if unknowingly, because what ultimately tortures us are contradictions built into the nature of selfhood (the purported fact that the self is both determined and free, finite and infinite, temporal and eternal, etc.), which makes us all want to be what we are not or not want to be what we are, that is, to be in *despair*. Hence his view that "despair is precisely the inability to die," where "to die means that it *is* all over" (Kierkegaard, *The Sickness Unto Death*, 48). In the end, Kierkegaard suggests that only faith in a God for whom "everything is possible" – even the resolution of such seemingly intractable contradictions – can save us. Secularizing Kierkegaard, Heidegger suggests that only the radically individualized Dasein can pass through existential death and *resolve* such contradictions for themselves. I would thus also suggest that what it means, phenomenologically, to "reside transparently in the power that created you" (Anti-Climacus's formula for the eradication of despair) is to reside transparently in your own *projecting* into projects, that is, to undergo existential death's projectless projecting and then, from the perspective that discloses, reconnect resolutely to worldly projects.

[92] (See Nagel, "Death," in Nagel, *Mortal Questions*.) Nagel, we might say, did not anticipate Heideggerian *anticipation* or "running-out" into death, in which (as Heidegger already wrote in 1925) "the world withdraws, collapsing into nothingness" (BH 265).

[93] The basic insight behind Heidegger's strange terminology here is that part of what connects (1) the charging-out into death to (2) resolve's reconnection to the world (in this *double* movement of *authenticity*) is that the nullity of worldly projects I discover at the core of my self in existential death is partly taken over in resolve, where (having experienced myself as *being* this "null-basis" of my projects in death) I embrace my defining existential finitude by lucidly affirming that to *be what I become* (when I project into projects) I must also *not be* (or *nullify*) every other live-option (life-project) that

1.6. FEAR OF DEMISE AND ANXIETY ABOUT DEATH

In order to confirm Heidegger's phenomenological analysis for ourselves, then, we would need to be able to attest to the fact that death conditions demise; that is, we would need to recognize that what we are really afraid of about demise is not just losing our world but also being here to experience that loss. So, is Heidegger right about this? I have suggested that this is a *phenomenological* matter and, as such, one that we must each decide for ourselves on the basis of our own experience, but here are some leading questions that I think help make Heidegger's case. In our fear of demise, do we not torture ourselves precisely by paradoxically imagining, that is, trying to project ourselves into, our own non-existence (for example, by imagining what the world will be like after we are gone from it)? Is this paradoxical projection into our own non-existence, perhaps, also what is ultimately so unsettling about *the very idea* of a world in which we no longer exist? (Indeed, so unsettling that, as films like Bay's "*Armageddon*" [1998] and von Trier's "*Melancholia*" [2011] suggest, it sometimes seems easier to imagine the end of all life on earth than to imagine others' living on after we are gone – an undeniably disturbing fact but one that unfortunately only begins to suggest the dangerous thanatological forces unleashed by our failure to confront our anxiety in the face of existential death.)[94] And, finally, does not this phenomenological notion of projectless projecting also help explain what is so dreadful about various forms of dementia such as Alzheimer's disease, which present us with the terrible possibility of being here to experience the gradual disintegration of our

---

I thereby forgo. In this way, ontological guilt encourages me to let go of the ordinary guilt I otherwise feel at not being able to be who I could have been had I projected into different projects (had I attended that other school, taken that other job, married that other person, etc.), much as ontological death encourages me to let go of my ordinary fear of demise, and this transformative epiphany is part of what makes these ontological analyses *convincing*, phenomenologically. Indeed, for Heidegger, ontological "death and guilt" explicitly come together in the *thrown project* of authenticity, where I lucidly affirm myself "as the null-basis of a nullity" (BT 354/SZ 306), that is, a being whose choices are partly shaped but not determined by a *thrownness* I can never fully understand (or get to the bottom of, such that the real power I do indeed have over my defining choices comes from rejecting the rationalistic fantasy of ever completely understanding myself from the ground up so that I could make the one correct or rationally optimal decision) and who, in projecting into projects, must *nullify* what I am *not* becoming in order to *be* what I *am* becoming instead. (Heidegger's recognition of these interconnections proves important to his phenomenological disclosure of temporality as well, as Section 1.7 will show.)

[94] I think we can also recognize this same dangerous thanatological imaginary at work in the increasingly common phenomena of weaponized nihilism that include not just those old fanatics longing for the war that will signal the apocalypse but also in the murderously suicidal "death by cop" of the "school shooter" and other public mass-murderers who seem only to be able to overcome their own fear of demise (and so of suicide) by taking as many others with them as they can (thereby expressing their nihilistic disdain of human life) and so forcing someone else to kill them in turn. (On suicide, see also n. 91.)

being-here, the slow-motion implosion of our worlds?[95] If we answer "Yes" to such questions, this suggests that the phenomenon Heidegger calls *death* is not only related to but actually conditions our ordinary relation to demise. Indeed, it suggests that projectless projecting, not terminal world-collapse, *is* what we are really afraid of about demise.

I think the best *confirmation* of Heidegger's phenomenology of death, moreover, would come if this existential recognition that death conditions demise can help us no longer to fear demise – which it should do, because *in demise* our own Dasein will not be here not to be here. Interestingly, I have repeatedly been told (after presenting earlier versions of this chapter as a talk) that those wracked by terrible fear on their deathbeds can often be helped by hospice workers, therapists, or others who guide them in visualizing their own demise; when the terminally ill imaginatively project themselves into such projectlessness, they reportedly experience a cathartic release of their mortal fear, which can thus turn into a wondrous openness to the unknown. This is very strong evidence in favor of Heidegger's initially strange but, I think, ultimately quite compelling view. For, part of what Heidegger's phenomenology of death and demise in *Being and Time* seeks to show us here is that, if we want to shed the mortal fear of demise that will otherwise pursue us throughout our lives, then we need to muster the courage to confront our anxiety about death, thereby learning calmly and simply to be here – instead of continuing to rush blindly toward the very thing we fear in our desperate attempts to evade it (BT 477/SZ 425). When we learn to be here in the finite disclosure of existential death, moreover, what we thereby encounter turns out to be those wondrous phenomena Heidegger will call *futurity* and the *nothing* (as we will now go on to see), potentially transformative phenomena that can help us learn to turn our anxiety about demising into a creative embrace of the inexhaustible source of phenomenological intelligibility – or so I shall seek to show in the chapters that follow.

1.7 Ontological Futurity: Situating *Being and Time*'s Phenomenology of Death

Now, revisiting an influential work as we approach the centenary of its publication should perhaps encourage us to take a step back and situate the part of the work we have been focusing on within the larger context of the text's overarching architectonic, understanding not just the pivotal role existential death plays therein (which we have already begun to address) but also existential death's connections to the loftiest philosophical ambitions of the work (which we have only mentioned briefly thus far), thereby examining

---

[95] We will come back to this issue in Chapter 7 (in part because it suggests that we can *demise* much more slowly than Heidegger recognized).

1.7. SITUATING DEATH: ONTOLOGICAL FUTURITY 63

some of the most provocative insights to which it helped give rise – all before going on to examine the subsequent influence of Heidegger's rethinking of death on some other important philosophers (to whom we will turn in Chapters 5 through 7). That kind of "big picture" portrait can be quite daunting (especially when it requires us to step back from and simplify a complex work we have been rereading and teaching for decades). But it can also help us "not to lose the forest for the trees," an old hermeneutic warning that rings true when one has primarily been focused on a single important issue within a text that ultimately leverages that issue for larger purposes that go well beyond both that issue and that text. So let me briefly situate *Being and Time*'s phenomenology of death within the context of this text's ultimate philosophical ambitions, thereby venturing beyond what I have said about its philosophical context thus far, before turning to examine these larger purposes and issues branching off from death in more detail in Chapters 2 and 3. Doing so will also encourage us to briefly explore two other difficult issues – namely, nothingness and futurity – which can be found at or beneath the very roots (to stay with the metaphor) of the fascinating tree we have been focusing on thus far.

Viewed in terms of *Being and Time*'s largest and most ambitious goals, Heidegger is primarily concerned to understand death *ontologically*. Put simply, he hopes to phenomenologically convince us of two interconnected ontological claims: First, that the phenomenon of existential death can help us uncover the deepest existential structures that ultimately condition our shared way of being ("existence"), namely, the "temporal horizons or ecstasies." (The main reason Heidegger thinks this is that "futurity," the "primary" aspect of this tripartite temporal structure, first becomes visible in the phenomenon of existential death, as I shall show momentarily.) The second, even bigger claim is that understanding these temporal structures that ultimately condition all phenomenological intelligibility can, in turn, enable us to discover "a fundamental ontology," that is, a *single* answer to *"the question of the meaning of being in general"* (BT 61/SZ 37). As Chapter 2 will show, that second and most ambitious hope – Being *and Time*'s ultimate goal of discovering "a fundamental ontology" that will finally *answer* "the question of being" – fails dramatically, and the later Heidegger will abandon it as an "errant" and unwitting last gasp of the very "metaphysical" tradition he characterizes as *ontotheology*.[96] Fortunately, the phenomenology of existential death originally yoked into the service of *Being and Time*'s failed metaphysical ambition to discover a fundamental ontology survives this death of metaphysics – a profound existential death through which Heidegger himself lives and thinks – and continues to be developed in important ways by the later Heidegger himself (as Chapter 3

---

[96] This is one of the main theses of Thomson, *Heidegger on Ontotheology*.

shows), while also fascinating, befuddling, infuriating, and inspiring some of *Being and Time*'s most serious and creative readers for generations.[97] Before examining at least a few important details from those readings (in Chapters 5, 6, and 7), let me very briefly explain these two big ontological claims.

The "*and*" in the title of *Being and Time* does not designate mere succession, as if Heidegger were naming two separate items in a very short list. It is, instead, the "and" of conjunction, designating the *intersection* between *Being and Time*, an intersection the text will name and describe successively as Dasein, *existence*, *being-in-the-world*, and, finally, *temporality*. "Temporality" is Heidegger's name for time as it enters into being by becoming intelligible, and also for being as it enters into time and so gets disclosed.[98] Indeed, one of *Being and Time*'s guiding insights is that *temporality* is the most primordial structure of Dasein's being-here that phenomenology can access. As *Being and Time* claims: "*Ecstatical temporality primordially clears the 'here'*" (BT 402/SZ 351). That is, the "ecstatico-horizonal" structure of temporality – or the way temporality opens and orients our intelligible worlds – is what most deeply discloses that practical understanding of being that originally structures and shapes Dasein's existential "being-here." (How exactly does temporality condition and shape our most basic understanding of being? We turn to that fraught question in Chapter 2.) *Being and Time* thus describes temporality as "the fundamental existential constitution of Dasein in the ultimate foundations of its own ontological intelligibility" (BT 351/SZ 304).

At this primordial layer of Dasein's intelligibility in which being and time most fundamentally intersect, moreover, Heidegger thinks that this *Ur-phenomenon* metaphysics dichotomizes into mind and world, spirit and matter, the mental and the physical, subjects and objects, etc., still remains fundamentally interconnected. Heidegger's thinking of temporality as the allegedly primordial unity of being and time is that deepest insight from which he thinks even "Kant shrank back" (BT 45/SZ 23) when he revised his *Critique of Pure Reason* in a way that effaced the role originally played there (in the first, "A edition") by the faculty of the imagination. In doing so (in his second, "B edition"), Kant abandoned his own earlier attempt to articulate the constitutive role that the imagination's *temporal* "schematism" plays in joining the faculties of understanding and sensibility, uniting the deliverances of "mind" and "world" in a

---

[97] (We can, of course, only examine a few of these noteworthy readers here.) I have tried to show that the way Heidegger lives and thinks through this "death of metaphysics" is what explains the most dramatic differences between his "early" and "later" work (his so-called turn), as the traumatic and transformative collapse of the metaphysical project that guides his early philosophy eventually gives rise to the post-metaphysical perspective of his later thinking. (See Chapter 3 and Thomson, *Heidegger on Ontotheology*.)

[98] See also B. Scott Rouse, "Retrieving Heidegger's Temporal Realism," *European Journal of Philosophy*, 30:1 (2022), 205–26.

1.7. SITUATING DEATH: ONTOLOGICAL FUTURITY

way that (Heidegger suggests) might have undercut modern Cartesian dualism. Heidegger's goal of undermining the modern ontological dualism of mind and world may be the most ambitious project that *Being and Time* successfully accomplished (as Dreyfus influentially argues), but it is not the most ambitious project the famous text pursues.[99] That honor (or dishonor, as it *turns* out) goes to Heidegger's ill-fated quest for a "fundamental ontology," in the vain pursuit of which he presents his phenomenology of death.

The main reason Heidegger's phenomenology of death plays that pivotal role in the text (as briefly suggested at the outset) is because, after all the other independently important twists and turns already examined, the phenomenon of death ultimately discloses the temporal horizon of "futurity," that is, the constitutive openness of our intelligible worlds to the perpetual *arriving* of what is not yet fully intelligible.[100] Such *futurity* is itself so important, moreover, because its discovery enables Heidegger to discern all three of the interconnected *temporal* structures that most deeply shape Dasein's being, and *Being and Time*'s ultimate hope is to show how this understanding of temporality's fundamental, constitutive role in shaping the intelligible worlds that we Dasein *are* will subsequently enable him to discover that "fundamental ontology" (or understanding of the meaning of being in general) for which he is searching during this early, pro-metaphysical period of his work. We will explore this attempt in detail in Chapter 2, but let us not skip over "futurity" too quickly, since Heidegger's way of conceptualizing this phenomenon can only be understood through its connection to existential death. Moreover, reconstructing the phenomenological connection between death and futurity is also important because it will help us to better understand the origins of Heidegger's initially strange and provocative insistence on the great philosophical importance of "the nothing," which first opens and begins to anticipate the later Heidegger's central phenomenological insight into being's apparently inexhaustible meaningfulness, as insight utterly at odds with *Being and Time*'s quest for a fundamental ontology (as Chapters 2 and 3 will explain in detail).[101]

---

[99] This is one of the main theses of Dreyfus's seminal work, Dreyfus, *Being-in-the-World*.

[100] Five years after that, Heidegger describes it as "the rift structure" at the intersection of "earth and world" (that is, of truth as phenomenological "dis-closure," *a-letheia*), though his later work most often calls this temporally dynamic phenomenon "the presencing of presence" (see Thomson, *Heidegger, Art, and Postmodernity*, ch. 3). Despite subtle and important differences, all these terms of art seek to draw our attention to the continual but (owing to that first law of phenomenology, "the law of proximity" or *the distance of the near*) typically unnoticed phenomenological arriving of what is not yet discretely intelligible as an entity, whereby "being as such" makes itself felt in its difference from the "being of entities" that metaphysics seeks to capture and doubly ground once and for all in an ontotheology. (We shall explore this still too often misunderstood issue in more detail in Chapter 3.)

[101] See also Thomson, *Heidegger on Ontotheology*, ch. 1.

In *Being and Time*, temporal "futurity" – or the "to-come" (*Zu-kunft*), that is, *futurity* in its sheer *coming toward* us – is first disclosed only by *enduring* the phenomenon of existential death. ("Enduring" such death in order to recognize the full depths of its disclosure requires phenomenologists neither to *inauthentically* rush back into reactionary conformity to escape anxiety in the face of death, nor to immediately find a way back to worldly projects in resolve by taking lucid ownership of themselves in *authenticity*.) By enduring such death phenomenologically, Heidegger suggests, we can uncover not only the bare existential structure of the understanding (as a projectless projecting) but also a deeper temporal horizon that is discernible beneath that core existential structure, conditioning it. *Being and Time*'s basic insight here is that, in enduring the desolate phenomenon of existential death, the "*solus ipse*" of projectless projecting finds itself rebounding back off the world of projects it cannot project into and so thereby *coming back toward* itself, a return from the world empty-handed or "naked" (that is, bereft of the clothing of worldly projects), which renders Dasein's own core structure perspicuous in its sheer "existing" (or *ek-sistere*). As Heidegger puts it (and we should now be better equipped to understand his philosophical terminology):

> Anticipatory resoluteness [or authenticity in its two interconnected moments as death and rebirth to the world] ... is only possible in that *in the first place* Dasein *can* come toward itself in its ownmost ability-to-be [namely, death], and can endure [*aushält*] this possibility as a possibility in thus letting itself come toward itself [that is, Dasein can endure existential death so as to encounter what this phenomenon discloses about itself], namely, that it exists. (BT 372/SZ 325)

Enduring existential death discloses to *Dasein itself* the brute fact that it "exists" or *stands-out* into the "nothingness of the world," a looming world of indifferent objects, rendered insignificant by Dasein's inability to project practically into any of the worldly projects that ordinarily disclose the significance and salience of those entities as practical equipment.[102] In other words,

---

[102] It may well seem like a jarring exaggeration to describe the totality of "de-worlded" present-at-hand objects as a "nothingness," but here we need to remember Heidegger's claim in *Being and Time* that: "*Readiness-to-hand is the way in which entities as they are 'in themselves' are defined ontologico-categorially*" (BT 101/SZ 71), which is why he holds that "the [existential] *possibility* of the ready-to-hand in general... is the world itself" (BT 231/SZ 187). Heidegger's early view of the being of entities as readiness to hand will become problematic from the perspective of his later history of being, where this (ontologically reductive) understanding of being as equipment looks like the penultimate stage in the history of nihilism (see Thomson, *Heidegger on Ontotheology*, ch. 1), as well as from a deep ecological perspective (see Iain Thomson, "Ontology and Ethics at the Intersection of Phenomenology and Environmental Philosophy," *Inquiry*, 47:4 [2004], 380–412). More to the point for us here, however, Heidegger's view of this *nothingness* evolves in subtle but important ways over the next few years and into his later work (as we shall see in Chapter 3).

1.7. SITUATING DEATH: ONTOLOGICAL FUTURITY

Dasein's being-bestowing rebound – off of the world it cannot project into and back toward itself – is rendered *perspicuous* by enduring existential death, that desolate situation in which I find myself utterly unable to be (that is, to project into and so implicitly *understand* myself in terms of) any worldly self at all.

When entirely unable to project into its practical, worldly projects, Dasein can phenomenologically encounter the way doing so ordinarily discloses the significance of its existence. That much should already be familiar. The new twist, however, is the deeper, temporal insight that Heidegger seeks to convey here – namely, that, in order for existential death to be able to show Dasein the structure of its own naked existing *phenomenologically*, Dasein's projecting must rebound off its failed projecting into worldly projects and so *come back toward itself*. In discerning this phenomenologically, Dasein can thereby encounter and recognize the fact that its experience of this (ordinarily) being-bestowing arrival of meaning is made possible by an even deeper structure conditioning its being, which Heidegger calls the *temporal horizon* of *futurity*. In his words:

> Enduring this distinctive possibility [existential death] in its letting-itself-come-toward-itself [and so recognizing how our being *comes back toward us* from the projects we project into] is the primordial phenomenon of the future as coming toward [*Zu-kunft*, the futural horizon in its *coming toward* us]. (BT 372/SZ 325)

Enduring death, in other words, discloses not only my naked existence, standing out into the nothingness of a world I cannot project into; in so doing, it allows the phenomenologist who endures existential death to recognize an even deeper structure built into its own being, the *temporal* horizon of "futurity" (as sheer *coming toward* me) that enables my projecting into projects to *rebound back upon me* and bestow my existence with significance (or, in death, the lack thereof).

That explains why Heidegger sets up his (admittedly abstract) descriptions of futurity by reminding us that: "The meaning of Dasein's being – is the self-understanding Dasein itself" (BT 372/SZ 325). As we saw earlier, Dasein "understands" (or, better, *takes a stand on*) the meaning of its own being by projecting into practical projects (namely, its embodied, existential "possibilities"). Ordinarily, we press-ahead or project into the practical world of our projects and the meaning of our being implicitly *comes back to* us as the meaningful world that we Dasein are.[103] In existential death, however, we can

---

[103] In teaching, for example, a teacher *implicitly* presses into a dynamically significant and holistically interconnected world of students to be taught, texts to be explained and explored, ideas to be clarified and questions and other opportunities for learning to be pursued, pens to write on the board in order to clarify such ideas, and so on, and in disclosing such a ready-to-hand world the meaning of the teacher's own being implicitly comes toward them as well. (It is tempting to think of this as Heidegger's secularization of the Christian view of the isomorphic relation between faith and grace.)

explicitly encounter this "coming back to" us, precisely because it is rendered *perspicuous* by its emptiness. In existential death (as a global collapse of Dasein's embodied "understanding" as a projecting into projects), Dasein rebounds off the world of projects it can no longer project into, yet its being still comes back to it (as a sheer existing in the face of that utterly *insignificant* nothingness of the world). No longer covered over (or filled in) by such worldly meaning, Dasein can recognize the deep "temporal" horizon conditioning this existential *rebound*, whereby the meaning of our being comes back to us. As Heidegger expresses the crucial insight:

> Anticipation [our projecting into the projectlessness of death] makes Dasein *genuinely* futural, and in such a way that the anticipation itself is only possible insofar as Dasein *as an entity* is in the first place always already coming-toward-itself, which means it is futural in its very being. (BT 373/SZ 325)

By experiencing our own being-bestowing existential rebound back onto ourselves in its emptiest form (in death), we can discern the temporal horizon underlying the existential structure of our "understanding" as a projecting into projects that, in return, discloses the significance of things and renders us meaningful to ourselves.

To sum up this difficult point, enduring a phenomenological encounter with death discloses the structural rebound whereby the meaning of Dasein's being *comes toward* its existence, and this ontological arrival (by which Dasein's being *comes toward* it) is made possible by the deeper temporal horizon Heidegger calls "futurity." As Heidegger explicitly defines the term: "Here 'futural' ['*Zu-kunft*'] means ... the coming [*Kunft*] in which Dasein, in its ownmost ability-to-be [death], comes toward itself" (BT 373/SZ 325). The basic idea, then, is that Dasein's reflexive return from the world (by which the projects we project into implicitly *come back* to bestow our existence with the meaning of our being) is itself made possible by a temporal horizon Heidegger calls "futurity" as this "coming toward" (*Zu-kunft*), that is, Dasein's constitutive openness to the *coming toward* itself of the meaning of being (the meaning of *its own being*, implicitly bestowed back upon it or disclosed for it by its projecting into worldly projects, as we have seen, but thereby also – according to the hopeful architectonic we can see Heidegger beginning to sketch out here – the *meaning of being in general*, as we will see in Chapter 2).

For the early Heidegger, the three temporal horizons come together to constitute the deepest substrate of Dasein's being that phenomenology can reach, and temporality's three horizons are just as inextricably interconnected as the three main existential structures that they underlie and condition. As a result, there can be no phenomenological encounter with "futurity" that does not also involve Dasein's "having beenness" and "making present" (BT 373–4/ SZ 373–4) – just as there is no "understanding" without its "affective attunement" (*Befindlichkeit*) and "conversance" (*Rede*), and hence no *death* without *anxiety* and *conscience*.[104] The temporal horizons intertwine, for example, in that what I am becoming (in the projects I project into) *comes back* to shape how I am making sense of who I have been (or, more precisely, of how I *continue* to become what I have been).[105] If a student resolutely chooses to become a philosophy major, to take a simple example, then their felt sense of who they are, as they throw themselves into particularly challenging reading assignment, might tend to be informed by half-forgotten stories they heard about their insatiable childhood curiosity and drive to understand, say, rather than about their prodigious business acumen or athletic talent.[106] In general, as we project into the practical world of projects that make (and remake) us who we are (in our repeated becoming), our future projects shape (and reshape) the way our past continues to shape us. This is what Heidegger has in mind when he sums up his view of Dasein's *temporality*:

> The character of having-beenness arises from futurity, and in such a way that that the coming-toward which has been (or, better, which is in the process of having been) releases from itself the present. This phenomenon has the unity of a coming-toward which makes-present in the process of having-been; we designate this unity as *temporality*. (BT 374/SZ 326)

According to this *unified* account of the three interlocking temporal horizons, Heidegger's vision of the way "futurity releases the present from itself" suggests that, after futurity has been disclosed in death (as the naked existence of the *solus ipse* rebounds off the practical world it cannot connect to and comes toward itself perspicuously), it also gets disclosed, second, through the

---

[104] We have discussed the role of anxiety in death at length. But it is "conscience" that silently calls us back from thoughtlessly doing *what one does* and so calls us into death as our ownmost ability-to-be (which itself turns out to be the source of the call [BT 320/SZ 275]), and thereby calls for (and enables) Dasein to resolutely reconnect to its world *in its own way*, and therefore become "answerable [*verantwortlich*]" or *responsible* for so doing (BT 334/SZ 288).

[105] Hence Heidegger's aforementioned view that authenticity also helps bestow Dasein with a sense of its own existential "constancy of the self in the dual sense of enduring steadfastness" (BT 369/SZ 322). In other words, Dasein's existential *self-constancy* comes not from staying the same but, instead, from the way we repeatedly continue to *become* what we are as we struggle to remain faithful to our defining projects and identity-bestowing commitments. (See n. 55. Chapter 4, and, on some of the fascinating complexities and challenges facing such commitments, see Chapter 9 and Iain Thomson, "Thinking Love: Heidegger and Arendt," *Continental Philosophy Review*, 50:4 [2017], 453–78.)

[106] As Heidegger expresses the underlying point: "Only insofar as it is futural can Dasein *be* authentically as having-been. The character of 'having-been' arises, in a certain way, from the coming of the future [*Zu-kunft*]" (BT 373/SZ 326). At the most primordial level of originary temporality, our "ownmost having-been [*eigenste Gewesen*]" is first disclosed in death, when death's sheer projecting comes toward our worldly selves as what we have always-already been (BT 373/SZ 326).

multiplicitous arriving of those self-world "possibilities" *coming toward* the *solus ipse* as the different selves we *can be* henceforth, coming toward us as largely inchoate live-options that require us to "open" (or "un-close," *ent-schlossen*) ourselves to and so let ourselves become just one of them as resolve (*Entschlossenheit*) thereby "releases the present [*die Gegenwart*] from itself," letting that originary present it is (literally) "waiting-toward [*Gegen-wart*]" arrive, letting-go of all inchoate others (BT 374/SZ 326).[107] In the desolate perspective first disclosed by the projectless projecting of existential death, then, we experience the multiplicitous and inchoate arriving of those futural selves and their partly glimpsed worlds in a maximally open and unmediated way. "Futurity" comes to describe this futural horizon whereby we phenomenologically encounter this sheer *coming toward us* in death (and then its repeated, *momentous* arriving in resolve, which "allows an unconcealed encounter with that [specific situation] which is seized upon in taking action"), rather than the usual (and "fallen") way in which one usually conceives of the future, as a distant "not yet" somewhere out ahead of us.

It is thus important to notice that, in these two different ways of thinking about the future – namely, as standing out there somewhere ahead of us, on the one hand, and as "always-already" *arriving*, on the other – we can now recognize the temporal conditions that underlie Heidegger's two different ways of relating to the phenomena of our own demise and death, respectively. In light of that first thinking of the future (as standing off somewhere ahead of us), recall the "inauthentic" understanding that "flees" death, vainly trying to radically separate existential death from the self by placing it far off in the distant future *as mortal demise*. This is the very same conflation of existential death with mortal demise that typifies our "falling" into the leveled-down intelligibility of the public world and so, unsurprisingly, shapes those same commonsensical expectations we initially bring to *Being and Time* (as we have seen). Then, in light of that second thinking of futurity (as the "coming" of the future in its perpetual *arriving*), consider the "authentic" existential view which *owns* the phenomenon of death by recognizing that existential death helps disclose the most basic structures definitive of our very selfhood by uncovering the radical existential solitude (or "*solus ipse*") of projectless projecting. This sheer structural "existing" is disclosed by Heidegger's phenomenology of existential death as the most ineliminable, individuating, certain, constant, and unsurpassable core of Dasein's intelligible world, a discovery that helps enable the authentic self-recovery accomplished in resolve. In Heidegger's terms, these different ways of "temporalizing" temporality thus "make possible the multiplicity of Dasein's modes of being,

---

[107] I am here simplifying Heidegger's phenomenology of Dasein's successful resolution of ontological guilt, whereby we "let go" of what we are not becoming (lucidly embracing our constitutive *nihilating* of those other live-option projects) in order to (wholeheartedly) become what we are. (See also n. 97, BT 330–4/SZ 283–8, and Chapter 4.)

above all the fundamental possibility of authentic or inauthentic existence" (BT 377/SZ 328)

Futurity thus names the *being* of the future as it is disclosed to existential phenomenology, the deep temporal-horizonal orientation whereby our intelligible worlds are fundamentally open to what is continually coming toward us (always arriving from partly beyond what is as already "having-been" and currently "making-itself-present"). Indeed, this phenomenon of *futurity* – as the temporal horizon conditioning our being's "coming toward" us (*Zukunft*) – discloses an otherwise overwhelming "coming toward presence" that our practical identities usually (1) enable us to navigate and orient ourselves within (with the help of our mooded attunements and embodied skills), but thereby also (2) dim-down and so eclipse futurity's perpetual arriving from sight in our ordinary lives.[108] By uncovering such ontological *futurity* from beneath its ordinary existential taming (into those public roles and established ways of doing things that thereby accomplish "a dimming down of the possible as such" [BT 239/SZ 195]), *Being and Time*'s phenomenology of existential death first grants Heidegger access to the most primordial structures of our Dasein, the temporal structures that delve as deeply into our being as Heidegger then believed phenomenology could reach, precisely because "futurity" is just the first of the three interlocking horizons of originary *temporality*, each of which directly underlies one of the three core existential structures (or *existentials*) set out in Division One (BT 479/SZ 426-7).

As that suggests, the three interconnected existential structures, working in concert, are what ordinarily allow Dasein to tame and navigate the broader openness of the temporal horizons beneath them, since these temporal "ecstasies" would otherwise bombard us with too much unorganized phenomenological information for us to cope with successfully.[109] *Understanding*, as the practical identities we "stand under," enables us to orient ourselves within futurity by charting a meaningful course through the continual and manifold arriving of what is *coming* into presence. *Befindlichkeit*, or our affective attunement, describes how our embodied sense of *what has been* continues to shape and circumscribe our intelligible worlds, helping us maintain a grip

---

[108] Nevertheless, Heidegger thinks the constant background hum of *Angst* in our lives shows that we can never be fully at-home in these ordinary worlds – that we cannot identify with our practical identities the way a chair can be a chair, in some unbroken substantive permanence or coincidence. Instead, we can only *be* something by continuing to *become* it, repeatedly transforming ourselves as our lives and situations continue to change (as subsequent chapters endeavor to show).

[109] Here one can perhaps begin to glimpse the radical neo-Kantianism of Heidegger's phenomenological approach in *Being and Time*. (See Blattner, *Heidegger's Temporal Idealism*.) But one can also begin to recognize another sense in which Heidegger conceives "primordial time as the condition of the possibility and necessity of the everyday experience of time" (BT 381/SZ 333), the ambitious *transcendental* project that, Blattner convincingly argues, fails.

on what *matters* to us.[110] And *Rede*, or our skilful *conversance* with things, articulates the embodied and linguistic ways we skilfully navigate the manifold significations of all that *makes itself present* in our intelligible worlds.

Among these three interlocking temporal "ecstasies," Heidegger thinks futurity is "primary" (BT 378/SZ 329). This is not because his existential phenomenology discovers it first but, rather, because "the present arises from futurity" (BT 479/SZ 427), in the sense that our life-projects orient and circumscribe what shows up for us while also helping attune us to what matters most from the having-been that we continue to be, as we repeatedly reshape that living past we always carry with us (a "having-beenness" that *tunes us in* variously, as Wrathall and Londen suggest, and so helps filter what is salient to and so discernible by us).[111] But we should not let this relative priority of futurity in orienting our existential odysseys through time lead us to forget that the three interconnected temporal horizons always work together as a whole (just like the three existentials they underlie and condition). Hence Heidegger's notoriously recondite formula, which does not describe the *linear* passage of time (as a future that slips through the present into the past) but, instead, the underlying horizons of primordial temporality that condition all our experiences in time (as we have seen): "Temporality temporalizes itself as a coming-toward that makes present in the process of having been [*Zeitlichkeit zeitigt sich als gewesende-gegenwärtigende Zukunft*]" (BT 401/SZ 350).[112] The fact that the three temporal horizons underlie the three main existential structures that *Being and Time* primarily focuses on explains why Heidegger mainly develops just these three essential existentials (*Befindlichkeit*, *Rede*, and *Verstehen*), even while frequently mentioning and partly describing numerous other existential structures. He does not think *Being and Time*'s three main

---

[110] See Mark A. Wrathall and Patrick Londen, "Anglo-American Existential Phenomenology," in *The Cambridge History of Philosophy: 1945–2015*, ed. by Becker and Thomson.

[111] "'As long as' Dasein factically exists [as a "thrown project"], it is never past [*vergangen*, that is, gone into the past], but is always already *having-been*, in the sense of 'I am-as-having-been'" (BT 376/SZ 328). Heidegger's prioritization of futurity over having-beenness (which Arendt famously criticized for opening the door to a historically dangerous *revisionism*) helps explain why he often makes such paradoxical-sounding pronouncements as: "What has been comes to meet us from out of the future," or: "Where we come from remains always still to come [*Herkunft stet bleibt immer Zukunft*]." Nevertheless, existentially, our mooded attunements accomplish "the primary discovery of the world," taking the deepest ontological cut out of what we encounter and in so doing reaching deeper than words can ever fully recapitulate (BT 176–7/SZ 137–8). See also Mark A. Wrathall and Patrick Londen, "An overview of *Being and Time*," in *The Cambridge Companion to Being and Time*, ed. by Mark Wrathall (Cambridge: Cambridge University Press, 2013).

[112] Book 4 of Division II even distinguishes our inauthentic, intermediate, and authentic modes of making sense of ourselves through these temporal horizons. (For a careful reconstruction and critique of Heidegger's complex view of their interrelations, see Blattner, *Heidegger's Temporal Idealism*.)

1.7. SITUATING DEATH: ONTOLOGICAL FUTURITY 73

existentials are *exhaustive* (or a *complete* list of all the constitutive structures universally conditioning Dasein's existential world) but, instead, that these three existential structures of Dasein play a crucial role precisely as the three "essential existentials" that directly emerge from and so help disclose the three primordial temporal horizons underlying them. Those three existentials are nothing more nor less than "the main structures of the most importance in the framework of this problematic" (viz., the pursuit of fundamental ontology) because they help disclose the temporal "horizon within which the concept of being in general becomes intelligible" [BT 133/SZ 100], or so the early Heidegger hopes.[113]

Such big picture sketches inevitably require us to proceed too quickly (tormenting our scholarly and pedagogical consciences, which rightly want to qualify and explain such fascinating issues in detail), but the biggest of several deep problems here is that, in *Being and Time* (and all the way through 1929's *Kant and the Problem of Metaphysics*), Heidegger also believes that the temporal horizons *constitutively condition* what shows up through the existential structures. Indeed, as we shall see in Chapter 2, it is the early Heidegger's neo-Kantian view – that the three temporal horizons fix some of the fundamental terms for any ontology we disclose through the three existential structures – that (temporarily) props up his false and politically disastrous belief that he will be able to disclose "a [*einer*] fundamental ontology" (a *single* "understanding of the meaning of being in general"), which will *answer* the question of being in a way that will enable Heidegger to reunify the university and, behind it, Germany itself (by answering the very question of what it means to *be* German).[114] It is to the philosophical foundations of this large problem that we shall now turn; for, doing so will also enable us to understand how the most important transformation in the development of Heidegger's own thinking required him to find his way through a prolonged and profound philosophical instance of such existential death and rebirth.

---

[113] This means that *Being and Time* does not at all preclude the possibility that sexuality, gender, ethnicity, class, etc., could be existentials. See my "Ontopoliticosexual Pro(-)vocations" (206–210; cf. Tina Chanter, *Time, Death, and the Feminine: Levinas with Heidegger* [Stanford, CA: Stanford University Press, 2002] and Marianna Ortega, *In-Between: Latina Feminist Phenomenology, Multiplicity, and the Self* [New York: SUNY, 2016]).

[114] See Thomson, *Heidegger on Ontotheology*, ch. 3.

2

The Death of Metaphysics and the Birth of Thinking, or Why Did *Being and Time* Fail to Answer the Question of Being?

Being and Time is a failed project.

Theodore Kisiel[1]

2.1 Introduction: Thinking Philosophical Failure

Let us add another item to the long list of lessons still to be learned from *Being and Time*: We need an ontology of philosophical failure. What *is* failure in philosophy? I am not asking about failing at philosophy either by failing to do it or by doing it badly. I mean the more deeply puzzling phenomenon of doing philosophy as well as it has ever been done and yet failing in that philosophy, nonetheless. What does it mean to say, rightly, that *Being and Time* fails, or that it is (in Kisiel's words) "a failed project"? In what way can and should the most influential philosophical work of the twentieth century be considered a failure, judged by the most sympathetic standards of an "internal" or immanent reading (that is, by its own lights or on its own terms) rather than by some measure "external" to the text itself?[2] What did *Being and Time* set

---

[1] Theodore Kisiel, *The Genesis of Heidegger's Being and Time* (Berkeley, CA: University of California Press, 1993), 3.

[2] There are, of course, a potentially infinite number of ways in which *Being and Time* fails. It fails to float, to be a couch, to make good eating, etc., but those are silly and trivial "failures," of little philosophical interest. One could also argue, nontrivially, that *Being and Time* fails to be an important feminist text, or a major contribution to Marxist thinking, or a visionary blueprint for a liberal-democratic political order, and so on. However significant those latter kinds of failure might be, I am not interested in them here because *Being and Time* is not explicitly and centrally trying to be a feminist text, or a contribution to Marxist thinking, or a blueprint for a liberal-democratic order, and so on. Instead, I am interested in the way *Being and Time* fails to do the very thing Heidegger most wants to do in that book, as well as the way this failure teaches him, and so potentially us, a profound lesson about what philosophy can and cannot be henceforth. I shall thus suggest that this failure – rather than taking away from the greatness of *Being and Time* – should instead be recognized as a crucial part of what makes it the seminal and uncircumventable philosophical work that it is.

out to accomplish, and why did it fail to achieve that goal? Is this a failure Heidegger could have avoided or rectified if he had had time to complete the book in the way he originally planned? Or is this a necessary failure, one that follows from some inexhaustibility inherent in the subject matter of *Being and Time* itself, and so from the impossibly ambitious nature of its attempt to answer "the question of being"? In what way must philosophy *fail itself* (to employ a polysemic locution), necessarily falling short of its own deepest, perennial ambitions? What is the lesson of such necessary philosophical failure?

Questions look easier than answers, but in fact our questions guide and circumscribe our search for answers. As Heidegger points out near the beginning of *Being and Time*: "Every question is a kind of seeking, and every search must be guided beforehand by what is sought" (BT 24–25/SZ 5–6). If we do not ask the right questions, we stand little chance of finding the right answers. Yet, sometimes philosophers get lucky (though at first such luck appears to be anything but), and our misguided questions lead to an *aporia* or impasse, requiring us to step back, *rethink*, and revise our earlier questions. This, we will see, is exactly what happened to "the question of being" Heidegger asked in *Being and Time*. He went looking for the wrong sort of answer and, failing to find it, eventually found something else instead, something better because more true. Or, in the terms of *Being and Time* set out in Chapter 1, we could say that the early Heidegger's ultimate project to answer the question of being had to *die*, to be reborn differently only in his later work. For, to *be* "a failed project" (as Kisiel fortuitously puts it) is precisely what *Being and Time* means by existential "death." (This is ontological death – our own *being* dead – as opposed to the mortal phenomenon of ontic "demise," which is something we can never *be* since mortal demise takes away our being, as Epicurus observed long ago.) With such allusions to existential death and rebirth – especially to that *philosophical* death and rebirth that used to be called Heidegger's "turn" (until that locution too died, prematurely, before being fully understood) – we are already "running out ahead" of ourselves, "anticipating" what is to come.[3]

Such death and rebirth also forms the path to what *Being and Time* famously calls "authenticity," though to begin to see this we must pass through and beyond the death of the project guiding that text, as Heidegger himself did. Following this path will suggest that the failure of *Being and Time* can be understood as the failure of philosophy itself as metaphysics, and thus the death of the most fundamental project that has shaped and driven Western

---

[3] On such "anticipation" (or "running out ahead," *vorlaufen*) into existential death (as "projectless projecting") and its relations to and differences from our common expectations about our *mortal demise*, see Chapter 1. On the meaning of the "turn" in and for Heidegger (and the current and older forms of *misunderstanding* it), see Thomson, *Heidegger, Art, and Postmodernity*, 179.

philosophy since it first began with Thales and Anaximander. In the end, I think, this death of philosophy is cause for celebration, even if reaching that point requires a period of mourning for the failed philosophical ambitions of what Heidegger will call metaphysics or, more precisely, *ontotheology*. For, philosophy's metaphysical failure – the death of philosophy as metaphysics in and through Heidegger – opens up the possibility of *thinking* in another way, an "authentic" thinking that learns to embrace the inescapable limits of our finitude by remaining creatively and responsibly grounded on this "earth" (which remains ontologically finite yet phenomenologically inexhaustible, as we will see), rather than escaping into philosophical metaphysics and its ontotheological castles in the sky.[4] To walk such a precarious path we first need to find our hermeneutic footing, so: "Back to the text itself!"

2.2 Fundamental Ontology as the "Onto-" of Ontotheology

According to "The Outline of the Treatise" that concludes *Being and Time*'s "Introduction" (see section 8, BT 63–64/SZ 39–40), the text published in 1927 (and reprinted with only minor alterations ever since) includes just the first two of the book's envisioned six divisions, or *one-third* of the treatise as originally outlined.[5] This means Heidegger published only the "preparatory" part of *Being and Time* (BT 38/SZ 17). The published text – the rightly famous "existential analysis" of the three main universal structures conditioning our "being here" or *Dasein* in Division I and the deeper analysis of the temporal foundations of those existential structures in Division II – was supposed to *prepare* Heidegger to delve into such temporality in order to disclose "a fundamental ontology [*einer Fundamentalontologie*]," that is, a *single* answer to "the question of the meaning of being in general [*die Frage nach dem Sinn von Sein überhaupt*]" (BT 61/SZ 37). As he plainly states: "The analytic of Dasein . . . is to prepare the problematic of fundamental ontology, *the question of the meaning of being in general*" (BT 227/SZ 183). The ultimate goal of the text is thus to answer "the fundamental ontological question of the meaning of being in general [*die fundamentalontologische Frage nach dem Sinn von Sein überhaupt*]" (BT 241/SZ 196). *Being and Time* analyzes the meaning of our own "being here [*Dasein*]" in order to *prepare* to answer this larger question of the meaning of "being [*Sein*] in general." In other words, the "existential

---

[4] On the history of these ontotheological castles in the sky, and the way their collapse opens up another kind of thinking and so a new historical age, see Thomson, *Heidegger, Art, and Postmodernity*, ch. 1.

[5] Of course, the fact that these alterations have been minor does not preclude their sometimes having been highly significant – as, to mention just the most notorious example, when Heidegger removed *Being and Time*'s opening dedication to his Jewish mentor Husserl during his own Nazi years.

analysis" of the meaning of our "being here" (as Dasein) is supposed to serve as a preliminary or propaedeutic bridge to understanding the meaning of "the *being* of entities [*das* Sein *des Seienden*]" *tout court* (BT 59/SZ 35), that is: What do *all* entities share in common insofar as they *are*? What is it simply to be? What, in the end or "after all" (*überhaupt*), does "being" *mean*? Heidegger's ultimate ambition in *Being and Time* is to answer this "question of the meaning of being in general" by uncovering a single "fundamental ontology" (BT 61/SZ 37), a bedrock ontological account of what it means for anything at all to be.

The fact that Heidegger thinks this "question of the meaning of being" is also "the fundamental question of philosophy in general" (BT 49–50/SZ 27) indicates the incredible magnitude of *Being and Time*'s ambition. For, Heidegger is seeking to answer what he takes to be to the most fundamental question of all philosophy (and, indeed, of human existence) – namely, *What does it mean to be?* – a question he believes has *never* been satisfactorily answered in the entire history of Western philosophy and has now "been forgotten," requiring him to "reawaken" it (BT 19–21/SZ 1–2). (*Hubris, nemesis*, as the Greeks taught. Or, in the Christian proverb: "Pride goeth ... before a fall.")[6] In *Being and Time*, "the question of being [*die Seinsfrage*]" takes shape as a quest for a "fundamental ontology"; indeed, these are the book's "guiding question [*leitenden Frage*]" (BT 49–50/SZ 27), "thematic object" (BT 49/SZ 27), and "cardinal problem" (BT 61/SZ 37). They are also, nonetheless, a question the text never answers, an object it never reaches, and a problem it never resolves. For, despite some potentially misleading suggestions to the contrary, Heidegger *never* uncovered a "fundamental ontology" that could answer "the question of being," not in *Being and Time* nor in any of his later work, published or unpublished.

Instead, his quest for a fundamental ontology reached its apogee in 1929 and then hit a dead end, and Heidegger began to *turn* away from it as deeply misguided, indeed, as an unwitting (or "errant") expression of the "metaphysical" tradition he now sought to transcend.[7] In his transitional middle period (from about 1929 to 1937), he began – slowly, sometimes reluctantly, and with significant and repeated backsliding – to profoundly rethink the way he had posed and pursued the "question of being" in *Being and Time*. Experiencing the failure of metaphysics firsthand, in the collapse of

---

[6] *Proverbs* 16:18: "Pride goeth before destruction, and an haughty spirit before a fall" (King James Version of the Bible.). (The Greek and Christian expressions are not strictly equivalent but remain interestingly similar.)

[7] (See, for example, P 250/GA9 328.) On the way fundamental ontology reached its apogee in 1929, in Heidegger's claim that the category of substance derived from the temporal horizon of making present, see Section 2.3 and Thomson, *Heidegger on Ontotheology*, 54, n. 15. On "errancy," see Chapter 5.3.

his own metaphysical ambitions, Heidegger began again, more thoroughly deconstructing the metaphysical tradition (which he came to understand more clearly as *ontotheology*) and developing another kind of thinking (with which he sought to transcend such ontotheology from within). From the perspective of this *later* thinking, "fundamental ontology" can clearly be recognized as an instance of the ontological side of *ontotheology*, that dual metaphysical ambition to "doubly ground" the entire intelligible order from its innermost (*ontological*) core to its outermost (*theological*) expression.[8]

[8] According to Heidegger's favorite formulation (of Western history's "fundamental metaphysical positions"), metaphysics seeks to understand "the being of entities" by grasping the truth about "the totality of entities as such." This involves two intertwined tasks: The attempt to grasp entities "as such" (by discovering the deepest ground that unifies them all) is *ontology*, while the attempt to comprehend their "totality" (by taking up some God's-eye view on the whole) is *theology*. The fact that metaphysics does both simultaneously is what makes it *ontotheology*. Thus, ontotheology does not mean merely treating God as the highest entity (as is commonly but erroneously supposed). Instead, in the simplest terms, *ontotheology* is the attempt to grasp reality *fundamentally*, from the inside out (or the bottom up) *and ultimately*, from the outside in (or the top down) *at the same time*, thereby comprehending reality floor to ceiling by uncovering its deepest microscopic depth and linking this to an account of its ultimate telescopic expression (on how that linkage between ontology and theology functions, see Thomson, *Heidegger, Art, and Postmodernity*, ch. 1). When successful, an ontotheology "doubly grounds" the entire intelligible order root to branch by (temporarily) grasping *both* its innermost ontological core (that fundamental ground all entities share in common) and its outermost theological expression (as if taking up some ultimate "view from nowhere" outside the totality of all that is). I shall focus on the early Heidegger's own ontological ambitions here, since that is what his quest for a *fundamental ontology* turned out to be. The fact that Heidegger himself frequently resists acknowledging his own ontotheological "errancy" (at least in any other terms) does not make it any less true (see nn. 16–17 and Chapter 5). We can see this, for example, from Heidegger's fascinating but deeply confused "Appendix" to 1928's *Metaphysical Foundations of Logic* (MFL 154–159/GA26 196–202). Reading this appendix in light of Heidegger's mature understanding of ontotheology suggests that the short-lived project of "metontology" he advocates there – "a special problematic which has as its proper theme entities as a whole" (MFL 157/GA26 199) – is best understood as Heidegger's attempt to jump from the sinking ship of "fundamental ontology" to that project's ontotheological complement, a type of "fundamental theology" or "theiology" (cf. HCE 135/H 195). Here in 1928, Heidegger still regards metaphysics as a positive "task," indeed, as "the one basic problem of philosophy itself," a task he still believes he will be able to *accomplish*. Nevertheless, he comes very close to his later recognition of metaphysics as ontotheology when he writes: "In their unity, fundamental ontology and metontology constitute the concept of metaphysics" (MFL 158/GA26 202). In *Kant and the Problem of Metaphysics* (1929), Heidegger again defines "metaphysics" in the very terms he will soon abandon as ontotheology: "Metaphysics is the fundamental knowledge of entities as such and as a whole" (KPM 5/GA3 8). What this all suggests, I take it, is that Heidegger had to recognize the fatal flaws in his own ontotheological endeavors – "fundamental ontology" and "metontology," respectively – before decisively rejecting metaphysics as ontotheology. (Nonetheless, by 1940 Heidegger is already recognizing Nietzsche's ontotheology as the metaphysical substructure of our nihilistic age of enframing [see, for

2.2. FUNDAMENTAL ONTOLOGY AS ONTOTHEOLOGY

Our main goal here is to understand the philosophical reasons for the early Heidegger's failure to deliver a fundamental ontology and his consequent turn against metaphysics as ontotheology and transformation of his own "question of being" (from *the meaning of the being of entities* to *the truth of being as such*), the notorious "turn" that most fundamentally distinguishes and divides Heidegger's early and later work (as I argued in *Heidegger on Ontotheology*). Reconstructing some of the *philosophical* reasons for this profound and dramatic transformation will help us address that misleading misreading (long common among orthodox Heideggerians) according to which *Being and Time* did not fail in this way; instead, Heidegger successfully delivered a fundamental ontology when he showed that our understanding of being is grounded in time (or, more specifically, in the temporal structures that fundamentally condition our "being here"). On this view, Heidegger's later thinking simply develops the consequences of *Being and Time*'s deepest insight that being is necessarily conditioned by temporality. This reading thus takes Heidegger's philosophical development to be fundamentally "unified," and so misses the way his thinking *turns* radically around a breakdown in the middle of his thought-path, a philosophical failure so profound that it constituted the death of the central philosophical (and, for Heidegger himself, existential) project from which his later thinking had to be reborn (and, with it, the philosophical tradition itself), as I shall here suggest.[9]

What that widespread, orthodox view gets right is that Heidegger did indeed recognize in *Being and Time* (and subsequently never stopped

---

example, N1 18–19, 63/NI 26–27, 76].) For a fuller account of ontotheology (and the historical role ontotheologies play founding and transforming historical "epochs" or constellations of intelligibility), see Thomson, *Heidegger on Ontotheology*, ch. 1; and, for a more detailed explanation of the relation between "ontology" and "theology" in ontotheology (and for how Heidegger sought to transcend ontotheology from within), see Thomson, *Heidegger, Art, and Postmodernity*, chs. 1 and 3.

[9] Otto Pöggeler is the most influential advocate of the thesis that Heidegger's development must be understood as fundamentally *unified* (and for the glaring problems with Pöggeler's view, see Thomson, *Heidegger, Art, and Postmodernity*, ch. 6), but more nuanced versions of this untenable claim have been defended by such major scholars as Gadamer, Kisiel, Olafson, and White. (For a critique of White, see Chapter 5. On Olafson's view, see n. 14. For a detailed critique of those other scholars' views, see Iain Thomson, "The End of Ontotheology: Understanding Heidegger's Turn, Method, and Politics" [University of California, San Diego: Philosophy Dissertation, 1999], 23–34.) When Heidegger finally published a text called "Time and Being" in 1962 (giving it the weighty name of *Being and Time*'s unpublished Third Division), he argued that time cannot explain being, no more than being can explain time. Instead, he refers to a mysterious "it" that gives us the "there is" (*es gibt*) of our world, an apparently inexhaustible source that bestows both being and time (in their changing historical intelligibility) (TB 5/GA14 9). This nonsubstantial "it" is another of Heidegger's names for "being as such," that is, for being in its *difference* from the being of entities that all "metaphysics" seeks to grasp, including the metaphysics of "fundamental ontology."

believing) that *being is conditioned by temporality* (although Heidegger's understanding of the way temporality conditions being changes dramatically between his early and later work).[10] What the view gets wrong is the further claim that this insight either is or somehow leads to the fundamental ontology for which *Being and Time* was searching. The view is also right that Heidegger never stopped asking "the question of being" (and this lifelong quest does indeed provide an important formal continuity to the path Heidegger's thinking, although this *Denkweg* has a dramatic "turn" on it, what Gadamer nicely called "a switchback" on that mountainous "thought-path" Heidegger followed in pursuit of being). But it is wrong once more not to recognize that the answer Heidegger was looking for changed dramatically in his later thinking, so much so that he came to reject *Being and Time*'s quest for a fundamental ontology as itself metaphysics. (To put it in Heidegger's own terms, *Being and Time*'s search for a fundamental ontology was an attempt to understand the meaning of "the being of entities"; like all metaphysics, it thus effaced the *truth* of "being as such," that is, the temporally dynamic "presencing" of that apparently inexhaustible Ur-phenomenon that informs and makes possible but is never completely captured by any metaphysical understanding of "the being of entities.")[11] To see all this, of course, we need to delve more deeply into the details of Heidegger's early project.

We saw that *Being and Time* hoped to uncover a "fundamental ontology" (an "understanding of the meaning of being in general") by way of an existential analysis of our "being here." (As that distinctive ontic entity who has an ontological understanding of being, we form the bridge between the

---

[10] There is thus an important difference even here. In *Being and Time* Heidegger thought of temporality as a *transcendental* condition on the possibility of any understanding of being, that is, a necessary and constitutive condition that is not itself conditioned by what it conditions and that (at least partly) informs what it conditions. But in his later work, he instead came to think of being and time as "reciprocally determining" or mutually conditioning one another (TB 3/GA14 7), that is, as equiprimordial or co-originary phenomena in the larger "play of space-time [*Zeitspielraum*]," neither of which can be treated as the unilateral foundation of the other.

[11] (See n. 8 and, on the way metaphysics denies and contradicts its own conditions of possibility, leaving it open to the immanent critique and deconstruction, see Thomson, *Heidegger on Ontotheology*, chs. 1 and 3.) Metaphorically, Gadamer's "switch-back" image (for the *Kehre* in Heidegger's *Denkweg* or "path of thought") might thus be better replaced with one capable of conveying Heidegger's dawning insight that the ontotheological mountain he was scaling did not lead to any single summit but, instead, disappeared into the fathomless ground as well as up into those same cloudy heights that had lured on Western metaphysicians since Thales went down and Anaximander up in pursuit of a final ground. (For the philosophical details, see Thomson, *Heidegger, Art, and Postmodernity*, ch. 1.)

2.2. FUNDAMENTAL ONTOLOGY AS ONTOTHEOLOGY

ontic and ontological domains.)[12] More specifically, interpreting the meaning of our "being here [*Dasein*]" in terms of temporality" was intended to establish "time as the transcendental horizon for the question of being [*die Seinsfrage*]" (BT 63/SZ 39). The climax of *Being and Time* comes in Division II, when Heidegger demonstrates that the three main existential structures of our "being here" articulated in Division I (*Befindlichkeit*, *Rede*, and *Verstehen*, or roughly our "affective attunement," our "conversance" with things, and our practical and self-guiding "understanding") are themselves grounded in more fundamental temporal horizons (of having-been, making-present, and futurity, respectively). Our "being here" or *Dasein* – that is, our making-intelligible of the world in which we find ourselves – is grounded in temporality, in that (1) the affective attunement that shapes our world-disclosure originates from our *always-already* "having been" (simply put, the past is always present as the mood that shapes our world, tuning us in to what matters to us in light of our shifting cares); (2) the conversance with things (prelinguistic and conceptual, practical and theoretical) that constitutes the *significance* of our everyday worlds comes from our way of "making present" (such that what we call "the present" is fundamentally a making-present that takes shape primarily through our skillful use of "hands-on" [*zuhanden*] equipment with which we are integrally and inconspicuously involved – the pen we write with, the shoes we walk in, and so on – and only secondarily through our express deliberations about a separate domain of objects "on-hand" [*vorhanden*]); and (3) the life-projects that we "understand" (that is, the practical projects we project into

---

[12] For the early Heidegger, our being (that is, the essentially distinguishing characteristic of the entity we are) *is* to understand being. Our failure to understand the meaning of being in general would thus be a failure not only of Heidegger's early philosophy, or even of philosophy as such (in its fundamental ontological ambitions), but of human beings to fulfill their very being (BT 35/SZ 15; BT 96/SZ 67). Or so it looked to Heidegger initially, before he realized that to try to understand the meaning of being in terms of fundamental ontology was precisely to fail to understand "being as such," and thus that to understand (and help *realize*) being as such (for example, by disclosing it in ways that show how "it" informs and exceeds all metaphysical conceptions of "the being of entities") is what truly fulfills human beings. (For more on this topic, see Chapter 6; Thomson, *Heidegger on Ontotheology*, ch. 4; and "Heideggerian Perfectionism and the Phenomenology of the Pedagogical Truth Event," in *Kevin Hermberg and Paul Gyllenhammer*, ed. by Phenomenology and Virtue Ethics [London and New York: Bloomsbury, 2013], 180–190.) We need not get into the ("animality") debate concerning whether Heidegger's ontological definition of Dasein is necessarily anthropocentric or whether it can and should apply in principle to all entities capable of understanding being, be they human or not. I take the latter view because it is more philosophically defensible, but there is ample textual evidence capable of supporting both readings. (For more on the issue of Heidegger and "animality," see, for example, Thomson, "Ontology and Ethics at the Intersection of Phenomenology and Environmental Philosophy"; and cf. Matthew Calarco, *Zoographies: The Question of the Animal from Heidegger to Derrida* [New York: Columbia University Press, 2008].)

and so come to *stand-under* – teacher, father, friend, philosopher, revolutionary, and so on – projects that shape and guide our basic sense of self) disclose and help orient us in our ongoing navigation of "futurity" or the "to come." (Futurity is here now too, in the way our life-projects help constitute and organize our basic sense of self, as we chart our way through this perpetual *arriving* of what is not yet.)[13] These three existential structures of our Dasein or "being here" are thus made possible by these interlocking temporal horizons, which come together – as "a future that makes present in the process of having been" (BT 401/SZ 350) – to constitute the temporally "ecstatic" ways we "exist" or "stand out" (*ek-sistere*) into a meaningful world.

Readers have often supposed that with this rather breathtaking demonstration – of the way our "being here" is grounded in temporality – Heidegger delivered the fundamental ontology he had been pursuing throughout *Being and Time*. Yet, the text itself makes clear that this is not in fact the case: "With this interpretation of Dasein as temporality, however, the answer to our guiding question about the meaning of being in general is not already given. But the soil [*der Boden*] will have been made ready to reap such an answer" (BT 38/SZ 17). By showing that our being here is grounded in temporality, Heidegger believes he has prepared "the soil" – namely, "temporality" – from which to "reap" an understanding of the meaning of being in general, but this reaping itself does not take place. *Being and Time* does not even show us *how* temporality constitutes the meaning of being in general, let alone *what* that fundamental ontology is supposed to be.[14]

---

[13] As we saw in Chapter 1, the collapse of these life guiding and identity bestowing projects is what Heidegger calls existential "death" (in distinction from mortal demise). In the projectless projecting (that follows the collapse of our projects), we encounter the sheer "futurity" of the future in the way that first we and then the world we can no longer inhabit come toward us nonetheless. *Being and Time* glimpses (and even names) this "nothing" of the world (for example, BT 321/SZ 276–277), but does not yet recognize it as the active "noth-ing of the nothing," the *ontological futurity* whereby that which *is not yet* repeatedly arrives, and so the first guise of that Ur-phenomenon of "being as such," which makes metaphysics possible (by informing it) and yet impossible (by always exceeding and so at least partly eluding its grasp). As we will see in Chapter 3, it is thus this "nothing" – along with its phenomenological descendants like "the earth" – that eventually undermines the metaphysics of "fundamental ontology" and, from out of the death of that project, helps give birth to Heidegger's later thinking. (See Thomson, *Heidegger, Art, and Postmodernity*, chs. 3 and 7.)

[14] I think there is more room for disagreement on the former point than on the latter. Indeed, the scholar who has done the most to show *how* exactly temporality is supposed to condition fundamental ontology in *Being and Time* concludes that the project fails. (See Blattner, *Heidegger's Temporal Idealism*.) For the clearest argument that Heidegger did deliver a fundamental ontology by showing that *the meaning of being in general is presence* (articulating this fundamental ontology in the lecture courses he gave right after *Being and Time* on Aristotle, Descartes, and Kant, thereby completing most of *Being and*

2.2. FUNDAMENTAL ONTOLOGY AS ONTOTHEOLOGY

In a later marginal note to the first sentence just quoted, Heidegger specifies that in trying to answer *Being and Time*'s "guiding question about the meaning of being in general," he is looking for what all entities share in common simply insofar as they *are*, that is, the fundamental ontological "unity, the thing itself [*katholoy, kath auto*]" (GA2 24, note a). As this use of the Greek suggests, *Being and Time* is still pursuing the question of what unifies all the different senses of being, the very same "question of being" Heidegger had been asking since 1907, when the eighteen-year-old teenager was given Brentano's 1862 dissertation ("On the Manifold Meaning of Being in Aristotle") by the Catholic headmaster of his boarding school in Constance, Dr. Conrad Gröber.[15] *Being and Time* was supposed to finally answer that "question of being" by uncovering the "meaning of being in general," but this fundamental ontology never materialized.

It is not surprising that this philosophical failure would prove to be so momentous for Heidegger (nor that he would struggle against acknowledging it throughout much of the 1930s), since it meant the collapse of the existential project and pathway he had been on ever since his first philosophical awakening in 1907. In 1946, however, a fifty-eight-year-old Heidegger forthrightly describes his early philosophy as "breaking against the hardness of the matter" he was trying to think (P 261/GA9 343), a dramatic admission made all the more telling by (what I have described as) "Heidegger's nearly constitutional incapacity to admit his own mistakes," the fact that he typically prefers to drastically reinterpret his own early works (often quite incredibly) in order to render them consistent with what he has come to believe, rather than admit he had previously been wrong.[16]

Time as originally outlined), see Frederick Olafson, "The Unity of Heidegger's Thought," in *The Cambridge Companion to Heidegger*, ed. by Charles Guignon (Cambridge: Cambridge University Press, 1993). But those familiar with the later Heidegger will recognize that the thesis Olafson believes *unifies* Heidegger's thought as a whole – viz., that *being means presence* – is deeply problematic at best, since in fact the later Heidegger famously *critiques* that equation of being with presence *as the metaphysics of presence* (see Thomson, *Heidegger on Ontotheology*, ch. 1). (Olafson obscures this point by collapsing the distinction between "presence [*Anwesenheit*]" and "presencing [*Anwesen*]" that is crucial to the later Heidegger; see Olafson, "The Unity of Heidegger's Thought," 101.) More importantly, even if Heidegger did believe that thesis in his early period (before turning decisively away from it in his later work), I shall go on to suggest that such an understanding of being as presence is not sufficiently detailed and robust to fulfill the philosophical function that the early Heidegger intended such a "fundamental ontology" to serve (as shown in detail in Thomson, *Heidegger on Ontotheology*, ch. 3).

[15] See Heidegger, "My Way to Phenomenology," in *On Time and Being*, 74.
[16] See also, for example, the later Heidegger's telling admission that "The Heidegger of *Being and Time* ... is still stuck in metaphysics" (GA102 94, explained at the beginning of Chapter 1); and see Chapter 5 for several dramatic examples of such incredible retroactive self-reinterpretation.

Nonetheless, Heidegger makes clear that he did abandon this early quest for a fundamental ontology in numerous places, including in another of the elliptical notes he wrote in the margins of his copy of *Being and Time* (this one next to his published outline's reference to the unpublished Division III on "Time and Being"). We saw that *Being and Time*'s analysis of Dasein's temporality was supposed to establish "time as the transcendental horizon for the question of being" (BT 63/SZ 39). This means that the "fundamental ontology" *Being and Time* seeks can be discovered only by way of an understanding of Dasein's temporality or, more specifically, the ecstatic "horizons" of intelligibility that Dasein's temporality constitutes.[17] Instead of trying to reap the fundamental ontological harvest of such temporal horizons, however, Heidegger's later note calls for "the overcoming of the horizon as such." Rather than thinking we can answer the question of being by understanding Dasein's temporal structures as constitutive conditions for the possibility of any understanding of being (including a fundamental ontological understanding of the meaning of being in general), he now suggests that we need to "turn back into the origin" and so discover "the presencing of the origin [*das Anwesen aus dieser Herkunft*]" (BT 37/GA2 53). Here we witness *Being and Time*'s "transcendental" approach – Heidegger's search for necessary "conditions of possibility" (heavily under the influence of Kant) – giving way to his later phenomenology.[18] For Heidegger is referring to the "presencing [*Anwesen*]" of "being as such" in its *difference* from "the being of entities" that metaphysics pursues (P 246/GA9 322), including the metaphysics of fundamental ontology. This temporally dynamic and seemingly inexhaustible phenomenological "presencing" is precisely what fundamental ontology cannot account for, a condition of possibility that all metaphysics (as ontotheology) must thus deny, obscure, and so contradict – or so I shall

---

[17] In his middle period, Heidegger often seems to recognize (though he rarely admits) that *Being and Time*'s guiding methodological claim that the path to being *must* pass through an existential analysis of the structure of our own "being here" is very close to the metaphysical "subjectivism" he increasingly critiques (see, for example, P 125/GA9 162 and n. 16 in Chapter 1).

[18] For some discussion on the issue of whether Heidegger abandoned the transcendental approach entirely or just complicated it (by, as I would say, recognizing "being as such" as that which makes all the different metaphysical ways of understanding "the being of entities" possible and yet also undermines them, as a condition of possibility they systematically deny), see n. 8 and, for example, the essays collected in Steven Crowell and Jeff Malpas, eds, *Transcendental Heidegger* (Stanford, CA: Stanford University Press, 2006); and Lee Braver, *A Thing of This World: A History of Continental Anti-Realism* (Evanston, IL: Northwestern University Press, 2007), esp. 273–275. For a detailed account of Heidegger's later phenomenological method, see Thomson, *Heidegger, Art, and Postmodernity*, ch. 3. On why recognizing that any understanding of being must be conditioned by temporality (something Heidegger never stopped believing) is not sufficient to establish a fundamental ontology, see below and n. 10.

suggest in what follows. Elsewhere I have shown how Heidegger's later phenomenology undermined that quest to uncover a fundamental ontology that lured him on throughout *Being and Time* (and many of the other texts that followed over the next decade).[19] Here I shall focus primarily on the prior question of why "time" or "temporality" *cannot* itself be the answer to the question of being that Heidegger was looking for in *Being and Time*. Why *must* such an answer fail to satisfy the deepest ambitions of *Being and Time*? Then we can ask: What are the main consequences of this failure? These are complex matters, but I shall try to address them briefly.

2.3 Beneath Fundamental Ontology: The Temporal Abyss of Being

Faced with the fact that he never finished *Being and Time*, Heidegger reluctantly deleted the words "First Half" from its title page in 1953, explaining (in his preface to its seventh edition) that "after a quarter century," the long-promised "second half could no longer be added unless the first were to be presented anew. Yet, the path [*Weg*] it follows remains a necessary one even today, if our being here is to be moved [*bewegen*] by the question of being" (BT 17/SZ vii). Here Heidegger exaggerates how much of the book he published.[20] But he often reiterates the sentiment that his formative passage through this unfinished book was "necessary" in order for him to develop his later thinking about being. In his preface to Father Richardson's *Heidegger* book, for example, Heidegger writes: "Only by way of what Heidegger I [that is, the "early" Heidegger] has thought does one gain access to what is to be thought by Heidegger II [or the "later" Heidegger]" (Pre xxii–xxiii).

---

[19] I have written two books that explain the motives and consequences of the philosophical transformation in Heidegger's thinking in great detail; I frequently refer to those throughout rather than merely repeating them or asserting their conclusions without references. (See esp. Thomson, *Heidegger on Ontotheology*, chs. 1 and 3.)

[20] He had really published only a third of his outline, since he had not published Division III of Part One on "Time and Being" or Divisions I–III of Part Two. Still, his (then unpublished) lecture notes on the contributions made by Aristotle (GA18, GA22, GA33), Descartes (BPP/GA24), and Kant (KPM/GA3) to the history of ontology can be recognized as drafts (more and less polished, as well as more and less successful) of the final three divisions he had planned. But treating his significantly later essay, "Time and Being" (1962), as a version of the unpublished Division III is a much more problematic move (even if Heidegger encouraged it by giving it that same name), since he wrote this essay long after rejecting *Being and Time*'s quest for a fundamental ontology (the explicitly "metaphysical" project that most of those earlier lectures still eagerly pursue) and in it he makes clear that he no longer believes that temporality constitutively conditions being, instead maintaining that both being and time are conditioned by an inexhaustible (and never finally nameable) "it," an irreducibly polysemic Ur-phenomenon that "gives" both being and time by informing and also exceeding our best ways of understanding them and, indeed, all else (see nn. 8 and 10).

Let me thus be clear: When I suggest that *Being and Time* failed *by its own standards*, I do not want to reinforce that other widespread misreading (of which Kisiel is the most influential purveyor) according to which Heidegger considered the book a simple *failure* and said as much by repeatedly referring to it in later years as a *Holzweg*. For Heidegger, a *Holzweg* is no mere "dead end" but (more carefully thought) instead designates a forest path that leads to a "clearing" (*Lichtung*), that is, a place in the forest from which the trees have been removed. Such a "clearing" affords us an ontological epiphany (that is, an insight into our understanding of being). Out of an encounter with *nothing*, initially, we come to notice the light through which we ordinarily see the forest. A clearing thus helps us "see the light" by redirecting our attention from entities to being, that usually unnoticed ontological light through which entities appear.[21] This clarification provides us with an important hint as to why *Being and Time* had to remain unfinished: Heidegger himself came to see the light (to redeploy that rich and revealing locution), and what he saw – although initially it looked like "nothing" at all – soon unfolded itself differently (as we will see in Chapter 3), in a way that prevented him from following through on *Being and Time*'s original plan. In other words, the impasse to which *Being and Time*'s question of being led is also what opened up the perspective from which all Heidegger's later works were born.[22]

---

[21] A *Holzweg* brings us to a "clearing [*Lichtung*]" (in which we can "see the light" through which we have been seeing and so recognize how "the open" is "lit up," to use Heidegger's dual terms for this *clearing* as both a noun and verb, an open and a lighting, respectively, that is, as the *open* of "being as such" in its apparent phenomenological inexhaustibility and as the *lighting* of the ontotheological "being of entities" that attempts to settle its meaning once and for all). By allowing us to see our own (metaphysical) way of seeing (the being of entities), such a "clearing" helps us glimpse and so begin to discern the ontological prescription on those unnoticed lenses through which we ordinary make sense of all that is. (See Thomson, *Heidegger on Ontotheology*, xiii, and the development of this point in Thomson, *Heidegger, Art, and Postmodernity*, 83–84.) Let me also be clear that the fact that *all* things tend to appear in the light of our current ontotheology does not mean that all things appear *completely* in its terms (as if the dominant ontotheology could exhaust the available phenomena and fully explain all things), for that would trap us in our current epoch and render epochal transitions impossible. (I critique this still common "fatalistic misreading" of Heidegger in Iain Thomson, "Ontotheology," in *The Bloomsbury Companion to Heidegger*, ed. by François Raffoul and Eric S. Nelson [London: Bloomsbury, 2013], 324–326 and 327, n. 10. But for Heidegger's dystopian view of how this "greatest danger" of technology could actually come to pass, see Iain Thomson, *Heidegger on the Danger and Promise of Technology, or What Is Called Thinking in the Age of AI*? [Cambridge: Cambridge University Press, forthcoming]).

[22] This is the most obvious sense in which *Being and Time* remains a *necessary failure*. As suggested earlier, however, there are other senses as well. Most importantly, the failure of fundamental ontology is also the failure of the tradition of Western metaphysics itself (as Heidegger understands it). It is, more precisely, the beginning of the collapse of the ontological component of *ontotheology* – a collapse Heidegger himself had to pass

To see clearly that the early Heidegger failed to answer the question of being in *Being and Time* (and subsequent texts), we need to understand how exactly that answer was supposed to allow Heidegger to fulfill the text's neo-Husserlian ambition to establish phenomenology as the queen of the sciences. As I showed in *Heidegger on Ontotheology* (2005), Heidegger sought to uncover the meaning of being in general in *Being and Time* in part because he believed that only such a fundamental ontology would prove capable of uniting all the different academic disciplines, reversing their "boundless and aimless dispersal" and thereby unifying the *University* (QA 9/GA16 111).[23] Heidegger's basic idea (inherited from Husserl's critique of the natural sciences but developed differently) is that every well-formed academic discipline must presuppose an ontological understanding of what the class of entities it studies *is* (BT 29–31/SZ 9–11): Research in biology presupposes some understanding of what "life" *is*; historical research presupposes some prior grasp of what history *is*; research in psychology presupposes a preexisting sense of what "consciousness" *is*; and so on. Practitioners in every field of research (or "positive science") need to be guided by such an ontological understanding (or "posit") simply to be able to pick out the relevant entities to study: Biologists must have some sense of what it means to *be* alive just to be able to distinguish living from nonliving entities; historians need some sense of what it means to *be* historical in order to sort those entities from the past destined for oblivion from those needing to be preserved in history books, museums, and so on. In Heidegger's early work, the distinctive role of philosophy (as phenomenological ontology) is to focus on these ontological presuppositions themselves: What is the *being* of life; that is, what does it mean to *be* alive?[24] What is the *being* of history; that is, what does it mean to *be* historical? (And so on.) Indeed, that last question (and this is still too

---

through to be able to elaborate his critique of the end of philosophy as ontotheology and his postmodern thinking of the other beginning of Western history. (See below and Thomson, *Heidegger, Art, and Postmodernity*.) On this crucial "noth-ing," around which Heidegger's philosophical development itself turned, see Chapter 3.

[23] See Thomson, *Heidegger on Ontotheology*, ch. 3, esp. 99–123.

[24] (And, as we saw in Chapter 1: What is the *being* of death; that is, what does it mean to *be* dead?) The early Heidegger (who remains avowedly "Ur-scientific" and prometaphysical) is still trying to redeem Husserl's ambitious goal of establishing phenomenology as the foundation of all the other sciences in order to avert the "crisis" arising from the sciences' lack of any unifying vision or guiding self-understanding. I have shown that Heidegger later abandons the commitment to fundamental ontology at the heart of this proudly "Ur-scientific" vision of philosophy, but he continues to develop his response to the larger problem of disciplinary fragmentation and its connection to cultural and historical nihilism. (That Heidegger refines rather than abandons his educational view – replacing his early task of recovering a fundamental ontology with his later one of discerning and transcending our age's reigning ontotheology – is a central thesis of Thomson, *Heidegger on Ontotheology*, chs. 3 and 4. See below and Chapter 4.)

infrequently recognized) is precisely the one Heidegger is trying to answer when he explicates the "historicality [*Geschichtlichkeit*]" of the historical in *Being and Time* [BT 424–455/SZ 372–404].[25]

It is not surprising that history is the ontological domain in which Heidegger made the most progress, given that it is the field to which Husserl originally assigned him, and the one he had last been working on the longest (since at least 1915, when he published "The Concept of Time in the Science of History" [see BH 77–85]). *Being and Time* does advance a fairly robust (and subsequently controversial) view of what it means to *be* historical, arguing (to simplify) that each generation of people constitutes its own defining historical mission through a creative and critical *inheritance* of "the tradition," in which the missions that guided heroic figures and movements from the past are updated so that they speak to the current generation's understanding of its own most pressing contemporary needs. We can probably imagine how such an account of historicality might guide the specific research of historians (and the dangers of *revisionism* clearly loom large here). But how does Heidegger's account of historicality answer such questions as the one he inherits from Dilthey's central concern with the relation between the natural sciences and the human or social sciences – namely: How should we understand the relation between the history of human beings and our social and cultural institutions, on the one hand, and the history of nonhuman entities and events, on the other? What, for example, do the history of cultures and constitutions have in common with the history of geological and even cosmological processes?[26] What understanding of the *being* of history can account

---

[25] "Historicity" suggests the fact that our understanding of being changes over time (that is, it suggests what Heidegger will later call "the history of being"). The word "historicity [that is, *Historicität*]" is thus a bad translation of *Being and Time*'s "*Geschichtlichkeit*," by which Heidegger does not mean the *history of being* but rather the *being of history*. (Those are not simply equivalent locutions; for the later Heidegger, the former is the ground of the latter; see Thomson, *Heidegger on Ontotheology*, 114, n. 76. Cf. BT 41-2/SZ 20, where Heidegger might seem to be doing the reverse, grounding historicity in historicality, but is in fact taking note of the historicity of our awareness of historicity itself, pointing out that our recognition that history changes us was itself a historical change in our understanding of what history is, and was thus made possible by the fact that we are beings shaped and transformed by changes in our historical self-understanding.) For, in *Being and Time*, Heidegger is clearly asking what history *is*: That is, what makes some entity or event "historical" (that is, historically significant or meaningful) in the first place? (How in other words, should we understand the being of this class of entities, that is, "the historicality of the historical"?)

[26] Interestingly, the controversy that initially greeted the very concept of the "Anthropocene" seems to have resulted not only from reactionary deniers of the relatively straightforward findings of natural science (establishing anthropogenic climate change) but also from natural scientific defenders made skeptical by the way this very notion (that the earth is entering a new geological age catalyzed in large part by humanity's growing use of fossil fuels) challenges our post-Diltheyan sense that the human and natural

for *both* human and nonhuman history by telling us what all history *is*? *Being and Time*'s treatment of historicality ends abruptly with the remark that no further progress can be made on this very question until Heidegger has succeeded in "clarifying, through fundamental ontology, the question of the meaning of being in general" (BT 455/SZ 403). Only by understanding what it means for anything to *be*, in other words, will Heidegger be able to say what anything historical *is*.

That, of course, is a proverbial leap from the frying pan into the fire. Heidegger is saying, in effect, "Before I can tell you what 'history' *is*, I have to tell you what 'Isness' itself *is*." This also turns out to be a strategy of endless deferral (since this *metaphysical* question of what "Isness" *is* will later get deconstructed rather than answered). But this helps make clear how much is riding on Heidegger's promise in *Being and Time* that his deconstruction of the philosophical tradition will allow him to uncover a fundamental ontology. Such an understanding of the meaning of being in general would tell us what *all* entities share in common, what unites the being of all things. If we could uncover such a fundamental ontology, Heidegger thinks we would then be able to understand how this general understanding of "being" divides into its three constituent "regional ontologies" of *history, nature,* and *language*, thereby allowing us to understand what unifies and distinguishes all historical entities, natural entities, and linguistic entities as such (and so answer Dilthey's question, among many others).[27]

As that suggests, Heidegger treats the regional ontologies of history, nature, and language as the three basic "ontological regions" of entities (the three most basic ways of slicing up the *being* pie, as it were). Fundamental ontology divides into these three regional ontologies of nature, history, and language, and then these three regional ontologies get sliced up further to yield the domains of being studied by all "mature" or well-formed academic disciplines.

sciences describe different ontological regions, which do not typically interact in such directly causal ways, a long-standing prejudice unlikely to survive our current technological age (in which it is becoming increasingly obvious that human artifacts can indeed fundamentally alter the nature of ontological domains previously assumed to be untouchable – a development by which Heidegger was philosophically quite troubled; see Thomson, "Post/Modernity?"). See also Fernando Flores and B. Scot Rousse, "Ecological Finitude as Ontological Finitude: Radical Hope in the Anthropocene," in *The Task of Philosophy in the Anthropocene: Axial Echoes in Global Space*, ed. by Richard Polt and John Wittrock (New York: Roman & Littlefield, 2018), 175–92.

[27] In his Rectorial Address ("The Self-Assertion of the German University"), Heidegger adds "language" (a category meant to map onto his understanding of the pre-Socratic *logos*) to the regional ontologies of nature and history (which he traces back to *phusis* and *alêtheia*, respectively), suggesting that the university should be reorganized into twelve academic disciplines (including "death," as mentioned in Chapter 1), which would be unified as four different ways of approaching and elucidating these three regional ontologies (Q&A 9/GA16 111). (See Thomson, *Heidegger on Ontotheology*, ch. 3.)

So, once we see how the three regional ontologies get divvied up into the particular ontological "posits" that guide each of the "positive sciences," we will have recognized the deeper unity connecting all the academic disciplines. For, we will have seen how all the academic disciplines' different ways of understanding the being of the classes of entities they study stem from regional ontologies that are themselves ultimately rooted in a single fundamental ontology or understanding of the meaning of being in general. Such a comprehensive, hierarchical vision might indeed help the philosopher who articulated it to unify the university – and perhaps even, behind it, the German nation, since it will also enable an answer to the politically momentous question of what it means to *be* German. (Indeed, as I have previously shown, Heidegger's metaphysical quest for a fundamental ontology explains the more authoritarian dimension of the political program he attempted to initiate in his Rectorial Address of 1933.)[28]

Being and Time pursues this fundamental ontology right to the end, where the book breaks off with leading rhetorical questions (veiled assertions that Heidegger knows he has not yet justified, but which clearly reveal how he hopes to proceed subsequently): "Is there a way which leads from primordial *time* to the meaning of *being*? Does *time* itself reveal itself as the horizon of *being*?" (BT 488/SZ 437). The text thus ends by reiterating Heidegger's metaphysical hope that by understanding how temporality constitutively conditions any understanding of being, he will be able to reconstruct a *fundamental ontological* understanding of the meaning of being in general. Here, however, the caution Heidegger expresses in an earlier passage from *Being and Time* proves to be far more prescient:

> The question of being [*die Seinsfrage*] will achieve its true concreteness only when we have carried through our deconstruction of the ontological tradition. ... In this domain where "the thing itself is deeply veiled" [as Kant wrote in his first *Critique*], every investigation should avoid overestimating its own results. For such questioning is constantly compelled

---

[28] For, "if a philosophical vision which recognized that and how all the different ontological posits fit together into a fundamental ontology could reunify the university (and, behind it, the nation), then Heidegger, as the unique possessor of just such a vision, would be the natural ('fated') spiritual leader of the university, and thus ... the nation. In this sense, Heidegger's neo-Husserlian ambition to restore philosophy to her throne as the queen of the sciences clearly helped fuel his political vision for the revitalization of the German University" (Thomson, *Heidegger on Ontotheology*, 116–117). If phenomenology can be the queen of the sciences, then the phenomenological fundamental ontologist can be "the philosopher king." Heidegger was thus not subordinating his philosophical vision of the university to the nation (as critics often mistakenly allege) but rather the reverse. (On the dangers and lessons of this vision, see Thomson, *Heidegger on Ontotheology*, 114–139.)

to face the possibility of disclosing an even more primordial and universal horizon from which to answer the question: What does "being" mean? (BT 49/SZ 26–27)[29]

In fact, Heidegger's quest for a fundamental ontology reaches its final apogee in 1929, in *Kant and the Problem of Metaphysics*, which Heidegger originally presented as "a first working-out of Part Two of *Being and Time*" (KPM xix/ GA3 xvi). As I mentioned briefly in Chapter 1, in the first ("A") edition of Kant's *Critique of Pure Reason*, Kant postulated a third faculty of the "imagination" that mediates between the faculties of sensation and understanding, explaining how mind and world become joined together through the temporal process of "schematization," by which the conceptual categories of the understanding get subconsciously applied to the empirical data of sensation to yield an intelligible world. Kant largely effaced this faculty of imagination (and with it the central role temporality plays in constituting the intelligible world) from the second ("B") edition of the *Critique* – hence Heidegger's dramatic charge in *Being and Time* that "Kant shrinks back ... in the face of something which must be brought to light as a theme and a principal if the expression 'being' is to have any demonstrable meaning" (BT 45/SZ 23).

Kant and the Problem of Metaphysics picks up this task (which, as *Being and Time* already emphasized, Kant valorized as the "duty of philosophers" [BT 45/SZ 23]). Indeed, at the very apogee of his own fundamental ontological ambition, Heidegger goes so far as to suggest that he can derive Kant's categories from the temporal structures of our "being here [or *Dasein*]" discovered in *Being and Time*. Heidegger even tries to derive the category of "substance" (that is, of what "stands beneath" and persists throughout all change) from the temporal horizon of making present. Time "shows its own permanence" in the fact that it "is always now," and in such temporal permanence, "time gives the pure look of something like lasting in general," thereby constituting the temporal "ground" of the metaphysical idea of something that persists beneath all change (KPM 75–6/GA3 106–107). Yet, what Heidegger thus inadvertently shows is that only one facet of temporality (namely, our sense that all our experience happens in the now) leads us to search for a single, unchanging ontological ground beneath all things, and

---

[29] (Notice that Heidegger's very quest for the most "primordial and universal" horizons already suggest the *ontotheological* ambition driving his early metaphysical project; see n. 8.) Heidegger convinced himself in *Being and Time* that beyond the being of entities there was "essentially nothing [*wesenhaft nichts anderes*, that is, essentially nothing else]" (BT 60/SZ 36), but we will see in detail in Chapter 3 that the meaning of this "nothing" soon crucially shifted in his own thinking, from an irrelevant nothing at all to the ontologically inexhaustible "noth-ing" of the nothing (his first name for being as such, that horizon beyond the metaphysical being of entities that ontotheology can neither account for nor encompass).

temporality has other facets that undermine that search for a fundamental ontology in that single underlying "sub-stance" that Western ontologists have been searching for since Thales.[30] Most important here is Heidegger's dawning recognition of that temporally dynamic "presencing" (*Anwesen*) referred to earlier, a subtle coming into and passing out of being which plays an even more important role in constituting our intelligible worlds than the final ontological foundations repeatedly sought by the metaphysics of substance.

As Heidegger deepens his analysis – proudly applying hermeneutic "violence" to uncover what Kant left "unsaid and force it into words" (KPM 141/GA3 202) – he works through this problem vicariously. Thus, instead of asserting that Kant "shrinks back" from the temporal foundations of being, Heidegger now writes that "Kant's falling back before the ground which he himself unveiled, before the transcendental power of imagination, is ... that movement [*Bewegung*] of philosophizing which makes manifest the breaking open of the foundation [*Bodens*] and thus makes manifest the abyss of metaphysics [*den Abgrund der Metaphysik*]" (KPM 150–151/GA3 215). In other words, the Western tradition of substance metaphysics (that is, the metaphysics that understands being only as that which has permanent presence) systematically overlooks that dynamic phenomenological excessiveness (the bottomless abyss of temporally dynamic "presencing") that is needed to explain how the metaphysical tradition can change over time (and, with it, the historical constellations of intelligibility that this ontotheological tradition helps constitute and transform). This temporally dynamic "presencing" (long-overlooked by metaphysics, Heidegger comes to realize) can never be completely captured by any single fundamental ontological understanding of the meaning of being.[31]

Heidegger later inscribed a brief handwritten note on the title page of his copy of the first edition of *Kant and the Problem of Metaphysics* (an undated note which he later included in the Preface of the fourth edition of 1973), admitting that his attempt to use Kant to develop the project of fundamental ontology "over-interpreted" Kant (here Heidegger finally rejects the excessive

---

[30] For a detailed explanation of this point, see Thomson, *Heidegger on Ontotheology*, ch. 1.
[31] By the late 1930s, Heidegger comes to realize that this history of being – that is, the history of different metaphysical ways of understanding the being of entities – should be recognized as neither a tragic *regress* away from an original fullness of being (achieved in the Greeks' understanding of being as presence or as readiness-to-hand), nor as a story of *progress* toward a single correct answer about what and how being is (as we tend to presume in our unreflective scientific optimism). Instead, being is best recognized as a temporally dynamic, ontological *excess* (which Heidegger designates with such names as "presencing," "being as such," the "truth of being") that partly informs and yet also exceeds (overflowing and so escaping) every metaphysical way of seeking to understand and so capture "the being of entities" in a single, unchanging conceptual account. (See n. 8 and, for example, CP/GA65, secs. 52–54, 87, and 116.)

2.3. BENEATH FUNDAMENTAL ONTOLOGY

hermeneutic "violence" of trying to read Kant as a forerunner of his own fundamental ontological project) and also led to a dead end: "The *Kant* book. With *Being and Time* alone—; soon clear that we did not enter into the authentic question [*die eigentliche Frage*]" of being; instead, "the particular path was blocked [*der eigene Weg versperrt*]" (KPM xvii/GA3 xiii). What this self-acknowledged aporia rightly suggests is that, during the 1930s, when Heidegger carried out the "deconstruction of the history of ontology" famously called for in *Being and Time*, he was not able to "recover" the fundamental ontology for which he had long been searching (BT 44/SZ 11). When Heidegger traces the regional ontologies of nature, history, and language back to the pre-Socratic Greek understanding of *phusis*, *alêtheia*, and *logos* (respectively), then traces this *phusis-alêtheia-logos* constellation back to a conceptually inexhaustible ontological "presencing," this is as close as he ever comes to actually "grounding" the regional ontologies in a fundamental ontology, and it is quite instructive. For it shows that the relations between the positive sciences, the regional ontologies, and fundamental ontology are too murky and indistinct to allow for a top-down, authoritarian reorganization of the University, in which the philosopher who has learned to be receptive to phenomenological presencing will be able to discern how the regional ontologies emerge out of this fundamental ontological presencing and so help build new academic disciplines around the distinct ontological posits that emerge from these regional ontologies.[32]

Instead, as Heidegger carries out his deconstruction of the history of ontology, he discovers that a series of metaphysical "ontotheologies" have temporarily grounded and justified a succession of ontological "epochs" or historical constellations of intelligibility. Each historical age in the West has been unified by such a basic metaphysical understanding of what and how entities *are*. This succession of dual, ontotheological understandings of "the being of entities" temporarily "doubly ground" the intelligible order only by denying "being as such" (the dynamic and inexhaustible source of intelligibility that both informs and exceeds every ontotheology). Heidegger will thus conclude that the ontological posits that guide each of our positive sciences come not from some unchanging fundamental ontology beneath all of Western history but, instead, from our contemporary age's reigning

---

[32] (See Thomson, *Heidegger on Ontotheology*, 117–118.) We have seen that these new disciplines were to have included one dedicated entirely to the study of *death*, pursuing wide-ranging investigations grounded in the ontology of death disclosed by *Being and Time*'s phenomenology of existential death. Today we would call this an *interdisciplinary* investigation, but Heidegger hoped his phenomenological disclosure of the being of death would prove sufficient to rigorously ground a broad-spectrum exploration of death's meaning and significance, a new discipline thus unified by his phenomenological ontology of death.

ontotheology. The later Heidegger would suggest that present-day biology, for example, takes over its implicit ontological understanding of what life *is* from the metaphysical understanding of the being of entities that governs our own epoch of technological "enframing." And indeed, one has to admit that when contemporary philosophers of biology proclaim that life *is* a self-replicating system, it certainly appears that they have unknowingly adopted the basic ontotheological presuppositions of Nietzsche's metaphysics, according to which life *is* ultimately the eternal recurrence of will-to-power, that is, sheer will-to-will, an ongoing struggle between competing forces by which life perpetuates itself.[33] In the same way, when contemporary philosophers of psychology suggest that consciousness *is* merely an emergent property, the fortuitous (but in itself meaningless) result of an evolutionary struggle to integrate all the various sensory modalities (vision, touch, taste, hearing, etc., each of which itself merely the result of random emergence which conferred adaptive fitness in the evolutionarily arms-race), does not this picture of the *being* of consciousness fit only too well with our Nietzschean ontotheology, according to which all entities are *nothing* but inherently meaningless forces endlessly competing with one another? Cannot the same be said of our historians' view that history *is* the study of the struggle between those forces that have most powerfully shaped our self-understanding (hence, paradigmatically, wars)? Or of the increasingly widespread view in literature departments that literature *is* an arena for representatives from different groups to give voice to the struggles that have most profoundly shaped their competing identities?

Because the later Heidegger comes to believe that *all* of the different disciplines' guiding ontological posits are implicitly taken over from this nihilistic Nietzschean ontotheology underlying our "atomic age," I have suggested that the first task of his mature understanding of *ontological education* involves making us reflective about the way in which our experience of what is commonly called "reality" has already been shaped by these fundamental conceptual parameters and ultimate standards of legitimacy. For, when we become aware of the way our late-modern age's reigning ontotheology implicitly shapes our understanding of the being of ourselves and our worlds – and thereby come to recognize the subtle but pervasive influence of this nihilistic, "technologizing" understanding of all things as nothing but meaningless resources to be efficiently optimized – we begin to open up the possibility of

---

[33] For an explanation and defense of Heidegger's reductive yet revealing reading of Nietzsche as the unwitting metaphysician of technological enframing who consummates the tradition of Western metaphysics and so also helps us move beyond it (into a more meaningful postmodern understanding of being), see Chapter 8 and Thomson, *Heidegger, Art, and Postmodernity*, chs. 1 and 7.

understanding ourselves *otherwise*, in much more meaning-full (and literally *post*modern) terms.[34]

2.4 Being Unfinished

Let us end this chapter by returning to one of the unanswered questions with which we began: How should we understand the unfinished nature of *Being and Time*? Heidegger had been developing the philosophical ideas he published in *Being and Time* for more than a decade, and intermittently writing the book itself since at least 1924.[35] Still, he had to finish the book under great time pressure (working furiously in a rented farm house near his famous "hut," where he could write all day long for months, away from the competing demands of his family, hoping finally to publish the major work he needed to secure a professorship). It is thus understandable that the question repeatedly arises: Could Heidegger have finished *Being and Time* in the way he originally envisioned if pressures coming from "outside" philosophy had not encouraged him to publish the text before he had time to complete it? I have tried to show that the answer to this question is *no*; when he had time to carry out the project over the next decade, he ended up deconstructing and transcending it. Instead of trying to deliver a fundamental ontological understanding of "the being of entities" that would finally *answer* the question of being, Heidegger recognized that all such answers are but temporary metaphysical dams in the ontohistorical river that shapes Western history. These ontotheological dams, when they prove temporarily successful (by uncovering and linking their age's most fundamental and ultimate ways of understanding the being of entities), allow an historical "epoch" to form by "holding back" (*epochê*) the floodwaters of historicity for a time. Heidegger came to see that these metaphysical ontotheologies are themselves made possible by something (which is not a thing but rather a "noth-ing," a dynamic phenomenological "presencing" he also calls "the earth") that they can never render fully intelligible and so permanently stabilize in the light of our historical worlds.

Still, I think the question remains interestingly problematic. It is true that the imperative to "publish or perish" led Heidegger to send off the manuscript of *Being and Time* before he could finish it in the way he had planned. Such mundane pressures to publish philosophical work in hopes of securing or

---

[34] This is the guiding thesis developed in Thomson, *Heidegger, Art, and Postmodernity*, chs. 1, 3, and 7. (On its important educational components and implications, see also Chapter 4 and Thomson, "Heideggerian Perfectionism and the Phenomenology of the Pedagogical Truth Event," 180–190.)

[35] See, for example, BH 77–85; and Heidegger's 1924 review essay, CT, which (as Farin emphasizes) Kisiel calls "the very first draft of *Being and Time*" (Kisiel, *The Genesis of Heidegger's Being and Time*, 323).

advancing a professional career are increasingly ubiquitous in the world of professional philosophy, and we are often right to bemoan the ways these pressures can rush and so undermine philosophical work. Indeed, we should recognize the growth of such pressures as a symptom of the optimization imperative that quietly rules our late modern age of technological "enframing" (as Heidegger himself began to recognize by 1938 [see, for example, OBT 64, 74]). Wittgenstein, who published very little (and yet proved almost as influential as Heidegger), might even have been right to suggest that philosophers should learn to greet one another with an emphatic reminder: "Take Your Time!"[36] Nonetheless, it would be false to imagine that there was ever some golden age in which philosophy was free of the pressures of time, and it is naïve to think of such pressures as simply "external" to philosophy itself – nostalgic mistakes Heidegger himself sometimes makes.

For the later Heidegger, Socrates was "the purest thinker of the West." Socrates was drawn into the withdrawal of being "all through his life and right into his death" – tirelessly asking, What *is* piety? What *is* justice? What *is* friendship? What *is* love? – yet never finding a satisfying answer about what any of our most important concepts *are*. This relentless pursuit of the being of what is, Heidegger suggests, is why Socrates never tried to *write down* any of his thoughts, leaving to his student Plato that impossible task of capturing his thinking's restless search for being (which led to Plato's famous doctrine of the eternal ideas, which sublated and influentially spread Parmenides' original equation of being with permanent and unchanging presence). Socrates preferred to be drawn by the winds of thought that issue from being's withdrawal (as Heidegger puts it), instead of fleeing this "draft [*Zugwind*]" into the refuge of writing down some fixed *answer* to these ontological questions.[37] Heidegger even suggests that "all great Western thinkers after Socrates, regardless of their

---

[36] See Ludwig Wittgenstein, *Culture and Value*, trans. by Peter Winch (Chicago: University of Chicago Press, 1980), 80: "*Laß Dir Zeit!*" For a close comparison of Wittgenstein with the early Heidegger, see Lee Braver, *Groundless Grounds: A Study of Wittgenstein and Heidegger* (Cambridge, MA: The MIT Press, 2012).

[37] How can Heidegger suppose that *writing* is somehow separate from all such drafts? If speech can do some justice to polysemy – rather than seeking to still its movement in one single correct answer (in an endless pursuit of that desolate impossibility Heidegger calls monosemic exactitude) – then why cannot writing? Rather than follow Heidegger's outdated prejudice here, let us instead acknowledge, after Derrida (and, ironically, after the example of Heidegger's own polysemic writing, as well as that of Derrida, Cavell, Irigaray, and so many others), that Heidegger's opposition here between the purity and immediacy of speech ("only when man speaks does he think; not the other way around" [WCT 16/GA8 19]), on the one hand, and the derivative artificiality of writing, on the other hand, remains naïve and simplistic ("phonocentric," as Derrida argues), at best the beginning rather than the end of the conversation – conversations to be written as well as spoken. (See esp. Jacques Derrida, *Of Grammatology*, trans. by Gayatri Spivak [Baltimore, MD: The Johns Hopkins University Press, 1976].)

greatness, had to be such fugitives and refugees [*Flüchlinge*]" (WCT 17/GA8 20). The great philosophers help focus, shape, and transform their ages' understanding of "the being of entities," yet their great *answers* to the question of being prove that they were unable to endure the unending onslaught of "being as such" in the manifest inexhaustibility of its "question-worthiness." (For it is, paradoxically, through the apparently inexhaustible excessiveness of its phenomenological "presencing" that being *withdraws*, eluding every attempt to capture and so still its polysemic movement in a single philosophical answer or metaphysical system.) This, Heidegger hints (twenty-five years after *Being and Time*), is "the secret of a still concealed history" (ibid.); Western philosophy is a history written by such fugitives and refugees from being, driven by their own greatness to try the impossible: To *answer* the question of being, once and for all. Heidegger seems loath simply to admit it here (preferring, out of a telling combination of modesty and pride, to keep his own secret), but the author of *Being and Time* knows (and so hints) that he too was in flight from being's temporally dynamic inexhaustibility when he pursued a "fundamental ontology" throughout his most famous book; he too knows the failure – the *necessary* failure – of such "great philosophy" (that is, *metaphysics*) firsthand.

Indeed, who could deny that Heidegger faced the pressures that led to the publication of *Being and Time* brilliantly when he submitted an unfinished book manuscript that nevertheless went on to become an overnight success and, eventually, the most celebrated philosophical work of the twentieth century? In thus negotiating the pressures of his own being in time, Heidegger provides a dramatic illustration of the constraints that inevitably condition *all* philosophy (and not just all metaphysics, but all thinking too). The notoriously compromised genesis of *Being and Time* reminds us that all philosophical work (from the greatest to the most humble) must find ways to respond to the unavoidable limitations that arise from our *finitude*, constraints we might indicate with such terms as *temporal scarcity*, *historical situatedness*, and *perspectival limitation*. Such ineliminable constraints condition (and always have conditioned) *all* philosophy, *all* thinking (even that of our noble Socrates), at least to some degree – a degree we can seek to minimize or negotiate in creative ways but can never completely control, let alone abolish.[38] Such constraining conditions make philosophy both possible and impossible (as Derrida liked to say); more precisely, they make philosophy possible in the only way it can ever be possible, namely, as impossible ever to perfect, finish, complete – impossible to somehow establish safely beyond all lack, absence, or imperfection – impossible to secure beyond all philosophical (in a word) *failure*.

---

[38] On such unavoidable limits and some of Heidegger's most ingenious strategies for handling them, see also chs. 6 and 8 of Thomson, *Heidegger, Art, and Postmodernity*.

The lessons of such failure (as I have only begun to suggest here) are endless, or so we may hope, as we too strive toward the impossible in our own inescapably mortal and finite projects. The necessity of such failure is not simply a tragedy. For us finite beings, a text survives only so long as it continues to provoke debate, discussion, critique, development, and so on. It can survive, in short, only so long as it *fails* to attain and maintain some unquestionable state of timeless perfection. I suspect, moreover, that even an immortal could never *finish* a text that would be perfectly complete. For, owing to the holism of meaning, one thing leads to another *ad infinitum*. As long as there is being *and* time, there will be genesis, emergence, and the new, as well as death, decay, and passing away, and thus instability, rearrangement, and transformation. Making sense of things generates more things to make sense of, so the work of philosophy is never done – though its seemingly endless doings and undoings might eventually drive an immortal to despair (an issue to which we shall return in our last chapter). Failure is thus a necessary part of even the greatest works.[39] The unavoidable nature of such failure suggests that we need to rethink its meaning in and for philosophy. In my own view, the fact that our otherwise tragic-seeming finitude makes meaning inexhaustible for us mortals is a crucial part of what allows us to embrace our mortality and finitude.[40]

What, then, is the main philosophical lesson of *Being and Time*'s failure? I have tried to suggest that the metaphysical failure at the very heart of the project is inseparable from the greater destiny of Heidegger's later thought – and, perhaps, our own, insofar as we remain inspired by his later critique of metaphysics as ontotheology – including Heidegger's prescient understanding of the nihilism of our late-modern age of limitless technological *enframing*, to which that critique of ontotheology gives rise. For, despite its halting and painful genesis (unavoidable for a mortal philosophy, which can never leap from our minds fully grown and formidably armored, like Athena from the skull of Zeus), Heidegger's deconstruction of metaphysics teaches us to

---

[39] I want to say that failure marks the best thinking in an endless variety of ways: In (and through) the impossibility of metaphysics; in the way the deathly collapse of that metaphysical project discloses the noth-ing (first to Heidegger and then, through him, to us); in the way that noth-ing permeates intelligibility, holding open its future possibilities (as the "to-come" of the not-yet-a-thing); in the way death permeates life, reminding us of its tender fragility, poignant transience, undeniable pain, and occasional sweet rebirths (including that rebirth of philosophy as "thinking"); in the way the greatest artworks preserve an overabundance of meaning that we can sometimes discern and yet can never render fully intelligible; perhaps even in the way the most tantalizing beauty remains marked by ugliness, as in the so-called beauty-mark. (I find it lovely, at any rate, to imagine failure as a beauty-mark of philosophy.)

[40] For an argument to this effect, see Chapter 9 and Thomson, *Heidegger, Art, and Postmodernity*, chs. 3 and 8, esp. 75–77, 217–220.

2.4. BEING UNFINISHED

recognize the creeping nihilism of our current age, helping us learn to discern the roots of this nihilism in our typically unnoticed metaphysical understanding of all things as nothing but intrinsically meaningless resources awaiting optimization. Understanding the failure of metaphysics *in* Heidegger can also help us find ways to transcend its nihilism ourselves. For, as I shall try to show in Chapter 3, it can help teach us to *rethink* the "noth-ing" that surrounds us not as nothing at all but as the not-yet-a-thing, the presencing of inchoate but meaning-full possibilities that have yet to come fully into being, thereby giving our impure thinking an ontologically maieutic task to which we can continue to creatively and responsibly attend – after Heidegger.

Renouncing the failure of metaphysics will not allow us to think from some place beyond failure. But we can seek to find other, more meaningful ways of rethinking failure, neither effacing nor denying failure but instead incorporating its unavoidability into our projects in more creative and meaningful ways. Beyond the failure of metaphysics, the failures of thinking beckon us on. It is in this hopeful half-light (where dusk turns into dawn) that we might hear again those oft-quoted words of Beckett: "All of old. Nothing else ever. Ever tried. Ever failed. No matter. Try again. Fail again. Fail better."[41]

---

[41] (Samuel Beckett, "Worstward Ho," in *Samuel Beckett: The Grove Centennial Edition*, Volume IV, ed. by Paul Auster [New York: Grove Press, 2006], 471.) To those famous words I would also add (as we turn to Chapter 3), a few other brilliant provocations from Beckett's same work (which would be worth explicating in detail): "When ever what else? Where all always to be seen. Of the nothing to be seen. Dimly seen. Nothing ever unseen. ... No saying what it all is they somehow say. ... Never by naught be nulled" (ibid., 477, 479). On "seeing (the nothing) differently" as the transformative gestalt switch from the midnight of technological nihilism to the morning of a more meaningful postmodernity, see also Thomson, *Heidegger, Art, and Postmodernity*, chs. 3 and 7. On the contemporary relevance of Heidegger's critique of technological enframing, see Thomson, *Heidegger on the Danger and Promise of Technology, or What Is Called Thinking in the Age of AI?*

3

Heidegger on Death and the Nothing It Discloses

> There, where matters of death and the nothing get treated, being and being alone is thought most deeply.
>
> Heidegger (N2 208/NI 471)[1]

3.1 Death: A Phenomenological Ontology

This chapter endeavors to explain Heidegger's intertwined thinking about death and "the nothing" and explore the ontological significance of this relationship. As we have seen, "death" (*Tod*) is Heidegger's name for a stark and desolate phenomenon in which *Dasein* (that is, our world-disclosive "being-here") encounters its *own* end, the end "most proper" to the distinctive kind of entity that Dasein is. *Being and Time*'s phenomenology of death is primarily concerned to understand Dasein's death *ontologically*. Heidegger is asking what the phenomenon of our own individual deaths reveals to us all about the nature of our common human *being*, that is, our *Dasein* (and what that discloses, in turn, about the nature of being in general). Understood ontologically, "death" designates Dasein's encounter with the end of its own world-disclosure, the end of that particular way of becoming intelligible in time that uniquely "distinguishes" Dasein from all other kinds of entities (BT 32/SZ 12).

In *Being and Time*, our ontologically distinctive manner of becoming intelligible in time (or "world-disclosing") is through Dasein's (purportedly

---

[1] Here at the conclusion of his 1937 lectures on Nietzsche, Heidegger continues (clearly still smarting from Carnap's critique, rather ironically echoed by Heidegger's fellow members of the Nazi party, who publicly dismissed his focus on the nothing as *nihilism*): "... while those who ostensibly occupy themselves solely with 'reality' flounder in nothingness" (N2 208/NI 471). Heidegger even proclaims that "the hardest and most infallible touchstone of the genuineness and forcefulness of thought in a philosopher is whether or not they experience in a direct and fundamental manner the nearness of the nothing [*die Nähe des Nichts*] in the being of entities. Whoever fails to experience it remains forever outside the realm of philosophy, without hope of entry" (N2 195/NI 460).

3.1. DEATH: A PHENOMENOLOGICAL ONTOLOGY

defining) "existential" structures. In terms of these most general "existential" structures, death has to do primarily with the "understanding" (*Verstehen*). *Understanding*, for Heidegger, is practical before it is cognitive, and so primarily designates the embodied life-projects we *stand under* (as it were) and understand ourselves in terms of (whether tacitly or explicitly). Existential *death* is thus encountered most directly as a global collapse in our embodied self-understanding. But the phenomenon of death also shows up in the registers of *Dasein's* other two defining existential structures, because Dasein's existential structure always forms an inextricably tripartite whole.[2] Thus, death also makes itself felt in *Angst* ("anxiety," "dread," or even "anguish"), which is death's affective attunement (or *Befindlichkeit*), with "reticent silence" and "conscience" as our (authentic and inauthentic) modes of discourse or conversance (*Rede*) with death.[3]

In the existential phenomenon of ontological death, our being-here encounters its *own* not-being; as Heidegger provocatively puts it, Dasein encounters its own "nothingness." Indeed, *Being and Time* famously describes the existential phenomenon of "death" in these deliberately paradoxical terms, as "the possibility of the *im*possibility of existence – that is to say, the utter nothingness of Dasein" (BT 354/SZ 306). Now, at first, the very idea that Heidegger is designating a meaningful *phenomenon* here might sound dubious, even absurdly self-undermining, because it is not initially clear how we could possibly encounter the complete and utter end of our own defining being, the end of that very world-disclosure that marks us out as the *unique* kind of entities we are.[4]

To put the worry sharply: What *is there* to encounter phenomenologically in our own "utter nothingness"? What could a phenomenological encounter with our own nothingness even be an encounter *with*? Why does Heidegger think that the self can *meaningfully* encounter its own nothingness? And what exactly does encountering our own nothingness *mean*; that is, what does Heidegger think his phenomenology of death "discloses" ontologically? (This turns out to be the literally *crucial* question, although Heidegger does not yet recognize it as such in *Being and Time*. We will return to this crucial *turning*

---

[2] See Haugeland, "Truth and Finitude."
[3] Cf. Blattner, *Heidegger's Being and Time*, 140; see also Chapter 6.
[4] The "animality" worry rightly arises here (that is, the question of the being of the nonhuman animal, along with the related question of whether Dasein really picks out a unique ontological type) because, throughout his life, Heidegger distinguishes Dasein from other kinds of entities (including *all* nonhuman animals) by appealing to our relation to death and the openness to language that this relation makes possible. (See Thomson, "Ontology and Ethics at the Intersection of Phenomenology and Environmental Philosophy"; Jacques Derrida, *The Animal That Therefore I Am*, ed. by M.-L. Mallet, trans. by D. Wills [New York: Fordham, 2008]; and Joachim L. Oberst, *Heidegger on Language and Death: The Intrinsic Connection* [London: Continuum, 2009].)

point between the "early" and the "later" Heidegger when we turn to "the nothing" in Section 3.4 below.) What philosophical lessons does Heidegger think this existentially *weighty* encounter with death can help teach us?[5] These are some of the deep and difficult issues with which Heidegger's existential phenomenology of death grapples.

3.2 What Does It Mean to Approach Death Phenomenologically?

Heidegger famously presents his phenomenological interpretation of death in *Being and Time* (1927), then subtly develops the view in his later work. For the early and middle Heidegger (and even, I have often sought to show, the later Heidegger), "phenomenology" is always a *hermeneutic* or interpretive enterprise (BT 61–2/SZ 37). The phenomenologist carries out this enterprise by focusing on (at least some of) the most significant structures that tacitly underlie – and so quietly work to constitute and condition – our ordinary, everyday ("ontic") experience of what-is.

The most famous examples of such phenomena in Heidegger's work from the late 1920s and early 1930s include our skilful use of equipment; our strong feelings of guilt, anxiety, and love; our subtler encounters with truth, art, death, and (*through* the encounter with death) even our most basic disclosure of temporality itself (since the existential phenomenon of death discloses "futurity," the first horizon of originary temporality as we have seen Chapters 1 and 2).[6] As a hermeneutic phenomenologist, Heidegger seeks to uncover the

---

[5] In *Being and Time*, Heidegger does recognize something of death's *weightiness*, at least as an important phenomenological issue. As we saw in Chapter 1, *Being and Time* goes so far as to suggest that taking up the topic of death (and so enduring the *Angst* that usually generates) seems to fly in the face of one of the most basic principles of the phenomenological school, viz., the requirement that we must experience or encounter a phenomenon *for ourselves* (gathering the relevant phenomenological *evidence*, to put it in Husserl's terms) to then be able to confirm or contest a phenomenological account directly, weighing in on the issue for ourselves as we seek to make a "contribution" to the field (or to, as Husserl and the early Heidegger thought of it, the "scientific" or *knowledge*-generating communal endeavor of phenomenology as a meta-academic discipline [see Thomson, *Heidegger on Ontotheology*, ch. 3]). The problem is that, in the case of death, the principle that we must experience the phenomena *for ourselves* generates "a fantastically unreasonable demand" (SZ 266; see also Chapter 1, n. 7). We will further explore the nature of this unreasonable demand in section 3. It is, however, an even more vexed question whether Heidegger reaches the right *conclusions* about death's true weight as an existential phenomenon. For, the conclusions he reaches in *Being and Time* lead him, allegedly, to downplay and diminish the significance of "death" as we ordinarily understand the term, viz., as the apparently irreversible end of life, and not just our own lives but (perhaps first and foremost) the lives of others. (On this Levinasian critique, see, for example, Critchley *Very Little ... Almost Nothing*; and Chapters 6 and 7.)

[6] I have often argued that Heidegger's "later" (c. post 1938) work also centers around less tightly focused but no less important *phenomenological* analyses of such matters as the way

3.2. APPROACHING DEATH PHENOMENOLOGICALLY 103

underlying ("ontological" and "existential") structures that tacitly condition, shape, and constitute our particular individual ("existentiell") lives in their ordinary everyday ("ontic") significance. When such interpretive phenomenology succeeds (indeed, as the very measure of and testament to its success), it *deepens* our understanding of our everyday lives by revealing the usually unnoticed structures that tacitly condition ordinary experience. And by thus making us aware of the underlying ontological structures that quietly shape and condition our ordinary lives, phenomenology often *transforms* our everyday experience as well (in various complex ways), as it does most dramatically in the case of the death (as we saw in Chapter 1).[7]

I risk rehearsing such a basic point – that hermeneutic phenomenology always takes as its point of departure *phenomena* that we can encounter or experience in our own everyday lives – because that rather obvious point proves to be extremely consequential for the case at hand.[8] Indeed, the very fact that Heidegger adopts a *phenomenological* approach toward death means that, to understand his view, we need to recognize the sense in which he thinks that we existing beings can experience or encounter our own deaths *while we are still alive*. Precisely that point sticks in the craws of many scholars (leading to the large controversy addressed in Chapter 1), but it remains textually undeniable. In Heidegger's view, as *Being and Time* clearly states (in a crucial passage too many interpreters ignore): "*Death is a way to be*, which *Dasein* takes over as soon as it is" (BT 289, my emphasis/SZ 245). In 1925 (two years before publishing *Being and Time*), Heidegger had already written: "I myself

---

our lives are pervasively shaped by art, education, politics, and – most profoundly and importantly for Heidegger – by our historical understanding of the *being* of what-is (see, for example, Thomson, *Heidegger, Art, and Postmodernity*, ch. 3).

[7] As *phenomenological*, Heidegger's existential descriptions are meant to be tested against his readers' own personal experiences, not taken on faith or, indeed, on any basis other than the disclosive power of the relevant phenomena themselves. These phenomena are *always* meant to be personally experienced and interpreted, so that they can be directly subjected to interpersonal contestation or verification, elaboration or redescription. Phenomenology is in this sense thus profoundly *secularizing*, continuing that "death of God" inadvertently begun (on Nietzsche's view) when Kant deliberately replaced God with human reason. (On this point see also Chapter 1, nn. 10 and 61; Thomson, *Heidegger on Ontotheology*, 20–1; and Chapter 8.)

[8] In Heidegger's terms, the "ontic" and the "ontological" (that is, the domains of entities, on the one hand, and of their meaning, sense, or intelligibility, on the other) are never completely separable, let alone dichotomous. Thus, despite widespread misunderstandings on this score, no phenomena are "too ontic" for phenomenological analysis, though the point of such analysis will always be to excavate beneath these ontic phenomena in order to reach the ontological structures that shape and condition our experience of them. Heideggerian phenomenology seeks to disclose the bridges connecting the ontic and ontological domains, bridges the phenomenologist can travel then back and forth on, to illuminating and even transformative effect (see Chapter 1 and Thomson, *Heidegger, Art, and Postmodernity*, ch. 3 for detailed examples).

am my death precisely when I live."⁹ And he expresses this provocative view even more clearly in 1959: "Mortals die their death in life" (GA 4: 165/190). To understand Heidegger's phenomenology of death, then, we need to understand the sense in which we can experience our own deaths while we are still alive (BT 277/SZ 234).

As Heidegger recognizes (BT 279–80/SZ 236), however, this phenomenological requirement (that we can experience our own deaths while we are still alive) leads to a paradox familiar to the Western philosophical tradition since Epicurus. The apparent annihilation of our individual existences that we ordinarily call "death" seems to be characterized by *the absence of all experience*. (The reasons for this now appear obvious: Experience is based on sensations, but death is what follows the cessation of our biological functions, without which there do not appear to be any sensations, at least not for long. Thus death, on this typical and long-standing view, appears to be some final and irreversible absence of experience.) Insofar as we cannot experience the absence of all experience, it would seem that we cannot experience "death" itself. We can experience death in its approach but not in its having arrived; there is thus no experience of "death" itself, ordinarily conceived. (Hence Epicurus' famous maxim of Stoic edification: Should your thoughts ever turn to your own death, simply remind yourself not to worry, since "where you are, death is not; and where death is, you are not.")[10] Heidegger's *phenomenological* interpretation of death – because it necessarily *begins* from the assumption that we can somehow undergo an *intelligible* encounter with our own death itself – would therefore seem to be a misguided nonstarter.[11]

In fact, however, recognizing this paradox – that it seems impossible to experience our own deaths themselves (so long as we understand "death" in the normal way) – helps us understand (1) what Heidegger himself means by "death" and also (2) why he approaches the phenomenon in the particular way

---

[9] BH 263; see also Blattner's aforementioned seminal paper, Blattner, "The Concept of Death in *Being and Time*."

[10] On how Heidegger draws the line between what we can and cannot possibly experience (and so what is and what is not a fitting subject for phenomenology), see Iain Thomson, "Transcendence and the Problem of Otherworldly Nihilism: Taylor, Heidegger, Nietzsche," *Inquiry*, 54:2 (2011), 140–59.

[11] As that suggests, Heidegger views our existential collision with death as more of a (sub- or pre-conscious) *encounter* than as a (subjective) "experience." That is, he thinks of death more as something that strikes us involuntarily than as something over which we can exert conscious control – for example, by following in the heroic style of modern Stoics like Spinoza (who proudly proclaimed that "the free man thinks of nothing less than death") or, more darkly, by emulating those romantic *Sturm und Drang* suicides who followed (supposedly in droves) in the wakes of Goethe and Schiller. Still, as I shall suggest below, the Stoic and Romantic movements left indelible marks on Heidegger nevertheless, in terms of what he appropriated as well as what he rejected. (I develop a neo-Heideggerian critique of Spinoza's neo-stoicism about death in Chapter 8.)

3.2. APPROACHING DEATH PHENOMENOLOGICALLY

he does in *Being and Time*, by distinguishing the phenomenon of existential *death* from the ordinary way of thinking about death he terms *demise*. Put simply, "demise" (*Ableben*) is the word Heidegger uses to refer to our normal understanding of death as the arrival of an apparently final absence of all experience, that is, as our mortal *demise* or becoming "deceased" – or, more colloquially and vividly, as "kicking-the-bucket," "taking a dirt nap," and so on. Most of us, most of the time (that is, as *das Man*), understand death *only* as "demise," as our collision with an apparently unremitting absence of all meaningful intelligibility which (as far as we can tell phenomenologically, from "this side" of the veil) seems fated to happen as the final event of our lives (if we are conscious and undeceived). Understood as this fatal collision with (or return to) a cosmic nothingness that remains ultimately incomprehensible (at least from "this side" of that great beyond, the only side to which *phenomenology* has direct access), demise itself remains inaccessible to phenomenology.[12]

It is precisely here, however, that Heidegger's distinction between ordinary "demise" and existential "death" is absolutely crucial, making it highly problematic that *Being and Time*'s way of drawing out the distinction is so subtle and complex. As we saw in Chapter 1, a great deal of confusion continues to be generated by the fact that Heidegger uses the term "demise" to refer to that terminal annihilation of experience most people call *death*, and then goes on to use the word "death" to name the existential phenomenon that implicitly structures and conditions our ordinary experience of such "demise." Nonetheless, Heidegger's view that the phenomenon of existential death underlies and conditions our experience of ordinary demise is, in my view, one of the deepest and most enduringly interesting parts of his existential analysis of death in *Being and Time*.[13] For, in the end (pun intended), the Stoics would seem to be right: Demise itself appears to be phenomenologically inaccessible (whether it is our own demise or that of another), and this is something Heidegger explicitly recognizes (BT 277/SZ 234), because he refuses to allow his underlying religious *faith* to override the phenomenological evidence that is directly available to us as living individuals (BT 292/SZ 247-8).

So, instead of just analysing our ultimately inaccessible relation to demise – a kind of phenomenological black hole – Heidegger goes two big steps further. He first analyzes the *structure* of our ordinary relation to "demise," seeking to

---

[12] Such a collision with our own nothingness would seem to follow ineluctably from the permanent cessation of our biological functions, should we be awake, conscious, and undeceived at the time (as we saw in Chapter 1).

[13] Other important aspects of his view (touched on below) include the way Heidegger thinks death discloses the deepest temporal horizon of "futurity" (as we saw in Chapter 1.7), as well as the tragic "aporia" inherent in our relation to demise, that is, the fact that demise stands as a kind of "necessary impossibility," something we cannot experience and yet, in some deeply problematic sense, seem fated to encounter or undergo nevertheless (see Derrida, *Aporias*).

characterize the sense in which this (ultimately inaccessible) phenomenon appears to us while we are still alive. Employing a phenomenological technique the early Heidegger calls "formal indication," *Being and Time* isolates the six structural characteristics that characterize our ordinary understanding of demise, then goes on to suggest, second, that these six formal structures also come together in a deeper way to "define" *Being and Time*'s "full existential-ontological conception of death": "Death, as [1] *the end of Dasein* [2], is *Dasein's ownmost,* [3] *non-relational,* [4] *certain and* [5] *as such indefinite,* [6] *non-surpassable possibility*" (BT 303/SZ 258–9, Heidegger's emphasis). These defining structures of existential death are thus *drawn from* a formal analysis of demise, and in this way Heidegger seeks to excavate beneath demise, disclosing a deeper phenomenon – existential *death* – which he thinks conditions our ordinary relation to demise.

This means that *demise* – *that* is, "death" understood in the normal sense (as our vexed relation to the apparently permanent absence of our individual experience) – maintains a direct connection to the phenomenon Heidegger himself calls *death*. Heidegger is thus not (*pace* Haugeland and White) renaming some other phenomenon "death" arbitrarily or merely using this loaded word metaphorically.[14] On the contrary, existential death is drawn from a formal analysis of ordinary demise (or kicking-the-bucket), and Heidegger thinks that the phenomenon he calls "death" *conditions and structures* our normal way of relating to our own demises. Indeed, because the phenomenon of existential death tacitly *shapes* our normal ways of understanding and so relating to demise, Heidegger suggests that encountering existential death phenomenologically can powerfully *transform* our ordinary relation to demise.

To put it simply, *Being and Time* ultimately suggests that the encounter with existential death can help liberate us from a confused and unnecessarily restrictive relation to our own demises, radically freeing up our ways of relating to the fact that our own lives come to an ineluctable end, and so helping us learn to shed the mortal fear of demise that will otherwise pursue us throughout our lives (as we saw in Chapter 1). I shall not fully reprise that view here, but it turns on recognizing that what our fear of demise is really afraid of is our own not being (or, to put the fear in a way which heightens its apparent paradoxicality, it is an *anxiety* about *being our own not being*), and our own not being is in fact something that we *can* encounter in practical life, in the "projectless projecting" of existential death. The idea that such an existential encounter with our own not-being can help liberate us from our fear of mortal demise is one of the most important and edifying conclusions of Heidegger's phenomenology of death in *Being and Time*. In what follows, we will seek to

---

[14] See Haugeland, "Truth and Finitude"; White, *Time and Death*; and, for critiques of their views, see Chapters 1 and 5.

better understand the philosophical motivations for that view. Doing so will also help us understand how Heidegger goes beyond this view after *Being and Time*, disclosing from the "nothingness" of existential death *an even more liberating and edifying* relation to being's apparently inexhaustible phenomenological plenitude for us mortal Dasein.[15] First, however, we need to directly address the question of how the self can meaningfully encounter its own *end*, thereby coming to see what such an encounter discloses for Heidegger as his thinking evolves.

3.3 Death and Existential Possibility

When *Being and Time* calls death "the possibility of the *im*possibility of existence – that is to say, the utter nothingness of Dasein," it is important to see that the *phenomenon* Heidegger is referring to is not merely our entertaining (conceptually or imagistically) the idea of our own no longer being here – as, for example, when we try to conceive or imagine what the world might be like after we are no longer a part of it. Whether such phantasmatic projections are voluntarily or involuntarily, disturbing or edifying, fleeting or enduring, scientific or fictional, silly or sanctified, the same basic problem remains: Any time we imagine a future after our own demise, we *are there* in some sense, if only as the ones doing the imagining, the ones *by whom* that particular fantasy is being played out. (We are the ones conceptualizing or imagining the future from some implicit perspective, reflecting just some particular cares and concerns, and so on.)[16] Insofar as such fantasies about life after our own demise have any content, moreover, they show that we still have an intelligible world while we are imagining them. Such fantasies thus do not constitute true encounters with our own nothingness. For, they do not bring us face to face with "the utter nothingness" of our own practical "being here" (or *Dasein*) that Heidegger calls *death*.

---

[15] On the crucial phenomenological connection between death and the plenitude of being, see also Chapter 9 and Thomson, *Heidegger, Art, and Postmodernity*, ch. 3.

[16] At the very least, imagining life after we are demised requires us to project ourselves into a kind of spectral project, even if it is just a vision of hovering over the world from which we are absent and watching it like a film or a dream. (Watching films and dreaming, or at least falling asleep, are also primordially practical projects into which we project, albeit often effortlessly.) However involuntary they might feel, such *acts of imagining* life after we are gone are thus not like merely staring at some decontextualized and so insignificant *object* (in its disconnected "on-handness" or sheer *Vorhandenheit*), unable to take up any project that would disclose its practical significance. Our projecting into some such project is already there implicitly, generating the details of that particular vision of what things might be like after our own demise and thereby bestowing such spectral scenarios with at least some minimal significance (whether as haunting, worrisome, serene, or satisfying).

To understand the phenomenon of death as "the possibility of the *impossibility* of existence," we need to remember that Heidegger means "possibility" in an *existential* rather than any merely *logical* sense.[17] Existential "possibilities" are the embodied life-projects that compose our particular ways of being (such as teacher and student, mother and father, son and daughter, man and woman, tall and short, fat and skinny, graceful and clumsy, brother and sister, skateboarder and bicyclist, friend and colleague, liberal and conservative, poet and revolutionary – and all the myriad other ways of being that Dasein takes up and lives in some particular, embodied way).[18] Such life-projects, taken together, help positively constitute our existences, allowing us to become intelligible to ourselves and to each other in worldly terms. Such existential possibilities are thus not merely the *logically* possible alternatives that can help us understand the structure of some conceptual space. Instead, existential possibilities are the embodied projects that we ordinarily *project* ourselves into, and so understand ourselves in terms of, as we go about charting the course of our everyday lives. This "charting the course" is primordially *practical*, usually carried out in that primary mode of Dasein's existence Dreyfus famously calls "skilful coping," but it can also be cognitive, as when we make explicit plans or formulate conscious ideas about our lives.[19]

As Heidegger thus provocatively asserts (inverting Aristotle): "Higher than actuality stands *possibility*" (BT 63/SZ 38). There would seem to be at least two reasons for *Being and Time*'s existential privileging of possibility over

---

[17] Heidegger does recognize death's logic, nevertheless, as the implacable logic of *necessity*. *Being and Time* even insists that our relation to death is always one of "certainty" (as explained in Chapter 1), because he views our ordinary *denial* about our own "death" (our denial about our own *demise*, more precisely) as a motivated flight from, and so an inauthentic testament to, the *certainty* we nevertheless maintain concerning our own deaths. It is ultimately existential death that our widespread repression of demise is seeking to escape – futilely, until after we come to understand the existential structures that condition our relation to demise. (On the relation of Heidegger's view here to those of Freud and Derrida, see Thomson, "Can I Die?" That early essay of mine unfortunately follows Derrida in conflating existential death with mortal demise; on how best to disentangle death from demise, and so how to distinguish death's definitive "certainty" from the "certainty" of demise – the formal structure from which it is drawn; see Chapter 1.)

[18] These projects and our ways of projecting into them are typically neither merely arbitrarily constructed nor entirely dictated to us by the objective facts of the case, and so leave some ineliminable "elbow-room" both for what we choose as well as for how we go about projecting into and so taking them up. What Heidegger calls *"das Man"* or "the anonymous anyone" levels pre- and proscriptions on *what one does* that work to repress that former freedom (by making us think there is a very limited array of acceptable choices about what to do with our lives) as well as that latter freedom (too often convincing us that there is a single right way to be whatever we have decided to be from that artificially narrow range).

[19] See Dreyfus, *Being-in-the-World*.

3.3. DEATH AND EXISTENTIAL POSSIBILITY

actuality.[20] First, existential possibilities are *more actual than actuality itself* (so to speak) in that they are what actually *actualize* whatever "actuality" our individual existences possess at any given moment. Metaphorically, existential possibilities are the "clothing" of the world (as Kierkegaard – or rather his pseudonymous clothing, "anti-Climacus" – put it in *The Sickness Unto Death*, the singular book that most deeply influenced Heidegger's understanding of death in *Being and Time*). In other words, existential possibilities are the roles, embodied self-understandings, and life-projects that allow an existence to recognize itself as something – and so not just as a sheer, naked existing, devoid of worldly content and so fully transparent to itself. Indeed, Heidegger's search for such a fully transparent self-understanding is what initially motivates his turn toward death in *Being and Time*, as he seeks an understanding of Dasein that is primordial and so, he thinks (problematically, in my view), complete.[21] Such "naked," sheer *existing* turns out to be our most primordial condition, although this irreducible core of the self is something that we can only *rediscover* after existential death strips us of the clothing of the world.

Remember that *Being and Time* seeks to help recognize and remedy one of the most basic and pervasive errors of modern philosophy by showing us that human "existence" is not really a physical *thing*, and so is not best understood as a thinking *substance* (as with Descartes' *res cogitans*). At a more primordial level of existence (which the understanding of the self as a *res* or spatially extended "substance" presupposes but cannot account for), *existence* is simply a "standing-out" (*ek-sistere*) into temporally structured intelligibility. At the most basic level, this "naked" core of the self – namely, existence as sheer *existing* – is primordially "uncanny" (*Unheimlich*), literally "not-at-home" in the world (BT 234/SZ 189), unable ever to finally be anything and instead tasked with repeatedly becoming who we are (as we will see in Chapter Four).[22] (Existence is thus "in but not of" the world, according to the Christian view Heidegger is creatively *secularizing* here, as scholars like Mulhall have long recognized.)[23]

---

[20] For a third reason, having to do with Heidegger's neo-romanticism, see Thomson, *Heidegger, Art, and Postmodernity*, 159.

[21] On the deep problems with Heidegger's view here, see Chapter 1, n. 51.

[22] Heidegger could almost agree with Sting that "we are spirits in the material world," were Heidegger not seeking to deconstruct and transcend such traditional metaphysical dichotomies as the one between "spirit" and "matter" (Thomson, *Heidegger on Ontotheology*, ch. 1).

[23] Authenticity is indeed a secularized "version of conversion," as Cavell nicely put it (in Stanley Cavell, *This New Yet Unapproachable America: Lectures after Emerson after Wittgenstein* [Albuquerque, NM: Living Batch Press, 1989].) Heidegger's phenomenological appropriation of Kierkegaard allows him to develop and convey his own sense of the significance of the *conversion* experience, that is, the experience of death and rebirth *in life* (an experience polysemically "crucial" to Christianity). Thus, Heidegger is able to appropriate (and transform) some of the deepest insights preserved in the Christian tradition by expressing them in the secularizing language of existential phenomenology.

This lack of fit between self and world (in which our naked existing can never be finally at home in any of the contingent clothing of the world), *Being and Time* suggests, is what ultimately motivates our existential *Angst*, whereby the lack of any permanently satisfying answers among the predetermined array of public options telling us what it means to be impels each of us to take an individual stand on what it means to be the self that we are – even if only by rushing into thoughtless conformism in order to abjure and repress the need for such resolute decisions. More generally, by recognizing the primarily *existential* nature of the self, *Being and Time* seeks to disabuse the philosophical tradition of the "category mistake" (as Ryle rightly called it) of trying to understand Dasein's intelligible world-disclosure in terms drawn from our understanding of physical objects.[24] Instead, we should recognize that: "*The 'essence' of Dasein lies in its existence*" (BT 67/SZ 42), and focus our phenomenological investigations accordingly, seeking to discover and display the distinctive structures that underlie Dasein's world-disclosive "existence" (Heidegger's term of art in *Being and Time* for Dasein's distinctive mode of being).

Existential possibilities "stand higher" than actuality not just because they *actualize* whatever actuality we might possess, but also, second, because these existential possibilities always *transcend* or stretch beyond our current actuality as well. Existential possibilities outstrip whatever actuality we possess, just as my way of being a teacher, a father, or a man all draw on a past that is no longer actual and project into a future that is not yet actual. We anxiously experience our own being (or the intelligibility of our selves) as exceeding what we can actually express in terms of the roles, goals, and life-projects through which we ordinarily understand ourselves, so that we are always more existentially than we are actually. *The clothing of the world is always too tight* (to use Kierkegaard's metaphor for this lack of fit), and yet as I find my own ways to take up, stretch, and transform this garb of worldly actuality, doing so also enables me to articulate and develop aspects of myself in ways I would not otherwise have been able to do. As I thus live through my existential

---

(See also Stephen Mulhall, *Philosophical Myths of the Fall* [Princeton, NJ: Princeton University Press, 2007].)

[24] (See Gilbert Ryle, "Heidegger, M. – Sein und Zeit," *Mind*, 38:355 [1928], 355–70.) We make such a *category mistake*, for example, whenever we erroneously approach the self as if it were a substance with properties (after Descartes), or otherwise fundamentally *miscategorize* the self by treating it as if it could be wholly understood in the same categories as physical nature, whether following Kant or those contemporary "naturalists" who advocate eliminative materialism or other forms of *scientism*, that is, the false view that natural science has a monopoly on legitimate forms of inquiry (including inquiry into the nature of the self). Phenomenology's famous "anti-naturalism" (which goes back to Husserl but is extended by Heidegger) is primarily directed against just such reductive and mistaken scientistic views (see Thomson, *Heidegger, Art, and Postmodernity*, ch. 2).

possibilities by *being* (for example) a teacher, a father, and a man in my own life – which I can only do "authentically" by continuing to *become* a teacher, father, and man – such existential possibilities help me *make sense* (again, primarily practically but thereby also cognitively) of who I have been and who I am becoming.[25]

In this way, existential possibilities help render temporality itself intelligible to us (as individual Dasein), because these possibilities work to concretely *constitute* the particular living worlds that make us intelligible to ourselves, shaping and reshaping these living worlds that we *are*. On those occasions when we *reconstitute* our living worlds (transforming central aspects of our embodied self-understandings) by, for example, sloughing-off an outdated, arbitrarily restrictive, unsatisfying, or otherwise unfree or no longer liveable way of being a father, man, teacher, philosopher, etc. (before taking up a more liberating or otherwise meaningful embodied self-understanding), existential death plays a crucial role in such transformations, as the very moment of that old world's collapse. Indeed, such periodic personal deaths and rebirths to the publicly intelligible world are precisely what Heidegger means by "anticipatory resoluteness" or, in a word, "authenticity" (as we shall see in Chapter 4). Unlike Heidegger, I do not think this process is always best thought of as a *complete* collapse and transformation of the self, but I do understand what drives him (both philosophically and autobiographically) toward that view. Put simply, Heidegger thinks such a global collapse of our life-projects will follow from the collapse of our *defining* life-project (what *Being and Time* calls our "ultimate for-the-sake-of-which"), as this collapse of what we care most about (or the end of that project we least want to abandon, "what we would give up last," as Dreyfus once memorably put it) sets off a chain reaction that brings all our other life-projects cascading down in its wake.[26]

In *Being and Time*, Heidegger (rather subtly) defines Dasein's *existential possibilities* in terms of our "being-possible" (*Möglichsein*) and our "ability-to-be" (*Seinkönnen*), that is (respectively), in terms of our *life-projects* and our *projecting* ourselves into or upon those projects as we go about being (by becoming) what we take ourselves to be, charting the course of our everyday being-here (BT 185–6/SZ 145). By repeatedly referring to death as "the possibility of an impossibility," then, Heidegger is deliberately designating a stark and desolate phenomenon in which we find ourselves (at least momentarily) unable to project ourselves into any of the existential projects that ordinarily disclose the practical significance of things and render us meaningful to ourselves. This

---

[25] See Dreyfus, *Being-in-the-World*; Iain Thomson, "Rethinking Education after Heidegger: Teaching Learning as Ontological Response-Ability," *Educational Philosophy and Theory*, 48:8 (2016), 846–61; and Chapter 4.

[26] On the painful existential collapse of the philosophical project guiding *Being and Time*, the avowedly "metaphysical" project of "fundamental ontology," see Chapter 2.

explains why Heidegger also repeatedly refers to death as Dasein's *"ownmost ability-to-be"*: In the phenomenon of existential death, our selves get stripped of the positive, worldly contents they ordinarily seem to possess (as we lose all the concretions of self conferred on us by the projects we can no longer project ourselves into in our lives). When we undergo this shipwreck of our life-projects in existential death, however, we do not simply disappear entirely; instead, we encounter ourselves as (what I am calling) a *projectless projecting*, that is, as a sheer *existing* that (at least temporarily) finds itself unable to exist *as* anyone or anything (teacher, man, father, and so on).

To encounter death as the existential "possibility of an impossibility" is thus (as Heidegger glosses it) to encounter a *positive* "nothingness" – that aforementioned "utter nothingness of Dasein." The nothingness we encounter in existential death is not the onrush of oblivion (although we can also encounter existential death – in *passing*, as it were – in the phenomenon of mortal "demise," if we are aware that our demise is approaching and it is not too sudden, because if we are conscious and undeceived when we demise we can die as well (though we can also die without demising, fortunately, since otherwise we would have to write out phenomenologies of death from beyond the grave, as we saw in Chapter 1, which is not something we mortal phenomenologists can do). Dasein's "utter nothingness" is instead the stark condition undergone by what Heidegger calls the "solus ipse" or *self alone* (BT 233/SZ 188), that is, the utterly desolate core of the self that survives the shipwreck of all its worldly projects. In this way, existential death discloses to Dasein its "ownmost ability to be," that projectless projecting that forms the very *sine qua non* of the self in *Being and Time* (and so defines the ultimate touchstone of Dasein's definitive "mineness").[27] The ontological core of the self disclosed in the phenomenon of existential death is not "alone before God" (as Kierkegaard has it). Instead, in existential death, Dasein is alone before its own sheer existing, standing out into a world of possibilities it cannot connect to, and so starkly encountering itself as "a naked 'that-it-is-and-has-to-be'" (BT 173/SZ 134).

As *Being and Time* shows, I can explicitly experience what my bicycle implicitly *is* when it breaks down, and so just stands there as (for example) a broken piece of equipment that was supposed to get me to school, so that I could get to my class on time, for the sake of being a good teacher, a responsible colleague (and so on). In the same way, Dasein can come face-to-face with itself as an embodied stand on the meaning of existence when its being-in-the-world breaks down in existential death and we find ourselves unable to be anything in particular at all, unable to exist as anyone or anything. This is what Heidegger means when he suggests that, in the attunement of radical *Angst* that accompanies such existential death, the naked "self"

---

[27] See Crowell, "Subjectivity."

of sheer "mineness" encounters "the 'nothing' – that is, the world as such, the world as world" (BT 232/SZ 187).

3.4 Existential Death and the Noth-ing of the Nothing

Rather than precipitously dismissing Heidegger's core idea of the self's encounter with its own nothingness as absurd or hopelessly paradoxical, we have tried to appreciate the deeper phenomenon that Heidegger deliberately risks such paradoxical formulations to try to help us see *for ourselves* (or to see, in the terms of phenomenology, *authentically*, in a way that makes it our own). The larger goal of the existential phenomenology of death in *Being and Time*, we have seen, is to understand "death" in its full ontological significance. However daunting that task remains, anyone seeking to understand Heidegger will eventually need to undertake it. Why? Because, as Haugeland recognized, "death, as Heidegger means it, is not merely relevant but in fact the fulcrum of Heidegger's entire ontology."[28] In other words, we cannot understand the early Heidegger's project of "fundamental ontology" without understanding what *Being and Time* means by death.

Indeed, I think we now need to go even further: Heidegger's phenomenology of death helps disclose something like the Ur-phenomenon of his later work, that irreducibly polysemic and multivocal phenomenon that he first calls "the noth-ing of the nothing," an ontological abundance that appears to be both conceptually and practically inexhaustible and so, as such, the ultimate source of whatever authentic and meaningful disclosure remains possible for us mortal beings, now and in the future.[29] This also means, however, that the phenomenon death discloses brings Heidegger face-to-face with the ontologically indigestible iceberg that spells the ruin of his central early project, namely, *Being and Time*'s ill-fated attempt to deliver a "fundamental ontology" (or a single "understanding of the meaning of being in general"). *Pace* Haugeland, then, I side with those who think Heidegger never delivered on that promised fundamental ontology, not in *Being and Time* or in any of the works that followed while he continued to pursue his ill-fated "metaphysical" project with a desperation that continued to grow until – in a philosophically profound instance of existential *death* – Heidegger was finally driven to abandon this metaphysical project, subsequently making its very impossibility the central pillar of his later thought (as we saw in Chapter 2).[30] In other words,

---

[28] Haugeland, "Truth and Finitude," 44.
[29] See Julian Young, *Heidegger's Later Philosophy* (Cambridge: Cambridge University Press, 2002); Thomson, *Heidegger, Art, and Postmodernity*, ch. 3.
[30] See also Daniel Dahlstrom, "The End of Fundamental Ontology," in *Division III of Heidegger's Being and Time: The Unanswered Question of Being*, ed. by Lee Braver (Cambridge, MA: The MIT Press, 2015), 83–103.

Heidegger's phenomenology of death catalyzed the philosophically and politically tumultuous "middle" period in his thinking (between 1929 and 1938), inadvertently setting off that philosophically (and politically) motivated transformation in Heidegger's thinking long referred to as his "turn."[31]

To understand how Heidegger's early phenomenology of death fits into the larger development of his thought, then, one needs first to understand what death discloses initially, as we have mostly done here by focusing on his famous phenomenology of death in *Being and Time*. Then, however, one also needs to understand how Heidegger's thinking about this ontological Ur-phenomenon that death first discloses transforms over time in his thinking. We cannot fully do that here (as that work is both immense and complex), but perhaps what remains most difficult and important to understand is the way *Being and Time*'s existential phenomenology of death first discloses the paradoxically positive "nothingness" that will soon become 1929's notorious "noth-ing of the nothing." This active "noth-*ing*" of that which is not-yet-a-thing – and yet nevertheless continues to make itself felt phenomenologically (by subtly beckoning to be disclosed responsively and creatively) – *turns* out to have been the first glimmering of "being as such" (in Heidegger's own retrospective self-understanding at least). How so?

If we remember what we said at the end of Chapter 1 about how death discloses futurity, we can begin to see how Heidegger thought existential death brings such inchoate possibilities toward Dasein: First, in the phenomenon of existential death, the *solus ipse* at the core of the self (our "ownmost ability-to-be" or projectless projecting) *comes toward* our ordinary worldly selves. Then, second, in resolve, those partly inchoate self-world unities Dasein could be (their details still fuzzy until one is chosen and so disclosed) *come toward* this *solus ipse* as Dasein reopens itself to the practical world in resolve.

Just briefly recall *Being and Time*'s phenomenological account of Dasein pursuing its essential "uncanniness" until it discovers its core self in existential death. As Heidegger develops his phenomenology of anxiety and death into his linked account of guilt and conscience (which lead to resolve and so the return to the world lost in death), he fleshes out his portrait of Dasein's core self as a desolate *solus ipse*, "a self which has been individualized down to itself

---

[31] (Thomson, *Heidegger on Ontotheology*, ch. 1; Julian Young, "Was There a 'Turn' in Heidegger's Philosophy?" in *Division III of Heidegger's Being and Time*, ed. by Braver [op. cit.].) To understand this changing phenomenon is thus to begin to understand the deep philosophical motivations behind the controversial "turn" that leads from Heidegger's early to his later work, philosophical motivations that remain closely tied up with his political struggles as well. The close and important connections between Heidegger's thinking and his politics have always been visible (as I showed two decades ago in Thomson, *Heidegger on Ontotheology*), but they have become glaringly obvious in light of his most recently published "Black Notebooks" and related work (see Thomson, "Heidegger's Nazism in the Light of His Early *Black Notebooks*").

in uncanniness and thrown into the nothing" (BT 322/SZ 277). Stripped by existential death of those practical projects that ordinarily clothe the self with the significance of its practical world (BT 231/SZ 187), Dasein encounters itself as "the naked 'that it is' in the 'nothing' of the world [*das nackte 'Daß' im Nichts der Welt*]" (BT 321–2/SZ 276–77). Two years later, in 1929, he goes further: "Being-here [*Da-sein*]" means "being held out into the nothing … beyond the totality of entities.… The nothing does not merely serve as the counter-concept of entities, but belongs originally [*ursprünglich*] to their essential unfolding [a later note specifies: 'the essential unfolding of being'] as such. In the being of entities, the noth-ing of the nothing happens" (P 91/GA9 115).

In other words, Heidegger's hermeneutic phenomenology of death helps disclose being in its ineliminable *difference* from any "metaphysical" understanding of "the being of entities," exposing being's seemingly ineliminable phenomenological "excessiveness," by which being escapes every attempt to capture what it means to *be* in some final understanding of "the being of entities" – including *Being and Time*'s self-avowedly *metaphysical* attempt to capture being in a fundamental ontology (as we saw in Chapter 2).[32]

What Heidegger's phenomenology of existential death discloses, then, is a paradoxically positive nothingness – "the noth-ing of the nothing" – that is, the inchoate phenomenological emergence of what is-not-yet but is actively becoming intelligible in time. Existential death thus discloses that subtle but dynamic Ur-phenomenon of being's phenomenologically primordial emergence into intelligibility. What Heidegger's phenomenology of death shows us is not merely the apparent oblivion of mortal demise. In an end that is not yet the end, existential death discloses what *Being and Time* already calls the very "futurity" of the future, its "incessant" coming to be, the temporally dynamic basis of all we can encounter phenomenologically so long as we *are here* (as Dasein), together, critically inheriting each other's projects and transformatively making them our own. So, let us thus turn to examine this "noth-ing" more carefully.

3.5 Understanding Heidegger's Phenomenology of Noth-ing

> The nothing is never nothing, and neither is it something in the sense of an object; it is the truth of being itself as it comes over human beings when they overcome themselves as subjects, that is, when they no longer represent entities as objects. (AWP 85/GA5 113)

---

[32] On the question of whether existential death is Heidegger's way of repressing mortal demise, see Chapter 1; and on the way death helps disclose "the noth-ing" (that turns out to be the first phenomenological glimmering of "being as such" in its difference from the metaphysical notion of "the being of entities") see Chapter 2 and below, where I explain these important transformations in Heidegger's very way of understanding, and so pursuing, the "question of being."

For Heidegger, "the nothing" does not designate brute nonbeing; what he calls "the nothing itself" is not nothing at all. In his words, the nothing is not "the *non-being of the null* [*das* Nicht-Sein des Nichtigen], which *is* not at all" (BT 181/GA36–37 236). Such a null or nugatory nothingness would have no force or effect, whereas the phenomenon Heidegger calls "the nothing" actively *does* something: "The nothing itself noths or nihilates [*Das Nichts selbst nichtet*]" (P 90/GA9 114).

Heidegger made that notoriously recondite pronouncement in 1929 and philosophers have disagreed vociferously about what it might mean ever since. It is even no exaggeration to say that, when Heidegger proclaimed, "The nothing itself noths," he thereby gave the Western philosophical tradition the single sentence most responsible for splitting it into its contemporary "continental" and "analytic" branches.[33] In effect, Heidegger divided subsequent philosophers into those who found such esoteric utterances at least potentially deep and important (namely, the "continentals") and those like Carnap (the arch-"analytic" logical positivist who attended Heidegger's original lecture), who would go on three years later to ridicule this very sentence as the paradigm example of metaphysics' tendency to produce "entirely meaningless ... pseudo-statements."[34]

By "pseudo-statements," Carnap does not mean *false* statements but *non*-statements, that is, statements that do not even qualify as proper "statements," because such meaningless assertions mimic the syntactical structure of ordinary propositions but turn out to be empty of semantic content, owing to their unknowing commitment of basic logical errors, in this case, to Heidegger's alleged hypostatization of the familiar act of negation. Put simply, Carnap is suggesting that we all know what subtraction is, and we know that if we subtract everything from everything, then we get nothing. But that does not mean nothingness is itself a thing (let alone that such a void reaches out like some satanic force to negate, erode, or undo all that has been done, nor to beckon us suggestively into a future beyond what is currently actual). Thanks to Carnap, "The nothing itself noths" became the single most infamous philosophical example of *philosophical nonsense*, and Heidegger's use of "nothing" has also been taken as an example of what Wittgenstein (in another context) famously characterized as "language gone on holiday" from common sense and established usage.[35]

---

[33] See Michael Friedman, *A Parting of the Ways: Carnap, Cassirer, and Heidegger* (Chicago, IL: Open Court, 2000).

[34] See Rudolf Carnap, "The Elimination of Metaphysics through Logical Analysis of Language," in *Logical Positivism*, ed. by A. J. Ayer (New York: Free Press, 1959 [original 1932]), 61, 69.

[35] (Ludwig Wittgenstein, *On Certainty* [New York: Harper and Row, 1969], 19; Wittgenstein, *Philosophical Investigations* [New York: Macmillan, 1958], 19.) Proudly "analytic" fans of Carnap and Wittgenstein have often enjoyed ganging up on Heidegger, but Wittgenstein's point is subtly different from Carnap's allegations of philosophical

3.5. HEIDEGGER'S PHENOMENOLOGY OF NOTH-ING

Wittgenstein himself understood Heidegger's proclamation more sympathetically (and accurately, we will see) as an expression of Heidegger's phenomenological inquiry running "up against the boundaries of language." But Wittgenstein similarly thought that all such efforts to put the extra-linguistic source of linguistic intelligibility into words were doomed "a priori" to "be nonsense," at best respectable but futile attempts to say what should instead be passed over in reverent silence.[36] Wittgenstein's own respect for Heidegger's attempt was subsequently silenced, moreover, omitted from the English translation of his remarks – a telling omission few seemed to notice, since the "analytics" went on to win the day politically in the English-speaking philosophical world, gaining hegemony over most of its leading academic institutions (and setting the taken-for-granted terms for most of the prejudice-confirming "common sense" of mainstream philosophy in the English-speaking world).[37] The deep irony, however, is that the continentals were in the right *philosophically* here. Heidegger's famous assertion that "the nothing itself noths" is not meaningless metaphysical nonsense, *pace* Carnap and the still common misreading of Heidegger as an "irrationalist."[38] As Wittgenstein intimated, "the nothing itself noths" is part of Heidegger's phenomenological attempt both to describe the prelinguistic source of linguistic and conceptual meaning and also to characterize the emergence of such meaning. Heidegger worked on this difficult phenomenological project throughout his career, from *Being and Time* to his last public presentation in 1974 (FS 93–7/GA15 401–7),

---

"nonsense." Rather than Carnap's "the emperor wears no clothes" charge that such a pseudo-statement actually says nothing at all (and not in a good, Heideggerian way), Wittgenstein's paradigm examples of "language gone on vacation" include many analytic epistemologists' ways of using "certainty," which set the bar for such *certitude* impossibly high rather than recognizing that our ordinary language games already have built-in procedures for determining when we are entitled to say we are "certain" of something. (Indeed, this is the central thesis of Wittgenstein's last book, *On Certainty*, a text which, I would argue, also sublates and subtly expresses Wittgenstein's existential struggle with his philosophical relation to his own impending mortality.)

[36] See Friedrich Waismann, *Ludwig Wittgenstein and the Vienna Circle: Conversations Recorded by Friedrich Waismann*, trans. by Brian McGuinness and Joachim Schulte (New York: Rowman and Littlefield, 1979); Ludwig Wittgenstein, "A Lecture on Ethics," in *Philosophical Occasions 1912-1951*, ed. by James Klagge and Alfred Nordmann (Indianapolis, IN: Hackett, 1993) (from 1929).

[37] See Jeffrey Bell, Andrew Cutrofello, and Paul Livingston, *Beyond the Analytic-Continental Divide: Pluralist Philosophy in the Twenty-First Century* (London: Routledge, 2015); Iain Thomson, "Rethinking the Analytic/Continental Divide," in Kelly Becker and Iain Thomson, eds, *The Cambridge History of Philosophy, 1945-2015* (Cambridge: Cambridge University Press, 2019), 569–89.

[38] This "irrationalist" misreading has been devastatingly refuted by Stephan Käufer, "The Nothing and the Ontological Difference in Heidegger's *What Is Metaphysics?*", *Inquiry*, 48:6 (2005), 482–506, building on Simon Glendinning, "Much Ado about Nothing," *Ratio*, XIV (2001), 281–8.

and leading philosophers influenced by the phenomenological tradition still continue to pursue it.[39]

To put my view more precisely, Heidegger's succinct, summarizing formulation, "The nothing itself noths" seeks to evoke both (1) that prelinguistic "origin" (the primal phenomenological source or *Ursprung*) from which all ordinary concepts and established linguistic meanings first arise (namely, "The nothing itself") and also (2) the manner in which this prelinguistic origin offers itself to language (by actively "noth-ing," so to speak). Heidegger's initially jarring reference to a dynamic "noth-ing" is thus not some illegitimate hypostatization of the act of negation (as Carnap's polemic falsely assumed) but, instead, one of Heidegger's earliest attempts to evoke the way in which what is currently outside linguistic and conceptual intelligibility ("the nothing itself") offers itself to us phenomenologically, enabling us to capture at least some aspects of it in words and concepts. In 1929, this "noth-ing of the nothing" is Heidegger's attempt to express what allows us to grasp and conceptualize that which, prior to such conceptualization, remains inchoate and unformed in our phenomenological experience, not yet recognized as a meaningful entity, and in this sense not yet a thing (but rather a "no-thing"), hence (rather naturally in English at least) a "nothing."

The active "noth-ing" of this "nothing" is thus a conceptual generalization that designates this not-yet-a-thing on its way to becoming a thing.[40] This temporal process of ontological becoming happens (to take the most germane example) when we (world-disclosive Dasein) conceptually disclose some inchoate phenomenon's hints about its nature (its active "noth-ing"), intimations which are largely preconceptual but still sensibly manifest and so phenomenologically accessible. (Think, for instance, of coming up with a way of describing and so communicating a new experience, feeling, or insight.) The linguistic and conceptual innovations whereby we seek poetically to capture aspects of this previously inchoate phenomenon in words can thus serve that phenomenon's coming-into-being (or becoming intelligible), allowing it to become a discrete thing for us by entering into our intelligible worlds in a relatively stable and meaningful way. Taken together, then, "The nothing itself noths" seeks *both* (1) to designate that background of preconceptual but phenomenologically accessible intelligibility ("the nothing itself") from which meaningful words and concepts are first drawn, and also (2) to convey the way our words and concepts can facilitate things' emergence from preconceptual intelligibility into conceptual sense – which is precisely what

---

[39] See, for example, Hubert Dreyfus and Charles Taylor, *Retrieving Realism* (Cambridge, MA; Harvard University Press, 2015).

[40] It is, we could say (in the terms I will now introduce and explain), a phenomenological conceptualization of what world-disclosive conceptualization *conceptualizes* – in other words, a *poietic* conceptualization of such conceptualization itself.

3.5. HEIDEGGER'S PHENOMENOLOGY OF NOTH-ING 119

happens when these words and concepts responsively disclose the nothing's suggestive "noth-ing," its beckoning phenomenological hints about its nature.

Thanks primarily to his subtly yet profoundly transformative engagement with the German romantic poet Friedrich Hölderlin, the "middle" Heidegger (c. 1929–37) comes to think that human beings first form meaningful words when we responsively conceptualize our preconceptual encounter with that which is not yet an entity. When we do this well, we disclose the beckoning, suggestive hints (or "noth-ing") of the world's preconceptual background intelligibility ("the nothing itself") into words and concepts. We could thus finish Heidegger's famous sentence as follows: "The nothing itself noths" *into meaningful words and concepts – with the help of Dasein's (poietic) acts of world-disclosure*. For, when we pick up on the inchoate hints of some emerging phenomenon and creatively disclose those hints in order to "name" this phenomenon "into being" conceptually (GA4, 33–48), what had previous been nothing (or no thing) for us *becomes* something (or some discretely intelligible thing).

This kind of poetic – or, more precisely, *poietic*, that is, world-disclosive – "naming into being" is accomplished when we attend carefully to and manage to express in words the particular way in which some phenomenologically accessible aspect of the previously unnoticed, background intelligibility (or "nothing") of our world suddenly "noths" (or shows itself to us as something beckoning to be put into words), calling on us to conceptualize it. "The nothing itself noths" into words and concepts, consequently, whenever a previously inchoate aspect of this background seems to beckon us to carve it (poetically) into some discrete sense or meaning that then comes to populate and structure our intelligible worlds. For the middle and later (post-1938) Heidegger, this distinctive act of "naming-into-being" makes Dasein essentially a "poietic" (or ontologically-maieutic) discloser of being. For, such poietic or disclosive acts are at the heart of all our most meaningful practices, from poetry and thinking to art, architecture, and education. (As that suggests, Heidegger will soon come to see that we disclose the nothing in our embodied practices as well as in our linguistic concepts.)[41]

Perhaps the most profound lesson Heidegger first learns from Hölderlin is that such poietic acts of world-disclosure do not merely make *explicit* those relations of preconceptual significance that were already *implicit* in our practical familiarity with our worlds, as 1927's *Being and Time* suggests, famously presenting the view that Dasein's prelinguistic, practical "significations grow or ripen into words" (BT 204/SZ 161).[42] Heidegger implicitly retracts this view

---

[41] See, for example, "The Origin of the Work of Art" and "Building Dwelling Thinking" in PLT, and Thomson, *Heidegger, Art, and Postmodernity*, ch. 3.

[42] But cf. BT 205/SZ 162, where Heidegger suggests that poetry can also deliberately explore the different ways in which our mooded attunements can shape and transform our very disclosure of intelligibility.

seven years later, in his first lectures on Hölderlin (in 1934–35), when he writes: "In language there occurs the revelation of entities, not just a post-facto expression of what is already unveiled" implicitly in our practical engagement with the world (HHGR 57/GA39 62). In other words, rather than simply making implicit practical relations of significance explicit conceptually (as we do, for instance, when someone in a workshop tells us that "the hammer hangs over there, on those nails next to the saw"), "poietic" naming-into-being more creatively discloses previously inchoate hints, bringing these hints together in new and suggestive ways that allow us human beings to come to see something where previously we saw nothing – or where, in the case of the poetic disclosers themselves, we previously encountered only the suggestive glimmering (or phenomenological "noth-ing") of that which we had not yet brought at least partly into the focused clarity of our linguistic concepts. To try to put this subtle but profound shift in Heidegger's philosophy of language simply, then, we might say that he passes from his earlier pragmatic view that language is about making implicit relations explicit to a later, neo-romantic and post-expressivist view that language is not just about expressing individual insights but, ultimately, about responsively opening up and creatively preserving an intelligible historical world in which we human beings can meaningfully dwell.[43]

Throughout Heidegger's later work, his crucial examples of this more ontologically disclosive (and literally *meaning-full*), poietic understanding of language turn – just like the very idea of the noth-ing of the nothing itself – on the crucial idea of learning to discern a subtly dynamic phenomenon in which something as of yet absent is coming-to-presence. (Heidegger's crucial examples all turn on learning to discern "the presencing of presence [*Anwesen des Anwesenheit*]," as he famously puts it later, which means learning to recognize something that is not a thing but rather "comes to presence in a coming that presses in upon us" [HHGR 101/GA39 111].) The great importance of learning this vigilant sensitivity to the subtle presencing of that which is not yet a thing is the most fundamental lesson Heidegger learned from Hölderlin, Nietzsche, and Van Gogh, all those "touched" thinkers whose descent into madness Romantically vouchsafed their contact with divinity and inspired something in Heidegger in turn – albeit something only mistakable as mere "irrationalism" by readers whose hermeneutic sensibilities were already blunted by an (in itself perfectly understandable) hostility toward Heidegger's

---

[43] "Bringing to language," Heidegger suggests, requires disclosing the inconspicuous happening of the nothing (as, for example, when we struggle to find words to express ourselves): "Being comes, clearing itself, to language. It is perpetually underway to language.... Ek-sistence dwells thoughtfully in the house of being. In all this it is as though *through thoughtful saying nothing happens*" (P 274–5, my emphasis/GA9 361–2).

3.5. HEIDEGGER'S PHENOMENOLOGY OF NOTH-ING

views on logic and politics.[44] Existentially, we could say, what Heidegger learned from Hölderlin's poetry was to not fear the nothing as an anxiety-inducing sign of death's approach but, instead, to learn to discern and affirm this "nothing of the nothing" as the source of all creative disclosure and new meaning (see HHGR 131, 184/GA39 149), as we will see in more detail in the last three chapters.

In his famous text on "The Origin of the Work of Art," Heidegger demonstrates how Vincent van Gogh paints "A Pair of Shoes" in a way that shows these shoes stepping forth from "the nothing," disclosively emerging from a richly suggestive background to which they continue to belong (as I have shown in detail elsewhere).[45] In Heidegger's contemporaneous lectures on Hölderlin (in 1934–35), however, the central example of an absence coming to presence is what Heidegger calls Hölderlin's "holy mourning." For Heidegger, to understand "holy mourning" is to understand Western humanity's current relation to God – that is, our relation to God in this age after that "death of God" which Nietzsche announced (as having already happened).[46] Heidegger's crucial idea here is that we need to recognize that absence of God which Hölderlin calls "God forsakenness" – that is, the nothing of God, the absence (or "abandonment") of any meaningfully unifying God from our modern historical world – not as a null or nugatory nothingness (a mere nothing at all) but, instead, as the phenomenologically inconspicuous way in which we learn to "stay faithful to the earth." When Heidegger proclaims that our "godless time is not nothing [at all], but an uprising [or rebellion, *Aufruhr*] of the earth" (HHGR 73–7/GA39 80), he means to suggest not only that the deliberate godlessness of modern enlightenment rationality results from the insurrection of modern *subjectivism* (or the axiomatic modern view of all reality as objects for subjects to master and control rationally, which makes human subjectivity the source of all value). Heidegger also means, more subtly and profoundly, that the absence of God in modernity is *itself* an active nothing, a "noth-ing" we need to learn to recognize *as* the concealed presencing of the earth.

Here we see Heidegger moving from his earlier language of the "nothing" to his slightly later terminology of "the earth," a terminological transition he also makes in his contemporaneous lectures on "The Origin of the Work of Art."[47]

---

[44] See Thomson, *Heidegger, Art, and Postmodernity*, ch. 3; Käufer, "The Nothing and the Ontological Difference."

[45] See PLT 33–4/GA5 19; IM 37–8/GA40 38; Thomson, *Heidegger, Art, and Postmodernity*, ch. 3.

[46] See the famous passage from Friedrich Nietzsche's *The Gay Science: With a Prelude in Rhymes and an Appendix of Songs*, trans. by Walter Kaufmann (New York: Vintage Books, 1974) (section 341).

[47] As detailed in Thomson, *Heidegger, Art, and Postmodernity*, 84–106.

This terminological change is not arbitrary but reflects Heidegger's dawning recognition that the word "earth" (beloved by Hölderlin and Nietzsche, Heidegger's central influences at the time) does a better job of communicating the specificity, particularity, and phenomenological *texture* whereby that which is outside our current language actively offers itself to our understanding. Unlike that nebulous haze suggested by "the nothing," the texture-riven "earth" better conveys Heidegger's crucial, phenomenologically realist view that there is a genuine source of partly subject-independent meaning to which we Dasein need to learn to respond (with the creative disclosure of our phenomenologically informed concepts). Heidegger's 1934–35 vision of "remaining true to the earth" is part of his complex and critical appropriation of the leading lesson of Nietzsche's *Thus Spoke Zarathustra*: "Stay faithful to the earth!"[48]

For, Heidegger will not be satisfied with Nietzsche's naturalistic understanding of the earth as "what is thinkable for humanity, visible for humanity, feelable by humanity," a naturalistic ideal of sticking to what is empirically accessible that, ironically, does not prevent Nietzsche himself from "thinking through his own senses to their [rather speculative] consequences" by postulating an empirically unprovable and even knowingly *unknowable* understanding of the earth (and indeed of the very cosmos itself) as the product of a competing play of basic forces (which Nietzsche famously terms "Dionysus" and "Apollo," chaos and order, or, when he names their endless struggle, "will to power").[49] In other words, Nietzsche's "earth" is not only a Darwinian arena for competing life forces (and the "value systems" by which human beings attempt to extend their dominance around the globe and beyond). The earth itself is thereby also the expression of a more fundamental "will to power" in the endless dynamism of its ceaseless cosmic becoming, an eternal *agon* of forces (in an *unknowably* endless play that the early Nietzsche suggests can *never* be accurately captured by any fixed or stable name).[50] Heidegger, as a hermeneutic phenomenologist, understands "the earth" differently, as a temporally dynamic yet still semantically supporting substratum of intelligibility. In 1934–35, Heidegger's "earth" designates an extra-linguistic reality that can meaningfully inform our best words and concepts even as it also inevitably overflows and so exceeds the words we discover to express some of its aspects. In sum, then, Nietzsche thinks "staying faithful to the earth" means sticking to what we can possibly experience and know (even though his own notions of *will to power* and *eternal recurrence* do not stay true

---

[48] Friedrich Nietzsche, *Thus Spoke Zarathustra*, in *The Portable Nietzsche*, ed. and trans. by W. Kaufman (New York: Viking Penguin Books, 1954), 125.
[49] Nietzsche, *Thus Spoke Zarathustra*, 198, 339, 226–7.
[50] Ibid, 42–7; John Richardson, *Nietzsche's System* (New York: Oxford University Press, 1996); Thomson, *Heidegger, Art, and Postmodernity*, ch. 1.

to that dictum), whereas Heidegger takes the slogan to mean that we should faithfully struggle to responsively disclose and patiently unfold the meaningfulness of that source of intelligibility which can be partly experienced but never exhaustively known.[51]

The basic difference between Heidegger and *his* Nietzsche (at least) comes from Heidegger's phenomenologically realist intuition that there is something outside language to which language itself needs to and can respond meaningfully. To respond meaningfully is not just to respond creatively (as we do for the early Nietzsche when we legislate names that usefully but illusorily still the stream of becoming in ways that bestow adaptive benefits on the organisms that innovate them).[52] For Heidegger, to disclose (or "world") the earth faithfully is to do so *responsively*, such that the poets' words do at least some justice to what they disclose or "name into being" (EHP 51–65/GA4 33–48). This difference between the early Nietzsche's linguistic idealism and the middle and later Heidegger's plural realism is important for us here because Heidegger's terminological transformation of "the nothing" into "the earth" was driven by his dawning recognition that language needs to be responsive to the "scarcely graspable beckoning" of something beyond it. (As he writes in 1935: "Poetizing as founding – as that creating that has no object and that never merely sings about what lies at hand – is always an intimating, a waiting, a seeing come" [HHGR 233/GA 257].) Heidegger will thus come to believe that language is at its best and most meaningful when it finds creative ways to respond faithfully to something arriving from at least partly beyond the horizon of our present experience.

In other words, the phenomenological lesson Heidegger ultimately learns from Hölderlin's poetry and Van Gogh's painting is to become sensitive to the promise of a more meaningful future that arrives in an "event of enowning" (or *Ereignis*), a momentous and overwhelmingly meaningful event (like falling in love, or coming to understand oneself as the member of an identity-defining group of "people") that can help unify the subsequent unfolding of our lives if we faithfully disclose the manifold truths toward which this event beckons us (HHGR 101/GA39 111).[53] Such ontological truth events offer human beings an abundance of hints that exceed the bounds of current sense and so need to be patiently unfolded and responsively disclosed in our subsequent lives, lives that this disclosive activity can thereby bestow with an evolving and thereby enduring sense of identity. (Such group identity is Heidegger's central political

---

[51] On this crucial difference, see Thomson, "Ontology and Ethics at the Intersection of Phenomenology and Environmental Philosophy," esp. 386–8.
[52] See Nietzsche, "On Truth and Lie in an Extra-Moral Sense" (Walter Kaufmann, ed. and trans., *The Portable Nietzsche* [New York: Penguin, 1954]), 42–7.
[53] On Heidegger's later view of love as such a momentous "event of enowning" (*Ereignis*), see Thomson, "Thinking Love: Heidegger and Arendt."

preoccupation at this time; it is the focus of his question of what means to be, or not to be, German.)[54] Here, then, we can begin to see how Heidegger's neo-Nietzschean ideal of "staying faithful to the earth" will itself evolve into his later neo-Hölderlinian vision of maintaining fidelity to an enduringly meaningful "event" of ontological truth (which we will explore further in Chapter 8), the thinking of which both emerges from and exceeds the terrible political maelstrom of 1933–34.

But the earlier and more basic terminological transformation of "the nothing" into "the earth" was also motivated by Heidegger's recognition that his discussion of the nothing had not been well received or understood. While briefly serving as the Rector of Freiburg University in 1933, Heidegger still bitterly recalls how, after delivering "What Is Metaphysics?" in 1929, "I was indignantly repudiated on every side" (BaT 62/GA36-7 78). (The fact that Heidegger felt so globally rejected also tells you how widely he had hoped to be heard.) Here Heidegger suggests that the widespread rejection he experienced was due primarily to the great importance he had assigned to the disclosive power of the fundamental attunement of profound "anxiety" or dread (the *Grundstimmung* of *Angst*). His *phenomenological* view was widely misunderstood as suggesting that some individual's morbid and idiosyncratic "personal mood" was being used to disclose universal ontological truths about the "nothing" as the origin of humanity's understanding of being.

Heidegger rejects those criticisms as a misunderstanding of his phenomenology, which he rightly presents as a philosophy of "engagement" that demands the active participation of each individual in the experience under discussion. We must personally partake in such phenomenological experiences ourselves in order to be able to affirm or contest the ontological truths these experiences are supposed to disclose (as we saw in Chapter 1). In Heidegger's phenomenological method, the route to the ontological passes *through* the ontic; only by engaging in an experiential encounter with the ontic phenomenon at issue will we be able to discern the form of any of the underlying ontological structures that such an experience might "formally indicate." In short, Heidegger recognizes that his view of how *Angst* discloses the nothing was roundly misunderstood, and he explicitly seeks to "*learn*" from that perceived failure of understanding by developing the ontological insights from 1929 in a language that would allow them to be heard better and expressed more fully. Phenomenologically (and politically) engaged "*teaching*" requires such "courage to stand there when the attempt does not succeed,"

---

[54] This is the question pursued throughout HHGR/GA39. I am often leaving Heidegger's troubling and complicated politics aside here, but I take up the difficult issue most directly relevant in our context when discussing Agamben in Chapter 7, and have dealt with the broader topic in detail elsewhere (see, for example, Thomson, *Heidegger on Ontotheology*, ch. 3; and "Heidegger's Nazism in the Light of His Early *Black Notebooks*").

3.5. HEIDEGGER'S PHENOMENOLOGY OF NOTH-ING 125

facing up to one's failures "courageously" by learning to make oneself better understood in the future (BaT 62–3/GA36–7 78–9). The phenomenological teacher must possess the Lutheran fortitude and martial "courage to stand there" firmly, weathering whatever storms may come, thereby "*learning*" to advance his or her phenomenological views even further in (and into) the future (BaT 63/GA36–7 79).

As this rather telling overemphasis on "courage" suggests, and as Heidegger's lectures from the following year (1934–35) confirm, he was worried – during this, his most militaristic, bellicose, political, and activist period – that his great emphasis on *Angst* might be "understood as the helpless trembling of a cowardice that loses its head," instead of being recognized (the way he would have it) as a heroic confrontation with the nothing, indeed, as Heidegger's own daring, vanguardist advance to the very front-lines in the historical collision between being and nothingness, a phenomenological *Kampf, polemos*, or *Auseinandersetzung* between knowing and the unknown. Eagerly volunteering for reconnaissance missions to the "outermost edge of understanding" (HHGR 225/GA39 248), this would-be heroic advance into the nothing allows his 1929 confrontation with *Angst* to be rightly "grasped as the metaphysical proximity to what is unconditional [*Unbedingten*, literally "non-thinged," not yet brought into intelligibility as a discernible thing], a nearness bestowed only to a supreme steadfastness and readiness" (HHGR 66/GA39 73). Heidegger's rhetoric is rather obviously compensatory (this was, after all, a man whose psychosomatic anxiety attacks prevented him from taking up the kind of front-line military service he philosophically romanticizes and rhetorically emulates).[55] But the deeper point behind the rhetoric remains true and important nevertheless: Heidegger is indeed learning, pushing *his own understanding of* the boundary between being and nothing ever further into the nothing.

Crucially, Heidegger is moving beyond his (now falsified) view from *Being and Time*, that "the being of entities can least of all ever be something such that 'behind it' stands 'something else' which does not appear. / Behind the phenomena of phenomenology there is essentially nothing [or nothing else, *nichts anderes*]" (BT 60/SZ 35–6). The later Heidegger's definitive recognition is that there is indeed something else standing behind "the being of entities" – albeit something that is not a thing but (initially) a "nothing." The noth-ing of that which stands beyond the current horizon of intelligibility is what makes it possible for human beings to conceive and transform our historical understanding of "the being of entities"; this nothing, in short, is Heidegger's first name for that Ur-phenomena that his later work most often calls "being as such." As he will put it, looking back in 1940: "What is needed beforehand is a

---

[55] See HHGR 66/GA39 73; Thomson, *Heidegger on Ontotheology*, 174–81.

recognition of the 'positive' in the 'privative' essence of *alêtheia* [that is, the essence of ontological *truth* understood as phenomenological "un-concealment" or "dis-closure"]. This positive [in the privative, that is, the concealed which *enables* any unconcealing] is to be previously experienced as the basic characteristic of being as such [*das Sein selbst*]. The need must first break in on us whereby what becomes worthy of questioning is not only entities in their being [that is, the being of entities] but, first of all, being itself" (P 182/GA9 238). What the later Heidegger now recognizes he needs, that is, is a recognition of being in its very difference from metaphysics' understanding of the being of entities – a recognition of that not-yet-a-thing which first shows up for Heidegger as a phenomenological "noth-ing."

Despite withering attacks from Carnap and others, Heidegger never gave up this difficult notion. Instead, he struggled his whole life to develop this phenomenological insight more clearly and meaningfully, continually seeking new names with which to evoke the way being gives itself which would not hypostatize this giving as if it were a given entity, names such as "noth-ing," "earth," "being as such," "beyng [Seyn]," the clearing (as the open that can be lit-up differently), being written under a "cross-wise striking-through," (which itself becomes) "the fourfold," "the difference," "presencing," "the promise," "the same," the "it" of "*es gibt Sein, es gibt Zeit*," and so on. Indeed, I have long argued that Heidegger's recognition that the "noth-ing" of the nothing is the *action* of being as such, an activity that exceeds and so cannot be explained in terms of the ontological difference between being and entities, is the defining experience at the heart of his so-called turn and the *sine qua non* of his "later" thought.[56] And while Heidegger is far from presenting "the nothing" as the final word on the matter, he never completely abandons this use of the "nothing" as his first name for the temporally dynamic *presencing* of being as such, and so will still succinctly tell his students as late as 1969 that: "The noth-ing of the nothing 'is' being" (FS 57/GA15 361). To the end, then, Heidegger still occasionally reaches for that first name he came up with, in 1929, to designate the phenomenological presencing of that which exceeds the ontological difference between entities and our current (ontotheologically stabilized) understanding of their being, which he had previously thought unsurpassable.[57]

---

[56] See Thomson, *Heidegger on Ontotheology*, ch. 1; Thomson, *The End of Ontotheology: Understanding Heidegger's Turn, Method, and Politics*.

[57] (Ibid.) For reasons I have explained elsewhere, Heidegger believes that Paul Klee paints "the nothing coming to presence [*Nichts Anwesendes*]" and that "Zen" painting (for example, the traditional "Enso" or circle painted by Zen masters in one continuous brush stroke) are concerned "with the approach of humanity to the enveloping nothingness" (Heidegger, quoted in Günter Seubold, "Heideggers nachgelassene Klee-Notizen," *Heidegger Studies*, 9 [1993], 11; see Thomson, *Heidegger, Art, and Postmodernity*, ch. 3).

3.5. HEIDEGGER'S PHENOMENOLOGY OF NOTH-ING

Heidegger's tumultuous middle period is marked by this deep tension between his early and later views, and in the 1929 essay which suggests that "The nothing itself noths" (viz., "What is Metaphysics?" [in P]), Heidegger is focused not just on the question of how (and from where) *entities* emerge into conceptual intelligibility; he is also focused on the more general question of how (and from where) the meaning of being (or of what it means to "be" in general) first emerges into intelligibility (before being stabilized in a metaphysical understanding of "the being of entities"). We thus see Heidegger struggling in the 1930s to move beyond the metaphysical ambitions to which his discussion of the nothing was directly linked in 1929's "What Is Metaphysics," in which he was still pursuing *Being and Time*'s guiding project of disclosing a fundamental ontology or understanding of the meaning of being in general (as we saw in Chapter 2). As Heidegger's thinking matures – passing through its tumultuous, pro-Nietzschean, pro-metaphysical, political middle-period from the early to mid 1930s (see esp. HHGR/GA39 and N1/NI) – he increasing emphasizes that, when human beings accomplish this poetic "naming into being" well, we do not merely *impose* concepts we have prefabricated onto the world. At our best, we instead respond to the particular solicitations of the inchoate phenomenon we are seeking to characterize, and what we are then seeking to disclose is not nothing at all, but the "noth-ing" of the not-yet a thing on its way toward language.

Let me conclude by suggesting that Heidegger may have initially chosen his own language of the nothing in part because – like his emphasis on "the mystery" or "the secret" (*das Geheimnis*, the secret gathering into and at the heart of the home) which begins in 1934–35 – such language avoids the Wittgensteinian pitfall of trying to say the unsayable. Instead, it draws our attention to the way what is sayable repeatedly emerges from what *remains* unsaid (indeed, from what can *never* be completely or exhaustively said), and so "leaves the unsayable unsaid, and does so in and through its saying" (HHGR 108/GA39 119).[58] To hear "the noth-ing of the nothing" in this way is to hear it as Heidegger's would-be *poietic* disclosure of *poietic* disclosure itself – that is, as a thinking of the being (nature and origins of) thinking, one inspired by and running parallel to Hölderlin's poetry about poetry and Van Gogh's painting of painting.[59] This also helps us see how Heidegger might

---

[58] The difficulty (as Heidegger concludes his second course on Nietzsche by hinting to his students) is "to say the matter in such a way that it is named in not-saying [*Nichtsagen*]: the saying of thinking is [such] a telling keeping silent [*Erschweigen*]" (N2 208/NII 471). Here what is said and yet left unexplicated and so thereby also kept silent is the moving beyond nihilism by (what Heidegger then calls) a "need-turning and necessary thinking" in which the nothing is thought not as nothing at all but, instead, as the temporally dynamic not-yet-a-thing whereby being as such comes toward us (N2 175/NII 438). (On *this* crucial turning, see Thomson, *Heidegger, Art, and* Postmodernity, ch. 7.)

[59] See Thomson, *Heidegger, Art, and Postmodernity*, ch. 3.

respond to Wittgenstein's more quietistic criticism that the origin of language should not be evoked and explored phenomenologically but only passed over in reverent silence. Heidegger too believes in the power of reticent silence to speak volumes in the right circumstances, but he also thinks that: "A mystery that is not known in the power of its veiling is no mystery" (ibid.). In other words, to preserve "the mystery" we have to show *that there is* a mystery. To *keep* the secret we have to tell *that* there is a secret by putting part of that secret into words and then showing that there is still (and for us always will be) more to this secret – that being can never be completely disclosed, because there always seems to be more for us to see and say about phenomena (including that ontologically polysemic Ur-phenomenon from which all phenomena emerge), at least as far as we *mortals* can tell phenomenologically (a complication we will return to in Chapter 9).

Heidegger thus suggests in the early 1930s that the mystery of the nothing, or the secret of the earth, is not will to power, eternally recurring (as *Zarathustra* suggests); instead, the secret of the earth is "an inexhaustible abundance of simple modes and shapes" (PLT 47/GA5 34) – an apparently inexhaustible source of all that is not-yet, a rich texture of phenomenological hints "in which all emergent happening trembles and remains held" (HHGR 97/GA39 107). To name this mystery "earth" is not to tell the secret or disclose the mystery *once and for all* – which, for Heidegger, is something we finite human beings can *never* do, our modern "subjectivist" pretentions and late-modern drive toward the endless optimization of technological *enframing* notwithstanding. We cannot have the last or final word about what it means to be. As Heidegger nicely puts it: "That silence preceding the world is more powerful than all human powers" (HHGR 199/GA39 218). That which keeps silent before and beyond language can never be exhaustively expressed, but it still *speaks* powerfully (in its beckoning hints), escaping exhaustive saying while partly giving itself to be said in all meaningful disclosure. *Pace* Wittgenstein's view, then, Heidegger thinks we keep the secret or preserve the mystery best not by staying silent before it but, instead, by sharing it in our own ways, as he himself did by repeatedly innovating multiple, evolving, and overlapping linguistic and poietic inventions, improvisations, and rediscoveries, which – taken as a whole that only begins with the nothing – forthrightly attest to the impossibility of ever exhaustively expressing this mystery in words once and for all time.

Indeed, each of the succinct philosophemes in Heidegger's succession of poietic names for this mysterious source of intelligibility disclose some of its aspects while missing others and sometimes even occluding them. This explains why Heidegger never simply rejects his earlier poietic names for the source of intelligibility and its ways of offering itself to our words and practices, just as he does not simply reject "the nothing of the nothing" when he begins referring instead to the "the rift structure of the earth."

3.5. HEIDEGGER'S PHENOMENOLOGY OF NOTH-ING 129

He recognized that "the nothing of the nothing" was almost universally misunderstood, and that it risks occluding the inchoate yet nevertheless real phenomenological *texture* of that to which we need to respond with phenomenological sensitivity and poietic, disclosive creativity. But we have also seen that "the noth-ing of the nothing" still nicely suggests (and better than "the earth" does) both (1) that the source of intelligibility is not a thing but should instead be recognized as the not-yet a thing on its way to becoming a thing, and also (2) that this "noth-ing of the nothing" calls to us from at least partly beyond the horizon of our current understanding of being – two central later insights that Heidegger never subsequently abandons.

We have thus seen how some of Heidegger's central philosophical innovations and contributions emerged from his rethinking of that "nothing" first disclosed by *Being and Time*'s phenomenology of existential death. As this nothing of temporal *futurity* developed into a "noth-ing" coming from beyond our current metaphysical understanding of the being of entities, its apparently inexhaustible meaningfulness overwhelmed and devastated the early Heidegger's guiding project of fundamental ontology, as we saw in Chapter 2. But the death of that life-guiding metaphysical project led to the rebirth of Heidegger's later vision of philosophical *thinking* as a series of overlapping efforts to help us recognize and transcend the ontotheological roots and nihilistic implications of our own, late-modern age of technological enframing (as we have begun to see here and I have shown in detail elsewhere).[60] I would thus like next to return to *Being and Time* to see how the formal structure for this kind of *existential death and rebirth of the self* – in which we die to an outdated self-understanding in order to be reborn into one whereby we can authentically understand ourselves – was already mapped out there, inchoately at least, with (what Chapter 4 describes as) *Being and Time*'s "perfectionist" vision of education providing a rather nice philosophical blueprint for the then still unknown radical transformation to come in Heidegger's own philosophical development. I shall suggest that this blueprint concerning how we become ourselves by repeatedly passing through different versions of existential death and rebirth remains important not only for understanding the trajectory of Heidegger's own subsequent thinking but also for all of us seeking to thoughtfully understand the philosophical meaning of education (and so the original meaning of Western philosophy itself, since Plato's *Republic* at least).

---

[60] This is the guiding thesis developed in both Thomson, *Heidegger on Ontotheology* and *Heidegger, Art, and Postmodernity*.

4

Death and Rebirth in *Being and Time*'s Perfectionist Philosophy of Education

4.1 *Being and Time*'s Philosophy of Education?

In *Heidegger on Ontotheology: Technology and the Politics of Education* (2005), I sought to establish and build upon the hermeneutic thesis that Heidegger's concern to reform education spans his entire career of thought. In my view, a radical rethinking of education – in a word, an *ontologization* of education, one that situates a transformative death and rebirth of the self at the very heart of the educational vision that founded the philosophical academy in Plato's *Republic* – forms one of the deep thematic undercurrents of Heidegger's work, early as well as late. We will come back to this "ontologization" of education at the end, but I want to begin by addressing a worry I did not previously thematize and confront.[1] If my interpretive thesis is correct, then we should expect to find some sign of Heidegger's supposed lifelong concern with education in his early magnum opus, *Being and Time*. The fact, then, that little or nothing had been written on *Being and Time*'s "philosophy of education" before my first book came out could reasonably be taken to cast doubt upon my thesis that a philosophical rethinking of education was of great

---

[1] In Thomson, *Heidegger on Ontotheology*, I do establish an important, indirect connection between Heidegger's philosophy of education and *Being and Time* by showing that his early magnum opus articulates the philosophical view of the relation between philosophy and the other sciences that motivates Heidegger's attempt to transform the German university in 1933–34. I show there that the controversial connection between Heidegger's philosophy and his politics cannot be understood apart from his radical philosophical efforts to rethink and reform higher education. Instead of using this connection as an excuse to dismiss Heidegger's later views on education, however, I suggest that his prescient critique of the university has only become more relevant since he elaborated it, and that, with the important philosophical corrections made (or suggested) to this philosophical research program by his so-called turn, the later Heidegger's mature vision for a reontologization of education merits the careful attention of those of us now seeking to understand the roots and implications of our own growing crisis in higher education.

4.1. *BEING AND TIME*'S PHILOSOPHY OF EDUCATION?

importance to Heidegger's work as a whole.[2] Such a worry, of course, does not arise deductively; even if *Being and Time* contained no philosophy of education, one might be able to explain such an omission in a way that would leave my general thesis intact. Rather than trying to preserve the thesis in the face of such a hermeneutic anomaly, however, I will instead demonstrate that no such anomaly exists. This chapter will seek both to show that Heidegger's philosophy of education deeply permeates *Being and Time* and to explain some of the context and significance of this fact, thereby coming to understand yet another interlocking set of philosophical implications arising from Heidegger's phenomenology of existential death.

Of course, if I am right that Heidegger's educational views are integrally entwined with some of the most essential themes of *Being and Time* (including existential death and authenticity), some may still wonder why these views so long went unheralded in the secondary literature. The short answer is that Heidegger does not present his philosophical views on education as such in *Being and Time*; in fact, he develops these views with an almost excessive subtlety.[3] As a result, if one does not already have a good sense for the shape Heidegger's views on education generally take in his work, their quiet presence in *Being and Time* is easy to miss. We thus need first to know something about

---

[2] Michael A. Peters only slightly overstates the matter when he recounts searching through two comprehensive digital archives in vain for "a single reference to [Heidegger's] educational thought or the educational significance of his philosophy" in August 2000. (See Michael A. Peters, ed., "Introduction," in *Heidegger, Education, and Modernity* [Lanham, MD: Rowman & Littlefield, 2002], 4.) Fortunately, things have changed for the better in the meantime; indeed, Dall'Alba and Barnacle generously credit my work with having helped inspire an "ontological turn" in the philosophy of education. See Gloria Dall'Alba and Robyn Barnacle, "An Ontological Turn for Higher Education," *Studies in Higher Education*, 32:6 (2006), 679–91.

[3] Why did Heidegger choose to present his views of education in *Being and Time* with such subtlety? It is tempting to suppose that he was trying to fly beneath the radar here, not because the "philosophy of education" would have been seen as a less serious subject than ontology, even for a famous teacher such as Heidegger (such an explanation would be anachronistic, since the disastrous marginalization of the philosophy of education took place between Heidegger's time and our own), but for the opposite reason, namely, that the philosophy of education was so central and highly charged a philosophical topic in 1920s Germany that Heidegger would not have wanted to look like he was jumping on the bandwagon. (I treat this historical background in Thomson, *Heidegger on Ontotheology*, ch. 3.) I suspect that the reason for Heidegger's subtlety (beyond general issues concerning the difficulty of his style, even in *Being and Time*) may be double: Both to shelter the content of the teaching from hostile (and so impatient) readers, and, conversely, to help ensure that these teachings would be received only by those willing to struggle with the ideas in order to make them their own, since only such an audience would be able to *understand* them in the immediate, practical sense in which, we will see, they are intended. (Other versions of this same worry often arise in reading Heidegger, and I take them up, for example, in Thomson, *Heidegger, Art, and Postmodernity*, 120, n. 74.)

the basic contours of Heidegger's broader philosophical views on education in order to be able to recognize these views in *Being and Time* and begin to understand the role they play there. This task is made trickier by the fact that Heidegger's philosophy of education did not remain static throughout his life; he developed and refined his educational views in important ways between 1911 and 1940, while working toward (what I have called) his "mature" philosophy of education (which he first presented in his 1940 essay, "Plato's Doctrine of [or Teaching on," *Lehre von*] Truth").[4] Throughout this entire series of transformations, however, Heidegger's philosophy of education remains within the broad framework of what has come to be called philosophical *perfectionism* (not to be confused with psychological "perfectionism," that neurotic inability to bring anything to a satisfactory completion).[5] A brief outline of philosophical perfectionism will thus help us recognize Heidegger's philosophy of education in *Being and Time*.

4.2 What Is Philosophical Perfectionism?

Although its Western roots go back at least as far as Pindar, the lineage of philosophical perfectionism derives mainly from Aristotle, and perfectionists

---

[4] I present a historical genealogy of the development of Heidegger's philosophical views on education in Thomson, *Heidegger on Ontotheology*, ch. 3, and develop his mature philosophy of education in ch. 4.

[5] Neuroses, of course, come in varying degrees, and in colloquial use, "perfectionism" often connotes merely a tendency not to be satisfied by one's own work. Even in colloquial use, however, this dissatisfaction is taken to derive less from the merits of one's work than from features of one's psychology. By "psychological perfectionism," then, I mean the extreme version of this neurosis, in which one is *never* satisfied by one's work, no matter how good it may be. Because psychological perfectionism tends both (1) to impede the completion of particular tasks and (2) to distort an accurate appreciation of the relative successes and failures of these tasks, and because both are required to fulfill the aim of philosophical perfectionism (viz., the development of our relevantly distinctive traits and capacities), *psychological perfectionism is in direct tension with philosophical perfectionism.* This tension remains even if the version of philosophical perfectionism under consideration abjures, or infinitely defers, the actual attainment of perfection (that is, the final completion or fulfillment of our relevantly distinctive traits or capacities), as is the case with Kant (for whom such goals as the kingdom of ends and the cosmopolis usually function as regulative ideals – unreachable, guiding stars by which we can chart our never-ending progress), Nietzsche (whose doctrine of the superman holds that "humanity [too] is something that must be superseded," since the one constant of "will-to-power," the essence of life, is to supersede all previous forms of itself, and so valorizes an endless becoming), and Cavell (who treats "perfection [only] as *perfecting*"). Other perfectionists, however, do believe that the perfection of our distinctive nature is attainable (however episodically), as did Aristotle, with his conception of intellectual virtue (outlined below) and the early Heidegger, albeit episodically, with his understanding of authentic resolve (which includes the resolution to keep repeating itself).

can still be recognized by their adoption of some version of three interrelated views Aristotle first set forth in the *Nicomachean Ethics*, views we could call the *ontological thesis*, the *ethical thesis*, and the *linking principle*. Perfectionism's ontological thesis holds that there is something essential or importantly distinctive about the form of life human beings embody, some set of significant talents or capacities that set us apart from (and, typically, above) all the other kinds of entities with which we are familiar. Perfectionism's ethical thesis maintains that our greatest fulfillment or flourishing follows from the cultivation and development (hence the *perfection*) of these importantly distinctive talents and capacities. Finally, the linking principle characterizes more precisely the connection between these ontological and ethical theses, specifying the nature of the link between the relevant ontological talents or capacities that distinguish us and our greatest possible ethical fulfillment or perfection. Aristotle provides the archetypal versions of these three perfectionist views when he argues: First (his ontological thesis), that we are most importantly distinguished from other living beings by our ability to employ *nous* or active intellect (we are, in effect, that entity able explicitly to comprehend the web of connections implicitly governing all entities); second (his ethical thesis), that the greatest human fulfillment comes from perfecting our distinctive theoretical nature (for Aristotle, the greatest human fulfillment comes from maximally actualizing our distinctive theoretical capacities); and third (his linking principle), that our ethical fulfillment follows directly from the unimpeded cultivation and development of our distinctive ontological nature (since this nature endows us with a desire to understand that both sets us on and inclines us along the path leading to our ethical fulfillment).[6]

Aristotle casts a long shadow over the subsequent history of philosophical perfectionism, but conceptual space remains within the framework he establishes for profound disagreements concerning how best to understand and instantiate the three different perfectionist theses. Perfectionists thus disagree, first, about what the importantly distinctive human essence is (the *ontological thesis*): Should human beings be distinguished by our possession of reason, intellect, soul, passion, freedom, culture, community, creativity, world-disclosure, self-interpretation, or merely by our continual supersession of each of our previous self-understandings?[7] Second, perfectionists disagree about

---

[6] See Aristotle, *Nicomachean Ethics*, trans. by H. Rachham (Cambridge, MA: Harvard University Press, 1934), I.vii.9–16, 31–4 (1097b22–1098a20); and Jonathan Lear, *Aristotle: The Desire to Understand* (Cambridge: Cambridge University Press, 1988), 160–4. For a detailed conceptual critique of the perfectionist tradition, and an innovative attempt to construct a naturalistically defensible, contemporary version of perfectionism, see Thomas Hurka, *Perfectionism* (Oxford: Oxford University Press, 1993).

[7] In the last case, does it even make sense to speak of our relevantly distinctive "essence" or "nature"? And if not, is Nietzsche really a perfectionist? Yes, I think, but a perfectionist who focuses on *life* in general, not on human life in particular. In fact, Nietzsche thought

how to understand the "perfection" of these distinctive traits or capacities (the *ethical thesis*): What constitutes the greatest human fulfillment? Can such fulfillment ever be achieved? Permanently, or only episodically? By individuals, within the finite span of their lives, or only by a historically enduring human community, projected indefinitely into the future? Does the advancement of humanity simply piggyback upon the perfection of individuals, or does it happen despite them, "behind their backs" (as Kant suggests)? Conversely, is individual development served by the development of humanity? Or does the development of the distinctive essence of humanity instead demand the supersession of existing humanity (as Nietzsche thought)?[8] Finally, perfectionists disagree about the connection between our distinctive human essence and our ethical fulfillment (the *linking principle*): Is it the case, as Aristotle thought, that what distinguishes us also naturally impels us toward our perfection, or must we not instead struggle against other important aspects of ourselves in order to achieve our fulfillment? (The former view represents a *positive* version of the linking principle, while the latter would be a *negative* version, in the terms I shall use.).

Thanks to the variety of perfectionist views that these three kinds of differences make possible, membership in the perfectionist lineage is quite diverse, cross-cutting better known philosophical divides. For example, perfectionism is often presented as if it were an ethical doctrine (Cavell and others write simply of "moral perfectionism"), but this can be misleading. It is true that perfectionism importantly includes what I have called the *ethical* thesis, but "ethical" is meant here in its original sense, having to do with what the Greeks called our *ethos* – *that* is, the way our habitual practice (ἔθος) shapes our general comportment (ἦθος) or way of being in the world – and not with the narrower contemporary understanding of "ethics" (better termed "morality") as centrally concerned with the formulation of action-guiding

---

that the cultivation and development of the essence of life in general (viz., "will-to-power") led inexorably toward the supersession of human life. (This is his rightfully controversial doctrine of the "superman," his claim that "humanity too is something that must be superseded." I discuss his call for the post-human in Thomson, *Heidegger, Art, and Postmodernity*, ch. 5 and in Thomson, "Ontology and Ethics at the Intersection of Phenomenology and Environmental Philosophy.") The penultimate doctrine on my list I associate with Rorty, an avowed "anti-essentialist" who nevertheless maintains a perfectionist view when he proclaims that we are basically self-interpreting animals (and so, he would have it, essentially inessential), and that we are at our best insofar as we maximally develop our interpretive capacities (letting "a thousand interpretations bloom" so as to replenish the field of historical intelligibility, in which even the brightest poetic blooms fade away with everyday use).

[8] On Kant's argument concerning humanity's *"unsocial sociability,"* see the "Fourth Thesis" of his "Idea for a Universal History with a Cosmopolitan Intent," Immanuel Kant, *Perpetual Peace and Other Essays*, trans. by Ted Humphrey (Indianapolis and Cambridge: Hackett, 1983), 31–2.

4.2. WHAT IS PHILOSOPHICAL PERFECTIONISM? 135

principles.[9] Indeed, the perfectionist lineage cuts across all the major Western ethical schools, its membership including not only the foremost virtue theorist (Aristotle), but also the main deontologist (Kant), the most famous consequentialist (Mill), and the most important existentialists (Kierkegaard, Nietzsche, and Heidegger).[10] This brings us back to the matter at hand.

---

[9] These formulaic moral imperatives most famously include the maximization principle of consequentialism (roughly: Do whatever brings about the greatest good for the greatest number) and the *categorical imperative* of Kantian deontology ("Act only in accordance with that maxim through which you can at the same time will that it become a universal law.") (Immanuel Kant, *Groundwork of the Metaphysics of Morals*, ed. and trans. by Mary McGregor [Cambridge: Cambridge University Press, 1998], 34.)

[10] Thomas Hurka suggests a distinction between "broad" and "narrow perfectionism," where the latter designates *moral* perfectionism, but this does not address the point that broad perfectionism cuts across – and, indeed, *beneath* – the standard cartography of the competing moral traditions (Hurka, *Perfectionism*, 4). Cavell does better to suggest that perfectionism "is not a competing theory of the moral life, but something like a dimension or tradition of the moral life that spans the course of Western thought," a tradition that itself suggests that "morality [or, better again, *ethics*] is not the subject of a separate philosophical study or field." (See Stanley Cavell, *Conditions Handsome and Unhandsome: The Constitution of Emersonian Perfectionism* [Chicago, IL: Chicago University Press, 1990], 2, 7.) Cavell's sprawling argument with Rawls over whether perfectionism is "elitist" rightly suggests that perfectionism possesses an ineliminable political dimension (see ibid., passim; and John Rawls, *A Theory of Justice* [Cambridge, MA: Harvard University Press, 1971], section 50, on "the principle of perfection," 325–32). The political implications of perfectionism are debated further in George Sher, *Beyond Neutrality: Perfectionism and Politics* (Cambridge: Cambridge University Press, 1997), and Steven Wall and George Klosko, eds, *Perfectionism and Neutrality: Essays in Liberal Theory* (Lanham, MD: Rowman & Littlefield, 2003); the debate centers on the question of whether perfectionism's political demands conflict with the formal neutrality often thought to be required by political liberalism. I suspect that in my own short list of philosophical perfectionists, the inclusion of Mill will be most controversial (at least to those familiar with Kant's political philosophy, where his perfectionism is obvious). There are interesting tensions between Mill's consequentialism and his perfectionism, but a strong perfectionist streak undeniably animates his work (and probably better accounts for its enduring appeal than do his staid utilitarian views). Mill writes, for example, that: "Among the works of man which human life is rightly employed in perfecting and beautifying, the first in importance is surely man himself.... It is not by wearing down into uniformity all that is individual in themselves, but by cultivating it and calling it forth, within the limits imposed by the rights and interests of others, that human beings become a noble and beautiful object of contemplation; and as the works partake of the character of those who do them, by the same process human life also becomes rich, diversified, and animating, furnishing more abundant aliment to high thoughts and elevating feelings, and strengthening the tie which binds every individual to the [human] race, by making the race infinitely better worth belonging to" (John Stuart Mill, *On Liberty* [Indianapolis: Hackett, 1978], 56, 60). Recall, too, that Mill opens this great work with an epigraph drawn from Wilhelm von Humboldt that stresses "the absolute and essential importance of human development [almost certainly Mill's translation of *Bildung*] in its richest diversity" and approvingly quotes (again in his own translation)

4.3 Heidegger's Perfectionism in *Being and Time*

4.3.1 *Being and Time*'s Ontological Thesis

In keeping with the preceding sketch, we will understand what kind of perfectionist the early Heidegger is when we know what versions of the ontological and ethical theses he advances and how he understands their linkage. We thus need to know, first, what is *Being and Time*'s version of perfectionism's ontological thesis? What does Heidegger think makes Dasein, the human form of life, distinctive? (I should specify that I am using the neo-Wittgensteinian locution, "human *form of life*," to respect the conceptual space opened up by Haugeland's admirably unorthodox argument that "Dasein" and "human being" are not coextensive. Haugeland suggests that not every Dasein need be a human being, while Dreyfus points out, conversely, that not every human being counts as a Dasein, such as human infants, as we saw in Chapter 1. These points are well taken, and remind us that we have to be careful to unpack the sense in which a human being *is*, or *becomes*, a Dasein in a way that will not undercut, in a single stroke, the force of Heidegger's perfectionist exhortation to "Become what you are!" – an injunction that, we will see, plays a subtle but crucial pedagogical role in *Being and Time*.)[11] To understand Heidegger's

---

Humboldt's dictum that "the end of man ... prescribed by the eternal and immutable dictates of reason ... is the highest and most harmonious development of his powers to a complete and consistent whole" (Mill, *On Liberty*, 55).

[11] As we saw in Chapter 1, and as Heidegger tells his students in 1939: "For us the word 'Dasein' names something that is by no means coterminous with human being ... What we designate with the word 'Dasein' does not arise in the history of philosophy hitherto" (N2 26/NI 278). Haugeland famously suggests that the reference of "Dasein" is, in principle at least, *broader* than that of "human being." I am sympathetic to this general strategy, and have argued elsewhere that *Being and Time*'s revolutionary reconception of the self not as a thinking substance, subject, ego, or consciousness but as a *Dasein* (a "being-here," that is, a temporally structured making-intelligible of the place in which I happen to find myself) suggests how we might develop a philosophically defensible and ethically indispensable argument for awarding "rights" (understood as political protections intrinsically merited by all agents capable of reflexively pursuing life-projects) to every Dasein, that is, to every entity who has a temporally enduring world that matters to it explicitly. (See John Haugeland, "Heidegger on Being a Person," *Nous*, 16 [1982], 6–26. For the argument that, Heidegger's intentions notwithstanding, his conception of Dasein promises us a philosophically defensible, non-speciesist way of making ethically and politically indispensable distinctions between what has long been problematically described as "lower" and "higher" forms of life, important distinctions missing from other avowedly non-speciesist ethical views, see Thomson, "Ontology and Ethics at the Intersection of Phenomenology and Environmental Philosophy.") In this context, however, I should add that I think any view of Dasein that would extend the category to corporations stands, *prima facie*, in serious need of rethinking, a rethinking nicely launched in Taylor Carman's critique of Haugeland. (See Taylor Carman, "Is Dasein People? Heidegger According to Haugeland," *Boundary*, 41:2 [2014], 197–212.)

4.3. HEIDEGGER'S EARLY PERFECTIONISM

perfectionism, we next need to know, second: What is *Being and Time*'s version of perfectionism's ethical thesis? That is, how does Heidegger conceive of Dasein's greatest possible fulfillment or perfection? Finally, how are Heidegger's answers to these two questions linked in *Being and Time* – positively or negatively? That is, does Heidegger think Dasein's fulfillment follows directly from the development of the capacities that make our form of life distinctive, or that our perfection instead requires us to struggle against a kind of inertial resistance intrinsic to the human condition?

Let us take the ontological question first: What essentially distinguishes Dasein, the human form of life, from all other kinds of entities? Strikingly, Heidegger not only explicitly answers this perfectionist question in *Being and Time* but does so thrice over in the space of a single paragraph. He writes:

> Dasein is an entity which does not just occur among other entities. Rather [1] it is ontically distinguished by the fact that, in its very being, that being is an issue for it.... [2] It is peculiar to this entity that with and through its being, this being is disclosed to it.... [3] Dasein is ontically distinctive in that it *is* ontological. (BT 32/SZ 12)

Dasein is "ontically distinguished" – that is, distinguished from all other kinds of entities – in that: (1) its being is an issue for it (in its very being); (2) its being is disclosed to it (with and through its being); and (3) it *is* ontological. These, for Heidegger, are three interconnected ways of unpacking the significance of the fact that only Dasein "has an understanding of being" (BT 32/SZ 12). Now, one can "have an understanding of being" in at least two different ways – theoretically or practically – and, as the qualifications I have put in parentheses indicate ("in its very being," "with and through its being"), Heidegger is concerned *to ground the theoretical* (the analyzing, entertaining, or developing of an understanding of being*) in the practical* (the embodying, living, or existing of an understanding of being), as we saw in Chapter 1. To bring out this emphasis on *the primacy of the practical*, we could restate Heidegger's version of perfectionism's ontological thesis as follows. Only Dasein: (1) lives in an intelligible world implicitly structured by the stand it takes on its own identity; and so, conversely, (2) tacitly encounters this self-understanding in and through the structure of its intelligible world; and in this dual sense (3) exists in, through, or even *as* an understanding of being.

What this restatement seeks to make clear is that when Heidegger singles out Dasein as the unique possessor of an understanding of being, he is referring primarily to the fact that Dasein is the only kind of entity that takes a stand on its being practically (embodying an ontological self-understanding in its everyday practices by projecting into projects), and only secondarily to the fact that Dasein alone can understand being theoretically (by formulating theses concerning what entities *are* – *itself* included). Put concretely,

Heidegger's point is not just that only a Dasein can formulate and entertain thoughts such as "Life is a self-replicating system," "Matter is composed of N-dimensional strings," "It is raining," or "I am a teacher" (although this is true). Rather, Heidegger is primarily concerned with the preceding fact that the very way reality shows up for us is filtered through and circumscribed by the stands we take on ourselves, the embodied life-projects that organize our practical activities and so shape the intelligibility of our worlds. For example, if the fundamental self-understanding implicitly organizing my practices (what Heidegger calls Dasein's ultimate "for-the-sake-of-which") is that of being a teacher, as opposed to, say, being a scholar, or a husband or father, then a student unexpectedly knocking on my office door in the late afternoon will tend to show up as an opportunity to teach, rather than as an unwelcome distraction from my scholarship or an impediment to my desire to get home to my family.

Conversely, as this example illustrates, I implicitly encounter my self-understanding, the fundamental stand I take on myself, through the very ways in which entities and events show themselves to me. Nevertheless, I may only notice this tacit filtering of my experience when something goes awry, for instance, when my different life-projects, and so my "worlds," collide, or break-down entirely, encouraging me explicitly to confront, in a way I usually do not, the fundamental self-understandings organizing my experience.[12] When this happens, I must find some way to accede to and affirm (or else disown and transform or relinquish) these self-understandings, and so take responsibility for myself, answering for or owning up to myself, if I am ever to make my life (and so my self) my own. Such a fundamental confrontation with oneself – in what we should now be able to recognize as the experience of existential death – is at the heart of what Heidegger calls *Eigentlichkeit* ("authenticity," or more literally "owndedness"), and there is an important sense in which these confrontations, however rare they may be, bring us explicitly into contact with what is implicitly a basic and constant structural characteristic of the human form of life, namely, the fact that (as Dreyfus succinctly summarizes *Being and Time*'s version of perfectionism's

---

[12] Conflicts between our personal and professional lives provide ready examples of this. If, for example, my young daughter has just told me that she is unhappy with how late I have been coming home from the office, then that same unexpected student visit may show up in a kind of dual, conflicting light, reflecting an ambivalence in my embodied self-understanding in virtue of which I am being pulled in two different directions. Moreover, although I suggest (in passing) a conflict between the life projects of "teacher" and "scholar," I do believe that, at its best, being a teacher and a scholar function synergistically, like two mutually reinforcing aspects of the same life-project, in which research emerges from teaching and feeds back into and informs it.

ontological thesis): "To exist is to take a stand on what is essential about one's being and to be defined by that stand."[13]

4.3.2 Being and Time's Ethical Thesis and Linking Principle

With this reference to authenticity, we get a glimpse of what I will argue is *Being and Time*'s version of perfectionism's ethical thesis. But to both clarify this ethical thesis and distinguish it from its main competitors in *Being and Time*, a contrast with Aristotle will again prove helpful. Aristotle holds that human beings are distinguished from all other entities by being that part of the *logos* which is able to turn around and theoretically understand the *logos*. Indeed, he calls this capacity to employ theoretical wisdom "the true self of each," and maintains that our lives reach their highest peaks – attaining "perfect fulfillment" (*teleia eudaimonia*) – in "intellectual or theoretical contemplation" (*theoretikê*). As he famously puts his perfectionist views:

> [T]hat which is best and most pleasant for each creature is that which is proper to the nature of each; accordingly, the life of the intellect is the best and most pleasant life for humanity, inasmuch as the intellect more than anything else is human, therefore this life will be the most fulfilled [*eudaimonestatos*]. The life of practical virtue, on the other hand, is fulfilled only in a secondary degree.[14]

Heidegger would not deny Aristotle's thesis that we, alone among entities, are capable of developing an ontology and situating ourselves within it. (Aristotle's thesis is either empirically true, as far as we know, or else trivially true, if "we" means "we Dasein" of any variety – be they human, alien, artificial – rather than solely "we human beings.") Without denying the great importance of our theoretical capacities, Heidegger's phenomenological approach inverts the priority Aristotle assigns to the theoretical over the practical. As *Being and Time* provocatively maintains: "Higher than actuality stands *possibility*" (BT 63/SZ 38). We have seen that the sense of "possibility" celebrated here is not "logical possibility," mere alternatives arrayed in a conceptual space, but rather existential possibility, "being possible" (*Möglichsein*), which is for Heidegger "the most

---

[13] See Dreyfus, *Being-in-the-World*, 23. Dreyfus expresses the converse point on p. 15: "Dasein's activity – its way of being – manifests a stand it is taking on what it is to be Dasein."

[14] See Aristotle, *Nicomachean Ethics*, X. viii, 7, p. 623 (1178b8); X.vii.9-viii.1, p. 619 (1178a1–10). To emphasize the contrast with Heidegger's perfectionism, my presentation of Aristotle simplifies his internally contradictory and therefore controversial views on the relative merits of our intellectual and practical virtues in his *Nicomachean Ethics*. I do, however, take the passage just quoted – in which Aristotle emphasizes the great importance of the practical virtues, even as he subordinates them to a conception of our greatest intellectual fulfillment – to represent his considered view.

primordial and ultimately positive way in which Dasein is characterized ontologically" (BT 183/SZ 247). Our existential possibilities are what we forge ahead into: the roles, identities, and commitments that shape and circumscribe our comportmental navigation of our lived environments. Dasein *exists* or "stands out" (*ek-sistere*) into intelligibility through such a charting of "live options," choices that matter and that are made salient to us by these fundamental life projects, this sense of self embodied and reflected in our worlds.[15]

For Heidegger, this practical embodiment of an understanding of our being both *precedes* and *makes possible* any explicit theoretical articulation or construction of an understanding of being. He thus clarifies his aforementioned ontological thesis – according to which "Dasein is ontically distinctive in that it *is* ontological" – by specifying that, strictly speaking, "ontological" should be heard here as "pre-ontological," since "being ontological is not *yet* tantamount to developing an ontology" (BT 32, my emphasis/SZ 12). This "not yet" is important; it indicates Heidegger's belief that the theoretical activity of developing an ontology does in fact follow from our "being pre-ontological" in the prior, practical sense. For he holds that:

> [W]henever an ontology takes for its theme entities whose kind of being is different than that of Dasein, this ontology has its own *foundation and motivation* in Dasein's own ontical structure, which includes a pre-ontological understanding of being as a definite characteristic. (BT 33, my emphasis/SZ 13)

If, like Aristotle, Heidegger believed that attaining a theoretical understanding of being fulfilled human existence, then he would be expressing here a positive version of perfectionism's linking principle, since he holds that the theoretical development of an ontology is founded in and motivated by the same ontological (or "pre-ontological") capacities that make Dasein, the human form of life, distinctive (including this "pre-ontological" fact that our way of being is "always already" mediated by our tacit understanding of what things are). Other passages in Division I reinforce the same point. Perhaps most clearly, Heidegger writes:

> [A]s an investigation of being, phenomenological interpretation brings to completion [*Vollzug*], autonomously and explicitly, that understanding of being which belongs already to Dasein and which 'comes alive' in any of Dasein's dealings with entities. (BT 96/SZ 67)[16]

---

[15] As we saw in Chapter 1. (I first developed this point in Thomson, "Can I Die? Derrida on Heidegger on Death" [1999], 31–2.)

[16] Heidegger applies the same point to Dasein's reflexive explication of its own existential structure as well, maintaining that: "If being-in-the-world is a kind of being which is essentially befitting to Dasein, then to understand being-in-the-world belongs to the essential content of its understanding of being" (BT 118/SZ 86). These passages

4.3. HEIDEGGER'S EARLY PERFECTIONISM

Have we thus uncovered *Being and Time*'s versions of perfectionism's ethical thesis and linking principle? Does Heidegger conceive of the greatest fulfillment, completion, or perfection of Dasein in terms of our development of a theoretical understanding of being? If so, then he maintains a positive version of the linking principle, since he holds that the development of any such theoretical understanding of being emerges "autonomously and explicitly" from the implicit, inchoate, and unarticulated ("pre-ontological") understanding of being that makes our form of life distinctive. Yet, if Heidegger does adopt such a positive version of the linking principle, then why does *Being and Time* so often stress the need to struggle against a kind of inertial undertow intrinsic to the human condition? Could it be that there are in fact two different sorts of ethical ideals at work in *Being and Time* – competing, practical and theoretical visions of *Dasein*'s fulfillment? If so, how does Heidegger fit these ideals together, and which represents *Dasein*'s greatest fulfillment?

The trick to answering these questions, it seems to me, comes from our previous recognition of the way Heidegger inverts Aristotle, elevating the practical above the theoretical without denying the great importance of the theoretical (no more than Aristotle himself denigrates the practical). Attaining a theoretical understanding of being is undeniably important in *Being and Time*. At one point, Heidegger even goes so far as to say that: "All our efforts in the existential analytic serve the one aim of finding a possibility of answering the [fundamental ontological] question of the *meaning of being* in general" (BT 424/SZ 372). As we saw in Chapter 2, however, Heidegger never fulfills *Being and Time*'s overarching theoretical aim (never arriving at the "fundamental ontology" he pursues like a mirage throughout the text and most of those that follow over the next decade), and I want to suggest that, despite the considerable influence Aristotle's intellectualist ideal exerts upon his thinking, Heidegger does not believe that human existence reaches its ethical apotheosis in the attainment of a theoretical or conceptual understanding of being. Rather, *Being and Time* conceives of *Dasein*'s greatest fulfillment practically, in terms of an embodied stand – "authenticity" – that each of us is capable of taking on our own being.[17]

(significant differences notwithstanding) show that Heidegger believed ontological theory-building follows directly from the ("pre-ontological," being disclosing) capacities that make our form of life distinctive.

[17] It may be slightly misleading to say that Heidegger celebrates a practical *rather than* an intellectual ideal of Dasein's greatest fulfillment, not only because Heidegger deconstructs the theory/practice dichotomy, but also because (according to Heidegger's conception of authenticity) Dasein often attains practical fulfillment by incorporating a kind of insight into its own being gained from its fundamental confrontation with itself in death. As Dreyfus puts the point, Dasein's "fully *authentic* way of acting [is] made possible by Dasein's understanding of its own *way of being*." (See Hubert L. Dreyfus, "Could

Although Heidegger holds that *Dasein*'s ontologically distinctive nature is fulfilled with the achievement of authenticity, it is his recognition of the difficulty we nevertheless have in attaining this practical ideal – the way we have to struggle against the inertial resistance of ubiquitous social norms that quietly enforce a kind of anonymous conformity (usually with our unnoticed complicity) if we are ever genuinely to repossess ourselves – that explains why *Being and Time* tends to maintain a positive version of the linking principle in Division I, and a negative version in Division II.[18] The remainder of this essay will delve a bit further into these complexities and explain their relation to Heidegger's philosophy of education in *Being and Time*.

4.4 How We Become What We Are: *Being and Time*'s Answer to the *Bildungsfrage*

The most direct intersection of perfectionism with the philosophy of education can be found in the *Bildungsfrage*, the pedagogical question of how best to cultivate and develop our importantly distinctive talents and capacities. This question animates Plato's *Republic* and Aristotle's *Nicomachean Ethics* and is kept alive in the Western tradition by philosophers as diverse as Plotinus, Aquinas, Spinoza, and Leibniz, but it gets its name from the German Idealist tradition, with which it enters the mainstream of philosophical modernity. Terry Pinkard glosses *Bildung* as "the self-determining self-cultivation and inwardly motivated love of learning and education."[19] This is a rather telegraphic gloss (Pinkard's rendering of one word by thirteen brings to mind Heidegger's own long-winded "translations" from Greek), and so suggests the telling lack of a synonym for *Bildung* in present-day English – despite Cavell's droll observation that the obsolete English "'upbuilding' . . . virtually pronounces *Bildung*." "Building" and "*Bildung*" are not etymologically related, however, so this phonetic resemblance is merely fortuitous.[20] Indeed, there is

---

Anything Be More Intelligible than Everyday Intelligibility? Reinterpreting Division I of *Being and Time* in the Light of Division II," in *Appropriating Heidegger*, ed. by Mark Wrathall [Cambridge: Cambridge University Press, 2000], 166.) Dreyfus's insightful essay also nicely sorts out the two different notions of "the moment" influencing Heidegger's conception of authenticity, viz., the Aristotelian *kairos* or "Greek act of seizing the occasion" and the Pauline *Augenblick* or "Christian experience of being reborn" (164).

[18] This also helps explain why (as Dreyfus observes) Heidegger seems to contradict himself methodologically in *Being and Time*, maintaining the necessity of a hermeneutic of suspicion for the most part only in Division II, where some of the ontological insight developed in Division I gets incorporated into the achievement of authenticity. (See Dreyfus, *Being-in-the-World*, 35–8.)

[19] See Hurka, *Perfectionism*, 4; Terry Pinkard, *Hegel: A Biography* (Cambridge: Cambridge University Press, 2000), 427.

[20] See Cavell, *This New Yet Unapproachable America*, 9; Raymond Geuss, *Morality, Culture, and History: Essays on German Philosophy* (Cambridge: Cambridge University Press,

no single word in English for the polysemic *Bildung* (even Pinkard leaves out such important meanings as "formation," "constitution," "culture," and "training"), but perhaps we can capture the perfectionist philosophy of education in a slogan. If so, it would be the original and most enduring one: "*How we become what we are.*"[21]

Nietzsche borrows the exhortation to "Become what you are!" from the second of Pindar's *Pythian Odes* (incorporating it, most famously, into the subtitle of his philosophical autobiography, *Ecce Homo*); Heidegger, in turn, appropriates it from Nietzsche (as well as from such other important early influences as Kierkegaard, Dilthey, and Husserl).[22] As you might already have noticed, there is a paradox at work in the imperative to: "Become what you are!" It is as if one were being told: "(Leave here immediately and) Go to the place where you are!" (Or simply: "Catch up to yourself!") I may be able to become what I am not, but what sense does it make to instruct me to become what I am? (Haven't I done that *already*?)[23] The perhaps obvious answer,

---

1999), 45, n. 9: Geuss points out that *Bildung* comes from *Bild*, "sign or image" (as in *Einbildungskraft*, literally, "the faculty for unifying images," or simply, "imagination"), while "building" comes from "a completely different Indo-European root having to do with 'dwelling.'"

[21] Hence the subtitle of Thomson, "Heidegger's Mature Vision of on Ontological Education, or: How We Become What We Are" (later revised and published as Chapter 4 of Thomson, *Heidegger on Ontotheology*).

[22] See E. Capps et al., eds, *The Odes of Pindar*, trans. by J. Sandy (New York: G. P. Putnam's Sons, 1915), 178–9; Friedrich Nietzsche, "Ecce Homo: How One Becomes What One Is," in *The Portable Nietzsche* ed. by W. Kaufmann (New York: Penguin, 1954); and Søren Kierkegaard, *Concluding Unscientific Postscript to the Philosophical Fragments*, trans. by D. F. Swenson (Princeton, NJ: Princeton University Press, 1941), 116. For a genealogy of Heidegger's likely sources for this trope, see Joachim Oberst, "Heidegger's Appropriation of Aristotle's *Dunamis/Energeia* Distinction," *American Catholic Philosophical Quarterly*, 78:1 (2004), 28–32, and Charles Guignon, "History and Historicity," in *The Blackwell Companion to Phenomenology and Existentialism*, eds. by Hubert L. Dreyfus and Mark Wrathall (Oxford: Blackwell, 2005), 545–58.

[23] Given the fairly obvious solution (offered in the next sentence of the text), it seems strange that Sher should so precipitously take this paradox to be a standing refutation of any perfectionism that stresses the development of our *essential* defining traits or capacities: "The problem lies in the nature of the essential human properties: because these are properties that every human already has,... their possession by humans is not anything that anyone can bring about or prevent. And, for this reason, no theory that identifies the human good with their possession seems capable of telling us anything about what anyone should *do*" (Sher, *Beyond Neutrality*, 221). Perhaps Sher does not consider the solution I offer because he does not distinguish perfectionism's ontological and ethical theses, and because his strong communitarian adherence to the Hegelian view that "each person defines himself through the eyes of the others" (206) leads him to ignore perfectionism's traditional commitment to a *radically individualistic* notion of the "absolute responsibility of the self to itself"; indeed, as Cavell points out, perfectionism traditionally turns on some notion of "being true to oneself – or to the humanity in

alluded to earlier, is that one can "become oneself" only if and insofar as one is not already oneself (in the relevant sense): If, for instance, one is alienated from oneself, living inessentially, under an illusion, in bad faith, caught up in the crowd (or even "the herd"), partaking in the tyranny of public opinion, or simply, as Heidegger puts it in *Being and Time*, acquiescing in "the real dictatorship of the one [*das Man*, the anonymous *anyone*]" (BT 164/SZ 126), a conformist and superficial hall of mirrors in which: "Everyone is the other, and no one is himself" (BT 165/SZ 128).

The point, then, is that I can indeed become who I am if who I am presently is not my own self (a self I have made my own), but merely a borrowed self, a self-understanding appropriated piecemeal from "everyone and no one" (to unpack one Nietzschean subtitle with another). Yet, if that explanation dispels one paradox, it leaves another, deeper one in its place: What sense does it make for Heidegger to exhort me to become myself when, on his view, I ultimately have no self to become? For, as Blattner and Dreyfus have long argued (and we saw in detail in Chapter 1), Heidegger's phenomenological interpretation of death reveals the anxiety-provoking fact that (as Dreyfus puts it) "Dasein can have neither a nature nor an identity, . . . it is the constant impossibility of being anything at all."[24] If I cannot *be* anything, then what sense does it make to exhort me to become *myself*? What strange kind of self am I being urged to become? To answer this question, we will need to look more closely into some of the details of Heidegger's view.

I mentioned that Heidegger appropriates the existential exhortation to "Become what you are!" from Nietzsche and others. As is usually the case with Heidegger's critical appropriations of the thinkers who have influenced him the most, this deconstructive critique takes the general form of going beyond (philosophically) by getting beneath (ontologically); that is, he articulates the ontological presuppositions conditioning their insights, thereby seeking to situate those insights within a broader and more encompassing interpretive framework. In this case, Heidegger maintains that what makes the imperative to "Become what you are!" meaningful is precisely the view I presented as his version of perfectionism's ontological thesis. We can see this if we unpack the following difficult but crucial passage (which I will refer to subsequently as *P1*):

> oneself, or of the soul as on a journey (upward or onward) that begins by finding oneself lost to the world, and requires a refusal of society" (Cavell, *Conditions Handsome and Unhandsome*, xxvii, 1).
>
> [24] (Dreyfus, *Being-in-the-World*, p. 312). Dreyfus adds: "Dasein has no possibilities of its own and . . . can never have any" (ibid.) As Carman points out, this "sounds dangerously close to saying that Dasein cannot *be* its own, that is, cannot be authentic (*eigentlich*). But this is not what Dreyfus has in mind" (see Carman, *Heidegger's Analytic*, 286). See also Blattner, "The Concept of Death in *Being and Time*," 321–39, and *Heidegger's Temporal Idealism*, 76–88.

[P1] Only because the being of the there receives its constitution through understanding and its character as projection, only because Dasein *is* what it becomes (or does not become), can it say to itself with understanding: "Become what you are!" (BT 186/SZ 145)

Here Heidegger seems to answer one paradox with another: The exhortation to "Become what you are!" makes sense only because "Dasein *is* what it becomes." How, then, are we to comprehend this strange (and rhetorically chiasmic) claim that *we can become what we are only because we are what we become*?

To answer this question, we need to remember that "understanding" is Heidegger's term for the basic stands we take on ourselves (the practical self conceptions we *stand under*, as it were), and that "projection" designates the way we press ahead into (or *project* ourselves upon) these roles, identities, and life-projects. When he says that "Dasein *is* what it becomes," then, Heidegger is drawing attention to the fact that the future constitutively informs my sense of self, since the roles, goals, and life-projects implicitly organizing my present experience stretch out into my future. In other words, "Dasein *is* what it becomes" does not record the truism that who I am now is a who I have become but, instead, registers the phenomenologically interesting fact that my basic sense of self has an ineliminably *futural* dimension. As Heidegger provocatively puts it, who I am now is a who I am "not yet."[25] Indeed, who I *am*, I may in fact never become. (The parenthetical in P1 brings home precisely this paradox.) Now, put abstractly, it sounds more than a bit strange to claim that I may in fact never become the who I already am. Thought phenomenologically, however, Heidegger's point is perfectly clear: A student, for instance, can "understand" himself as a teacher by committing himself practically to this life-project, in which case this fundamental self-understanding will implicitly shape and organize much of what he does, notices, thinks about, remembers, plans for, and cares about, and so also the sorts of skills and sensitivities to the practical situations of teaching he develops. In short, understanding himself as a teacher will shape much of what he *is*, even while he is not yet in fact a teacher, and even if (for whatever reason) it should turn out that he never in fact becomes a teacher. Heidegger's "Dasein *is* what it becomes (or does not become)" calls attention to the important sense in which this student, who may never in fact *become* a teacher, nevertheless already *is* a teacher: Being a teacher is the stand he takes on himself, and the intelligibility of his world is now fundamentally shaped and structured by this self-understanding (and will always have been so shaped, come what may).[26]

---

[25] "Dasein always exists in such a manner that its 'not yet' belongs to it.... Dasein must, as itself, *become* – that is to say, *be* – what it is not yet" (BT 287/SZ 243).

[26] Hermeneuts might consider another example: Heidegger understands himself in *Being and Time* as searching for a fundamental ontology, but this is a destination at which he in

To see that this is what Heidegger means, it helps to know that the immediate context for P1 is Heidegger's introduction of a subtle (and often overlooked) distinction between two senses of existential possibility, namely, "being-possible" (*Möglichsein*) and "ability-to-be" (*Seinkönnen*). This crucial distinction (detailed in Chapter 1) turns on our "being-possible" stretching further into our lived sense of the future than our "ability-to-be" does. (Indeed, the sentence immediately preceding P1 above reads: "Dasein, as being-possible . . . *is* existentially that which, in its ability-to-be, it is *not yet*" [BT 185–6/SZ 145].) Our *being-possible* is composed of our long-term identities, goals, commitments, and life-projects, while our *ability-to-be* names our basic ability to develop the capacities and skills we exercise precisely by committing ourselves to and pressing ahead into such life-projects. As Blattner puts it, "there are two functions here: opening up the range of possibilities, and pressing ahead into one of them."[27] We become what we are "not yet," then, by pressing ahead – or practically projecting ourselves – into our projects.

So, how does the fact that *we are what we become* (or do not become) make it possible to *become what we are*? One way to read this claim is as a fairly traditional answer to the *Bildungsfrage*, as if Heidegger were simply pointing out that we can meaningfully develop our defining capacities only because our inherently futural life-projects constitutively inform our present self-understanding. In his terms, only because our being-possible gives us a practical direction or orientation, the pursuit of which enables us to exercise and develop our abilities-to-be, can we in fact become the who we already implicitly understand ourselves to be. *Being and Time* says things that clearly support this interpretation. For example, Heidegger writes that when Dasein makes the world discovered in the light of its self-understanding explicit, and

---

fact never arrives, and which later he will explicitly reject. Still, this fundamental textual self-understanding allows Heidegger to press forward into and develop all manner of phenomenological and hermeneutic analyses and insights, many of which remain meaningful and important even in the absence left by the collapse of the overarching project in the service of which they were originally presented. (Combined with what we learned in Chapters 1 and 2, this helps suggest the *authenticity* of the later Heidegger's work, with which he finds a way to reconnect to the world after the collapse of *Being and Time*'s fundamental project.)

[27] (See Blattner, *Heidegger's Temporal Idealism*, 41.) Blattner suggests the further difference that as ability-to-be we always press into one possibility rather than another (SZ 285), while our being-possible is always multiple, since "Dasein is never just one for-the-sake-of-which" (Blattner, *Heidegger's Temporal Idealism*, 41, n. 14). Although I think Blattner is right about *us* today (and thus more right than Heidegger on this point), I called this aspect of his view into question as a reading of Heidegger in Chapter 1 (see Chapter 1, n. 55).

4.4. HOW WE BECOME WHAT WE ARE

so "works out" the possibilities implicitly disclosed by its self-understanding, Dasein "does not become something different. *It becomes itself*" (BT 188–9, my emphasis/SZ 148).[28] Such an interpretation fits well, moreover, with those passages in Division I quoted earlier, where Heidegger stresses that the theoretical activity of ontology building merely consummates the understanding of being implicit in our practical self-understanding. This interpretation is thus not so much wrong as incomplete. For it does not help us answer the crucial questions we posed earlier: If, for Heidegger, I cannot *be* anything (that is, if there is nothing about Dasein's defining structure that can tell any of us which particular life-projects we should pursue), then what sense does it make to exhort me to become *myself*? What kind of self is Heidegger encouraging me to become? And how does the fact that my future constitutively informs my present make it possible to become that kind of self?

To see how Heidegger solves these problems, we need to recognize the functional independence of our being-possible (the overarching life-projects we press ahead into: teacher, husband, father, son, brother, scholar, colleague, friend, and so on) from our ability-to-be (our pressing ahead into, or projecting ourselves upon, these projects). We have seen that "Dasein *is* what it becomes (or does not become)" makes sense, because we can press into possibilities, and so develop our abilities-to-be, even if we never in fact become the life-project we were pressing into. But is the obverse true as well? Can we become what we are no longer? To recognize that we can, think of the case of someone who (unlike the student we considered earlier) was in fact a teacher (or a husband, son, father, communist, pet owner, soccer-player, or any other identity-defining self-understanding), but who then experiences the catastrophic collapse of this life-project. What is crucial to recognize is that, when such world-collapse occurs, we do not instantly forfeit the skills, capacities, and inclinations that this identity previously organized. Indeed, in such a situation, we tend to continue projecting ourselves into or upon an absent project (for a time at least – the time it takes to mourn that project or else replace it, redirecting or abandoning the practices it organized). Even after that world collapses, we will keep pressing blindly ahead, even though the project that previously organized this projection is no longer there for us to press ahead into. It is this paradoxical situation, in which we do indeed continue to become what we no longer are, that Heidegger calls "being toward death" (as we saw in Chapter 1) – and it forms, as we will see by way of conclusion, a crucial part of what allows him meaningfully to exhort a self who cannot ultimately be *anything* to: "Become what you are!"

---

[28] "In interpretation, understanding does not become something different. It becomes itself" (BT 188/SZ 148).

4.5 Philosophical Education as Preparation for Existential Death – and Rebirth: Authenticity

I mentioned earlier that we would need to unpack the sense in which a human being *is* a Dasein carefully, so as not to undercut, with one stroke, the force of the perfectionist injunction to "Become what you are!" Here, to cut to the chase, is how Heidegger does it: "Dasein becomes 'essentially' Dasein in that authentic existence which constitutes itself as anticipatory resoluteness" (BT 370/SZ 323). Put simply, we "become what we are" by (repeatedly) becoming *authentic*.[29] Now, authenticity is a complex and important notion (well deserving of the attention it has often received as a separate topic of study), but the distinction we have drawn between being-possible and ability-to-be can help us sketch the two basic components of Heidegger's full formal conception of "authenticity" as *anticipatory resoluteness*, and thereby get a sense for the kind of self Heidegger exhorts us to become. I draw further textual support for this reading from one of Heidegger's undated marginal comments to *Being and Time*, where he writes that "anticipatory resoluteness" is "[a]mbiguous: existentiell [that is, particular and individual] project and existential [universal to all Dasein] self-understanding projecting itself into that project belong together here" (BT 372/SZ 325; GA2 430 note a). In "anticipation" (*Vorlaufen*), or "running-out" toward death (we saw in Chapter 1), we experience ourselves as an existential projecting without any particular existentiell projects to project ourselves upon, and so come to understand ourselves as, at bottom, an existential projecting, a projecting that is more basic than and independent of any of the specific projects that usually give our lives content and meaning. Making Heidegger's use of this point clear, however, will take a bit more explaining.

The difference between being-possible and ability-to-be, we have seen, is the difference between our life-projects and our projecting ourselves upon those life-projects. Usually we project ourselves upon our projects by skillfully coping through, rather than by theoretically deliberating over, the live-options these projects delimit and render salient for us – except in cases when something goes wrong or breaks down. Heidegger thinks it is possible, however, for all of my projects to break down simultaneously; indeed, this is precisely what he thinks will happen to anyone who endures a true confrontation with their existential *Angst*. Chapter 1 showed that Heidegger's existential phenomenology demands that we endure our existential anxiety rather than flee it back into *das Man*'s "indifferent tranquility as to the 'fact' that one dies," a flight by which we transform "this anxiety into fear in the face of an

---

[29] As Heidegger writes: "The meaning of Dasein's being is not something free-floating which is other than and 'outside of' itself, but is the self-understanding Dasein itself" (BT 372/SZ 325).

4.5. PREPARATION FOR DEATH – AND REBIRTH

oncoming event" that remains somewhere off in the future (BT 298/SZ 254), which is precisely what we do when we reduce our anxiety about death to fear of our mortal demise. Confronting and enduring our anxiety instead makes it possible, *Being and Time* suggests, for us to trace this anxiety back to its source in our basic "uncanniness" (*Unheimlichkeit*), that existential *homelessness* that follows from the fact that there is no life-project any of us can ever be finally at home in, since there is ultimately nothing about the ontological structure of the self that could even so much as suggest that we should become grief counselors rather than gossip columnists (as Dreyfus provocatively puts it). This phenomenological scenario – in which I pursue my anxiety to the point where my life-projects founder on the reef of their own unrecognized and unquestioned contingency and thereby break down or collapse – is the first component of authenticity Heidegger calls "anticipation" (or "running-out") toward death.[30]

To grasp what Heidegger thinks the self ultimately boils down to (in his existential version of the phenomenological reduction), it is crucial to remember that when my projects all break down or collapse, leaving me without any life-project to project myself upon, projection itself does not cease.[31] When my being-possible becomes impossible, I still am; my ability-to-be becomes blind, unable to connect to the world, but not inert. My projects collapse, and I no longer have a self to be, but I still *am* this inability to be. Heidegger calls this paradoxical condition revealed by anticipation "the possibility of an impossibility," or *death*. In his words:

> Death, as possibility, gives Dasein nothing to be "actualized," nothing which Dasein could itself actually *be*. It is the possibility of the impossibility of every way of comporting oneself toward anything, of every way of existing. (BT 307/SZ 262)

We can see the phenomenon Heidegger has in mind if we again generalize from the breaking down of one project to the catastrophic collapse of them all. A student can explicitly encounter his computer, a carpenter his hammer, and a commuter his car as a tool with a specific role to play in an equipmental nexus organized by his self-understanding, when this tool breaks down – when the hard-drive crashes the night before a paper is due, the hammer breaks and cannot be fixed or replaced in the middle of a job, or the car breaks down on the way to an important meeting, leaving the commuter stranded by the side of the road. Just so, Dasein can explicitly encounter its structure as the embodiment of a self-understanding when its projects all break down in death. Dasein, stranded (as it were) by the global collapse of its projects, can come explicitly to recognize itself as, at bottom, not any particular self or project but

---

[30] See Chapter 1, n. 75.
[31] See Stephen Crowell, "Subjectivity," 433–54.

rather as a *projecting* into projects, and so (in Heidegger's version of perfectionism's ontological thesis) as a being who takes an embodied and practical stand on its being and whose very world is defined and rendered significant by that stand.

This, moreover, helps us see why, for Heidegger, death is something I can live through. Heidegger himself stresses the paradox that Dasein lives through its death when he writes: "Death is a way to be, which Dasein takes over as soon as it is" (BT 289/SZ 245). Heidegger's point, I take it, is that the projecting we experience when we are unable to connect to our projects is what is most basic about us; this existential projecting is implicit in all of our ordinary *projecting* upon projects, but it also inalienably survives the loss of Dasein's any and every particular project (which is why Heidegger frequently refers to death as Dasein's "ownmost ability-to-be"). How, then, can we "live through" death? The passage through death is what Heidegger calls "resoluteness," and it is the second structural moment in his phenomenological account of *authenticity*.

Resoluteness is at least as complex a phenomenon as anticipation, but at its core is Dasein's accomplishment of a reflexive reconnection to the world of projects lost in death, a recovery made possible by an encounter of the self with itself in death. On the basis of the insight gained from this explicit self-encounter, it becomes possible for us to recover ourselves and reconnect to the practical world we are usually connected to effortlessly and unreflexively. As I understand it, this reconnection turns on our giving up the unreflexive, paralyzing belief that there is a single correct choice to make, because recognizing that there is no such correct choice (because there is no substantive self to determine such a choice) is what gives us the *freedom* to choose between whatever live options we face. As Heidegger puts it (in an important passage we will have reason to return to in Chapter 6):

> If Dasein, by anticipation, lets death become powerful in itself, then, as free for death, Dasein understands itself in its own *greater power*, the power of its finite freedom, so that in this freedom, which "is" only in its having chosen to make such a choice, it can take over the *powerlessness* of abandonment to its having done so, and can thus come to see clearly what in the situation is up to chance [and, correlatively, what is up to Dasein].
> (BT 436/SZ 384)

"Resoluteness" (*Entschlossenheit*) is Heidegger's name for such free decisions, by which we recognize that the self, as a (projectless) projecting, is more powerful than (that is, *survives*) death (the collapse of its worldly projects), and so become capable of "choosing to choose," making a lucid reconnection to the world. The freedom of such meta-decisions is "finite" because it is always constrained – by Dasein's own *facticity* (our inherited talents, cares, and predispositions, which can be altered piecemeal but not simply thrown off in some Sartrean "radical choice"), by the preexisting concerns of our time and

4.5. PREPARATION FOR DEATH – AND REBIRTH

"generation" (to which we cannot but respond in one way or another), by the facts of the specific situation we confront (which of these facts can be altered, Heidegger stresses, we cannot fully appreciate until we act and so enter into this situation concretely), as well as by that which remains unpredictable about the future (including the responses of others). Nevertheless, it is by embracing this finitude – giving up our naïve desire for either absolute freedom or a single correct choice and instead accepting that our finite freedom always operates against a background of constraint (in which there is usually more than one "right" answer for us, rather than none at all) – that we are able to overcome that paralysis of our projects experienced in death. It is thus important that Heidegger sometimes hyphenates "*Ent-schlossenheit*" (literally "un-closedness") to emphasize that the existential "resoluteness" whereby Dasein freely chooses the commitments that define it does not entail deciding on a particular course of action ahead of time and obstinately sticking to one's guns come what may but, instead, requires an "openness" whereby one continues to be responsive to the emerging solicitations of, and unpredictable elements in, the particular existential "situation," the full reality of which only the actual decision itself discloses.

In resolve's decisive "moment of insight," Dasein is (like a gestalt switch) set free rather than paralyzed by the indeterminateness of its choice of projects, and so can project itself into its chosen project in a way that expresses its sense that, although this project is appropriated from a storehouse of publicly intelligible roles inherited from the tradition, it nevertheless matters that this particular role has been chosen by this particular Dasein and updated, *via* a "reciprocative rejoinder" (BT 438/SZ 386), so as, ideally, to develop its particular ontic and factical aptitudes as these intersect with the pressing needs of its time and generation. Instead of simply taking over our projects from *das Man* (by going with the flow, following the path of least resistance, or simply doing what one should do the way one should do it), it thus becomes possible, through resolve, to take over a project reflexively and make it our own, and thus to reappropriate oneself, to "become what we are" by breaking the previously unnoticed grip arbitrarily exerted upon us by *das Man*'s ubiquitous norms of social propriety, its pre- and proscriptions on *what one does* and *how one does it*.

Indeed, *Being and Time* describes the perfectionist recovery of the self in just these terms:

> With Dasein's lostness in the one [*das Man*], ... Dasein makes no choices, gets carried along by the nobody, and thus ensnares itself in inauthenticity. This process can be reversed only if Dasein specifically brings itself back from its lostness in the one.... When Dasein thus brings itself back from the one, the one-self is modified in an existentiell manner so that it becomes *authentic* being-one's-self. This must be accomplished [enacted, or fulfilled, *vollziehen*] by *making up for not choosing*. But "making up" for not choosing signifies *choosing to make this choice – deciding* for an ability-to-be [that is, pressing into a particular existentiell

possibility], and making this decision from one's own self. In choosing to make this [particular] choice, Dasein *makes possible*, first and foremost, its authentic ability-to-be. (BT 312–3/SZ 268)[32]

This literally "revolutionary" image of repossessing oneself by first turning away from and then turning back to the world is implicit in many of Heidegger's most direct descriptions of authenticity – as, again, when he emphasizes that in resoluteness we do indeed reconnect to the same public world we first turn against:

> The authentic existentiell understanding is so far from extricating itself from the way of interpreting Dasein which has come down to us, that *in each case it is in terms of this interpretation, against it, and yet again for it*, that any possibility one has chosen is seized upon in one's resolution. (BT 435/SZ 383)

In these authentic moments in which we pass through existential death to a resolute rebirth of our guiding self understanding, Heidegger is not suggesting that we merely throw off one confining, superficial, and conformist understanding of what and how to be in favor of another, nor (at the opposite extreme) that we need to invent entirely new ways of existing in order to live authentically. Rather than requiring us to innovate our own new roles, goals, and life-projects whole-cloth (which, were they absolutely new, would make no sense to other people or even to ourselves):

> The resoluteness in which Dasein comes back to itself discloses current factual possibilities of authentic existing *in terms of the heritage* which that resoluteness *takes over* as thrown. (BT 435, first emphasis mine/SZ 383)

---

[32] As this quote suggests, there are at least two ways in which one can achieve resoluteness, viz., explicitly or lucidly. Out of the confrontation with ourselves made possible by the total collapse of the inauthentic "one-self" (our unthinking obedience to superficial and confining social norms that "dim down" our sense of what is possible), we can become explicitly aware of our ontological structure as beings who implicitly take a stand on our own being. (Indeed, Heidegger himself had to explicitly experienced authenticity in this way to be able to articulate and describe the two moments of anticipatory resoluteness in *Being and Time*. We, moreover, also need to be able to experience authenticity explicitly, if we are to be able to reconnect to the reality Heidegger's analysis discloses and so find it *phenomenologically* convincing, or not, rather than merely authoritative, suggestive, or fanciful.) On the other hand, this reconnection with one's everyday world can take place *lucidly* rather than *explicitly*. That is, one need not have read *Being and Time* and explicitly understood his analysis of the structure of existence to be able to shake off the arbitrary grip of social norms, lucidly repossess oneself, and so become authentic, however transiently. (On this issue, see David Cerbone, "Distance and Proximity in Phenomenology: Husserl and Heidegger," *The New Yearbook for Phenomenology and Phenomenological Philosophy*, III [2003], 1–26.)

4.5. PREPARATION FOR DEATH – AND REBIRTH

That is, even as we inevitably draw upon the historical "tradition" of existentiell possibilities that have always already come down to us through the time and place we are born into, resoluteness demands that we take genuine ownership of our own lives by owning up the fact that we are each choosing (that is, lucidly and creatively disclosing) who and how to be – and are therefore responsible for this embodied existential stand we continue to take and retake on the meaning of our own being (BT 334/SZ 288).

Indeed, as these passages indicate, it is through "becoming ourselves" in authenticity that we accomplish what Heidegger calls the "handing down of the heritage," the "reciprocative rejoinder" by which we critically appropriate and so update select aspects of the "tradition" in order to meet the needs of our own time, thereby transforming an otherwise dying tradition into a living "heritage" and so helping to constitute the communal "destiny" of our "generation" (BT 435-6/SZ 384-5). It is precisely thus that, as Young puts it, "*Being and Time* tries to mark out a conception of the flourishing life, the life lived in the light of an 'authentic' facing up to death and commitment to communal 'destiny.'" For, as Guignon writes, "To 'become who you are' ... is to identify what really matters in the historical situation in which you find yourself and to take a resolute stand on pursuing those ends."[33]

In sum, then, authenticity, as anticipatory resoluteness, names a double movement in which the world lost in anticipation is regained in resolve, a (literally) revolutionary movement by which we are involuntarily turned away from the world and then voluntarily turn back to it, in which the grip of the world upon us is broken in order that we may thereby gain (or regain) our grip on this world.[34] Let me conclude by quoting, as one last bit of textual support for the interpretation of authenticity as existential death and resolute rebirth advanced here, an intriguing marginal note Heidegger appends to the exhortation to "Become what you are!" (in passage P1). The note reads: "But who are 'you'? He, as who you are *without* project – as who you *become*. [*Aber wer bist 'du'? Der, als den du dich* loswirfst – als *welcher du* wirst.]" (GA2 194, note a.) I take this note to be an oblique reference to *authenticity*, understood in terms of its two constituent moments as *anticipatory resoluteness*. The words before the hyphen ("He, as who you are *without* project") designate "anticipation" (or, more suggestively, "running-out" into death), which we have understood as *projectless projecting* (that *solus ipse* disclosed in existential death as Dasein's "ownmost ability-to-be"). The words after the hyphen ("as who you *become*")

---

[33] See Julian Young, *Heidegger's Philosophy of Art* (Cambridge: Cambridge University Press, 2001), 131; Charles Guignon, *On Being Authentic* (London and New York: Routledge, 2004), 134.

[34] Of course, Heidegger's construal of this transition has seemed overly voluntaristic to critics ever since Levinas, *Time and the Other* (1946), hence the famous but, in my view, mistaken charge of *decisionism* (see Chapter 1, n. 56).

suggest resoluteness, choosing to choose and so, (re)appropriating oneself from the conformist undertow of *das Man*, becoming yourself (anew). The hyphen itself thus stands for the transition through and beyond death, the existential rebirth that resoluteness is as a reawakening to and reconnection with a world previously lost or rejected.

Authenticity's double movement of death and rebirth has often been thought of as Heidegger's phenomenological *version of conversion*, since it is a movement in which we turn away from the world, recover ourselves, and then turn back to the world, a world we now see anew, with eyes that have been opened. What is crucial for our purposes here, however, is that this "conversion" – or better, this revolutionary return of the self to itself – is at the very heart of Heidegger's mature *ontologization* of education.[35] Indeed, to come full circle myself, I have argued at length (in *Heidegger on Ontotheology: Technology and the Politics of Education*) that the later Heidegger seeks to effect nothing less than a reontologizing revolution in our understanding of education. As he puts it in 1940: "Real education lays hold of the soul itself and transforms it in its entirety by first of all leading us to the place of our essential being and accustoming [*eingewöhnt*] us to it." This, for the mature Heidegger, is what it means to "become what we are." Genuine education leads us back to ourselves, to the place we *are* (the *Da* of our *Sein*), teaches us "to dwell" (*wohnen*) "here," and transforms us in the process. This transformative journey back to ourselves is thus not a flight away from the world into thought but a reflexive return to the fundamental "realm of the human sojourn [*Aufenthaltsbezirk des Menschen*]" (P 168/GA9 219).[36] The goal of this

---

[35] Is this the *same* "conversion" I argued (in Thomson, "Ontology and Ethics at the Intersection of Phenomenology and Environmental Philosophy") was required by Heidegger's "transcendental, eco-phenomenological ethical realism"? They are not identical (as we saw in Chapters 1 and 2), although the orthodox Heideggerians were right to notice a deep continuity between his early and later work, even if they were wrong to exaggerate that continuity into a false equivalence (as we will see in Chapter 5). We saw in Chapters 1 and 3, for example, that (1) the "nothing" of (1A) the core self and of (1B) the world uncovered phenomenologically in death in *Being and Time* is not yet identical to (2) the nothing revealed in 1929's "What Is Metaphysics?" nor to (3) the nothing Heidegger recognizes *circa* 1937 as the way "being as such" appears to all of us when we view it through the unnoticed lenses of Nietzsche's metaphysics (since Nietzsche's ontotheology of eternally recurring will-to-power dissolves being into *nothing* but becoming; see Thomson, *Heidegger, Art, and Postmodernity*, ch. 7). But for an attempt to develop just such an orthodox Heideggerian argument (which very much follows in the spirit of her teacher, the arch-orthodox Heidegger scholar and editor von Herrmann), see Daniela Vallega-Neu, *Heidegger's* Contributions to Philosophy: An Introduction (Bloomington, IN: Indiana University Press, 2003), 1–51. For a critique of such orthodox readings, see Chapter 5.

[36] *Aufenthalte* ("abidance, sojourn, stay, or stop-over") is an important term of art for the later Heidegger; it connotes the temporal *finitude* of that journey through intelligibility which is human existence. Because *Aufenthalte* is also the title Heidegger gave to the

educational odyssey remains simple but revolutionary: To bring us full circle back to ourselves, first by turning us away from the world in which we are most immediately immersed, then by turning us back to this world in a more thoughtful, sensitive, and profound way.

The later Heidegger, moreover, develops a surprisingly specific set of pedagogical suggestions concerning how teachers might actually help students effect such a revolutionary recovery of the self – a pedagogical question about which *Being and Time* says little directly, leaving us to wonder if Heidegger thought teachers should actively seek to foment anxiety attacks, identity crises, or other forms of world-collapse in their students. That the answer to this question is "No" is strongly suggested by *Being and Time*'s primary pedagogical insight, namely, the distinction between a "leaping ahead" that "liberates" and a "leaping in" that "dominates" (BT 158–9/SZ 122). From a teacher's perspective, this is the distinction between doing it for students (rewriting their papers for them, for example) – as opposed to helping them learn to do it for themselves – a distinction which for Heidegger maps onto the difference between authentic and inauthentic methods of pedagogical "being-together" (*Mitsein*). That, however, still leaves us wondering what the early Heidegger thought teachers might do *directly* to help students achieve authenticity, and this pressing pedagogical problem may have encouraged Heidegger temporarily to shift his phenomenological focus from anxiety to *boredom*, an attunement he could seek to evoke in his students – as he in fact does (for more than one hundred pages!) in his 1929–30 lectures on *The Fundamental Concepts of Metaphysics* – without putting their psychological stability at risk (FCM 78–167/GA29–30 117–249). This does not solve the problem, unfortunately, since Heidegger's short-lived evocation of boredom has a quite different pedagogical effect than anxiety; the phenomenology of boredom helps students learn to step outside the totality of entities and so take up the perspective from which *metaphysics* (as onto*theology*) becomes possible, the very perspective Heidegger decisively turns against in his later work (as we saw in Chapter 2).

That reference to Heidegger's *turn* against metaphysics brings us to the most important difference between his mature thinking of education and the views presented in *Being and Time*. Although both share the sense that the work of philosophical education turns, finally, on a kind of self-recovery, and both stress that this critical recovery must be won by recognizing, confronting, and overcoming a preexisting source of resistance, in *Being and Time* this basic resistance to self-recovery is exerted by the inertial undertow of *das Man*, whereas in the later work such resistance comes, ultimately, from the

---

journal in which he recorded his thoughts during his first trip to Greece in the Spring of 1962, it is tempting to render it as "odyssey" to emphasize Heidegger's engagement with the Homeric heritage and the crucial sense of coming full circle back to oneself.

unnoticed effects exercised upon us by a set of historically specific metaphysical or, more precisely, *ontotheological* presuppositions. In this way (I have tried to show), the philosophical goal of Heidegger's early educational views – an edifying, empowering, and liberating reconnection to the world (which is not without a historically transformative element) – becomes more precise in his later work, which seeks to effect the transformation of our particular historical self-understanding by teaching us to recognize, contest, and so work to transcend the reigning ontotheology of the age and its increasingly nihilistic effects on us and our worlds.[37]

We have now reached the end of what is roughly the first part of this book, namely, our rethinking of the meaning and importance of death *in* Heidegger's work. Let us thus turn to the second part suggested by my title, beginning our rethinking of the meaning of death *after* Heidegger. In doing so, what we will in fact see is that these two projects should not be kept separate, because understanding the ways Heidegger's views on death were taken up, contested, and transformed by later philosophers helps us continue to deepen and refine our understanding of the meaning and significance of death in Heidegger's thought – and, I shall suggest, the reverse holds true as well, enabling the two parts of this book to form a mutually enriching hermeneutic feedback loop for our existential understanding of death.

---

[37] See chs. 3–4 of Thomson, *Heidegger on Ontotheology*.

PART II

Rethinking Death after Heidegger

5

White's *Time and Death*
On the Advantages and Disadvantages of Reading Heidegger Backward

In *Time and Death: Heidegger's Analysis of Finitude*, Carol White pursues a strange yet once common hermeneutic strategy, namely, reading Heidegger backward by reading the central ideas of his later work back into his early magnum opus, *Being and Time*. White follows some of Heidegger's own later directives in pursuing this hermeneutic strategy, and this chapter critically explores these directives along with the original reading that emerges from following them. The conclusion I reach is that White's creative book is not persuasive as a strict interpretation of Heidegger's early work, yet it remains extremely helpful for deepening our appreciation of Heidegger's thought as a whole. Most importantly, I shall suggest, White helps us sharpen and extend our understanding of the pivotal role that thinking about death played in the lifelong development of Heidegger's philosophy.

5.1 Introduction

Carol White's *Time and Death: Heidegger's Analysis of Finitude* is a book rich in thought, dense in original interpretive claims, and overflowing with supporting textual references.[1] Indeed, there is so much going on in White's text that a reader might be excused for initially feeling a bit like a hungry mosquito upon discovering an elephant, that is, excited and daunted at the same time, since there is more food for thought here than a single reading can hope to digest. It is fortunate, then, that Dreyfus has written a magisterial "Foreword" to White's book, in which he introduces his former student's work by focusing on her original and provocative interpretation of Heidegger's phenomenology of death. White's view, put simply, is that "death" is Heidegger's name for the

---

[1] White, *Time and Death* (unprefixed page references throughout this chapter are to this work). It is perhaps worth nothing that, besides being a wonderfully creative reader of Heidegger and legendary teacher, White was also quadriplegic and wrote much of this book by typing "with the handle of a wooden spoon" that she held in her mouth. (Later, her student I would come to inherit, now Professor Mark Ralkowski, helped type it for her and subsequently saw it though to publication after White's unfortunate demise in 2000 [xxxvii].)

collapse of an historical understanding of being, a collapse that creates the space for a rare authentic individual to disclose a new historical understanding of being and so inaugurate a new age. Dreyfus, after critically but sympathetically reconstructing White's interpretation, goes on to situate it within a panoramic overview of eight different ways in which eleven well-known interpreters have understood – or, more commonly, misunderstood – what Heidegger means by death. Providing a critical synopsis of each of these eight different interpretations of death, Dreyfus organizes them into an almost dialectical progression of increasingly satisfying interpretations, a progression that, he argues, reaches its fulfillment in the complementary work of White and John Haugeland.[2] Although I cannot recapitulate the detailed arguments from Dreyfus's (28 page) essay here, I shall build upon several key points from his analysis in what follows.[3]

If the inclusion of Dreyfus's important Foreword in White's book is itself already sufficient to make White's book significant for the scholarly community, Dreyfus, in turn, argues for the independent importance of White's work by suggesting that – once some minor interpretive reconstruction distances White's interpretation of death from Nietzsche and brings it closer to Haugeland – her work on the long-vexed topic of what exactly Heidegger means by death should be recognized as one of the twin peaks of more than a half century of scholarship on this difficult topic. Since Dreyfus has already made a forceful case for a slightly reconstructed version of White's interpretation of death, what I propose to do here – in hopes of expanding the critical discussion of White's original and provocative book beyond that text itself and into the larger issues it raises – is to step back and examine her more general hermeneutic strategy of reading Heidegger's early magnum opus, *Being and Time*, back through the interpretive lens of his later work. This strategy of "retrospective reading" forms the background for White's interpretation of

---

[2] See Dreyfus, "Foreword"; Dreyfus nicely summarizes his interpretive overview on p. xxxi.
[3] Heidegger scholars will want to read Dreyfus's Preface for themselves, because this comprehensive work by the philosopher who was at the time the world's leading expert on *Being and Time* critically synthesizes almost every major interpretation of Heidegger on death then extant, thereby providing a significant contribution to our understanding of Heidegger – one with respect to which many interpreters of Heidegger's views on death will need to situate themselves. Apropos of which, my own view of what the early Heidegger means by "death" in *Being and Time* remains closest to Blattner's (though I would also reconstruct Blattner's view differently than Dreyfus does, and take myself to have develop Blattner's original insight well beyond the point at which Blattner himself left it) Still, I agree with Dreyfus that the later Heidegger's more mature view was (in 2005) most helpfully approached in terms of the hybrid, White–Haugeland view Dreyfus recommends. For me a crucial question, then, is: Can we not have the best of both views, simply by recognizing the real and important differences between Heidegger's early and later work and critiquing both accordingly? (I try to motivate this idea in what follows, but see also Chapters 2 and 3.)

death, as Dreyfus recognizes (ix), and by explicitly focusing on this background here, I shall be able say more about what White's original method of reading Heidegger backward reveals as well as what it conceals, and then conclude by suggesting how we might develop the best of these insights while eliminating the blind spots that still accompany them in White's path-breaking work.[4]

5.2 White's Reading: Unorthdox Orthodoxy

Despite my title, White does not actually take herself to be reading Heidegger backward, for that would require the later Heidegger to have said something that the early Heidegger did not already say, some philosophical insight unique to his later work that would be capable of casting a new and revealing light on his early work. As White puts it, however: "There is no distinct 'early' and 'late' Heidegger, in my view, only earlier and later ways of saying the same thing" (2). Surface similarities notwithstanding, White's claim that the early and later Heidegger *say the same thing* is not a reflexive application of Heidegger's provocative claim that "all great thinkers think the same," his idea that great thinkers think from (and so circle around) an "unthought" insight (viz., their own unique view about the meaning of being) that they never fully manage to put into words. Nor is it a version of his closely related but more mystical idea that all the great thinkers were really struggling in this way to put *the same* ultimate reality into words, but that this reality is "so essential and so rich that no single thinker exhausts it" (N1 36/NI 46).[5]

---

[4] François Raffoul, *Heidegger and the Subject*, trans. by D. E. Pettigrew and G. Recco (Amherst, NY: Humanities, 1999) provides another example of this surprising hermeneutic strategy of reading Heidegger backward, perhaps not surprisingly, since Raffoul is a student of Derrida, who, despite his own anti-orthodox predilections, also employs this very same orthodox strategy when reading Heidegger, creatively but often misleadingly reading the later Heidegger back into *Being and Time* (see, for example, Jacques Derrida, *Heidegger: The Question of Being and History* [Chicago: University of Chicago Press, 2016], a book based on lectures originally delivered in 1964-65). I return to Derrida's fascinating but problematic readings of Heidegger in Chapter 7 (though the topic is rich and complex enough to merit its own book).

[5] For Heidegger, "the same" (*das Selbe*) is distinguished from "the identical" (*das Gleich*) by the fact that there is always some *difference* between two things that are the same. (I explain Heidegger's puzzling but important claims about "the same" in Thomson, *Heidegger on Ontotheology*, 23-8.) To be clear, then: The orthodox Heideggerians labor under the illusion that the early and later Heidegger think being in ultimately identical ways (which is false and misleading, as we saw in Chapter 2). They do not merely point out that the early and later Heidegger both think "the same" in the later Heidegger's special sense (which would be true only *if* taken to mean that both early and later Heidegger think *being*, albeit under crucially *different* descriptions, such that the early Heidegger makes the metaphysical mistake *par excellence* of reducing "being as such" to

White's claim – that Heidegger's early and later works are "saying the same thing" – is more mundane and yet just as provocative: White really means that there is no essential difference between Heidegger's early and later philosophy. Heidegger's later works obviously look different from *Being and Time* (most obviously, by employing a more poetic style), but White maintains that "this is not because of a change of mind but rather because of a change of method and a change of language to one not so easily accommodating of the metaphysical misreading that has plagued the early work" (47). In other words, the later Heidegger never changed his mind philosophically, he just changed his method and style so that he could present *the same philosophy* in a way that would resist the "metaphysical misreading" (by others) that befell his initial presentation of this philosophy in *Being and Time*.

What, then, was the disastrous metaphysical misreading that motivated Heidegger's drastic stylistic metamorphosis shortly after *Being and Time*? White's answer is again surprising; the problem to which Heidegger's later style is a response was the "personalistic misreading of the whole text of *Being and Time*" (117). Or, as White provocatively puts it: "Reading [Heidegger] as any sort of an existentialist was a mistake on our part" (2). The common view that *Being and Time* seeks to describe, and so help readers to achieve, genuine individuality or personal authenticity is a "metaphysical misreading," White thinks, because this reading of Heidegger as an existentialist follows from (what Heidegger himself later called) the metaphysics of *subjectivism* (or metaphysical "humanism"), that is, the historical process by which conscious self-awareness became so foregrounded in our philosophical analyses that the human "subject" was first divorced from and then eventually came to eclipse the independent significance of the broader reality of which this human being was originally an integral part. Just so, White believes, a reader like Sartre so foregrounds Heidegger's existential analyses of the meaning of human being that these analyses come to eclipse the ("fundamental ontological") understanding of the meaning of being in general that they were ultimately meant to illuminate (as we saw in Chapters 1 and 2).[6] White thus holds that "it is a mistake to understand Heidegger's discussion [of matters such as death, conscience, and authenticity] as dealing only *or even directly* with the personal level" (101, my emphasis). The hard-line White takes here, in other words, is

---

"the being of entities," a mistake the later Heidegger dedicates his thinking to helping us recognize and transcend).

[6] Although this is too large a topic to develop here, I do not think this standard Heideggerian reading of Sartre is entirely fair, because even in Sartre's *Being and Nothingness*, Sartre too meant his analyses of the individual subject to reveal the structure of a more encompassing reality. But it is true (as we will see in Chapter 7) that Sartre remains within the subject/object dichotomy *Being and Time* undermines, and thus (from a Heideggerian perspective) seems to disastrously re-Cartesianize Heidegger's work in his creative appropriations of it.

that, however illuminating Heidegger's discussions in *Being and Time* might be about such recognizably existential topics as the significance of death, the meaning of conscience, and the achievement of individual authenticity, such illumination is only incidental, an indirect flash at best, borrowed from a light Heidegger is really casting elsewhere. Less metaphorically put, the existential analytic of Dasein is intended merely to be propaedeutical to the discovery of the meaning of being in general (or "fundamental ontology"). And, if the existential analytic of Dasein is important *only* as preparatory to fundamental ontology, then, White suggests, "[t]he ontological level of the whole discussion in the second half of *Being and Time* [needs to be] shifted from the personal and subjective to the cultural and historical" (l).[7]

---

[7] A lot turns here on the thorny question of how exactly one understands the role that Heidegger's analysis of Dasein is supposed to play in his broader investigation of the question of being: Is that analysis merely propaedeutical (like a Wittgernsteinian ladder to be climbed up and then kicked away), as White rather narrowly construes it, or is Dasein not rather the pathway supposed to lead directly to (or open out upon, via temporality) the meaning of being in general? If the latter (as some of White's own analyses suggest), that is, if the existential phenomenology of Dasein (or being-here) is supposed to disclose the temporal horizons that constitutively condition the broader meaning of being in general, then we need not choose between the individual and ontological readings of *Being and Time*, for we can affirm (with the early Heidegger, as we saw in the first two chapters) that the experience of the individual provides the only possible phenomenological path to that fundamental ontology Heidegger was indeed searching for – fortunately, since that search was itself in vain (as we saw in Chapter 2). But then we would also need to acknowledge, as Heidegger himself was typically loath to do (but see Chapter 2, nn. 16–17), that *Being and Time* failed to deliver on its main promissory note; the pathway Heidegger thought would lead directly from Dasein to the meaning of being in general crumbled away beneath him as he walked along it. As we saw in Chapter 2, in fact, the high water mark of the project of "fundamental ontology" is reached in 1929's *Kant and the Problem of Metaphysics*, where Heidegger tries to show how Kant's categories of being can be derived from the way Dasein experiences time, such that, for example, we *necessarily* experience the world in terms of the category of substance – that idea of something unchanging which "stands beneath" everything that changes – because our experience of the world is always conditioned by our sense that it is "now." (Notice that, if true, that view would make *the metaphysics of substance* unavoidable, rather than something that, in fact, the later Heidegger repeatedly seeks to deconstruct and help move us beyond.) In the mid-1930s, Heidegger abandons this "temporal idealism," which sought to generate the constitutive conditions of intelligibility out of Dasein''s self-temporalizing, as "subjectivism" (as Blattner suggests in his aptly titled book, *Heidegger's Temporal Idealism*). Once the path from Dasein's temporality to fundamental ontology crumbled, Heidegger had either to admit that he had been wrong (which he rarely does) or else provide revisionist reinterpretations of what he had originally been saying back in *Being and Time* (the path he usually takes, and on which White follows him, as do all those called *orthodox* Heideggerians for this very reason). The middle Heidegger even tries for a time to imagine a path leading directly to being itself which need not pass through the privileged site of Dasein (a seemingly "quietistic" path on which all individual agency threatens to disappear, absorbed into the greater "destiny" of the history of being). But this is a temporary

It is this attempted hermeneutic shift – from the personal to the historical – that paves the way for White's original and creative interpretations of Heidegger's famous discussions of such phenomena as "death," "authenticity," and "conscience," phenomena White reads not as existential descriptions of experiences shared by many individuals but, instead, as Heidegger's somewhat "convoluted" way of articulating "cultural and historical" phenomena that are of the greatest ontological importance (li), since they transform a culture's historical understanding of what is and what matters, and are also extremely rare, since only a handful of Promethean individuals have ever experienced the phenomena of death and authenticity directly. Remember that, as I mentioned at the beginning, White takes "death" to be Heidegger's way of describing the collapse of an historical understanding of being which creates the space for Dasein authentically to disclose a new historical understanding of being and so inaugurate a new age.[8] As she puts it, "Heidegger regards authentic

and untenable view (itself an overreaction against his early reduction of being to "the being of entities" [BT 29/SZ 9]), and thus a deeply problematic moment in the transitional middle period of Heidegger's development recently rediscovered and hypostatized by the (avowedly) "metaphysical" interpretation advanced in Richard Capobianco's *Heidegger's Being: The Shimmering Unfolding* (Toronto: University of Toronto Press, 2022). (Capobianco is also overcorrecting here, but not, like Heidegger, in response to *Being and Time*'s metaphysical conflation of "the being of entities" with "being as such" [that inexhaustible phenomenon Heidegger first called "the nothing," as we saw in Chapter 3] but, instead, in response to the recent reassertion of the orthodox view that Heidegger *never* changed his mind philosophically in Thomas Sheehan, *Making Sense of Being: A Paradigm Shift* [London: Rowman & Littlefield, 2015].) Indeed, by 1940, Heidegger decisively rejects the untenable view from the 1930s that Capobianco seizes upon, making clear that "Being is not segregated off by itself, nor does it also keep away; instead, the staying-away of being as such [in the metaphysical tradition that understands being only as the being of entities] is being itself" [N4 214/NII 353, see also N4 217/NII 357]; that is, being's historical disclosure happens through metaphysics and its overflowing excess is encountered *as* "the noth-ing" metaphysics misses. Heidegger's critique of subjectivism thus began as a critique of *Being and Time*, and only later broadens into a critique of the "errancy" of the history of being, which Heidegger thought he too had earlier been caught up in. (I return to these points in Section 5.3 below, but see also Thomson, *Heidegger on Ontotheology*, 54, n. 15.)

[8] "Being toward the ownmost possibility of death discloses Dasein's ownmost being as the entity which makes an issue of being, and it frees Dasein from its current cultural understanding of human nature and the things with which we deal; as Heidegger puts it, Dasein is freed from its lostness in the Anyone. ... Dasein is thrown back upon its ownmost self to determine what can be" (88–9). There are some obvious problems with this as a reading of "death" in *Being and Time*. For instance, White cannot explain the "certainty" of death, although this is one of death's formal-ontological characteristics, according to Heidegger. On White's view, "existential death ... is by no means a certain or inevitable actuality or eventuality for everyone" (84); on the contrary, it is exceedingly rare (experienced only by world-historically transformative thinkers like Jesus and Descartes). Moreover, White's interpretation of another of death's formal-ontological features, viz., that it cannot be "overtaken" (77), turns on her creative but untenable transformation of

5.2. WHITE'S READING: UNORTHODOX ORTHODOXY

disclosedness as something quite rare and ... not just a matter of adopting a certain attitude toward one's life or behaving in a certain way" (119). For White, the linked phenomena of death and authentic disclosedness do not directly concern the individual person at all but, rather, seek to describe the way a few rare individuals experience the collapse of the ontological self-understanding that had been guiding the age. White, quoting Heidegger's work from the 1930s, says that death is the collapse of a historical world that uncovers a "reservoir of the not-yet revealed" (55), the ontological "well" of history from out of which this same Promethean individual authentically discloses a new understanding of being and so inaugurates a new age.[9]

This "well" of history, encountered in death, is being, and White describes this revolutionary encounter with a poetic, almost visionary elegance:

> Authentic Dasein is the one who reaches into the depths of this well to find a new star, a new way of understanding the being of what-is, that becomes the culture's new starting point as it navigates the twilight between its old world and the new way of disclosing its world that glimmers on the horizon. Nietzsche could see in a lightning flash that God was dead, that will to power ruled what-is, but it took the thunder, the shattering impact of this revelation, another half century to reach the ears of the anyone. (75)

White is virtually channeling Heidegger here, and her powerfully evocative description lets one who has studied Heidegger's late essay on Georg Trakl see how Heidegger himself probably understood the symbolism of the starred well outside his famous "hut" in Todtnauberg. Still, one might wonder why White thinks that the same rare individual who experiences the collapse of the ontology previously guiding their age should be fortunate enough also to be

---

"overtaken" (*überholen*), which for Heidegger means *surpassed*, that is, moved past or left behind, into "taken over," that is, *appropriated*. As she has it: "what lies beyond that possibility [that is, death] cannot be 'fetched over' by Dasein into its clearing, that is, the possibility cannot be overtaken" (77). Although ingenious as a hermeneutic attempt to reconcile early and later Heidegger and suggestive for thinking about the significance of death in his work as a whole, I shall suggest that this is untenable as a strict reading of *Being and Time* (a fact which will not surprise anyone who has read the preceding chapters of this book).

[9] Here White is quoting from Heidegger's "The Origin of the Work of Art" ([OWA], from 1935), which I classify as a transitional "middle" work, since in it Heidegger has discovered the history of being (at least a simplified version which has only three epochs) but he is still attempting to square this ontological history (or epochal *historicity*) with his earlier idea of a fundamental ontology. He thus explains the historical epochs in terms of a *regress* from an original ontological plenitude – a halfway story (on the way to his later understanding of being's inexhaustibility), but one that White projects all the way to the end of Heidegger's career, thereby generalizing the philosophically unstable views of the middle Heidegger. (See Thomson, *Heidegger, Art, and Postmodernity*, ch. 3, esp. 66–72.)

the one to disclose a new understanding of being for the next age. Why not think instead, for example, that lots of individuals will temporarily experience the more or less total collapse of their world, but only a very few will respond by disclosing a whole new world for themselves and for their ages, rather than just finding some new and more reflexive way to reconnect to their old world?[10]

White's considered view seems to be that the authentic discloser of a new world recognizes the death of the old world precisely by recognizing the new understanding of being waiting in the wings to replace the old; that is, the death of the old is seen only in the birth of the new.[11] As White thus puts it (drawing explicitly from the later Heidegger's readings of Hegel [56–60] and Trakl [22]), "death is not decay but rather a matter of leaving behind the form of man that has decayed. In Western history, the rational animal died for Dasein to become the image of God; God's favorite creature died for Dasein to become the conscious subject" (22), and, we should add (to update White's story), the conscious subject is now dying as Dasein becomes merely another intrinsically meaningless "resource" (*Bestand*) standing by to be optimized; and, moreover, this "technological" understanding of Dasein as a mere human resource will need to die in order for Dasein to be reborn once again in a non-nihilistic form (on the far side of our late modern age of enframing).[12]

Heidegger's philosophical vision of historical salvation is much more easily described than accomplished, however, since on White's view: "Exhorting someone to 'Be authentic!' makes as much sense, or as little, as exhorting them to be another Plato or Nietzsche" (43). White still finds reason for hope, nonetheless, because she reads *Being and Time*'s discussion of "conscience ... as what has kept Dasein continually questioning what it is to be for over 2500 years and has prevented us from remaining satisfied with any one answer" (112). Conscience, on her reading, testifies to our perennial

---

[10] For such a view of death, see Chapter 4. (See also the complex account articulated in Charles Spinoza, Fernando Flores, and Hubert L. Dreyfus, *Disclosing New Worlds: Entrepreneurship, Democratic Action, and the Cultivation of Solidarity* [Cambridge, MA: The MIT Press, 1997], and the neo-Freudian one developed by Lear in *Radical Hope*.)

[11] See also 160: "The new world which is coming to be is disclosed to authentic Dasein as already there."

[12] (I explain and defend the later Heidegger's philosophical vision of a more meaningful *postmodern* age beyond modern subjectivism and late-modern enframing in Thomson, *Heidegger, Art, and Postmodernity*.) Trakl (1887–1914) was a young German poet (supported, like Rilke, by Wittgenstein) who killed himself during World War I and whom Heidegger seems to have understood as a visionary whose poetry transmutes the tragic cataclysm of war into a historically redemptive experience by offering a vision of the historical emergence of a unified human "race" (*Geschlecht*). See Heidegger's 1952 essay, "Language in the Poem" (OWL 159–98/GA12 31–78). See also Ian Alexander Moore, *Dialogue on the Threshold: Heidegger and Trakl* (Albany, NY: SUNY, 2022).

5.2. WHITE'S READING: UNORTHODOX ORTHODOXY

ontological *restlessness*. Such restlessness might seem uniquely well-fitted to our current technological understanding of all entities as intrinsically meaningless resources awaiting optimization, the agitated late-modern ontology of a "constant becoming" (Nietzsche) that is accelerating all entities into "a state of pure circulation" (Baudrillard), but in fact the phenomenon of conscience suggests that *this too shall pass* (into the *postmodern*).[13] White, looking at the inner structure of "the conflict in the interpretation of the being of what-is," finds hope in the idea that this ontological conflict of interpretations "cannot be put to rest. Every interpretation leaves out something about the appearance of being and thus leaves something unsaid that the next creator will try to say" (164).

There is a final complication, however. Until now, these Promethean creators found something new to say about being by returning to the well of untapped possibilities left over by the Greek inception of metaphysics, but this well is now tapped dry; as White says, "we have run out of possibilities for new metaphysical conceptions of the being of what-is" (164). White adopts Heidegger's claim that metaphysics is coming to an end (although to be able to explain *why*, White would need to discuss Heidegger's crucial view of metaphysics as *ontotheology*, which she leaves out of her account). Nevertheless, White reasons, because "being always prepares a path for itself over and beyond whatever is at any particular time" (160), we can still learn to understand being in a new, non-nihilistic way. Indeed, we will once again be able to recognize and restore the intrinsic meaning to entities, if only we can learn to practice a phenomenological comportment sensitive to the "Appropriation" (her somewhat old-fashioned translation of *Ereignis*), an ontological truth *event* that – even after the end of ontotheology – still "takes away that which is its own from boundless unconcealment" (as Heidegger puts it in the 1962 essay, "Time and Being," in a passage White quotes [162]).

Obviously, such ideas ring rather differently from the measured tones of *Being and Time*. (White's quasi-agential interpretation of being, most notably, is redolent of a conflation of Heidegger's "being" with a benevolent and omniscient God, a rather telling misinterpretation long common among Heidegger's orthodox readers.) Yet, for White there is nothing new to be found even in the later Heidegger's famous notion of *Ereignis*, which she reads simply as Heidegger's later way of spelling out the implications already contained in the early notion of *Eigentlichkeit*. *Ereignis* might be the later Heidegger's preferred name for a genuine ontological "event," a revolutionary insight that can help inaugurate the next stage in the history of being (its postmodern "other beginning"), but White suggests that *Being and Time*

---

[13] See Jean Baudrillard, *The Transparency of Evil: Essays on Extreme Phenomena*, trans. by J. Benedict (London: Verso, 1993), 4.

already understood the authentic *Augenblick* as a "moment of insight" that "discloses the being of what-is" (114). With the support of some of Heidegger's most spectacular etymological acrobatics, White reads *Ereignis* back into *Eigentlichkeit* and maintains that, already in *Being and Time*, the authentic moment of resolute "[i]nsight is in fact the 'happening' in which Dasein lets itself be taken up into the Appropriation of being" (159).[14]

5.3 Reading White

Although I find White's views creative, insightful, and extremely suggestive, they are not without some deeply problematic presuppositions and implications that need to be more critically explored.[15] White's ingenious

---

[14] Guided by Heidegger's own later remarks, White connects the *Augenblick* of authenticity to the ontological truth event of *Ereignis* not, as one might expect, by emphasizing that *Eigentlichkeit* and *Ereignis* both stem from *eigen*, "own or proper" but, ironically, by denying this derivation in the case of *Ereignis* in favor of a more speculative etymology that roots *Ereignis* in the "eye" (*Auge*), deriving it from the archaic verb *eräugnen*, "'to place before the eyes' or 'to catch sight of'" (158). White also draws on marginalia Heidegger appended to his 1946 "Letter 'On Humanism'" in which he suggests that we need "to think of *Eigentlichkeit* as the '*Eignen des Er-eignens*,' that is, as the belonging to the coming to pass of the *Ereignis*" (159). Although, in fact, the meaning of Heidegger's use of *Ereignis* changes over time (as Polt has clearly shown), White does pick out one of his main ways of using this crucial term during his middle period especially, viz., to designate the revolutionary insights that effect epochal breaks in the history of being. (See Richard Polt, "*Ereignis*," in *A Companion to Heidegger*, eds. by Hubert L. Dreyfus and Mark A. Wrathall [Oxford: Blackwell, 2005] and Thomson, *Heidegger, Art, and Postmodernity*, ch. 6.)

[15] Problems emerge when one puts White's interpretations of death and conscience together; on White's view, new understandings of being are decaying on arrival, such that only the questioning which generates new understandings of being is genuinely authentic – all new answers are not. As she writes: "Authentic insight lies deeper than the spoken or written word, and it has already become the banal chatter of the Anyone by the time it can be stated in mere words" (167). Once expressed, even such revolutionary insight "ceases to be authentic and becomes commonplace"; it remains "authentic insight ... [only] when it still involves the same fundamental questioning of what it is to be" (126). Insofar as this idea of "continuous questioning" forgets epochality (that is, Heidegger's claim that the history of intelligibility divides into three ages made up of at least five overlapping historical epochs), it sounds more like Levinas than Heidegger (treating being as *ineffable* instead of *inexhaustible*), and insofar as it forgets "preserving" (that is, Heidegger's idea that we are called upon to try to creatively disclose the most meaningful insights from older understandings of being in order to help inaugurate a new one beyond modernity), it sounds more like Nietzsche (or even Derrida) than Heidegger. (On the crucial role of such creatively disclosive "preserving," see Thomson, *Heidegger, Art, and Postmodernity*, ch. 3). Dreyfus brings out the latter problem in his Foreword and suggests that White's Nietzschean emphasis on constant creativity should be synthesized with Haugeland's emphasis on the importance of *preserving*, according to which resolute Dasein is called to "stick with" an understanding of being "without getting stuck with it."

5.3. READING WHITE

readings of Heidegger's discussions of death, authenticity, and conscience in *Being and Time* allow her to present Heidegger's early *magnum opus* as if it were already primarily concerned with the history of being. By creatively reading Heidegger's later insights into the history of being back into *Being and Time* (which is what I mean by "reading Heidegger backward"), White is able to make a completely uncompromising claim for the unity of Heidegger's thought. And indeed, if Heidegger was already illuminating the structure of the history of being in Division II of *Being and Time* – and thus already distinguishing between the different epochal understandings of "the being of entities" that metaphysical ontotheologies stabilize historically, on the one hand, and, on the other, that conceptually inexhaustible "noth-ing," "earth," or "being as such" that enables metaphysics to do so and yet is constantly overlooked by metaphysics (just as it is also overlooked by the early Heidegger's own metaphysical quest for a fundamental ontology, as we saw in Chapters 2 and 3) – then there would not be two separate halves of Heidegger's work to try to connect. Instead, the simple unity of Heidegger's entire career of thought would become clear.

Now, anyone who has studied the voluminous literature on the contentious question of how to understand the relation between the early and the later Heidegger will know that enthusiastic assertions of the fundamental unity of Heidegger's work are a dime a dozen among the Heideggerian faithful. But what gives White's untenably monistic view of Heidegger its substance and traction is her unqualified claim that, even when we adopt the perspective of Heidegger's later work, "no retreat from or retraction of the basic points of *Being and Time* is necessary" (35). White thus thinks it a problem that "Heidegger seems to have no a priori guarantee that his own philosophy is not another episode in the history of being" (29), and she even understands the consecutive epochs in Heidegger's history of being as a series of "new orientation[s] to the ready-to-hand" (155). As Dreyfus rightly points out, however, Heidegger's ontology of the ready-to-hand in Division One of *Being and Time* looks, from the perspective of the later Heidegger's "history of being" (his historical account of the different ways metaphysics understands the being of entities), like the penultimate stage in this history of growing *nihilism*, because understanding the being of entities in terms of their practical use by Dasein is almost as instrumentalizing as their current reduction to meaningless resources awaiting optimization (in our own late-modern epoch

(It should also be noted that Haugeland does not read later Heidegger back into early, since he does not have much interest in the later Heidegger; instead, he reaches conclusions very similar to White's *via* the more straightforward hermeneutic path of a highly creative rereading of *Being and Time* itself, one that merits its own careful and critical reading in turn.)

of *enframing*).¹⁶ But by reading Heidegger backward – by reading the later notion of *Ereignis* back into the early notion of *Eigentlichkeit*, for example – White eliminates any need to account for what most interpreters would take to be the glaring philosophical differences between Heidegger's early and later views, including, most centrally, his radically transformed understanding of being (which only emerged from the death of Heidegger's own early metaphysical ambitions, as we saw in Chapter 2).

Now, for many of us, I suspect, White's uncompromising defense of Heidegger – a figure who, on her reading, never changes his mind, never needs to retract or fundamentally transform the claims he set forth in *Being and Time* (as if his philosophy were born full-grown in his early and *unfinished* text, like wisdom from the head of Zeus) – all this will sound too hagiographic, too excessively faithful, almost more Heideggerian than Heidegger himself.¹⁷ In my view, it is in this orthodox disposition of White's reading that her important work most problematically shows its age, the mark of that incredibly polarized scholarly audience for which White first conceived and began writing her book forty years ago, in which one had to be either for or against Heidegger.¹⁸ That absurdly simplistic imperative is finally giving way to more balanced approaches (in Heidegger scholarship, if not, sadly, in American politics). Indeed, who among Heidegger's most ardent admirers today would deny that he was a philosophical giant with feet of clay? In the right mood and company, we might even debate which of Heidegger's character flaws was the greatest.¹⁹ The most philosophically significant of these

---

[16] See Hubert L. Dreyfus, "Heidegger's History of the Being of Equipment," in *Heidegger: A Critical Reader*, eds., by H. L. Dreyfus and H. Hall (Cambridge, MA: Basil Blackwell, 1992), 173–85, and Thomson, *Heidegger on Ontotheology*, ch. 1.

[17] I document this in Thomson, "The End of Ontotheology" (see esp. pp. 23–35: "Unity, Teleology, and Other Illusions of Hermeneutic Hindsight"). One is reminded of the French saying, "*Il ne faut pas être plus royaliste que le roi* [one need not be more royalist than the king]." Yet, is not such excessive orthodoxy one of the subtler forms a certain *independence* can take? (And so, in the political context, the path to a certain form of treason, or in religion, to heresy?) We might recall, moreover, that even Athena modified her views over the course of time, or so Euripides suggests in the *Bacchae*.

[18] I address this point in more detail in Thomson, *Heidegger on Ontotheology*, 78–84.

[19] Megalomania, mendacity, unquenchable philosophical ambition, unbridled lasciviousness – perhaps these form a recognizable cluster ("narcissism," or the "narcissistic self disorder") and follow from a common root: in the typical case for a man, abundant (perhaps even excessive) love from his mother, building and strengthening his ego, coupled with an emotionally distant father, undermining the son's ego strength and thereby leaving him with a recurring sense that nothing he does will be good enough to please his father (and the patriarchal authorities the father often first stands in for and represents), hence the so-called "superiority complex," which is really a bipolar superiority–inferiority complex. Of course, Heidegger had considerable virtues as well, including first and foremost his truly exceptional philosophical talent, creativity, and dedication (for which I remain profoundly grateful, my own strong criticisms notwithstanding).

faults, however, was surely Heidegger's nearly constitutional incapacity to admit his own mistakes. The damage done to Heidegger's philosophical reputation by his refusal ever to apologize publicly for his Nazi affiliation is only the most disturbing consequence of this fault. Another, less obvious (and occasionally even amusing) consequence can be found in Heidegger's frequent later attempts to provide revisionist reinterpretations of his earlier views, retroactively rereading them so that they will not contradict his later insights (offering creative rereadings that White accepts at face value and follows enthusiastically).[20]

A large question that critical interpreters of Heidegger's body of work must eventually face is: How should we approach Heidegger's retrospective remarks concerning his earlier work? Because these frequent rereadings run the gamut from plausible and insightful, to suggestive but dubious, all the way to bizarre and ridiculous, the only general hermeneutic principle we can rely on is to approach these retrospective reinterpretations individually and with caution. Still, a student of Heidegger's retrospective remarks could be forgiven for taking them as evidence for the once controversial but now widely accepted view that authors' self-interpretations never settle difficult questions concerning the meaning of their work, since authors are only their own first readers, and not even necessarily their own *best* readers. Indeed, reading Heidegger's own violent attempts to fit the square peg of his early philosophy into the round hole of his later thought would make anyone hesitate to assent to the received view that an author has privileged access to the meaning of his or her own words. This issue leads to some large hermeneutic questions, such as whether the "best" interpretation is the scholarly one that most faithfully captures the meaning of the original in its original context, even at the price of showing it to be wrong, or, on the contrary, the more charitable interpretation that most forcefully asserts the truth of the original by updating its context and creatively altering its meaning.[21] Rather than discuss the matter in the abstract (or in another context), however,

---

[20] Again, these rereadings are much less amusing in the political context, as, for example, when the later Heidegger writes to a young admirer insisting that what many of us took to be the worst line he ever published – viz., the rightly infamous "The Führer alone *is* the present and future German reality and its law" – can be restored to its true but hidden meaning and so vindicated politically once those who have learned the task of reading notice the stress he in fact placed on the "*is*" ... Indeed, staring too long into such a rhetorical abyss will make anyone question Heidegger's reliability as a guide to the meaning of his own earlier work. (See Heidegger, "German Students," in Richard Wolin, ed., *The Heidegger Controversy* [New York: Columbia University Press, 1991], 47.)

[21] Those to whom the answer seems obvious might pause to consider the example of Michael Friedman's and Henry Allison's different ways of interpreting the relation between Kant's view of space (in Immanuel Kant, *The Critique of Pure Reason*, eds. and trans. by Paul Guyer and Allen W. Wood [Cambridge: Cambridge University Press, 1998], second analogy) and Newtonian science. Friedman (in Michael Friedman, *Kant and the Exact Sciences* [Cambridge, MA: Harvard University Press, 1998]) situates Kant's

let us examine one of the main examples White relies on to justify her strategy of reading Heidegger backward.

Heidegger's famous 1935 essay, "The Origin of the Work of Art," contains several retrospective reinterpretations of *Being and Time*, published eight years earlier. Eight years might not seem like a lot of time (and this lends Heidegger's remarks more plausibility), but in fact a great deal transpired between 1927 and 1935, not just politically but philosophically as well. Of the transformations in Heidegger's philosophical views during these years, the single most consequential is Heidegger's dawning recognition of the profound importance of *historicity*, the fact that being, and so our being-in-the-world, has a changing history in terms of which it must be understood. Heidegger's recognition of the profound importance of the fact that humanity's most basic sense of reality shifts profoundly over time is a lesson hard-won from the "deconstruction" of the history of ontology that *Being and Time* called for, yet Heidegger's insight into historicity turns out, ultimately, to be incompatible with such central doctrines of *Being and Time* as Heidegger's belief in and pursuit of a historically immutable *fundamental ontology* (or "meaning of being in general"), his apparent attribution of an a priori, ahistorical status to the three main existential structures of Dasein, and his ahistorical understanding of being in terms of readiness-to-hand.[22] Taking such incompatibilities as expressions of the irreconcilable differences between the early and later Heidegger, most contemporary scholars would now agree that Heidegger's insight into the historicity of being – and so his recognition that being cannot be reduced to any metaphysical understanding of the being of entities – constitutes the *sine qua non* of his "later" work.[23]

---

philosophy firmly in its historical context and thereby argues that Kant's Euclidean understanding of space has been falsified by the non-Euclidean space of relativity theory, while Allison pries Kant loose from this context to "reconstruct and defend" his thought as a viable position in the contemporary landscape (see Henry Allison, *Idealism and Freedom* [Cambridge: Cambridge University Press, 1996], 80–1). For a thoughtful consideration of this hermeneutic continuum in relation to the specific question of how best to read Heidegger in particular, see Wrathall and Londen, "Anglo-American Existential Phenomenology."

[22] (*"Readiness-to-hand is the way in which entities as they are 'in themselves' are defined ontologico-categorially"* [BT 101/SZ 71].) To recognize this incompatibility, it helps not to confuse *historicity* (the later Heidegger's insight that our bedrock sense of what-is changes over time) with *Being and Time*'s attempt to define *historicality* (the ontological issue of what history *is*, with which the early Heidegger hoped to found and unify the disciplines that study history, as we saw in Chapter 1), despite the fact that Heidegger sometimes uses the same word, *Geschichtlichkeit*, to designate both his later thinking of historicity (as the history of being) and his early thinking of historicality (or the being of history); see Chapter 2, n. 25.

[23] (Sheehan is the most influential exception here.) Further complicating matters is the fact that Heidegger himself would later date his "turn" to 1929, to the essay "On the Essence

For the same reason, however, Heidegger himself would certainly reject this contemporary scholarly consensus (at one point he even denigrates the view that he changed his mind this way as "insidious" [OWL 20/GA12 104]), and in this White is entirely in agreement with Heidegger. White (110) thus quotes Heidegger's 1935 remark that:

> The resoluteness [Heidegger hyphenates *Ent-schlossenheit*, thereby connoting "un-closedness," as we saw in Chapter 4] intended in *Being and Time* is not the deliberate action of a subject but rather the opening up of Dasein, out of the captivity to entities [*Befangenheit im Seienden*], toward the openness of being. (PLT 67/GA5 55)

Heidegger's explanation is slightly overloaded; let us grant that *resoluteness* is not the action of a "subject," since *Being and Time* seeks to undercut the subject/object dichotomy and replace it with a recognition of Dasein as a being-in-the-world (a more basic dimension of human practice in which self and world are integrally interconnected and mutually constituting). Setting that rather large issue aside, Heidegger's main retrospective claim here in 1935 is that when *Being and Time* describes that "resoluteness" whereby a Dasein whose practical world has collapsed in existential death finds a way to reconnect to its world, this reconnection is not the result of a deliberate *decision*. Dasein, confronting the "nothing" in being-toward-death, does not reconnect to its world by "choosing to choose" (as Heidegger did in fact say several times in *Being and Time*); instead, Dasein reconnects to its world by opening up to its futural being in a way that allows our "being here" to transcend the uncanny captivity of its *solus ipse* to the worldless nothingness of insignificant, objective entities (BT 231-2/SZ 187). As suggested earlier (at the end of Chapter 1 and in Chapter 2), I think Heidegger is making a deep point here (a point that White's connection of *Eigentlichkeit* and *Ereignis* helps suggest) – namely, that the "nothing" discovered in being-toward-death was, it turned out, Heidegger's first phenomenological glimpse of the "presencing" of being as such, that is, of the way being as such makes itself felt within our current metaphysical age of enframing, in which, as White rightly puts it, "Being reveals itself by holding itself back" (160), showing up only as a *nothing*, albeit an active *nothing*

---

of Truth"; his reference is to an unspoken transformation that he claims takes place in the background between the end of Section 5 and the beginning of Section 6, and not, as one might expect, to the history of being which he begins to trace there in terms of the historical transformations in our concept of truth. This reflects Heidegger's own sense that the most crucial difference between his early and later work was his recognition of the "nothing" or concealment as the way being as such makes itself felt (as we saw in Chapter 3), a difficult idea central to his later work, and one that he himself doubted he had ever expressed with sufficient clarity. (See Heidegger, "On the Essence of Truth" [P 148 note a/GA9 193 note a], and also Thomson, *Heidegger, Art, and Postmodernity*, ch. 7.)

whereby (Heidegger only recognized later) being exceeds its reduction to nothing but meaningless stuff to be optimized.[24] In *retrospect*, we can say that Heidegger did indeed first (unknowingly) glimpse the way being itself exceeds the current understanding of the being of entities in his existential analysis of death in *Being and Time*, but to say (as Heidegger himself and White like to) that Heidegger already understood this back in *Being and Time* is to succumb to a retrospective illusion of hermeneutic hindsight and so to read him anachronistically, that is, timelessly, without sufficient sensitivity to the very real breaks, ruptures, and discontinuities through which his work passed as it underwent its often painful evolution – including, most importantly, that existential death and rebirth Heidegger's own thinking had to pass through, reluctantly *dying* to its metaphysical ambitions so as to be reborn as a "thinking" dedicated to transcending metaphysics – a philosophical turn from which that painful personal dimension cannot be entirely shorn (as we saw in Chapter 2).[25] In Heidegger's own case, moreover, his frequent attempts to erase the real *differences* that give his thought its irreducible texture are often neither convincing nor necessary but instead follow from an obsessive desire to have been right all along. I think we can see this if we look a little more closely at the context of the remark from "The Origin of the Work of Art" that White quotes (a context White herself does not mention).

The immediate context for the revisionist rereading of *Being and Time* explored above is Heidegger's extremely provocative claim, in 1935's "The

---

[24] There is some confusion in White's account of the later Heidegger's crucial notion of "presencing" (*Anwesen*). White rightly notes that "[p]resencing is not simply the way that all things show up in Dasein's present, as many commentators seem to suggest" (148, n. 9), but then goes on to make the same conflation of presencing with "presence" (*Anwesenheit*) herself, falsely maintaining, for example, that "[s]cience both ancient and modern is founded on the understanding of the being of what-is as presencing" (149).

[25] Another particularly telling example is that, when Heidegger wrote in *Being and Time* that "the being of entities can least of all ever be something such that 'behind it' stands 'something else' which does not appear. / Behind the phenomena of phenomenology there is essentially nothing [or nothing else, *nichts anderes*]" (BT 60/SZ 35–6), he clearly meant this "nothing" in the sense of nothing at all. Indeed, it was probably only in rereading this line later that Heidegger realized that his words had said something true that he had not meant at the time (indeed, something he had then meant to deny), viz., that humanity's historical understanding of "the being of entities" (established by metaphysical ontotheologies) is made possible by that Ur-phenomenon of his later work which he first calls "the noth-ing of the nothing" (in 1929), then "the earth," then "being as such," and so on (as Chapter 3 showed). I suspect that rereading and retrospectively reinterpreting such lines (and so seeing that, read otherwise, they suggested something true instead of the false claim he had clearly meant them to say at the time) encouraged Heidegger's famous later view that *language speaks us*, rather than the reverse. (But it is still very poor *scholarship* to imagine, on the basis of such suggestive ambiguities, that Heidegger's early view already deliberately articulates insights he in fact only develops later.)

Origin of the Work of Art," that: "He who truly knows what is, knows what he wills to do in the midst of what is [*Wer wahrhaft das Seiende weiß, weiß, was er inmitten des Seienden will*]" (PLT 67/GA5 55). In other words, knowing how to act follows from truly knowing what entities are. The obvious implication is that a genuine philosopher (or "great metaphysician" in Heidegger's sense, that is, someone who genuinely understands "the being of entities") knows what to do in any situation. If one thinks about it a little, it is pretty astounding that Heidegger would reiterate the view that *right practice follows from right ontology* in 1935, the year immediately following his resignation from his failed Rectorate. If one thinks about it a little more, however, then the underlying worry to which he is responding becomes obvious. If right practice follows right ontology, then does not wrong or false practice – as evinced, for example, by a disastrous political decision – entail a false ontology? If he who truly knows (the being of) entities knows what he will do in their midst, then (by *modus tollens*), he who has just been very publicly shown not to have known what to do in their midst looks like he did not truly know entities in the first place. Beneath the surface, in other words, Heidegger seems to be struggling here with a recognizable version of the worry, later debated *ad nauseum* by critics and defenders alike, that his political decision constituted a practical refutation of his philosophical views. Heidegger's response is quite telling, too. Rather than admit that his political decision did in fact follow from a philosophical confusion – indeed, a philosophical confusion (namely, his earlier belief in a transhistorically binding fundamental ontology) that his disastrous political misadventure helped uncover (as I show in *Heidegger on Ontotheology: Technology and the Politics of Education*) – Heidegger instead deconstructs the relation between a historical ontology and a decision of the will. He writes:

> The willing here referred to, which neither merely applies knowledge nor decides beforehand, is thought of in terms of the fundamental experience of thinking [*der Grunderfahrung des Denkens*] in *Being and Time*. Knowing that remains a willing, a willing that remains a knowing, is the existing human being's ecstatic entrance into and compliance with the unconcealedness of being [*ist das ekstatische Sicheinlassen des existierenden Menschen in die Unverborgenheit des Seins*]. (PLT 67/GA5 55)

To will, in other words, really means opening yourself to the way being reveals itself historically.[26] One who seeks to act on history needs first to understand

---

[26] We do this (as we saw in Chapters 1 and 3) by passing through the nothing that existential death discloses and then resolutely reconnecting to that which comes toward us through this noth-ing of futurity (as the self we thereby become). The other big here problem is that Heidegger writes here as if there were only one correct path, project, or existential possibility to be glimpsed within such futurity, rather than an inchoate hinting that always requires our own creative response to disclose it and hence our responsibility

the direction in which the history of being is moving; for, willing against the historical tide of being is like spitting into the wind.

White thinks that "we may well take this language of [being] 'giving' and 'sending' [itself] with a grain of salt, but it seems relatively harmless," since Heidegger's way of making reference to being's "destiny does not indicate some mechanical determinism but rather the way being is revealed to us in the Appropriation" (159). White is right that Heidegger's view does not entail "some mechanical determinism," but that is not the only issue at stake. For critics from Arendt and Löwith to Habermas, Wolin, Zimmerman, Rockmore, and Olafson, we have here evidence for the "burnt fingers thesis," the idea that Heidegger, having scorched his fingers on the stove of ontic political action, subsequently retreated into an ontological quietism, as if taking refuge in the excuse that "being made me do it" – or, as Heidegger really did say, in the closest he ever came to a public apology (and it is not very close), "He who thinks greatly errs greatly."

White thinks such "errancy" [*die Irre*] is Heidegger's later name for an attempt to swim against the tide of the history of being and, reading this idea back into *Being and Time*, White takes errancy to be just a later name for "inauthenticity." This is a mistake, however, since to "err" in Heidegger's ontological sense is not to swim *against* the tide of the history of being but, on the contrary, to be unknowingly carried along by this tide so as to inadvertently develop the understanding of being implicitly guiding one's own historical epoch, just as Heidegger's own middle-period work initially extended Nietzsche's ontotheology instead of contesting and transcending it, as his later work seeks to do. The idea underlying Heidegger's notorious "He who thinks greatly errs greatly," then, is that the only way out of a historical understanding of being is to think it through to its end and so pass beyond it.[27]

I have argued elsewhere that the line of criticism begun by Löwith, amplified by Habermas, and taken over by many others rests on a misunderstanding of

---

for having done so in just that way – a responsibility we cannot simply foist off onto being the way Heidegger himself seeks too often seeks to do.

[27] White reads her misunderstanding of errancy back into "inauthenticity" when she explains inauthenticity as follows: "We do not want to place our understanding of being in question so we try to keep things the way they are, maintain the status quo, and ignore the changing understanding of being even if we are in the midst of it" (136). For Heidegger, however, "[e]rrancy is that within which a particular understanding of being [*Seyn*] must err, which erring alone truly traverses the clearing of refusal – traverses in accord with the clearing of what is lighted up." Errancy does not mean swimming upstream historically, then, but rather following the stream all the way to its end, where it turns into something else, as Heidegger thought his own extreme Nietzscheanism in the 1930s developed Nietzsche's technological ontotheology to exhaustion and, in so doing, opened a path leading beyond it (M 229/GA66 259). Ontohistorically, that is, *the only way out is through* (as we saw earlier). On the middle Heidegger's "errant" extension of Nietzsche, see Thomson, *Heidegger on Ontotheology*, ch. 3.

the real complexity of Heidegger's later thought, but it does present a rather large obstacle to simply accepting his self-understanding, the now seemingly politically compromised view that (as White sympathetically puts it) different existential "situations are made 'possible' by revelations of being" (123).[28] White frequently adopts such apparently quietistic views, asserting, for instance, that "Dasein is rooted in the temporality of being. The changing revelation of being gives Dasein its possibilities: what it is able to be" (14).[29] Since for White the different revelations of being emerge out of Dasein's changing cultural practices, however, there is a circularity problem here. (Which comes first, the revelation of being or the practices of Dasein? Is there not a feedback loop running between human agency and the historical unfolding of intelligibility that prevents us from simply grounding one in the other?) I think White does better to finesse the issue in more carefully wrought statements such as the following: "for Heidegger the motivating force behind history is ... the creative insight of Dasein as the vehicle for the changing disclosure of what it is to be" (123), a statement that does not simply efface the role of creatively disclosive human agency in the historical transformation of intelligibility. Thus, when White asserts that "what is at issue in both notions [of death and authenticity] is not the personal responsibility for individual actions ... but rather Dasein's relationship to being" (112), I want to ask: Why not *both*? Why should sensitivity to the history of being preclude, rather than refine, individual responsibility?

White perhaps comes closest to the view I would recommend when she writes: "For Heidegger, ... the particular person is always the one who understands, makes decisions, and acts, whether these decisions and actions simply define us or help bring about a change in the significance of the culture as a whole, as did Nietzsche's self-reflection," but she immediately goes on to add that: "Only in the [culture transforming] case they are decisions within the realm of authenticity" (37). Remember that, on White's view:

> Heidegger regards authentic disclosedness as something quite rare and ... not just a matter of adopting a certain attitude toward one's life or behaving in a certain way. For example, in his *Introduction to Metaphysics* [1935] he suggests that authentic Dasein creates great works of art, the political organization of the state, and poetry as well as 'thinking' or philosophy. Such works come to focus a new understanding of being. (119)

Notice, however, that, from the suggestion that one must be authentic in order to be the discloser of a new historical world, it does not follow that one must

---

[28] See Thomson, *Heidegger on Ontotheology*, esp. chs. 2–3.
[29] See also 146: "In Dasein's world the paths that guide its resolute decisions about what it is to be are already cleared by being itself through the ways things show themselves to us in our dealings."

be the discloser of a new historical world in order to be authentic. Not only is that inference invalid but it sets the bar much too high for authenticity, with the result – a seeming *reductio* of the view – that only a handful of individuals throughout Western history have ever been authentic! Would it not be more plausible for White instead to maintain that, of the many individuals who have achieved authenticity, only some small subset did so in a way which disclosed a new world for a subsequent historical age? This is, I think, a view once suggested by Dreyfus, who used to think of the relation between authenticity and disclosing a new world as something like the relation between expertise and mastery: An expert, like an Aristotelian *phronimos*, does the right thing at the right time and in the right way (and will be immediately recognized by his or her community as having done so); but a true master inaugurates a new discursive practice, often transforming the old standards of success in the process and so requiring more time to be recognized.[30]

Still, even this reconstructed version of White's view, which makes historical world-disclosure a subset of the class of authentic actions, assumes that only authentic Dasein can focus a new understanding of being, and that is not obviously true. Think of the founding figures of our current technological understanding of being: Was Darwin authentic? Adam Smith? What about Nietzsche himself? White's answer is that authenticity has nothing to do with the "personal" characteristics of an individual, so Nietzsche's insights into will-to-power need not be reflected in his life – but, in fact (*pace* White's explicit consideration of Nietzsche's "sickly, shy personal life" [43]), they were, in *negative*. Nietzsche knew this about himself and generalized from his own case, suggesting that philosophy is always obliquely autobiographical and that these oblique angles can be charted by "the psychologist" who recognizes that the heights of philosophical idealization are often a direct but inverted reflection of a philosopher's unhappy recognition of the depths of failure, weakness, and suffering in his or her own life.[31]

---

[30] Dreyfus himself abandoned the view that world-disclosure is the highest level of mastery and came to think, instead, that there are two fundamentally different accounts of decisive action – viz., the Aristotelian and Pauline understandings of the *kairos* and *Augenblick* – which Heidegger blurs together in his account of resolve in *Being and Time*. As Dreyfus puts it: "A satisfactory interpretation requires clearly distinguishing two experiences of the source, nature, and intelligibility of decisive action," viz., "the Greek act of seizing the occasion" in a virtuoso performance and "the Christian experience of being reborn" that is generalized in historical world-disclosure. See Dreyfus, "Could Anything be More Intelligible than Everyday Intelligibility?" (165–6).

[31] White seems to think that here *authenticity* designates a willing that genuinely knows what is (in the sense just problematized). But as Heidegger recognized, all metaphysics "begins by knowing something unknowable" (N3 5–6/NI 47477), since in fact being can never be reduced without remainder to the being of entities, as metaphysics always seeks to do. The problem, put simply, is that *authenticity* did not yet mean a recognition of being's apparently inexhaustible phenomenological excessiveness, whereby it both

We need not go along with Nietzsche, however, to resist reading the history of being back into *Being and Time*. We do better to acknowledge that in *Being and Time* authenticity does not require the disclosing of a new historical understanding of being, even as we praise White for both glimpsing the crucial link between Heidegger's early insights into Dasein's world-disclosure and his later dawning recognition of the fuller history of being, and also for helping to suggest how to articulate the pivotal role death plays in the development of Heidegger's thought as a whole. Death first reveals the nothing, and later the nothing turns out to have been the way being as such first shows itself to us (because our current ontotheological understanding of the being of entities as eternally recurring will to power reduces being to nothing, dissolving it into "constant becoming").[32] Although she did not grasp all the details, White still deserves a great deal of credit for helping us to glimpse such esoteric but crucial connections in the development of Heidegger's thought, and I think we best pay her insights forward by refining and incorporating them into an interpretation of Heidegger's philosophy more willing to acknowledge the important discontinuities in the fascinating development of his thinking throughout his life (as we have sought to do in this book).[33]

As I have tried to suggest, then, we do well to adopt a slightly reconstructed version of White's view of death as the pivot around which Heidegger's philosophical development turns. Even if, in the end, I do not find White's interpretation of phenomena such as death, authenticity, and conscience convincing as a close reading of *Being and Time*, her views remain extremely suggestive for how we should think about where Heidegger's philosophy went after the implosion – indeed, the existential death – of the fundamental ontological project guiding that early work. I would thus want to treat those portions of White's book in which she reads Heidegger's later views back into *Being and Time* as an ingenious exercise in creative interpretation, a kind of Heideggerian Midrash – that is, a faithful and often fascinating attempt to

---

beckons for and partly informs also yet always also exceeds even our best conceptual and practical efforts to do it justice. (We return to this crucial later Heideggerian insight in Chapters 8 and 9.)

[32] See Thomson, *Heidegger, Art, and Postmodernity*, ch. 1.

[33] Heidegger famously offered Father Richardson the following guidelines for understanding the relationship between his early and later work. "Only by way of what [my early work] has thought does one gain access to what is to be thought by [my later work]. But [my early work] becomes possible only if it is contained in [my later work]" (Pre xxii/ GA16 152). Orthodox readers like White seem to reverse Heidegger's advice and suggest that Heidegger's later thought was already *contained in* his early work, just waiting to be recognized and articulated. I instead read Heidegger, more straightforwardly, as favoring his later work over his earlier and suggesting that, although the later work can only be understood as developing out of the earlier, the early views can only be maintained if they do not contradict the later insights.

dissolve the contradictions in his thought – which, even if it is not always persuasive as a strict interpretation of Heidegger's early work, remains extremely suggestive for deepening our appreciation of his thought as a whole and the scholarly traditions still seeking to work through or come to terms with it.

We have thus seen in this chapter that White downplays the differences between Heidegger's early and later thinking out of an abundance of sympathy toward his work. Given my own efforts to practice a hermeneutic wisdom of the middle way (and so avoid both one-sided extremes of apologetic and dismissal), I think it will be revealing to turn in Chapter 6 to engage with a famous thinker – Levinas – who employs nearly the opposite hermeneutic strategy as White. Critically engaging with Levinas's reading of Heidegger on death, we will see that – out of an abundance of understandable anger and dissatisfaction with Heidegger and his thinking – Levinas exaggerates his own differences from Heidegger's existential phenomenology of death, thereby innovating some important and influential philosophical insights into existential death that (I shall suggest) are better understood as philosophically subtle and precise contestations whereby Levinas seeks to reorient and revise this Heideggerian inheritance.

6

Rethinking Levinas on Heidegger on Death

What are the basic coordinates of the dispute between Heidegger and Levinas over the phenomenology of "death" and its larger ontological or ethical significance? Or, put in the "perfectionist" terms developed in Chapter 4, in what ways do Heidegger and Levinas disagree about how we human beings become genuinely or fully ourselves? Examining the convergences and divergences of Heidegger's and Levinas's phenomenologies of death, this chapter suggests that Heidegger and Levinas both understood themselves as struggling to articulate the requisite ethical response to the great traumas of the twentieth century. By comparing their thinking at this level, I contend, we can better understand the ways in which Levinas genuinely diverges from Heidegger even while building critically on his thinking.

6.1 Heidegger and Levinas: Beyond the Standard View

The explosion of interest in Levinas at the turn of the twenty-first century followed in the wake of a large wave of "post-Farías" furor over Heidegger's Nazism, and not by chance: That earlier eruption of "the Heidegger controversy" cooled into the received view that Heidegger's inability to articulate an ethics demonstrated the blind spot of this otherwise uncircumventable thinker of the twentieth century, and Levinas – a Jewish philosopher who developed his ethical perspective precisely as a post-Heideggerian response to the Holocaust or *Shoah – appeared* to many to be just the right thinker to fill this ethical gap. The standard view here is that Heidegger's own early affiliation with the regime responsible for the horrors of Auschwitz, combined with his subsequent failure ever to even try to come to terms with this great trauma of the twentieth century, render the ethical deficiencies of his ontological perspective obvious and so demonstrate the need to ground Heidegger's ontological thinking in the allegedly more "fundamental" ethical perspective opened up by Levinas. Now, this received view of the relation between Heidegger and Levinas makes for a dramatic narrative, and one with reassuringly unambiguous moral contours, but there are at least two things wrong with it: It gets Heidegger wrong, and, in so doing, it gets Levinas wrong as well.

That the received view misreads Heidegger I shall not dwell on here, except, no doubt a bit too provocatively, to make two minor but controversial points of correction and then draw out some of their admittedly contentious implications. First, it is true that Heidegger, to the end, obstinately refused to publicly repudiate or apologize for his early Nazi affiliation, instead insisting, with forlorn pride, on the self-serving illusion that a very different National Socialism had been possible in the early 1930s, if only more intellectuals had been willing to get their hands dirty – a fantasy Sluga thoroughly vitiates by showing that Hitler never cared a whit for the views of *any* living intellectual.[1] At the same time, however, we also know now that Heidegger's supposedly damning "silence" on the Holocaust is in fact something of a myth.[2] Heidegger, at least, thought he had articulated the philosophical perspective necessary for understanding Auschwitz, as we can tell from the public remarks he made about the death camps in 1949. Quite understandably, it has not been easy for readers to see the point behind Heidegger's shockingly callous and abbreviated treatment of so momentous an issue. Heidegger's nearly constitutional incapacity to admit his own mistakes apparently sat too uncomfortably with the "growing shame" he privately confessed to Jaspers the following year (1950) for him to be able to develop his analysis in any detail.

Nonetheless, as I show in *Heidegger on Ontotheology: Technology and the Politics of Education*, the later Heidegger's central critical insight is that our "technological," Nietzschean ontotheology, which preconceives the being of entities as "eternally recurring will-to-power" – that is, as mere forces coming-together and breaking-apart with no end other than their self-perpetuating increase – works tacitly to shape (or "enframe") our sense of reality, leading us increasingly to transform all entities, human beings disastrously included, into intrinsically meaningless "resources" (*Bestand*) standing by merely to be used with optimal flexibility and efficiency (2005). Once we recognize this, I think we cannot help but acknowledge that Heidegger's 1949 evocation of the way "the gas chambers and the death camps" reduce human beings to mere "resource materials standing by for the manufacture of corpses [*Bestandstücke eines Bestand der Fabrikation von Leichen*]" indicates that he

---

[1] See Hans Sluga, *Heidegger's Crisis: Philosophy and Politics in Nazi Germany* (Cambridge, MA: Harvard University Press, 1993), 186–93.

[2] It is true that Heidegger never made a public apology for his Nazi affiliation, a deeply unfortunate matter I discuss, for example, in Thomson, *Heidegger on Ontotheology*, ch. 3 (see esp. 82–4 and n. 288). Traditionally, however, critics of Heidegger's notorious "silence" advance the broader allegation that Heidegger *never* addressed the significance of the Holocaust or *Shoah* in any of his later public speeches or writings and, as I show below, this potentially more damning allegation is false.

understood Auschwitz as an extreme symptom of the "technological" ontotheology undergirding our age (GA79, 56).

Because Heidegger's later work as a whole seeks to help us think beneath and beyond this nihilistic ontotheology, enthusiastic Heideggerians might be tempted to conclude that, rather than simply ignoring Auschwitz, Heidegger, in his own way, dedicated his later career to contesting what he understood to be the ontotheological roots of such devastating historical effects. Yet, whether one finds Heidegger's ontotheological understanding of Auschwitz convincing or not (and I shall suggest strong reasons for finding his view unconvincing in this crucial case, both here and in Chapter 7), such an aggressive strategy of hermeneutic de-Nazification would be rhetorically excessive and misleading, too similar to and so potentially complicitous with the now discredited exculpatory narratives long disseminated by Heidegger and his orthodox apologists. More importantly, such a reading risks obscuring the fact that, even if Heidegger's critique of ontotheology does help us to understand the Holocaust, it does so seemingly only as an afterthought, and certainly not, as with Levinas, as the fundamental philosophical motivation for learning to think *ethically*.

This brings me to the second problem with the received reading of Levinas's relation to Heidegger, which, being less controversial, I shall simply state: Heidegger characterized his later endeavor to address the ontotheological roots of contemporary nihilism as his own "originary ethics," by which he meant that he was developing an *ethics* pitched at the level of the original sense of the Greek word *êthos*, our basic existential comportment or way of being-in-the-world (P 271). Yet, if we connect the first point to this one, then the conclusion that undermines the standard view of Heidegger and Levinas seems to follow inexorably: The later Heidegger's "originary ethics" sought to develop a comportmental attunement he hoped would help us transcend the underlying ontotheology that he held responsible for the greatest traumas of the twentieth century. To be clear, this is precisely not to claim that Heidegger took himself to be articulating an ethical response to the Holocaust in particular. For, Heidegger clearly understood the death camps only as an extreme expression of the same underlying ontotheology that he also saw revealed in such phenomena as Russia's postwar blockade of Germany (which sought to starve human beings for the sake of political leverage) and, much more shockingly, in mechanized agribusiness (by which we treat the earth itself merely as another intrinsically meaningless resource to be optimized). To many of us, Heidegger's comparison of the death camps with mechanized agribusiness sounds almost obscene, and clearly reveals an incredible insensitivity to the real suffering of human beings, whose cries seem almost inaudible from the lofty perspective of the history of being – drowned out, perhaps, by the swan song of the earth itself, to whose somber notes Heidegger's ear remains so singularly trained. As I explain elsewhere, however:

For Heidegger, the traditional farmer is a paradigmatic figure, an exemplary embodiment of the *poietic* mode of disclosure that patiently struggles with the earth in order to creatively bring forth what is hidden there [as we saw in relation to "the nothing" in Chapter 3]. This romantic figure contrasts most starkly with the technological mode of revealing that imposes predetermined ends on nature with minimal regard for any of its meaningful solicitations or inherent possibilities. The technologization of such farming in "mechanized agribusiness" is thus for Heidegger a sacrilegious profanation, and so a particularly ominous sign of our ongoing desecration of the source of genuine meaning, a technologization of the *poietic* itself, as it were. This helps explain, but does not at all excuse, Heidegger's scandalously insensitive (indeed, rather inhuman) comparison of this technologization of farming with the murder of millions of human beings in the Nazi death camps. His own sense of 'shame' got in the way, but he should instead have recognized the death camps as by far the most sacrilegious and devastating form of technologization ever devised.[3]

We return to this fraught issue in Chapter 7 (when we turn to Agamben), but whatever the reason for Heidegger's inability to recognize the horror of Auschwitz in its historical uniqueness (including his own anti-Semitic beliefs), we can conclude that this failure prevents his own "originary ethics" from ever providing a genuinely ethical response to the Holocaust as such. That, however, is not because Heidegger fails to formulate the kind of clear and unambiguous action-guiding principles we need in order to preempt future genocides. That objection is not without merit, but in our context it misses the point that Levinas's own "ethics" – widely celebrated precisely as providing the requisite ethical response to the Shoah or Holocaust – remain "ethical" only in the same sense as Heidegger's "originary ethics." Indeed, Levinas and Heidegger pitch their "ethics" *at precisely the same level*, addressing the basic existential comportment that shapes our everyday interactions rather than providing moral decision procedures. Thus, while their ethical views remain different (in some obvious and some surprisingly subtle ways), neither thinker can simply claim to be the sole proprietor of a more "fundamental" *ethical* perspective, as Levinas liked to do.[4] In the end, of course, it might well turn out that Levinas's ethics represent the more appropriate lesson to be drawn from Auschwitz, in the sense that what I shall call Levinas's *metaphysical humanism*

---

[3] See Thomson, *Heidegger, Art, and Postmodernity*, 106–7, n. 57.
[4] When Levinas claims that his ethical perspective is more fundamental than Heidegger's ontological thinking, his main target is Heidegger's *Being and Time* claim that our only access to "entities" – that is, to anything that in any way "is," including other people – comes through a prior understanding of the *being* of those entities. This, however, is an avowedly metaphysical claim that the later Heidegger definitively rejects and seeks to help us learn to think beyond, as we saw in the first two chapters.

might make for a better firebreak against future genocides than the later Heidegger's ethics of dwelling, but that view needs to be argued for rather than simply asserted, and, I shall suggest at the end, the case for it is less obvious than the received views assume.[5]

In fact, as I have argued elsewhere, Heidegger's and Levinas's ethical views – as two different kinds of *transcendental ethical realism* – remain surprisingly similar. The main difference between them is that Levinas's metaphysical humanism restricts the ethical domain to relations between human beings, whereas Heidegger's ontological humanism more broadly concerns our relations to other nonhuman realms. Levinas himself recognizes this and repeatedly dismisses the Heideggerian concern for our relations to other animals and to nonhuman "things" (including the earth itself) as a return to a pre-Judeo-Christian "paganism." As a consequence, however, Levinas's own metaphysical humanism leads politically to a "speciesism" that remains both phenomenologically problematic and ethically tractionless in a wide range of cases, unable to recognize, let alone resist, what an increasing number of contemporary ethicists now recognize as the almost indiscriminate slaughter of nonhuman animals as well as the broader ecological catastrophe.[6] In other words, if thinking about the Holocaust helps motivate Levinas's humanism, worrying about other kinds of ethico-political disasters reveals the continuing suggestiveness of Heidegger's ethical "paganism," Heidegger's belief that what Levinas calls "alterity" can also be discovered in our relations to things that are not human.

So as to avoid any unnecessary controversy here at the outset, let me make clear that I am not claiming that Heidegger actually succeeded in working through the Shoah, let alone that his limited understanding of it should be accepted or even privileged – for example, as providing philosophical antibodies cultivated from the very subject originally infected with the totalitarian virus, as Lacoue-Labarthe and Dallmayr influentially suggest.[7] I am more inclined to conclude the very opposite, namely, that the Shoah is precisely what Heidegger's critique of ontotheology *cannot* explain, and what thus reveals the limits of the critical perspective distinctive of his later thought. I think Heidegger's understanding of Auschwitz as an extreme expression of

---

[5] The later Heidegger is not the "antihumanist" he is often taken to be; see Chapter 8 and Thomson, "Hearing the Pro-Vocation within the Provocation."

[6] I develop the former argument in Thomson, "Ontology and Ethics at the Intersection of Phenomenology and Environmental Philosophy."

[7] The seminal text here is Philippe Lacoue-Labarthe, *Heidegger, Art, and Politics: The Fiction of the Political* (Oxford: Basil Blackwell, 1990), but the most plausible version of the view can be found in Fred Dallmayr, *The Other Heidegger* (Ithaca, NY: Cornell University Press, 1993). Nonetheless, the metaphorics of *infection* remains alarming here, given the central role of such tropes in the paranoid and biologistic eugenic views at least partly responsible for the Shoah.

our nihilistic Nietzschean ontotheology does help shed a revealing critical light on both (1) the inhumanly rational system the Nazis developed to carry out their attempted genocide and (2) the broader framework behind the "biologistic metaphysics" of racial indigeny that Heidegger discerned (and consistently contested, as even his most serious critics acknowledge) in the Nazi pursuit of a eugenically purified "master race." But what jumps out as conspicuously absent from Heidegger perspective is that it cannot explain why the Nazis focused so obsessively on the Jewish people in the first place.[8] Put simply, there is still quite a leap required to get from the idea of the earth as a historical arena for the struggle between races (an idea that Heidegger's longstanding critique of Nietzsche's metaphysics helps us to uproot and reject) to the idea that the supposed Jewish "race" in particular had to be eradicated, and this is a leap about which Heidegger's view leaves us entirely in the dark, as far as I can see. Or, to approach the same problem from another angle, one may conclude that Heidegger's critique of our Nietzschean, "technological" ontotheology compellingly illuminates the deeper historical logic behind the "total mobilization" of the Nazi war machine (and the global arms race it catalyzed, in which we remain caught to this day), but one must still recognize, with Hannah Arendt, that the resources the Nazis poured into the Holocaust did not in fact serve this total mobilization but, instead, undermined it,

---

[8] But does not the same criticism also hold true of Arendt's remarkably similar views concerning the "industrialization of death" (in Hannah Arendt, *The Origins of Totalitarianism* [New York: Harcourt, 1968]) and "the banality of evil" (in Hannah Arendt, *Eichmann in Jerusalem: A Report on the Banality of Evil* [New York: Penguin, 1963]), as well as of Horkheimer and Adorno's understanding of Auschwitz as the terrible result of enlightenment rationality gone mad through its own fulfillment (in Max Horkheimer and Theodore Adorno, *Dialectic of Enlightenment: Philosophical Fragments* [Stanford: Stanford University Press, 2002])? I find more convincing Horkheimer and Adorno's suggestion (in the same text) that Nazi anti-Semitism should be understood as the scapegoating of a symbolic figure in whom were concentrated the worst excesses of capitalist-industrial modernization, so that the elimination of "the Jew" could substitute for a critique of the techno-capitalist system actually responsible for the worst suffering associated with industrialization (a view that is at least partly telling against Heidegger). Still, the question Arendt (among many others) raised as to why the Nazis fixated on the figure of "the Jew" remains an important one, and Adorno's views on the historical role Jewish figures played both in spreading Roman jurisprudence and, later (owing to the Christian prohibitions on usury) in international banking, while problematic, at least address the question in its specificity and (along with the infamous, forged "Protocols of the Elders of Zion" and various other biographical influences) help explain Heidegger's own anti-Semitic beliefs, the full details of which recently came to light, often most horrifyingly on this very issue (see, for example, PXII-XV 45–45/GA96 56–57 and GA97 20); see Thomson, "Heidegger's Nazism in the Light of his Early *Black Notebooks*." For an interesting development of Arendt's initial analysis of the historical dimension of this question, see Enzo Traverso, *The Origins of Nazi Violence* (New York: The New Press, 2003).

diverting valuable resources from the war effort right to the end, such that the Holocaust stands out as a terrible exception to the Nazi's otherwise total mobilization.[9] From the perspective of Heidegger's critique of ontotheology, in short, Auschwitz as such remains a dark and terrible anomaly.[10]

My own less controversial thesis here, then, would only be that Heidegger and Levinas both understood themselves as struggling to articulate the requisite ethical response to the great traumas of the twentieth century, and that if we compare their thinking at this level, we can better understand the ways in which Levinas – like all other important post-Heideggerian thinkers – genuinely diverges from Heidegger even while building on his thinking.[11] I began by suggesting that the received view of the relation between Heidegger and Levinas has impoverished our understanding not only of Heidegger but also of Levinas himself, and one of my main goals in what follows will be to suggest that if we want to fully understand Levinas's own views, then instead of treating his ethical thinking simply as a propaedeutic or groundwork to Heidegger's ethically impoverished ontological perspective (a reading that authorizes Levinasians to ignore or dismiss Heidegger), we do much better to appreciate Levinas as a post-Heideggerian thinker, that is, as someone often working critically against the background and within the perspectives opened

---

[9] On Heidegger's view of America's military–industrial complex as a fulfillment of the underlying logic of enframing also driving the Nazis' "total mobilization" for war, see Thomson, *Heidegger, Art, and Postmodernity*, ch. 7. On Arendt's important point (in Arendt, *The Origins of Totalitarianism*) that by the end of the war the resources the Nazis poured into the Holocaust were clearly undermining rather than serving their war effort, see the insightful essay by Robert Pippin, "Hannah Arendt and the Bourgeois Origins of Totalitarian Evil," in *The Persistence of Subjectivity: On the Kantian Aftermath* (New York: Cambridge University Press, 2005). Levinas tries to make some philosophical sense of this troubling question (without making explicit that he is doing so) in his discussion of the relation between "murder" and the "face," suggesting that Nazi genocide reached such terrible proportions because it was desperately trying to do the impossible, namely, to eliminate the very possibility of a different future (in this case, a future in which Nazi power would have come to an end and the Nazis would be judged for their murderous crimes, and so a future for which, Levinas suggests, the persecuted figure of "the Jew" represented the privileged witness). (See Emmanuel Levinas, *Totality and Infinity: An Essay on Exteriority*, trans. by A. Lingis [Pittsburgh, PA: Duquesne University Press, 1969], 197–201.)

[10] And the debate continues as to which would be worse: If the *Shoah* could not be understood rationally, or if it could – a divisive issue that pits, for example, Adorno against Agamben and the earlier Arendt of *The Origins of Totalitarianism* against the later Arendt of *Eichmann in Jerusalem*.

[11] Doing so, moreover, bestows the traditional philosophical advantage of allowing us to understand their important disagreements by situating them against the background of the still too infrequently recognized common ground that, I shall try to show here, underlies their philosophical projects as a whole. (Of course, I can only develop a few important pieces of that project here.)

up by Heidegger's work. If, with a few notable exceptions, Levinas scholarship has been slow to emerge from hermeneutic insularity and isolation (even within "continental" philosophy), Levinas is at least partly responsible, because his growing hostility to Heidegger, visible in the notoriously "un-Levinasian" spirit of some of his Heidegger interpretations, helped convince many Levinasians that they could understand Levinas without recognizing just how integrally entwined the essential themes of Levinas's thinking are with Heidegger's work, especially (though by no means exclusively) *Being and Time*, the great philosophical importance of which Levinas, to his credit, never ceased insisting upon. However understandable this hostility was in Levinas's own case (a more extreme case of Bloom's "anxiety of influence" would be difficult even to imagine), its effects have not served Levinas scholarship well. The main problem, I think, is that Levinas's rhetorical exaggerations of his distance from Heidegger have obscured their common ground in existential phenomenology, thereby blocking the recognition that Levinas was not only one of the earliest but also one of the most faithful and creative interpreters of *Being and Time*.

I am not claiming that the only way to be hermeneutically faithful to a creative philosopher like Heidegger is to betray him or, more precisely, to betray the letter of his text in order to respect its spirit by creatively developing its insights well beyond anything to which Heidegger himself would or could have assented, but such creative betrayal is certainly preferable to the myrmidonian devotion and jargonistic paraphrasing that still passes for "thinking" in some circles. In fact, even Heidegger's own notion of "repetition" (*Wiederholung*) suggests that such hermeneutic betrayal is justified when it is motivated by a deeper fidelity to the phenomenon whose attempted description we have "inherited" (where *inherited* means actively taken up from the otherwise ossified "tradition" and updated, via a "reciprocative rejoinder," to meet the deepest needs of the contemporary world), just as Heidegger insisted he had broken with Husserl out of a greater faithfulness to the phenomenological project itself – that is, the attempt to describe the matters that matter without distorting these things themselves by reading them back through our unnoticed metaphysical categories and frameworks (Pre xiv–xv).[12] If this is right, then rather than trying to gauge Levinas's faithfulness to Heidegger, we need instead to understand the phenomenon both seek to describe, see exactly where they disagree and what is really at stake in their disagreement, and then

---

[12] (These metaphysical prejudices included that unextruded Cartesianism Heidegger repeatedly objected to in Husserl.) This distinguishes Heideggerian repetition (concerning which, see Thomson, *Heidegger, Art, and Postmodernity*, ch. 5) from Benjaminian-Marxian messianic repetition, which stresses the need to actualize potentials in history that were betrayed by their own development (as, for example, liberalism supposedly betrayed the universal liberation glimpsed in the French revolution).

independently evaluate the phenomenon for ourselves. To begin to do this here, I shall focus on that crucial existential phenomenon Heidegger calls "death," which Levinas rightly insisted was at the heart of his disagreement with Heidegger.

As we saw in Chapter 1, to say that what Heidegger means by "death" is controversial strains the limits of understatement. Rather than devote this entire chapter to reiterating and defending my interpretation, I shall instead briefly reiterate aspects of it rather schematically, then go on to emphasize the elements of Heidegger's account most relevant to Levinas's critique.[13] It is my hope that the decidedly nonstandard interpretation of existential death developed throughout this book will gain further plausibility from the way it allows us to recognize just how profoundly Heidegger's existential phenomenology of death influenced Levinas's own view of the matter, as well as from the way such "death" was subsequently interpreted and contested in the "continental" tradition stretching from Levinas and Sartre to Derrida and Agamben (as well as White, Haugeland, Lear, and others), to which we will turn in Chapter 7.[14]

6.2 From Heidegger to Levinas: The Basic Terms of the Dispute

I made the case in Chapter 4 that Heidegger develops a "perfectionist" philosophy of education in *Being and Time*, a phenomenological account that links his *ontological* understanding of what most importantly distinguishes our human form of life to his *ethical* view of the way developing this distinctive "essence" enables human life to reach its greatest "fulfillment" (*Vollendung*). Building on that account (which itself builds on the work of Blattner, Dreyfus, Cavell, and others), I would like to show here that the deepest and most interesting set of disagreements between Heidegger and Levinas concerns precisely this central perfectionist question: *How do we become genuinely or fully ourselves?* Heidegger's and Levinas's competing phenomenological descriptions of what authentic self-fulfillment entails, I shall now show, follow from their quarrel over the meaning of "death." This famous disagreement concerns not only the proper phenomenology of death but also its relation to

---

[13] See Chapter 1 and the detailed treatment of Levinas as a "transcendental ethical realist" in Thomson, "Ontology and Ethics at the Intersection of Phenomenology and Environmental Philosophy."

[14] What I will suggest is that one of the philosophical questions most fundamentally at issue, first between Heidegger and Levinas, and then between the other important continental thinkers influenced by their disagreement, is this: What does it mean to become oneself, to become *genuinely* or *fully* oneself? One of the larger philosophical questions I am interested in concerns how the great traumas of the twentieth century have changed the political implications of this *perfectionist* question, and so transformed our ways of thinking about it.

the ultimate meaning of life, and owing to its formative influence on thinkers such as Sartre, Beauvoir, Derrida, and Agamben, this *gigantomachia* over the phenomenology of death remains one of the most fascinating disputes in twentieth-century continental philosophy.[15] (This means that, even if this interpretation turned out to be wrong about what Heidegger really means by "death," it would still help us to better understand how Heidegger's analysis of death influenced some of the leading continental thinkers who followed, however critically, in his footsteps, often taking his existential phenomenology of death as their own philosophical point of departure.)

What, then, are the basic coordinates of the dispute between Heidegger and Levinas over the phenomenology and, consequently, the ontological significance of "death"? Otherwise put, in what ways do Heidegger and Levinas disagree about how we become *genuinely* or *fully* ourselves? Their competing answers to this perfectionist question diverge sharply; Heidegger and Levinas disagree both about what self-fulfillment *is* and about *how* it can be achieved. As we saw in Chapter 4, *Being and Time* Heidegger conceives of self-fulfillment in terms of *becoming authentic*, contending that we achieve authenticity by traversing its two structural moments, "anticipation" (*Vorlaufen*) and "resolve" (*Entschlossenheit*). As he succinctly puts it: "Dasein becomes 'essentially' Dasein in that authentic existence which constitutes itself as anticipatory resoluteness" (BT 370/SZ 323).[16] In other words, Heidegger thinks we become ourselves through a two-step process of, first, "anticipating" or "running out" toward what he calls "death" – an experience of radical individuation in which we die to the world of our self-defining

---

[15] My main goal will simply be to try to set out its terms as clearly as possible. Immediately complicating matters, however, is the fact that, although Levinas usually criticizes "Heidegger" as if thereby designating a fixed philosophical view or position, there are really at least three different views of what is entailed in genuinely or fully becoming oneself at issue here. For, not only do Heidegger's and Levinas's phenomenological descriptions of self-fulfillment diverge radically from one another (as we will see), but Heidegger's own view undergoes a profound transformation between his early and later work (as we saw in Chapters 2 and 3). Still, I shall bracket the later Heidegger's understanding of self-fulfillment here (set out in detail in Thomson, *Heidegger on Ontotheology*, ch. 4), not only for reasons of space but also because I think the best way to understand this three-way disagreement is to situate it against what is in fact its common background in the early Heidegger's phenomenological description of how one becomes authentic, and of the roles played by "death" and "resolve" in the secular conversion whereby one becomes such an authentic self (as we saw in Chapter 4).

[16] Anticipation is to expectation as anxiety is to fear, so we can begin to understand the former terms (in each pair) by thinking of the latter ones deprived of an object, as in an expectation that does not know what it is so nervously expecting, or a fear that is afraid of (the) *nothing*, as it were. (On how Heidegger thinks art can help teach us to turn our tragic fear of the nothing into a heroic embrace of the possible, see Chapters 8 and Thomson, *Heidegger, Art, and Postmodernity*, ch. 3.)

6.2. THE BASIC TERMS OF THE DISPUTE   191

practical projects – and then, on the basis of the insight gained by this encounter of the remaining core of the self with itself in existential death, we find a way, through what he calls "resolution," to reflexively reconnect to the practical world lost touch with in death. Authenticity, as anticipatory resoluteness, thus names a double movement in which the world lost in anticipation is regained in resolve, a literally *revolutionary* movement by which we are involuntarily turned away from the world and then voluntarily turn back to it, a movement in which the grip of the world upon us is broken in order that we may thereby gain (or regain) our grip on this world.[17]

Levinas, I now want to suggest, builds his own account of how we become fully ourselves upon the structure of Heidegger's phenomenology of authenticity, indeed, so much so that Levinas's phenomenology of existential self-fulfillment simply cannot be understood without this Heideggerian background, which Levinas continually presupposes but never explicitly acknowledges or clearly explains.[18] We can begin to see this if we recall that authenticity's double movement of anticipation and resolve, death and rebirth, has long been thought of as Heidegger's phenomenological version of *conversion*, since it is a movement in which we turn away from the world, recover ourselves, and then turn back to the world, transformed by the process.[19] Levinas too is centrally concerned to provide a phenomenological description of such "death" and its role in what he goes so far as to call the self's

---

[17] I should perhaps qualify my claim that we are "involuntarily" turned away from the world. In an illuminating discussion of existential death, Pippin observes that: "We are simply not 'in charge' of whether care fails or not or how to think our way into or out of such an experience" (Pippin, "Hannah Arendt and the Bourgeois Origins of Totalitarian Evil," 71). I shall suggest that Pippin's view is actually closer to Levinas than Heidegger, because Heidegger thinks we can precipitate world-collapse by unflinchingly confronting our anxiety. (We cannot directly make our worlds collapse, no more than we can directly make ourselves sneeze, but just as we can indirectly make ourselves sneeze, say by exposing ourselves to something to which we are allergic, so Heidegger thinks we can indirectly make our worlds collapse by confronting our anxiety and tracing it back to our basic existential homelessness or "uncanniness" (*Unheimlichkeit*), the fact that there is nothing about the ontological structure of the self that can tell us what specifically we should do with our lives. Moreover, Heidegger also believes that there are indeed things we can do to help get beyond this world-collapse through resolve (as we saw in Chapters 1 and 2). Between these two important moments of undeniable agency, however, Heidegger recognizes that the experience takes on a momentum of its own, whereby we reach a point of no return in our confrontation with anxiety after which we can no longer successfully choose to flee this anxiety back into the tranquillizing hurry of everyday busyness, but are instead "forced" to confront it (BT 308/SZ 263).

[18] If this is right, however, it constitutes a fairly devastating objection to the many Levinasians who seek to understand Levinas without recourse to Heidegger.

[19] This reading of Heidegger, most prominently developed by Cavell and Mulhall (as we saw in Chapter 3), can also be traced back to the early Heidegger's theological colleagues in the Marburg circle around Bultmann (see Oberst, *Heidegger on Language and Death*).

"resurrection," and the structure of Levinas's account is almost identical to Heidegger's, in the following way.[20] Just like Heidegger, Levinas thinks we become fully ourselves only when we confront our "death" and then – on the basis of the transformative realization afforded by this confrontation with death – we find a way back to the world, a world which we thereby come to understand and inhabit quite differently.[21] Only if we keep this Heideggerian structure of Levinas's phenomenology of self-fulfillment in mind, I submit, will we be able to recognize their genuine *substantive* disagreements, understanding exactly where, and why, Levinas breaks with Heidegger and seeks to elaborate his alternative account of how we become truly or fully ourselves.

For, in what amounts to a formidable immanent critique of Heidegger's phenomenology of authenticity, Levinas challenges four interconnected aspects of Heidegger's account and offers his own positive alternatives. I shall quickly sketch these four differences, then devote the rest of this chapter to exploring them in more detail. *First, Levinas objects to Heidegger's phenomenological description of the self confronting itself in "death."* According to Levinas's famous critique, what Heidegger calls "death" reveals the self's indomitable "virility" and "lucidity," whereas Levinas himself thinks that death delivers the stroke of a paralyzing passivity that this self is unable to surmount of its own power. *Second, Levinas disputes the nature of the crucial insight afforded by the self's confrontation with death.* For Heidegger, confronting death enables us to discover something about ourselves that remains more powerful than death, an aspect of the self (the *projectless projecting* he calls our "ownmost ability-to-be") that does not go down with the shipwreck of our life-projects but rather survives for as long as each of us do. By contrast, Levinas thinks that death renders us utterly powerless and passive, thereby revealing the other person as providing our only chance to pass through death toward a future this death has placed beyond our reach. Levinas holds, moreover, in perhaps the definitive claim of his work, that recognizing the other person as the only vessel capable of transporting us through such "death" into the future allows us to understand the other person as the sole bearer of "what is not yet," that is, of *alterity*.

Third, Levinas contests Heidegger's account of how it is that the self lives through death and thereby reconnects to the world. What Heidegger calls "resoluteness" relies upon the lucidity and virility of the core self that death reveals, incorporating its newfound power over existential death into a second-order decision that frees the self to reconnect to its world by choosing (or

---

[20] Levinas, *Totality and Infinity*, 56, 284. (Originally published in 1961, *Totality and Infinity* is Levinas's central and most famous work.)

[21] This is central to Levinas's broader philosophical project (see n. 28); indeed, he calls this confrontation with death "the ineluctable moment of my dialectic" (Levinas, *Time and the Other*, 92).

opening itself to the arrival of one of) the identity-defining life-projects that constitute it.[22] Levinas, for his part, believes that the self can reconnect to the world only by acknowledging its own powerlessness and so giving itself over to another person – paradigmatically a "teacher" or "master" – with whom this self can grope, in conversation, toward a future it cannot comprehend. *Fourth, and finally, Levinas opposes Heidegger's description of how the self who finds a way back to the world is transformed by the adventure.* Heidegger's authentic self becomes itself fully by seizing its "fate" and thereby helping to shape the communal "destiny" of its generation, a heroic feat it accomplishes through a creative "repetition" of a project drawn from the past, thereby enabling this self to establish the coherent and in this sense relatively continuous identity of both itself and its community. Levinas, by contrast, thinks that we fully become ourselves only by being reborn as another person, becoming radically different from our previous self-conception. Through a process Levinas calls "transubstantiation," we are transformed into wholly other-directed selves, becoming committed to a community of those dedicated entirely to alterity (that is, to what is not yet), and so to the future, to continual transformation, even to the "permanent revolution" of "incessant death and resurrection," as Levinas rather dramatically puts it.

Of course, Levinas, an avowed enemy of all "totalizing" systems, would never present his immanent critique of Heidegger's secularized phenomenological account of the conversion to an authentic existence so schematically. The four "moments" just sketched remain tightly interwoven, moreover, both in Heidegger's phenomenology of authenticity and in the alternative "dialectic" of self-fulfillment Levinas develops through his immanent critique of Heidegger. For the sake of clarity, I shall nevertheless endeavor to explain these points in turn in this chapter's final Section 6.3.[23]

6.3 Thinking through Levinas's Challenge

Let us begin with Levinas's challenge to Heidegger's phenomenological description of the self confronting itself in "death." Levinas emphasizes that, in Heidegger's phenomenology of authenticity, "death" reveals Dasein's indomitable "virility" and "lucidity." As he puts it in his 1946 lectures on *Time and the Other*:

---

[22] On the subtle but important difference between *resoluteness* as "choosing to choose" (as Heidegger puts it in 1927's *Being and Time*) and as "un-closedness" (as he revises the view in 1934–35's "Origin of the Work of Art" [P]), see Chapter 5.3.

[23] It is also my hope that doing so will help us to understand Levinas's differences from Heidegger in a way that leaves room for the fact that some of these views – both his criticisms of Heidegger and his own positive alternatives – remain more plausible than others.

Being toward death, in Heidegger's authentic existence, is a supreme lucidity and a supreme virility. It is Dasein's assumption of the uttermost possibility of existence, which precisely makes possible all other possibilities, and consequently makes possible the very feat of grasping a possibility – that is, it makes possible activity and freedom.[24]

I think Levinas's point, however strangely put, is basically sound. For Heidegger, existential death allows Dasein to experience its ownmost ability-to-be, an inalienable *projecting* or *existing* (from *ek-sistere*, "standing out" into temporally structured intelligibility) that survives the shipwreck of all one's practical life-projects. This core volitional self that survives the collapse of its own practical life-projects then finds itself able *resolutely* to reconnect to the world, lucidly choosing to project itself into (or open itself to the arrival of) a defining project once again.

Levinas contests precisely this view, contending that the global collapse of life-constituting projects we experience in existential "death" should instead be understood as a paralyzing stroke that undoes the self's power entirely, reducing this self to a state of radical passivity.[25] Levinas nicely suggests that we can capture the basic difference between his view and Heidegger's through a simple inversion of Heidegger's famous formula: Whereas Heidegger understands death as "the possibility of an impossibility," for Levinas death is instead "the impossibility of ... possibility."[26] This is no mere rhetorical chiasmus; for Levinas, "[t]his apparently Byzantine distinction has a fundamental importance," and not just because the two phrases are not logically equivalent.[27] The significant difference between Heidegger's "the possibility of an impossibility" and Levinas's "the impossibility of all possibility" is *phenomenological*, although this will take some explaining.

We can see how Heidegger's and Levinas's phenomenologies of "death" initially part ways if we remember that, for Heidegger, when my projects all break down or collapse, leaving me without any life-project to project myself upon, projection itself does not cease.[28] When my being-possible becomes impossible, I still *am* this inability-to-be. My ability-to-be becomes stranded,

---

[24] Levinas, *Time and the Other*, 70.
[25] Ibid.
[26] Levinas, *Totality and Infinity*, 235.
[27] (Levinas, *Time and the Other*, 70, n. 43.) As one can see most by formalizing the two phrases, "the possibility of impossibility" is not logically equivalent to "the impossibility of possibility." (The latter is logically equivalent to "*necessarily* not possible," which is obviously not the same as the former's logical equivalent, "*possibly* not possible.") Still, one should not be misled by this, instead remembering that Heidegger has *existential* rather than *logical* possibility in mind here (as we saw in Chapter 1).
[28] To be clear, I am not claiming that this is the starting point of Levinas's critique of Heidegger; strictly speaking, his critique begins with an interesting but rather implausible challenge to Heidegger's notion of *thrownness*: Levinas seeks to get back behind our

6.3. THINKING THROUGH LEVINAS'S CHALLENGE 195

unable to connect to my world, but not *inert*. This strange condition – in which, stranded by the collapse of my life projects, I experience myself as a *projecting* deprived of any life-projects to project into – is precisely what Heidegger characterizes as "the possibility of an impossibility," or *death*. In Heidegger's words: "Death, as possibility, gives Dasein nothing to be 'actualized,' nothing which Dasein could itself actually *be*. It is the possibility of the impossibility of every way of comporting oneself toward anything, of every way of existing" (BT 307/SZ 262). As we have seen, in Heidegger's phenomenological account of existential "death" I experience myself as cut off from a world I nevertheless strive desperately to reach, and so encounter my self as a naked "thrown *projection*," a brute "that-it-is-*and-has-to-be*."

As Dreyfus suggests: "In non-terminal breakdown [that is, death not accompanied by demise or other apparently permanent forms of world collapse], Dasein as an ability-to-be does, indeed, collapse, but something remains aware of the collapse and survives to open the new world."[29] As Dreyfus sees, this "raises the difficult question: Just what survives world or identity-collapse so as to be aware that collapse has occurred" and subsequently reconnect to the world? Dreyfus's answer to this question of what survives in Heideggerian "death" is "naked thrownness or [in Heidegger's words] the that-it-is-and-has-to-be." Of course, "that-it-is-*and-has-to-be*" (my emphasis) is not only "naked thrownness" but also naked *projection*, in other words, pure "ability-to-be" (*Seinkönnen*) deprived of all "being possible" (*Möglichsein*), all the positive projects one usually projects oneself into and understands oneself in terms of (teacher, husband, father, citizen, pet-owner,

---

thrownness so as to begin his own account from a foundationless *Il y a*, an "anonymous" existing without an existent. It is in this sense that, as Hoy recognizes, "Levinas still aspires to 'first philosophy,' that is, to a foundationalist account of human existence" (David Hoy, *Critical Resistance: From Poststructuralism to Post-Critique* [Cambridge, MA: MIT Press, 2004], 149). What Hoy (like most commentators) does not notice is that, in so doing, Levinas is seeking to redeem the ontological wisdom he is implicitly drawing from his creative reading of the first book of the Hebrew Bible (*Genesis*, i.e., the entrance of being into time), the successive moments of which (creation, the garden, eating of the tree of knowledge, nakedness and shame, and so on) provide the skeletal framework of the original phenomenological "dialectic" Levinas unfolds and develops in his three main philosophical works (viz., Levinas, *Time and the Other*; *Totality and Infinity*; and *Otherwise than Being or Beyond Essence* [Kluwer, 1991]), thereby suggesting that the dialectical movement portrayed in the first book of the Torah symbolically portrays the path of the self's spiritual evolution toward its own fulfillment (by, ultimately and perhaps paradoxically, becoming radically other-directed, or at least fundamentally other-responsive). I think Levinas's still largely unnoticed attempt to read the *Torah* as containing a progressive account of the ontological fulfillment of self (one which Levinas thinks leads the self beyond itself) is what ultimately explains what Hoy recognizes as Levinas's attempt "to be even more fundamental than phenomenology" (Hoy, *Critical Resistance*, 162).

[29] Dreyfus, "Foreword" to White, *Time and Death*, xxxv; xxxv, n. 59.

and so on) – hence my description of this existential core of the self as *projectless projection*. In Heidegger's words, what survives the "death" of its projects is Dasein as "an individualized *solus ipse* [a "self alone," or as Dreyfus puts it] ... pure, isolated, world-needy mineness."[30] Again, if we do not fail to notice Dasein's *having-to-be*, its *world-neediness*, then we will see that Dasein's sheer "ability-to-be," its *projecting*, is precisely what does *not* collapse (*pace* Dreyfus's incautious formulation), but merely gets stranded, separated from its "being-possible," its self-constituting *projects*. Dasein is "collapsed" in death in the sense that it cannot do what it normally does (it cannot reconnect to its collapsed world of practical projects [BT 231/SZ 187]), not in the sense that it stops trying or gives up entirely.

As Guignon nicely expresses the crucial point, for Heidegger death reveals "that what I *am* at the most basic level is a reaching forward into possibilities, not an actualizing of possibilities" (2011, 197).[31] I have thus suggested that we can get a sense for the phenomenon Heidegger is describing as "the possibility of an impossibility" by generalizing from more common experiences such as an identity crisis, an anxiety attack, the work of mourning, a serious case of writer's block, an experience of genuine philosophical *aporia*, or even (as Pippin rightly suggests) the lonely isolation of old age, insofar as each of these experiences is characterized by a desperate striving for a practical identity that no longer seems possible to inhabit, a struggle to project oneself into identity-bestowing existential possibilities experienced as no longer within one's reach.[32]

By contrast, I would like to suggest, we can approach the phenomenon Levinas calls "death" – which he describes as "the impossibility of every

---

[30] Ibid.

[31] Guignon continues: "I exist as a 'running ahead toward' or 'directedness forward to,' which Heidegger calls 'fore-running' or 'anticipation' (*Vorlaufen*). Human existence is defined by a futurity or future-directedness, a standing out into an open space of possibilities, where actualizing specific possibilities, while generally important, is not what is crucial to our being" (Guignon, "Heidegger and Kierkegaard on Death," 197). Indeed, as we saw at the end of Chapter 1, we only *discover* "what is crucial to our being" in the phenomenon of existential death, when the shipwreck of our existentiell life-projects reveals this future-directed, world-hungry mineness as its sole survivor, thereby allowing us to recognize this core self – our existential projecting shorn of its specific existentiell life-projects – as the volitional and intentional core of existence (therein and thereby first recognizing futurity, as we saw in Chapter 1.7).

[32] (See Pippin, "Hannah Arendt and the Bourgeois Origins of Totalitarian Evil," 165.) As Pippin explains, Arendt saw totalitarianism as a "suicidal escape" from this dead end. (As a Hegelian more committed to than alienated by the modern world, Pippin contests Arendt's Heideggerian tendency to equate such deadening experiences with modern bourgeois society in general.) For the early Heidegger, we have seen, the "way out" of this deadlock is practical *action* (a view obviously influential on Arendt, who, as the muse of *Being and Time*, knew it well); for Levinas, it is, ultimately, creatively disclosive *teaching*. (Levinas's critical alternative to Heidegger here perhaps gives a new, phenomenological meaning to the old saw, "Those who cannot do, teach.")

6.3. THINKING THROUGH LEVINAS'S CHALLENGE 197

possibility, the stroke of a total passivity" – by considering a severe depressive episode, in which the depressed person completely gives up and, for a time at least, no longer even tries to reconnect to her world.[33] For Levinas, in a revealing critique of Heidegger on this very point, death is not "the inanity" of "a paralytic's freedom" – that is, the ability to *try* to do what has become impossible – but rather a kind of "suffocation in the impossibility of the possible."[34] For Levinas, the experience of "death" delivers the stroke of a paralyzing passivity, rendering the self utterly powerless, helpless even to "assume" death.[35] Desperately unable to cross, under my own steam, "the infinitesimal – but untraversable – distance" that now separates me from the future, I suffer death's *impossibility*: "The death agony is precisely this impossibility of ceasing," that is, of eradicating the paralyzed remainder of self left over in existential death.[36] It is thus telling that Levinas translates Heidegger's *Angst* not as *anxiété*, "anxiety," but rather as *"angoisse,"* "anguish," which suggests a deeper torment, and one suffered more passively: "No exit," but also no hope of ever finding one by oneself.[37] (In his early work, moreover, Levinas suggests another phenomenon remarkably similar to the anguish of being unable to cease – namely, "insomnia," an experience in which I remain riveted to the world, unable even to let go, and increasingly without hope of ever getting beyond or escaping the experience.)[38]

What, then, are we to make of this subtle but important disagreement between Heidegger and Levinas over the phenomenology of "death"? One tempting supposition would be that Levinas, as a phenomenologist similarly trained in the Husserlian school, also underwent and so experienced firsthand the same existential phenomenon Heidegger had described in *Being and Time*, only to find himself stuck in what Heidegger called *anticipation* (or running-out) into the projectless projecting of existential death, completely unable to pick himself up, as it were, and accomplish that radically autonomous reconnection to the world that Heidegger called resoluteness. So, when an

---

[33] Levinas, *Totality and Infinity*, 235.
[34] Ibid, 241, 57.
[35] Ibid, 57.
[36] Ibid, 56–7.
[37] See Emmanuel Levinas, *God, Death, and Time*, trans. by B. Bergo (Stanford: Stanford University Press, 2000) (to which we return in Chapter 7; unfortunately, the translator decided to override Levinas's far from irrelevant decision (see 251, n. 3).
[38] In Levinas, *Time and the Other*, however, the phenomenon of insomnia is supposed to attest to an experience in which the (post-hypostasis) subject, who has individuated itself from the anonymous "existing without an existent" of the *Il y a*, nevertheless maintains some experiential access to that presubjective experience of anonymous existing, and so can attest to it phenomenologically. Insomnia is thus the lynchpin in Levinas's attempt to get back behind Dasein's *thrownness* to a more radical (neo-Cartesian) starting point, seeking thereby to undercut Heidegger's *Being and Time* famous claim that Dasein cannot get back behind its thrownness.

alternative (*Torah* inspired) route back to the world occurred to Levinas (perhaps taking shape during his intensive tutelage with his famous Talmudic teacher, master Chouchani), Levinas made it the basis of his own competing phenomenological account of self-fulfillment. (Moreover, the way Levinas challenges Heidegger's secular, neo-enlightenment ideal of autonomous salvation implicitly raises the question of the relation in Levinas's work between his phenomenological descriptions and his religious commitments, a question I shall leave in parentheses here.)[39] Alternatively, those of us inclined to psychology as well as phenomenology might suppose that, rather than treating Heidegger's *active but paralyzed striving* and Levinas's *passive and suffocating collapse* as offering us competing descriptions of the same phenomenon, we should instead recognize these as powerfully evocative descriptions of two different existential experiences involving world-collapse, namely (to put it in the most brutally simplified terms), Heideggerian *anxiety* and Levinasian *depression*. (That explanation, moreover, opens another set of difficult questions about how to understand the relationship between phenomenology and psychology.)[40] Nonetheless, however we account for it, we are witness here to a subtle but important fork in the road of the tradition of continental phenomenology, one which, we will see, continues to diverge until it becomes a major parting of the ways between Heidegger and Levinas (and which will continue to exert a competing pull on such subsequent continental wayfarers as Derrida and Agamben).

To trace and examine this growing divide, let us turn to their second major difference, visible in Levinas's alternative understanding of the nature of the crucial insight afforded by the self's confrontation with death. I pointed out that for Heidegger, confronting death enables us to discover something about

---

[39] That is, the specific way Levinas's phenomenology challenges Heidegger's neo-enlightenment ideal of self-salvation obliquely raises the issue of the integral relation between his phenomenological works and his Talmudic scholarship – domains Levinas rather misleadingly claimed to have kept separate (see n. 28). Foucault points out, however, that the idea of "[n]ot being able to take care of oneself without help from someone else was a generally accepted principle" among the ancient Epicureans, Cynics, and [even] Stoics (Michel Foucault, *The Hermeneutics of the Subject: Lectures at the Collège de France, 1981-1982*, ed. by Frédéric Gros, trans. By G. Burchell [New York: Palgrave Macmillan, 2005], 496). Indeed, the early Heidegger's idealization of this radical existential individualism seems to suffer from the same rather obvious masculinist biases as the other modern fantasies of radical autonomy, self-sufficiency, and self-reliance. Beauvoir's famous critique of Levinas in Simone de Beauvoir, *The Second Sex*, trans. By H. M. Parshley (New York: Knopf, 1953) – for his explicit figuring of woman as the other (see below) – should not obscure this important affinity between their shared critiques of the early Heidegger on this important point.

[40] Do phenomenology and psychology range over the same experiences? If so, do they have the same "object domain"? Can one be subordinated or reduced to the other? What is the place of the *unconscious* in phenomenology? And so on.

us that remains more *powerful* than death (BT 436/SZ 384), an aspect of the self – our basic existential *projecting* – which does not go down with the shipwreck of our life-projects but rather survives for as long as do each of our individual Daseins. Levinas, by contrast, thinks that when the approach of death renders us utterly *powerless*, what we discover – in the "passion" of this radical passivity – is that it is only through another person that we have any chance of passing through death into the future that death places beyond our reach.[41] According to Levinas, to recognize the other person as the only vessel capable of transporting us through "death" into the future is, at the same time,[42] to understand other people as the sole bearers of "what is not yet," that is, of *otherness* in general. Now, Levinas is usually misunderstood here and taken to be insisting that, pace Heidegger's explicit claim in *Being and Time*, we do have access to death itself through the death of other people (our closest loved ones, for example). In fact, however, Levinas's critique of Heidegger is basically the reverse: Levinas is not claiming that we have access to death through other people but, instead, that we gain access to the crucial dimension of alterity – including the alterity of the other person – through the experience of death. Here we encounter perhaps the most difficult and distinctive claim of Levinas's phenomenology: Death reveals "alterity" (*altérité*), the link invisibly "connecting" (*religio*) the "other person" (*autrui*) with "otherness" (*autre*) in general.

---

[41] As Levinas's metaphors suggest, at this point in his "dialectic" he is articulating a phenomenological account easily amenable to *Christian* appropriation (since the other who saves you might be Christ rather than the Talmudic teacher Levinas himself apparently has in mind), which probably helps explain his later attraction of Catholic followers such as Jean-Luc Marion. In Levinas's larger "dialectic of being," "death" constitutes "the ineluctable moment," but I suggested that the earlier moments of his dialectic – in which Levinas seeks to get back behind thrownness to the anonymous existing which precedes existents (that is, God before the creation) – are inspired by *Genesis*, and it is here that Levinas explicitly seeks to attain a deeper foundation (for his "first philosophy") than Heidegger thought was possible (see n. 28). Nevertheless, Levinas's next move establishes the metaphysical *humanism* definitive of his work (the view, put simply, that God *is* only in the ethical relationship between human beings), which places his phenomenology in the closest proximity to atheism, at least as traditionally conceived (but see n. 43). Moreover, although the Christian paradigm of the salvation Levinas describes may be Christ, for Levinas it is exemplified by the "master" or "teacher" more generally, and can clearly happen inadvertently as well (for example, when the unrelated comments of a passing music teacher to his student – "Too tight and the strings will break; too loose and the instrument will not play" – legendarily enabled Prince Siddhartha finally to attain the enlightenment of the middle way, an example we return to in Chapter 7).

[42] "The time of an impossible diachrony," Levinas likes to say, so as to suggest the splitting of the subject in two, father and son, and the "transubstantiation" by which I survive only in (and as) my own existential (not biological) son.

Levinas's defining claim, in other words, is that *through the experience of death we encounter the alterity of the other person.*[43] This "alterity" of the other person is what Levinas famously refers to as the "face" (*visage*), which is his

---

[43] I think Levinas's distinctive claim concerning the relation between other people and otherness has not been well understood, especially in its relation to death. In his implicitly "religious" phenomenology (*religious* because it discerns and describes *connections* that, Levinas insists, remain invisible – even non-*phenomenal* – and yet paradoxically "reveal" themselves nonetheless, and thus constitute a kind of *non-phenomenal revelation*, a problematic notion to be sure from the perspective of Heideggerian phenomenology, which restricts itself to phenomena we can experience or encounter directly ourselves), the key insight, put simply, is that *only the other person reveals otherness in general.* This is the claim at the heart of Levinas's *metaphysical humanism*, a view by which he seeks to negotiate a safe path between what are for him the Scylla and Charybdis of *idolatry* and *atheism*. As Levinas describes these dual dangers, to approach the absolute *as* absolute, that is, as *non-relative*, would be to have no *relation* to it; and this would be "atheism" (Levinas, *Totality and Infinity*, 58). Conversely, to have a relation with the absolute is to risk the *idolatry* of treating that through which we relate to the absolute as if it were itself the absolute. (Levinas variously refers to the "absolute" as "infinity," "alterity," "exteriority," and even "God.") Now, what makes this dual danger of atheism or idolatry look like an inescapable double-bind is Levinas's metaphysical humanism, his distinctive claim that *otherness is revealed only through "the face" of the other person*. That is, because he holds that otherness "is" only through the other person – that the absolute "is" only in its relation to us; that God "is" only in and through relations between human beings; that otherness "is" only when the other person alters my world – it is not clear how Levinas can avoid both atheism and idolatry, and, indeed, his metaphysical humanism seems to enter into a perilous proximity to both. Reconstructing Levinas's interesting but rather tortuous logic would take us too far afield here, but it is clear that "the face of the other" – which essentially connects, and yet somehow does not conflate, the other person and otherness in general – acts as the fulcrum for Levinas's extremely delicate balancing act between atheism and idolatry. Still, Levinas's *humanism* looks like (a more traditional conception of) "atheism" in that he refuses to conceive of *infinity* as a noun. ("Infinity does not first exist, and *then* reveal itself. Its infinition is produced as revelation" [Levinas, *Totality and Infinity*, 26].) For Levinas, the infinite *is* only in the act of "*infinition*" (ibid.) – that is, it exists only by breaking the plane of the currently existing finite *totality* (i.e., of what has already been understood) so that something new may enter into the world. *Infinity* is, in other words, a version of Heideggerian futurity, but transcendentalized so as to emphasize what has *not* yet arrived (its alterity) rather than its phenomenological *arriving* (as in Heidegger). The reason for this is that Levinas thinks the *totality* of what is (a totality he calls "history") immediately assimilates anything new; for, even to appear it must appear for us, here, within what is. As a result, "God" exists only in the (nonhistorical) time of "diachrony," in which the instant opens the existing totality to something that exceeds it (that "face" of the other that the totality almost immediately *effaces* by trying to make sense of it in existing terms). What is most important for us here, however, is to recognize that Levinas's metaphysical humanism – his view that *otherness is revealed only through "the face" of the other person* – is both (1) the crucial insight he thinks the experience of existential death reveals and (2) the thesis that most clearly distinguishes his ethical thinking from that of the later Heidegger, who held that human beings have access to alterity (or at least the *arriving* of what is not yet) not only through other people, but also (and, indeed, paradigmatically, in his thinking about the

name for the intersection of otherness and the other person. His term "face" is misleading, however, because he insists that this alterity is not experienced visually but rather linguistically, through what Levinas calls "discourse" or "apology." That is, the "face" is not what I see when I look at you (and even less when I look in the mirror, since Levinas thinks, rather implausibly in my view, that – except by becoming an other person – I cannot be other to myself, no more than I can deliberately tickle or surprise myself). Instead, the face is what I experience when you speak to me – or otherwise communicate your viewpoint or perspective and thereby add something new or different to the discussion and so to my sense of the world. When the other person thus explains, clarifies, or defends her views (hence "apology"), she *brings something new into existence* for me, and in this sense shows herself (to be made, as it were) "in the *image* of God," the *Creator* – hence Levinas's choice of the misleading term "face."

For Levinas, in sum, otherness "is" only when it is revealed through the other person, and this is a revelation I can experience only when this other person says or does something that alters my world. With this background in place, we are positioned to see that when Levinas makes his crucial claim that *through the experience of death we encounter the otherness of the other person*, his point is twofold: First, that through existential death we explicitly experience the capacity of the other person to change us, to alter our world, and second, that through such death we experience ourselves becoming other to ourselves, that is, we experience our self become another, different self.[44] In the strange experience of existential death, as Levinas elaborates it, these two points are connected; I become other to myself through the experience of that which remains different, surprising, able to change me – or, as Levinas says simply, "other" – about the other person, who helps me find a way back to the world that I could not have found on my own. It is thus through this experience of the otherness of the other person in death that I learn to become other

---

poietic essence of art) through a relationship to nonhuman "things" (see Chapter 3 and Thomson, *Heidegger, Art, and Postmodernity*, ch. 3).

[44] This is what Levinas means when he writes that: "An event happens to us ... without our being able to have the least project. This approach of death indicates that we are in relation with something that is absolutely other, something bearing alterity not as a provisional determination we can assimilate through enjoyment, but as something whose very existence is made of alterity. My solitude is thus not confirmed by death but rather broken by it. Right away this means that existence is pluralist. Here the plurality is not a multitude of existents; it appears in existing itself. A plurality insinuates itself into the very existing of the existent ... In death the existing of the existent is alienated" (Levinas, *Time and the Other*, 74–5) Or as he later puts it: "Death ... is *present* only in the other person, and only in him does it summon me urgently to my final essence, to my responsibility" (Levinas, *Totality and Infinity*, 179).

to myself, to become another person. So, how exactly does Levinas think this happens?

Here we reach the third major difference between Heidegger's and Levinas's competing phenomenologies of authentic self-fulfillment. Levinas challenges Heidegger's account of how the self can live through the death of its world and then come to reconnect to the world of life-defining projects which disclose the significance of things and render us meaningful to ourselves. For Heidegger, "resolve" builds upon the bare projecting revealed by death; in a second-order decision (in resolve's *choosing to choose* or *self-unclosedness*), this unsinkable core of the self is able to reconnect to a world by lucidly or explicitly projecting into a self-constituting project.[45] If Heidegger thereby suggests that the best response to the anxiety-like phenomenon he describes is basically to "tough it out," that is, to confront and endure it, and then (on the basis of the core self it painfully discloses) find my own way back to the world, then Levinas himself insists that one simply cannot get oneself out of the depression-like phenomenon he evokes, indeed, that here one's only hope is to be saved by someone else, through what he calls "love" or *Eros*.[46] Levinas thus suggests that the self can reconnect to the world only by giving itself over to another person – paradigmatically a "teacher" or "master" – with whom this self can "grope," in conversation, toward a future it cannot yet comprehend.[47] I think the pedagogical, religious, and psychoanalytic implications of Levinas's

---

[45] How is this supposed to work, and how does Heidegger's account of such resolve avoid the charge of arbitrary decisionism? The account is complex, but as I explained in Chapters 1 (esp. n. 56) and 4, the recognition that (1) there is nothing about the structure of the self laid bare in death that can tell me specifically what project to choose is what enables me (2) to give up the paralyzing idea that there is a single correct choice to make, thereby (3) freeing me to select and update an exemplary life-project from the tradition, one that allows me (4) to employ (or seek to revise) my factical skills, aptitudes, and affective dispositions in a way that (5) helps me to play a role in shaping the issues that matter to and define my generation.

[46] It is perhaps tempting nonetheless to explain this "triumph over death" ("love, stronger than death") in terms of an experience, in death, of alterity as the "sublime" (*Erhaben*), which "lifts up," out of depression (Levinas, *Totality and Infinity*, 79), and Heidegger does perhaps move more in this direction later, as he learns to turn anxiety in the face of death into wonder before the seemingly inexhaustible source of intelligibility (as we saw in Chapter 3 and will see in another light in Chapters 8 and 9).

[47] As Levinas puts it: "The relationship with the other will never be the feat of grasping a possibility" (Levinas, *Time and the Other*, 76), rather, the relationship should be understood in terms of "the erotic relationship," as a groping in the dark (or "the caress") rather than a masterful grasping: "The caress does not know what it seeks. This not knowing, this fundamental disorder, is the essential. It is like a game with something slipping away, a game absolutely without project or plan, not with what can become ours or us, but with something other, always other, always inaccessible, and always still to come [*à venir*]. The caress is the anticipation of this pure future [*avenir,*] without content" (Levinas, *Time and the Other*, 89).

6.3. THINKING THROUGH LEVINAS'S CHALLENGE 203

view remain extremely suggestive, but what remains confusing and off-putting for many readers here is that, in good Platonic fashion, Levinas's descriptions of this process of transformation trade heavily on erotic metaphors, which his feminist critics especially have long insisted on taking literally, thereby obscuring Levinas's ultimate point.[48] When Levinas describes the way the "caress" – which "gropes" toward something it cannot reach or understand rather than *grasping* something it can – allows me to find a way through the "fecundity" of the "feminine" so as, ultimately, to live on in my "child" (indeed, my "son"), Levinas is not simply using sexist language to describe from his own masculine perspective the way that, as Plato suggested, those "impoverished in soul" seek to live on in their children. Levinas's erotic metaphors do work on that level, which he explicitly characterizes as the level of "biology," but – as he repeatedly emphasizes – this biological substrate of human life is only Levinas's version of what Heidegger calls our *ontic* everyday reality, the deeper *ontological* meaning of which both thinkers seek to describe phenomenologically, and to almost the same effect.[49] In other words, Levinas uses his initially sexist and biologically grounded metaphors to try to describe his philosophical vision of how the self, rendered powerless by existential death, can only with the help of the other find a path to the future, in which this self will be reborn as a radically different person.[50] But different *in what way* exactly?

This question brings us to their fourth and final difference, in which Levinas opposes Heidegger's description of how the self who finds a way through existential death back to the world is transformed by the adventure. Although Dreyfus rightly suggests that there are actually degrees of self-fulfillment that

---

[48] This tendency toward a reductive misunderstanding of this crucial point is almost as old as second-wave feminism itself, since it originated in the preface to Simone de Beauvoir, *The Second Sex*. Nonetheless, Beauvoir seems to agree with at least one of Levinas's criticisms of Heidegger, sharing (and developing) the view that "No man can save himself alone" (Beauvoir, *Ethics of Ambiguity*, 67), not least because freedom demands its own universalization, both logically and historically (a German Idealist principle Beauvoir shares with Sartre at this time, as we will see in Chapter 7).

[49] See Levinas, *Totality and Infinity*, 277, 279.

[50] As Levinas says with respect to his concepts of the "son" and "fecundity": "the son is not me, and yet I *am* my son. The fecundity of the I is its very transcendence. The biological origin of the concept nowise neutralizes the paradox of its meaning, and delineates a structure that goes beyond the biologically empirical" (Levinas, *Totality and Infinity*, 277). "If biology furnishes us the prototypes of these relations ... these relations free themselves from their biological limitations" (Levinas, *Totality and Infinity*, 279). "*To be* one's son means to be I in one's son, to be substantially in him, yet without being maintained there in identity. Our whole analysis of fecundity aimed to establish this dialectical conjuncture, which conserves the two contradictory movements. The son resumes the unicity of the father and yet remains radically exterior to the father" (Levinas, *Totality and Infinity*, 278–9). Cf. Marcel Proust, *In Search of Lost Time*, vol. 5, trans. by C. K. S. Moncrieff and T. Kilmartin (New York: Random House, 2003 [original 1969]), 805.

Heidegger has yet to recognize in *Being and Time*, Heidegger's early view is that the authentic self becomes itself fully by seizing its "fate" and thereby helping to shape the communal "destiny" of its generation. It does this through a creative "repetition" of projects drawn from the past which enable this self to establish the coherent and so relatively continuous identity of itself and its community. Levinas, by clear contrast, thinks that we become ourselves fully only by being reborn as another person, a person who is radically different from his or her previous self-conception. This is accomplished through a "transubstantiation" in which I am reborn as the "son" of myself and thereby transformed into a radically *other-directed* self. Levinas thinks that this newborn *ethical* self will recognize the paramount importance of the alterity of the other person (glimpsed in and understood as salvific through existential death, as we have seen), and so become committed to a dispersed community of ethical individuals dedicated to serving, eliciting, and respecting the alterity of other people. We fully become ourselves only by entering into this *ethical* community committed to bringing the otherness of what is not yet into the world, and so dedicated to the future, to continual transformation (as we vigilantly struggle against the reassertion of our own egocentrism), and, ultimately, to serving others as "teachers" of this "permanent revolution" of "incessant death and resurrection."[51]

What this all shows, in the end, is that the endpoints of the structurally analogous processes of death and rebirth described by the early Heidegger and by Levinas remain worlds apart. Indeed, their visions of self-fulfillment are almost inverted images. For the Heidegger of *Being and Time*, we genuinely become ourselves, realizing our greatest possible ethical fulfillment, through the self's *revolutionary* return to and repossession of itself. For Levinas, by contrast, we become ourselves fully only by making a literally *eccentric* passage in which the center of our being is moved outside our selves: I become myself only by "incessantly" learning to be for others. Early Heideggerian self-fulfillment describes the path of an existential odyssey that brings us full circle back to ourselves by first turning us away from the world in which we are usually immersed and then turning us back to this world is a more reflective way. By contrast, the "victory over death" Levinas evokes through his "phenomenology of Eros" – whereby I become "resurrected," "transubstantiated"

---

[51] (This vigilance means that both Heidegger and Levinas maintain an ethical perfectionism with a *negative* version of the "linking principle" discussed in Chapter 4.) As Levinas describes this definitive transformation through which we repeatedly become ourselves by endlessly struggling against our own egocentric self-interest in order to dedicate ourselves to alterity: "The I, ... the center around which [the subject's] existence gravitates, is confirmed in its singularity by purging itself of this gravitation, purges itself interminably, and is confirmed precisely in this incessant effort to purge itself. This is termed goodness. Perhaps the possibility of a point of the universe where such an overflow of responsibility is produced ultimately defines the I" (Levinas, *Totality and Infinity*, 244–5).

6.3. THINKING THROUGH LEVINAS'S CHALLENGE 205

into the son of myself, and thereby dedicated to alterity – contrasts sharply with Heidegger's circular odyssey. As Levinas thus puts it, through *"Eros,"* "a subject ... goes toward a future which is *not yet* and which I will not merely grasp but I *will be* – it no longer has the structure of the subject which from every adventure returns to its island, like Ulysses."[52]

How, then, should we begin to *evaluate* all of these differences (which become even more complicated if we introduce the later Heidegger into the discussion)? I hope others will help me with that rather large question. But since my expression of that hope might be taken as a kind of inadvertent confirmation of Levinas's ethical perspective (since Levinas suggests that we can be helped through genuine philosophical aporias only by another person), I shall also conclude by proposing – so as to bring us back into the vicinity, at least, of the political issues with which we began – that Levinas's most famous criticism of Heidegger also rebounds upon his own view as well.[53] Levinas famously objects that Heideggerian authenticity fails to secure itself against totalitarian violence, but it is hard to see how Levinas's own indiscriminate embrace of alterity – by which he means all as of yet unknown experiences of human otherness – can itself rule out *anything* different, new, or creative.[54] Unfortunately, *pace* Levinas, not everything different, creative, or new is good (although the temptation to think so is a perennial danger for those of us on the Left).[55]

In other words, Levinas's equation of ethics with alterity is much too quick. His indiscriminate ethicizing of everything human beings create that is new, original, unheard, different, or surprising is too broad to serve ethics very well, for it fails to distinguish between good and bad surprises, to put it simply. It does not help us distinguish, for example, between those intense surprises which, even if they wound us initially, eventually help us grow, and those that

---

[52] Levinas, *Totality and Infinity*, 271 (the implicit contrast is between Ulysses and Moses).
[53] "'I think' comes down to 'I can' ... Ontology as first philosophy is a philosophy of power. It issues in the State and in the non-violence of the totality, *without securing itself against the violence from which this non-violence lives*, and which appears in the tyranny of the state. Truth, which should reconcile persons, here exists anonymously" (Levinas, *Totality and Infinity*, 46; my emphasis). We return to this highly charged point in Chapter 7.
[54] "The face to face is ... the primordial production of being on which all the possible collocations of the terms [or different ways of placing them together] are founded. The revelation of the third party, ineluctable in the face, is produced only through the face. Goodness ... consists in going where no clarifying – that is, panoramic – thought precedes, in going without knowing where. An absolute adventure, in a primal imprudence, goodness is transcendence itself" (Levinas, *Totality and Infinity*, 305).
[55] One thinks here, for example, of Foucault's initially enthusiastic reaction to the rise of Islamic theocracy (for seeming to at least offer something new), as well as of our own home-grown reactionaries celebrating the surprise attacks of September 11 (albeit not in the Islamophobic way our disgraced former President infamously imagined).

traumatize us, never to heal, permanently stunting our growth.[56] The problem here, to put it provocatively, is that if the Holocaust or *Shoah* was historically unique, that is, if through it something new, surprising, or unprecedented was indeed introduced into human history (as many of us believe), then the question with which we began returns with renewed insistence: Is Levinas's ethical perspective really the most appropriate philosophical response to the Holocaust or *Shoah*? And, however inspiring his view remains, what ethical traction does it provide with which we might help combat or resist the outbreak of *other* political horrors, now and in the future?[57] Rather than

---

[56] An interesting test case can be found in Levinas's famous exchange with Father Richardson. The basic story runs as follows: Levinas generously accepted Richardson's invitation to sit as an outside examiner on Richardson's thesis committee for his doctoral degree at Louvain, where Richardson defended the text that would become his renowned treatise on Heidegger (William J. Richardson, *Heidegger: From Phenomenology to Thought*, 2nd ed. [The Hague: Martinus Nijhoff, 1967]). During the long defense Levinas never raised the issue of Heidegger's Nazism, about which Richardson told me he had been prepared to respond. Afterward, during the rush of customary congratulations, Levinas came up behind Richardson, poked him sharply in the back, and then, when Richardson turned around, expecting to shake Levinas's hand in the customary way, Levinas instead kept his hand firmly at his side and interjected something like: "You say in your thesis that '1942 was a very prolific year' ... In 1942, my mother was in one concentration camp and my father was in another. It was a very *prolific* year indeed!" Levinas then spun on his heel and walked away, never to speak to Richardson again. (Richardson recounts the story in several places – albeit with notable variations – including in William J. Richardson, "Heidegger's Fall" (in *From Phenomenology to Thought, Errancy, and Desire: Essays in Honor of William J. Richardson, S.J.*, ed. by Babette Babich [New York: Springer, 2005], 277–300); I remain grateful for our extended conversation about it.) Perhaps the lesson to be drawn from this exchange is that, rather than representing a bizarre aberration to be explained away as an uncharacteristic outburst of anger on Levinas's part, Levinas's response to Richardson should instead be understood as an exemplary embodiment of his ethical view, a powerful example of what Levinas called "the traumatism of the other." (And anyone who ever read or listened to Richardson's narration of these events will recognize that this is a trauma he never fully worked-through.) Of course, one should also recognize that, as Malka points out: "It is nevertheless easy to imagine how reading a book of 700 pages on the evolution of Heidegger's thought without the least reference to his political involvement ... could have been painful for Levinas," especially when this bitterly galling sin of omission was committed by a Jesuit priest (see Salomon Malka, *Emmanuel Levinas: His Life and Legacy*, trans. by M. Kigel and S. M. Embree [Pittsburgh, PA: Duquesne University Press, 2006], 166). Indeed, it is easy to imagine Levinas's indignation piqued by the then prevailing norms of scholarly propriety which long worked to preclude any public discussion of Heidegger's complicity with the Nazis.

[57] I am not the only one to raise such worries. Even Derrida – long one of Levinas's most sympathetic critics (indeed, Derrida's famous 1964 essay on Levinas, "Violence and Metaphysics" [collected in Derrida, *Writing and Difference* (Chicago: University of Chicago Press, 1978)] originally helped generate the broader philosophical interest in Levinas' work) – would later (in 2006) sharply object to the troubling ethical insensitivity evident in Levinas's treatment of nonhuman animals: "The animal remains for Levinas

6.3. THINKING THROUGH LEVINAS'S CHALLENGE 207

smugly imagining we can easily solve or dismiss such questions, we do well, in my view, to allow them to continue to haunt us and so provoke our continued thinking. For this too remains part of the unsettled and still unsettling legacy of Heidegger's existential phenomenology of death – as we will see when we pan out to take in more important moments of this legacy in Chapter 7.

> what it will have been for the whole Cartesian-type tradition: a machine that does not speak, that does not have access to sense, that can at best imitate 'signifiers without a signified,' ... a monkey with 'monkey talk,' precisely what the Nazis sought to reduce their Jewish prisoners to." In Derrida's (rather harsh) view, Levinas's failure of moral empathy or imagination when it came to humanity's treatment of nonhuman animals prevented the great ethicist from responding to what Derrida recognized as that "industrial, mechanical, chemical, hormonal, and genetic violence to which man has been submitting animal life for the past two centuries," a violent "war against the animal" that Derrida only hesitates to describe as *genocide* (even though "there are also animal genocides: the number of species endangered because of man takes one's breath away") because much of the "torture" involves "the organization an exploitation of an artificial, infernal, virtually interminable survival" (see Derrida, *The Animal that Therefore I am*, 26, 101, 117) – that is, a terrible *keeping alive* (in horrifying conditions like "factory farms") as well as a brutal *making die* (and hence a further *biopolitical* mutation of technological *enframing*, to put it in the terms of Foucault and Heidegger).

7

Critical Afterlives of Heidegger's Phenomenology of Existential Death in Sartre, Beauvoir, Levinas, Agamben, and Derrida

7.1 Existential Death in Sartre's Look of the Other and Beauvoir's Crisis of Adolescence

Let us start with Sartre, whose creative appropriation of *Being and Time*'s phenomenology of death came to prominence first – in 1946's *Being and Nothingness* – and probably remains the most widely known in its own right. If Sartre's vision of existential death is rarely recognized as his alternative to Heidegger's account, that is both because what *Being and Time* means by death is not widely understood and because Sartre's alternative represents the furthest departure from Heidegger's own view.[1] In general, Sartre's adoption of a subject/object dualism leads him to pervasively re-Cartesianize *Being and Time*, as if he were completely oblivious to Heidegger's overarching efforts to

---

[1] Sartre's creative appropriation of Heidegger's phenomenology of death in Sartre, *Being and Nothingness* (1946) appeared just months before Beauvoir published her own portrayal of the existential "crisis of adolescence" in *The Ethics of Ambiguity* and Levinas first sketched his own view of such death in Levinas, *Time and the Other* (1946–47). Let me explicitly note that Sartre does also appropriate Heidegger's views on death more directly (see Sartre, *Being and Nothingness* [Richmond translation], 692–718), but when Sartre does so, he too reduces existential death to a relation to mortal demise (see, for example, ibid., 692, 700, 704–5, 711) and so, like Derrida, Sartre cannot understand Heidegger's phenomenology of existential death as Dasein's way of *being at the end* of its own distinctive being. Sartre writes, for example: "As death escapes from my projects because it is unrealizable, so I myself escape from death in my very project" (ibid., 711), which might be true of mortal demise (to some degree at least) but, crucially, not of existential death (as we saw in Chapter 1). Indeed, Sartre clearly expresses his Epicurean view in a later interview: "For me, it's simple: death is nothingness, hence not part of life, so I do not think of death" (John Gerassi, *Talking with* Sartre: *Conversations and Debates*, ed. and trans. by J. Gerassi [New Haven: Yale University Press, 2009], 15). Sartre's grasp of *futurity* is nevertheless surprisingly strong, and he at least seems to understand what Heidegger is arguing (if not the phenomenological evidence for Heidegger's view): "That is the very structure of ipseity [or *selfhood*]: to be a self is to come-toward oneself" (Sartre, *Being and Nothingness* [Richmond translation], 698). Although this false conflation of existential death with mortal demise pervades the explicit thinking about "death" in Sartre's *Being and Nothingness*, I shall suggest that his phenomenology of "the look of the other" comes much closer to Heidegger's phenomenology of existential death and so restrict my focus to that phenomenon here.

undermine Cartesian dualism.² (This obliviousness is already clear from Sartre's oft-quoted but nonetheless false claim that the "existentialism" he shares with Heidegger can be *defined* by their shared insistence "that *subjectivity* must be the starting point.")³ Sartre's phenomenology of the objectifying "look of the other" transforms Heidegger's phenomenology of existential death so dramatically that Sartre can easily appear to be describing a different phenomenon altogether. Read carefully, however, it becomes clear that Sartre's account of the "the look" allows him to articulate his own version of an existential phenomenon in which I experience "the death of my possibilities" – even though "I *am* my possibilities" – and yet I live through that experience to tell the tale phenomenologically.⁴

Recall Sartre's famous example of a person who, "whether moved by jealousy, curiosity, or vice," has just "looked through a keyhole." As this jealous lover, nosy neighbor, or peeping Tom becomes absorbed in the "spectacle to be seen" on the other side of the door, he "loses himself" in that world unfolding before his gaze, completely "drunk in by [the] things [he sees] as ink is by a blotter." Then something unexpected happens to Sartre's spectator, whose thinking Sartre narrates: "But all of a sudden I hear footsteps in the hall. Someone is looking at me!"⁵ In this instant of being seen by another, the spectatorial experience is completely inverted: No longer a subject objectifying another in his gaze, he suddenly becomes the objectified being, utterly transfixed by the gaze of this other person who has caught him in a shameful act of voyeurism. Frozen in this other's gaze, Sartre suggests, all the living "possibilities" that ordinarily "I *am*" instantly get reduced to one objective "probability which is outside of me" – a *voyeur* – and "my shame is an [involuntary] confession" that "I *am* this being," an objectively

---

² Repeating the "disastrous" Cartesian error that Division One of *Being and Time* deconstructs (BT 46/SZ 25), Sartre ontologically bifurcates the subjective "for-itself" and the objective "in-itself." Interestingly, Sartre's definition of the "for-itself" as "being what it is not and not being what it is" (Sartre, *Being and Nothingness* [Barnes translation], lxv) enables Sartre to inscribe Kierkegaard's "formula for despair" from *The Sickness Unto Death* (namely, "wanting to be what you are not or not wanting to be what you are") into the very structure of subjectivity itself (and this despite Sartre's own deathbed confession – or perhaps hollow boast: "Personally, I have never despaired, not for one moment" [Jean-Paul Sartre and Benny Levi, *Hope Now: The 1980 Interviews*, trans. by A. van den Hoven (Chicago, IL: University of Chicago Press, 1996), 55; cf. 108]).

³ (Jean-Paul Sartre, *Essays in Existentialism* [New Jersey: Citadel Press, 1965], 34, my emphasis.) Sartre may be paraphrasing Kierkegaard again here, but Kierkegaard too remains problematically Cartesian in his ontological prejudices. As Sartre unambiguously expresses the same point in *Being and Nothingness*: "Any study of human-reality [Sartre's term for his problematic recartesianization of 'Dasein'] must begin with the *cogito* [that is, the Cartesian 'I think']" (Sartre, *Being and Nothingness* [Richmond translation], 136).

⁴ Sartre, *Being and Nothingness* (Barnes translation), 240, 247.

⁵ Ibid., 235–6.

reprehensible being who is unlivable and even *unknowable* by me.[6] Transfixed by this "look of the other," in other words, the living possibilities that I am instantly evaporate, and I find myself petrified into this one shameful object, as though I had been caught in the mythical gaze of Medusa.[7]

As Sartre explains, "the *Other's look* ... is not only a transformation of myself but a total metamorphosis of the world" as I ordinarily live and experience it, a profound existential mutation by which "I am stripped of my distanceless presence to my world."[8] This collapse of my world is (in Sartre's terms) an entirely subjective experience, since no one but me directly experiences this deathly mutation in which the objectifying gaze of the other completely strips me of the holistic network of living possibilities that I was just a moment before. Sartre thus describes it as a "hidden death":

> The other is the hidden death of my possibilities, insofar as I live this death as hidden in the midst of the world.... In the look, the death of my possibilities makes me experience the other's freedom; ... and I am myself, inaccessible to myself and yet myself, thrown and abandoned within the other's freedom.[9]

This hidden death effected by the "look of the other" is thus clearly recognizable as Sartre's own version of existential death, in which I experience the collapse of all the living "possibilities" I ordinarily embody into one unlivable, objective "probability," that is, a "dead-possibility," "*simply given*" by the look of the other.[10]

For Sartre, then, it is not the affective attunement of anxiety that discloses the existential "death of my possibilities" but, instead, the attunement of *shame*. As he puts it: "Pure shame is not a feeling of being this or that guilty object but in general of *being* an object; that is, of *recognizing myself* in this degraded, fixed, dependent being which I am for the other." For Sartre it is also shame, and not Heidegger's guilt, that discloses "that I have 'fallen' into the world in the midst of things and need the mediation of the other in order to be what I am."[11] Here, unfortunately, Sartre's reinscription of subject/object dualism back into existential phenomenology sets up what then becomes for

---

[6] In Sartre's thinking of "the Other" as "this pure subject which by definition I am unable to know," we can recognize some of the seeds that would germinate in Levinas's own thinking of radical alterity.
[7] Sartre, *Being and Nothingness* (Barnes translation), 237, 240–1.
[8] (Ibid., 245.) This "distanceless presence to my world" is Sartre's interpretive appropriation of what Heidegger calls Dasein's "readiness-to-hand" (*Zuhandenheit*), that is, our skillful integration into the practical world disclosed by our defining existential projects, a world which collapses in existential death (as we saw in Chapter 1).
[9] Sartre, *Being and Nothingness* (Richmond translation), 362, 369.
[10] Sartre, *Being and Nothingness* (Barnes translation), 264.
[11] Ibid., 245, 247, 265.

him a fundamental and inescapable dialectic, in which we are all fated to oscillate back-and-forth between either living as masterful subjects whose gaze objectifies others, or else having our living worlds objectified by the gaze of others and thereby finding ourselves "enslaved" by their objective appraisals.[12]

Sartre's dystopian vision of intersubjectivity presents us with a dark, Kojèvean mutation of the Hegelian dream of a public world constituted to enable satisfying mutual recognition. (Indeed, as Judith Butler has shown, Sartre's view was deeply influenced by Kojève's Heidegger-inflected reading of Hegel's *Phenomenology of Spirit*, which foregrounded Hegel's "master/slave dialectic" and read it as centrally turning on two fundamentally different ways of relating to death: namely, with either the *terror* of a slave or else the *fearlessness* of a master.)[13] As a Cartesian dualist, Sartre reduces the thinking subject to sheer negativity, and as a Hegelian, he argues that we need the mediation of others in order to exist in *any* positive terms at all. Combining these views, *Being and Nothingness* argues that we must enter the public world in order to exist meaningfully, but that to do so is to enter the terrain of an endless power struggle, in which we inevitably oscillate between affixing objectifying and reductive scarlet letters to others and experiencing ourselves brought up short by such unlivable categorizations. *Being and Nothingness* is at its most original as Sartre seeks to chart and describe the different existential strategies he thinks we have developed and adopted to navigate the ever-shifting battlefield of intersubjectivity – strategies that, Sartre concludes darkly, all inevitably fail to achieve their desired ends.[14]

---

[12] Ibid., 243.

[13] See Alexandre Kojève, *Introduction to the Reading of Hegel: Lectures on the Phenomenology of Spirit* (Ithaca, NY: Cornell University Press, 1980); and Judith Butler, *Subjects of Desire: Hegelian Reflections on Twentieth Century France* (New York: Columbia University Press, 1987), which examines Kojève's massive influence on Sartre's entire generation.

[14] (See Sartre, *Being and* Nothingness [Richmond translation], 479–566.) Although partly anticipated by earlier existential critiques of the public world (such as Kierkegaard's "public," Nietzsche's "herd," and Heidegger's anonymous "anyone [*das Man*]"), the complete identification of the public world with inauthentic conformity and oppression in Sartre's *Being and Nothingness* remains extreme. It was probably more compelling in the immediate aftermath of Nazism, which both politically and literally reduced its victims to such unlivable objective categories, and in which all resistance had to be carried out in underground movements (in which to be seen by the public world meant death). But a similarly alienated vision reemerges in later critical thinkers such as Foucault, with his influential rejection of all public markers of identity as "policing" tactics in a "carceral" society (to which we return in Chapter 8), as well as in some leading contemporary thinkers of transgender and nonbinary sexualities, which they argue should not be seen as emerging existential categories struggling for intersubjective recognition but, instead, as living rejections of the inherent repressiveness of all such objective categorizations of sexuality (see, for example, Paul Preciado, *Countersexual*

Sartre's elaborate depictions of the ultimately doomed existential strategies he thinks we employ to navigate our ways through intersubjectivity's continually shifting power dynamics remain provocative. But *Being and Nothingness*'s dualistic thinking of intersubjectivity in terms of an inescapable master/slave dialectic leads directly to Sartre's notoriously reductive depiction of all sexuality as *sadomasochistic*, an account Simone de Beauvoir subtly contests and replaces with a more nuanced, resonant, and ultimately hopeful account of intersubjectivity in *The Ethics of Ambiguity* (1947).[15] In the process of doing so, Beauvoir's own early, postwar work demonstrates a deep and original understanding of Heidegger's phenomenology of existential death, one which comes through most clearly in her critical examination of the reasons why (and various ways in which) too many of us flee our anxiety in the face of the death back into a reactionary embrace of the dogmatic and authoritarian moral and political worlds of *das Man* (Heidegger's anonymous "anyone"). Such conformist public worlds are characterized by an epistemically brittle (and so aggressively defensive) faith in the absolute standing of their own pervasive normative prescriptions about what *one should do and how one should do it*. Because they provide "ready-made" answers to life's most difficult questions, they appeal to those who cannot endure the anxiety-provoking process of having to struggle repeatedly in life to develop their own "genuine" (Beauvoir's version of *authentic*) answers to the basic existential questions of what to do and how to do it, questions that (as *Being and Time* taught) do not lend themselves to once-and-for-all-time answers or one-size-fits-all solutions.

Manifesto [New York: Columbia University Press, 2018]). In their problematic tendency toward *totalizing* critique, such views are more Levinasian than later Heideggerian, in that they tend toward thinking being – for example, the being of the sexual (that is, *sexuality*) – as *ineffable* (that is, as not capable of being meaningfully captured in concepts) rather than as *inexhaustibly excessive* (and so as both informing but also overflowing all such conceptual and practical categorizations). We return to this important point in Chapter 8 (but see also Iain Thomson, "Ontopoliticosexual Pro(−)vocations," *Gatherings: The Heidegger Circle Annual* XII [2022], 206–10).

[15] Sartre and Beauvoir developed their thinking *together* at this time (as both often stressed), yet differences remain, and I take this to be one of the most philosophically profound and suggestive ones. Although Beauvoir too believes that "[t]here is no way for a human being to escape from this world" (Beauvoir, *Ethics of Ambiguity*, 75), Beauvoir's optimistic realism – her view that humanity's greatest intersubjective achievements were genuine and important but remain contingent and fragile and so in need of our continued defense, improvement, and development – comes through clearly in such passages as the following (germane to the topic we are about to discuss): "Human beings do not like to feel themselves in danger. Yet, it is because there are real dangers, real failures, and real earthly damnation that words like victory, wisdom, or joy have meaning. Nothing is decided in advance, and it is because humanity has something to lose and because human beings can lose that we can also win" (ibid., 34–5).

Exploring an issue Heidegger remains almost entirely silent about, Beauvoir examines some key stages of our psychological development and argues that it is typical for young children to assume that there is an absolute truth about how to live. Indeed, naïvely taking their parents and other adult authority figures as representatives of such a "serious world" – an *adult* world, filled with unambiguous values and rules that adults seem to understand and follow – provides children with a kind of reassuring psychological backstop, helping carve out a safe space for the young to develop their own creative capacities as they explore various existential possibilities in imaginative play. As children "passionately pursue and joyfully attain goals" they have freely set for themselves in these worlds of play, they learn to develop the rudiments of an authentic life, such as "vitality, sensitivity, and intelligence," which "are not ready-made qualities but [rather develop from] a way of casting oneself into the world and of disclosing being."[16]

Of course, this ideal of children playing with "happy irresponsibility" and so developing a rudimentary understanding of what an authentic life entails can often fail to obtain in actual life (as when such responsible parents are absent, for whatever reasons, or when the parents' own behavior does not give the child the credible illusion of a serious world), and the practice can even lend itself to oppression (as in patriarchal efforts to permanently infantilize women – and, especially under contemporary technocapitalist *enframing*, men as well). But Beauvoir's deepest insight here is that, even in the best-case scenarios, such a childhood is still fated to end in a profound *existential*

---

[16] (Beauvoir, *Ethics of Ambiguity*, 38, 44.) As Beauvoir explains her *radically constructivist* view, what looks like ingrained character is only the sedimented residue of earlier free actions: "The child does not contain the man he will become. Yet, it is always on the basis of what he has been that a man decides upon what he wants to be. He draws the motivations of his moral attitude from within the character which he has given himself and from within the universe which is its correlative. Now, the child sets up this character and this universe little by little, without foreseeing its development. He was ignorant of the disturbing aspect of this freedom which he was heedlessly exercising. He tranquilly abandoned himself to whims, laughter, tears, and anger which seemed to him to have no morrow and no danger, and yet which left ineffaceable imprints about him. The drama of original choice [Sartre and Beauvoir's term for the "always-already" of the existential *projecting into projects* that constitute and transform our meaningful worlds in their "thrownness"] is that it goes on moment by moment for an entire lifetime" (ibid., 43). The child's development of such proto-authentic traits requires the right kinds of inter-subjective social life as well, for: "There is vitality only by means of free generosity. Intelligence supposes good will, and, inversely, a man is never stupid if he adapts his language and his behavior to his capacities, and sensitivity is nothing else but the presence that is attentive to the world and itself. The reward for these spontaneous [that is, *freely* disclosive] qualities issues from the fact that they make significances and goals appear in the world. They discover reasons for existing. They confirm us in the pride and joy of our destiny as man" (ibid., 44–5). Here, moreover, the contrast with Sartre's more darkly cynical view of intersubjectivity as *hell* stands out clearly.

death, a fraught transition each of us must pass through on the way to *genuine* adulthood. As she puts it, "the deepest reason for the crisis of adolescence" *is* "the collapsing of the serious world."[17] Genuinely growing up means growing out of the child's simplistic and illusory vision of a "serious world" of adults who have attained the correct answer about how to live.

There is thus a profound existential death at the heart of "the crisis of adolescence," Beauvoir suggests, one that requires each of us to confront and pass through a difficult psychological stage that mirrors the historical one Nietzsche famously called "the death of God," a momentous historical event in which human beings "unchained this earth from its sun" by realizing that our moral views about how to live cannot credibly be anchored in some absolute foundation outside the world of human experience.[18] As a result, when the adolescent experiences "the collapsing of the serious world":

> Men stop appearing as if they were gods, and at the same time the adolescent discovers the human character of the reality about him. Language, customs, ethics, and values have their source in these *uncertain* creatures. The moment has come when he too is going to be called upon to participate in their operation; his acts weigh upon the earth as much as those of other men. He will have to choose and decide.[19]

Successfully finding our way through this profound existential death, in other words, requires giving up the childish fantasy of there being one correct answer about how to live and instead resolutely coming to terms with the fact that we human beings are the only ones deciding such questions, and that these admittedly collective decisions are, in the end, made by individuals who either go along with and reinforce or else contest and transform the "ready-made" answers passed down to us and transmitted through us to the next generation.[20] I have elsewhere critiqued the problematic *subjectivism* of Beauvoir's early view – that is, its overemphasis of the transformative power of individual agency and correlative underemphasis of more hidden structures perpetuating oppression (not only those patriarchal forms of domination to which Beauvoir herself would soon turn but also their embeddedness within and reinforcement of the technocapitalist superstructures of what Heidegger

---

[17] Beauvoir, *Ethics of Ambiguity*, 42.
[18] (See Nietzsche, *The Gay Science*, section 125.) For Nietzsche, it was primarily Kant who "killed God" in this way (see Thomson, *Heidegger on Ontotheology*, 20–1).
[19] Beauvoir, *Ethics of Ambiguity*, 41–2 (my emphasis).
[20] To be clear, the critical point here is not that we should police the imagination (a problematically invasive move typical of Catholicism and psychoanalysis, as Foucault often observed) but, instead, that taking mythological fantasies *literally* is childish and often makes for dangerously regressive politics among adults.

calls *ontotheology* and Derrida fleshes out as *carnophallogocentrism*).[21] Here, however, I would simply like to emphasize how close Beauvoir's insight into the existential death of adolescence that is required for a birth to genuine adulthood brings her to some of the central Heideggerian insights we have been examining in this book.

For Beauvoir (like Kierkegaard and Heidegger), we existing beings can only "be" something by repeatedly *becoming* it.[22] Genuinely *becoming* an adult means facing up to "the anguish of freedom" from which the child has (ideally) been spared, acknowledging the existential *ambiguity* with which our own freedom repeatedly confronts us (when we find ourselves faced with more than one path forward, for example), and yet still genuinely taking responsibility for the actions (and inactions) by which we decide what and how to be.[23] "But the fact is that conversions are difficult," she emphasizes, and what makes such an authentic passage through this crucial existential death possible is that we learn to recognize and respond to (rather than deflect and deny) this positive *ethical ambiguity*, that is, the fact of there being more than one way for us to live well. (As Beauvoir thus explains her key term: "To declare that existence ... is ambiguous is to assert that its meaning is never fixed, that it must be constantly won.")[24] Beauvoir's irreducible ethical pluralism stems from her seemingly deeply (later) Heideggerian insight that there is no one correct way to capture the real of being within the always finite perspectives and projects of human existence. In her words:

> My freedom must not seek to trap being but to disclose it. The disclosure is the transition from being to existence. The goal which my freedom aims at is conquering existence across the always inadequate density of being.[25]

The point, I take it, is that the reality of what-is remains "inadequate" to tell us what to do or how to live. When we face important ethical questions about who and how to be, the being of what-is only provides us with *ambiguous* hints (that is, hints that could be resolved in *irreducibly multiple* ways), thereby always leaving room for the freedom of our own creative ways of disclosing being's inchoate possibilities. For Beauvoir (again sounding much like Heidegger), such creative and responsive *disclosure* constitutes the very

---

[21] See Chapter 8 and, for example, Thomson, *Heidegger on Ontotheology*, ch. 2 (esp. 48–51); Thomson, "From the Question Concerning Technology to the Quest for a Democratic Technology: Heidegger, Marcuse, Feenberg."

[22] (See Chapter 4.) As Beauvoir expresses the idea, "existence ... *is* only by making itself be" (Beauvoir, *Ethics of Ambiguity*, 24–5). Or, in what would become her most famous exemplification of this idea (from the following year): "One is not born, but rather becomes, [a] woman" (Beauvoir, *The Second Sex*, 267).

[23] Beauvoir, *Ethics of Ambiguity*, 38, 41, 42.

[24] Ibid., 139.

[25] Ibid., 30.

nature of our *existence* (in its difference from sheer objective factuality).[26] In narrating humanity's repeated struggles to assume the disclosive freedom that defines our existence, Beauvoir's *The Ethics of Ambiguity* elaborates her own perfectionist vision of *how we become what we are*.

Our very nature foists such freedom upon us (we are "condemned to be free," as Sartre famously put it, that is, we are not free not to be free), but Beauvoir argues that far too many of us recoil in horror from the irreducible ambiguity our existences must repeatedly face.[27] When the death of childhood's illusions about the adult world discloses the anxiety-provoking absence of any single correct answer about how to live, not everyone is able to genuinely grow up and accept "the agony [or endless *struggle*] of our freedom."[28] Instead, many so-called adults choose "to live in an infantile world," running back into the arms of one-sided dogmatisms that dishonestly deny any "ambiguity" concerning *what we should do and be*.[29] Rather than taking

---

[26] As Beauvoir puts it: "To wish for the disclosure of the world and to assert oneself as freedom are one and the same movement." Or, "the free man wants freedom in order to desire being," and "he wants the disclosure of being by freedom. These are two aspects of a single reality" (Beauvoir, *Ethics of Ambiguity*, 23, 75).

[27] Indeed, much of Beauvoir's *Ethics of Ambiguity* is dedicated to critically analyzing and cataloguing a series of characteristic ways in which human beings distort and deform their lives by seeking to deny, repress, minimize, or manipulate such ambiguity, which enables Beauvoir to develop fascinating philosophical caricatures of such unattractive figures as "the sub-man," "the serious man," "the tyrant," "the demoniacal man," "the nihilist," "the adventurer," "the passionate man," and "the intellectual" (45–78), all of whom represent various ways of failing to become "the free man" (or genuine existentialist), who realizes "that human freedom is the ultimate, unique end to which man should destine himself" (52) and so builds their own "existence upon the indefinite unfolding of time" (73). Beauvoir says "destined" here because, as *condemned* to be free, she argues that the free existentialist "*must* [I emphasize the word] disclose the world with the purpose of further disclosure and by the same movement try to free men, by means of whom the world takes on meaning" (79). Creatively combining Kant, Hegel, and Heidegger, Beauvoir argues that the genuine existentialist comes philosophically to understand "the requirements of his own freedom, which can will itself only by destining itself to an open future, by seeking to extend itself by means of the freedom of others. Therefore ... the freedom of other men must be respected and they must be helped to free themselves" (65).

[28] (Beauvoir, *Ethics of Ambiguity*, 55.) "Ethics does not furnish recipes"; instead, "morality resides in the painfulness of an indefinite questioning" (ibid., 144–5).

[29] (Beauvoir, *Ethics of Ambiguity*, 51.) Because they thus disavow their own freely disclosive nature, Beauvoir calls such people "sub-men" (a derogatory term which has not aged well), arguing that their eager embrace of authoritarian regimes follows from their reactionary desire to return to the child's comforting faith in an adult world of absolute values. For, were there such a world, then it could provide these childish adults with the correct answers about how to live, thereby protecting them from the anxiety-provoking struggle to repeatedly carve out livable answers for themselves. As Beauvoir thus describes this (so-called) "sub-man" type: "He is afraid of engaging himself in a project as he is afraid of being disengaged and thereby being in a state of danger before the future,

7.1. EXISTENTIAL DEATH IN SARTRE AND BEAUVOIR 217

up the endless struggle to be *authentically* (or "genuinely") right "in their own eyes," such inauthentic reactionaries flee into ready-made worlds of "extrinsic justification," adopting these "foreign absolutes" in vain hope of reassuring themselves and each other that the authoritarian system of values by which they live are absolute and invulnerable, and so not in fact fundamentally shaped and maintained by our individual and collective ways of freely projecting into such projects and thereby conserving, contesting, or transforming them.[30]

Beauvoir points out that human ideals and institutions can survive only by being passed down through time, which means they are in fact being repeatedly extended, developed, forgotten, or transformed. Our individual and collective visions about how to live can never simply be perpetuated in an unaltered form, because "the ambiguity of [the human] condition which is the most fundamental of all" is the fact "that every living movement is a sliding toward death." Fortunately (as we have seen throughout this book), those who "are willing to look [death] in the face ... also discover that every movement toward death is life." The fact that every individual and collective way of life is inevitably caught up in a process of historical entropy means that our best accomplishments can survive only by being repeatedly reborn. When old ways of living become outdated and begin dying off, our increasingly painful collective awareness of this death (an awareness shown not only in the suffering of those forced to live in unlivable categories and conditions, but also in that growing desperation with which the reactionaries seek to bring back a past that is already gone or existed only in their imaginations) is thus also an opportunity calling for our creative disclosure of a future that is more free, just, and livable than that dying present sent down to us from the past. The last word of *The Ethics of Ambiguity* is "death [*la mort*]," but to emphasize what for Beauvoir remains its ambiguous other side, we can end our brief treatment by resounding another resonant chord: "In the past people cried out, 'the king is dead, long live the king'; thus the present must die so that it may live; existence must not deny this death which it carries in its heart; ... humanity fulfills itself within the transitory or not at all."[31]

Let us turn, then, to briefly examine the two contrasting visions of the kind of human fulfillment we can reach by passing through such existential death and rebirth developed in the early Heidegger and in Levinas. As we will see,

---

in the midst of possibilities. [That is, he is afraid to try because he is afraid to fail and so have to confront the truth of not knowing what to do. He is, in Heidegger's terms, afraid of the nothing, that is, anxious about existential death.] He is thereby led to take refuge in the [superficial illusion of the] ready-made values of the serious world" (Beauvoir, *Ethics of Ambiguity*, 47).

[30] Beauvoir, *Ethics of Ambiguity*, 13–15.
[31] Ibid., 137, 173.

Levinas's foundational thinking of alterity ultimately makes his ethical perfectionism even more other-centered than Beauvoir's view that we cannot genuinely exist in free and meaningful ways without also helping to free others (for the Hegelian reason that we can only ever be truly satisfied by intersubjective recognition given freely by others).[32] The early Heidegger's perfectionist thinking is more individualistic (as we saw in Chapter 6), but he does ultimately come much closer to such views in his later thinking of education, which emphasizes both that the most meaningful form of individual ontological disclosure can be found only in an other-liberating pedagogical practice, and also that ultimately only a *collective* transformation of Western humanity's implicit understanding of being (as intrinsically meaningless resources) can save us from the growing nihilism of our late-modern age of technological *enframing*.[33]

7.2 Levinas's "Other" Phenomenology of Existential Death: Political Afterthoughts

Although undoubtedly Heidegger's most critical heir, Levinas was also the first creative interpreter who seems to have thoroughly understood Heidegger's phenomenology of existential death in *Being and Time*, as is shown by the way he contests so many of its crucial details. We have seen that Levinas, a former student of Heidegger, implicitly builds much of his own larger dialectical account of how we become ourselves ethically by contesting and revising the specific structure of *Being and Time*'s phenomenological account of "authenticity."[34] Recall that Heidegger defines *authenticity* (*Eigentlichkeit*, more literally "ownedness," an owning up to that takes ownership over my own existence) as "anticipatory resoluteness" (BT 370/SZ 323). As *anticipatory resoluteness*, authenticity is accomplished – temporarily, and so repeatedly – through an intrinsically double movement in which the practical world of one's defining projects is lost in "anticipation" (*Vorlaufen*, "running out"

---

[32] For Beauvoir, as we saw, "each individual ... must disclose the world with the purpose of further disclosure and by the same movement try to free men, by means of whom the world takes on meaning," through "concrete" actions. We successfully "realize our freedom" when we "engage" ourselves in collective or intersubjective projects – but "without losing" ourselves (a difference from Levinas, whose rather extreme goal is to ceaselessly combat our own self-concern) – for instance, "in political action, in intellectual or artistic research, [and] in family or social life" (Beauvoir, *Ethics of Ambiguity*, 59, 79).

[33] For the details, see Thomson, *Heidegger on Ontotheology*, ch. 4.

[34] As we saw in Chapter 6, Levinas's phenomenology of self-fulfillment simply cannot be understood without this Heideggerian background, which Levinas continually presupposes but never explicitly acknowledges or explains (and which then becomes a large but often unrecognized hermeneutic obstacle for the many Levinasians who seek to understand Levinas without recourse to Heidegger).

into existential death) and then regained in "resolve" (*Ent-schlossenheit*, that "un-closedness" by which the *solus ipse*, the radically finite solitude of existential death's projectless projecting, opens itself to the inchoate possibilities coming toward it from out of the nothingness of the future and thereby finds a way to project itself back into the world of self-constituting life-projects). We have thus seen that Heideggerian authenticity is a circular movement in which the world's grip on us is temporarily broken so that we may gain (or regain) our grip on the world, a literally *revolutionary* movement in which we are first involuntarily turned away from our world and then voluntarily turn back to it, thereby understanding our world and ourselves anew.

In *Being and Time*, we are turned away from the world of our life-constituting projects when confronting our *Angst* encourages us to discover our essential "uncanniness" or "not-being-at-home" in this world (that is, the ineliminable lack of fit by which our sheer existing inevitably overflows the worldly projects through which it understands itself). This discovery of our *uncanniness* shatters our superficial good conscience, leading to the collapse of any guiding life-project we had been pursuing with the blithe confidence that it was the sole right answer to the question of what we should do with our lives. Upon discovering that the core of the self is a projectless projecting that survives this existential death of its life-projects (and so "understands itself in its own *superior power*" [BT 436/SZ 384], as stronger than death), we can then turn back to the world by lucidly opening ourselves to and decisively projecting into a life-project. Such "authenticity" requires owning our ineliminable ontological "guilt," which stems from the fact that we can be anything specific only through an always finite and contingent projecting into an indeterminate future. Owning such ontological guilt means learning to tolerate the "nihilation" of all the other live-option life-projects that we could project into but choose not to in order to project into our defining existential project, thereby letting-go of what we are *not* becoming in order to *become what we are*. For Heidegger, moreover, such authenticity is not a permanent achievement; instead, striving to exist authentically means committing ourselves to repeatedly *becoming* who we are, periodically repossessing ourselves from the self-alienating grip of the public world and its superficial answers to existential questions about what and how to be that can never be answered once and for all.

Despite its temporary nature, authenticity's double movement of anticipation and resolve, existential death and rebirth, has long been thought of as Heidegger's phenomenological version of *conversion*, since it is a movement in which we turn away from the world, (re)discover the core of ourselves, and then turn back to the world, transformed by the process. When Levinas articulates, develops, and modifies his own core philosophical project (published in works like *Time and The Other* [1946]; *Totality and Infinity* [1961]; and *Otherwise than Being* [1974]), he too is centrally concerned to provide a phenomenological description of "death" and its role in what he goes so far as to call the self's "resurrection," and the structure of Levinas's account remains almost identical to Heidegger's, in the following way.[35] Just like Heidegger, Levinas thinks we become fully ourselves only when we confront "death" and then – on the basis of the transformative realization afforded by this confrontation with death – we find a way back to the world, a world which we thereby come to understand quite differently.[36] What, we can thus ask, are the basic coordinates of the dispute between Heidegger and Levinas over the phenomenology and, consequently, the ontological significance of "death"? (Those who have read the previous chapter and do not want a quick refresher should feel free to skip the next three paragraphs.)

In what amounts to a formidable *immanent critique* of *Being and Time*'s phenomenology of the existential death and rebirth that together constitute authenticity (and so tell the story of how we repeatedly become what we are), Levinas challenges four interconnected aspects of Heidegger's account and offers his own alternatives. Here I will briefly summarize their four major differences (explored in detail in Chapter 6), before going on to summarize Levinas's later development of this critique. *First, Levinas objects to Heidegger's phenomenological description of the self confronting itself in "death."* According to Levinas's famous critique, Heidegger thinks "death" reveals the self's indomitable "virility" and "lucidity," whereas Levinas himself thinks that such existential death delivers the stroke of a paralyzing passivity that this self is unable to surmount solely under its own power. *Second, Levinas disputes the nature of the crucial insight afforded by the self's confrontation with death.* For Heidegger, confronting death enables us to discover something about ourselves that remains more powerful than death, an aspect of the self (which Heidegger calls our "ownmost ability-to-be") that does not go down with the shipwreck of our life-projects but rather survives for as long as do each of our individual Daseins. By contrast, Levinas thinks that when death renders us utterly powerless and passive, it reveals *the other person* as providing our only bridge to pass through death toward a future that death has placed beyond our reach. Levinas thus holds, in perhaps the definitive claim of his work, that recognizing the other person as the only vessel capable of transporting us through such "death" into the future allows us to understand the other person as the sole bearer of "what is not yet," that is, of *alterity*, Levinas's famous term for an (allegedly) "infinite" otherness that repeatedly breaks into our worlds only through other people.

Third, Levinas contests Heidegger's account of how it is that the self lives through death and thereby reconnects to the world. What Heidegger calls

---

[35] See Levinas, *Totality and Infinity*, 56, 284.
[36] Although Levinas's view is not phenomenological all the way down (but also draws fundamental inspiration from the Torah and Talmud; see Chapter 6, n. 28), this moment is central to the broader philosophical narrative of ethical development that Levinas spends his life developing and revising; indeed, Levinas calls this confrontation with existential death "the ineluctable moment of my dialectic" (Levinas, *Time and the Other*, 92).

"resoluteness" draws upon the lucidity and virility discovered in death as our "ownmost ability-to-be" in order to reconnect to the world by "choosing to choose" or otherwise opening itself to a futural life-project that thereby comes to define it. Levinas, for his part, believes that the self can reconnect to the world only by giving itself over to another person – paradigmatically a "teacher" or "master" – with whom this self can grope, in conversation and learning, toward a future it cannot yet comprehend. (In this vision of existential learning as creative, dialogical interpretation, Levinas himself has Talmudic learning foremost in mind, but we could also think here of one popular version of the drama of Prince Siddhartha, who had collapsed beneath the Bodhi tree, exhausted by the successive failures of both princely hedonism and rigorous asceticism to alleviate his suffering, but then hears the fateful words of a music teacher instructing a student while drifting by in a boat: "If the strings are too tight, they will break; if the strings are too loose, they will not play," words of an other teacher that enabled Siddhartha to creatively discover his own "wisdom of the middle way" and so "awaken" as Buddha.)

Fourth, and last, Levinas opposes Heidegger's description of how the self who finds a way back to the world is transformed by the adventure. In *Being and Time*, Heidegger's authentic self becomes itself fully by seizing its "fate" and so entering into the history-defining struggle to shape the communal "destiny" of its generation, which is accomplished by creatively and critically "repeating" and updating a project drawn from a past "hero" or role-model in a way that enables this authentic self to intervene meaningfully in its time while also establishing its own relatively continuous identity as an engaged individual, its "existentiell constancy or steadfastness" (BT 443/SZ 391).[37] Levinas, by contrast, thinks that we fully become ourselves only by being reborn as another person, radically different from our previous self-conception. Through a process Levinas calls "transubstantiation," the passage through existential death via the other should transform us into wholly other-directed selves, no longer egocentrics but (literal) eccentrics committed to an open-ended community of those dedicated entirely to alterity, and so to the future, to continual transformation, even to the "permanent revolution" of "incessant death and resurrection" (as Levinas dramatically puts it).[38]

---

[37] It is in the context of this view about how we appropriate the living heritage from out of the dying tradition (and so help shape the collective identity of our generation as well as our own identity as part of that larger community) that Heidegger comes closest to the view advanced by Beauvoir, Guignon, and Wrathall (see Chapter 1, n. 55). But even here I would emphasize the *transformative* potential inherent in these repetitions, in which the self repeatedly reconstitutes its own identity by owning up to the embodied stand it is (re)taking on the meaning of its being (by becoming) in time, place, and history.

[38] Heidegger too thinks that authentic Dasein helps others achieve authenticity (although the meaning of such death and rebirth remains quite different, as we saw in Chapter 6). We do this, in *Being and Time*, by becoming "the conscience for others," which for Heidegger involves gently showing others (by "leaping ahead" to help liberate their existential

So, the heart of their disagreement or divergence is that, whereas existential death discloses the nothing for Heidegger, *death discloses alterity* for Levinas. Levinas does not assert the converse, that the other discloses death, or that we can somehow experience our own death directly in the demise of another person (although Levinas's critique of Heidegger has been influentially misread that way). As Levinas himself clearly states: "My death is not deduced from the death of the others by analogy; it is inscribed in the fear I can have for my being."[39] Although neither thinker addresses this point directly, Heidegger and Levinas should agree that the demise of an other person can indeed catalyze my own existential death – especially if my commitment to caring for that other person was what Heidegger calls my "ultimate for-the-sake-of-which," or that singular life-project implicitly organizing all my other life projects. (For Heidegger, the collapse of such an ultimate project is precisely what sends all my other supporting projects cascading down in its wake, leading to the *complete* world-collapse of existential death.)

Instead, their fundamental disagreement is suggested by Heidegger's later view that, for a phenomenologist, pure, absolute, or infinite *alterity* is a paradoxical (if not simply contradictory) concept, because it is a concept for

possibilities rather than "leaping in" to dominate them and close off their sense of what is possible) that there is no one right answer to the difficult and important questions we face in life, and thus no possible *righteous certainty* that one is doing the only morally or politically correct thing, or as he succinctly puts it (in a line Derrida loved to paraphrase): "The [so-called] 'good' conscience [that is, morally righteous self-certitude] is not a conscience phenomenon at all" (BT 338/SZ 292), but instead a reactionary flight from conscience into what one does. For Heidegger, "conscience is a knowing [*Gewissen ist ein Wissen*]," but what it knows is one's ineliminable *guilt* (stemming from our defining finitude, the fact that we *cannot* be all that we could actually be, as we saw in Chapter 1, n. 54). For Levinas too, our guilt defines us (my "*Sein*" is always in someone else's "*Da*," he liked to say; that is, ontologically, we cannot help taking up space that an other would have occupied differently). Ethical development means leaving behind the reassuring certainties of the various moral fundamentalisms and instead ceaselessly responding to one's own infinite responsibilities for others, an ethical life in which progress only *heightens* one's awareness of one's ethical shortcomings, rather than ever leaving one righteously certain of having fulfilled one's duty. (I return to these issues in Chapter 8.)

[39] (Levinas, *Totality and Infinity*, 233.) See, for example, Critchley, whose creative reading conflates existential death with mortal demise and so concludes that "there can be no phenomenology of death because ... Death is radically resistant to the order of representation" (Simon Critchley, *Very Little ... Almost Nothing: Death, Philosophy, Literature* [London: Routledge, 2004], 31.) As we saw in Chapter 1, that is true of *demise* itself, but were it true of existential death then Heidegger's phenomenological descriptions of our being at our own distinctive end in such death would be fantastic hallucinations and, moreover, his central later view of poetry's ability to responsively and creatively disclose the nothing that death reveals (examined in Chapter 3) would indeed be merely a cover for his own "arbitrary" and "unjustifiable decisions," as Derrida alleges on the basis of his own competing axiomatic commitments (as we will see in Section 7.3).

which there can be no convincing phenomenological evidence, not even in existential death (which first discloses being, albeit only in the guise of the nothing, as we saw in Chapters 1, 2, and 3). Merely for something to be intelligible to us, we must have some sense of it, in which case it will not be "infinitely other." As I thus have often emphasized, Heidegger's later thinking of "the noth-ing" as the dynamic presencing of "being as such" should not be conflated with Levinas's thinking of "alterity" (a common mistake), since for Heidegger being is not phenomenologically *ineffable* but rather *excessive*, "inexhaustibly given to human beings to think" (CPC 156/GA77 239), partly informing but also inevitably overflowing and so escaping all the meaningful efforts by which we successfully disclose aspects of it in words and actions, concepts and practices.[40] In his philosophical works, Levinas repeatedly embraces the paradoxical conception of pure alterity somehow making itself felt in the phenomenal field of "the same" (as an invisible "trace" of the other, for instance, or as a wounding irruption of "trauma," or as a relation between two things that have no relation, and so on). But Levinas forthrightly acknowledges that his views are not phenomenological all the way down but, instead, ultimately remain "dialectical," by which he means they are based on creative, masterful teacher-mediated readings of the Torah and Talmud as a living dialogical testament of the stages through which a human life can and should proceed in order to realize its *ethical* fulfilment.[41]

Revealing the ethical and political subtext of his critique, Levinas famously suggests that Heidegger's phenomenology of death (as "the *possibility* of impossibility"), precisely because it discloses the ontological core of the self as a virile and powerful agency, "leads inevitably" to Heidegger's own embrace of a fascist tyrant.[42] I have argued that there is no *inevitable* connection between Heidegger's thinking and his horrifying embrace of Nazism. The connection between Heidegger's thinking and Nazism is neither *arbitrary*, as Sluga suggests, nor *necessary*, as Levinas does, but, instead, *contingent*, turning on a number of important factors and so leaving behind a complex legacy for his critical heirs to think through carefully.[43] But we might well wonder how Levinas's alternative phenomenology of death (as "the *impossibility* of possibility") – which discloses an utterly powerless self that can find its way through

---

[40] Heidegger's (self-styled) "Guide" asks the pointed phenomenological question: "But has it really been established that the absolutely nameless is given [to us]? For us much is often ineffable, but only because its name has not yet come to us" (CPC 77/GA77 119).
[41] Indeed, in ways Levinas's theological works often help show more clearly; see Chapter 6, n. 28 and Claire Katz, "Jewish Philosophy and the Shoah," in Becker and Thomson, *The Cambridge History of Philosophy* (op. cit.), 709–22.
[42] Levinas, *Time and the Other*, 70 and *Totality and Infinity*, 46.
[43] See Sluga, *Heidegger's Crisis*, and Thomson, *Heidegger on Ontotheology* (ch. 3) and "Heidegger's Nazism in the Light of His Early *Black Notebooks*."

death and back to the world only with the help of a great "teacher" or "master" – can itself rule out any possible embrace of fascism.

Indeed, if we could prevent all future ethico-political atrocities simply by adopting the correct foundational principle (as if choosing between *being* and *alterity* were like choosing between consequentialism and deontology, and as if such a choice could actually settle those concrete existential questions that cannot be settled once and for all, rather than trying to short-circuit or dodge them), then we would not have as much need as we do for the kind of complicated ethical responses Levinas and the later Heidegger both give us, which address not just our faculties of *moral* reasoning but also the *ethical* dimension of our broader, comportmental being-in-the-world, as we saw in Chapter 6. More generally, I argued there that, while it is important to appreciate the many differences between Heidegger and Levinas and think through them carefully, these differences are too often exaggerated by overly uncharitable readings of Heidegger, which follow the hermeneutically problematic lead of Levinas himself, who held that it is not possible "to forgive" even a brilliant teacher like Heidegger – to whom a student owes so much ("often ... to his regret," Levinas poignantly adds), but who never asked for forgiveness and, even if he had, could *never* be granted absolution, since Levinas holds that one must first understand what one has done wrong in order to be able to be forgiven, and Heidegger could never possibly comprehend the full extent of his own wrongdoing (given his "intellectual" contributions to the *immeasurable* horrors of the Shoah, including millions of *unforgivable* murders), and who really, above all, should have known better.[44] But this completely understandable refusal of forgiveness did not prevent Levinas from continuing to critically engage with Heidegger's thinking for the rest of his life – albeit "unjustly," by Levinas's own standards and admission, since he could never overcome his "allergy" to the political "climate of Heidegger's thinking."[45]

Indeed, in Levinas's last lectures at the Sorbonne (begun in 1975, the year of Heidegger's demise), Levinas once again confronts Heidegger's phenomenology of death, as if to have it out for a final time. Here Levinas again emphasizes the "this-sidedness" of Heidegger's treatment of death while stressing, for his part, death's unknowability and alterity, even polemically suggesting that because Heidegger's *phenomenological* approach confines itself to the "this-sidedness" of death (or to the way we can experience death while still alive), Heidegger reduces death to "annihilation" – that very same "*negative* character of death ... inscribed in hatred or the desire to murder," Levinas

---

[44] Emmanuel Levinas, *Nine Talmudic Readings*, trans. by A. Aronowicz (Bloomington: Indiana University Press, 1990), 19–25.
[45] See Emmanuel Levinas, *Existence and Existents*, trans. by A. Lingis (Pittsburgh: Duquesne University Press, 1978), 3; Levinas, *Totality and Infinity*, 303.

adds, that is, an ultimately impossible desire to be rid of the judgemental other once and for all – a desire whose very impossibility works to motivate overcompensatory "reaction-formations" like genocidal mass-murder. This remains a jarring, seemingly political misreading of what Heidegger means by the "nothing" that *death* discloses (since, as we have seen, the active "nothing of the nothing" is not negative *annihilation* but positive *futurity*, the arrival of the not-yet, repeatedly beckoning to be disclosed in resolve). Levinas's late objection that Heidegger reduces death to *annihilation* may well hold true of the way *Being and Time* presents our ordinary relation to *demise* (which might seem to suggest that Heidegger thought of *das Man* as atheistic rather than agnostic, as relating to demise itself as if it were a known absence rather than as an unknowable mystery).

In fact, however, Heidegger's *phenomenological* approach to demise simply follows from the methodological *agnosticism* of his phenomenological method, which must restrict itself in principle to first-personal evidence available to all of us (and so cannot pretend to know what might or might not happen after demise). Unfortunately, Levinas's apparent late conflation of death with demise allows him to present the difference between Heidegger and himself as a stark alternative: "Is that which opens with death nothingness, or the unknown?"[46] That, however, is a false alternative for the phenomenology of existential death, where the answer should really be: *Both*. Existential death discloses nothingness *and* the unknown *together*, eventually even recognizing that nothingness (of the self and its practical world in existential death) as the futural arriving of the never entirely known (although not the entirely unknowable), as we saw in Chapter 1.

7.3 Agamben on How Existential Death Discloses the Phenomenon of "Bare Life"

Another student of Heidegger (this time from almost half a century after Levinas), Agamben's creative and scholarly appropriations of Heidegger's thinking about death are deeply woven into many of his own works.[47] But just how fundamentally Agamben's mature perspective was shaped by his engagement with Heidegger becomes clearest from *Remnants of Auschwitz*, Agamben's moving and deeply critical re-reading of Heidegger's phenomenology of death through the eyes of Primo Levi. Although I cannot reconstruct the view with the full detail it deserves here, I shall suggest that Agamben demonstrates, more convincingly than anyone before or since, not only how

---

[46] See Levinas, *God, Death, and Time*, 8–9.
[47] See, for example, Giorgio Agamben, *Language and Death: The Place of Negativity* (Minneapolis, MN: University of Minnesota Press, 1991) and *The Open: Man and Animal* (Stanford, CA: Stanford University Press, 2004).

Heidegger failed to confront and think through the reality of life and death in the Nazi concentration camps, but also what beginning to do so might actually entail.

In 1949, when Heidegger finally broke his public silence on the Holocaust or Shoah, his now infamous remarks included the horrifying suggestion that the millions of innocent Jewish men, women, and children systematically murdered in Nazi death camps like those around Auschwitz did not "die" in his existential sense of the term, but only "demised," meaning that they were killed in ways that precluded them from genuinely experiencing the collapse of their worlds, a horrific treatment which, Heidegger suggests, now calls for thinking to confront "the immense misery of innumerable, atrocious deaths [of those Dasein] who have not died."[48] Some may find Heidegger's view so offensively ignorant as not to merit any detailed and thoughtful response, but that is precisely what Agamben provides, thereby seeking to answer Heidegger's call for us to think the truth of all these "terrible undying deaths [*grausig ungestorbener Tode*]" better than Heidegger himself did when he provocatively suggested that this deliberate industrialization of death should be understood as the most extreme expression of technological *enframing*.[49] Agamben thus offers a profoundly critical and yet deeply Heideggerian immanent critique of Heidegger, carefully showing what Heidegger should have said but failed to think. Reminding readers of Heidegger's cherished line from Hölderlin's late hymn "Patmos" – "But where the danger is, / that which saves [from it] also grows [*Wo aber Gefahr ist, wächst / das Rettende auch*]" – Agamben takes up Heidegger's suggestion that the death camps embody that "greatest danger" of technological enframing and so looks unflinchingly into the horrifying reality of the camps themselves for that promised salvific insight.[50]

Drawing primarily on the stark, deeply disturbing, and profoundly moving eye-witness testimony of his Italian compatriot, the death camp survivor Primo Levi, Agamben builds a careful and complex case. He shows that, even if we acknowledge that the Nazis deliberately murdered many of their victims by employing terrible ruses, subterfuge, and trickery that might have prevented some of their victims from understanding that they were being murdered (meaning that some might not have realized that they were demising and so also died existentially as a result), that is irrelevant, because they

---

[48] Giorgio Agamben, *Remnants of Auschwitz*, trans. by D. Heller-Roazen (New York: Zone Books, 1999), 74; quoting GA79 56; cf. BFL 53–4.

[49] See Chapter 6, Thomson, *Heidegger on Ontotheology*, 82–4 and *Heidegger, Art, and Postmodernity*, 106–7.

[50] Friedrich Hölderlin, *Poems and Fragments*, ed. by M. Hamburger (London: Anvil, 1994), 550–1. (On Heidegger's view of the danger and the promise, see Thomson, *Heidegger, Art, and Postmodernity*, ch. 7.)

7.3. AGAMBEN ON DEATH AND "BARE LIFE"

had *already* experienced the existential collapse of their worlds through the earlier arrests and ghettoization that stripped them of their practical lives and citizenship. But Agamben's most sustained and powerful arguments focus on the many who survived the brutal labor and systematic starvation of the death camps long enough to become (what those in the camps called) "*Musselmänner*, the drowned," human beings submerged into "bare life" and so barely subsisting with the sole compulsion of finding enough food to stay alive for one more day.[51] If these "living dead" were not experiencing a prolonged state of existential death, Agamben forcefully suggests, then no one ever does. (Indeed, if Heidegger's thinking of existential death lacked any real phenomenological reference, then his depiction of *complete* world-collapse would represent, at best, an exaggerated generalization from partial world-collapse. Agamben's powerful critique thus begins to show its cards as a defense of Heidegger's view.) In fact, Agamben argues, these victims submerged into bare life were the living embodiment of existential death, the true horror of its deliberate and systematic infliction and perpetuation.[52]

Heidegger's ignorant failure to recognize any of this looks symptomatic of his inability to face the horrors of the Shoah, but Agamben, for his part, seeks to think this horror all the way through. Focusing on the *Musselmänner* as the "moving threshold in which man passed into non-man" (as the systematic starvation in the Nazi death camps reduces human Daseins to sheer animal life), Agamben argues that the Nazi's deliberately dehumanizing infliction of such a living death should be recognized as "the 'core' of the camp, the fatal threshold that all prisoners are constantly about to cross," an existential death in which "the Jew is transformed into a Muselmann and the human being into

---

[51] (Agamben, *Remnants of Auschwitz*, 69.) In 1936, Heidegger describes hunger in ways that reinforce Agamben's analysis of the *Musselmänner* as the prolonged embodiment of existential death: "Hunger, for example, is a sheer compulsion and striving, a compulsion toward food for the sake of nourishment" (N1 54/NI 66). I should thus be clear that Agamben's understanding of the *Musselmänner* as subsisting in a prolonged state of existential death holds true only insofar as these horribly victimized prisoners have been reduced to a state of radical passivity (or the "sheer compulsion and striving" of a fruitless instinctive drive), no longer even capable of engaging in any minimal practical (*Zuhanden*) project of trying to find some food to eat, and so instead utterly dependent on others (that is, on their fellow prisoners who, as Levi informs us throughout *Survival in Auschwitz*, do not receive enough food to arrest their own systematic starvation even when they can still work, let alone enough to share with others, whose terrible state they thus hasten to join if they do share – a terribly cruel and deliberate destruction of human empathy and community that still did not entirely succeed in preventing acts of astounding generosity).

[52] As we saw in Chapter 1, what is really so anxiety provoking about death is being our own not being, which the Musselmänner is forced to *endure*, often until their very demise (when the Nazi's systematic starvation and forced work regimen accomplishes its horrifying task and its victims are finally "selected" for murder in the gas chambers).

a non-human."[53] Yet, if it is not simply grotesque to try to discover any possible salvific lesson here, Agamben suggests, it is that bearing witness to this terrible human power to reduce another human being to "bare life" also teaches us the very essence of "the political," revealing what politics *is* at what Agamben argues is its ontological core, namely, the sovereign determination of who and what counts as a "human being," that is, as an inviolable life with dignity worthy of political protection. Indeed, to think beyond our entrenched metaphysical anthropocentrisms, Agamben suggests, that same "bare life" revealed to us by the horrors of the Shoah must henceforth become the common foundation for all future ethico-political responsibility, a solidarity of the living that should supplement (if not supplant) such criteria as rationality, dignity, and even species membership as the new common basis for the progressive struggle to extend political and ethical responsibility to all lives (in the most inclusive and encompassing ways possible). In Agamben's words, this is "the thesis that summarizes the lesson of Auschwitz: the human being is the one who can survive the human being."[54] In other words, the "bare life" of that which does not die in existential death is exactly what human beings should henceforth struggle to sanctify and preserve *in all its forms*.

As an insightful critique of Heidegger that shows how he *should* have rethought his phenomenology of existential death in the terrible light of the death camps, Agamben's reading remains strikingly original and largely compelling. Moreover, although the connection is not often appreciated, Agamben's resulting ontopolitical suggestions about "bare life" certainly merit the more careful and extended treatment they have elsewhere begun to receive.[55] But I shall also return to criticize some of the more extreme and politically pessimistic positions Agamben takes in Chapter 8 (which remain considerably bleaker than even Sartre's most pessimistic postwar views).[56] Let us turn now to the more extensive engagement with Heidegger's thinking of death in the work of Derrida, whose even more radical deconstruction of selfhood could be said both to complement and to complicate Agamben's thinking of the political core of a life worth protecting.

---

[53] Agamben, *Remnants of Auschwitz*, 47, 51, 52.
[54] Ibid., 133.
[55] See, for example, Andrew Norris, ed., *Politics, Metaphysics, and Death: Essays on Giorgio Agamben's Homo Sacer* (Durham, NC: Duke University Press, 2005); Matthew Calarco and Steven DeCaroli, eds., *Giorgio Agamben: Sovereignty and Life* (Stanford, CA: Stanford University Press, 2008); and Susanne Claxton, *Heidegger's Gods: An Ecofeminist Perspective* (London: Rowman and Littlefield, 2017), ch. 5.
[56] (See n. 14.) The problematic exaggerations generated by Agamben's wholly negative view of the contemporary Western world came to rather unfortunate prominence with his controversial readings of the public health responses to the global Coronavirus pandemic as the triumph of Foucaultian *biopower* (or our post-sovereign regime of "making live and letting die"), collected in Giorgio Agamben, *Where Are We Now? The Epidemic as Politics* (London: Eris, 2021).

7.4 Derrida's Deconstructive Thinking of Demise as Aporia and Death as *Survivance*

Derrida's critical engagements with Heidegger thoroughly pervade his own work, and Heidegger's thinking about death is one of Derrida's central preoccupations, making Derrida's view complex and resistant to summary. "And yet."[57] I shall nevertheless try to briefly convey some of Derrida's main thoughts on Heidegger and death from what Derrida tellingly calls "my life of reading Heidegger."[58] I mentioned earlier that Derrida never fully grasps Heidegger's crucial distinction between existential *death* and mortal *demise*. Instead, in *Aporias*, Derrida's most sustained engagement with *Being and Time*'s treatment of death, Derrida analyzes what Heidegger says about death the way most readers do, by falsely assuming that Heidegger's entire discussion concerns mortal demise.[59] Developing that aforementioned Epicurean paradox – that demise and I can never coincide (since where I am, demise is not, and where demise is, I am not) – Derrida brings this non-coincidence of my demise and myself into a collision with Heidegger's thesis that existential death (misread as mortal demise) is the "most certain" of all certainties, a move whereby Derrida makes our experience of our own demise both necessary and impossible, unavoidable and yet also unreachable, certain but still unknowable.[60]

Instead of dismissing this as absurd, however, Derrida concludes that this paradox – according to which our own mortal demise is both *necessary and impossible* – is actually a faithful description of the strange fate to which all of us mortals remain consigned. As "mortals," demise is something we each seem fated to undergo somehow and yet also something none of us can experience "as such." (Remember that we cannot experience demise "as such" because we cannot *be* demised; we Dasein cannot coincide with our own demise or *be here* once our own demise has fully arrived.) Derrida concludes that our own mortal demise should thus be understood as a paradigmatic instance of the "aporia" or *necessary impossibility*. Derrida's *Aporias* raises fascinating issues (as I have tried to show elsewhere), but the main problem is that the aporia he articulates only concerns the experience of demise, not of death. For Heidegger, there is no certainty that we will *experience* our own demise.[61] There is not even any certainty that we will ever experience existential death.

---

[57] "And yet" is a crucial Heideggerian locution to which Derrida was keenly attuned; see Jacques Derrida, *The Truth in Painting* (Chicago: University of Chicago Press, 1987), 320; Thomson, *Heidegger, Art, and Postmodernity*, 90–120 (esp. 91).
[58] Derrida, *The Beast and the Sovereign, Volume II*, 279.
[59] See Derrida, *Aporias*.
[60] This move turns on a conflation of death and demise. (On the two *different* kinds of certainty definitive of death and demise, respectively, see also Chapter 1.)
[61] For some of those fascinating issues, see Thomson, "Can I Die?"

That is not what the "certainty" of either mortal demise or of existential death means for Heidegger.

As we saw in Chapter 1, Heidegger thinks of demise and death as "certain" in two different ways: "*Demise* is empirically certain: We know no exceptions to the proposition that 'all men are mortal.' *Das Man* reduces this to the certainty that *one dies* (someday), or that *we all die* (but not me, not now)." Heidegger reads our typical flight from demise as a testament to our repressed certainty about it (because you must be aware of demise somehow in order to run away from it). Nonetheless, this repressed certainty of demise does not make it certain that everyone will experience demise (as Derrida assumes). For example, if someone demises in their sleep and does not wake up, or demises without ever realizing it (by mistakenly thinking they were only falling asleep, for instance), then they might not experience anything of the terminal world-collapse of mortal demise.[62] For those who are aware as they demise that they are demising, however, the paradox Derrida articulates does seem to hold; we do not appear to be able to live all the way through our own demise in order to experience our being demised. But that is something Heidegger clearly realized. As *Being and Time* explicitly writes, existential death must be "distinguished from" any "*Erleben* des *Ablebens*" – distinguished, that is, from any ultimately impossible "living-through of [our own] ceasing to live" (BT 295/ SZ 251).

Indeed, Heidegger adopts a version of the Epicurean insight that we cannot experience our demise *itself* when he argues that Dasein can never understand itself as a "whole or totality" (*ganz*) so long as we think of death as demise. For, if we think of Dasein's "end" as mortal demise, then our Dasein will not be whole until we have demised, but once we have demised we will not *be* whole, since we will no longer "be here" at all (at least as far as we can tell phenomenologically). Heidegger's (rather unconvincingly motivated) quest for a complete understanding of Dasein (one which will get "Dasein as a whole" into its hermeneutic "fore-having") is the primary reason he gives for

---

[62] How many of those who demise are aware that they are in fact demising? This is in principle an empirical question, but one about which it would be very difficult to gather much reliable evidence without being horribly intrusive. Of course, our sometimes over-fastidious fear of intruding upon the demise of another can easily reinforce that widespread denial of demise that Ivan Ilych famously illustrates, where those surrounding the person who is demising even attempt to deny the reality of the situation with reassuring platitudes like, "Do not worry; you'll be back on your feet in no time!" Such notorious denials of demise not only make demising more traumatic, but can go so far as to deprive us of our once in a lifetime chance to experience whatever there is to experience in demising. (We have made some progress since the days when paternalistic medical doctors regularly let their patients demise in ignorance, but I have repeatedly suggested that we still have a long way to go here as well.)

taking up the topic of death and also for distinguishing mortal demise from existential death (as we saw in Chapter 1). For, only in existential death can Dasein reach the kind of end that is appropriate to its distinctive nature as the entity that *exists* (or "stands out" toward an intelligible world by projecting itself into projects). Heidegger maintains that Dasein, as an existing entity, "ends" differently than a "present-at-hand" (*vorhanden*) entity such as an unfinished road: "Dasein does not have an end at which it just stops or drops-off [*ein Ende, an dem es nur aufhören*] but, instead, [Dasein] *exists finitely* [*existiert endlich*]" in existential death (BT 379/SZ 329). In other words, Dasein can experience its own being-ended only when it encounters itself as an "authentic whole" (BT 379/SZ 329), which we can do only when our own existence has become fully "transparent" (*durchsichtig*) to itself in the phenomenon of existential death. For, in death's projectless projecting, Dasein has no outstanding life-projects it can project itself into practically and so has no futural aspects of its existence that it cannot see coming.

Now, given Derrida's pervasive skepticism about Heidegger's strategic appeals of the experience of "death *as such*," I think we can anticipate what his response to Heidegger's phenomenology of existential death would be, had he ever clearly articulated it. Derrida would likely seek to deconstruct any claim that Dasein can ever exist as a whole or totality, whether in the experience of mortal demise or of existential death. Echoing his arguments about demise from *Aporias*, I imagine that Derrida would focus on *Being and Time*'s rather sketchy defense of Dasein's supposed "wholeness" as "existing finitely" in existential death, a view Derrida could then trace back to its ultimate ground in Heidegger's even sketchier defense of "the finitude of primordial temporality" itself (BT 379/SZ 330). These remain difficult issues worthy of debate, and I sought to contribute to clarifying them phenomenologically in Chapter 1. But like Levinas (albeit for different reasons), Derrida is not a phenomenologist "all the way down" (as it were). Instead, Derrida's own axiomatic commitments are to a neo-Saussurian view in which the meaning of all words, concepts, and significations derive not from their reference to some extra-linguistic reality we can partially experience and describe phenomenologically but, instead, from their holistic relationship to the endlessly interwoven webs of difference between and among such significations. That is why Derrida's *Of Grammatology* famously rejects Heidegger's thinking of "being" as a nostalgic faith in "the myth of the transcendental signified," instead insisting that "There is nothing outside the text," no way to get outside the myriad differences between significations which give them their ever-shifting meaning in order to check or compare that meaning against some reality beyond it. In his final lectures, Derrida concludes that Heidegger's appeal to "being as such" as an inexhaustibly polysemic Ur-phenomenon that partly lends itself to meaningful language and practice is little more than an attempt to hide his own "arbitrary" and "unjustifiable decisions" on ultimately undecidable issues that should instead be kept open, for us to work through and take responsibility for ourselves.[63]

This deepest difference between Heidegger and Derrida thus remains crucial. Replacing Heidegger's "being" with his own "*différance*," Derrida's motivating idea is that words, concepts, marks, signs, traces, etc., derive their meaning not from some anchoring in being's phenomenological unconcealment in time but, instead, from their never fully chartable relations to vast and ever-shifting holistic webs, diffuse semantic and syntactic networks composed of all the other relevantly different marks, signs, concepts, traces, etc. (so that the concept "cat" gets its meaning not from any referential relation to actual cats but, instead, from cats *not* being rats, bats, hats, dogs, frogs, hogs, cogs, and so on, and on, and on). This non-foundational philosophy of endless and irreducible differences leads Derrida to a generalized skepticism about every "as such," any faith in a "pure" concept or experience uncontaminated by what it excludes. Derrida backs up this skepticism by strategically deconstructing (what he takes to be residually *metaphysical*) attempts by Heidegger and others to rigidly delineate and defend the borders around their own foundational terms. This generalized skepticism about any perfectly delineable dichotomy between mutually defining concepts enables Derrida to strategically challenge Heidegger's own reliance on such rigid dichotomies in his work, including *Being and Time*'s attempts to dichotomize "demise and perishing" as well as Heidegger's later attempts to sharply distinguish Dasein's distinctive mode of *existence* from the life of "*the* animal."

Despite the explanation advanced in Chapter 1, I think Derrida is partly right to be troubled by *Being and Time*'s claim that Dasein is "imperishable," or that while Dasein might die or demise, "Dasein never perishes" (BT 291/SZ 247).[64] If we remember that "croaking" is a common colloquialism for *demise* (and that a frog or lizard "basking in the sun" on a rock feature among Heidegger's examples of the "world-poor" animal that demises but does not die [FCM 193–6/GA29–30 285–90]), then we can summarize Heidegger's view with a simple formula: "Pear trees *perish*, frogs *croak*, but Daseins croak and die." In other words, the *perishing* of our biological systems leads to our mortal *demise* (that is, our "croaking"), and if we are aware of our mortal demise as it befalls us, then that experience of undergoing demise can also lead to our existential "death," if it catalyzes the collapse of any remaining practical projects making our individual existence meaningful. But (as we saw earlier), Heidegger is clear that we can *demise without dying* (for example, if we demise in a dreamless sleep and never wake up, as in that euphemistic "good death" which is actually no experience of demise at all), and also that we can *die*

---

[63] Derrida, *The Beast and the Sovereign, Volume II*, 61.
[64] Derrida, *Aporias*, 40.

without demising (if our identity constituting life-projects collapse while we are still alive), as in that phenomenological experience of existential death which plays such a fundamental and pivotal role in *Being and Time* and in the development of Heidegger's later thinking.

Whereas Derrida himself embraces the paradoxical, impossible "experience" of an aporetic encounter with our own annihilation in demise, Heidegger's phenomenological approach and Epicurean worries combine to lead him to conclude that our Dasein cannot *be demised* and therefore to focus instead on existential death, that phenomenon in which we can experience ourselves as *being ended* (that is, as being our own not being anything practical or worldly, but merely a naked, world-hungry, *solus ipse*) and live through the experience (of such *projectless projecting*) to be able to tell the tale phenomenologically.[65] We saw in Chapter 1 that, while crucially different, mortal demise and existential death remain formally connected for Heidegger, whereas *Being and Time* erects a rigid border between the *perishing* of the organic systems keeping us alive and the various ways we Dasein might encounter or experience the collapse of our worlds in demise and death.[66] In challenging Heidegger's claim that "Dasein never perishes," then, Derrida helps draw our attention to the truth that such borders are in fact experientially criss-crossed in myriad ways, as is particularly obvious in the strokes, heart-attacks, cancers, etc., that can lead to our demise, but also in the slower degradations and transformations of our Dasein inevitably brought about by those more and less devastating failures of cell replication we call aging (such as our phenomenological experience of memory loss, degradations of balance, coordination, and motor skills, progressive hearing and vision loss, and even in the slow-motion existential death or world-collapse typical of Alzheimer's and other forms of dementia), in other words, by the fuller and more complex realities of our own mortal being in time. (In more ways than one, then, we are reminded that *Being and Time* was the work of a relatively young man.)

---

[65] Such worries about the necessary impossibility of experiencing demise (paradoxes about "the existence that is mortal but incapable of passing away ... [or of being] present after its death" [Levinas, *Totality and Infinity*, 57]) are frequently and eloquently articulated by Blanchot, whose work forms a common link between Levinas and Derrida – indeed, these worries are perhaps nowhere more poignantly conveyed than in the powerful passages Derrida excerpts from his own eulogy for Blanchot (see Derrida, *The Beast and the Sovereign*, Vol. II, esp. 183–90).

[66] This border might be thought to be merely a consequence of a rigid "ontological difference" *Being and Time* allegedly draws between entities and their being or meaning. As we saw in Chapters 1, 2, and 3, however, it is in fact crucial to Heidegger's phenomenological method that *the ontological difference is a bridge rather than a wall*, designating intersecting rather than dichotomous domains. (Indeed, only in that way can Heidegger's phenomenological method be epistemically nonarbitrary.)

It is also precisely here, moreover, where Heidegger seeks to draw a bright red line between Dasein's distinctive mode of existing and any merely organic life or even animal drives, that Derrida and others rightly raise objections to Heidegger's still overly dualistic and anthropocentric prejudices in his treatments of "animality" (that is, his many and varied attempts to think about the *being* of the animal) as well as worries over the alleged "ableism" entailed by his views. Does "Dasein" refer only to human beings, or even only to "normally" developed, *neurotypical*, adult human beings? Does "Dasein" even successfully pick out the distinctive ontological type Heidegger intends? (And if so, at what *exclusionary* cost?) We might slightly offset the ableism worry by pointing out (as Derrida suggests) that Heidegger in fact thinks Dasein's "ownmost ability-to-be" as an *inability*, namely, that projectless projecting in which I *cannot* be anything practical or worldly – making the very core of the self a practical disability "hidden" from us by our ordinary projecting into projects, which thereby "alienate" us from our "ownmost Dasein" disclosed in "genuine break-down" (BT 222/SZ 178). Still, the underlying worry reemerges later, when Heidegger tries to distinguish Dasein from all (other species of) animals by appealing to our allegedly unique relation to death and the way this relation makes disclosive words and thus language possible. Heidegger's later view (as we saw in Chapter 3) is that words are born as poetic insights that reach into that phenomenon of the "nothing" that death uncovers, successfully disclosing (or "naming into being") the suggestive "noth-ing" whereby that which is not yet a thing offers itself to be (partially) disclosed and shared. Heidegger is thus not repeating the typical claim that humanity's linguistic concepts give us a unique relation to death but, rather, the reverse, the more original and provocative view that the phenomenon uncovered by existential death is what enables Dasein to articulate linguistic concepts in the first place.[67]

Moreover, Heidegger's increasingly infamous claim that animals "are poor in world" is typically misunderstood, since Heidegger is claiming that animals live in a kind of permanent connection to being's polysemic openness, a connection they cannot extricate themselves from in order to partially conceptualize any aspects of that openness with words. Their "world-poverty" is the paradoxical poverty of over-richness, much like that of the Christian Monk (who is poor in worldly terms but spiritually rich), an essential "poverty" that (as Heidegger says) lacks only what is unnecessary (and so lacks only lack itself). Hence, despite Heidegger's romantic, spiritual-elevation of its world-poverty, Heidegger's "animal" is still (as Derrida aptly puts it) "deprived of

---

[67] See also Thomson, *Heidegger, Art, and Postmodernity*, ch. 3; Derrida, *The Animal that Therefore I Am*; Oberst, *Heidegger on Language and Death*; John Haugeland, *Dasein Disclosed: John Haugeland's Heidegger*, ed. by Joseph Rouse (Cambridge, MA: Harvard University Press, 2013); and Carman, *Heidegger's Analytic*.

7.4. DERRIDA ON APORIA AND *SURVIVANCE*

privation itself."[68] For Derrida, the real problem with Heidegger's romantic thinking of "the being of the animal" is not its romanticism but its untenably monolithic thinking of "*the* animal," a thinking of "animality" ignorant of the irreducible differences between different animals – and not only between different species but between different animals of the same species, and even between the "same" animals at different moments in their lives (and, perhaps, afterlives), a brutal simplification of endless differences which, ironically, thoughtlessly betrays the same kind of "beastly asinanity [*bêtise*]" that Derrida thinks the philosophical tradition endlessly tries to attributes to nonhuman animals in one untenable way after another.[69]

None of that, however, is Derrida's last word on Heidegger. Like Levinas before him, Derrida devotes his own final lecture course to articulating yet another reading of Heidegger on death, this time focusing on isolation and individuation, through the suggestive lens of Dafoe's *Robinson Crusoe*, a fantastic existential story of shipwreck, isolation, and survival that allows Derrida to articulate his own view of how we – and, indeed, he – might live on after demise. For, unbeknownst to most of his audience, Derrida wrote these final lectures after having been diagnosed with late-stage pancreatic cancer, a fact that lends them an evocative depth and poignancy (well worthy of the close, careful, and creative rereadings for which they call). Deconstructing the decision about whether to be buried or cremated, Derrida presents both rituals as prophylactic attempts to enforce the death of the other, to keep the dead one dead and out of play. Rejecting such a binary alternative, Derrida instead develops his own axiomatic thinking of *différance* in a way that deconstructs the dichotomy between life and death by reconceiving selfhood in terms of that aforementioned holistic web of differential significations. Such webs of difference can and often do survive demise, for example, by being inscribed in a text and then read or reread. Naming this "life death" or "survival ... of the living dead" *survivance*, Derrida describes how a reread "book lives its beautiful death," not as "my survivor but as the survivor of me, the there beyond my life" (where what was once most vital in me is reanimated by the creatively disclosive reading of another), a "being there" or Dasein that survives demise (in "a survival that is not, " Derrida provocatively contends, "less alive than life").[70] In such an "alliance of the dead and the living," a reread text is "a dead thing that resuscitates each time a breath of

---

[68] Derrida, *The Beast and the Sovereign*, Volume II, 283.
[69] (Derrida, *The Animal that Therefore I Am*, 31.) As Derrida's repeated critiques of Heidegger's thinking of "animality" show almost in spite of themselves, however, Heidegger's thinking on this topic is far less homogeneous, consistent, and repressive than is generally acknowledged.
[70] Cf. Levinas on "the child," who is "not me" and yet who "I am" (see Levinas, *Totality and Infinity*, 277, and Chapter 6).

living reading, each time the breath of the other ... makes it live again by animating it."[71] In other words, Derrida's last will and testament, written here, is that there can and should be no last will and testament; it is neither possible nor desirable for us to seek to determine how our texts will be taken up and creatively reappropriated by others. For, if we could dictate how we should be read, then we would be foreclosing the critical engagements and creative reappropriations that keep our thinking alive in the thinking of others.

As if leading by example, Derrida uses his own final reading of Heidegger to reread Levinas's final reading of Heidegger in a way that brings it back to life and reopens it to future readings. Derrida mobilizes his thinking of the *survivance* of the differential webs of signification that he thinks we *are* in order to transform Levinas's previously implausible reading of Heidegger's nothing as *annihilation* in a way that brings it back into a direct engagement with Heidegger's texts. As Derrida ceatively rereads him, Levinas's point is that "to transform death into annihilation ... is to deprive the dead one of everything through which he or she can still affect, from the outside, from such exteriority, affect our sensibility ... in time and space." For Levinas, "the dead person is not annihilated but is what no longer responds."[72] The point is no longer just that painful truth that the demised can no longer literally respond but, now, much more broadly, that as long as someone can creatively disclose the responses of another by rereading their texts, then these demised others *are here*. Derrida means both "reading" and "texts" in the most expansive ways possible, including everything in any way readable (from published and unpublished works, to the visitations of others in memories and dreams, to the claw marks of a bear on a tree or a bird in the sand, and so on); as long as we read and reread their texts and traces, their being or *différance* is not gone but *survives*, "living on" in a different kind of Dasein after demise, a *survivance*.

To the end of his own life, then, Derrida keeps Heidegger alive (in a creative dialogue with Levinas, Blanchot, Defoe, and many others), repeatedly "resuscitating" Heidegger's thinking though his creative and often highly critical rereadings. That these readings are both creative and critical is essential to their faithfulness, Derrida argues, since the only way to keep a thinker who has demised alive is to continue to contest, develop, and so transform the texts in and as which they (and henceforth we) can live on – *in some sense*, at least. I think there are good reasons to find this somewhat consoling (as we saw in Chapter 1).[73] *And yet*, hopeful provocations aside, even Derrida himself did not believe that the living on of our differential traces in others was a satisfyingly substitute for our own first-personal being here. As Derrida told

---

[71] Derrida *The Beast and the Sovereign, Volume II*, 130–31.
[72] Ibid., 166, 168.
[73] See especially Chapter 1, n. 46.

his philosopher friend, Jean-Luc Nancy, as the end of Derrida's life drew near: "You know, what I would prefer is a good old resurrection." Nancy suggests that Derrida's ironic gallows "humor conveyed both the impossibility of believing in another life and a bitter regret that it had to be this way."[74] Nancy's simplification is a bit misleading, however, since Derrida did believe in another kind of afterlife (as we have just seen), a *survivance* whereby the living webs of differential signification that we were live on in other forms as they are repeatedly reanimated and transformed by the creative and unpredictable appropriations of others. That is clearly not the same as the survival of our relatively continuous sense of our own first-personal identity, a first-personal persistence that many people seem *never* to want to end. I shall argue against the desirability of our own first-personal Dasein living on *forever* in Chapter 9, but I also agree with the basic intuition Derrida's joke facetiously expresses: Demise does indeed involve the *loss* of something worth caring about – namely, my Dasein. My first-personal existence as a significance-disclosing projecting into projects that shapes and reshapes my practical identity and repeatedly structures and restructures what I care about is something that can be, for a time at least, profoundly significant and worthwhile, certainly to me and hopefully also to others, and the importance of its loss is not something to be overly downplayed or denied.

Mark Johnston defends a more extreme position than Derrida in *Surviving Death*, going so far as to conclude that "there is no persisting self worth caring about."[75] Whether defended by rationalists or Buddhists, however, such a nihilistic view of the self looks (from the perspective of Heidegger's existential phenomenology) like an overcompensatory reaction to our fear of demise, an attempt to short-circuit such fear by denying that there is anything rationally care-worthy about the persistence of our individual selves. Such denials that we should care about the persistence of our individual selves thus seem not to acknowledge or seriously try to come to terms with the reality of profound loss that our mortal demise often represent (to ourselves and others). I shall thus defend a less rationalistic but more reasonable middle ground between wanting our individual selves to live forever, on the one hand, and denying that our persisting selves are even worthy of our care, on the other, in the final chapter.

But we can steer clear of such nihilistic views of the self, I would suggest, by facing up to our normal fear of demise and tracing that fear back to our deeper anxiety in the face of existential death. For, doing so allows to recognize that the persisting self of individual existence is made up of *both* the core *solus ipse* that stands revealed in existential death *and* the clothing of worldly

---

[74] See Jean-Luc Nancy, "Scandalous Death," trans. by M.-E. Morin and T. Holloway, *Angelaki* 27:1 (2022), 8.
[75] Mark Johnston, *Surviving Death* (Princeton, NJ: Princeton University Press, 2010), 358.

significance that this self repeatedly projects into and so discloses in resolve. "Care [*Sorge*]" is the name Heidegger uses to characterize the nature of this *connection* (since the self's defining *care* for the living world it is forms the ontological condition of all our specific, individual cares and worries – making "care" a name for the very "being of Dasein" [BT 225/SZ 180]). Identifying narrowly with the core self in rationalism, or trying to dismiss or dissolve its futurity-laden "nothingness" into mere emptiness in (some forms of) Buddhism, both miss the way the care-worthiness of the self involves a dynamic union of this core self with its temporally shifting world. To recognize this, moreover, is to acknowledge the complex existential fact that "I am both myself and my circumstances, and if I do not save them then I do not save myself [*Yo soy yo y mi circumstancia, y si no la salvo a ella no me salvo yo*]," as Ortega y Gasset famously suggested in his *Meditations on Quixote*.[76] Dasein's care-full intertwinement of self and world – as the ontological condition of the very care-worthiness of the living selves that we are – thus brings us back inexorably to the ethico-political dimensions of our existence, and so to the pressing question of what light our existential phenomenology of death might help bring to such matters.

---

[76] See Carlos Alberto Sánchez, *A Sense of Brutality: Philosophy after Narco-Culture* (Amherst College Press, 2020).

8

Heidegger's Mortal Phenomenology of Existential Death and the Postmetaphysical Politics of Ontological Pluralism

Proposition 67 of Spinoza's hyper-rationalistic *Ethics* proudly proclaims that: "A free man thinks of nothing less than of death."[1] Well, in this book I have thought a great deal about existential death, and a good bit about the "noth-ing of the nothing" that such death discloses. Still, I have probably thought of noth-ing less than of death, so Spinoza might have to count me "free" on a technicality.[2] There are, at any rate, worse things than being freed on a technicality. One can be *convicted* on a technicality, for example, or even convicted *by* technicality. Indeed, the later Heidegger suggests that we have *all* been convicted by technicality, technicity, or technologicity, that is, by "the essence of technology." According to his view of our late modern age of technological *enframing*, we have all been *thrown* by Western history into the prison city-state (or *polis*) of nihilistic technologicity.[3]

In developing Heidegger's seemingly foreboding view, however, I have reached more hopeful conclusions than such post-Heideggerian heirs as Foucault and Agamben. I cannot agree with Foucault that we must remain forever trapped within the panoptical walls of a "carceral society," an endless

---

[1] See Benedict de Spinoza, *Ethics*, ed. and trans. by E. Curley (New York: Penguin, 1996), 151.

[2] Adding some further irony here is the fact that I *hope* my other work shifts these facetious scales of "freedom" against me. For, although it is existential death that first discloses the nothing to Heidegger (and death remains a great *deal*, in that sense at least), the "noth-ing" of that "nothing" turns out to be accessible in numerous other ways than through the practical world-collapse of existential death (in which, moreover, Heidegger did not immediately recognize the future-laden, inchoate positivity of this nothing himself, as we have seen in Chapters 1 and 3). This noth-ing can also be disclosed through art and poetry, for example (as I show in Thomson, *Heidegger, Art, and Postmodernity*, ch. 3). Indeed, this "noth-ing" gives us a good bit more to think about, even turning out to be a more suggestively disclosive phenomenon to attend to than the existential death that first reveals it. (Thus, we perhaps uncover some unintentional kernel of truth hiding beneath Spinoza's untenably heroic proclamation, to which I return in Section 8.5.)

[3] For a detailed interpretation and defense of Heidegger's understanding of ontotheology as the metaphysical substructure driving such nihilistic technologization, see Thomson, *Heidegger on Ontotheology*, ch. 2.

sadomasochistic prison in which knowledge is never more than "power."[4] Nor could I simply assent to Agamben's even starker view that in the advanced technological societies of our late-modern world, "the true horror of the [concentration] camp ... continues as if uninterrupted."[5] I take the point behind such hypertrophic rhetoric, and strongly agree that we need to do much more to address and redress the terrible injustices of mass incarceration (disproportionately directly against society's most disempowered members in ways that continue to worsen their marginalization), that more sustained critical attention should be paid to the growing problems of technological surveillance, and so on. (Not long ago there was yet another ominous sign, when researchers smugly announced they had successfully redeployed tele-technological surveillance and advanced computational techniques – a combination meant to help prevent outbreaks of infectious disease, catch serial killers, and so on – to identify Banksy, the previously anonymous guerrilla street artist famous for his graffiti critiques of technocapitalism.)[6]

It would be foolish not to heed such warnings by taking seriously the most dangerous futures that our current historical trajectory seems to imply.[7] Still, for me, those remain dark visions of a dystopian future – a future we increasingly threaten to realize and yet can still avert, not merely remediate, by

---

[4] It is not clear that Foucault himself was entirely repelled by this vision; rather, both he and Sartre seem to have had strongly ambivalent relations of erotic attraction and intellectual repulsion to such sadomasochistic stalemates, as we can see in Foucault's creative engagements with sadomasochistic power relations as well as in *Being and Nothingness*'s commitment to the inescapability of Hegel's master/slave dialectic. See Butler, *Subjects of Desire*; and James Miller, *The Passion of Michel Foucault* (New York: Anchor, 1994).

[5] (See Agamben, *Remnants of Auschwitz*, 26.) Foucault and Agamben were deeply concerned to critically develop the political implications of Heidegger's ontological view of technological "enframing," as we can recognize in Foucault's important late critiques of "power/knowledge" and "biopower," as well as in Agamben's guiding concern to elaborate the politics of "bare life" (as we saw in Chapter 7). Near the end of his life, Foucault seems to have had glimmers of a way of passing through and out of power/knowledge and biopower, but tragically died before he was able to develop it very far. (See, for example, Foucault's last three years of lectures at the Collège de France, between 1981 and 1984; and, on Foucault's experience with hallucinogens that may have played a role in this breakthrough, see Miller, *The Passion of Michel Foucault*; Simeon Wade, *Foucault in California* (Heyday: Berkeley, CA: 2019)].)

[6] See, for example, Lisa Guenther, *Solitary Confinement: Social Death and Its Afterlives* (Minneapolis: University of Minnesota Press, 2013); then contrast the attention grabbing but deeply unethical, artistically clueless, and politically alarming "proof of concept" of their work by Michelle V. Hauge et al., "Tagging Banksy: Using geographic profiling to investigate a modern [sic] art mystery," *Journal of Spatial Science*, 61:1 (2016)

[7] How could I, when I first wrote this in the midst of what I then rightly recognized and (at the time controversially) described as the rise of political "fascism" into the American mainstream? (See Thomson, "Heidegger's Nazism in the Light of his Early *Black Notebooks*," 206–9.)

addressing its deep causes and not just its painful symptoms. (Moreover, as Heidegger suggests, *the greatest danger* of technological enframing is not the one popularly expressed by our dystopian nightmares of creating a true "artificial intelligence" that, upon becoming genuinely self-conscious, deliberately sets out to exterminate humanity – that fear expressed in such influential Hollywood franchises as *The Matrix* and *Terminator* series. Technologization's greatest danger is rather the reverse: that we are becoming as *thoughtless* and *careless* as our unthinking and uncaring technologies. Indeed, the realization of that greater danger is partly confirmed by the increasingly common phenomenon in which people mistake computer-generated simulations of genuine intelligence for high-level human creations, or even think that such products of a simulated intelligence suggest a true intelligence within.)[8] Still, to argue, as I have often done, that we both can and should recognize the deepest roots of the nihilistic technologization sweeping our world (roots that turn out to be deeply embedded in the ontotheological substructure of our metaphysical tradition) is also to confess an unfashionable faith in the dangerous yet indispellable dream of "spiritual revolution," the belief that the steering wheel of history can still be *turned* in a meaningful way.[9] *Human history is not yet over*, in other words, and the mad desire to believe that it is – or worse, to work (whether deliberately or more or less unconsciously) to bring human history to an end – these eschatological visions look to me like symptoms of a deep thanatological impulse that still beats in the millennial heart of Western philosophy.[10]

In a sense, then, Foucault and Agamben have not carried their critical deconstructions of nihilistic technologization far enough; for, they have not developed the logic underlying such technologization to the point where it

---

[8] I return to address such issues in Iain Thomson, *Heidegger on the Danger and Promise of Technology, or What Is Called Thinking in the Age of AI?* (Cambridge: Cambridge University Press, forthcoming).

[9] To put the point in the terms of that wily late-modernist often mistaken as a postmodernist: We need not crash (by letting the endless fine-tuning of the engine continue to steer the car) into Lyotard's "Pacific Wall." (See Jean-François Lyotard's deliberately provocative and still prescient work, *Pacific Wall* [Venice, CA: Lapis Press, 1990]; and, on Lyotard, Thomson, *Heidegger, Art, and Postmodernity*, ch. 4.)

[10] See the great late work by Herbert Marcuse, *Eros and Civilization* (Boston, MA: Beacon Press, 1974). I do not identify as a Marxist materialist but as a post-Hegelian, social-democratic postmodernist who thinks – with Heidegger and Derrida – that we need to deconstruct the metaphysical dichotomy increasingly setting a trendy "materialism" *against* all idealisms, and instead recognize (in a true Hegelian spirit) what both exaggerated positions get right so that we can preserve those insights in a broader view. (The still unjustly underappreciated legacy of Mexican existentialism also has much to teach us here; see, for example, Carlos Alberto Sánchez, *Contingency and Commitment: Mexican Existentialism and the Place of Philosophy* [New York: SUNY Press, 2016].)

leads beyond itself. We have explored Heidegger's Dante-inspired view that *the only way out is through* and, among the paradoxes Derrida loved to intone (before explicating at length), one of my favorites remains: "What they do not realize is that the only way to untie the knot is to tie it tighter." Following the hints of Derrida, Gadamer, and Vattimo, I have tried to show that once we really understand technology's ontotheological essence, we also discover that the so-called prison of technological enframing has wide-open doors in all sorts of unexpected places.[11] I shall even seek to show here that some of the most immobile looking walls in our ever-expanding city of technicity or technologicity turn out to be doors opening onto a more meaningful future. In the face of technologization, once again, *the only way out is through*; here that means that we need to recognize enframing's ontotheological roots so that we can learn to use particular technologies against such nihilistic technologization.[12]

8.1 The Serious Issue of Philosophical Facetiousness

Now, I began a bit facetiously, even opening with a joke. We sometimes recognize that "when a serious thing is a joke, a joke can be a very serious thing" (hence fascist leaders' common repression of all political humor). But we might suppose that, given the seriousness of our subject – namely, the political implications of a Heideggerian or post-Heideggerian phenomenology of technology (a subject that inevitably raises the specter of Heidegger's Nazism) – all such facetiousness should really be set aside. But is that even possible? As the later Heidegger teaches us to recognize, human beings *are* "facets of being," unique and finite perspectives on the historically shifting constellation of intelligibility, a temporally unfolding intelligible order which itself fails to exhaust the being it discloses and that, together we finite, world-disclosive beings constitute and transform. As long as we *exist*, "standing-out" into our being in time, we can never leave all our facetiousness behind; only if and when we cease to be entirely will we abandon our own particular perspectives in and on being's ontohistorical disclosure.

So long as we are, then, each of us will *be partial* in the double sense of the word, that is, both *limited* and *partisan*. The finite and care-full worlds of disclosure that we Dasein are remain partial both in that we can never exhaust the ontological riches of that which we disclose and also that we are never wholly disinterested in our myriad efforts to do so. For, as partial or non-exhaustive, our intelligible worlds inevitably remain selective; and as selective, we remain partial to or somehow implicated in the worlds we disclose – both

---

[11] See below and Thomson, *Heidegger, Art, and Postmodernity*, ch. 7.
[12] See, for example, ibid., 211–2.

responsive to and responsible for the worlds we thereby help transmit through time (as Beauvoir recognized). Our constitutive and never entirely eliminable existential *partiality* immediately raises concerns about prejudice, and rightly so, but it should also remind us of a central lesson of the hermeneutic tradition (a lesson which does not make this tradition *politically* conservative): We *need* prejudices; we cannot even function without relying on at least some such "prior judgments." Prejudices remain necessary to all skill, agency, and intelligibility; even our basic comportmental navigation of the life world requires us to employ prior judgments. (Try to imagine what it would be like if we had to figure out how to open a door every time we approached one. And we could not even approach doors if we did not rely on prior judgments about what a "door" is, about how to identify and move toward doors, how to open and pass through them, and so on.) Such guiding prejudices are only *bad*, then, insofar as the particular prejudgment embedded within and so perpetuated by them are themselves bad. Here "bad" cannot simply mean "limiting," moreover, since we finite beings are all inevitably limited in innumerable ways. Prejudice in the bad or objectionable sense must mean something more like "limiting in an unnecessary, problematic, and harmful way."

Such bad kinds of prejudice include the familiar "-isms" of racism, sexism, classism, ableism, neurotypicalism, neo-conservativism (or global free-marketism), fundamentalism, authoritarianism, and so on. Such widespread and often mutually reinforcing systems of unjustified prejudice continue to harm our societies and ourselves despite what, especially among the young, seems to be a growing intellectual and political consensus dedicated to uprooting and transcending *all* such harmful, unnecessary, and (I shall try to show again here) ultimately *unjustifiable* views. At the same time, as if working in concert, I think we also need to address the even more ubiquitous prejudices of what Derrida (rather cheekily) calls "ontotheo-carno-phallogocentrism," an interconnected set of harmful, unnecessary, and objectionable prejudices that are still too often treated as if they were natural or innocuous truths. Here I shall primarily be concerned with the two-chambered, *ontotheological* heart of this baleful network of "carnophallogocentric" prejudices. My goal will be to direct our critical attention to that nexus of ontotheological prejudgments that negatively impact our understanding and treatment of almost all entities, pervasively and perniciously distorting our thinking about identities and differences at the deepest and most general levels.[13]

By adopting this approach, then, I am not discounting the necessity or importance of confronting all our other objectionable ethical and political prejudices. On the contrary, my hope is that focusing on our *ontotheological*

---

[13] Heidegger taught us to recognize being as enabling our thinking of both identity and difference. (See ID and Thomson, *Heidegger on Ontotheology*, ch. 1.)

prejudices will help us learn first to discern and then to move beyond these still very widely shared but harmful and unnecessary prejudgments about what it means for anything and anyone to *be*. Though not completely universal, these ontotheological prejudices have nevertheless become so general and pervasive that our critical efforts to discern and move beyond them can often prove helpful to other important struggles for freedom within more specific domains. Some of the most obviously relevant emancipatory struggles include our efforts to rethink the ontotheological prejudices that distort the fields of education, technology, ecological ethics, and erotic love (to name some of the domains I have sought to address).[14] But, as Derrida's neologism linking *ontotheology* directly to *carnophallogocentrism* means to suggest, the deconstruction of ontotheology also has important emancipatory implications for our ongoing efforts to rethink the ethico-politics of eating, of animal liberation, as well as our important efforts to disclose post-phallogocentric ways of understanding and embracing those rapidly emerging forms of transgender, poly-, queer-, and asexualities.[15]

Our time seems marked by such proliferations of emergent particularities (as well as the repressive reactions against them), and I will return to the profoundly hopeful light in which I view this historical eruption of differences. But even as I celebrate difference, I would never deny that our concrete and specific struggles are often pervaded by often intolerably painful forms of existential suffering (especially when particular groups are forced to suffer harmful wrongs in silent despair, or in isolation from communities of political solidarity and support).[16] I only want to suggest that the more general

---

[14] See Chapter 4.

[15] The last point, at any rate, is the way I read such rich works as Jacques Derrida, *Spurs: Nietzsche's Styles* (Chicago: University of Chicago, 1981) and "Geschlecht I: Sexual Difference/Ontological Difference" (in Jacques Derrida, *Psyche: Inventions of the Other*, Vol. II [Stanford: Stanford University Press, 2008]), viz., as creative, post-Heideggerian works of hermeneutic phenomenology that seek to disclose an originary protosexual plenitude that both precedes and exceeds its repressive subjection to the metaphysical dichotomies of sexual difference (a topic especially fascinating in the context of transgendered thinking, which Derrida not only presciently anticipates but often participates in as well). (See also Derrida, "'Eating Well,' or the Calculation of the Subject," in Jacques Derrida, *Points … Interviews, 1974–1994* [Stanford, CA: Stanford University Press, 1995]; Paul Preciado, *Countersexual Manifesto* (New York: Columbia University Press, 2018), 57–73 ("Derrida's Scissors: The Logic of the Dildo"); and Thomson, "Ontopoliticosexual Pro(−)vocations.")

[16] The magnitude of the problem is powerfully suggested by the landmark study in which the results of a national survey showed that 41 percent of trans- or gender nonconforming respondents had attempted suicide. (See A. Haas et al., "Suicide Attempts Among Transgender and Gender Non-conforming Adults: Findings of the National Transgender Discrimination Study," *American Foundation for Suicide Prevention and the Williams Institute, UCLA School of Law* [2014]. Retrieved from https://williamsinstitute.law.ucla.edu/wp-content/uploads/AFSP-Williams-Suicide-Report-Final.pdf.) Research suggests

suffering our ontotheology reinforces remains quite real as well, if perhaps less obvious. For, as Heidegger argued, our ontotheological prejudices contribute to that already very general (and some say increasingly global) intellectual and even "spiritual" malaise most often called "nihilism," the historical phenomenon of a growing sense of existential *meaninglessness*.[17]

8.2 Disclosing Technological Nihilism through Hermeneutic Phenomenology

One of the deepest lessons of Heideggerian phenomenology is that most of the Western world has been socialized into a basic set of interconnected prejudgments about what it means to *be*, and this ontological (or, more precisely, *ontotheological*) prejudice seems to be spreading across the globe along with the ever-expanding reach of technology – indeed, *as* "the very essence of technology." When Heidegger writes that "the essence of technology is nothing technological," he means not only that we cannot find the essence of technology in any particular technological device but also that this essence, when we really discover it, turns out not to be *technological* at all. The essence of technology is our historical understanding of being, the metaphysical substructure driving the late-modern epoch Heidegger calls "enframing" (*Gestell*). Still, too few recognize that this technological understanding of being follows from the ontotheology that forms the dual metaphysical foundation of our current age. Indeed, the growing phenomena of nihilistic *technologization*

---

that transgender youth whose emergent identifies and gender transitions are affirmed and supported by their families and larger communities do not seem to suffer such terrible outcomes. (See K. R. Olson et al., "Mental Health of Transgender Children who are Supported in Their Identities," *Pediatrics*, 137 [2016], 2015-3223.) None of this prevents political reactionaries from increasingly targeting such vulnerable minority populations in order to intensify, manipulate, and mobilize prejudices in ways that divert attention away from the real causes of the existential suffering they thereby sadistically intensify. (On this point, see also Thomson, "Ontopoliticosexual Pro(−)vocations," 206–208.)

[17] This growing sense that existence is meaningless (visible in everything from burgeoning rates of anxiety and depression to the weaponized nihilism of school shootings and other forms of "suicide by cop") continues unabated, I think, despite what I have called "the problem of the happy enframer," that is, the fact that many of those most deeply inculcated into the technological understanding of being see nothing objectionable about it, or else believe that whatever problems they continue to experience will eventually be solved by the endless advance of technological innovation. I suggest that we can begin to address this problem with the tripartite response of confronting anxiety, deploying immanent critiques, and even using "Trojan horse" strategies to help show happy enframers the enduring appeal of postmodernity. (See Thomson, *Heidegger, Art, and Postmodernity*, 103, 200, and 215.) On the increasingly global reach of technologization, see, for example, Mustapha Chérif, *Islam and the West: A Conversation with Jacques Derrida* (Chicago, IL: University of Chicago Press, 2008).

result from our increasing thoughtless application of this ontotheology to our worlds, each other, and ourselves.

Fortunately, as I suggested at the beginning, we cannot truly understand our current technological ontotheology without thereby being led beyond it. For, to understand ontotheology *is* to be led beyond it (or so I shall try to show again here). This hopeful idea that our technological understanding of being leads beyond itself is what Heidegger meant by "the freeing claim" of technology, an idea he later developed with his view that the "danger" of technologization, seen otherwise, discloses the "promise" of the postmodern "event." (Or, in his provocatively analogy: "Enframing is like the photographic negative of enowning" [FS 60/GA16 366].) We are well prepared to understand Heidegger's difficult idea here, because it is basically a later development of the same transformative insight we traced in the first three chapters, in which what originally shows us as nothing at all (in *Being and Time*'s denial that there is any further phenomenological horizon to discover beyond the being of entities, for example) *turns* out to be the subtle and inchoate hinting of futural possibilities (that dynamic "noth-ing" of the nothing or "presencing" of the conceptually inexhaustible "earth") that thereby solicit our creative and responsive disclosures. In the later Heidegger's crucial vision of just such a phenomenological conversion, the nihilism of technological nothingness is transformed into the genuinely meaningful experience of a postmodern understanding of being. In a transformative moment of insight, we experience a gestalt switch in which we pass from understanding being as nothing but resources awaiting optimization to realizing, instead, that what looks like sheer nothingness from within enframing is really the "noth-ing" of the nothing, that is, the not-yet-a-thing of those inchoate possibilities still on their way to be being disclosed and so brought maieutically into our shared worlds of meaning.[18]

To understand how the later Heidegger rethinks and develops his earlier thinking of such a disclosive death and rebirth to a meaningful world, we need to at least briefly recall his philosophical reasons for understanding our contemporary, "late-modern" age as a time of technological *enframing*. Like all the other relatively coherent epochs in the Western "history of being" (or what I have called "the different historical constellations of intelligibility"), our late modern epoch of technological enframing is unified by its underlying understanding of the being of entities – that is, by what Heidegger frequently calls our "fundamental metaphysical position," or "the truth concerning the totality of entities as such." These metaphysical *ontotheologies* "doubly ground" an historical understanding of being by linking their grasp of reality's innermost *ontological* core (its deepest microscopic depth or final component

---

[18] See especially Thomson, *Heidegger, Art, and Postmodernity*, ch. 7.

part) with their account of reality's outermost, *theological* expression (its highest ground or ultimate, telescopic manifestation). By joining that *ontological* "as such" and *theological* "as a whole" into an ontotheological "truth concerning the totality of entities as such," these metaphysical ontotheologies grasp reality from the outside-in and the inside-out simultaneously. When these ontotheologies succeed in uncovering and linking our innermost and our outermost ways of grasping what-is, their *dual foundationalisms* dam the floodwaters of ontological historicity for a time – the time of an "epoch" (from the Greek *epochê*, "holding back" or "putting in parentheses").

Ontotheologies thus put the parentheses around an epoch's understanding of being, temporarily holding back the overwhelming excessiveness of being's seemingly inexhaustible phenomenological riches and so allowing the particular and coherent metaphysical understanding of being that unifies an age to take shape and spread, becoming the tacit ground for that age. Such ontotheological understandings of being are able to proliferate and unify an age thanks to what I call *ontological holism*: Everything intelligible "is" in some sense, so when an ontotheology changes our understanding of "Isness" itself, that sets off an historical transformation in our understanding of everything, rippling throughout a historical world until it eventually gives way to another ontotheology, one even deeper and more far reaching in its understanding of the being of entities (thereby allowing this historical process of punctuated equilibrium to repeat itself in its successive ontotheological forms as the Western "history of being"). In the end, then, ontotheologies are simply an existing epoch's deepest and ultimate, but nonetheless temporary, bulwarks against the seemingly inexhaustible excessiveness of being

To come to the point that is crucial for our purposes here, Heidegger thinks that our current, "technological" understanding of being follows directly from an underlying ontotheology that Nietzsche was the first to recognize and name when he understood being as nothing but "eternally recurring will to power." Nietzsche was able to first name the ontological foundation of our late-modern epoch not by legislating from his own creative imagination but, instead, because he extracted and generalized the common ontological insight he saw shared by the cutting-edge biology, economics, chemistry, and physics of his time. Basically, Nietzsche appropriated the Darwinian understanding of biological life as an endless struggle between competing life forms – a struggle often to the death (as with the lion chasing the gazelle) that nevertheless works to keep life itself alive (by generally selecting for organisms better adapted to their environments than their competitors). In ontologizing Darwin, Nietzsche drew further inspiration from Adam Smith's *laissez-faire* understanding of economics as fundamentally a conflict between the forces of supply and demand, a conflict that generates maximal economic growth when those competing forces are unfettered and allowed to vie against one another without external interference. Nietzsche also read keenly from contemporary work in chemistry and physics that similarly seemed to understand the domains of the chemical and the physical as essentially fields composed of complex interactions between opposing forces, and all of these views reinforced Nietzsche's preexisting Heraclitean intuitions and his love of the Homeric *agon* or struggle, a competition (like Patroclus's mythological funeral games in the *Iliad*, paradigmatically enshrined in the Olympics) in which competing opponents drive each other to push the limits of the possible with endlessly self-surpassing achievements.[19]

Nietzsche disclosed (what he took to be) the core ontological view shared across all these different fields, calling that "will to power," then drew out the ultimate cosmological implications of this ontology, giving rise to his view of "eternal recurrence," or "the doctrine of the eternal return of the same." In the philosophical notebooks from the last year of his productive life, Nietzsche hypothesized that, if we assume finite matter and finite space, then it seems to follow ineluctably that: "In infinite time, every possible combination [of matter] would at some time or other be realized," entailing that every empirically possible state of affairs will occur and "recur endlessly" in the infinite expanse of time.

Heidegger's reading of Nietzsche as a secret ontotheologist rightly remains controversial (precisely as an overly systematic reading of the irreducible complexity of Nietzsche's thought), but we should still acknowledge the deep insight at its core.[20] Heidegger's great insight is that Nietzsche was a hermeneutic phenomenologist who rightly discerned the ontotheology underlying our historical period; we do indeed increasingly tend to understand the being of all entities as "eternally recurring will to power," that is, as an unending disaggregation and reaggregation of forces with no end beyond the perpetuation of force itself. (If I press you on what this table really *is*, for example, you will usually end up saying that it is an arrangement of subatomic particles moving so fast that the table appears solid despite the fact that it is really just a rather temporary and mostly empty form that these underlying forces have taken.) Here we reach the ontotheological roots of the problem of technological nihilism, the real motor of *technologization*. For, when we implicitly understand what-is through such an ontotheological framework, we tend to dissolve

---

[19] See Iain Thomson, "Interpretation as Self-Creation: Nietzsche on the Pre-Platonics," *Ancient Philosophy*, 23:1 (2003), 201–5; and Julian Young, *Friedrich Nietzsche: A Philosophical Biography* (Cambridge: Cambridge University Press, 2010), especially 536–8.

[20] I address this controversy in Thomson, *Heidegger, Art, and Postmodernity*, ch. 1. I would also refer those still tempted to reject Heidegger's reading of Nietzsche out of hand to the deeply Heideggerian interpretation advanced and defended in John Richardson's *Nietzsche's System* (New York: Oxford University Press, 1996).

8.2. DISCLOSING TECHNOLOGICAL NIHILISM

being into nothing but endless collisions of forces that work only to maximally perpetuate force itself. Insofar as we understand being in these "nihilistic" terms – dissolving being into *nothing* but endlessly competing forces – the result is that we tend to relate to and so transform all entities into mere "resources" (*Bestand*), intrinsically meaningless stuff standing by to be optimized, ordered, and enhanced with maximal efficiency. This technologizing worldview is nihilistic, then, precisely insofar as it leads us to treat all things as devoid of any inherent worth or enduring meaning – ourselves included (as we saw in Agamben's poignant analysis in Chapter 7).

This problem of growing historical nihilism is exacerbated by the fact that, as our technological ontotheology becomes more entrenched, the historical transformation of beings into mere resources it generates becomes more pervasive, and so – according to the first law of phenomenology, *the distance of the near* – it increasingly eludes our critical notice. In this way, we late-moderns come to treat ourselves in the very same nihilistic terms that underlie our technological reframing of the world. No longer even modern "subjects" seeking to master and control an objective world, we late-moderns have turned the techniques and tools developed for controlling that objective world back onto ourselves. This ongoing *objectification of the subject* is transforming human beings into just another intrinsically meaningless resource to be optimized – whether cosmetically, psychopharmacologically, genetically, aesthetically, educationally, politically, or otherwise "technologically."

In sum, then, the deepest problem with our ongoing "technologization" of reality is the nihilistic understanding of being that underlies and drives it. This underlying ontotheology dissolves being into *nothing* but "sovereign becoming" (as Nietzsche put it), merely an endless circulation of forces, and in so doing, it denies that things have any inherent nature, any genuine meaning that could prove capable of resisting this slide into nihilism. This technologizing worldview cannot account for the very idea of *qualitative* "worth," for example, and so increasingly tends to reject the cogency or meaningfulness of anything that cannot be quantified and so represented in terms of "values." (Like "net worth," "intrinsic value" is an oxymoron; both make the category mistake of trying to quantify qualities.) Instead, we get trained to follow enframing's optimization imperative, endlessly quantifying all qualities as we flexibly and efficiently seek to get the most for the least. Under the sway of this technological understanding of being, *nothing is invaluable*. Heidegger's crucial move here is simply to help us hear the full polysemy of that phrase and so learn to disclose this *nothing* otherwise (as we have seen).[21]

---

[21] See Chapter 3; Thomson, *Heidegger, Art, and Postmodernity*, ch. 3; and Thomson, *Heidegger on the Danger and Promise of Technology*.

8.3 From the Righteous Lure of Good Conscience toward the Creative Peace of Ontological Pluralism

In the way just briefly recounted, then, Heidegger draws our attention to the ontotheological roots of that widespread prejudice I have called nihilistic *technologization*. But we still need to show that this prejudice is not in fact a necessary one, or that we can indeed legitimately and meaningfully understand what-is otherwise than merely as resources to be optimized. In pursuing this critical task of hermeneutic phenomenology, however, we are not engaging in yet another quest for a good ethico-political conscience. Levinas, we have seen, taught that our progressive ethical development leads us to a heightened awareness of our own ethical shortcomings, a growing recognition of our inevitable failures to respond to the real needs of others, not as an alibi for inaction or cynicism but as a spur to continue developing our own infinite responsibility to the other. Emphasizing that view, Derrida used to provocatively tell his students (in English): "The good conscience is not!" He probably should have said instead that "the good conscience is neither," since he was amplifying Heidegger by lamenting rather than denying that the phenomenon of good conscience exists and asserting that its symptomatic expressions are neither good nor expressions of a genuine ethical conscience (BT 338/SZ 292).

I also hear this in the spirit of *Zarathustra*'s keen psychological observation that the most righteous "teachers of virtue" always seem to be those individuals most desperately in need of a clear conscience themselves. Just think of William Bennett, the former US Secretary of Education and best-selling author of *The Book of Virtues*, inveterately gambling away millions of the dollars he was paid for preaching about the importance of autonomy and self-control. Or if you want an even more obvious example, recall that pathetic parade of firebrand preachers of homophobia, inevitably caught "with their pants down," secretly soliciting gay sex in public bathrooms. (Although striking, such hypocrisy is no longer surprising, since it reminds us that homophobia often just *is* a symptomatic expression of repressed homosexuality, as Sartre argued in *Being and Nothingness* and empirical psychology confirmed decades ago.)[22] Do not such hypocrisies suggest that the most righteous purveyors of their one final Truth lack clear consciences themselves, that they are first and foremost trying to convince *themselves* of the truth of their own final Truths, and *failing* to do so, no matter how loudly they shout these alleged Truths at the rest of us?

Listening to such symptoms of bad conscience echoing across centuries of moral and political philosophy, Nietzsche concluded that a truly clear conscience remains impossible for any living thinker. Nietzsche recognized that

---

[22] See Sartre, *Being and Nothingness* (Barnes trans.), 407. See also the empirical study by Adams et al., "Is Homophobia Associated with Homosexual Arousal?," *Journal of Abnormal Psychology*, 105:3 (1996), 440–445.

8.3. GOOD CONSCIENCE OR PLURALISTIC PEACE? 251

life always involves a struggle between competing forces and interests, a struggle that often forces us to take sides. This means we will remain haunted by some of these roads not taken (as Heidegger too recognized and inscribed into his concept of *ontological guilt*).[23] We will know in our hearts (even if we try to deny it in our minds) that things would look very differently to us – that we would in fact *be* very different selves – if we had taken, or been *thrown* into, different paths. Zarathustra concludes that the only possible fulfillment of these virtue preachers' vision of a perfectly clear conscience would be "the sleep without dreams" – that is, *being demised* (a phenomenological impossibility, as we saw in Chapter 1). The hopeless quest for righteous purity thus fuels our thanatological drive to make that "one fatal leap" into "an otherworldy beyond," *a leap into the void* whereby we could leave behind our bad consciences, albeit along with everything else about us.

For Nietzsche, then, there are no truly clear consciences among the living, and all those righteous preachers who "knew no better meaning of life" than the dreamless sleep of demise turn out to be *nihilists*. For, by valorizing nonexistence over existence, the righteous preachers of virtuous purity are really stating that our inevitably impure *life is worth less than the purity of sheer non-existence*.[24] This, ironically, puts the preachers of virtue on the side of the Devil. As Derrida nicely suggests (in a creatively disclosive reading of Paul Valéry), Satan is that archetypal nihilist who prefers the purity of the "void of non-being," which he personally witnessed as God's first creation (the mythological angel Lucifer, the "light-bringer" created by God's first command: "Let there be light!"). Longing for a return to the perfect purity of that void which originally surrounded him, the Devil pursues the nihilistic dictum that everything that exists "deserves to have an undoing" (as Mephistopheles famously put it in Goethe's *Faust*), and so works tirelessly to negate and destroy everything that exists in a vain and so desperate hope of returning to that state of pure nonbeing.[25]

---

[23] As we saw in Chapter 1 (n. 54), *Being and Time* calls this phenomenon *ontological guilt*, thereby naming the existential fact of our ineliminably anxious being-guilty (hence his aforementioned description of Dasein as "null-basis of a nullity," an ontological structure of finite Dasein's necessary lack that underlies every specific instance of regret for what we do or fail to do, as a felt lack in ourselves that leads to a lack in another).

[24] See Nietzsche, *Thus Spoke Zarathustra*, 142.

[25] Here I am developing Derrida's suggestive reading of Valéry's poem, "Silhouette of a Serpent," in which Satan memorably declares that "the universe is merely a blot / On the pure void of Non-being!" See Derrida, *The Animal That Therefore I Am*, 65–68 (quotation from 66, perhaps appropriately). (On the animality topic, see also Kelly Oliver, "Tropho-Ethics: Derrida's Homeopathic Purity," *The Harvard Review of Philosophy*, 15 (2007), 37–57 and *Animal Lessons: How They Teach Us to Be Human* [New York: Columbia University Press, 2009]; and Cynthia Willett, *Interspecies Ethics* [New York: Columbia University Press, 2014].)

We sought phenomenologically to deconstruct the dubious motivations of this nihilistic desire for a final metaphysical escape from the bonds of finitude and mortality in Chapter 1 (and I critique the nihilism of this theological drive in detail elsewhere).[26] So let me just add one more post-Heideggerian twist to Derrida's Nietzschean provocation here. Is not the righteous dream of *being unprejudiced* just another version of the fantasy of *being unlimited*, that perennial philosophical daydream in which we mortal beings find some way to shed our finite skin and adopt a God's-eye view-from-nowhere? Freud called this paradoxical drive to *be nothing* "the nirvana principle," thus deriving humanity's dangerous thanatological drive from our deep sense of loss connected to the pain of individuation (as Schopenhauer originally suggested). The child's inevitable loss of "the oceanic feeling" of primordial wholeness in the womb fuels the adult's impossible wish for a permanent return to that feeling of undifferentiated oneness. And did not Kierkegaard discern something similar in the suicidal person's contradictory desire to *be* demised? Diagnosing suicide as a desire to continue to exist, just without this particular self that suffers, Kierkegaard described this impossible desire for a purely *selfless* existence as a form of "despair."[27] According to Kierkegaard's spiritually elevated pseudonym, "Anti-Climacus," the *serious* Christian's goal should be to struggle to assume, rather than to escape, our individual differences and always unique particularities.

In the history of Western philosophy, the dream of *being demised* most typically takes the form of a wish to completely transcend our particular point of view in order to speak from the aperspectivalism of the whole.[28] Such

---

[26] See Thomson, "Transcendence and the Problem of Otherworldly Nihilism" and Chapter 9.

[27] See Sigmund Freud, *Beyond the Pleasure Principle* (New York: Norton, 1961); Arthur Schopenhauer, *The World as Will and Representation*, Vol. 1 and 2 (Cambridge: Cambridge University Press, 2014, 2020); and Kierkegaard, *The Sickness Unto Death*.

[28] We will critique a contemporary technological version of this theological fantasy in Chapter 9. As we saw in detail in Chapter 1, the early Heidegger already suggests that what we despairingly fear (or thanatologically desire) from demise (viz., an impossible state of being our own nonbeing) is something we can attain only in his phenomenological vision of *being dead*, a desolate experience of the radical existential solitude of the "*solus ipse*" or self alone that emerges when we live through the global collapse of all the particular existentiell projects that give our lives their worldly significance. I suggested that we need not find that vision compelling in its extremity (as a *total* collapse of one's life-projects), but that we can still attest to the phenomenological cogency of Heidegger's idea of "ontological death" (as the existential death of Dasein's constitutive "being-in-the-world") by generalizing from the collapse of a particular life project (something virtually all of us will have experienced) to the idea of a catastrophic collapse of them all. Heidegger thinks we will at least begin to experience such a global collapse of our projects if we are awake and undeceived when we demise, but that (owing to our inability to live all the way through our demise) the only phenomenological way to fully undergo such existential death is if our most fundamental existential project (or "ultimate for-the-sake-

of-which") collapses, bringing down the rest of our other projects like a house of cards (see also Chapter 1, n. 57). It is perhaps not too surprising that Heidegger would thus describe an experience that can be found by passing through and beyond the perennial theological temptation in his early work, since (as we saw in Chapter 2) his critique of metaphysics as ontotheology emerged out of the failure of his own early ontotheological ambitions.

Interestingly, an account similar to Heidegger's discovery of the *solus ipse* in the phenomenon of existential death seems to have reemerged (albeit in a psychoanalytically informed version distorted by the residual metaphysics of modern "subjectivity") in Slavoj Žižek's neo-Freudian vision of "the pure internality of the 'autistic' subject detached from external reality, disengaged, reduced to the persisting core deprived of its substance" (see Slavoj Žižek, *Disparities* [London: Bloomsbury, 2016], 338). "Autistic subject" is a doubly problematic term, both because *autism* has often been misunderstood as an isolated (or even cognitively impoverished) self largely if not entirely split off from the world when, in fact, it is better understood as a too-intensive encounter of a self with that world (an intensity maintained in an overcharged surface that complicates the traffic between self and world), and also because Žižek's "autistic subject" seemingly seeks to describe the emergence of the *solus ipse* through existential death (and its ensuing confrontation with the *nothing*) in the metaphysically reductive categories of "subjectivity." Nonetheless, Žižek similarly suggests that "what appears as the brutal destruction of the subject's very (narrative) substantive identity is the moment of its birth. The post-traumatic autistic subject is the living proof that [the] subject cannot be identified (does not fully overlap) with [the] 'stories it is telling itself about itself,' with the narrative symbolic texture of its life: when we take all this away, something (or, rather, *nothing*, but a *form* of nothing) remains, and this something is the pure subject of [the] death drive" (ibid.). Unfortunately, Žižek miscognizes his own proximity to Heidegger here by following Badiou and so repeating the common misunderstanding that conflates existential death with our relation to mortal demise. To wit, Žižek symptomatically dismisses "the standard Heideggerian topic of finitude," that is, the human being's "relating to its own finitude and unavoidable death (ibid., 339, 343), showing that he and Badiou both fatally conflate mortal demise with existential death, since such death is not "unavoidable" (as we saw in Chapter 1). Indeed, Heidegger thinks most people flee from their anxiety about existential death (into a common fear of demise that they "tranquillize" by keeping busy) and so remain "alienated" from their ownmost Dasein" (BT 222/SZ 178). Few find the fortitude to face up to and live through death, thereby encountering the world-disclosive lessons of its suggestive "noth-ing" for themselves (as recounted in Chapter 3). Still, Žižek similarly emphasizes the very thing that, Heidegger reminds us, standard post-Cartesian accounts of subjectivity miss, viz., that the self was originally connected to its world before being cut off from it (with the emergence of the objective thematization or *Vorhandenheit*). Without going further into the problems generated by Žižek's paradoxical employment of the same metaphysical categories of subjectivity that his descriptive analysis itself undermines, let me just emphasize his insightful Freudian suggestion that what tends to make existential death *traumatic* is precisely the way it repeats the self's originary loss of integration with the world, a traumatic loss of that originary self-world integration Freud characterized as "primary narcissism." Lacan identifies this loss with "*the birth of subjectivity itself*" in its emergence into the symbolic order, making this traumatized residue of the self (or, perhaps, *solus ipse*) the actual "realization" of the Cartesian *cogito* (ibid., 338). While Žižek's suggestion remains intriguing (if largely undeveloped), I doubt we need Lacan's "metapsychological" terminology visions of perfect union with universality itself can be beautiful (as in art and music), or terrible (as in totalitarian politics), or some mixture of terror and beauty both (as in some forms of religious devotion and drug intoxication). The point I want to suggest is that these unfulfillable dreams of total escape repeatedly reanimate the Western philosophical tradition of metaphysics as *ontotheology*. For, this haunting dream of total escape is a paradoxical vision of *being completely outside everything that-is*, a contradictory theological vision of reaching an absolute exteriority or alterity and then somehow bringing this absolute outside back into the whole as what secures its totality from beyond. Here, with this haunting but paradoxical vision of a return from demise, we thus find that core metaphysical fantasy that we could finally secure our knowledge of reality by coming to know its ultimate, self-caused cause. The discovery of such a miraculous *causa sui* would provide the ultimate anchor for our telescopic thinking, securing its outermost extension in an immovable foundation outside space and time. In all its interconnected forms, this impossible dream of reaching an absolute exteriority and then returning again (to ground and secure the ultimate borders of the known) provides the rocket fuel that seems historically to endlessly expand the "theological" ambitions of metaphysics, driving our desire not only to get outside all that-is but thus to discover above and beyond all that-is some foundation that can never again be dislodged by subsequent thinking.

Sartre was right to call this "the desire to be God" (a desire this proud "atheist" nevertheless struggles with in *Being and Nothingness*). But Nietzsche had already observed that this "God is dead," that we killed the god of metaphysics when "we unchained this earth from its [metaphysical] sun," coming to realize historically that it was impossible permanently to anchor our understanding of reality in something outside itself.[29] As if reluctantly waking up from a once comforting dream (as it turns increasingly into a

---

(with all its undeconstructed metaphysical baggage and nihilistic implications) in order to understand why Dasein tends to experience its loss of (*zuhanden*) self-world integration in existential death as traumatic, since that loss entails both the break-down of Dasein's skillful engagement in its significance-bestowing life-projects and also brings it before the initially bewildering "nothingness" of its core self and futural worlds in their manifold "coming toward" this *solus ipse* (as we saw at the end of Chapter 1). It is not surprising that we (like Heidegger himself, as we saw in Chapter 3) would initially find such an encounter traumatic and anxiety-provoking, before we learn to creatively open ourselves to and disclose meaning from the initially overwhelming excess of possibilities this dynamic "noth-ing" primordially discloses (which Heidegger will later come to recognize *retrospectively* as the first glimmering of being as such).

[29] Heidegger's view is that, just as Kant *thought* Descartes' ontological "unthought," so *Nietzsche thinks Kant's unthought*, developing the heretofore unrecognized consequences of Kant's establishment of subjectivity as the metaphysical foundation for morality, politics, and art. By making the rational subject the ground of what is good, right, and beautiful, *Kant kills God*, in Nietzsche's terms; that is, Kant finally severs this human

nightmare), humanity is gradually coming to see that there is no way to construct an unbroken cognitive chain anchoring our finite world in that ultimate foundation beyond the sky that metaphysics has been searching for since even before Plato postulated his good "beyond being."[30] We realize the impossibility of metaphysics' ultimate theological ambition when we realize that *we* cannot be such a God. Indeed, that seems to be the deep point behind *Zarathustra*'s facetious proof for the nonexistence of God: "*If* there were Gods, how could I stand not to be a God! *Therefore* there are no Gods."[31] Nietzsche's point is not that we cannot be God because there is no God but, instead, that there is no God because we finite human beings can never be God.

For many, the death of the metaphysical God still seems too bitter a pill to swallow.[32] So let me hasten to acknowledge that we finite beings do seem to be able to at least partly attain a paradoxically aperspectival perspective in some limited domains of investigation, deducing or disclosing some apparently aperspectival truths in restricted domains within mathematical logic and natural science, for example. While rightly abjuring the reductiveness of all scientisms, we seem to be able to extend the quest for perspective-neutral, universal truths to yield some structural guidelines in some neighboring domains of human self-understanding (stretching from psychiatry to urban

---

world from all its traditional ("otherworldly") metaphysical foundations. (On this point, see Thomson, "Post/Modernity?")

[30] See Sartre, *Essays in Existentialism*; Nietzsche, *The Gay Science* (*The Portable Nietzsche*), 95–6; and Plato, *Republic* (New York: Books, Inc., 1943), VI, 509b8. When Heidegger calls this metaphysical vision of a self-caused cause "the God of philosophy," by "philosophy" he means metaphysics understood as "ontotheology." (On this incredible God of the metaphysicians, which goes back to Anaximander and the beginnings of Western metaphysics, see ID 72 and Thomson, "Ontotheology.")

[31] Nietzsche, *Thus Spoke Zarathustra*, 198. Here Nietzsche also seems to be offering a metaphysical analogue of the Hobbesian argument that the *bellum omnium contra omnes* (or "war of all against all" in his mythological state of nature) motivates even the most powerful to give up their licentious freedom and instead adopt a social contract that protects everyone from the worst abuses. Similarly, *Zarathustra* suggests, no one may legitimately legislate their fundamentalist morality for all because, if they could, then how could he (or any of us) stand not to be that tyrannical legislator, maintaining an unjustified dominance over the rest? *The death of God spells the death of all such moral tyranny*, because it permanently severs the metaphysical foundations that allegedly justified the imposition of such unjustifiable fundamentalisms.

[32] When Nietzsche's "madman" first announces the death of God, he famously asks how we were able "to drink up the sea" of prior human values, and also worries that the death of metaphysics leads to nihilism, such that we are now "straying as through an infinite nothing" (Nietzsche, *The Portable Nietzsche*, 95). But what Nietzsche's madman misses (perhaps the very thing that marks him as "mad" for Nietzsche) is that the God of metaphysics helped cause, rather than prevent, the nihilism of our own historical age. Here, however, Nietzsche's and Heidegger's diagnoses of nihilism crucially diverge (see Thomson, "Transcendence and the Problem of Otherworldly Nihilism").

planning). But do these domains include ethics and politics, as repeatedly assumed within the modern Enlightenment tradition of cosmopolitan universalism that stretches from Descartes – through Spinoza – to Kant?

Today, are we not witnessing the dramatic historical spectacle of a historical *return of the repressed* by the Enlightenment, that is, a multifaceted reemergence of numerous differences of parochial belonging and tribal identity that continue to stubbornly resist cosmopolitan assimilation – and for good as well as for bad reasons? In my view, these sometimes destructive and disturbing signs of a burgeoning resurgence of difference and particularity follow from and feed back into a deeper ontohistorical transformation from late-modernity to postmodernity.[33] I would thus like to take this broad-spectrum resurgence of particularity as an auspicious sign that we are approaching a genuinely *postmodern* understanding of being. As we saw in Chapter 3, Heidegger hopes to teach us to understand "the death of God" otherwise, *as* the concealed presencing of the conceptually inexhaustible earth – that is, of what he originally called the "noth-ing" of that ambiguous "nothing" existential death first disclosed in *Being and Time*. In other words, "the death of God" seems to be opening up Western humanity to the progressive realization that the only truly secure "foundation" for our ethical and political thinking is the irreducible *ontological pluralism* that populates the phenomenological horizon beyond which our metaphysicians sought to find their God.[34]

---

[33] The idea that we are in the midst of such a profound ontohistorical transformation is one of the central theses of Thomson, *Heidegger, Art, and Postmodernity* (esp. chs. 3 and 8) and that post-Heideggerian hope remains in the background of the arguments presented here.

[34] By "ontological pluralism" (a concept which, owing to a paradox of reflexivity, cannot be one thing and so can have no single exhaustive definition), I also mean that being-many or being-multiple that Heidegger teaches us to think as a "nonidentical sameness" that pulsates throughout what-is as the temporal unfolding of all things, an endlessly "presencing" *sameness* (in the Parmenidean sense) or ontological interconnectedness that subtly gathers-together while also remaining actively riven and driven by differences. As we saw in Chapter 3, the nothing first disclosed in death soon develops into the earth's temporally dynamic "rift-structure" of real textures and edges that can never be finally captured and laid to rest in any singular conceptual account or practical understanding. Being's nonidentical sameness remains so internally differentiated that to *think* such an ontological pluralism, I suggest, means becoming attentive and sensitive to the ongoing emergence of unique particularities, even dedicating oneself to the open-ended task of becoming and remaining creatively receptive to those real differences that seem to be endlessly manifest in our encounters with and experiences of what is coming into being (whether we describe such dynamic emergence via *futurity*, the *nothing*, the *earth*, *presencing*, and so on). To think ontological pluralism is thus to learn to dwell in a vigilant and creative receptivity to being's conceptually underdetermining phenomenological texture and overabundant hermeneutic significance. This means learning to embrace that responsive and creative world-disclosure in and as which we Dasein are, an existential sojourn we can take up both as "meaning farmers" (see Thomson,

8.3. GOOD CONSCIENCE OR PLURALISTIC PEACE?

The proliferating phenomenological rainbow of ontological pluralism is a sign not of God but of an emerging, postmodern understanding of being, in which we no longer prejudge and so relate to all things as if they were modern objects to be controlled, nor merely late-modern "resources" awaiting efficient optimization, but instead as postmodern "things," ontologically rich phenomena that can only ever be understood partially. To embrace the irreducibly plural truth of postmodern phenomenology, in my view at least, is to realize that the temporal source of historical intelligibility not only precedes and informs our fullest conceptions of things but also continues to overflow them as a never entirely conceptualizable phenomenological excessiveness, a temporally dynamic emergence into our intelligible worlds that seems inevitably to at least partly escape even our best concepts – thereby repeatedly revealing the limits of these concepts as well as of the sense of self such concepts help shape and transform.

Yet, welcoming the emerging plenitude of particularities – in their irreducible diversity – also means recognizing and rejecting the excessive forms they can take whenever one of them proclaims itself to be the new (or old) one final Truth in ethico-political matters and so strives to drive out all competing perspectives.[35] A genuine commitment to this postmodern vision of ontological pluralism thus requires us to learn to maintain a critical vigilance in the face of all the more and less alarming manifestations of reactionary extremism,

---

Heidegger, Art, Postmodernity, 116-9) and as restless "ontological fugitives or refugees" (as we saw in Chapter 2), thereby sublating that most terrible dichotomy of Heidegger's own disastrous politics (see Thomson, "Heidegger's Nazism in the Light of His Early *Black Notebooks*").

[35] Hazarding some simple and straightforward definitions, I would say that a *conservative* is someone who thinks that new solutions are usually worse than the old problems they mean to solve, and is therefore skeptical of and resistant toward efforts to effect wide-ranging political changes. The risk-averse slogan of traditional conservativism (going back to Edmund Burke) is probably best captured in the homely epigram: "If it ain't broke, don't fix it." At the other, less risk-averse end of the political spectrum, a *revolutionary* is someone who thinks that our problems have become so terrible, generating so much entrenched suffering – that the system is already so broken, in other words – that just about anything would be better than continuing to perpetuate the status quo. Located between these two extremes of conservation and revolution, a *progressive* is someone who thinks that the severity of our problems, while undeniable to anyone paying attention to real suffering, still does not justify indiscriminately throwing out the baby of past political achievements with the bathwater of our enduring and even intensifying problems. Heidegger himself may have been a revolutionary conservative, swinging back and forth between the excessive poles of quietism and revolution, but the post-metaphysical political orientation I espouse as the more authentic heritage of his thinking is resolutely progressivist. My progressivist (post-Foucaultian) slogan might be: "*Cheer up! There is something wrong with just about everything.* So there will always be lots of work for us to do to help make some of these things better – which we really can do! (Just not everything, everywhere, or all at once.)"

in which particular groups from across the political spectrum (from ISIL to PETA) assert their own individual counter-perspectives as the new Truth of the whole.[36] (*Because none of us can be God, therefore there is no God.*)

8.4 Wrestling with Nietzsche and the Mortal Politics of Ontological Technologization

In the face of such fundamentalist demands (old and new), we should thus ask once again how amenable ethics and politics really are to pure reason's unconditional dictates. Nietzsche has *Zarathustra* starkly proclaim that: "Never yet has truth hung on the arm of the unconditional."[37] Did Nietzsche mean by this that there never have been *and never will be* any truly unconditional foundations for our ethico-political systems, although such metaphysical foundations have often been falsely announced? Or does the word "yet" in his "Never yet has truth hung on the arm of the unconditional" instead suggest that there were no such unconditional foundations until Nietzsche's own discovery of "the will to power" as the ultimate motor driving the universe, an endlessly conflictual agon of forces that secretly underlies all the different attempts to discern and install some unconditional ethico-political "tablet of values"? We find strong evidence for that second reading in *Zarathustra*'s own *unconditional* assertion that: "A tablet of the good hangs over *every* people. Behold, it is the tablet of their overcomings; behold, it is the voice of their will to power."[38]

We know Heidegger reads Nietzsche in that second way – as a secret metaphysician who proclaims "the will to power" as our new fundamental ontology (that is, as our most basic ontological "understanding of the meaning of being in general"). Between 1938 and 1946, while painfully working through the aftermath of his own neo-Nietzschean embrace of National Socialism (that would-be "revolution" Heidegger pretty consistently tried – but still utterly failed – to transform from within), Heidegger is admittedly not very sensitive to what gets missed and obscured by his reductive yet revealing reading of Nietzsche as the unthought ontotheologist of nihilistic technologization. By 1951, however (with the postwar reemergence of his public philosophical

---

[36] For example, when those who would challenge the scientific consensus that global warming has anthropogenic causes seek funds for their research, there might be good philosophical reasons to support them (even if those reasons fail to tell against the overwhelming preponderance of empirical evidence standing against them in the face of limited research funds). But when the same groups refuse to acknowledge the possibility that they are wrong, and so seek to block all human actions which seek to help ameliorate global warming in the future, such reactionary efforts to enact a totalizing account must be stopped.

[37] Nietzsche, *Thus Spoke Zarathustra*, 164.

[38] Ibid., 170 (my emphasis).

8.4. NIETZSCHE AND TECHNOLOGIZATION

voice), Heidegger is once again straining his hermeneutic ear to hear the message of "the other Nietzsche," a post-metaphysical thinker whom Heidegger now suggests can help us find our way beyond the very nihilism bequeathed us by the "technological" metaphysics on display in Nietzsche's notebooks, with their terrible call for a "superhuman" project to deliberately "breed" a world-dominating "master race" by taking control of evolution and setting out to reshape human beings "the way artists sculpt clay."[39]

Of course, one need not agree with Heidegger's reading of Nietzsche to be skeptical about how far even the most uncontroversial principles of universal reason can take us in our attempts to address the most pervasive and pressing

---

[39] (On Heidegger's disastrous political Nietzscheanism, see Thomson, *Heidegger on Ontotheology*, ch. 3, esp. 119–23.) Here I leave aside the famous final words of that problematic, posthumously edited and published selection of Nietzsche's notes known as Friedrich Nietzsche, *The Will to Power: Selections from the Notebooks of the 1880s*, ed. by R. Kevin Hill, trans. by R. K. Hill and M. Scarpitti (London & New York: Penguin Classics, 2016), a source Heidegger relies on frequently (along with other unpublished writings), in a way that remains controversial. We can certainly argue about the importance Nietzsche attributed to such ideas as "will to power," "eternal recurrence," and the "superman" (let alone his call for the "breeding" of a new "race," "the future masters of the earth" – a breeding that Nazi eugenics took solely "biologistically" and so terribly narrowly, as Heidegger publicly argued throughout the political period of his Nazi Rectorship (throughout N1 and N2, for example). An anti-Semite who nevertheless argued forcefully against the biologistic eugenics that led directly to the Holocaust or *Shoah*, Heidegger repeatedly called for an ongoing transformation of the revolution from within, frequently insisting that the "Nazi revolution" was far from over, and that it was the duty of philosophers to help "liberate" Germany from the falsely self-evident obviousness of all the political buzzwords of 1933 ("struggle," "community," blood and soil," and even "breeding"), dangerously racist buzzwords that Heidegger presented as superficial biological "shadows" on the walls of the political cave and so sought to transform in terms of his own philosophical views. (We can see this throughout much of Heidegger's important public lectures from 1933–34 (see BaT and LQ) as well as in Heidegger's remarks to his smaller seminar (see NHS).) Perhaps Heidegger's philosophical search for the "inner truth and greatness" of National Socialism was doomed from the start. (But I wonder if we would still say the same thing – that it is *impossible* to transform an authoritarian dictatorship from within – if Donald Trump 2.0, the slicker and less obviously horrifying version, should ever be democratically elected and then proceed to systematically eliminate his critics and oppositional parties and journalists, successfully consolidating a fascist regime in America?) Regardless, no one can credibly deny that the notebooks in which Nietzsche advanced those views as far as he could were influentially published as Nietzsche's *The Will to Power* on the eve of the First World War, where they unfortunately did considerable damage to the world as well as to Nietzsche's subsequent philosophical reputation. Despite apologistic attempts to minimize the importance of those ideas to Nietzsche himself (understandable in the context of trying to get this important thinker taken seriously in English-speaking philosophy departments), I think Heidegger's reading of their importance to the late Nietzsche (at least) is largely vindicated by the latest scholarly work on Nietzsche's most infamous text; see esp. R. Kevin Hill's careful and important "Introduction" to Nietzsche, *The Will to Power*.

ethico-political questions of our own time. Nonetheless, my post-Heideggerian vision of a postmodern ethico-politics remains guided by at least one universal principle, which we could call *the principle of ontological pluralism*. The guidance this principle gives us, while extremely rudimentary, nevertheless remains enduringly important. For, this universal principle of ontological pluralism (or the anti-reductive insight that being can never be exhaustively captured by any single conceptual framework) underwrites an ethico-politics of strong tolerance, that is, a robust, universal tolerance that is intolerant only of intolerance. However minimal, this postmodern principle still has some real teeth, because it allows us to reject most would-be ethico-political purveyors of the one final Truth, all the competing fundamentalisms still seeking to take God's place.[40]

Looking back at the manifest failure of all the ontotheological fever dreams of a rationality drunk on itself – and so aggressively heedless of its own ineliminable limitations – we seem to be learning finally to reject all such final Truths. To put the point in logical terms, human reason has reached the point in history where we realize that the axioms that ground a system cannot be grounded by the theorems they ground (on pain of vicious circularity), so that the very idea of a self-grounding axiom has rightly become incredible. Let me risk another expression of hope and suggest that this incredulity about absolute foundations seems to be spreading across the globe. That sounds Pollyannish until we recognize that this incredulity about the one right Truth is visible not only in the cynical relativism and unbearable-lightness-of-being *ennui* experienced by so many young people in our most technologically advanced societies (which too often sell stimulating technological simulations in place of inexhaustibly and so enduringly meaningful events). The same anti-foundationalist incredulity can also be discerned in those symptomatic outbreaks of righteous "good conscience" mentioned earlier. Just as an exaggerated braggadocio unintentionally reveals the underlying insecurity for which it is overcompensating, can we not also detect an irrepressible uncertainty in the reactionary violence with

---

[40] I cannot hope to fully develop or motivate this view here, but let me just say that I think there are two main kinds of arguments which, taken together, strongly support humanity's progressive adoption of the principle of ontological pluralism and the robust tolerance it underwrites. First, as we have seen, there are historical and logical arguments about the foundations we cannot have, largely negative arguments with an important positive conclusion. Second, there are phenomenological arguments that show us this ontological pluralism directly, by repeatedly disclosing some of its apparently inexhaustible manifestations in such domains as philosophy, poetry, art, music, and literature. Thomson, *Heidegger, Art, and Postmodernity* focuses on providing the second kind of phenomenological evidence for ontological pluralism, whereas we have been more concerned here to understand the "death of God" as the historical collapse of all metaphysical foundationalisms (along lines developed in detail in Thomson, *Heidegger on Ontotheology*, ch. 1).

which so many of today's fundamentalisms try to insist upon the exclusive righteousness of their one Truth?[41]

We are coming to know, albeit in starts and stops, progressive insights and entrenching reactions, that no consistent system of ethico-political mores can be closed from without. Perhaps that helps explain why Spinoza could not bear to think about "death" (even after reducing it to Heidegger's *demise*). Remember that Spinoza's *Ethics* is an incredibly ambitious attempt to demonstrate mathematically that the final truths about nature, God, and the good life follow deductively from a strict conception of rationality itself.[42] Today, such efforts finally to establish such an ethical and political geometry look like metaphysical eruptions of an unacknowledged Western mysticism of the *logos*. Spinoza drank deeply from that intoxicating spring, like all the other fantasists of pure reason stretching from Pythagoras to Badiou and beyond. When we instead take seriously the serious question of what philosophical seriousness requires, however, we find that we cannot pre-answer that question with obsolete prejudices about the limitless power of reason. When we think seriously, I have suggested, we find that we cannot follow those mystical rationalists who falsely believed that ethics and politics require us to completely abdicate, rather than struggle to assume, the partiality of our finite perspectives. We cannot follow them because they provide only part of the story at best, a part dangerously (and, we can now recognize, irrationally) seeking to stand in for the whole.

So, instead of seeking to set our facetiousness aside, let us continue to experiment existentially with what happens when we forthrightly foreground our finite particularity and embrace finitude and partiality as limitations we can never entirely understand, let alone escape – an endless tissue of beliefs we must nevertheless relentlessly question in the pursuit of historical *justice*, by which I mean our efforts to critically update and thereby vindicate what remains (or becomes) true from our own defensible sense of the best (for example, most meaningful, livable, inclusive, and inspiring) hopes of our past.[43]

---

[41] As Žižek nicely suggests, those more genuinely confident in the Truth of their ethico-political worldview – like Tibetan Buddhists or the Amish – do not seem to feel such an overwhelming need to force their view on others. (See Slavoj Žižek, *Violence: Six Sideways Reflections* [London: Verso, 2006], 85; and see also the immanent critique of philosophical "violence" carefully developed in Ann Murphy *Violence and the Philosophical Imaginary* [New York: SUNY Press, 2012].)

[42] For a sympathetic view of Spinoza's incredible *equation* of happiness with rationality, see Steven Nadler, "Baruch Spinoza," in *The Stanford Encyclopedia of Philosophy*, ed. by Edward N. Zalta (Fall 2013 Edition). http://plato.stanford.edu/archives/fall2013/entries/spinoza/.

[43] See Jacques Derrida, "Force of Law: 'The Mythical Foundations of Authority,'" in *Deconstruction and the Possibility of Justice*, eds, by Drucilla Cornell, Michel Rosenfeld, and David Gray Carlson (New York and London: Routledge, 1992), 3–67.

Acknowledging our "thrownness" does not require us to reject whatever aid the rationalist traditions can still offer us. But perfectionism's existential-ontological imperative to *become what we are* does encourage us to continue working to become the best selves we are capable of becoming in and through time, rather than outside it. This means critically and creatively receiving (or *inheriting*) what the past tradition has given us and so paying forward (at least some of) its most promising insights in order to help form and inform our future-directed heritage in the here and now of our concrete phenomenological existence.

8.5 The Future beyond Spinoza: Toward a Free Thinking of Death and the Nothing

Mindful that our ontohistorical embeddedness places unavoidable limits on our ethical and political thinking – and with the goal of better understanding the nature of these limits, and so the nature of our freedom with respect to our ontohistorical situatedness – let us come back to Spinoza's blunt proclamation that: "A free man thinks of nothing less than of death." When we hear that the way Spinoza intended, it suggests that "the free man" (that is, the human being who "lives according to the dictates of reason alone") thinks of death less than of any other matter, and so ideally demises without ever having given death a single thought, having thought all his life only of life, of staying alive and so "preserving his being." Spinoza's free man thinks only about how best to preserve and enhance his life ("seeking his own advantage"), and for Spinoza that means ignoring death (or demise) as much as possible. Behind the bravado of Spinoza's heroic answer, the superficial fearlessness of this allegedly free refusal to think freely about death at all, do we not hear yet another hypocritical confession of death's repression?[44]

Spinoza's free man – driven by his proto-Nietzschean, metaphysical *conatus essendi* (his essential struggle to persist in being) – can think freely only of endlessly increasing his powers. What is this but a valorization of that repression of death which haunts the West? Spinoza's claim freely not to think of death is a *denegation*; it really means: "I think of death only long enough to reassert my 'freedom' by repressing my thinking about it!" And yet, a *free repression* is a contradiction in terms; Spinoza's allegedly free repression of

---

[44] Spinoza, *Ethics*, 151. Proposition 67 reads in its entirety: "A free man thinks of nothing less than of death, and his wisdom is a meditation on life, not on death." An older translation by R. H. M. Elwes renders proposition 67 as: "A free man thinks of death least of all things; and his wisdom is a meditation not of death but of life." Cf. Derrida's post-Freudian insight about "what the word 'courage' means," viz., "the courage to think courage, and therefore [to think] fear [since there is no true courage without the fear it confronts], to think in general, [freely] to say what comes to thought and first of all to tell oneself what one is thinking" (Derrida, *The Beast and the Sovereign, Volume II*, 148).

death is really just a repression of the freedom of thinking. Such repressions of demise have the unfortunate effect of foreclosing all the important philosophical lessons we can learn when we confront our fear of demise and so begin to think with true freedom about death (as we saw in Chapter 1), lessons about how to make peace with our common finitude and ineliminable mortality by living freely and so acknowledging rather than denying our shared vulnerability, interdependence, and other constitutive *existential* limitations. Showing its age in the face of the existential tradition of hermeneutic phenomenology, Spinoza's allegedly "free man" now looks like a compensatory fantasy of masculine bravado, a neurotic and rather pathetic figure of repression, proudly going to his death without ever realizing that death confronts each one of us (and so *all* of us) with something we can neither control nor comprehend, namely, the inchoate reality of something outside our own selves (that "nothing" of futurity) that bluntly defies the powers of subjectivity to master and control, to comprehend once and for all. Freely thinking demise and so death thus starkly reveals the limits of all our modern "subjectivistic" fantasies of absolute freedom and control, and so helps encourage us instead to creatively disclose genuinely postmodern ways of understanding the meaningfulness of our lives, not just alone but with and among one another, as we take up the struggle to stop denying and start assuming the initially discomforting (but ultimately liberating) realities of our shared condition of existential finitude.

Indeed, when we can get beyond the terror of demise that drives us to repress our common existential finitude – disclosed in existential death, as we have seen – it becomes possible to acknowledge the true existential bonds that deeply unite us all, learning to embrace our shared condition of vulnerable finitude as the very condition for the ongoing possibility of our creative disclosures of meaning. Indeed, such a creatively responsive and thus responsible but still finite disclosure of meaning is what we human beings *are*, individually and together, when we live our best, most fulfilling and meaning-full lives. Rather than seeking with growing desperation to take control over even demise itself – an impossibility that, taken to its ultimate extension, actually becomes profoundly undesirable, since (as we will see next chapter) such individual immortality would inevitably become a horrible nightmare of unremitting endlessness – it is better to be spurred by our end (as a likely moment of radical passivity and world collapse) to find ways of making peace with and affirming the inescapable reality of our shared condition of ontological finitude. For, what initially looks like the tragedy of our common finitude turns out to be what enables us to creatively disclose the apparently inexhaustible meaningfulness of our being in time. Indeed, as we will see next chapter, it is only because each of us dies that reality seems to show itself to human beings ever anew; it is thus such existential death that bestows humanity with a future other than nihilism's ultimate extinction of meaning.

Of course, it would be self-defeating to reject reason – rather than seeking to learn from, contextualize, and supplement it (for example, by understanding the historical emergence of modern subjectivism and acknowledging the epistemic contributions of our mooded attunements, as *Being and Time* already began to do) – just as it would be ridiculous to deny the truth of power (or the deep and pervasive role power relations play in shaping the perceived contours of our worlds and the futures they delimit or at least imply). Yet, if the later Heidegger is right that our technological ontotheology of power is profoundly nihilistic in its implications (as I think he is), then we need to acknowledge the partial truth of its optimization imperative only in order to help find ways beyond its narrow and reductive limits, creatively disclosing pathways into more meaningful futures. It is precisely here that I part ways which some of my closest ethico-political philosophical allies, those would-be "postmodern" (but really *late-modern*) heirs of Heidegger, Richard Rorty and Gianni Vattimo. For, I do not think that unconditionally embracing nihilism in return for the freedoms that such an embrace gives us in ethics and politics is the wisest response to our ontohistorical situation.[45] I think we can preserve the most important of those freedoms while also helping to creatively disclose philosophical paths opening out beyond nihilism. To do so, we do need to begin by acknowledging that neither reason nor power has a monopoly on the truth. Moreover, even "truth" has no monopoly on being. And, in the end, even "being" has no monopoly on that apparently inexhaustible source of phenomenological intelligibility which the name "being" seeks to disclose – always partially. (Such are the basic lessons of ontological pluralism.)

In the end, then, we have not engaged in a philosophical search for ethico-political purity but instead for "peace" (or *peacefulness*, as Heidegger came to think it, viz., as an irreducible ontological fullness rather than merely the absence of conflict or war). We realize that any such quest for peace obliges us to work for justice. But we also realize – as denizens of the epoch of an increasingly global technological understanding of being – that we can no longer claim that our ancestry can determine our identity once and for all. For those of us looking for a meaningful sense of communal belonging, Heidegger thought the best we could hope for was to learn to build a home not on our geographical location but, rather, in our shared sensitivity to being, our mutual openness to its never exhaustively conceptualizable possibilities and inevitable

---

[45] See Giorgio Vattimo, *Nihilism and Emancipation: Ethics, Politics, and Law* (New York: Columbia University Press, 2003); Richard Rorty, *Take Care of Freedom and Truth Will Take Care of Itself* (Stanford: Stanford University Press, 2006); and, for a succinct statement of our differences, see Iain Thomson, "Review of Santiago Zabala, *The Remains of Being: Hermeneutic Ontology after Metaphysics*," *Notre Dame Philosophical Reviews*, October 12, 2010. https://ndpr.nd.edu/reviews/the-remains-of-being-hermeneutic-ontology-after-metaphysics/ (accessed June 6, 2023).

8.5. FREELY THINKING DEATH AND THE NOTHING

overflowing of all reductive frameworks. To become ontologically rather than geographically indigenous (DT 53–4), in other words, human beings have to learn to become "at-home in our not-being-at-home" (HHI 125/GA53 155), getting beyond our neurotic anxiety (and compensatory desires for finality and control) and embracing the fact that we world-disclosers can never have some fixed and settled identity that could be established once and for all time.[46] After Nietzsche (and Kierkegaard), we can only "be" something insofar as we continue to *become* it. But after Heidegger, we can only become the selves we are most meaningfully capable of becoming when we learn to be attentive to those meanings that exist in partial independence from our preexisting plans and designs.[47]

One of Heidegger's most long-standing ways of expressing this crucial insight (as we saw in Chapter 3) was to suggest that we need to learn to discern and disclose those inchoate hints of the noth-ing, that is, the suggestive glimmers of that which is not-yet-a-thing but only coming to be, finding (and innovating) ways to receptively tune into and creatively disclose this "futurity" of the future, and thereby helping to bring this postmodern future into being by poietically and maieutically participating in its repeated arrival (like good philosophical midwives, who all of us heirs of Socrates should aspire to become and inspiringly remain). Moreover, this futuristic, postmodern response emerging from Heidegger's later work reinforces the idea that we need to find ways to freely use our technologies, especially since we human beings have never been and will never be entirely free of technologies. The goal is to learn to use technology without being used by it, that is, to employ technologies in ways that recognize, resist, and help transcend (rather than merely reinforce) our becoming self-optimizing resources ourselves. That, in the simplest terms, is what it means to use technologies against nihilistic technologization of enframing: Learning freely to use technologies in ways that creatively and responsibly *disclose* the inexhaustible meanings of, rather

---

[46] I have tried to show that this postmodern understanding of being helps encourage us to maintain a comportmental, *ethical* openness to the momentous events that continue to emerge and unfold their meanings within and across our most stable and coherent ways of making sense of things. Such new events of meaningfulness expand and contest our intelligible worlds from within and without, sometimes overturning even our most seemingly incontestable claims to having already exhausted the truth of our existential situation, but they also thereby help us disclose larger patterns of significance unfolding across our lives, thereby discerning more enduring meanings which we would not otherwise have recognized. Thinking through and across such events can thus help us *repeatedly* to creatively disclose the meaning of our own lives, defining commitments, and identities. (For more on this point, see Chapter 9; Thomson, "Heideggerian Perfectionism and the Phenomenology of the Pedagogical Truth Event"; and Thomson, "Thinking Love.")

[47] See Thomson, *Heidegger on Ontotheology*, ch. 4 and *Heidegger, Art, and Postmodernity*, ch. 3.

than *impose* preexisting meanings on, things, each other, and ourselves.[48] Such a free relation to technology, however, is not something on offer in the technological pursuit of immortality via "mind up-loading" (still largely confined to the "imagineering" stage); quite the contrary, as I shall suggest in Chapter 9.

---

[48] This is what it means to become (post-metaphysical) "thinkers," ontologically-disclosive beings whose sensitive thinking (*Besinnung*) creatively composes being's polysemic hints into meaningful compositions, and because we can never do so finally, we instead *learn* to do so repeatedly, in ways that also help creatively disclose and coherently (re)constitute the meaning of our unfolding existences in time. I develop this crucial point in Chapter 9 and in Thomson, *Heidegger on the Danger and Promise of Technology*.

9

Why It Is Better for a Dasein Not to Live Forever, or Being Pro-Choice on the Immortality Question

In this penultimate chapter, we take up the philosophical question of whether immortality is truly desirable, seeking to establish an important difference between existing for a finite and for an infinite stretch of time by introducing the following important consideration.[1] If it remains possible for an event to occur, then even an extremely unlikely event is certain to occur, given infinite time. I shall suggest that this consideration leads to insuperable problems with the most popular scenarios currently being envisioned for achieving immortality by techno-scientific means. These problems, moreover, motivate us to think more deeply about death and thereby rethink the requirements of a genuinely meaningful human life. Drawing on Kierkegaard, Heidegger, and other existential thinkers, I suggest that human beings' most abiding sources of meaningfulness come not from endlessly repeating certain profound experiences (which sometimes does wear out their appeal) but, instead, from our struggle to stay true to and so continue to creatively and responsibly disclose what such momentous events, often rare and singular, only partly reveal to us in the first place, as we often come to realize only in retrospect – much as Heidegger came only *retrospectively* to recognize and then spend his life creatively disclosing the seemingly inexhaustible ontological riches of that ambiguous "nothing" *Being and Time* first glimpsed in the momentous experience of existential death, but in a way that Heidegger only partly understood at that time.[2]

As that central philosophical example of this book suggests, we keep the meaning of such profound events alive by struggling to continue to unfold and so stay true to their meaning in our lives. Such struggles can and do sometimes fail (a fact I argue is essential to their *remaining* meaningful to us), and yet the potential meaningfulness of these kinds of profound experiences seems to remain inexhaustible for us mortals. We have no way of knowing whether truly *immortal* beings might not eventually exhaust such sources of meaning, however, and I shall supply some worrying reasons for thinking that they might

---

[1] I originally wrote this chapter with the generous editorial and research assistance of James Bodington, hence my occasional employment of the royal hermeneutic "we."
[2] As we saw in Chapters 1, 2, and 3.

indeed exhaust them (and so themselves) in the endlessness of time. Rather than rejecting our mortality in pursuit of the kinds of immortality that technology currently encourages us to imagine, then, I instead suggest that we should recognize and embrace the existential finitude of mortal life (a finitude most clearly revealed in existential death) as crucial to its meaningfulness. Rethinking death in order to embrace our mortality in this way can help encourage us to remain receptive to the profound philosophical lessons that humanity's perennial quest for immortality might still afford – despite the many dangers and even apparent impossibility of that quest (which we began to discuss in Chapter 8). Come what may, then, such an approach serves the interests of a maximally ecumenical philosophical dialogue about immortality, even while making the case that we should be resolutely *pro-choice* rather than blithely *pro-life* on this philosophical question of the desirability of immortality.

9.1 To Be or Not to Be – Forever?

What do you say? North or South? Shall I atone for old sins or make some new ones?

Tyrion Lannister (in George R. R. Martin's *A Dance with Dragons*).[3]

Imagine facing the following stark but simple choice. Either you can undergo a quick and painless procedure that will grant you immortality, thereby making it *impossible* for you to cease to exist subsequently. Or else you can refuse the procedure and continue to exist with your inevitable demise in your future, as well as the ineliminable possibility of demising at any moment.

Which would you choose?

I think this overlooked question is crucial for determining whether you are for or against immortality.[4] Why? Imagine any techno-scientific procedure that might actually be able to grant you an immortal existence some day. You might be able to upload your neural net, for example, in some sufficiently dispersed way that you could exist on-line without the possibility of being

---

[3] George R. R. Martin, *A Dance with Dragons Book Five of A Song of Ice and Fire* (New York: Bantam Books, 2011), 24.

[4] A 2013 Pew research poll found that when people are asked "whether they, personally, would choose to undergo medical treatments to slow the aging process and live to be 120 or more," 56 percent of US adults say "no" (and only 38 percent say "yes"), despite the fact that 68 percent of those polled believe "most people" would say "yes" to this question (see Pew 2013). The most obvious problem here is that the presumption that life extension will be accomplished by medical procedures that "slow the aging process" suggest an extended old age (with at least some of its attendant health problems) rather than an extension of peak health and fitness (with all their benefits and attractions). But life extension presents some different issues than immortality (as we will see), and it is the latter that I have chosen to focus on here.

accidentally or maliciously deleted. Or you might be able to back up your consciousness continually and store it in a secure location (or locations) so that, in the event of a catastrophic destruction of your current body (or avatar), your saved consciousness would be automatically (re)uploaded onto the internet or downloaded into cloned, synthetic, robotic, or cybernetic replacement bodies (or parts) that have been made ready for that purpose, allowing you to pick right up where you left off. (Many other scenarios remain conceivable as well, though variants on these two seem to be the most popular.) Let us grant, *concesso non dato*, that some such science-fiction scenario for achieving immortality could one day become commonplace, both a feasible and an affordable part of our everyday reality. Of course, I would not concede this point without considering the seemingly insurmountable empirical, economic, ethico-political, ecological, and other difficulties all such scenarios entail.[5] For the sake of argument, however, let us hypothetically set all such doubts aside in order simply to ask whether such immortality would really be desirable if we could somehow actually achieve it. Setting aside all immortality's seemingly unavoidable extrinsic problems, in other words, let us simply consider the intrinsic merits and demerits of immortality itself.

---

[5] In order to address the strongest and most appealing version of such admittedly still science-fictional scenarios, I am granting (*concesso non dato*), for example, that the re-downloading of one's memories could somehow be made both invulnerable (to avoid the kinds of obvious problems explored in Mostow's "Surrogates" [2009]) and also instantaneous, despite the fascinating problems that could be introduced by even a minor "disruption of services" that interrupts one's relatively continuous sense of their own experience (an idea nicely explored in Kalogridis's "Altered Carbon" [2018]). But Hackers usually find ways to stay one step ahead of security, which is one of the reasons I would wager that true immortality will never be empirically achievable by technological means. Another more telling reason is that it is not clear how consciousness can survive infinitely in a universe in which all particular combinations of matter (at least) only exist for finite spans of time. But I recognize that it is much too early in the game to consider such objections decisive; and I even feel relatively confident that considerable life-extension will be achieved if humanity (or our post-human descendants) survive long enough. (The fact that some shorter-range challenges, like anthropogenic climate change, seem more pressing calls into question the immense resources already being devoted to the development of life-extension technologies by affluent individuals fearful of their own demise. But perhaps the two challenges will yet prove synergistic rather than antagonistic, as proponents of humanity's need to become interplanetary to stave off accidental extinction sometimes suggest, for instance.) Still, I think such life extension may be indefinite but not infinite: Conscious beings will never truly banish the threat of demise. But I shall also argue that this turns out to be a good thing. I worry, moreover, that the longer we survive the less likely our existences are to continue to resemble the human lives that so matter to us now. (Once again, the real threat of technology is not that it will become like us but rather the reverse, as Heidegger suggests and Dreyfus argues in Dreyfus, *On the Internet*, a suggestion I develop further in Thomson, *Heidegger on the Danger and Promise of Technology, or What Is Called Thinking in the Age of AI?*)

Even granting that some techno-scientific procedure capable of bestowing immortality could one day become real and extrinsically unobjectionable, then, here is the rub. All such procedures could *guarantee* you immortality (completely banishing the threat of involuntary demise or nonexistence) only by making it *impossible* to permanently delete your dispersed or backed-up self, whether accidentally or deliberately, by malicious strangers or by you yourself. Why? Well, think about it: If, after undergoing such a procedure, you could ever delete yourself – that is, if you could *choose* to bring your existence to an end subsequently – then someone else could delete you too, or it could happen by accident. This possibility is ineliminable in principle. If it remains possible for you ever to wipe out your existence, then it remains possible for someone else to do so or for it to happen by accident. In that case, however, you would still be subject to the threat of demise and so would not truly be *immortal*. For, "immortal" simply means "not mortal," not subject to demise, *mors*. And you are either subject to demise or you are not. That mortals are subject to demise in varying degrees of intensity, immediacy, etc., does not change the fact that, conceptually, there is a fundamental dichotomy that divides mortals from immortals (such that the two categories share no intersecting members). An "immortal" who can demise or permanently cease to exist is not truly an *immortal*.[6]

---

[6] Cf. the Gods in Wagner's Ring cycle (who are described as immortal but then learn to die) with the "immortal" protagonist in Gaiman's *Sandman* comic series – viz., "Dream, the endless," who arranges for his own death only to have another version of himself reborn. (Moreover, Gaiman's central character, as an immortal driven toward suicide by his endless existence, represents a telling rejoinder to his "Hob Gadling" side character, a human who has not yet chosen to demise after more than 600 years of life.) Of course, one might falsely believe oneself to be immortal, only to discover that one was wrong. (This seems to be what happens to the Gods in Wagner's Ring cycle, and if a creature who had stopped aging, like a vampire, *falsely* thought themselves "immortal" (*pace* Paul, Transformative Experience, 2), they too might be quite surprised by demise. Indeed, so-called clinical or "biological immortality" (like that of the allegedly "immortal jellyfish," *Turritopsis dohrnii*, which can duplicate its cells without the replication errors that cause aging, but which can still be eaten by a shark or other predator) seems like a much more probable achievement for us mortals than true *immortality* (which would require somehow becoming *invulnerable* to demise). Moreover, even a truly immortal being might still remain subject to "death" in Heidegger's sense; that is, its particular projects could collapse into meaninglessness (as happens to the immortal character Dream in Neil Gaiman, *The Sandman* [New York: Vertigo/DC Comics, 1988–1996]). The likelihood of such existential world-collapse might decrease as one's life-span increases, assuming one learns to cope with disasters better for having gone through them many times. But the opposite is possible too; think for example of an immortal being exhausted to the point of brittle frailty by an endless existence that has long since grown torturous in its inexorability (as often portrayed in Anne Rice's vampire novels, for example). All such complications notwithstanding, an *immortal* cannot "die" in the ordinary sense, that is, demise; and conversely, anyone (or thing) that can demise is not, strictly speaking, *immortal*.

In sum, then, if you could ever choose to undergo a procedure (such as mind uploading) that would give you true immortality by banishing the threat of demise, then after such a procedure you would be unable to die or cease to exist. This means you cannot be rid of the threat of involuntary demise while also keeping voluntary demise around as an option, should you become hopelessly sick of an existence without end. True immortality, once granted, cannot be rescinded. So, your choice about whether or not to undergo any techno-scientific procedure capable of granting true immortality would literally be a once and for all time decision.[7] Given the unrescindable permanence of your choice, would you choose mortality or immortality, an existence with or without demise? This, I submit, is the true question of whether immortality is desirable, and it is a much more difficult question than the simple one too often substituted in its place, which merely asks if you would like to be able to live for as long as you desire. That is the much simpler question of the desirability of life-extension (not of immortality), an option that many of us would happily affirm under the right circumstances.

In thinking about the difficult question of whether true immortality is desirable, I think we need to consider the following. Am I so concerned to avoid the supposed eternal nothingness of demise that I would instead rush to embrace the eternal "somethingness" of an existence without end, come what may? Is Poe's "Nevermore" so haunting that I would rather choose to plunge into an immortal "Forevermore"?[8] Or is the vertiginous prospect of actually existing for all eternity, once taken seriously, disconcerting enough to help me overcome what philosophers from Lucretius to Bernard Williams have recognized as our "fear of sheer nothingness"?[9] That the alternatives – demise or immortality – both seem to be *eternal* (in the sense of *temporally infinite*) makes the decision especially difficult; eternity is so immeasurably vast as to exceed quantification, if not comprehension. Eternity is not "a long time," no more than infinity is "a large number." Just as infinity is larger than any number, so eternity is longer than any span of time. Eternity cannot end, not because it is outside of time (as in those theological fantasies examined in

---

[7] Nietzsche famously countenances a similar scenario (in Nietzsche's interconnected works, *The Gay Science* and *Thus Spoke Zarathustra*), in which one must decide for all time whether to affirm the endless repetition of one's own life. But Nietzsche's scenario presupposes circular rather than linear time and so leads to paradoxes about free will (among other difficulties) which we need not discuss here.

[8] Don Delillo, *Zero K* (New York: Scribner, 2016), 53.

[9] (Bernard Williams, "The Makropulos Case: Reflections on the Tedium of Immortality," *Problems of the Self* [Cambridge: Cambridge University Press, 1973], 92; reprinted in Fischer [1993].) Our fear of nothingness is a "misplaced" but "not unfounded" fear, since it can indeed happen to us that we come to our own distinctive end while still existing, and anxiety about this is for Heidegger the real source of our fear of demise (as we saw in Chapter 1).

Chapter 8) but because it is a name for the endlessness of time, just as infinity is not a number but a name for the endlessness of number. To become truly *immortal* would thus be to become endless; similarly, we mortal beings, once we meet our mortality, seem to *remain* demised for all eternity.[10]

This apparently inexorable endlessness makes it surprisingly difficult to think about what we should prefer to do for eternity, even if the choice is as simple as: "Something or nothing?" And yet, as abyssal as an endless future might be, is it not necessarily *nihilistic* to choose nothing over something? No, because only a being who exists can face this choice. Such a being would thus not be choosing sheer nothingness over something. Instead, the choice would still be between the finite life of a mortal, a life that ends at some point, and the infinite life of an immortal, a life that never ends.[11]

Futurists and philosophers of a pro-immortalist bent often overlook this crucial complication – the fact that immortality would necessarily be endless – in order to argue that immortality would be *desirable*. Instead of trying to confront the full ramifications of a future without demise, some simply assume that if you could choose to undergo a techno-scientific procedure granting you immortality, you would still be able to retain the possibility of ending your existence at your own discretion. According to Nick Bostrom, for example, in the future in which "immortality" is achieved by uploading the mind, demise will become a "voluntary" decision (albeit a "regrettable" one).[12] This is a philosophical mistake, however. For the reasons already explained, any mind-uploading scenario that can leave room for the possibility of voluntary demise

---

[10] Gaiman's *Sandman* rightly recognized the former (see n. 6) even while taking some liberties with the latter (esp. through Gaiman's wonderfully imagined "Death" character) – understandably, since a work of fantasy need not be bound by the phenomenological requirement to stay faithful to what we mortal Dasein can experience.

[11] We can thus embrace mortality and reject the quest for immortality as part of our struggle against nihilism. Nietzsche himself taught that if we want to avoid nihilism, then we should learn to embrace our lives in their finitude, rather than believing that our lives must be extended into an immortal beyond in order to be meaningful. But Nietzsche's view presupposes that such immortality is impossible actually to achieve, so that the vain quest for it obscures the meaning inherent in our finite lives. Nietzsche might turn out to be right about this, but I prefer to take a different tack here so as to make a direct rather than an indirect argument against immortality. (For Nietzsche's critique of any appeal to a "transcendent beyond," see Thomson, "Transcendence and the Problem of Otherworldly Nihilism.")

[12] (Nick Bostrom, "The Transhumanist FAQ: A General Introduction," Version 2.1 [2003]. www.transhumanism.org/resources/FAQv21.pdf [accessed September 2, 2013], 37.) Fischer often makes a similar move when defending "immortality" to popular audiences, trying to bootstrap his way into the desirability of an infinite life by arguing for the desirability of a very long one. But we will see that making a strong case for even extreme life-extension (so long as we retain the possibility of demise) is far easier than doing so for true immortality.

9.1. TO BE OR NOT TO BE - FOREVER?

cannot eliminate the possibility of unexpected or unintended demise. In order fully to safeguard against unexpected or unintended demise, it cannot be possible to voluntarily go offline permanently, or else that possibility could also be triggered accidentally or maliciously. (There is simply no way to rule this out with techno-scientific immortality scenarios.) So, any decision about whether to become truly *immortal* by techno-scientific means must instead include a version of the choice with which we began: Either you choose to forego such a procedure and so continue to remain vulnerable to demise, or else you choose to undergo the procedure and subsequently live forever, without the possibility of ever ceasing to exist.

Instead of overlooking this crucial complication, a philosopher interested in defending the desirability of immortality can try to deny that it makes a decisive difference. This is the tack John Fischer takes:

> I do not see exactly why the indisputable differences between very long but finite life and immortal life would *make a difference* as regards desirability. I consider this one of the most difficult and challenging issues surrounding immortality. I have argued that, properly understood, immortal life would involve a mix of activities that could propel us into the future with genuine engagement; and I do not see exactly why this engagement would disappear as we move from a very long finite life to an immoral [*sic*, he means *immortal*] life.[13]

Here Fischer suggests that the endless life of an immortal would be just as desirable as the very long but finite life of a long-lived mortal. The problem, however, is that many of us, under the right circumstances, would love to significantly extend our (currently rather pathetically short) lives by a few decades, centuries, or even millennia, but we nevertheless balk at the prospect of existing for all eternity.

To his credit, Fischer acknowledges that this is "one of the most difficult and challenging issues surrounding immortality." But Fischer sticks to his guns and suggests that his argument that a significantly extended life could be desirable (a conclusion few would disagree with) shows that an endless life could be desirable as well: A very long but finite life and an infinite life would both "involve a mix of activities that could propel us into the future with genuine engagement." So, is Fischer right that an endless life could be just as desirable as a very long one? Why do I think, conversely, that being able to demise - or at least die existentially - makes such a crucial difference? Why would a continuous individual existence that could never come to an end necessarily be bad? These are the questions the remainder of this chapter seeks to answer.

---

[13] John Martin Fischer (ed.), *The Metaphysics of Death* (Stanford, CA: Stanford University Press, 1993), 17.

9.2 The Finitude of Being within the Infinitude of Time

Tyrion Lannister had lived all his life in a world that was too big for him, but in the manse of Illyrio Mopatis the sense of disproportion assumed grotesque dimensions. *I am a mouse in a mammoth's lair*, he mused, *though at least the mammoth keeps a good cellar*.[14]

The "imp" Tyrion Lannister experiences a "grotesque ... sense of disproportion" during his brief stay in a giant mansion built for a corpulent tycoon. But what monstrous sense of disproportion might a being like us feel if, after aspiring to little more than a century of life, we were suddenly to find ourselves living *forever*? How might it feel to live not merely as mice in a mammoth's lair but as self-conscious beings stretching forever into the infinitude of time? What could continue to get us out of bed in the morning? What sort of "cellar" would we need to discover to help pass the time? And what might we pass the time *toward*? What meaningful ends could we hope to reach, if our existences were truly endless?

When Fischer argues that the unending life of an immortal would be just as desirable as the finite life of a very long-lived mortal, he is responding to Bernard Williams's "The Makropulos Case: Reflections on the Tedium of Immortality." Inspired by the fictional story of a woman (Elina Makropulos) who has already become despondent after a mere 300 years of life extension, Williams argues that an immortal life would necessarily become "meaningless" and "intolerable" for beings like us, leading us inevitably to "boredom and inner death."[15] He therefore suggests that, faced with a choice between mortality and immortality, we should not allow our (aforementioned) "fear of sheer nothingness" to override our rational capacities and drive us blindly to embrace an endless life. Instead, we should think about it carefully, asking ourselves: Is the unending life of an immortal one that I myself would actually want? This is a difficult question to think through, as we have seen. Indeed, how can we finite beings think *through* eternity?

Williams' rather ingenious strategy is to argue as follows. We would not happily embrace even an extended life if we knew that this extended life was going to be filled with pain, sickness, and suffering. We might still reluctantly choose to extend a life filled with suffering if there was some very powerful, overriding reason to do so (for instance, if we believed we were close to curing some terrible disease or completing some very important work, or if I had a

---

[14] Martin, *A Dance with Dragons*, 26.
[15] Williams, "The Makropulos Case," 73, 82.

family member or loved one who could not live without us, and so on).¹⁶ But in order for extending my life to be attractive to me in its own right, that extended life itself must be attractive to me. That initially sounds like an obvious tautology, but Williams analyzes it as entailing the far from trivial consequence that the entirety of my future life has to be attractive to the person who I am now. In other words, my entire future life must be a life that I would embrace now, given my existing character.

This is a controversial move, however, because it turns on two implicit presuppositions that, once made explicit, are not widely shared. First, it assumes that we know enough about what an immortal life would actually be like to make a meaningful decision for or against it now. Second, it assumes that living a meaningful life requires each of us to build and maintain a unified sense of self with a strong and consistent ethical character. (For, it is only this second assumption that would justify our current, ethically mature self in making a decision that will be binding on all our possible future selves.) Today, however, Williams's famous view that no one can have a truly meaningful sense of self without developing and maintaining a robust core of ethical "integrity" is often seen as old-fashioned, and his commitment to such a view (which he shares with the early Kierkegaard and Heidegger, as we have seen) seems to be getting less popular in our increasingly fractured and fragmented (but only allegedly "postmodern") world.¹⁷ The truth is that our lives often unfold in unpredictable ways, and Fischer forcefully objects (against the second assumption) that it is unreasonable to insist that the self I am now should get the right to reject, ahead of time, the different selves I might become in the future as the result of a series of rational decisions I will make in response to circumstances I cannot currently envision. (We will come back to this point.)

---

[16] Francis Ford Coppola's beautiful film, "Youth Without Youth" (2007), meditates thoughtfully on a version of the second scenario, ultimately suggesting that, in the quest to live a meaningful life, finding love is more important than completing a great work.

[17] (See Chapter 1, n. 55.) To be fair, we should note that Williams's "The Makropulos Case" was originally published as part of his book, *Problems of the Self*, in which he argues for the premises (like his integrity requirement) that essay presupposes. (On the widely shared understanding of "postmodernity" in terms of the fragmentation of subjectivity – a sense of postmodernity that Heidegger, like Williams, would resist – see Thomson, *Heidegger, Art, and Postmodernity*, ch. 4.) I should note again here (see Chapter 1, n. 55), however, that the later Heidegger gives us good reasons to be suspicious of any supposed requirement that a life should possess some single overarching narrative unity (since he came to recognize that being, and hence our own being, exceeds and overflows every conceptual framework). Late in his life, moreover, Kierkegaard himself is said to have remarked that if he had more *faith* he would have married Regina (and trusted in God to help it work out somehow), instead of thinking he had to choose between becoming *either* a philosopher *or* a husband. (I thank Eric Kaplan for sharing that intriguing anecdote.)

Fischer's objection to the first assumption is even more forceful: Williams has no argument that an immortal life would be less desirable than the kind of long mortal one that many of us would happily embrace. Here Fischer rather boldly accepts one of Williams's own arguments but turns it to the opposite conclusion. Williams writes: "perhaps, one day, it will be possible for some of us not to age. If that were so, would it not follow then that, more life being per se better than less life, we should have a reason so far as that went ... to live forever?"[18] But where Williams would reject both a very long life and an immortal one, Fischer embraces both. I shall argue that we should embrace the former and reject the latter.

Even without presupposing that we must maintain a consistent character to live a meaningful life, I think we can show that immortality would necessarily be highly undesirable. My argument thus seeks to establish the undesirability of an infinite life but not the undesirability of a very long but finite one. For, there is another crucial difference between the two cases, one that makes the loss of demise as an option into what epistemologists like to call a "defeater" of the pro-immortality view. That crucial difference between existing for a finite and for an infinite stretch of time is this: If it *remains* possible for an event to occur, then even an extremely unlikely event is certain to occur, given infinite time. For example, assume that with every keystroke you type, it remains possible but astronomically unlikely that the tip of your finger could pass right through the surface of your keyboard. If that exceedingly unlikely event remains genuinely possible, and you were to keep typing forever (obviously we would have to postulate that neither you nor your keyboard would ever wear out, etc.), then no matter how unlikely that scenario is, it is *certain* to happen eventually.[19] That is not the case, however, if we assume finite rather than infinite time; so this kind of consideration applies to an immortal life but not to a very long mortal life. The reason this generates insuperable problems for immortality is that, given infinite time, various dead-end scenarios that would make an eternal existence into a living hell become inevitable. The converse – eventualities that would turn eternal existence into a kind of permanent heaven that beings like us would forever desire – are not possible, not even conceivable (for reasons Heidegger and Williams help suggest), and

---

[18] Williams, "The Makropulos Case," 81.

[19] To be clear, I am not asserting that this specific scenario *is* actually an empirically plausible example of an astronomically unlikely event that remains genuinely possible but, instead, merely imagining that it is in order to dramatically illustrate the point. One could think more prosaically and plausibly of an immortal playing the exact same weekly lottery numbers in some endless and genuinely random drawing (with a finite number of winning numbers): In the infinity of time, our immortal would be *certain* to win this lottery – and, indeed, *to win it an infinite number of times*, thereby very likely wearing out the initial thrill of winning (to anticipate the next big problem that pro-immortalists like Fischer need to face).

so will never happen even in an infinitely long life. As a result, there is nothing to stop an endless life from necessarily becoming torturous eventually, which is why we should reject immortality. Or so I shall now argue, building on some of Williams' insights and supplementing them with Kierkegaardian and Heideggerian considerations.

Think of it this way: If I live forever, then either (1) I will remain the same person throughout eternity or (2) I will not. Let us start with alternative one. If I will remain the same person, then Williams thinks I am doomed to boredom and meaninglessness eventually. Fischer tries to resist this move by arguing for the idea of endlessly "repeatable pleasures," experiences that supposedly could be repeated endlessly without ever ceasing to give us pleasure. As possible examples, Fischer mentions "the pleasures of sex, of eating fine meals and drinking fine wine, of listening to beautiful music, of seeing great art, and so forth."[20] Unfortunately, we have probably all had the experience of playing our favorite music, watching our favorite film, or reading our favorite book until we could not stand it any longer, and Fischer himself points out that we quickly get sick of even the finest meal if we eat it too often. As if anticipating Fischer's faith in the endless "pleasures of sex," moreover, Williams invokes George Bernard Shaw's suggestive image of "Don Juan in Hell," the implication being that where an immortal life is concerned, there would probably be a kernel of truth in that cynical old adage, "Show me the most sexually attractive person in the world, and I'll show you someone who is tired of having sex with them."[21]

Fischer responds by suggesting that we will not tire of such experiences if we can vary and space them out sufficiently, periodically abjuring from and then eagerly rediscovering such pleasures so that they can keep us satisfied throughout an endless life. The problem here is that, as Fischer admits, we might not be able to vary and space out such experiences sufficiently to keep them fresh and appealing forever. At some point, we might become permanently sick of such experiences or they might become permanently unavailable to us. And if it remains even possible that such experiences might disappear or permanently cease to satisfy us for other reasons, then, no matter how improbable such an outcome may seem to us now, it will *necessarily* occur, given infinite time.

Fischer responds by asserting that, even if the pleasure of some experiences can become exhausted (or, I would add, if those experiences can become unavailable or otherwise impossible for us to engage in), there are still other meaningful experiences that cannot ever become exhausted. Fischer writes: "[S]urely, the deep and resonant rewards of spiritual and religious experience

---

[20] Fischer, *Our Stories: Essays on Life, Death, and Free Will*, 85.
[21] See Williams, "The Makropulos Case," 87; George Bernard Shaw, *Man and Superman* (Virginia: Wilder, 2008), 72–109.

would not somehow become wooden or etiolated, if part of an endless life."[22] The problem, again, is that there is no way to be *sure* about this. (Indeed, it is difficult not to read Fischer's "surely" as a *denegation*, that is, a public attempt to exorcise a doubt that in fact thereby reveals it – as in the famous Freudian example: "I have no idea what my dream means, Doctor; I only know that it was *not* about my mother.") We cannot eliminate the possibility that we might eventually exhaust the meaning of even the most profound experiences we know of, if we lived forever.

As I mentioned earlier, Kierkegaard and Heidegger suggest that human beings' most abiding sources of meaningfulness come not from endlessly repeating certain profound experiences – which, sadly, sometimes does wear out their appeal – but, instead, from our struggle to stay true to what those experiences only partly disclose to us in the first place. As in the experience of falling in love, for example, or of being profoundly moved by a work of art, or becoming committed to a political cause or to some particular calling, way of life, or practical identity, we keep the meaning of such profound events alive by *struggling* to continue to unfold and so stay true to their meaning in our lives, and such struggles can and sometimes do fail. This, I take it, is why Heidegger famously insists that *being is finite*; as far as we can tell, the meaning of such profound experiences is inexhaustible for us mortals, but we have no way of knowing that truly immortal beings might not eventually exhaust their meaning in the endless infinitude of time. In my view, the fact that the otherwise tragic finitude of life helps make meaning inexhaustible for us mortals is part of what allows us to embrace our mortality and the meaning-disclosing finitude of the self disclosed by existential death.[23]

Unfortunately, Fischer fails to take seriously the challenge he raises when he mentions Kierkegaard's famous example of the "aesthete" who pursues a complex strategy of "crop rotation," deliberately cycling through new experiences in varying combinations, both pursuing new and remixing old pleasures in hopes of keeping his life endlessly fresh and exciting. Ironically, Fischer agrees with the youthful aesthete's optimistic view that we can successfully manage our pleasures so that we never become tired or bored of them, apparently unaware that Kierkegaard's deeper point is that even such a clever strategy can only postpone the profound disillusionment that comes from the pursuit of pleasure, since we can and do get sick of even the most novel and intensely pleasurable experiences. What the aesthete is supposed to learn from the implosion of this clever but ultimate naïve strategy is that we need more from life than the intense feeling of being alive. The lesson of this painful disillusionment, for Kierkegaard, is what catalyzes the aesthete's

---

[22] Fischer, *Our Stories: Essays on Life, Death, and Free Will*, 89.
[23] I develop these points in Thomson, "Thinking Love" and *Heidegger, Art, and Postmodernity*, 75–77, 217–20.

transformation into a higher "stage" on life's path, namely, the "ethical" sphere of existence, in which one instead looks for life's meaning through an unconditional commitment to some ruling moral principle (such as deontology or consequentialism). As Aristotle already recognized, however, the most challenging moments in life require a skillful responsiveness that transcends the application of all such life-guiding principles.[24] So unconditional adherence to any *moral* principle fails as well, and this implosion of this "ethical" stage leads to the "religious" sphere of existence, in which one puts unconditional faith in God, who can work miracles to resolve the otherwise irresolvable contradictions that would otherwise make our lives absurd and so lead us to despair. Because the kind of techno-scientific immortality scenarios we are considering (such as mind-uploading) need to obey the rational dictates of programming, they seem to rule out such miracles. So, Kierkegaard's religious solution (or the one suggested by his successive pseudonyms in his *Concluding Unscientific Postscript*) is not likely to be of much help here.[25]

In sum, then, however improbable it might be that we would eventually exhaust even our most profound sources of meaning if we lived forever, if that remains possible (and I can see no credible way to deny it), then it will necessarily occur, given infinite time. This, I take it, is the deep point behind Williams's assertion that: "Nothing less will do for eternity than something that makes boredom *unthinkable*."[26] To the best of my knowledge, no one in the world of science fiction (let alone science fact) has yet credibly imagined how the infinitely long life of an immortal individual could be desirably arranged so as *to rule out the very possibility* of its eventually becoming unbearable tedious (if not even more overtly terrible), further reinforcing my suggestion that such an enduring likelihood (even if it seems vanishingly small to the most willfully optimistic among us) would indeed necessarily obtain in the infinity of time.

Still, Williams's own argument that eternal life would necessarily become boring is not convincing because of his aforementioned presupposition that living a meaningful life requires us to build and maintain a mature, relatively unchanging ethical character. What remains right about his view, however, are the weaker presuppositions (shared with Heidegger) that beings like us cannot live meaningful lives without some guiding project or hope about the future

---

[24] This is also why consciousness cannot be programmed by the traditional means of trying to reduce such skill to rules or propositional content; see Hubert L. Dreyfus, *What Computers* Still *Cannot Do: A Critique of Artificial Intelligence* (Cambridge, MA: The MIT Press. 1992).

[25] At least as it stands, in this form not yet secularized by a creatively disclosive phenomenological appropriation. (See also Mark A. Wrathall, "Trivial Tasks that Consume a Lifetime: Kierkegaard on Immortality and Becoming Subjective," *The Journal of Ethics*, 19 [2015], 419–41.)

[26] Williams, "The Makropulos Case," 87.

that can organize our lives and so disclose the meaning of our being-in-the-world, and that in order for such a guiding hope or life-project itself to be meaningful, it has to be possible for it to succeed or fail. As Williams expresses that second point: "If he can regard this future life as an object of hope, then equally it must be possible for him to regard it with alarm, or depression, and – as in the simple pain case [that is, the scenario in which one faces a future filled with overriding pain] – opt out of it."[27] Williams shares this basic premise with Heidegger, for whom our defining "commitments are essentially risky" (as Haugeland nicely sums up the view).[28]

Williams never makes the following consequence of this point explicit, but if it is indeed possible for our defining hope or life-project either to succeed or fail, then, in the infinite expanse of our time as an immortal, it necessarily will *either* succeed, leaving us first fulfilled and satisfied and then bored and restless, or *else* fail, leaving us bereft and hopeless. When the constitutive hope or project that had been disclosing the meaning and significance of my life either fails or is fulfilled, then that defining life project has to be able to come to an end and give rise to another – in precisely the kind of existential death and resolute rebirth we have been examining – or else we would remain trapped in hopeless meaninglessness forever. Is that sufficient to show that I must be able to demise in order to avoid the torment of eternal despair? Only if we accept Williams's controversial presupposition that my character must remain unified – and then point out that it was my old pursuit of a life-project or defining hope that unified my character and made my life meaningful. But why not instead allow – with Kierkegaard, Heidegger, Levinas, Eric Erickson, and others – that a new or transformed life project, and so a new meaningful sense of self, can emerge out of the fulfillment or collapse of my old self's defining hope?[29] When we allow for this possibility of existential death and resolute rebirth – as we should, since such "authentic" death and rebirth of the self happens within even some mortal lives (as we have seen), and actuality entails possibility – then we can conceive of an immortal life continuing to be meaningful even after the fulfillment or collapse of its previous life-project or defining hope.[30] As a result, an immortal being could conceivably cycle through an endless succession of such selves, each organized into a coherent and meaningful identity by the new life-project born out of the collapse of the old one. This possibility (neglected by Williams) brings us to alternative two

---

[27] Ibid., 85.
[28] BT 443/SZ 391; Haugeland, *Dasein Disclosed*, 186.
[29] Although we now often have multiple projects, the collapse of an ultimate project (if we have one) can still catalyze the collapse of all the others. (See Chapter 1, n. 57.)
[30] See also the convincing argument to this effect in Jonathan Lear, *Radical Hope: Ethics in the Face of Cultural Devastation* (Cambridge, MA: Harvard University Press, 2006).

above, in which *I do not remain the same person* throughout all eternity (as required by Williams's commitment to the unified "integrity" of the self).

The problem is that this second alternative lands us onto the horns of a new dilemma: If I do not remain the same person throughout the infinity of time, then at least one of two other undesirable outcomes becomes inevitable. First, it is possible that (2A) I will become no self at all; for instance, I might immediately or eventually dissolve into pure flux or meld into some kind of "oneness" with all things as my consciousness is dispersed across time or cyberspace. In such a case, however, I will no longer be "a person but [merely] a phenomenon," as Williams nicely puts it.[31] Williams's implication is that such a dispersed non-self would not count as an immortal life in any desirable sense, and he seems right about this. Consider: If you are asked whether you would like to undergo a procedure (some mind-uploading scenario, for example) that would make you "one with the universe" – but at the price of losing all the definition and distinctiveness that allows you to exist *as a self* – would you accept that offer?

Why would you, unless you believed the rest of your life likely to be filled with suffering, or were already convinced (with many Buddhists, anti-natalists, Anaximander, and other nihilists) that all finite existence is meaningless (with the consequence that it is always better *not* to exist than to exist as an individual with life-defining cares and commitments)? I have rejected that nihilistic view of a finite human life throughout this work, instead arguing that our lives can be made meaningful not despite but because of their defining finitude, through the courage and commitment to repeatedly undergo the kinds of existential deaths and resolute rebirths that help us creatively and responsibly disclose new meanings to replace the worn-out, overly restrictive, or otherwise no longer livable self-understandings to which we otherwise find ourselves shackled (both as individuals and as collectives). At any rate, those of us not already committed to a nihilistic view of our existence will likely find the permanent annihilation of the self too high a price to pay for the immortality supposedly granted by such self-annihilation. For, *to whom* would such immortality be granted? Not to "*me*."[32] Indeed, the paradoxical logic of such an exchange is a bit like O. Henry's *The Gift of the Magi*, taken to an existentially absurd conclusion: You can buy immortality, but the cost is the very self who wanted it as well as the possibility of ever having any meaningful

---

[31] (Williams, "The Makropulos Case," 86.) Although not our target here, on those religious versions of immortality that would invoke God as a *Deus ex machina* capable of resolving this problem, see nn. 34 and 38.

[32] Can such an *unbounded oneness* even be called a "self"? I would say no, since such a boundless oneness lacks that self-conferring temporal rebound from the practical world of life-projects that gives the core "mineness" of our *solus ipse* the existential space in which to disclose a meaningful world for itself (as we saw at the end of Chapter 1).

sense of selfhood again.[33] Why choose such a self-undermining alternative? (For the same reasons, the offer of an eternity spent frozen in some amazing feeling would ordinarily be no better deal.)[34] Granted, it might well be worth experiencing the *becoming* one with the universe (at least up to the point where such a process can meaningfully be experienced). But my own best guess (with Epicurus and Heidegger) is that this is what undergoing demise will probably be like anyway, so long as we are awake and aware of what is happening, and in so far as it can be meaningfully experienced. So, while it might even be worth giving up some life (at the very end) in order to undergo this ultimately paradoxical experience of demise, that is quite different than doing so in order to live forever without a self.

Instead of permanently losing the self through dispersion (into either oneness or nothingness), there is a second way I might maintain a meaningful sense of self throughout eternity without remaining the same self forever. Through an unending succession of defining life-projects (in which a new or transformed life-project emerges out of the collapse of my old one, repeatedly giving my life new or renewed purpose), I could (2B) cycle through all the selves that prove possible for me to become during the endless eternity of time. This brings us to the second horn of the aforementioned dilemma, however, because here too problems abound. For example, if it is possible for me to evolve into someone whom the person I am now would reject as (2B1) ethically despicable or (2B2) otherwise abhorrent, then in the infinity of time such a possibility, no matter how remote, will eventually become an actuality. (2A could be one example of 2B2; other examples would include all manner of dead-end scenarios in which eternity becomes an endless hell of suffering without hope of remission.) For, in order for eternity not to become hopelessly tedious, I might well eventually have to pursue the kind of radically novel experiences that would eventually lead me far away from the defining commitments of the self I am now (indeed, far away even from the kind of self I could ever ethically countenance myself endorsing in the future), radically

---

[33] Delillo portrays a scenario in which a newly "immortal" uploaded consciousness immediately finds itself trapped in a hellish existence (Delillo, *Zero K*, 157–62), its former hope for an eternal "all-oneness" [*All-einheit*] replaced instead with an apparently endless loop of torturous "alone-ness" [*Allein-heit*] (67–8).

[34] I think this is true whether such frozen immortality is conferred via a science-fictional "experience machine" or a medieval vision of Heaven as an eternal moment spent basking in the perfect radiance of divine goodness (and thereby "deprived of privation itself," like that aforementioned lizard sunning itself on a rock [see Chapter 7, n. 68]). But such calculations become a bit different if the gift is offered at the very end of one's individual existence, as I shall suggest next. If only a nihilist would accept such an offer of eternal selfless pleasure in the midst of a reasonably good life, then perhaps only a nihilist would reject it at the very end of one, since that would be more like *choosing nothing over something*.

different and even abhorrent kinds of projects which would eventually prove hopelessly tedious (or otherwise terrible) in turn, nonetheless. I can see no way to rule out such possibilities on principle without reintroducing Williams's untenably strong presuppositions about the underlying stability and overarching unity of the self's positive commitments, problematic (and arguably even proto-ontotheological) presuppositions that would take us back to the problems of the first alternative, which has already been shown to be a dead-end.

As for 2B1, Fischer himself comes close to biting this bullet when he suggests that, if we can become a person we would now despise one step at a time, where each step toward that self was reasonable given the step that preceded it, then we have no reason to resist becoming that despicable person ahead of time.[35] Fischer could even argue (though he does not) that, just as even a terribly shameful moment diminishes but does not necessarily ruin an otherwise meaningful mortal life, so a shameful millennia or two might not ruin the life of an immortal.[36] But, again, if an evolution of the self into a person so abhorrent that having become that kind of person would spoil eternity remains *possible*, then, in the infinity of time, it will happen. Here we can feel the force of Williams's point: Who would knowingly embrace such an evolution of the self and agree to undergo it ahead of time? How afraid of the nothingness of demise would you have to be to choose to embrace a life in

---

[35] Fischer, *Our Stories: Essays on Life, Death, and Free Will*, 89–91.

[36] Thinking of the legendary example of King Priam of Troy, who lived long enough to see the flourishing family and kingdom he had built up and cared for all his life utterly destroyed and brought to ruin, Aristotle's *Nicomachean Ethics* famously cautions us against ever confidently counting a life good, happy, or fulfilled before it has ended. But Aristotle also reminds us that, just as the arrival of one swallow does not make it summer, so even a terrible event need not ruin a life, though it is often thought to have done so in Priam's tragic case. As if taking Aristotle's logic even further than Aristotle himself, Lear unambiguously asserts that "*once the kalon* [that is, the good that constitutes our ethical happiness of fulfillment] *has been achieved, nothing can completely destroy it in us. A kernel remains that is inalienable*" (Jonathan Lear, *Imagining the End: Mourning and Ethical Life* [Cambridge, MA: Harvard University Press, 2022], 43, italics in the original). Lear's inspiringly optimistic point, I take it, is that even when tragedy utterly destroys the flourishing of a life, some indestructible kernel of that happiness will survive nevertheless, if not in the person brought low then in those aspects of their memory that survive as exemplars to inspire others to live ethically themselves, in search of their own flourishing, well-being, or goodness. Indeed, after Heidegger, Derrida, and Levinas, we can also recognize that such inspiring traces can sometimes survive in our own reborn selves as well as in those others who reanimate them in their own unique ways. (Lear's optimism brings him close to Derrida here, who similarly wants to believe that the trace of an other can never be completely erased. Unfortunately, I am far from certain that this is really always the case. Is there really no once flourishing person whose inspiring goodness was destroyed while they were still alive and has since been or will be utterly and completely forgotten? Though that would be nice to believe, it seems highly unlikely to me.)

which you are doomed to become an evil or otherwise despicable person (by the lights of your own, mature judgment)?[37]

Most of us are familiar with the terrible example of the death camp inmate who is able to survive only so long as he helps his captors murder his fellow prisoners. Obviously the urge to survive at any cost is strong enough that people sometimes do choose such a horrific life, but few of us would argue that they are right to do so, nor would we agree ahead of time to voluntarily undergo such a fate ourselves merely in order to survive. There are fates worse than demise, as Socrates famously taught (in the *Apology*), and becoming a person we despise or abhor are classic examples of such a hellish fate. Why would someone choose immortality knowing they were fated to such hells?[38] Why indeed, other than a powerful but irrational fear of nothingness, or a false belief that more life is better even if the addition is bad?

---

[37] Part of what makes Fischer's analogy misleading is that a young person's resistance to future changes in their own character may be arbitrary in a way that such resistance in a mature person with a stable character need not be. I might even suggest that the "Freudian typo" in the long quotation from Fischer above (his perhaps telling substitution of "immorality" for "immortality") suggests a repressed awareness of the real force of this problem (viz., that an immortal version of our self will eventually become someone whom the self we are now would reject on good moral grounds).

[38] I have occasionally used the terms "heaven" and "hell" in a colloquial sense. But if I am right that an immortal life would necessarily be undesirable, then this presents a prima facie challenge to widespread conceptions of the Christian "Heaven" as an eternal afterlife. How, exactly, could any kind of endless individual existence fail to become torturous eventually? In Christian terms, how can Heaven avoid turning into Hell? Of course, theologians sometimes try to bake endless happiness into the very definition of an eternal afterlife: for example, by simply stipulating that being in God's presence is blissfully timeless (a very different conception of "eternity" than the one we have been employing) or otherwise intrinsically satisfying (solutions which risk simply begging the question); or else by appealing to a mysterious, omniscient, and omnipotent God who would play the ultimate party host (as it were), endlessly varying our experiences or even altering our natures so that we never grow tired of Heavenly existence. Our primary target here has been techno-scientific immortality scenarios, but even with these more fantastic scenarios, it is difficult to conceive of an immortal life as attractive without depriving immortal individuals either of their identity or of their knowledge that they are immortal, and this seems fairly telling against the appeal of immortality for a particular individual. (Theologians may also worry that such scenarios risk turning the omnipotent God into a deceiver, benevolent or otherwise. But they also need to explain how the eternal existence of such a God could itself fail to become torturous, without falling into a infinite regress.) Here, indeed, one can see why the Christian affiliated Templeton Foundation awarded Fischer five million dollars (!) to develop his argument that immortality is not necessarily bad. For, if he were right, then Heaven need not necessarily become Hell. If I am right, however, then giving individuals an endlessly protracted, immortal existence would inevitably doom them to a living hell (a conclusion that cannot be altered by any amount of money and its associated signal-boosting but only by convincing counterarguments, which I at least have not thus far encountered).

I think it is still worth hoping, nonetheless, that conscious life (or at least life in some form) will find a way to survive forever. Of course, the provisional "immortality" of life on earth thus far – or, more precisely, the fact that life seems to have found ways to stay alive ever since first appearing on earth – is based on life's endless perishing, demise, and rebirth, rather than displaying some kind of unbroken identity. Still, it is unclear how life could possibly continue its impressively unbroken record of staying alive indefinitely, given the finitude of matter and the infinitude of time (and, in the shorter term, the ticking clock of our own solar system's apparently *temporary* hospitability to life as we know it). But it is still early in the game, and some of the axiomatic assumptions of our best science could turn out to be incorrect, or we might creatively disclose workable solutions to such currently fatal problems. Such hope, even if it is ultimately misplaced, might help us continue to find ways of extending the limits of a life worth living, continuing to push the always finite limits of what currently seems possible. Such worthwhile hopes notwithstanding, I have argued in this concluding chapter that the endless life of an immortal individual would necessarily fail to qualify as such a life worth living. So, were you ever to face that choice with which we began, I think living with demise remains preferable to the alternative. Pun (and its ethico-political implications) intended, I have thus characterized my position as the "pro-choice" rather than the "pro-life" stance on these questions of the desirability of immortality and, thus, demise.[39]

---

[39] In the end, the thesis I have advanced here gets rather brilliantly summarized by the title of the subsequent essay by Shimon Edelman, "Identity, Immortality, Happiness: Pick Two," *Journal of Ethics and Emerging Technologies*, 28:1 (2018), 1–17 (although I would substitute "meaningfulness" for the slipperier and potentially more misleading term, "happiness").

10

Concluding Recapitulations
Lessons from Rethinking Heidegger's Phenomenology of Existential Death and the Irreducible Nothings It Discloses

Here, facing the end, we might well ask: What have we learned from this *rethinking of death in and after Heidegger*? By way of a concluding – and inevitably partial – recapitulation, I shall restate some of the main lessons we have drawn in this work, even while acknowledging (as we did in the preface) that the difficult existential questions we have explored here are not the kinds of issues that can be finally settled or uncontroversially summarized, once and for all.

We have seen that Heidegger's methodological approach to understanding "death" in *Being and Time* is *phenomenological*. That might sound obvious, but phenomenologists take "the risk of discussing the obvious" (BT 81/SZ 55) because important truths can often be found hiding in plain sight, owing to that "first law of phenomenology," *the distance of the near* (BT 69/SZ 43), or the fact that what shapes us most pervasively and profoundly is often the most difficult for us to notice and understand. Like the proverbial water for a fish, "the meaning of being" is rendered invisible by its very ubiquity; we see *through* it and tend not to notice our doing so. This hiding in plain sight also applies the meaning of our own distinctive kind of being, "existence" (BT 359/SZ 311), which is part of what makes it difficult to understand the correspondingly distinctive kind of "end" that Heidegger thinks our existence can undergo in the phenomenon of existential death.

Nonetheless, what exactly it means that Heidegger approaches death *phenomenologically* turns out to be crucial for understanding both his own thinking about death and the way it helped inspire and provoke other important thinkers to take up this core existential concern in his wake, including Sartre, Beauvoir, Levinas, Derrida, White, and Agamben. As we have seen, each of these post-Heideggerian philosophers contests, modifies, and develops Heidegger's phenomenology of death in their own original and thought-provoking ways. To recognize that, however, we first had to understand the fundamental contours of Heidegger's own existential phenomenology of death, which retains that odd philosophical privilege of being both highly influential and yet also widely misunderstood. I shall thus conclude this book by recapitulating some of the main points from our rethinking of death in and after Heidegger.

We saw that *Being and Time*'s loftiest goals are *ontological*. Situated in the context of the text's largest ambitions, Heidegger is primarily concerned to understand death *ontologically*: to understand what death most fundamentally *is* for us by phenomenologically describing and analysing how it shows up within, and so what it comes to mean for, our own distinctive way of "being here" as *Dasein*. Beyond this ontology of death itself, however, *Being and Time* ultimately hopes to convince us of two further interconnected ontological claims: First, that the phenomenon of existential death helps uncover the deepest constitutive structures that condition our shared way of being ("existence") – namely, those three interconnected "temporal horizons or ecstasies" that most originarily condition our intelligible worlds.[1] The reason Heidegger thinks death discloses temporality is that "futurity," the "primary" aspect of this tripartite temporal structure, first becomes visible in the phenomenon of existential death (as we saw at the end of Chapter 1). Second, Heidegger's even larger hope is that understanding these temporal structures that ultimately condition all phenomenological intelligibility will, in turn, enable us to discover "a fundamental ontology," that is, a *single* answer to *"the question of the meaning of being in general"* (BT 61/SZ 37).

That second and most ambitious hope – *Being and Time*'s ultimate goal of discovering "a fundamental ontology" that will finally *answer* "the question of being" – fails dramatically, however, and the middle Heidegger painstakingly works through the death of his own avowedly metaphysical project before definitively abandoning it in his later work as an "errant" and unwitting last gasp of the very "metaphysical" tradition he characterizes as *ontotheology* (as we saw in Chapter 2).[2] Fortunately, the phenomenological ontology of existential death originally yoked into the service of *Being and Time*'s failed metaphysical ambition to discover a fundamental ontology survives this death of metaphysics and continues to get developed in important ways in his later work (as we saw in Chapter 3), while also fascinating, befuddling, infuriating, and inspiring some of *Being and Time*'s most serious and creative readers for generations (as we saw in Part II of this book).

Although *Being and Time*'s ultimate ambitions are thus ontological, Heidegger maintains that the *only* way to do ontology is through phenomenology. *"Ontology is possible only as phenomenology"* (BT 60/SZ 35), he emphasizes. That sounds like an untenably strong claim until we realize that (here) it simply means that the only possible access to an understanding of being is through an entity who has such an understanding.[3] This

---

[1] To be more precise (since there are different ways of being fundamental), these are the most originary structures *accessible to phenomenology* (as we saw in Chapter 1). These early claims from *Being and Time* are complicated and called into question by Heidegger's later discovery of the history of being and the ontotheological structures at its core (as Chapters 2 and 3 showed).

[2] See also Thomson, *Heidegger on Ontotheology*, chs.1 and 3.

[3] Heidegger is not suggesting that natural scientific methods, for example, can have no access to ontology but, rather, that even the natural sciences must presuppose some prior phenomenological encounter with and understanding of the meaning of the being of the

entity who has an understanding of being is, by definition, *Dasein*, that is, our "existence" as a world-disclosive "being-here" that phenomenology can encounter and describe.[4] "Dasein" is the maximally open term of art Heidegger employs as he seeks to designate and *describe* the distinctive mode of "existence" we exemplify – an *ek-sistere* or "standing-out" into a phenomenologically intelligible world – without importing the *prescriptive* metaphysical baggage of "uninterrogated" ontological concepts of what a self *is*, such as "the *ego cogito*, the subject, the 'I,' reason, spirit, person, ... soul, consciousness" (BT 44, 72/SZ 22, 46). Such traditional metaphysical concepts of selfhood carry with them unintentionally "prejudicial" ontologies that need to be carefully deconstructed, Heidegger argues, precisely because they all miss or misdescribe the phenomenological "existence" of the self in ways that obscure our distinctive, world-disclosive mode of being.[5]

We could thus say that *Being and Time*'s phenomenological ambition is minimally prejudiced ontological description. Still, calling Heidegger's method "descriptive phenomenology" would be *tautologous* or pleonastic (BT 59/SZ 35), he holds, because phenomenological ontology *always* seeks to understand the way things are by *describing* the way they show up and become intelligible for us, in order to test these descriptions against the phenomenological experience of others and thereby contest, confirm, and develop them (as we have seen). At the same time, however, a "pure" or unbiased ontological description of the being that all entities share in common is a phenomenological ideal that seems forever out of reach (although Heidegger resists that conclusion in *Being and Time*).[6]

(class of) entities that these natural scientists study, simply in order to be able to pick out the appropriate kinds of entities to focus on in their empirical investigations (even though that presupposition remains tacit in the normal course of their research, becoming explicit only in times of scientific revolution within or across the disciplines, the Kuhnian point Heidegger already made in 1927 [BT 29/SZ 9]). Nonetheless, *Being and Time*'s specific view of how all the other sciences *presuppose* phenomenology turns out to be far from merely trivial. (For the details of the early Heidegger's audacious – and, I argue, untenably ambitious – understanding of the priority of phenomenology over all the other sciences, see Thomson, *Heidegger on Ontotheology*, ch. 3, esp. 104–14.)

[4] Indeed, "by definition" in *Being and Time*, but even there Heidegger begins to recognize and argue that *becoming what we are* is an important accomplishment, one with increasingly revolutionary consequences developed in his later work (see Chapter 1, n. 16 as well as Chapter 4, and see also Thomson, *Heidegger on Ontotheology*, ch. 4).

[5] *Being and Time* only begins this deconstruction of the ontological tradition by taking on the "disastrous prejudice [*verhängnisvollen Vorurteils*]" of the modern "subject," a dualistic conceptualization of the self as ontologically separated from an "external world" of objects (BT 44–7, 85–90, 122–34/SZ 22–6, 58–62, 89–101), but the later Heidegger carries it much further, developing his deconstruction of metaphysics in bold and insightful ways (see, for example, Thomson, *Heidegger on Ontotheology*, ch. 1 and *Heidegger, Art, and Postmodernity*, ch. 2).

[6] (On this resistance, see Thomson, *Heidegger on Ontotheology*, 92–104.) In fact, Heidegger himself never gives up his hope for a purely descriptive insight (something for which I have frequently criticized him). Nonetheless, the more sober (and proto-postmodern)

Instead, phenomenology remains necessarily *hermeneutic* or interpretive, critically struggling against the phenomenologist's unrecognized ontological prejudices (and other historical blind-spots) and so inevitably having to "wrest" a fuller ontological truth from the *partial* experience of us *finite* beings (BT 61–2/SZ 36–7), whose experience and understanding always remains *partial* (in both senses).[7]

The phenomenological ontologist pursues this progressive hermeneutic enterprise by focusing on some of the most significant of the universal existential structures that tacitly underlie our intelligible worlds, conditioning and constituting our ordinary, everyday experiences of what-is. *Being and Time* focuses predominantly, though not exclusively, on the three interconnected "existential" structures of *affectivity* (or mooded-attunement), *conversance*, and *understanding* (or *Befindlichkeit, Rede*, and *Verstehen*).[8] Heidegger calls these "existential structures," or "*existentials*" for short (preferring the plural Latinate "*existentialia*"), precisely because "existence" is his technical term for Dasein's *distinctive* kind of being, that aforementioned *ek-sistere* or "standing-out" into a phenomenologically intelligible world. As he provocatively emphasizes: "*Dasein is its disclosedness*" (BT 171/SZ 133) and "Dasein *is* its world existingly" (BT 416/SZ 364). That is, we *are* our intelligible worlds, and such world-disclosive "existence" is our distinctive mode of being.[9]

 conclusion that all phenomenological insight remains doubly *partial* (see Kelly Becker and Iain Thomson (eds.), "Introduction," *The Cambridge History of Philosophy: 1945-2015* [Cambridge: Cambridge University Press, 2019], 1–2) is further suggested both by Heidegger's failure ever to reach the fundamental ontology for which *Being and Time* is ultimately searching (as we saw in Chapter 2) and also by the proliferation of *different*, post-Heideggerian interpretations of death (as *partially* addressed here).

[7] See Becker and Thomson, "Introduction," 1–4.

[8] "Conversance" might sound like a heavy-handed translation of *Rede*, but "*Rede* is the articulation of intelligibility" (BT 204–4/SZ 161), and *Being and Time* shows that we responsively disclose the structure of what is *intelligible* (or *"understandable" in the widest sense* [BT 193/SZ 151]) first *practically*, with our embodied skills, before we do so linguistically, with our words and theoretical insights.

[9] This means that *only Dasein "exists"* in the technical sense of the term, and also that *all Dasein always exist* (so long as we are not in a dreamless sleep or otherwise entirely unaware). In *Being and Time*, to "exist" simply means to be the kind of entity that has Dasein's distinctive kind of being (BT 32/SZ 12), with all the radical implications of that seemingly simple view (as we saw in Chapter 4). In sum, then, *all and only Dasein "exist."* But the consequence that chairs, for example, do not technically "exist" does not mean that there are *no such things as chairs*. *For us* (Dasein), *there are* chairs (that is, chairs frequently show up in our intelligible worlds), but there is no *us* for a chair (as it were), because a chair has no intelligible world of its own. As Heidegger provocatively puts it, chairs come equipped with legs and might physically touch tables (if there is no distance separating them), but "strictly speaking" only Dasein can *have* legs and *touch* tables (BT 81/SZ 55). When Heidegger further glosses such "existing" as "thrown projecting," he draws attention to the dual structural fact that by the time we become aware of ourselves we already have selves to become aware of, and that as long as we are here we have to continue projecting into the projects that help render us intelligible to ourselves – the very

This brief background should help us recognize and recall that in *Being and Time*, "death" (*Tod*) is Heidegger's name for a stark and desolate *phenomenon* in which our *Dasein* – our *existence* as a world-disclosive "being-here" – encounters its *own* end, the end "most proper" to the particular kind of entity that Dasein *is*. "Death" thus designates Dasein's phenomenological encounter with the end of its own world-disclosure, the "end" of that particular way of becoming intelligible in time which (as we saw in Chapter 4) uniquely "distinguishes" Dasein from all other kinds of entities (BT 32/SZ 12). Our ontologically distinctive manner of becoming intelligible in time – Dasein's "existing" or phenomenological "world-disclosing" – takes place through Dasein's "existential" structures. In terms of the three interconnected existentials *Being and Time* mainly focuses on, death has to do primarily with the "understanding" (*Verstehen*). Understanding, for Heidegger, is practical before it is cognitive, and so principally designates the embodied life-projects we *stand under* (or project ourselves into practically) and understand ourselves in terms of (whether tacitly or explicitly), like teacher, father, husband, friend, pet-companion, biker, and so on (and on). Consequently, existential *death* is encountered most directly as a *global* collapse in our embodied self-understanding (as Chapter 1 showed in detail). But the phenomenon of existential death also shows up in the registers of *Dasein*'s other two main existential structures, because these three existentials always form an inextricably tripartite whole.[10] Accordingly, death also makes itself felt in *Angst* ("anxiety," "dread," or even "anguish"), which is death's affective attunement (or *Befindlichkeit*), with "reticent silence" and "conscience" as our (authentic and inauthentic, respectively) modes of discourse or conversance with death, that is, our ways of articulating death's intelligibility.[11]

In this phenomenon of existential death, our being-here as a primordially practical being-in-the-world that projects into constitutive projects comes to an *end* (the only end it can reach phenomenologically) and thereby encounters its *own* not-being; or, as Heidegger provocatively puts it, Dasein encounters its own "nothingness." Indeed, *Being and Time* famously describes the phenomenon of existential "death" in these deliberately paradoxical terms, as "the possibility of the *im*possibility of existence – that is to say, the utter nothingness of Dasein" (BT 354/SZ 306). Now (as we saw in Chapter 3), the very idea that Heidegger is designating a meaningful *phenomenon* here initially sounds dubious, even absurdly self-undermining, because it is not clear how we could possibly encounter the complete and utter end of our own defining being, the

---

process that breaks down in existential death and then gets resolved in resolve, where Dasein lucidly projects into a chosen project in a way that takes over its being the groundless ground of its embodied, practical world.

[10] Haugeland, "Truth and Finitude."
[11] See Blattner, *Heidegger's Being and Time*, 140.

quintessential end of that very world-disclosure that marks us out as the *unique* kind of entities we are (BT 231/SZ 187). What *is there* to encounter phenomenologically in our own "utter nothingness"?[12] In other words, what exactly does Heidegger mean by "death"?

I began this recapitulation by belaboring an obvious point – that hermeneutic phenomenology always takes as its point of departure *phenomena* that we can encounter or experience in our own lives – because that rather rudimentary point proves extremely significant for understanding Heidegger's treatment of existential death.[13] For, the very fact that *Being and Time* adopts a *phenomenological* approach to death means that, to understand Heidegger's view (and so begin to take the measure of its complicated influence), we need to recognize the sense in which he believes that we existing beings can somehow undergo an encounter with our own deaths *while we are still alive*. Understandably, that highly provocative point represents a bridge too far for many scholars (leading to the hermeneutic divide addressed in Chapter 1), but it remains textually undeniable. As *Being and Time* clearly states: "*Death is a way to be*, which Dasein takes over as soon as it is" (BT 289, my emphasis/SZ 245). Indeed, in 1925 (two years before *Being and Time* was published), Heidegger had already written: "I myself am my death precisely when I live" (BH 263). And he expresses this provocative view even more clearly in 1959: "Mortals die their death in life" (GA 4: 165/190). To understand Heidegger's phenomenology of death, then, we need to understand the sense in which he thinks we can encounter our own deaths while we are still alive (BT 277/SZ 234).

As Heidegger recognizes (BT 279–80/SZ 236), moreover, this phenomenological requirement – that we can somehow experience our own deaths while we are still alive – leads to a paradox familiar to the Western philosophical

---

[12] Chapter 3 provides a detailed answer to this question.
[13] In Heidegger's terms, the "ontic" and the "ontological" (that is, the domains of entities, on the one hand, and of their meaning, sense, or intelligibility, on the other) are never completely separable, let alone dichotomous. Despite widespread misunderstandings on this score (entrenched misunderstandings rooted in the desire of Heidegger apologists to dichotomize the ontic human being, Heidegger, from his ontological insights, so as to avoid the difficult work of understanding the relation between his politics and his thought; see Thomson, *Heidegger on Ontotheology*, ch. 3), *no phenomena are "too ontic" for phenomenological analysis*, though for Heidegger the point of such analyses will always be to excavate beneath these ontic phenomena in order to reach the ontological structures that shape and condition our experience of them, and in the case of the existential structures that constitute Dasein's world, such structures will then feedback into and transform our experience of our everyday lives as well. In short, Heideggerian phenomenology seeks to disclose the bridges connecting the ontic/existentiell and the ontological/existential domains, bidirectional bridges the phenomenologist can travel then back and forth on, to illuminating and even transformative effect. (See Chapter 1 and Thomson, *Heidegger, Art, and Postmodernity*, ch. 3, for detailed examples.)

tradition since Epicurus. Put simply, the apparent annihilation of our individual existences that we ordinarily call "death" seems to be characterized by *the absence of all experience*.[14] Insofar as we cannot experience the absence of all experience, it seems that we cannot experience "death" *itself* (so understood). We can experience such "death" in its approach but not in its having arrived; there is thus no experience of "death" itself, ordinarily conceived. (Hence Epicurus's famous maxim of Stoic edification: Whenever your thoughts circle anxiously around your own death, simply remind yourself not to worry, since "where you are, death is not; and where death is, you are not." You and your death will never meet, since the two cannot occupy the same place simultaneously.)[15] Heidegger's *phenomenological* interpretation of death – because it necessarily *begins* from the assumption that we can somehow undergo an *intelligible* encounter with our own death itself – can therefore easily seem to be a misguided nonstarter.

In fact, however, recognizing this paradox – that it seems impossible to experience our own deaths themselves *so long as we understand "death" in the ordinary way* – helps us recognize both what Heidegger really means by "death" and also why he approaches the phenomenon in the particular way he does in *Being and Time*, by (eventually) distinguishing the phenomenon of existential *death* from the normal way of thinking about death he terms *demise*. Put simply, "demise" (*Ableben*) is the term Heidegger uses to refer to our typical understanding of "death" as our experiential undergoing of an apparently permanent absence of all experience. *Demise* refers to that seemingly final foreclosure of our intelligible worlds that accompanies what Heidegger calls the "perishing" (*Verenden*) of our biological systems; that is, we undergo *demise* when the organic systems supporting our lives *perish* (BT 291/SZ 247). In other words, such mortal *demise* (or becoming "deceased") is what our language more colloquially and vividly refers to as "kicking-the-

---

[14] The reasons for this now appear obvious: Experience is based on sensations, but what we ordinarily call "death" (Heidegger's "demise") is what follows the cessation of our biological functions (Heidegger's "perishing"), without which there do not appear to be any sensations, at least not for long. Thus "death" (reduced to *demise*), on this typical and long-standing view, appears to be some final and irreversible absence of experience.

[15] In other words, Dasein cannot *be* demised. Although we often say that "he or she is dead," in fact "no Dasein *is* demised" since our being and demise cannot coincide without one destroying the other. For, if it turned out somehow that we could *be* demised – if there was an afterlife, for example, such that we Dasein could still be here (or there) in demise – then we could not demise; for we could not experience anything of our being at an end by becoming nothing (although we could still encounter the "noth-ing of the nothing" that death discloses, as we saw in Chapter 3, which itself shows that Heidegger's views of the nothing in 1927 and 1929 are not identical). In sum, we cannot enter finally into mere nonbeing and still keep being us. (For Heidegger's fuller response to this view that we can never "die" because we cannot *be demised*, and my response to a related paradox espoused by Nagel, see Chapter 1 as well as the remarks below.)

bucket," "taking a dirt nap," "croaking," and so on. Most of us, most of the time (that is, as *das Man*, the anonymous anyone), understand death *only* as "demise," as that apparently unremitting absence of all our meaningful, first-personal experience, a permanent cessation of worldly intelligibility that seems to follow the final moment of our lives (at least as far as we can tell while we are still alive). Understood as a fatal collision with (or return to) a cosmic nothingness that remains ultimately incomprehensible from where we stand on "this side" of the veil (the only side to which *phenomenology* has direct access), demise itself remains inaccessible to phenomenology. Phenomenology cannot describe what it is like to be *at an end* in demise, since as far as we can directly tell from experience there is nothing that it is like to *be demised*.[16]

It is thus precisely here, we saw, that Heidegger's distinction between ordinary mortal "demise" and the phenomenon of existential "death" becomes absolutely crucial, making it unfortunate and problematic that *Being and Time*'s way of drawing out the distinction between demise and death is so subtle and complex. Walking readers through the implications of the paradox that we cannot access our own demise phenomenologically, because there is no "'living-through' of [our own] ceasing to live [*"Erleben" des Ablebens*]" [BT 295/SZ 251], Heidegger gets about thirteen pages into his treatment of death before finally proclaiming that "the analysis [of death] cannot keep clinging to an idea of death which has been devised accidentally and at random" (BT 292–3/SZ 248), then immediately signals that he will remedy this problem by extracting the six formal structural features of existential "death" from the "average everyday" understanding of "demise." Still, a thick cloud of confusion gets generated by the fact that Heidegger deliberately uses the term "demise" to refer to that annihilation of experience most people call "death," then uses the word "death" to name the existential phenomenon that implicitly structures and conditions our normal experience of such "demise." Indeed, we even saw in Chapters 6 and 7 that, while Levinas, Sartre, Beauvoir, and Agamben all grasp something of Heidegger's crucial distinction between mortal demise and existential death, even as careful a reader as Derrida misses it – at least until his own final reflections on existential shipwreck and *survivance*.

Despite its hastily composed and confusing presentation, Heidegger's view that the phenomenon of existential death underlies and conditions our ordinary experience of mortal demise remains one of the deepest and most

---

[16] To be clear: being demised is not some unique experience, or even an experience of the nothing. As far as those of us who have not yet demised can tell, *being demised is not an experience at all*. This is part of what makes the experience of *demising* seem so paradoxical or aporetic; demising appears to be an experiential undergoing that cannot be fully undergone, an experience of approaching an endpoint that experience itself cannot reach. (Whenever I am struck by the thought that "it is *strange* to be alive," I thus ask myself, *"Compared to what?"*)

enduringly insightful aspects of his existential analysis of death in *Being and Time*. For, in the end (pun intended), the Stoics would appear to be right: Demise *itself* seems to be phenomenologically inaccessible; demise as such cannot be directly experienced, whether in our own demise or through the demise of another Dasein. (This is something Heidegger explicitly recognizes [BT 277/SZ 234] because he refuses to allow his underlying religious *faith* to override the phenomenological evidence that is directly available to us as living individuals [BT 292/SZ 247-8].) This explains why, instead of just analyzing our own ultimately inaccessible relation to demise (a kind of phenomenological black hole), Heidegger goes two big steps further.

First, he analyzes the *structure* of our ordinary relation to "demise," seeking to characterize the way in which this ultimately inaccessible phenomenon appears to us while we are still alive. Employing the phenomenological technique the early Heidegger calls "formal indication," *Being and Time* isolates the six structural characteristics that characterize our ordinary understanding of demise. Then, second, he goes on to suggest that these six formal structures that characterize our ordinary understanding of demise also come together in a deeper way to "define" *Being and Time*'s "full existential-ontological conception of death": "Death, as [1] *the end of Dasein* [2], is *Dasein's ownmost*, [3] *non-relational,* [4] *certain and* [5] *as such indefinite,* [6] *non-surpassable possibility*" (BT 303/SZ 258-9, Heidegger's emphasis). The six defining structures of existential death are thus *drawn from* a formal analysis of demise, where those six structures have subtly but importantly different meanings (as we saw in Chapter 1.5). In this way, then, Heidegger seeks to excavate beneath mortal demise, disclosing a deeper phenomenon – existential *death* – which he thinks *conditions* our ordinary relation to demise. That *conditioning claim* is something we must phenomenologically "enact" in (and thereby test against) our own individual experience in order to be able either to confirm and develop or else contest and transform Heidegger's phenomenological description of existential death. That is precisely what his subsequent philosophical heirs sought to do (as we saw in Chapters 5, 6, and 7), reminding us that existential phenomenology was never meant to be a spectator sport but, instead, presents us with a complex series of conversations centered around these thinkers' own overlapping and subtly conflicting insights into the meaning and significance of existential death, which together help constitute the living legacy of this still unsettling and inspiring philosophical tradition.

What we have also seen, moreover, is that *demise* – that is, death understood in the normal sense (as our experiential undergoing of an apparently permanent absence of individual experience) – maintains a direct connection to the phenomenon Heidegger calls "death." Heidegger is not (*pace* Haugeland and White) renaming some other phenomenon "death" arbitrarily or merely using this loaded word metaphorically.[17] On the contrary, existential death is drawn from a formal analysis of ordinary mortal demise (our ultimately paradoxical experience of croaking or kicking-the-bucket), and Heidegger thinks that the phenomenon he calls "death" *conditions and structures* our normal way of relating to our own demises. Specifically, because he thinks that our *repression* of the phenomenon of existential death tacitly shapes our normal ways of understanding and so relating to mortal demise (and thereby "alienates" Dasein from its "ownmost" self [BT 222/SZ 178]), he suggests that encountering existential death *phenomenologically* can powerfully *transform* our ordinary relation to demise. As we saw in Chapter 1, *Being and Time* ultimately suggests that such an encounter with existential death can help liberate us from a confused and unnecessarily repressive relation to our own mortal demise, radically freeing up our ways of relating to the fact that our own lives come to an ineluctable end and thereby helping us learn to shed the mortal fear of demise that will otherwise pursue us throughout our lives.

Without fully reprising that view, recall that it turns on recognizing that what really drives our fear of mortal demise is an unrecognized anxiety about our own *not being*. Heidegger thinks we ordinarily "flee" and repress our fear of demise, "tranquillizing" it by *keeping busy*, but that such fear of demise is itself a way of fleeing and repressing our deeper anxiety about death.[18] In other words, *we repress our fear of mortal demise so as to repress our deeper anxiety about existential death*, a phenomenon which is thereby doubly repressed and concealed – a deep repression of the phenomenon that unfortunately also suggests that even its painstaking articulation is likely to be met with various

---

[17] After Blattner (in Blattner's "The Concept of Death in *Being and Time*"), Haugeland and White (early students of Dreyfus) were among the first to distinguish death and demise (a very important step), but both interpret Dasein as a necessarily *collective* understanding of being, of which individuals are merely cases or instances. This misinterpretation (based in part on a misreading of "mineness" as well as a once common "orthodox" conflation of early and later Heidegger) generates hermeneutically untenable consequences (which we saw, in Chapter 5, White bites the bullet and accepts), like the conclusion that only a handful of people have ever achieved what Heidegger calls "authenticity," viz., those like Jesus, Copernicus, and Descartes who directly experienced the collapse of the entire historical understanding of being that previously guided their cultural ages or epochs *and* went on to disclose a new collectively livable historical world. Lear's *Radical Hope*, influenced by this reading from his colleague Haugeland (as well as by his own creative appropriations of Freud), presents the Iroquois Chief Plenty-Coup in the same terms (while suggestively defending *dream interpretation* as a potentially helpful way through existential death and back to the world).

[18] We might thus wonder: Is tranquillizing anxiety what Levinas and Derrida are doing, from Heidegger's perspective, by suggesting that we can live on in the lives of others, surviving in all those living worlds in which we come to play a role? (Would this make our afterlives like some influential person's social media account that never closes, even after they demise?) We return briefly to this question at the end (as is perhaps appropriate).

forms of *hermeneutic resistance*, which can range from bewildered incredulity to outright hostility. If, in the face of such resistance, we want to express the deeper existential motive behind our fear of mortal demise in a way that heightens its apparent paradoxicality, we can say that it is an *anxiety* about *being our own not being*. What really drives our fear of demise, in other words, *is* our anxiety about existential death, an experience of *losing our world and still being here to experience that loss*. Our fear of demise is thus misplaced but not irrational (*pace* Epicurus and Nagel), because our own not being is indeed something we *can* encounter *in life*, precisely in that phenomenon Heidegger calls existential "death" – that is, in a desolate, world-bereft experience of what I have called *projectless projecting*.

Heidegger's insight that an existential encounter with our own not-being can help liberate us from our fear of mortal demise is one of the most edifying implications of *Being and Time*'s phenomenology of death.[19] But it also provides evidence in favor of the view, because Heidegger thinks that when hermeneutic phenomenology succeeds (indeed, as the very measure of and testament to its success), it *deepens* our understanding of our everyday lives by revealing the usually unnoticed structures that tacitly condition ordinary experience.[20] And by thus making us aware of the underlying existential

---

[19] Heidegger then goes beyond this view after *Being and Time*, disclosing from the "nothingness" of existential death an even more liberating and edifying relation to being's apparently inexhaustible phenomenological plenitude for us mortal Dasein. On the crucial phenomenological connection between death and the plenitude of being, see Chapter 3 and below.

[20] Some of the most fascinating examples of such phenomena in Heidegger's work from the late 1920s and early 1930s include our skillful use of equipment, our strong feelings of guilt, anxiety, and love (see my Thomson, "Thinking Love"), our subtle encounters with truth, death, and (*through* the encounter with death) even our most basic disclosure of temporality itself (since the existential phenomenon of death discloses "futurity," the first horizon of originary temporality, as we saw in Chapter 1). I have often shown that Heidegger's "later" work also centers around less methodologically explicit but no less important phenomenological analyses of such matters as the way our existence is pervasively shaped by art, education, politics, and (most profoundly and importantly for Heidegger) by our historical understanding of the *being* of what-is (see, for example, Thomson, *Heidegger on Ontotheology*, chs. 3–4). To understand Heidegger's central later views of art and poetry, for example, one has to recognize them *as phenomenological* (albeit post-Husserlian, in fact they already were in *Being and Time* [BT 62–3/SZ 38]). Indeed, Heidegger's crucial encounter with Vincent van Gogh only becomes plausible once we recognize it *as phenomenological*, and he even understands great poets like Hölderlin phenomenologically, as poetically disclosing things in ways that at least partly escape (and so help teach us how to transcend) the prejudicial confines of the metaphysical tradition of Western ontotheology (on both points, see Thomson, *Heidegger, Art, and Postmodernity*, ch. 3).

structures that quietly shape and condition our ordinary lives, existential phenomenology *transforms* our everyday experience as well, as it does quite dramatically in the case of death (as well as in other important and illustrative cases such as Heidegger's later phenomenological ontology of art, which also profoundly transforms the ordinary "aesthetic" experience from which it first sets out).[21]

As we sum up the lessons of Heidegger's existential phenomenology of death, we should not fail to mention some other important distinctions it encouraged him to draw. Recall that, in order to understand Heidegger's *phenomenology* of death as "the possibility of the *im*possibility of existence," we needed to recognize that he means "possibility" in an *existential* rather than any merely *logical* sense. Existential "possibilities" are the embodied life-projects that compose our particular ways of being (such as teacher and student, friend and colleague, queer and nonbinary, liberal and conservative, son and daughter, poet and revolutionary – and all the other myriad ways of being that each individual Dasein takes up and lives in its own particular, embodied, "*existentiell*" ways). Such practical life-projects, taken together, help positively constitute our existences in worldly terms, allowing us to become intelligible to ourselves and each other as we encounter the holistically interwoven significance of the things disclosed in the tacit light of these practical projects. Existential possibilities are these embodied *projects* that we ordinarily *project* ourselves *into*, and so understand ourselves in terms of, as we go about charting the course of our everyday lives. As we do so, we thereby implicitly take (and retake) an embodied stand on the meaning of being, both the meaning our own being and of (the "significance" of) those things disclosed in the light of these embodied worlds that we Dasein *understand* ourselves to be as we make our ways through time.[22]

---

[21] (See Thomson, *Heidegger, Art, and Postmodernity*, ch. 2.) As Heidegger expresses this crucial point: "The interpretation which is more primordial existentially also discloses *possibilities* for a more primordial existentiell understanding [that is, such interpretations disclose deeper and more encompassing ways for individuals to embody those existential structures in our everyday lives], so long as our ontological conceptualization [of the structure of Dasein's being] does not let itself get cut off from our ontical experience [that is, separated from our worldly experience of entities]" (BT 341/SZ 295). That methodological mistake Heidegger warns against happens, for example, when phenomenologists postulate a false dichotomy between the ontic and ontological domains, a radical split between entities and their being or meaning (see also n. 10 in Chapter 1 and n. 13 above).

[22] These ways we "chart the course" *understandingly* are "usually and ordinarily" practical, carried out in that primary, "hands-on" (*zuhanden*) mode of existence Dreyfus famously calls "skilful coping," but they can also be cognitive and thematic ("hands-on" or *vorhanden*), as when we deploy them to make explicit plans or formulate conscious ideas about our lives (see Dreyfus, *Being-in-the-World*).

For that reason, Heidegger rather subtly distinguishes two different kinds of *existential possibilities*: our "being-possible" (*Möglichsein*) and our "ability-to-be" (*Seinkönnen*); that is (respectively), our *life-projects* and our *projecting* ourselves into or upon those projects as we go about charting the course of our existential "being-here" and so *become* what we "understand" ourselves to be (BT 185–6/SZ 145). I "project" myself practically into the project of being a *teacher*, for example, by preparing for and teaching classes, talking with and advising students, answering their emails, reading and responding to their work, and so on; the existential project of being a teacher organizes the intelligibility of all such practical activities. Taken *in toto*, projecting into all my existential projects provides my world with its significance, shape, and coherence – or *lack thereof*. For, by repeatedly referring to death as "the possibility of an impossibility," Heidegger is deliberately designating a stark and desolate phenomenon in which we find ourselves (at least temporarily) unable to project into (or connect with) any of the existential projects that ordinarily disclose the significance of things and render us meaningful to ourselves. This is also why Heidegger repeatedly refers to death as Dasein's "*ownmost* ability-to-be." In the phenomenon of existential death, our selves get stripped of "the clothing of the world" (as Kierkegaard put it), losing all the worldly life-projects that ordinarily render us intelligible to ourselves. But when we undergo this shipwreck of our life-projects in existential death, we do not simply disappear entirely.[23] Instead, we encounter ourselves as a *projectless projecting*, that is, as a sheer "*existing*" which finds itself unable to exist *as* anyone or anything (teacher, man, father, and so on).

To encounter death *phenomenologically* as the existential "possibility of an impossibility" is thus also to encounter a *positive* "nothingness" – that aforementioned "utter nothingness of Dasein." This "utter nothingness" we encounter in the phenomenon of existential death is not the onrush of oblivion – although we can also encounter existential death (*in passing*) in undergoing mortal "demise," if we are aware that our demise is approaching. For, if we are conscious when we demise and aware that we are demising then we will likely die existentially as well, experiencing the collapse of all the remaining life-projects that rendered us intelligible to ourselves.[24] But we

---

[23] Unless, of course, we also demise at the same time (see below).
[24] I have suggested that this is likely true even if we have authentically come to understand others as carrying on some of our own defining projects (cf. Derrida's *survivance*), or have faith in reincarnation or some other afterlife (since, regardless, we will still not be eating that next meal, taking any more visitors or phone calls, making any more appointments, trying to get some sleep or make it through another day, etc.; that is, I think we will probably always leave some project unfinished when we demise). But if we can imagine someone as having no defining life-projects at the time of their demise (perhaps not even that final project of being there for their own paradoxical experience of

can also *die* existentially without mortally *demising*. Experiencing this nonfatal phenomenon of existential death may often be traumatic (though it can also be profoundly liberating, as when the dead self from it which it frees us had become oppressive or unlivable), but it is also fortuitous for phenomenology. (As Kierkegaard's "Anti-Climacus" observes, what seems "luckiest" from a worldly perspective – namely, *never* falling into "despair" or dying to the world while still alive – is the "most unlucky" from a spiritual perspective, and so from a phenomenological one, given Heidegger's secularizing appropriation of Kierkegaard's view.).[25]

Instead of the approach of annihilation, the "utter nothingness" Dasein encounters phenomenologically in existential death is actually the bedrock condition of what Heidegger calls the *solus ipse* or "self alone," that is, the utterly desolate core of a self that has survived the shipwreck of all its worldly projects. Such an existing self remains more *powerful* than death, a "superior power" (*Übermacht*) capable of *overpowering* death's power (BT 436/SZ 384), not only by surviving the collapse of its worldly projects in existential death (which might only make this self *as powerful as* death) but also by revealing this core self that can subsequently break the grip of such existential death by reconnecting to the world of projects in "resolve [*Entschlossenheit*]." In order to discover that "superior power" (in *resolve*), existential death must first disclose to Dasein its "ownmost ability to be [*eigenste Seinkönnen*]," that unsinkable projectless projecting which forms the very *sine qua non* of the self in *Being and Time* (since Dasein cannot forfeit it and still *be here* at all).[26] This ontological core of the self disclosed in the phenomenon of existential death is thus our own Dasein reduced to sheer *existing* (from the Latin "*ek-sistere*"), "standing out" into a world of practical possibilities we cannot connect to, a projectless projecting in which Dasein starkly encounters itself as "a naked 'that-it-is-and-has-to-be,'" an anxious "mineness" (BT 173/SZ 134) hungry to return to the world of practical projects.

In this extreme phenomenon of existential death (Heidegger's version of what his early collaborator Karl Jaspers called a "limit situation

---

demise, as Derrida himself quite inspiringly hoped to do), then such a being might not die when they demise, but perhaps only because they would *already* be in existential death, merely a projectless projecting having no practical world the collapse of which to undergo. (On the way Heidegger's thinking about this difficult issue evolves in his later thought, see n. 46 in Chapter 1.)

[25] "Unluckiest," both because *the only way out is through* (for both thinkers) and also, for Heidegger, because we cannot describe the phenomenon (or test the adequacy of the phenomenological descriptions of others) unless we have undergone the experience ourselves. (We explored the unequalled influence of Kierkegaard's *The Sickness Unto Death* on Heidegger's phenomenology of existential death in Chapter 1.)

[26] See also Crowell, "Subjectivity."

[*Grenzsituationen*]"), we thus find ourselves temporarily unable to be anything in particular at all.[27] We still *exist* ("standing out" toward the world) and yet find ourselves incapable of existing *as* anyone or anything, unable to project into any of our life-projects and so exist in any "actual" or "positive" terms. As Heidegger puts it: "Death, as possibility, gives Dasein nothing to be 'actualized,' nothing which Dasein, as actual, could itself be. It is the possibility of the impossibility of every way of comporting oneself toward anything, every ["actual"] way of existing" (BT 307/SZ 262). Since Dasein exists *as* its intelligible world of practical significance, this phenomenological "nothingness of Dasein" is also "the 'nothing' of the world" (BT 393/SZ 343). Heidegger thus adds that, in the attunement of radical *Angst* which accompanies existential death, the naked "self" of sheer "mineness" encounters "the 'nothing' – that is, the world as such, the world as world" (BT 231-2/SZ 187).

We have seen that Heidegger does not mean entities within the world vanish or become conceptually unintelligible in existential death; the *solus ipse* or "self alone" does not suddenly find itself transported into the "undifferentiated emptiness" of a worldless Cartesian vacuum (BT 233/SZ 188). I do not find myself suddenly unsure if I exist among alarm clocks or coffee machines; instead, all entities lose the practical significance and salience they had formerly as holistic and interconnected webs of equipment that implicitly elicited my engagement and so fleshed out my world. In existential death, the world of indifferent objects looms before me in its "empty mercilessness" (BT 393/SZ 343), confronting me with the now useless detritus of all those previously defining existential projects I can no longer connect to (no matter how desperately I might want to).[28] How, then, does

---

[27] Thornhill and Miron explain Jaspers's early view (from the *Psychology of World Views* [Karl Jaspers, *Psychologie der Weltanschauungen* (Berlin: Springer, 1919)], for example) in a way that helps suggest its influence on Heidegger's own phenomenology of existential death (and the empowering resolve such death enables): "Limit situations are moments, usually accompanied by experiences of dread, guilt or acute anxiety, in which the human mind confronts the restrictions and pathological narrowness of its existing forms, and allows itself to abandon the securities of its limitedness, and so to enter [a] new realm of self-consciousness." (See Chris Thornhill and Ronny Miron, "Karl Jaspers," in *The Stanford Encyclopedia of Philosophy*, ed. by Edward N. Zalta [Spring 2022 Edition], https://plato.stanford.edu/archives/spr2022/entries/jaspers/ [accessed May 29, 2023].)

[28] As we saw in Chapter 1, this "de-worlded" objective detritus no longer solicits my practical engagement and yet stands there nonetheless – almost as if, suddenly deprived of its practical significance, it now tauntingly reminded me of what I have lost. Precisely here, moreover, we discover what is for Heidegger the primordial unity of existential guilt and anxiety, an essential union between discovering ourselves as a "null basis" (the "thrownness" at the root of existential guilt that leaves our choice of life-projects undetermined) and that uncanny lack of fit between self and world (that world-exceeding projection which is the source of existential *Angst*. In existential death, we find ourselves

this nothingness of self and world bring Dasein face-to-face with "the world as world" (BT 233/SZ 188)? As *Being and Time* shows, I can explicitly experience what my bicycle implicitly *is* in my everyday use of it when it breaks down, and so just stands there as, for example, a broken piece of equipment that was supposed to get me to school, so that I could get to my class on time, for the sake of being a good teacher, a responsible colleague, and so on. In an analogous way, Dasein can come face-to-face with itself as an embodied stand on the meaning of existence when its being-in-the-world breaks down in existential death.

What is perhaps most fascinating here from a scholarly perspective (as we saw in Chapters 2 and 3) is the way *Being and Time*'s phenomenology of existential death first helps disclose something like the Ur-phenomenon of Heidegger's later work, that irreducibly polysemic phenomenological "presencing" he initially calls "the noth-ing of the nothing" (in 1929), a temporally dynamic ontological abundance that turns out to be both conceptually and practically inexhaustible and so the ultimate source of whatever authentic and meaningful disclosure remains possible for us mortal beings, now and in the future.[29] This also means, however, that the phenomenological "nothing" death first discloses brings Heidegger face-to-face with the ontologically indigestible iceberg that spells the *death* of his central early project, *Being and Time*'s ill-fated attempt to discover and articulate a "fundamental ontology" (that is, "an understanding of the meaning of being in general"). It takes Heidegger a decade to recognize and work through the significance of this discovery, however, since doing so requires him to let the metaphysical project that defines his own early work *die* and then *resolutely* commit himself to uprooting and transcending all such metaphysics in his later work. In this way, the existential death of his early metaphysical project (his fundamental ontological quest to discover a unified understanding of being) gives birth to the post-metaphysical project that comes to define his later thinking, namely, to help humanity learn this same lesson about the impossibility of metaphysics (an initially painful and yet ultimately liberating

---

in our fundamental uncanniness (or *Unheimlichkeit*, our not-being-at-home in the world), utterly unable to be anyone (teacher, father, husband, friend, and so on). And yet we still exist, standing out *toward* all the self-world unities we can no longer connect to and understand ourselves in terms of, thereby *"nullifying or nihilating"* them all (as we saw at the end of Chapter 1). Ordinarily we nullify only those live-options we have not projected into, hence our ordinary ontic and existentiell guilt; in existential death, we project into none and so *nullify them all*, existing in the empty (and so transparent) nullity of our own "finite existing." Here, moreover, we also exist as "the null basis" we are as the groundless ground of *having to exist*, that is, in being a "thrown project" or existing entity that did not choose to be and yet must go on somehow, nevertheless.

[29] See Young, *Heidegger's Later Philosophy*; and Thomson, *Heidegger, Art, and Postmodernity*, ch. 3 and "Post/Modernity?"

lesson for him as well as for us), so that we can begin to find our collective way beyond the metaphysical substructure responsible for the growing nihilism of our age.[30]

In spite of itself, then, *Being and Time*'s existential phenomenology of death first discloses the paradoxically positive "nothingness" that will soon become 1929's notorious "noth-ing of the nothing." This active "noth-ing" of that which is not-yet-a-thing – and yet nevertheless continues to make itself felt phenomenologically (by subtly beckoning to be disclosed) – eventually *turns* out to have been the first glimmering of (what Heidegger most frequently later called) "being as such" (as Chapter 3 showed). Yet, as we also saw (in Chapters 2 and 5), Heidegger's later claims to have already recognized as much in *Being and Time* are demonstrably false and misled generations of orthodox readers into minimizing or even erasing the fundamental philosophical differences between his early and later work. Put in the terms of his later thought, Heidegger's hermeneutic phenomenology of death first helped disclose what he would only later recognize as "being as such" in its ineliminable *difference* from any "metaphysical" understanding of "the being of entities," exposing that seemingly ineliminable phenomenological "excessiveness" by which being not only informs but also escapes every meaningful attempt to capture what it means to *be* in some final understanding of "the being of entities," including *Being and Time*'s self-avowedly *metaphysical* attempt to capture the meaning of being in a fundamental ontology.

More specifically, we saw, Heidegger's phenomenology of existential death discloses a paradoxically positive and dynamic nothingness that soon became that notorious "noth-ing" of "the nothing." "The nothing itself noths [*Das Nichts selbst nichtet*]" (P 90/GA9 114), as he so infamously put it in 1929, seeking phenomenologically to describe the inchoate emergence of what is-not-yet fully or discretely intelligible but is actively beckoning to become intelligible – with the help of Dasein's responsive and creative disclosures. In this rather complicated way, existential death first inadvertently uncovers what later becomes the subtle but dynamic Ur-phenomenon of being's phenomenologically primordial emergence into intelligibility, a conceptually and practically inexhaustible "presencing" that seems likely to make itself felt for as long as mortal Dasein exists (as

---

[30] *Pace* Haugeland, I have sided with those who think Heidegger never delivered on that promised fundamental ontology, not in *Being and Time* nor in any of the works that followed while he continued to pursue his ill-fated "metaphysical" project with a desperation that continued to grow until – in a philosophically profound instance of existential *death* and rebirth – Heidegger was finally driven to abandon this metaphysical project, subsequently making its very impossibility the central pillar of his later thought (as we saw in Chapter 2).

we saw in Chapter 9). In other words, what Heidegger's phenomenology of death shows us is not merely the apparent oblivion of mortal demise. In an end that is not yet *the* end, existential death discloses what Heidegger already calls the very "futurity" of the future, its "incessant" coming to be, the temporally dynamic basis of all we can encounter phenomenologically so long as we *are here* as Dasein.

We have seen in this book that, for Heidegger and all the thinkers in the existential tradition of hermeneutic phenomenology who take his work as their own point of departure (in one way or another), this creative and responsive disclosure is something we do primarily by critically inheriting our predecessors' projects and transformatively making them our own. Such predecessors of course include Heidegger himself – just as, for the early Heidegger, they included Kierkegaard and others, and for the later Heidegger, they included (creatively disclosive rereadings of) his own earlier work. But we have also seen that seeking to do justice to the complex ethico-political and other implications of the irreducible ontological pluralism that turns out to be entailed by being's inexhaustible phenomenological excessiveness (that very anxiety-provoking excessiveness first disclosed by existential death, then developed as the "noth-ing," the "earth," "being as such," "presencing," and so on) – remains an important and ongoing project, one that continues to provoke the post-Heideggerian thinkers of yesterday, today, and tomorrow to develop such insights well beyond the narrow limits they sometimes assumed in Heidegger's own work.

It was in that liberating hermeneutic light that we turned (throughout part two) to critically examine some of the most important and influential ways Heidegger's philosophical heirs sought to rethink, transform, and develop his phenomenology of existential death. Rethinking White, Levinas, Sartre, Beauvoir, Agamben, Derrida, and others in this way let us begin to understand some of the most important moments in the critical afterlife of Heidegger's existential phenomenology of death. At the same time, doing so showed how all these post-Heideggerian thinkers critically complicate and creatively develop different aspects and implications of Heidegger's phenomenology of existential death, thus helping us understand what he recognized and what he missed, and so also how we might continue to build on these insights ourselves.

As a result, these thinkers' various efforts to rethink existential death and authentic rebirth help make a strong case for the diverse and enduring philosophical relevance of this deep issue at the heart of existential phenomenology. Putting this living legacy to the test in Chapters 8 and 9, we explored just some of the broader contemporary implications of this manifold rethinking of death in and after Heidegger, thereby helping to illustrate its enduring importance. In the end, then, I think it perfectly reasonable to hope that the philosophical heritage of this rethinking of existential death and authentic rebirth will continue to survive – and, indeed, that it will do so precisely by being repeatedly reborn in different forms, as called for by those emerging challenges that thinking inevitably confronts as we find ourselves called upon to help creatively disclose more meaningful paths through time, place, and history. In the progressive historical spirit of all the foregoing, let us thus end with our own echo of Beauvoir's appropriation of existential death as necessary for the repeated rebirths of a more authentic self and world: *Viva la mort!* "Long live death!"

REFERENCES

Adams, H. E., L. W. Wright, Jr., and B. A. Lohr, "Is Homophobia Associated with Homosexual Arousal?" *Journal of Abnormal Psychology* (1996) 105:3, 440–5.
Agamben, Giorgio, *Language and Death: The Place of Negativity*. Minneapolis, MN: University of Minnesota Press, 1991.
  The Open: Man and Animal. Stanford, CA: Stanford University Press, 2004.
  Remnants of Auschwitz, trans. D. Heller-Roazen. New York: Zone Books, 1999.
  Where Are We Now? The Epidemic as Politics. London: Eris, 2021.
Allison, Henry, *Idealism and Freedom*. Cambridge: Cambridge University Press, 1996.
Arendt, Hannah, *Eichmann in Jerusalem: A Report on the Banality of Evil*. New York: Penguin, 1963.
  The Origins of Totalitarianism. New York: Harcourt, 1968.
Aries, Philippe, *The Hour of Our Death: The Classic History of Western Attitudes toward Death over the Last One Thousand Years*, trans. H. Weaver. New York: Vintage, 2008.
Aristotle, *Nicomachean Ethics*, trans. H. Rachham. Cambridge, MA: Harvard University Press, 1934.
Babich, Babette, ed., *From Phenomenology to Thought, Errancy, and Desire: Essays in Honor of William J. Richardson, S.J.* New York: Springer, 1995.
Badiou, Alain, *Being and Event*. New York: Continuum, 2005.
Baudrillard, Jean, *The Transparency of Evil: Essays on Extreme Phenomena*, trans. J. Benedict. London: Verso, 1993.
Beauvoir, Simone de, *Ethics of Ambiguity*. New York: Open Road, 2018.
  The Second Sex, trans. H. M. Parshley. New York: Knopf, 1953.
Becker, Ernest, *The Denial of Death*. New York: Free Press, 1973.
Becker, Kelly, and Iain Thomson, eds., "Introduction," *The Cambridge History of Philosophy: 1945–2015*. Cambridge: Cambridge University Press, 2019.
Beckett, Samuel, "Worstward Ho," in *Samuel Beckett: The Grove Centennial Edition*, Vol. IV, ed. Paul Auster. New York: Grove Press, 2006, 471–85.

Bell, Jeffrey, Andrew Cutrofello, and Paul Livingston, *Beyond the Analytic-Continental Divide: Pluralist Philosophy in the Twenty-First Century*. London: Routledge, 2015.
Blattner, William, "The Concept of Death in *Being and Time*." *Man and World* (1994) 27:1, 49–70.
  Heidegger's Being and Time: A Reader's Guide. London: Continuum, 2006.
  Heidegger's Temporal Idealism. Cambridge: Cambridge University Press, 1999.
Bloom, Harold, *The Anxiety of Influence: A Theory of Poetry*. Oxford: Oxford University Press, 1997.
de Boer, Karin, *Thinking in the Light of Time: Heidegger's Encounter with Hegel*. Albany, NY: SUNY Press, 2000.
Böhme, Jakob, *Mysterium Magnum*, trans. John Sparrow. San Rafael, CA: Hermetica, 2007 [original 1623].
Bostrom, Nick, "The Transhumanist FAQ: A General Introduction," Version 2.1 (2003). www.transhumanism.org/resources/FAQv21.pdf (accessed September 2, 2013).
Braver, Lee, *Groundless Grounds: A Study of Wittgenstein and Heidegger*. Cambridge, MA: The MIT Press, 2012.
  A Thing of This World: A History of Continental Anti-Realism. Evanston, IL: Northwestern University Press, 2007.
Burke, Edmund, *Reflections on the Revolution in France*. Oxford: Oxford University Press, 2009.
Butler, Judith, *Subjects of Desire: Hegelian Reflections on Twentieth Century France*. New York: Columbia University Press, 1987.
Calarco, Matthew, *Zoographies: The Question of the Animal from Heidegger to Derrida*. New York: Columbia University Press, 2008.
Calarco, Matthew, and Steven DeCaroli, eds., *Giorgio Agamben: Sovereignty and Life*. Stanford, CA: Stanford University Press, 2008.
Capobianco, Richard, *Heidegger's Being: The Shimmering Unfolding*. Toronto: University of Toronto Press, 2022.
Capps, E. et al., eds., *The Odes of Pindar*, trans. J. Sandy. New York: G. P. Putnam's Sons, 1915.
Carman, Taylor, *Heidegger's Analytic*. Cambridge: Cambridge University Press, 2003.
  "Is Dasein People? Heidegger according to Haugeland." *Boundary 2* (2014) 41:2, 197–212.
Carnap, Rudolf, "The Elimination of Metaphysics through Logical Analysis of Language," in *Logical Positivism*, ed. A. J. Ayer. New York: Free Press, 1959 [original 1932], 60–81.
Cavell, Stanley, *Conditions Handsome and Unhandsome: The Constitution of Emersonian Perfectionism*. Chicago, IL: Chicago University Press, 1990.
  This New Yet Unapproachable America: Lectures after Emerson after Wittgenstein. Albuquerque, NM: Living Batch Press, 1989.

Cerbone, David, "Distance and Proximity in Phenomenology: Husserl and Heidegger." *The New Yearbook for Phenomenology and Phenomenological Philosophy* (2003) III, 1–26.
Chanter, Tina, *Time, Death, and the Feminine: Levinas with Heidegger*. Stanford, CA: Stanford University Press, 2002.
Chérif, Mustapha, *Islam and the West: A Conversation with Jacques Derrida*. Chicago, IL: University of Chicago Press, 2008.
Claxton, Susanne, *Heidegger's Gods: An Ecofeminist Perspective*. London: Rowman and Littlefield, 2017.
Critchley, Simon, *Very Little ... Almost Nothing: Death, Philosophy, Literature*, revised edition. London: Routledge, 2004.
Crowell, Steven, "Metaphysics, Metontology, and the End of *Being and Time*." *Philosophy and Phenomenological Research* (2000) 60:2, 307–31.
  "Subjectivity: Locating the First-Person in *Being and Time*," *Inquiry* (2001) 44:4, 433–54.
Crowell, Steven, and Jeff Malpas, eds., *Transcendental Heidegger*. Stanford, CA: Stanford University Press, 2006.
Dahlstrom, Daniel, "The End of Fundamental Ontology," in *Division III of Heidegger's Being and Time: The Unanswered Question of Being*, ed. Lee Braver. Cambridge, MA: The MIT Press, 2015, pp. 83–103.
Dall'Alba, Gloria, and Robyn Barnacle, "An Ontological Turn for Higher Education," *Studies in Higher Education* (2006) 32:6, 679–91.
Dallmayr, Fred, *The Other Heidegger*. Ithaca, NY: Cornell University Press, 1993.
Delillo, Don, *Zero K*. New York: Scribner, 2016.
Derrida, Jacques, *The Animal That Therefore I Am*, ed. M.-L. Mallet, trans. D. Wills. New York: Fordham, 2008.
  Aporias: Dying – Awaiting (One Another at) the "Limits of Truth," trans. T. Dutoit. Stanford, CA: Stanford University Press, 1993.
  "Force of Law: 'The Mythical Foundations of Authority,'" in *Deconstruction and the Possibility of Justice*, eds, Drucilla Cornell, Michel Rosenfeld, and David Gray Carlson. New York and London: Routledge, 1992, 3–67.
  The Gift of Death. Chicago, IL: University of Chicago Press, 1996.
  Of Grammatology, trans. Gayatri Spivak. Baltimore, MD: The Johns Hopkins University Press, 1976.
  Heidegger: The Question of Being and History. Chicago, IL: University of Chicago Press, 2016.
  Points... Interviews, 1974–1994. Stanford, CA: Stanford University Press, 1995.
  Psyche: Inventions of the Other, Vol. II. Stanford, CA: Stanford University Press, 2008.
  Spurs: Nietzsche's Styles. Chicago, IL: University of Chicago, 1981.
  The Truth in Painting. Chicago, IL: University of Chicago Press, 1987.
Dreyfus, Hubert L., *Being-in-the-World: A Commentary on Heidegger's Being and Time, Division I*. Cambridge, MA: The MIT Press, 1990.

"Could Anything Be More Intelligible than Everyday Intelligibility? Reinterpreting Division I of *Being and Time* in the Light of Division II," in *Appropriating Heidegger*, ed. Mark Wrathall. Cambridge: Cambridge University Press, 2000, 155–74.

"Foreword" to Carol J. White, *Time and Death: Heidegger's Analysis of Finitude*, ed. Mark Ralkowski. Aldershot: Ashgate, 2005.

"Heidegger's History of the Being of Equipment, in *Heidegger: A Critical Reader*, ed. H. L. Dreyfus and H. Hall. Cambridge, MA: Basil Blackwell, 1992, 173–85.

On the Internet, 2nd ed. London: Routledge, 2008.

What Computers Still Cannot Do: A Critique of Artificial Intelligence. Cambridge, MA: The MIT Press. 1992.

Dreyfus, Hubert, and Charles Taylor, *Retrieving Realism*. Cambridge, MA; Harvard University Press, 2015.

Dreyfus, Hubert L., and Mark A. Wrathall, eds., *A Companion to Heidegger*. Oxford: Blackwell, 2005.

Edelman, Shimon, "Identity, Immortality, Happiness: Pick Two," *Journal of Ethics and Emerging Technologies*, 2018 (28:1), 1–17.

Edwards, Paul, *Heidegger's Confusions*. New York: Prometheus, 2004.

Elgat, Guy, "Heidegger on Guilt: Reconstructing the Transcendental Argument in *Being and Time*." *European Journal of Philosophy* (2020) 28:4, 911–25.

Foucault, Michel, *The Hermeneutics of the Subject: Lectures at the Collège de France, 1981–1982*, ed. Frédéric Gros, trans. G. Burchell. New York: Palgrave Macmillan, 2005.

Fischer, John Martin, ed., *The Metaphysics of Death*. Stanford, CA: Stanford University Press, 1993.

Our Stories: Essays in Life, Death, and Free Will. Oxford: Oxford University Press, 2009.

Flores, Fernando, and B. Scot Rousse, "Ecological Finitude as Ontological Finitude: Radical Hope in the Anthropocene," in *The Task of Philosophy in the Anthropocene: Axial Echoes in Global Space*, Richard Polt and John Wittrock. New York: Roman & Littlefield, 2018, 175–92.

Freud, Sigmund, *Beyond the Pleasure Principle*. New York: Norton, 1961.

Friedman, Michael, *Kant and the Exact Sciences*. Cambridge, MA: Harvard University Press, 1998.

A Parting of the Ways: Carnap, Cassirer, and Heidegger. Chicago, IL: Open Court, 2000.

Gaiman, Neil, *The Sandman*. New York: Vertigo/DC Comics, 1988–96.

Glendinning, Simon, "Much Ado About Nothing," *Ratio* (2001) XIV, 281–8.

Gerassi, John, *Talking with Sartre: Conversations and Debates*, ed. and trans. J. Gerassi. New Haven, CT: Yale University Press, 2009.

Geuss, Raymond, *Morality, Culture, and History: Essays on German Philosophy*. Cambridge: Cambridge University Press, 1999.

Guenther, Lisa, *Solitary Confinement: Social Death and Its Afterlives*. Minneapolis, MN: University of Minnesota Press, 2013.
Guignon, Charles, *On Being Authentic*. London and New York: Routledge, 2004.
"Heidegger and Kierkegaard on Death: The Existentiell and the Existential," in *Kierkegaard and Death*, eds. Patrick Stokes and Adam Buben. Bloomington, IN: Indiana University Press, 2011, pp. 184–203.
"History and Historicity," in *The Blackwell Companion to Phenomenology and Existentialism*, eds. Hubert L. Dreyfus and Mark Wrathall. Oxford: Blackwell, 2005, 545–58.
Haas, A., P. Rodgers, and J. Herman, "Suicide Attempts Among Transgender and Gender Non-conforming Adults: Findings of the National Transgender Discrimination Study," *American Foundation for Suicide Prevention and the Williams Institute, UCLA School of Law* [2014]. [Retrieved from https://williamsinstitute.law.ucla.edu/wp-content/uploads/AFSP-Williams-Suicide-Report-Final.pdf.].
Hauge, Michelle V., Mark D. Stevenson, D. Kim Rossmo, and Steven C. Le Comber, "Tagging Banksy: Using Geographic Profiling to Investigate a Modern Art Mystery," *Journal of Spatial Science* (2016) 61:1.
Haugeland, John, *Dasein Disclosed: John Haugeland's Heidegger*, ed. Joseph Rouse. Cambridge, MA: Harvard University Press, 2013.
"Heidegger on Being a Person," *Nous* (1982) 16, 6–26.
"Truth and Finitude: Heidegger's Transcendental Existentialism," in *Heidegger, Authenticity, and Modernity: Essays in Honor of Hubert L. Dreyfus*, Vol. 1, eds. Mark Wrathall and Jeff Malpas. Cambridge, MA: MIT, 2000.
Hegel, G. W. F., *Phenomenology of Spirit*, trans. A. V. Miller. New York: Oxford University Press, 1979.
Hoffman, Piotr, "Death, Time, History: Division II of *Being and Time*," in *The Cambridge Companion to Heidegger*, ed. Charles Guignon. Cambridge: Cambridge University Press, 1993, 195–214.
Hoffman, Yoel, *Japanese Death Poems: Written by Zen Monks and Haiku Poets on the Verge of Death*. Rutland, VT: Tuttle, 1986.
Hölderlin, Friedrich, *Poems and Fragments*, ed. M. Hamburger, London: Anvil, 1994.
Horkheimer, Max, and Theodore Adorno, *Dialectic of Enlightenment: Philosophical Fragments*. Stanford, CA: Stanford University Press, 2002.
Hoy, David, *Critical Resistance: From Poststructuralism to Post-Critique*. Cambridge, MA: MIT Press, 2004.
Hurka, Thomas, *Perfectionism*. Oxford: Oxford University Press, 1993.
Jaspers, Karl, *Psychologie der Weltanschauungen*. Berlin: Springer, 1919.
Johnston, Mark, *Surviving Death*. Princeton, NJ: Princeton University Press, 2010.
Jünger, Ernst, *Storm of Steel*, trans. M. Hofmann. New York: Penguin, 2004.
Kant, Immanuel, *The Critique of Pure Reason*, eds. and trans. Paul Guyer and Allen W. Wood. Cambridge: New York, Cambridge University Press, 1998.

Groundwork of the Metaphysics of Morals, ed. and trans. Mary McGregor. Cambridge: Cambridge University Press, 1998.
Perpetual Peace and Other Essays, trans. Ted Humphrey. Indianapolis, IN and Cambridge: Hackett, 1983.
Katz, Claire, "Jewish Philosophy and the Shoah," in Becker and Thomson, *The Cambridge History of Philosophy* (op. cit.), 709–22.
Käufer, Stephan, "The Nothing and the Ontological Difference in Heidegger's *What Is Metaphysics?*" *Inquiry* (2005) 48:6, 482–506.
Kaufmann, Walter, ed. and trans., *The Portable Nietzsche*. New York: Penguin, 1954.
Kierkegaard, Søren, *Concluding Unscientific Postscript*, trans. Alastair Hannay. Cambridge: Cambridge University Press, 2009.
  Concluding Unscientific Postscript to the Philosophical Fragments, trans. D. F. Swenson. Princeton, NJ: Princeton University Press, 1941.
Kisiel, Theodore, "The Demise of *Being and Time*: 1927–1930," in *Heidegger's Being and Time: Critical Essays*, ed. Richard Polt. Lanham, MD: Rowman & Littlefield, 2005, 189–214.
  The Genesis of Heidegger's Being and Time. Berkeley, CA: University of California Press, 1993.
Kojève, Alexandre, *Introduction to the Reading of Hegel: Lectures on the Phenomenology of Spirit*. Ithaca, NY: Cornell University Press, 1980.
Kuhn, Thomas, *The Structure of Scientific Revolutions*. Chicago, IL: University of Chicago Press, 1986.
Lacoue-Labarthe, Philippe, *Heidegger, Art, and Politics: The Fiction of the Political*. Oxford: Basil Blackwell, 1990.
Lear, Jonathan, *Aristotle: The Desire to Understand*. Cambridge: Cambridge University Press, 1988.
  Imagining the End: Mourning and Ethical Life. Cambridge, MA: Harvard University Press, 2022.
  Radical Hope: Ethics in the Face of Cultural Devastation. Cambridge, MA: Harvard University Press, 2006.
Levi, Primo, *Survival in Auschwitz*. New York: Orion Press, 1959.
Levinas, Emmanuel, *Existence and Existents*, trans. A. Lingis. Pittsburgh, PA: Duquesne University Press, 1978.
  God, Death, and Time, trans. B. Bergo. Stanford, CA: Stanford University Press, 2000.
  Nine Talmudic Readings, trans. A. Aronowicz. Bloomington, IN: Indiana University Press, 1990.
  Time and the Other, trans. R. A. Cohen. Pittsburgh, PA: Duquesne University Press, 1987.
  Totality and Infinity: An Essay on Exteriority, trans. A. Lingis. Pittsburgh, PA: Duquesne University Press, 1969.
Lyotard, Jean-François, *Pacific Wall*. Venice, CA: Lapis Press, 1990.

Malka, Salomon, *Emmanuel Levinas: His Life and Legacy*, trans. M. Kigel, and S. M. Embree. Pittsburgh, PA: Duquesne University Press, 2006.
Marcuse, Herbert, *Eros and Civilization*. Boston, MA: Beacon Press, 1974.
Martin, George R. R., *A Dance with Dragons. Book Five of A Song of Ice and Fire*. New York: Bantam Books, 2011.
Mill, John Stuart, *On Liberty*. Indianapolis, IN: Hackett, 1978.
Miller, James, *The Passion of Michel Foucault*. New York: Anchor, 1994.
Moore, Ian Alexander, *Dialogue on the Threshold: Heidegger and Trakl*. Albany, NY: SUNY, 2022.
Mulhall, Stephen, "Human Mortality: Heidegger on How to Portray the Impossible Possibility of Dasein," in *A Companion to Heidegger*, eds. Dreyfus and Wrathall. Oxford: Blackwell, 2005, 297–310.
  Philosophical Myths of the Fall. Princeton, NJ: Princeton University Press, 2007.
Murphy, Ann, *Violence and the Philosophical Imaginary*. New York: SUNY Press, 2012.
Nadler, Steven, "Baruch Spinoza," *The Stanford Encyclopedia of Philosophy*, ed. Edward N. Zalta (Fall 2013 Edition), http://plato.stanford.edu/archives/fall2013/entries/spinoza/.
Nagel, Thomas, *Mortal Questions*, Cambridge: Cambridge University Press, 1979.
Nancy, Jean-Luc, "Scandalous Death," M.-E. Morin and T. Holloway, trans., *Angelaki* 27:1 (2022), 8–13.
Nietzsche, Friedrich, "Ecce Homo: How One Becomes What One Is." In *The Portable Nietzsche*, ed. W. Kaufmann. New York: Penguin, 1954.
  The Gay Science: With a Prelude in Rhymes and an Appendix of Songs. Walter Kaufmann, trans. New York: Vintage Books, 1974.
  Thus Spoke Zarathustra, in *The Portable Nietzsche*, ed. and trans. W. Kaufmann. New York: Viking Penguin Books, 1954.
  The Will to Power: Selections from the Notebooks of the 1880s, ed. R. Kevin Hill, trans. R. K. Hill and M. Scarpitti. London and New York: Penguin Classics, 2016.
Norris, Andrew, ed., *Politics, Metaphysics, and Death: Essays on Giorgio Agamben's Homo Sacer*. Durham, NC: Duke University Press, 2005.
Oberst, Joachim, "Heidegger's Appropriation of Aristotle's *Dunamis/Energeia* Distinction" *American Catholic Philosophical Quarterly* 78:1 (2004), 25–51.
Oberst, Joachim L., *Heidegger on Language and Death: The Intrinsic Connection*. London: Continuum, 2009.
Olafson, Frederick, "The Unity of Heidegger's Thought," in *The Cambridge Companion to Heidegger*, ed. Charles Guignon. Cambridge: Cambridge University Press, 1993.
Oliver, Kelly, *Animal Lessons: How They Teach Us to Be Human*. New York: Columbia University Press, 2009.
  "Tropho-Ethics: Derrida's Homeopathic Purity," *The Harvard Review of Philosophy* 15 (2007), 37–57.

Olson, K. R., L. Durwood, M. DeMeules, and K. A. McLaughlin, "Mental health of transgender children who are supported in their identities." *Pediatrics* 137:3 (2016), 2015–3223.

Ortega, Marianna, *In-Between: Latina Feminist Phenomenology, Multiplicity, and the Self*. New York: SUNY, 2016.

Ortega, Y. Gasset José, *Meditations on Quixote*. New York: Norton, 1961.

Paul, L. A., *Transformative Experience*. Oxford: Oxford University Press, 2016.

Peters, Michael A., ed., *Heidegger, Education, and Modernity*. Lanham, MD: Rowman & Littlefield, 2002.

Pew, "Living to 120 and Beyond: Americans' Views on Aging, Medical Advances and Radical Life Extension," *Pew Research Religion and Public Life Project*, 6 August 2013. www.pewforum.org/2013/08/06/living-to-120-and-beyond-americans-views-on-aging-medical-advances-and-radical-life-extension/ (accessed August 6, 2013).

Pinkard, Terry, *Hegel: A Biography*. Cambridge: Cambridge University press, 2000.

Pippin, Robert, "Hannah Arendt and the Bourgeois Origins of Totalitarian Evil," in *The Persistence of Subjectivity: On the Kantian Aftermath*. New York: Cambridge University Press, 2005.

Idealism as Modernism. Cambridge: Cambridge University Press, 1997.

Plato, *Republic*. New York: Books, Inc., 1943.

Pöggeler, Otto, *Martin Heidegger's Path of Thinking*. D. Magurshak and S. Barber, trans. Atlantic Highlands, NJ: Humanities Press International, 1989.

Polt, Richard, "*Ereignis*," in Hubert L. Dreyfus and Mark A. Wrathall, eds, *A Companion to Heidegger*. Oxford: Blackwell, 2005.

Preciado, Paul, *Countersexual Manifesto*. New York: Columbia University Press, 2018.

Proust, Marcel. *In Search of Lost Time*, Vol. V, C. K. S. Moncrieff and T. Kilmartin, trans. New York: Random House, 2003.

Raffoul, François, *Heidegger and the Subject*, D. E. Pettigrew and G. Recco, trans. Amherst, NY: Humanities, 1999.

Rawls, John, *A Theory of Justice*. Cambridge, MA: Harvard University Press, 1971.

Rorty, Richard, *Take Care of Freedom and Truth Will Take Care of Itself*. Stanford, CA: Stanford University Press, 2006.

Rouse, B. Scott, "Retrieving Heidegger's Temporal Realism." *European Journal of Philosophy* 30:1 (2022), 205–26.

Richardson, John, *Nietzsche's System*. New York: Oxford University Press, 1996.

Richardson, William J., *Heidegger: From Phenomenology to Thought*, 2nd ed. The Hague: Martinus Nijhoff, 1967.

"Heidegger's Fall." In *From Phenomenology to Thought, Errancy, and Desire: Essays in Honor of William J. Richardson, S.J*, ed. Babette Babich, 277–300. New York: Springer, 2005.

Ryle, Gilbert, "Heidegger, M. – *Sein und Zeit*." *Mind* 38.355 (1928): 355–70.

Sánchez, Carlos Alberto, "Authenticity and the Right to Philosophy: On Latin American Philosophy's Great Debate." In *The Cambridge History of Philosophy,* eds. Becker and Thomson (op cit.), 679–91.
  Contingency and Commitment: Mexican Existentialism and the Place of Philosophy. New York: SUNY Press, 2016.
  A Sense of Brutality: Philosophy after Narco-Culture. Amherst College Press, 2020.
Sartre, Jean-Paul, *Being and Nothingness: A Phenomenological Essay on Ontology,* H. E. Barnes, trans. New York: Philosophical Library, 1956 [original 1943].
  Being and Nothingness: An Essay in Phenomenological Ontology, Sarah Richmond, trans. New York: Washington Square, 2021 [original 1943].
  "The Desire to Be God," *Essays in Existentialism.* New Jersey: Citadel Press, 1965.
Sartre, Jean-Paul and Benny Lévy, *Hope Now: The 1980 Interviews,* A. van den Hoven, trans. Chicago, IL: University of Chicago Press, 1996.
Schopenhauer, Arthur, *The World as Will and Representation,* Volumes 1 and 2. Cambridge: Cambridge University Press, 2014, 2020.
Seubold, Günter, "Heideggers nachgelassene Klee-Notizen," *Heidegger Studies* 9 (1993), 5–12.
Shaw, George Bernard, *Man and Superman.* Virginia: Wilder, 2008.
Sheehan, Thomas, *Making Sense of Being: A Paradigm Shift.* London: Rowman & Littlefield, 2015.
Sher, George, *Beyond Neutrality: Perfectionism and Politics.* Cambridge: Cambridge University Press, 1997.
Sluga, Hans, *Heidegger's Crisis: Philosophy and Politics in Nazi Germany.* Cambridge, MA: Harvard University Press, 1993.
Spinosa, Charles, Fernando Flores, and Hubert L. Dreyfus, *Disclosing New Worlds: Entrepreneurship, Democratic Action, and the Cultivation of Solidarity.* Cambridge, MA: The MIT Press, 1997.
Spinoza, Benedict de, *Ethics,* ed. and trans. E. Curley. New York: Penguin, 1996.
Stokes, Patrick and Adam Buben, eds, *Kierkegaard and Death.* Bloomington, IN: Indiana University Press, 2010.
Taylor, Charles, *A Secular Age.* Cambridge, MA: Harvard, 2007.
Thomson, Iain, "Can I Die? Derrida on Heidegger on Death," *Philosophy Today* 43:1 (1999), 29–42.
  The End of Ontotheology: Understanding Heidegger's Turn, Method, and Politics. University of California, San Diego, CA: philosophy dissertation, 1999.
  "Hearing the Pro-Vocation within the Provocation: Heidegger on the Way to Post-Metaphysical Humanism." *Gatherings: The Heidegger Circle Annual* XII (2022), 187–97.
  Heidegger, Art, and Postmodernity. Cambridge: Cambridge University Press, 2011.

Heidegger on the Danger and Promise of Technology, or What Is Called Thinking in the Age of AI? Cambridge: Cambridge University Press, forthcoming.

Heidegger on Ontotheology: Technology and the Politics of Education. Cambridge: Cambridge University Press, 2005.

Heidegger: A Philosophical Biography (Cambridge: Cambridge University Press, in progress).

"Heidegger's Mature Vision of on Ontological Education, or: How We Become What We Are," *Inquiry* 44:3 (2001), 243–68.

"Heidegger's Nazism in the Light of His Early *Black Notebooks*: A View from America." In Alfred Denker and Holger Zaborowski, eds, *Zur Hermeneutik der 'Schwarzen Hefte': Heidegger Jahrbuch 10.* Freiburg: Karl Alber, 2017.

"Heideggerian Perfectionism and the Phenomenology of the Pedagogical Truth Event," in Kevin Hermberg and Paul Gyllenhammer, eds, *Phenomenology and Virtue Ethics.* London and New York: Bloomsbury, 2013.

"Interpretation as Self-Creation: Nietzsche on the Pre-Platonics," *Ancient Philosophy* (23:1) 2003, 195–213.

"Ontology and Ethics at the Intersection of Phenomenology and Environmental Philosophy," *Inquiry* 47:4 (2004), 380–412.

"Ontopoliticosexual Pro(−)vocations." *Gatherings: The Heidegger Circle Annual* XII (2022), 206–10.

"Ontotheology," *The Bloomsbury Companion to Heidegger*, ed. François Raffoul and Eric S. Nelson. London: Bloomsbury, 2013.

"Post/Modernity? How to Separate the Stereo from the Styrofoam." *Gatherings: The Heidegger Circle Annual* XI (2021), 183–97.

"From the Question Concerning Technology to the Quest for a Democratic Technology: Heidegger, Marcuse, Feenberg," *Inquiry* 43:2 (2000): 203–16.

"Rethinking Education after Heidegger: Teaching Learning as Ontological Response-Ability," *Educational Philosophy and Theory*, 48:8 (2016), pp. 846–61.

"Review of Santiago Zabala, The Remains of Being: Hermeneutic Ontology after Metaphysics." *Notre Dame Philosophical Reviews*, 12 October 2010. https://ndpr.nd.edu/reviews/the-remains-of-being-hermeneutic-ontology-after-metaphysics/ (accessed June 6, 2023).

"The Silence of the Limbs: Critiquing Culture from a Heideggerian Understanding of the Work of Art," *Enculturation* 2:1 (1998) www.enculturation.net/2_1/thomson.html (accessed January 22, 2023).

"Thinking Love: Heidegger and Arendt," *Continental Philosophy Review* 50:4 (2017), 453–78.

"Transcendence and the Problem of Otherworldly Nihilism: Taylor, Heidegger, Nietzsche," *Inquiry* 54:2 (2011), pp. 140–59.

Thornhill, Chris and Ronny Miron, "Karl Jaspers," *The Stanford Encyclopedia of Philosophy* (Spring 2022 Edition), Edward N. Zalta, ed. https://plato.stanford.edu/archives/spr2022/entries/jaspers/ (accessed May 29, 2023).
Traverso, Enzo. 2003. *The Origins of Nazi Violence*. New York: The New Press.
Vallega-Neu, Daniela, *Heidegger's Contributions to Philosophy: An Introduction*. Bloomington, IN: Indiana University Press, 2003.
Vattimo, Giorgio, *Nihilism and Emancipation: Ethics, Politics, and Law*. New York: Columbia University Press, 2003.
Wade, Simeon, *Foucault in California*. Heyday: Berkeley, CA: 2019.
Waismann, Friedrich, *Ludwig Wittgenstein and the Vienna Circle: Conversations Recorded by Friedrich Waismann*, Brian McGuinness and Joachim Schulte, trans. (New York: Rowman and Littlefield, 1979).
Wall, Steven, and George Klosko, eds, *Perfectionism and Neutrality: Essays in Liberal Theory*. Lanham, MD: Rowman & Littlefield, 2003.
White, Carol J., *Time and Death: Heidegger's Analysis of Finitude*, ed. Mark Ralkowski. Aldershot: Ashgate, 2005.
Willett, Cynthia, *Interspecies Ethics*. New York: Columbia University Press, 2014.
Wittgenstein, Ludwig, *On Certainty*. New York: Harper and Row, 1969.
  Culture and Value, Peter Winch, trans. Chicago, IL: University of Chicago Press, 1980.
  "A Lecture on Ethics," in *Philosophical Occasions 1912–1951*, ed. James Klagge and Alfred Nordmann. Indianapolis, IN: Hackett, 1993.
  Philosophical Investigations. New York: Macmillan, 1958.
Williams, Bernard, "Liberalism and Loss," in Mark Lilla, Ronald Dworkin, and Robert B. Silvers, eds, *The Legacy of Isaiah Berlin*. New York: New York Review of Books, 2001.
  "The Makropulos Case: Reflections on the Tedium of Immortality." Reprinted in Fischer (1993); originally published in Williams, *Problems of the Self*. Cambridge: Cambridge University Press, 1973.
Wolin, Richard, ed., *The Heidegger Controversy*. New York: Columbia University Press, 1991.
Wrathall, Mark A., "Trivial Tasks that Consume a Lifetime: Kierkegaard on Immortality and Becoming Subjective," *The Journal of Ethics* 19 (2015), 419–41.
Wrathall, Mark A., and Patrick Londen, "Anglo-American Existential Phenomenology." In *The Cambridge History of Philosophy: 1945–2015*, eds. Becker and Thomson (*op. cit.*), 646–63.
  "An Overview of *Being and Time*." In *The Cambridge Companion to Being and Time*, ed. Mark Wrathall. Cambridge: Cambridge University Press, 2013.
Young, Julian, *Friedrich Nietzsche: A Philosophical Biography*. Cambridge: Cambridge University Press, 2010.
  Heidegger's Later Philosophy. Cambridge: Cambridge University Press, 2002.

Heidegger's Philosophy of Art. Cambridge: Cambridge University Press, 2001.

"Was There a 'Turn' in Heidegger's Philosophy?" In *Division III of Heidegger's Being and Time*, ed. Braver (op. cit.).

Žižek, Slavoj, *Disparities*. London: Bloomsbury, 2016.

Violence: Six Sideways Reflections. London: Verso, 2006.

INDEX

ability-to-be, 37, *See* also possibility, existential
ableism, 234
Abraham, 6
absurdity, 59, 279
adolescence, crisis of, 214
adulthood, 214
aesthetics, 249
afterlife, xi, 4, 26, 59, 237, 284, 292, 298, 303
Agamben, Giorgio, 225, 227–228, 240–241
agency, 191
agnosticism, 27, 59, 225
agony, 197, 216
alêtheia, 89, 93, 126
alienation, 56, 219
Allison, Henry, 171
all-oneness, 282
alterity, 185, 192–193, 199, 204–205, 220
   phenomenological critique of, 222
Alzheimer's disease, 61, 233
ambiguity, 215–217
America, 8, 170, 187, 240
Anaximander, 76
anguish, 5, 101, 197, 215
animal, rational, death of, 166
animality, 185, 206, 234–235, 251
animals, 15, 185, 234
annihilation, 224, 236, 281, 299
anthropocentrism, 81, 228, 234
anthropology, 16
anticipation, 40–41, 46, 68, 148–150, 153, 190
anti-foundationalism, 260
anti-natalism, 281

anxiety, 5, 31, 35, 38, 43, 47, 49, 69, 101, 110, 114, 124–125, 148, 155, 191, 198, 202, 212, 216, 265, 290, 295–296, 300
   as death's affective attunement, 101
   distinguished from boredom, 155
   of influence, 35, 188
aperspectivalism, 252, 255
aporia, 75, 229
Aquinas, 142
Arendt, Hannah, 72, 186, 196
Aristotle, 52, 132–133, 139–141, 279, 283
Armageddon, 61
arrival, ontological, xiii, 67–68, 70, 193–194, 200, 225, 265
art, 239, 254, 277, 297
artificial intelligence, 241
asinanity, 235
atheism, 26, 59, 200, 225
authenticity, 40, 46, 48, 61, 66, 111, 138, 141, 146, 148, 150, 152, 154, 162, 168, 178, 190, 192–193, 205, 217–218, 221, 280
   as anticipatory resolve, 48
   as conversion, 154
   defined, 153
authoritarianism, 217, 243
autism, 253

Badiou, Alain, 253, 261
balance, 233
Banksy, 240
bare life, 227–228
Baudrillard, Jean, 167
beauty, 98, 254
Beauvoir, 30, 198, 203, 212, 214, 217

Becker, Ernest, 57
Beckett, 99
becoming, 147–148, 201, 215, 219, 249, 265, 282
being, 76, 264
  as abundance, 301
  as becoming, 69
  by becoming, 37, 71
  conflated with God, 167
  as difference, 79
  of entities, 12, 78, 80, 86, 125, 302, *See also* ontotheology
  as excess, 92, 178, 247, 257, 302
  history of, 66, 92, 177, 246
  as inexhaustible, 223, 301
  is finite, 278
  of life, 16
  meaning of, 76, 91, 286
  as postmodern, 94
  postmodern understanding of, 256, 263
  as presencing, 80, 84, 92, 97, 120, 173, 301–302
  question of, 80, 90, 287
  as question-worthy, 97
  understanding of, 11
  as Ur-phenomenon, 64, 80, 82, 85, 113–115, 125, 128, 231, 301–302
being as such, 79, 97, 125, 173, 231, 302
being-in-the-world, 14
being-possible, 37
being-together, 155
Bennett, William, 250
beyond, the, 251
biologism, 186
biologism, Heidegger's critiques of, 15
biology, 17, 87, 94, 203, 247
Blanchot, 22
Blattner, William, 5, 8, 29, 50, 82, 144, 146, 160, 295
Bloom, Harold, 35
Böhme, 33–34
boredom, 155, 277, 279
Bostrom, Nick, 272
brain death, 25
breeding, 259
Brentano, 83
Buddha, 221

Buddhism, 237–238, 281
burial, 235
Burke, Edmund, 257
Butler, Judith, 211

cancer, 233, 235
Capobianco, Richard, 163
care, 43, 238
caress, the, 203
Carman, Taylor, 136
Carnap, 116–118, 126
carnophallogocentrism, 215, 243
causa sui, 254
Cavell, Stanley, 109, 132, 134–135, 142
cell-replication, failures of, 233
chemistry, 248
child, 203, 213, 215
childhood, 213, 216
choice, original, 213
Christ, 199
Christianity, 34, 252, 284
Churchill, Winston, 45
circularity, 260
classism, 243
clearing, 86, 126
  as open and lighting, 86
climate change, 269, *See also* global warming; Anthropocene
community, 48, 204, 221, 244, 264
competition, 248
conceptualization, 118
conscience, 31, 40, 69, 101, 166, 168, 219, 221, 250–251, 260, 290
consciousness, 269
consequentialism, 224
conservative, defined, 257
constructivism, 213
contingency, 47, 149, 223
contradiction, 279
conversation, 193
conversion, 34
coordination, 233
Copernicus, 295
Coppola, Francis Ford, 275
courage, 125
cremation, 235
crisis, 130
  historical, 13

INDEX

Critchley, Simon, 222
critique, immanent, 74, 193
Crowell, Steven, 14, 44

danger, the greatest, 226, 241, 246
Dante, 45, 242
Darwin, 247
das Man, 13, 38, 46–48, 142, 144, 151, 154, 211–212, 225, 230, 293
Dasein, 15, 37, 64, 76, 137, 234, 237–238, 289, 298, 301
  as constantly dying, 33
  defined, 10–11
  existential structures as incomplete, 28
  existential structures of, 11, 13, 27, 43
  as imperishable, 232
  as imperishable, explained, 22
  as more powerful than death, 46, 299
  incompatible with demise, 26
  solus ipse as core of, 112
  virility and lucidity of, 193
  as a whole, 27, 29
  wholeness of, 30
  why cannot be demised, 26
dead-end, xxi, 276, 282–283
death, 4–5, 9, 24, 37, 40, 45, 63, 67, 75, 147, 150, 154, 164, 173, 179, 190–192, 194, 197, 212, 217, 227–228, 232, 237, 239, 246, 262, 268, 278, 280–281, 286–287, 294, 297, 301, 304
  alleged phenomenological incoherence of, 42, 101
  anxiety about, 17, 57, 59, 61–62, 237, 295
    as motivating fear of demise, 62
  as anxiety attack, 196
  as aporia, 196
  as being ended, 233
  being-toward, 29
  being-toward, defined, 19
  biological accounts of, 15, 23
  as certain, 53, 108, 230
  as collapse of historical world, 165
  collective awareness of, 217
  as conditioning demise, 19, 24–25, 52, 58, 62, 294
  conflated with demise, 8, 222, 229
  controversy surrounding meaning of, 3
  and crisis of adolescence, 214
  as Dasein's ownmost ability-to-be, 45, 112, 298–299
  defined, 48, 53, 60, 100, 290
  discloses alterity, 222
  discloses futurity, 67
  discloses the nothing, 222
  as disclosing alterity, 199
  as disclosing being, 115
  as disclosing future beyond nihilism, 263
  as disclosing futurity, 69
  as disclosing *solus ipse*, 44, 66, 112
  as disclosing the limits of subjectivism, 263
  distinguished from demise, 27–28, 32–33, 293
  distinguished from perishing, 20–21
  as end, 14, 53
  as end of being-in-the-world, 15, 19
  as end of Dasein, 15, 19, 24, 32
  as existential possibility, 108
  as existential version of phenomenological reduction, 41
  as finite existing, 29–32, 231
  formally defined, 3
  full existential-ontological conception of, 17, 50, 294
  genuine or authentic, 49
  as global world-collapse, 31, 39, 111, 227, 252
  and the grossest of hermeneutic perversions, 59
  as identity crisis, 196
  as impossibility of possibility (Levinas), 194
  as indefinite, 54
  industrialization of, 226
  as isolation, 196
  liberating us from fear of demise, 295
  as limit situation, 299
  as loss of significance, 42
  and mercilessness of world, 300
  as mourning, 196
  new academic department dedicated to study of, 17–18, 93
  as non-relational, 53
  ontological interpretation of, 15–16, 75, 100

death (cont.)
  ontology of, 17, 287
  as ownmost, 53
  phenomenological approach to, 17, 100, 103, 224, 286, 291
  of philosophy as metaphysics, 76
  as primarily relating to understanding, 101
  as projectless projecting, 29, 31, 41, 45, 62, 106, 112, 148, 150, 153, 219, 231, 299
  as something I am, 33, 291
  as something I can live through, 45
  as spiritual wretchedness, 35
  as the null-basis of a nullity, 29
  as the possibility of an impossibility, 149, 195
  as the possibility of impossibility, 40–41, 107, 111, 290
  and the ready-to-hand, 15
  relation to anxiety, 43
  relation to demise, 50, 294
  relation to guilt, 61
  relation to language, 234
  relation to life, 15, 17
  repression of, 295
  rethinking in and after Heidegger, xiii, xv–xvi
  role of in *Being and Time*, xi
  self as stronger than, 192, 219
  spiritual, 34
  as transforming demise, 106
  as unsurpassable, 54
  as way to be, 103, 291
  as writer's block, 196
  as a way to be, 45
death camps, 182–184, 227–228, 284
death of God, 121, 214, 255
  as presencing of the earth, 256
deathbed, 62, 209
decisionism, 31, 202
deconstruction, xiv, 90, 93, 144, 163, 172, 228, 232, 235, 241, 288
deferral, 89
Delillo, Don, 282
dementia, 61, 233

demise, 9, 20, 23, 48, 75, 149, 195, 229, 232, 236–237, 251–252, 271, 273, 282, 292, 294–295
  as certain, 53, 229–230
  as conditioned by death, 49
  as das Man's relation to death, 58
  in the death camps, 226
  defined, 53, 105, 292
  distinguished from perishing, 21
  as end, 53
  as experience of perishing, 21, 23
  fear of, 57–62, 237, 295
  as final appointment in Samarra, 24
  flight from, 230
  as inauthentic understanding of death, 70
  as indefinite, 54
  as intermediate phenomenon between perishing and dying, 24
  as non-relational, 53
  as ownmost, 53
  pain and suffering, 24
  paradox of, 18, 21, 26–27, 30, 104, 229, 292
  as passing away, 23
  as repression of death, 38
  return from, 254
  as unsurpassable, 54
  visualizing, 62
demise…paradox of, 233
demising without dying, 24–25, 49
demising without perishing, 25
Demme, Jonathan, xiii
denegation, 262, 278
deontology, 224
depression, 32, 59, 197–198, 202
Derrida, 16, 22, 47, 96, 161, 206, 215, 222, 229, 231–232, 235–236, 242–243, 250–251, 283, 293
  nothing outside the text, 231
Descartes, 44, 109, 211, 254, 300
desolation, 31, 299
despair, 60, 98, 209, 252, 279
destiny, 153, 193, 204, 221
Devil, the, 251
diachrony, 199–200
dialogue, 221, 268
différance, 232, 235–236
difference, 126, 243–244, 256, 302

dignity, 228
Dilthey, 88, 143
disclosedness, 289
disclosure, 165, 215, 218, 236, 242, 263, 265, 288, 290
  rather than imposure, 266
disease, 240
disenfranchisement, 31
diversity, 257
dogmatism, 216
Don Juan, 277
dread, 38, 101, 124
Dreyfus, Hubert, 10, 39, 44, 111, 141, 144, 160, 168, 178, 195
drowned, the, 227
drugs, 240, 254
dualism, 11, 31, 64, 209–210, 288
duty, 222
dying while demising, 32
dying without demising, 25, 32, 49, 299
dying, genuine or authentic, 19, 22
dystopia, 240

earth, 76, 95, 121, 123–124, 126, 128, 183, 247, 285, 303
eating, 44, 244, 277
ecology, 244, 269
economics, 247
education, 94, 129–130, 142, 146, 154, 156, 218, 244, 249
  crisis, 130
  ontologization of, 130
egocentrism, 204, 221
Einstein, Albert, xv
embodiment, 28
emptiness, 300
end, the, 286
endlessness, 263, 272
enframing, 12, 32, 96, 98, 128–129, 166, 170, 173, 182, 213, 226, 239, 241–242, 265
  death camps as, 183
  defined, 245
  global, 245
  quantification of quality, 249
enlightenment, 198, 256
ennui, 260
Epicurus, 22, 26, 59, 104, 292, 296
epoch, 247

equipment, 300–301
Erickson, Eric, 280
errancy, 176
eschatology, 241
eternity, 271, 273, 282
ethics, 134, 181, 183–184, 204–205, 224, 260, 275
  ambiguity, 215
  ethical realism, 185
  pluralism, 215
  postmodern, 260
Euripides, 170
event, 123, 167, 176, 214, 246, 267, 278
existence, 40, 286, 288–289, 299, 301,
  See also Dasein
  as transparent to itself, 30
existential structures, 5, 101, 172, 289
  affective attunement, 69, 71, 81
  as conditioned by temporal horizons, 71
  conditioned by temporal horizons, 81
  conversance, 68, 72, 81
  as incomplete, 73
  as inextricably tripartite, 101
  understanding, 67, 71, 82
existentialism, 6, 162, 241, 263
existentiell, 6
  defined, 297
  distinguished from existential, 6
expertise, 178
exteriority, 236, 254
extremism, 257

face, the, 200
facetiousness, 242, 261
facticity, 46, 150
failure, existential, 280
failure, philosophical, 74, 76, 81, 83, 85–86, 97–99
faith, 39, 105, 275, 294
fantasy, 214
farmer, 184
fascism, 223, 242
fate, 204
fear, 222
fecundity, 203
feminine, the, 203
film, xiii, 107, 241, 275

finitude, 31, 47, 60, 76, 97, 150, 231, 261, 263, 268, 272, 278, 281, 289
  of matter, 285
Fischer, John, 273, 276–278, 283
flourishing, 283
forgiveness, 224
formal indication, 51, 106, 294, See also phenomenology
Foucault, 211, 214, 239, 241
foundationalism, 247, 260, See also ontotheology
fourfold, 126
fragility, 98
freedom, 46–47, 150, 215–216, 263–264
Freud, 252
Friedman, Michael, 171
fundamentalism, 216, 243, 250, 258, 260–261
futurists, 272
futurity, 62–63, 66–68, 70, 72, 114–115, 175, 200, 225, 263, 265, 287, 303, See also arrival, ontological
  defined, 65
  as primary, 72
  relation to death and demise, 70

Gadamer, 80, 242
Gaiman, Neil, 270, 272
Gelassenheit, 62
gender, 28
generation, 48, 88, 151, 153, 193, 204
genetics, 249
genocide, 185, 225
Germany, 73, 90, 124, 183
gestalt switch, 246
Geuss, Raymond, 143
global warming, 258
God, 12, 60, 78, 167, 199, 201, 255, 279, 284
God forsakenness, 121
Goethe, 104, 251
graffiti, 240
Guignon, Charles, 30, 37, 153, 196
guilt, 29, 31, 61, 70, 219, 222, 251, 300
  relation of ontic to ontological, 61

Habermas, Jürgen, 56, 176
hackers, 269
hatred, 224
Haugeland, John, 4, 8, 50, 113, 136, 302

hearing, 233
heart-attack, 233
heaven, 276, 282, 284
Hegel, 166, 211
  on thinking death as tarrying with the negative, xii
Heidegger
  alleged atheism of, 26
  authoritarian dimension of politics, 90
  fatalistic misreading of, 86
  fundamental differences between early and later, 6, 11, 14, 26, 66, 80, 82, 84, 120, 125, 127, 155, 165, 170, 172, 174, 179, 218, 267, 302
  on *Holzweg* as clearing, xxi
  idealism, 11, 163
  metaphysical decade, 14
  Nazism, 7–8, 76, 100, 114, 131, 171, 175, 181, 185, 223, 258–259
  philosophy of language, 120
  realism, 11
  as romantic, 184
  similarities between early and later, 12, 14, 80, 155
  thinking as thanking, xviii
Heideggerian, orthodox, 154, 161, 169–170, 179, 188
hell, 45, 276–277, 282, 284
Heraclitus, 248
heritage, 153, 180, 188, 221, 262, 304
  contrasted with tradition, 153
hermeneutic, 171
hermeneutic faithfulness, 236
hermeneutic resistance, 296
hermeneutics, 74, 102, 145, 159, 164, 170, 172, 174, 188, 236, 243, 263, 289, 297, 303
  illusion of hindsight, 174
  Midrash, 179
  revisionist, 171
  and wisdom of the middle way, 180
hero, 125, 193, 221
historicality, 88
historicity, 172, 247
history, 88–89, 94
Hoffman, Piotr, 9
Hölderlin, 119–121, 123–124, 226
holism, 98
Hollywood, 241

Holocaust, 181–185, 187, 206, 224, 226, 228
Holzweg, as leading to a clearing, 86
Homer, 248
homophobia, 250
hope, 239, 244, 246, 280, 303
hopelessness, 280
horror, 216, 240
Hoy, David, 195
humanism, 162, 184–185, 199–200
Humboldt, 135
humility, 55
hunger, 44, 227
Hurka, Thomas, 135
Husserl, 18, 41, 76, 87–88, 102, 110, 143, 188

identity, 69, 71, 73, 137, 145, 147, 155, 196, 221, 237, 243, 256, 281–282
  as dimming down of the possible as such, 71
idolatry, 200
Ilych, Ivan, 230
immortality, 47, 98, 263, 267, 269, 276–277, 283, 285
  being pro-choice rather than pro-life about, 268
  being pro-choice versus pro-life about, 285
  defined, 270
  distinguished from life-extension, 271–272
  technological, 268
incarceration, 240
indigeny, 265
individual, the, 165
individualism, 218
individuation, 190
ineffablility, 223
infinity, 200, 272
injustice, 240
insight, moment of, 47, 151
insomnia, 197
integrity, 275, 281
intelligibility, constellations of, 246
interdisciplinarity, 93
intersubjectivity, 211

Jaspers, Karl, 17, 299
  limit-situation, 299

Jesus, 295
Johnston, Mark, 237
joke, 237, 242
Jünger, Ernst, 149
justice, 261, 264, 303

Kant, 28, 64, 91–92, 134, 171, 254
  categories grounded in temporality, 91
  as God killer, 254
Kaplan, Eric, 275
Kierkegaard, 6, 32, 34–35, 38–39, 55, 60, 109, 112, 209, 252, 275, 278–279, 298–299
  crop rotation, 278
  on infinite self, 35
  stages on life's way, 279
Klee, Paul, 126
Kojève, Alexandre, 211
Kuhn, Thomas, 288

Lacan, Jacques, 253
language, 89
last will and testament,, 236
late-modernity, 249, 257, See also enframing
  distinguished from modernity, 249
Lear, Jonathan, 283, 295
learning, 62, 204
Leibniz, 142
Levi, Primo, 225–227
Levinas, 6, 26, 168, 180–181, 184, 187, 192, 204, 218–219, 222–223, 236, 250
life
  after demise, 107
  ontology of, 17
  as a whole, 30
life death, 235
life-extension, 269, 271–273
life-project, See possibility, existential
limitations, 261
literature, 94
logic, 255
Londen, Patrick, 72
look, the, 6, 209–210
love, 202, 244, 296
Löwith, Karl, 176
Lucifer, 251
luck, 75, 299

Lucretius, 271
Luther, 125

Makropulos case, the, 274
Martin, George R. R., 268, 274
masculinism, 263
mastery, 178
Matrix, the, 20
McDowell, John, 31
meaning, 223
meaningfulness, 263, 267, 278, 302, 304, *See also* being, postmodern understanding of
Melancholia, 61
memory, 233, 236
metaphysics, *See* ontotheology
    abyss of, 92
    death of, 301
    of substance, 92
metontology, 78
Mill, J. S., 135
mind-uploading, 279
mineness, 44, 112, 196, 299–300
miracles, 279
misery, 226
modernity, 11, 249, 257, *See also* subjectivism
morality, 134, 250, 254
mortality, 98, 104, 229, 267, 272, 291
Mulhall, Stephen, 109
murder, 224
music, 254, 277
mystery, 127–128, 225
mysticism, 33–34, 45, 261
    central teaching of, 34

Nagel, Thomas, 59–60
Nancy, Jean-Luc, 237
narcissism, 170
nature, 89
near death experiences, 33
neo-conservativism, 243
neurosis, 32, 132, 263, 265
neurotypicalism, 234, 243
Nietzsche, xvi, 78, 94, 120, 122, 134, 143–144, 165–166, 176, 178, 214, 247, 250, 254, 258, 272
    death of God, 254
    eternal recurrence, 248, 271
    on creation requiring destruction, xii
    as ontotheologist, 248
    as ontotheologist of enframing, 259
    ressentiment driven by inability to change past, xvi
    will to power, 247, 258
nihilation, 219
nihilism, 66, 94, 99, 127, 169, 237, 241–242, 245, 248–249, 251, 263–264, 272, 277, 281, 285, 302
    and infinite time, 279
nirvana, 252
No exit, 197
nothing, the, xiii, 56, 60, 62, 65, 86, 95, 99, 113–116, 124–125, 127–128, 173, 184, 225, 234, 239, 246, 249, 265, 267, 300–302
    as concealed presencing of the earth, 121
    defined, 118
    difference between early and later, 125
    disclosed by death, 129
    distinguished from the earth, 122
    as presencing of being, 223
    as source of meaning, 121
    as splitting Western philosophy, 116
    as touchstone of thinking, 100
nothingness, 39, 66, 101, 105, 107, 112, 115, 225, 238, 246, 271–272, 290, 293, 298–300, 302

objectivity, 6
oblivion, 112, 298
Olafson, Frederick, 83
old age, 196
oneness, 252, 281
ontic, 102, 151
ontic and ontological, relation between, 56, 124
ontological
    as conditioning ontic, 52
ontology, 140–141
    only possible through phenomenology, 287
    ontological holism, 247
ontology, fundamental, 13, 63, 65, 73, 76–77, 79, 89, 93, 97, 113, 129, 163, 172, 287, 301–302
    as ontotheology, 78
ontology, regional, 89

ontotheo-carno-phallogocentrism, 243
ontotheology, xiv, 28, 63, 76, 78, 86, 92, 94–95, 156, 167, 169, 179, 182, 185, 215, 241, 243, 248, 253–255, 264, 283, 287
  as ground of enframing, 94, 98, 179, 246, 248
  defined, 78, 246
oppression, 213
optimization, 47, 249, 265, *See* also enframing
otherness, *See* alterity

paganism, 185
painting, 127
pandemic, 228
pandemic, mortality as, xii
paralysis, existential, 32
Parmenides, 96
partiality, 92, 242, 261, 289
particularity, 256
passivity, 194, 199, 263
patriarchy, 213
Paul, L.A., 47
pedagogy, 155
perfectionism, 129, 133, 137, 143, 150–151, 189–190, 218, 262
perfectionisms, disambiguated, 132
perishing, 20, 23, 232
perishing without demising, 24–25
perishing, defined, 292
phallogocentrism, 244
phenomenological attestation, 56, 62
phenomenological movement, the, 18
phenomenology, 5, 7, 64, 68, 102, 104, 125, 198, 200, 220, 245, 260, 262–263, 286, 288, 291, 293–294, 296–297, 299
  of demise is impossible, 29
  early transcendental approach, 84
  as engagement, 8, 124
  existential, 6
  feedback loop with personal experience, 8
  first law of, 249, 286
  formal indication, 51–52
  formal indication, defined, 51
  as methodologically agnostic, 27, 105
  necessarily hermeneutic, 289
  not a spectator sport, 294
  as only approach to ontology, 287
  phenomenological method, 5, 51, 124, *See* also phenomenological attestation; formal indication
  priority of, 16, 18
  relation to ontology, 6
  as queen of the sciences, 18
  as transforming everyday experience, 62, 103, 296
  as transforming our ordinary experience, 106
phenomenology, hermeneutic, 102–103
philosophy
  continental, 117, 188–189, 198
  as mortal, 98
  as obliquely autobiographical, 178
philosophy, defined, 6
phonocentrism, 96
physics, 248
Pindar, 143
Pinkard, Terry, 142
Pippin, Robert, 57, 187, 191, 196
Plato, 34, 36, 96, 130, 142, 166, 203, 255
pleasure, 277
Plotinus, 142
pluralism, 215
pluralism, ontological, 256–257, 260, 303, *See* also postmodernity
  defined, 256
  principle of, 260
Poe, 59, 271
  Nevermore versus forevermore, 271
poetry, 119, 127, 184, 234, 239
political, the, 228
politics, 249, 254
  postmodern, 260
polysemy, 12, 75, 85, 96–97, 109, 113, 128, 143, 231, 234, 249, 301, *See* also being, as postmodern
possibilities, existential
  ability-to-be distinguished from being-possible, 111
  being-possible distinguished from ability-to-be, 298

possibility
    existential, 108
    higher than actuality, 108
    and necessity, 276
possibility, existential, 36, 70, 111, 139, 147, 280, 297
    ability-to-be distinguished from being-possible, 45, 146
possibility, existential, defined, 19
possibility, logical, 37
postmodernism, 30, 241
postmodernity, 12, 14, 76, 95, 256–257, 275, 288
power, 205, 264
practical, primacy of, 137
Preciado, Paul, 211
prejudice, 243, 288
presencing, *See* being, as presencing
pride, 77
privation, 235
progressive, defined, 257
projecting into projects, 19
projecting, existential, defined, 19
projection, existential, 41
promise, the, 226, 246
psychiatry, 255
psychology, 20, 87, 94, 198, 213
psychopharmacology, 249
publish or perish, 95
purity, 251, 264
Pythagoras, 261

questioning, 75

race, 186, 259
racism, 243
Raffoul, François, 161
Ralkowski, Mark, 159
rationalism, 47, 237–238, 261
rationality, 260–261
Rawls, John, 135
reaction-formation, 225
Reality Bites, 54
reanimation, 235
reason, 264
receptivity, 268
reciprocative rejoinder, 188
refugees, 97
rejoinder, reciprocative, 48, 151

relativism, 260
religious experience, 254
repetition, 188, 193
repressed, return of, 256
repression, 295
resolve, 29, 31, 46–47, 55, 70, 150–152, 173, 190, 192–193, 221, 280, 304
    as living through death, 46
    as more powerful than death, 299
    and repetition, 55
responsibility, 47, 228, 232
restlessness, 280
resurrection, 192–193, 204, 221, 237
revelation, 200
revisionism, 88
revolution, 152, 193, 204, 221, 241, 258, 288
revolutionary, defined, 257
Richardson, Father, 206
righteousness, 222
Robinson Crusoe, 235
Rorty, Richard, 264
Russia, 183
Ryle, Gilbert, 110

sadomasochism, 212, 240
Saint Paul, 34
same, the, 161, 223
Sartre, 6, 47, 162, 208–210, 216, 254
Satan, 251
science, 255, 285, 287
science fiction, 279
sciences, positive, 90
scientism, 110
secret, 127–128
secularization, 34
self, 30, 32, 35, 39, 42, 112, 145, 147, 154–155, 220, 237, 265, 275, 281–282, 288
    as more powerful than death, 299
selfhood, 52, 147, 228, 282
sending, 176
serial killers, 240
seriousness, 261
sex, 28, 277
    transgender, 244
sexism, 243
sexuality, 212, 244
shame, 182, 184, 209–210, 283

Shaw, George Bernard, 277
Sheehan, Thomas, 163
Sher, George, 143
shipwreck, 298–299
significance, 8, 40, 44, 67, 300
signified, the transcendental, 231
silence, 101, 127–128, 182, 290
Silence of the Lambs, the, xiii
situatedness, 262
situation, 151
situation, the, 47
skepticism, 232
Sluga, Hans, 182, 223
Smith, Adam, 247
Socrates, 96, 284
soil, 82
solidarity, 244
solitude, 70, 201, 219
solus ipse, 299, See Dasein, solus ipse as core of
son, 203
space-time, 80
speciesism, 185
Spinoza, 17, 142, 239, 261–262
  repression of death, 262
stoicism, 104, 294
stroke, 194, 197, 233
subjectivism, 56, 121, 162, 214
suffering, 183, 244
suffocation, 197
suicide, 19, 60
superhuman, the, 259
surveillance, 240
survival, 235–237

teacher, 37, 193, 202, 221, 224
teaching, 124, 138, 298
technology, 269, 273, See enframing
  free use of, 265
  freeing claim of, 246
  mind uploading, 268
temporality, 4, 11, 13, 27, 61, 64–65, 69, 79–82, 84, 231, 287
  futurity, See futurity
  having beenness, 68
  making present, 68
  as transcendental condition of intelligibiity, 11

terror, 254
texture, 122, 128–129
Thales, 76
thanatological drives, xvi, 61, 241
theism, 27
theology, 252, 254, 284, See also ontotheology
thinking, 76, 97, 129, 263, 304
thrownness, 29, 31, 46, 61, 197, 262
time, infinite, 267, 272, 276, 285
tolerance, 260
Torah, 195, 198
totalitarianism, 205, 254
trace, 223, 236
tradition, 48, 88, 153, 188, 221, 262, 294
tragedy, 263, 278
Trakl, Georg, 165–166
transitory, the, 217
transubstantiation, 193, 204, 221
trauma, 25, 206, 223, 230
truth, ontological, 15, 126
turn, the, 14, 75, 79–80, 102, 114, 174
  as death of metaphysics, 75

Ulysses, 205
uncanniness, 38–40, 114, 149, 219, 301
  as lack of fit between Dasein and world, 39
undecidability, 47
understanding, 145, 290, 297
university, 17, 73, 87, 93
unknown, the, 62, 225
unthought, 161

Valéry, Paul, 251
values, 258
Van Gogh, 29, 56, 120, 123, 296
Vattimo, Gianni, 242, 264
view, 221
violence, 205, 207
violence, hermeneutic, 50, 52, 92–93
virtue, 250
vision, 233
visitation, 236
void, the, 251
voluntarism, 31
vulnerability, 55, 263

Wachowski sisters, 20
Wagner, Richard, 270
White, Carol, 8, 50, 159, 169, 177, 179
will, 175
Williams, Bernard, 48, 271, 274–275, 279–281, 283
Wittgenstein, 96, 116–117, 127–128
world, 300
  mercilessness of, 300
world, secular, 34
worldlessness, 300
world-poverty, 234
worth, 249
Wrathall, Mark, 21, 26, 43, 72, 172

y Gasset, Ortega, 238
Young, Julian, 153

Zen, 33
Žižek, Slavoj, 253

For EU product safety concerns, contact us at Calle de José Abascal, 56–1°,
28003 Madrid, Spain or eugpsr@cambridge.org.